The Two Frank Thrings
by Peter Fitzpatrick

Winner of the 2013 National Biography Award

'In exploring what made each man tick, and so adroitly placing them in their personal and professional contexts, Fitzpatrick gives a vivid sense of the shifting contours of Australian cultural life across most of a century... humorously and elegantly written.'

Brian McFarlane, the *Age*

'In Fitzpatrick's expert hands, their stories count among the saddest as well as the most scintillating in our annals.'

Ian Britain, *Australian Book Review*

'[I]nformed and immensely readable... Their detailed and engrossing double biographies are a welcome contribution both to regional history and to international studies of twentieth-century entertainment careers.'

Theatre Research International (Cambridge)

'Fitzpatrick has drawn on an exhaustive range of sources, from public records and surviving promotional materials from the day, to his own interviews, in researching this book... with subjects as ostentatious as these, his book certainly doesn't want for incident or appeal.'

Gerald Elson, *Bookseller + Publisher*

'An often fascinating, meticulously researched, and sometimes speculative biography of two key, closely related figures in Australian theatrical and cinematic history.'

Journal of Australian Studies, vol 37:3

'Few books gave me more pleasure this year than Peter Fitzpatrick's *The Two Frank Thrings*, not because of any particular veneration for either Frank, but because it is a superbly executed biographical account of them. It is elegantly written, spiked with wit and insight, immaculately researched, and structured with a style and originality that enable the reader to get inside the lives of these two disparate Thrings.

Brian McFarlane, 'Best Books of 2013', *Australian Book Review*

'This detail is painstakingly researched and should provide a useful resource for students of the early Australian film industry… fascinating stuff.'

Andrew Shaw, *Gay News Network*

'A well-paced and clearly written biography in which the author brings to life two very different and determined self-mythologisers, and gracefully deals with what can be known about them and what cannot.'

Judges, National Biography Award 2013

THE TWO FRANK THRINGS

PETER FITZPATRICK

MONASH University Publishing

Monash University Publishing
Building 4, Monash University
Clayton, Victoria 3800, Australia
www.publishing.monash.edu

First published as a hardback, 2012.

Monash University Publishing brings to the world publications which advance the best traditions of humane and enlightened thought.

Monash University Publishing titles pass through a rigorous process of independent peer review.

National Library of Australia Cataloguing-in-Publication entry:

Author:	Fitzpatrick, Peter, 1944-
Title:	The two Frank Thrings / Peter Fitzpatrick.
Edition:	1st paperback ed.
ISBN:	9781922235657 (pbk.)
Notes:	Includes index.
Subjects:	Thring, Francis William, 1882-1936;
	Thring, Frank, 1926-1994;
	Actors--Australia--Biography;
	Motion picture producers and directors--Australia--Biography.
Dewey Number:	920.710994

www.publishing.monash.edu/books/thrings.html

Design: Les Thomas
Cover images:
Front cover, left: Portrait of Frank junior by David Parker, c.1984. Courtesy of the Performing Arts Collection, Melbourne
Front cover, right: Portrait for Frank senior, c.1930. Courtesy of the Performing Arts Collection, Melbourne
Back cover: Frank junior looking at photo of his father, 1937. Courtesy of the Performing Arts Collection, Melbourne
Author photo: Les Thomas © 2011

Printed in Australia by Griffin Press an Accredited ISO AS/NZS 14001:2004 Environmental Management System printer.

MIX
Paper from responsible sources
FSC® C009448

The paper this book is printed on is certified against the Forest Stewardship Council ® Standards. Griffin Press holds FSC chain of custody certification SGS-COC-005088. FSC promotes environmentally responsible, socially beneficial and economically viable management of the world's forests.

CONTENTS

PART TWO: FRANK THE SON

ACKNOWLEDGEMENTS

The Two Frank Thrings took up seven years of my life, on and off, and over such a long time benefited from the contributions of so many people that inevitably many will go unacknowledged here. While there were very few living witnesses to the life of Frank Thring senior, it sometimes seemed that everyone of a certain age had an indelible memory (and a favourite anecdote, and maybe a minute or so of credible mimicry) of his son.

Some people, though, were especially important to its development. From the beginning, Peter Eyers and Frank Van Straten were wonderfully ready to share their own Thring materials. And there were the witnesses: Googie Withers and John McCallum at Bayview, and Peter Cooke in Sydney; Bill (once Wee Willie) Kerr in Perth, who remembered 'old Mr Thring' so vividly; Joan Harris and Fred Parslow in Melbourne, and friends of mine like John Preston and Peter Oyston who turned out to have Thring stories of their own. In England in 2004–5 I talked at length with Peggy Cummins, Trader Faulkner and Joanna McCallum, and, in particular, with Joan Thring and John Sumner, who gave very generously of their time and their memories. Minty Lalanne (formerly Creightmore), the younger Frank's cousin, who now lives in Paris, was another great resource. And I tracked down Hugh Rule in Kenya, whose emails offered not only detailed reminiscences, but some very shrewd insights into the man he knew. One of the nice things about being on the trail of the Thrings was that nobody I talked with seemed concerned with concealment. Perhaps the fact that both were dead, and that the younger of the Frank Thrings had lived his life so spectacularly without shame, freed the custodians of the memories of them to be candid. Or perhaps I was just lucky in the witnesses I talked with.

Much of my work for this double biography would have been impossible without the support of the Australian Research Council, which funded me through a Discovery Grant from 2004–8. I am very appreciative of the opportunities that it offered me, as I am of the support of the university that employed me throughout that time (and indeed for the thirty years before it); Monash University, and especially the School of English, Communications and Performing Arts in which I taught, was always a good place to begin an adventure.

Three people in particular had a special role in the development of this project. Two of them acted as research assistants, though that term seems hardly adequate in defining their contribution. Chris Long, who I believe knows more about Australian film than anyone I have met, lent all his erudition, his unrelenting curiosity, and his vast personal collection of materials and memorabilia to the enterprise from the beginning; he asked only that the book should include his definitive Efftee filmography, as it does. It also includes a number of photographs from his personal collection, obtained directly from two of Thring senior's right-hand men, Bert Nicholas and Jack Murray. Betty Hanner, who made many important connections on my behalf and brought to the project just the right balance of passion and persistence, was in her own way every bit as crucial to its evolution. I will always owe a great deal to both of them for what they gave to *The Two Frank Thrings*.

The third person is the one whose contribution to this book is at once the greatest, and the hardest to explain. To my wife Gay Baldwin, who has read it already more than anyone else ever will, who has been throughout so formidably incisive in her criticism while so wonderfully in tune with the things that I tried to achieve, I owe more than I could ever publicly explain. Some things, like love, are best kept private, I think; but that doesn't mean they shouldn't be acknowledged. A little bit. Or, maybe, quite a lot.

Peter Fitzpatrick
September 2011

AUTHOR'S NOTE

The two Frank Thrings were not inclined to put their thoughts on paper. They kept no diaries, wrote letters only when they had to, and managed to ensure that no self-revealing correspondence survived them at all. In this book I have tried to address that lack of the supposedly off-guard voice in the biographical materials through the 'Travelling' interludes. These monologues are wholly fictional, though the journeys to which they are linked all took place. They are exercises in impersonation that seek to create a distinctive voice for each of the Thrings, and a sense of how they might have talked to themselves. These sections of the text are clearly separated from the historical narrative by the use of italics.

PART ONE

FRANK THE FATHER

Chapter One

THIS MAN'S FATHER

They shared a name, of course, and the physical resemblance was startling. And both Frank Thrings spent their working lives in film and theatre, where each of them blazed some trails and achieved some fame.

But the contrasts between the father and son are more striking than the points of similarity. They were there in seemingly superficial things like their speech and their mannerisms, and the ways in which they presented themselves in public; more importantly, they were evident in the choices about the directions of their lives that lay behind those points of difference.

Some of those contrasts would be readily apparent in a *Who's Who* entry, though one of the things that the two Frank Thrings had in common was the fact that, for all their celebrity, neither ever appeared there. Frank the father, who had a keen interest in establishing or buying that kind of status, might have been denied it because of the ambiguities of his background; though he lived in a mansion in patrician Toorak, and was conspicuously a big spender, there were things about his early years on the carnival circuit and the ways in which he had acquired his wealth that may have made his past too colourful to be celebrated in such distinguished company. Perhaps he was offered the opportunity, after all, and found the business of creating a suitably respectable history too tricky a challenge, even though it was something he was always tinkering with.

In 1936, his fifty-fourth year and the year of his death, a *Who's Who* entry provided by Frank Thring senior might have looked rather like this:

> THRING, Francis William. Cinema and theatre entrepreneur, director. Born December 2, 1882 at Wentworth, NSW. *Parents:* Francis William and Laura (McKenzie) Thring. *Schooling:* privately educated. *Married*: Grace Wight (dec 1920), 1904: one daughter, Viola (Lola), born 1911. *Married:* Olive Marguerite Kreitmayer, 1921: one son, Francis William,

> born 1926. Performance artist, film exhibitor with Biograph Pictures, Tasmania, and Brunswick Theatre, Melbourne. Set up Paramount Theatre, Melbourne, 1915. Managing Director, J.C. Williamson Films, 1918–23, Hoyts Theatres, 1924–30. Established cinema houses in all Australian states. Founded Efftee Films, Melbourne, 1930, Efftee Players, 1933. Feature films: *A Co-Respondent's Course* (1931), *Diggers* (1931), *The Haunted Barn* (1931), *The Sentimental Bloke* (1932), *His Royal Highness* (1932), *Harmony Row* (1933), *Diggers in Blighty* (1933), *A Ticket in Tatts* (1934), *Clara Gibbings* (1934), *The Streets of London* (1934). Produced stage plays, inc. *Collits' Inn* (1933) and *The Cedar Tree* (1934). Founded Radio 3XY, Melbourne, 1935, Mastercraft Films, Sydney, 1936. *Hobbies:* reading, music. Address: 'Rylands', Toorak Road, Toorak, Victoria.

It wouldn't have told everything, or even what was most important in his life. Presumably such biographical sketches never do. It would have left out his sensitivities about his origins, and the shadowiness that surrounded the time of his first wife Grace's death and his remarriage to Olive. It would have indicated very little of the driving ambition and dogged resilience behind his achievements, and nothing at all of the continual frustrations and bitter disappointments that filled the times between them. There would be no suggestion there of his skill in bending or evading the rules, or of the ruthless calculation and, intermittently, the disarming kindness, that characterised his dealings with others. In the space provided for 'interests', the line allowed for a glimpse of the private man, Frank would doubtless have offered 'reading and music' as his pastimes because these were the civilised things a man of substance would appropriately and safely say. A man like Frank, whose business was his passion, had no room or time for a hobby.

It would tell the reader nothing, of course, of what mattered to him or moved him, of his capacity to give and inspire love, of the things that made him happy or brought him pain. Perhaps those things would be left to the biographer that a man so demonstrably a big fish in the small pond of Australian cinema and theatre in the 1920s and 1930s must surely attract. Frank Thring the father was aware of that possibility, and accordingly devoted a lot of energy to covering his tracks.

That hypothetical *Who's Who* entry would not have told the truth about a number of things, either. Among the 'facts' about Frank that appeared in it, several, as we will see, were the habitual lies and ornamentations that he was increasingly inclined to offer about himself and his history.

Frank Thring the son would certainly have had his chance to be recognised among the *Who* who mattered. He was one of the handful of Australian actors to establish an international reputation in film in the 1950s and 1960s, and, when he discarded that career, he found another at home as a perennial star on the stage; he cultivated, too, a high public profile through his advertisements, his regular appearances in television variety shows, and his guaranteed capacity to say outrageous things on cue. This Frank Thring was certainly a household name. And he suffered from none of the questionable family connections that might have made his father a doubtful starter for *Who's Who*. A generation further on, the Thrings of Toorak had become thoroughly respectable. His father, having died so prematurely, was posthumously a hero in the sorry tale of Australian film; Olive his mother was a socialite with a flair for philanthropy, and had ensured that Frank attended (however ingloriously) one of the prestigious schools that assumed and assured social advantage.

Yet this Frank, too, never appeared in *Who's Who*. Perhaps he was black-balled because of all his high-campery, and the air that surrounded him of delicious decadence, of scandals that dared not speak their name. More probably, Frank the son's acute sense of absurdity inclined him not to bother. The comedy and futility of life, from his point of view, meant that a lot of the games that other people played just weren't worth the candle.

Had Frank had his fifteen lines of fame in 1994, the year in which he died at sixty-eight, they would have read something like the following.

> THRING, Francis William. Stage and screen actor, critic. Born Melbourne, 11 May 1926. Parents: Francis William and Olive Marguerite (Kreitmayer) Thring. Schooling: Melbourne Grammar School, Taylor's College. War service, RAAF, 1944–5. Married: Joan Cunliffe, UK, 1955, no issue. Divorced 1956. Director-manager, Arrow Theatre, Middle Park, 1951–4. Member, Shakespeare Memorial Theatre Company, Stratford-upon-Avon, UK, 1955, 1957. Feature film roles include *The Vikings* (1958), *Ben Hur* (1959), *King of Kings* (1960), *El Cid* (1961), *Mad Max: Beyond Thunderdome* (1985), *The Howling III* (1987). Theatre productions: more than 40 productions with the Union Theatre Repertory/Melbourne Theatre Company since 1959, including *Moby Dick – Rehearsed* (1959), *The Homecoming* (1965), *Henry IV Part One* (1969), *Life of Galileo* (1971), *The Cherry Orchard* (1972). Other productions include *Robert and Elizabeth* (1966), *Hadrian VII* (1969). Television critic, *The Argus*

(1950s), *TV Week* (1960s). Book: *The Actor Who Laughed* (1985), with Roland Rocchegiolli. *Hobbies:* reading, music. *Address*: 'Rylands', Toorak Road, Toorak, Victoria.

His homosexuality, and his tendency to parade it at a time when most other men of that persuasion were still securely in their closets, would not have been part of the entry, obviously. And that absence in turn precluded any sense of the emotional texture of his life; there were no public attachments later than his parents to record, other than the fleeting marriage, no affectations of a happy family. The list of his starring roles certainly denotes a big fish in a pool that was still a modest one, but suggests nothing of the size of his persona, the role that most people who thought they knew Frank Thring regarded as his finest. Although mythologising his life was central to that persona, nothing in that summary of it would have been untrue.

The bare facts of Frank Thring senior's career leave no doubt as to his ambitions and motives: this is patently a man on the move, climbing from success to success until his career ends abruptly at its zenith with his sudden death. The bare facts of his son's career, though, leave plenty of questions. An inexplicably quick rise to a measure of acclaim in the West End and in Hollywood is terminated by an inexplicable return to Melbourne, where he stayed. Frank Thring the son made news, in his home country at least, for some forty years. But on the public record his life is as mysterious as that of his father, who schemed and gambled his way to prominence for just the last decade of his. Father and son were both, in their quite different ways, intensely private men, though the son bought his privacy by a flamboyant public performance of a self that nobody could live full-time. For him 'reading and music' were genuine interests, the indispensable elements of a solitude that he claimed, at least, to prize.

Like his father, Frank would consider himself a very suitable subject for a biography, indeed a compulsory one. For him, though, this meant determining very entertainingly the self that should be recorded, by generating a host of myths and funny stories. Where Frank the father sought to shape his place and history by leaving strategic gaps, his son in some areas left too much information.

For some years, indeed, there were rumours that Frank Thring junior was hard at work on his autobiography. When it finally appeared in 1984, *The Actor Who Laughed* turned out to be a slim volume of theatre anecdotes, some allegedly based in his own experience, but most of them jokes or humiliations involving people he had known.[1] It added nothing to our sense of Frank Thring the man that hadn't already been seen in a moment of preposterousness on television, or heard in a witty aside boomed across a foyer.

Both Frank Thrings would be a little disappointed, I suspect, with the form in which the anticipated biography has come at last into being. It wouldn't surprise them that it set out to get behind their defences; that is what biographies routinely do, and they would hardly have put so much energy into pre-emption if they hadn't assumed some kind of challenge. But it might disconcert them to find that they are required to share a spotlight, which was something that neither of them, certainly, was accustomed to doing.

There are good reasons for a dual focus. The contrast is intriguing in itself, and so are the elements of the father-son relationship: while their lives overlapped for just ten years, and you could argue that each hardly knew the other at all, the psychological dimensions of that interrupted relationship have resonances that last much longer. And beyond that there is another, broader, story. Both Frank Thrings, in those carefully crafted public selves, made their very distinctive marks across a century of the performing arts in Australia, and their story is part of that wider one. This means that in the chapters that follow they not only share centre stage, they concede a little space as well to those around them who were also setting the directions that Australian film and theatre would take.

It's a big story. And this telling of it widens its scope a little further, briefly at least, because its real beginnings lie in the colony of South Australia, somewhere around the middle of the nineteenth century, with another father and another son.

Biographers have a habit of doing this, of course. A glance at the grandparents is a comfortable way of easing the reader into the narrative, a gentle clearing of the throat before getting down to business. At the same time, it is always more than just a ritual. Biographers love genealogies partly because a family tree looks such a wonderfully unambiguous thing, even though we know that the real relationships are always more complicated than they look on the branch. The fact that those connections seem so demonstrable among all the speculative messiness of a life-story is one of the reasons, certainly, why biographies tend to start a generation or two before their subjects were born. This tree is hung with plenty of documents

---

1 Frank Thring and Roland Rocchecciolli, *The Actor Who Laughed*, Melbourne, Hutchinson, 1985.

recording 'hatches, matches and dispatches', too. But all of them are more interesting for what they try to hide than what they seem to prove.

There is usually, as well, an assumption about the ways in which the family context is much more than a backdrop. Whether the supposed connections take the form of inheritances of disposition, or environmental influences, or some kind of collective domestic unconscious, or all of these things, the routine look backwards implies that in some degree the die is cast for any of us before we make our first appearance.

All those motives and assumptions are in play here. They may turn out to be persuasive, or they may raise more questions than they answer. And there is a further dimension to the shaking of the Thring family tree, which invokes a very old riddle – 'Brothers and sisters have I none, but this man's father is my father's son' – and explores in relation to both Frank Thrings the question in its punch-line: 'Who am I?'

Once there was a William Thring, who had a legitimate son, Francis William, and an illegitimate son, Francis William, usually known as William Francis. The Francis William usually known as William Francis had one son, born William Francis but usually known as Francis William, who had in turn one son, Francis William. The last two Francis Williams were the two Frank Thrings who primarily concern us here, and the line stopped dead with Frank the son.

The repetition of the names was inconsiderate – it's a constant inconvenience to the biographer, and potentially infuriating to the reader. It must have been a source of confusion even for members of the family. It does tell us something about the Thrings, however. The pattern might just reflect an abysmal lack of imagination, but it seems reasonable to infer a sense of the importance of patrimony, the continuation of the male line.

This emphasis on the filial bonds between the fathers and their namesakes dominates the family tree, but there is not much evidence of it among the Thrings in terms of practical relationship, the tricky hands-on stuff of living with, caring for, talking to a son. By choice or misfortune, all three of the Thring fathers spent much less time with their sons than fathers normally do. This was understandable enough in the case of the first of the relevant

Williams, the man who fathered two Francis Williams; his son, the illegitimate second, appeared in circumstances that could hardly have been less convenient for the father, or less propitious for his son.

The first of the Williams (1812–1887) had emigrated to South Australia in 1849, complete with wife and young family. He had been a publican at Wilton in Wiltshire, where he had married his wife Elizabeth in 1835. She was well-educated enough to have done some teaching in schools before they left England, and within a month of their arrival in the colony she announced the opening of a suitably selective school at their new home in Jermingham Street, North Adelaide:

> Mrs Thring proposes, after the 1st January, 1850, to undertake the instruction of a limited number of Daily Pupils, under twelve years of age, in the rudimentary branches of an English education, which would be conducted in concert with that of her own children of about the same age. Terms – One guinea and a half per quarter, Writing and Arithmetic included.[2]

When 'her own children' disembarked with their parents from the *Duke of Wellington* on 8 November 1849, Ann Elizabeth was thirteen, Francis William twelve, John eleven and Emma Sophie nine. The transportation of the family to the colonies at that stage in the children's lives was a root-and-branch operation that must have appeared without motive or justification. Most new colonists left Britain because they didn't have much to leave, and dreamed of wealth and station. But William and Elizabeth were hardly a couple of newlyweds in need of an adventure, and their circumstances in Wilton were much more than comfortable. Forton Farm, the Thring home that William left in July 1849 and would never see again, was a gracious two-storey Georgian residence looking out on extensive lawns; its façade had five windows upstairs and three downstairs, and a short distance from the house were imposing stables and servants' quarters.[3] William would never live in such style again.

Thring family lore has it that the apparently inexplicable decision to emigrate had, as others like it must often have had, a dark secret behind it. The secret is so dark that no-one can quite see what it might have been, but

2 Margaret Blacker, *Things About Thrings: An Anthology of the Thring Family Tree, 1849–1985*, Millicent, S.A., privately published, 1985.

3 An unsigned oil painting of Forton Farm is in the possession of Gwen Davis, great grand-daughter of William and Elizabeth, in her home in Wentworth.

William was a man who generated throughout his life a number of stories about scandalous behaviour with women; the odds very strongly favour an indiscretion in that area. His parents seem to have paid him handsomely to go, and to stay, away; perhaps it was a spectacular lapse, perhaps just the final straw. Legend has it that he was responsible for the pregnancy of his children's nursemaid on the voyage out, but no record of that birth, or indeed of that woman, has survived.

William and Elizabeth had been painted in 1836 by J.C. Milns, 'Principal Painter in ordinary to W.Thring Esq. and family'.[4] The matching portraits confirm their rank and substance. Elizabeth, holding the new-born Anne, is dressed in voluminous grey satin, decorated with delicate lace; her hair falls in carefully fashionable ringlets. She is painted looking directly at the artist, her attractive, intelligent face looking enquiringly, if a bit apprehensively, at him. William is painted in right profile, a prosperous chap in kid waistcoat and dark dress jacket. His expression gives away nothing at all. William is handsome in a running-to-seed way; his wavy brown hair is receding, his face is fleshier than his bones intended it to be, and the striking flush in his cheek is a shade brighter than would be produced by rude good health. This is a portrait of a sybarite. William must have been much relieved that Milns was no Hogarth.

Whatever had happened in its old home far away, the family quickly found its feet in the new one: William made the most of a series of land speculations by investing in a brewery and hotel at Middleton, Francis and John were prepared for a life on the land and Emma to follow her mother into teaching. Ann took an early opportunity to become Mrs Liptrott. The pub was at least as good as a goldmine, and the family seemed securely on course for the dream of status and prosperity that came with a one-way ticket to the new world.

In 1857, there was a most unexpected complication. Perhaps it was not, after all, absolutely a surprise to Elizabeth. Catherine Canfil, an Irish woman who had arrived on board the *Admiral Boxer* in March, appeared suddenly at the edges of respectable William's life. She was thirtyish, an illiterate woman with no skills and no connections, looking for a chance of something better than she had left at home. William's pub was as likely a place as any to find it.

In July of the following year, Catherine registered the birth of a son:

4 These portraits, too, are privately held by Gwen Davis. Milns' signed proclamation of his status is written on the back of both canvasses.

Birth in the District of Adelaide
1 July 1858
Francis William TRING
Father: William TRING
Mother: Catherine CANFIL

There were no Trings at all recorded as living in Adelaide that year. There was a family of Thrings, however, the ones at the Middleton pub, and it is very likely that Catherine knew her lover's name as Thring but pronounced it, with her Irish accent, without sounding the 'Th'. And spelling was the least of Catherine's worries. The father's address was not given either, though the mother's, at the Destitute Asylum, did appear. Catherine's circumstances had probably always been fairly grim, but as a pregnant woman with no husband and then as an unmarried mother with an infant the colony would have had nothing better to offer her.

It was strange, though, even mischievous, to call the child by a name that was, leaving aside the mispronunciation, identical to that of William's eldest son. If William proposed or approved the naming of this unexpected addition to his offspring, it was a perverse touch of sentiment; the missing 'h' in Tring offered him little security, and it would surely be hard to pass off as a bizarre coincidence, even though William's legitimate first son Francis William was now twenty-one, and almost a generation away. Perhaps Catherine, by giving the baby William's family name and symbolically supplanting his child with hers, was making a bid for a more enduring kind of connection. The thought that there was enough in a surname to bring an aging roué to moral responsibility was touchingly naïve. The thought that William might choose a girl from the poorhouse over all that he and Elizabeth had built in the colony was a desperate delusion.

Two weeks after Catherine registered the birth of little Francis William, she did another very curious thing. She registered the baby's arrival again, this time under her own surname, thus confirming his illegitimacy to posterity, though still acknowledging William's part in the affair:

Birth in the District of Adelaide
18 July 1858
Francis William Canfil
Male
Father: William TRING, Labourer
Mother: Catherine CANFIL

Residence of Parents: of Mother, Destitute Asylum
Registered 29 July 1858

What kind of pressures and motives led Catherine to do this? The recognition that the child must bear the name of Canfil after all suggests that something or someone had persuaded her that he was to be entirely his mother's responsibility. The father's address was still omitted, his occupation disguised, and there is an implication that the claim on him has been withdrawn. She gave the baby a new birth-date, and might even have seen it as a new beginning.

Little Francis William from the Destitute Asylum had been dealt a poor hand, though not as disastrous as the one dealt to his mother. The baby Francis had one valuable card, his father's name, and because of it, in time, he recovered surprisingly well. At some point, probably fairly early given Catherine's dire circumstances, his father chose to take responsibility for him. He was always known thereafter as William, not Francis, and as Thring, not Canfil or Tring. That way, there could be no confusion with legitimate Francis.

In the process, though, there was an affirmation of the connection between father and son, however scandalous its origins. William had his father's name, and the way in which their lives were subsequently intertwined suggests at least an intermittent bond between them.

When William and Elizabeth, apparently inexplicably, sold the pub in 1858 and left the comforts of Middleton to travel up the Murray River to Wentworth, on the other side of the New South Wales border, they left the married Anne and their unmarried sons Francis and John behind. It would have seemed to their neighbours an odd decision to take when the family was doing so well, but it was a smart move for an embarrassingly reconstituted family making a fresh start. A husband who wanted to avoid scandal, and to get away from a woman with whom he had made a serious mistake, could find relocation in another state a quite attractive option. Whatever Elizabeth's feelings about the matter, she acquiesced in the change of scene. The younger of their daughters, eighteen-year-old Emma, went with William and Elizabeth to Wentworth. And so, then or soon after, did the little boy now known as William Thring, William Thring's illegitimate son.

What the three oldest of William and Elizabeth's children thought of it is a mystery. But they showed no inclination to join their parents at Wentworth. All three would live out their lives in South Australia: Francis became a famous explorer as well as a reputable stock agent, married in

1868, and produced over the next two decades thirteen children, including the inevitable William Francis, his second son, in 1873; John became a prosperous farmer at Tumby Bay, and showed a maverick streak by naming his first two sons Francis John and Frederick William.

Catherine Canfil, like a number of the women who were crucial in shaping the story of the Thrings, disappears from it as soon as she has played her part. There is no record of anyone of that name after 1858, in South Australia or in any of the other colonies. But there is an appearance in the South Australian archives of a woman declared destitute at Kapunda in 1884 who has too much in common with Catherine Canfil for coincidence:

> CANFELL, Bridget
> Age 59
> Ship: Admiral Boxer
> How long in Colony: Aust. 27 years, 1857 SA
> Nationality: I [Irish]
> Now living at Kapunda
> Occupation: Domestic duties
> No relations in colony
> Totally blind. This woman has been in receipt of out door relief since August 1875 at Kapunda.

It is a reasonable supposition that, though her name had changed, most other things in Catherine's life hadn't changed at all. The similarity of the surnames and the fact that Bridget Canfell came out from Ireland in the same year on the same boat are reasonably persuasive; her history fits the prognosis that was depressingly predictable when Catherine had her baby in 1858. She had 'no relations in the colony'. If Bridget Canfell was Catherine Canfil, it is extremely doubtful that she knew the whereabouts of her only son, by 1884 a married man in Wentworth with a little boy of his own named Francis William. There are not many signs of relations of any kind in Catherine's uphill battle of a life, apart from that fleeting connection with William that had, for a little while, left her with a child.

And so young William Thring, once Francis Canfil, grew up in Wentworth, where his father turned his hand to a spot of stamp-selling here, a bit of maltstering there, and – most improbably – the serious business of educating the youth of Wentworth, with his wife Elizabeth who ran the school. Nothing is known about how all this was managed. Who cared for whom, who was indulged, resented or forgiven – those of us who are left to look at the sketchy and deceptive public records are wonderfully free to imagine, on the basis of what we might have done had we been in that excruciating position ourselves.

In Wentworth, Elizabeth again set up a small private boarding school, and was also active in establishing the local National School opposite the Thring house in Darling Street, backing on to the Darling River, in 1860; she became its principal, assisted by her daughter Emma, in the middle of the following year, and closed the school she had been running at home. For a while, the arrangement worked quite well. A local newspaper reported positively on the mild festivities that followed the visit of the District Inspector, Mr Ross (and his four-hour examination of the students), though in a way that suggested that it would not, and should not, last:

> In the evening the children were entertained at tea, provided for them by the kindness of Mrs and Miss Thring. It is a matter of great regret that these ladies, who have so faithfully discharged their duties as teachers of this school, should have found it necessary to intimate their intention of resigning their charge, in consequence of ill-health ... What is required in a locality such as this is a male teacher to instruct the boys in the usual branches of an English education, and a lady to impart to the girls a knowledge of those matters in which they are more peculiarly interested.[5]

At the end of 1862, Elizabeth gave up the position. Though she cited her own ill health as the reason, Emma's approaching marriage to John Davie, a local draper, and the report of the new District Inspector Mr McCann that the school's building was 'unsuitable', its curriculum 'very elementary and inappropriate', and its students' proficiency 'very small', may have played a part in her decision.[6]

What William was doing through these years is uncertain, but it was much less conspicuous than the glory days at Middleton. It seems likely that, most of the time, he wasn't doing very much at all. But he did acquire real estate. There was prime land along the river in Wentworth, and William bought an entire block on Darling Street, opposite the National School, between Helena Street and Arthur Street. Some of the properties were commercial, but William owed two quite large houses – a four-room cottage

5 *Observer*, 17 July 1861.
6 Blacker, *Things about Thrings*, p.20.

at number four with an eight-room boarding house (which became the school) attached, and a three-room cottage next door.

Where William's bastard son was living through most of this period is not much clearer. Thring family tradition has it that the boy had lived in the little cottage next to his father's house from the time they arrived in Wentworth. Certainly no renters are recorded for the neighbouring cottage until 1885, the year of Elizabeth's death; in that year William Thring's tenant was his son, 'F.W. Thring', at an undisclosed rental. Young Francis had lived since his marriage to Angelina and the birth of his son in 1882 in a slab cottage owned by Richard Perring, a ten minute amble from his father's house. Three years later, the story goes, he came back to the cottage in which he had grown up. There is no evidence that it was; but the lack of any other recorded occupier for such a pleasant and central property until then encourages a hypothesis that Francis William may well have been accommodated there through his childhood, very near but not with his father.

One family myth gives implicit support to this notion, though it is predicated on a spectacularly public bigamy that would surely have been too outrageous for even Wentworth and Elizabeth to countenance; Gwen Davis recalls hearing her aunt Florence, Emma Davie's grand-daughter, talk about 'how embarrassing it must have been for poor Grandma, having to live with another Mrs Thring in Wentworth'.[7] But 'another Mrs Thring' is not recorded anywhere in the records of the town. It certainly wasn't poor, desperate Catherine Canfil from the Destitute Asylum; probably it was an anonymous woman of sufficiently good repute who was employed to look after William's inconvenient legacy from Middleton, and who was cast by the locals in the much more interesting role of the boy's mother.

In 1871, Elizabeth returned to the head teaching position at the local school, but this time it was held jointly by 'Mr and Mrs Thring'. William the publican had found an unlikely second string to his bow. The School Board had had a good deal of trouble filling the position, and the Thrings were something of a last resort:

> Their qualifications except in the point of respectability are not of high order. Mr and Mrs Thring are old but active people without a family at home. Their character is irreproachable.[8]

---

7 Gwen Davis, interview with the author, 3 July 2007.

8 Blacker, *Things about Thrings*, p.20.

The Thrings might fairly have objected to the reference to their age, but it would have been reassuring to have such a strong testimony to their character; especially since the presence of the twelve-year-old boy they had so generously, if conditionally, adopted, but who didn't count as legitimately part of their 'family at home', had so compromised their respectability in their previous home over the South Australian border.

Elizabeth's return to the National School was probably a mixture of altruism and a need to give William something to do. It could hardly have been seen as a brilliant career move. The school had closed in early 1871, following the disastrous tenure of Mr Gordon; despite his panicky telegram in September 1870 that the disappearance of his students was due entirely to natural causes ('TOWN FLOODED STOP NO ATTENDANCE AT SCHOOL IN CONSEQUENCE STOP MAY BE SO FOR SOME WEEKS STOP'), the Board discharged him for the 'very unsatisfactory way in which Mr Gordon has conducted the school'.[9]

The Wentworth school was a challenging posting, and would remain one. Its troubled history in later years gives a sense of the primitive conditions that confronted Elizabeth Thring in her two stints at the school-house across the road. In 1879 the teacher, Carl Meyer, noting that 'the thermometer while I write is at 114 degrees', requested a new water tank, since the existing underground one had cracked and held no water at all. The inspector that year had already reported that 'the river water which is often muddy and very poor to drink, is all the schoolmaster and scholars have to drink. It is poisoned by the woolwashings up above during the hottest part of the year'.[10] Meyer's request, in the great tradition of government bureaucracies, was neither approved nor denied. The tank, of course, continued leaking.

As late as 1883, plumbing in the schoolhouse remained a critical issue. The principal, Mr Stokes, was presumptuous enough to ask that a bath should be installed; the Board found the advice of its regional inspector much more persuasive:

> Mr Stokes' residence stands on the brink of the Darling, into which he may plunge daily without going 20 yards from his door.[11]

---

9 David J. Tulloch, *History of Wentworth: Sunraysia's Oldest Town*, Red Cliffs, Sunnyland Press, 1984, p.62.

10 ibid, p.63.

11 ibid, p.62.

Mr Stokes' request was, accordingly, declined. The Wentworth school, with all of its perceived advantages and actual horrors, was never a priority with the bureaucrats in Sydney.

The Thrings, though, had their own bathroom just over the road, and access to water that was fit to drink. The new joint principals re-opened the school in August 1871. They lasted only four months, however, before the Board found a better qualified incumbent, and Elizabeth re-established the boarding school at home. The Thrings' replacement, Mr Alcock, turned up for the first day of classes on January 17, but found that, 'owing to the inclemency of the weather there was no attendance'.[12] The Thrings had evidently been very busy enticing pupils to their own establishment over the summer.

Elizabeth seems to have handled the task of running the private school on the other side of Darling Street alone. Emma's husband, John Davie, died suddenly in that year, leaving her with four small children, so she was unlikely to have had much time to help her mother with other people's offspring. And there seems, unsurprisingly, to have been little call for prolonging William's teaching career.

Emma's presence in Wentworth, and her need for support, was clearly a strong determinant in her parents' decisions as to where to live and what to do. The young widow's difficult circumstances were worsened when two of her children, eleven-year-old Elizabeth and seven-year-old James, died in 1876 and 1877. When Elizabeth, her mother, died at Wentworth in 1885, Emma was administrator and sole beneficiary of her small estate. Two years later, when William died there at seventy-five, Emma was the only one of the Thring children to be named in the will; there was no reference to Anne, Francis or John, all now settled comfortably into middle-age in another state, and none to Francis William, formerly Canfil, the illegitimate son on the edge of the family.

William, who unlike the others was there in Wentworth and had recently acquired some dependants of his own, could certainly have done with a share of the three hundred pounds that his father left behind. Perhaps, though, he had learned to be thankful for small mercies, and not to expect to be treated as a fully fledged child of the family like the others.

William and Elizabeth Thring died as distinguished citizens of Wentworth. An article by a local historian on its cemetery gives them pride of place:

> Inside the gate is noticed a stone to the memory of Elizabeth, beloved wife of William Thring, born March 28, 1812; also W.Thring, born

12 ibid, p.61.

> August 16, 1812. These were a couple of the earliest colonists, and, as it should be, buried side by side.[13]

Not everyone finds the symbolism so apt. Gwen Davis, William's great grand-daughter, is particularly unconvinced by his epitaph – 'In certain hope of a joyful resurrection'; her judgement is that the confidence of 'Old Bill', 'after all he'd done', may well have been seriously misplaced.[14]

The next piece of evidence is a marriage certificate.

> Marriage Certificate, New South Wales, 1882/6725
> 15 February 1882 at St Francis Xavier Church, Wentworth
> William Frank THRING, 23 years, bachelor, sawyer, usual place of residence Wentworth
> Angelina McDONALD, 18 years, spinster, domestic servant, usual place of residence Wentworth
> in Rites of the Catholic Church
> Witnesses: Patrick J. KELLY & Agnes CAVANAGH

The document is unusually informative. Francis William, now William Frank, had completed his apprenticeship. He had a trade, and a place in the Wentworth community. Although his family was solidly Anglican, his marriage to Angelina was a Catholic ceremony; perhaps he cared about her so deeply that it didn't matter, or possibly religion didn't matter much to William anyway. The McDonalds were a poor family from the outback town of Hay, and Angelina had a swarm of siblings. As the oldest girl, she had been sent 'into service' at Wentworth, about a hundred miles from home, in 1881. It is tempting, of course, to imagine that she might have been engaged by the Thrings, the respectable family that ran the local school. Sometimes things actually do work out neatly, after all.

Like most of the public records that mark milestones in the story of the Thrings, this one is also less than honest. Angelina was not eighteen when she married William Thring, but fifteen; she had just turned sixteen when later in the year she had their child, but again she chose to be a little older:

> Birth Certificate, New South Wales, 1882/28827
> 2 December 1882 at Wentworth

13 W.B.O. in the *Murray Pioneer*, 14 November 1924.
14 Gwen Davis, interview with the author, 3 July 2007.

William Frank, male
Father: William Francis THRING, labourer, aged 24, born South Australia
Mother: Angelina formerly MCDONALD, aged 18 years, born Wagga Wagga
Married: 1882 at Wentworth. No previous issue
Informant: William Francis THRING, father, Wentworth
Witness (to birth) Mrs BUTCHER

This William Frank was the older of the two Francis Williams that are the subject of this book. The marriage was legal, and the birth occurred respectably enough nine-and-a-half months after the wedding. But William and/or Angelina obviously felt a touch of embarrassment about her age; it was decidedly at the lower end of the scale that the law and her church decreed acceptable. The young mother was far enough from Hay to adjust the facts without much risk of contradiction.

William and Angelina seem to have stayed in Wentworth for at least five more years, until the death of his father William in 1887. Then they, and their son William Frank, known henceforth as Francis William but less formally as Frank, slip from view. People do that quite often in the early part of this story. It's partly a matter of inadequate public documents and perishable private ones, but it is also indicative of a time in Australia when it was quite common, as well as relatively easy, to bury the past and invent a future. What Geoffrey Blainey called 'the tyranny of distance' was certainly, throughout the nineteenth century and for much of the twentieth, a mighty obstacle to those who wanted to connect and communicate, but at the same time it was a blessing to those who would prefer not to. A movement interstate was a new chapter, perhaps a new identity, even a brand-new history.

Young Frank certainly moved. That might be him, so some people say, glimpsed fleetingly at fifteen on the west coast of Tasmania, a jack-of-all-trades with a travelling carnival who quickly learned how to run a reel of film and so is improbably credited with 'starting Biograph pictures in Tasmania'.[15] There he is again at nineteen, now inexplicably a skilled tradesman, making boots in Hindmarsh, South Australia, in 1902, and then marrying at the age of twenty-two a woman seven years his senior. That looks like him there, too,

15 J.P.Holroyd, entry on 'THRING, Francis William', *Australian Dictionary of Biography* Volume 12: 1891–1939, Smy-Z. Melbourne University Press, 1990, p.221–2.

back over the border in New South Wales in 1907. And that is unmistakably him in 1909 showing films in dance halls and Masonic lodges in Tasmania. Frank in this period is the quintessential rolling stone: there is no sign of his father or mother in any of those places, and, apart from his marriage to Grace Wight, hardly any moss.

His father William moved, too, but in more mysterious ways. There are no public records of him anywhere until he pops up at the altar, metaphorically at least, for a second time, in South Australia. Again, the certificate leaves open more questions than it answers:

> Marriage in the District of Adelaide, book 212, page 565
> Francis William Thring, 43, Widower, maltster, usual residence Adelaide. Father: Francis William Thring
> Leonora Comley, 44, Widow, usual residence Norwood.
> Father: James Saville
> Office of the registrar-General, Victoria Square, Adelaide
> 20 August 1902

Having himself reverted to Francis William for the occasion, William also re-christened his father. The slippage was so habitual among the Thrings that it may have no significance at all. But there may still have been some residual subterfuge about his parentage, though William Francis his father had been dead for fifteen years and was perhaps past the need for protection. The bridegroom also understated his age by a year, which was another fine family tradition, if ungallant in the circumstances.

The Comely Widow brought to her second marriage four children from her first, ranging in age from twenty-five to thirteen. Probably only the youngest, Mary, lived with the newlyweds at Leonora's previous marital home at Norwood, where William appears in directories as a maltster in 1904, the year of his son's marriage to Grace at Gawler. After 1904, though, William slips out of all the records again, until his death in 1920, when he makes a spectacular and very significant return. He and Leonora, though living in a state that was at the time probably the most advanced democracy in the world, never bothered to register as voters, wherever it was that they went.

Young Frank his son, nineteen at the time of his father's remarriage, was not far away from him for some of this period. He was in Gawler between 1902 and 1905, and in Hindmarsh in 1906 and 1907, so there was at least an opportunity for contact with William. But Frank had established his independence very early, and his mobility had ensured that his life and his father's would proceed along separate, and quite different, lines.

The most conspicuous of the unanswered questions left by the 1902 marriage of William and Leonora, however, is the fate of Angelina. Leonora described herself as a widow, and the records confirm that her first husband Charles had died at Glenelg eleven years earlier. William declared himself as Francis William, widower, and there is no evidence to dispute the claim. But there is no evidence, either, of Angelina's death: no record of her living, come to that, after the document which disguises the fact that she had given birth to a child while still virtually a child herself.

And when in 1921 her son married, for the second time, he consigned his mother to irrelevance in a startling way by naming her on the certificate not as 'Angelina McDonald' but as 'Laura McKenzie'. The National Archive in Australia still faithfully records as Frank's mother's name the fictitious one that he came up with in that moment of deception or whimsy. Olive, his second wife, duly recorded it so when she supplied the information for Frank's death certificate; it was not the sort of thing a husband would lie about, after all.

What, then, could Frank have been thinking? Did he really not remember his mother's name, or was he being strategically misleading? At least he recalled or retained a vaguely Scots connection. But it seems poor justice to Angelina, thrust so quickly into adulthood and destined for such a short and unacknowledged life.

Angelina joins Catherine Canfil, dimly lit at the edge of the stage on which the male Thrings strut their stuff. It is not a story that offers rich roles for its women, and there are others in the wings whose parts in the plot further confirm the fact. It is a story dominated, in fact, by the quests of sons to find their fathers, every one of them answering to Francis or William or usually both, and every one of them frustrated in one way or another in their efforts to match or repudiate a man they never really knew. William Thring born in 1858 had little choice about his relationship with his father; he might even have counted himself lucky to have gathered a few crumbs by sitting not too far from the patriarchal table. Frank Thring born in 1926 was ten when his father died; he may never have forgiven Frank senior for letting him down like that, but neither could he do anything about it. Frank Thring born 1882 had the best chance of all of them to know his father, but spent quite a lot of his life choosing not to do so.

On the marriage certificate of the mysterious Mr Thring in 1921, alongside the name of his newly invented mother Laura, he entered his father's name and occupation: 'Francis William Thring, Gentleman'. William, once Francis Canfil/Tring from the Destitute Asylum, would have richly appreciated the irony, even if it came at the cost of being in a way disowned.

Touchingly, though, Frank made some last-minute reparations for his lack of connection with his father, most of them after William had died. Part of that story is intimated in the certificate that records William's death:

> Death Certificate, District of Melbourne East, 1920/2769
> 27 March 1920, Swanston Street, Melbourne, Gipps ward,
> City of Melbourne, County of Bourke.
> Francis William Thring
> Occupation: Storekeeper
> Usual Residence: Hindmarsh, SA
> Male, 61 years
> Cause: Old tubercular peritonitis; adhesions, asthenia; heart failure, 5 months
> Dr J Croon, 27 March 1920.
> Father: John Thring, occupation unknown
> Mother: unknown
> Born: Adelaide, SA, 5/12 years in Victoria
> Married: Wentworth, NSW at age 24 to Angelina MacDonald
> Issue: Francis William, 37

Some things were recorded accurately there; William is returned to the sequence of his forenames at birth, and Frank chose, unusually, to name his mother and record his own age and his father's correctly. Angelina was publicly acknowledged for the last time before her reinvention ten months later as Laura McKenzie. The uncertainty about how long William had spent in Victoria (somewhere between five and twelve years) reflects the periods in which father and son had lost touch, and the lack of some compensating conversations that might have filled the gaps. Frank wouldn't have known the identity of his father's mother, either; it is quite possible that William himself had never heard Catherine Canfil's name.

Inventing a new grandfather, John, is a creative touch, though; Frank, having spent his early years in Wentworth, would surely have known his father's true connection with the William Thring who ran the local school with his wife. Perhaps there was still a sense of secrecy in the family about some things.

When Leonora, his second wife, died in 1919, William, a sick man with no-one else to turn to, came to Melbourne to be with his son. Frank put him up in the hotel in Bourke Street that he himself had lived in for much of his time in Melbourne, and when William died in the following year, Frank buried him in a double plot that he had purchased in the Presbyterian section at Burwood Cemetery.

Sixteen years later that curious choice was explained, when the son was buried, in accordance with his wishes, at Burwood, beside the father he had been ashamed of, had run from, and had tried to reinvent. It was a reconciliation of sorts, and a reflection of the importance in Frank's life of a relationship that he spent quite a lot of time treating as an inconvenience. He would have felt keenly the recurrence of that pattern in the life of his son.

Chapter Two

THE GREAT DEXTER

Frank Thring's childhood passed without leaving a trace. We know that he was born in Wentworth late in 1882 to William, the young labourer whose first home had been Adelaide's Destitute Asylum, and his sixteen-year-old wife Angelina. We're told that, some time before his fifteenth birthday, Frank was moving around Tasmania as a carnival rouse-about, fetching, carrying, doing clever things with cards, and showing primitive moving pictures on the new-fangled magic lantern equipment that his elders almost certainly knew would be just another passing fad.

The rest is lost. Not a document, not even an anecdote, to build on. It is not possible to know now whether Frank grew up in the town where he was born and where his grandparents had become quite prominent citizens, or how much schooling he received, or whether his childhood was relatively deprived or relatively comfortable. His father William disappears almost completely from the public record until he remarries as a widower in Adelaide in 1902, and Angelina goes missing from it altogether. Frank himself bobs up in Adelaide two years later, registers on the electoral roll for which he is newly eligible, and celebrates his adulthood by marrying Grace Wight. It is as though his boyhood never happened at all.

There are two stories, though, to give those years some shape. Frank told them both, and there's a fair chance that one was mostly true; but which of them can we trust?

The first story, which became the authorised version, has Frank growing up in Wentworth, and then hitting the road at fourteen, working the carnival circuit down the wild west coast of Tasmania as Dexter the conjuror, and somewhere along that journey 'running Biograph pictures' in Tasmania in the late 1890s. Or even, as the *Australian Dictionary of Biography* has it, 'starting' the whole operation.[16] Ina Bertrand, in her monograph on Thring and Efftee Productions, has the young Frank performing Herculean feats for a lad of fifteen:

> He entered the film world … in 1898 as the owner of a touring plant in Tasmania, playing all the roles (billposter, house-manager, operator and orchestra) himself.[17]

Where the facts are few, the sky's the limit.

It's an impressive tale, this one about the lad who shakes off the dust and security of his home town to live on his wits in a place where he has no home. And although it's short on detail, it implies quite a lot about its hero. A boy who is on the road at fourteen, as Frank said he was, has missed out on the advantages, both social and personal, that an education can supply. He has had to learn, very quickly, how to behave like an adult; in emotional as well as practical terms, that has surely involved some disengagement, at least, from his parents. He has come to face the need to do things on his own, and he has started to do them. He is a boy who is no longer a child.

We can assume some other qualities in this particular boy on the road, who, as the Great Dexter, was fooling grown-ups with his sleight of hand, and in the newly invented occupation of projectionist was dispensing another kind of magic. He is a very smart lad, certainly, quick to learn and astute in finding out what it pays to know. He is not much hampered by fear, or deference, or self-doubt either. He can't afford to waste much time in homesickness, even if there was much of a home to miss. If we were to tell him, consolingly, on his way out of Wentworth, that his childhood is over without leaving a trace, he would doubtless have thought it about time. Frank's own son, though pampered and quite possibly loved, would have understood. It was lucky, all things considered, that both Frank Thrings were always big for their age.

---

16 J.P. Holroyd, entry on 'THRING, Francis William', *Australian Dictionary of Biography* Volume 12: 1891–1939, Smy-Z. Melbourne University Press, 1990, p.221–2.

17 Ina Bertrand, *Australian Film Studies 7: Efftee Productions*, Media Centre Papers, Centre for the Study of Educational Communication and Media, La Trobe University, Bundoora, n.d. (1979), p.1. Margaret Blacker, in her privately published family history *Things About Thrings: An Anthology of the Thring Family Tree, 1849–1985*, Millicent, South Australia, 1985, repeats this claim verbatim.

On the face of it, there should have been plenty to keep an ambitious boy in Wentworth in the late 1890s. The town had prospered, certainly, since William and Elizabeth had sold the Thrings' pub in Middleton in the year Frank's father was disreputably born, and made their trek up the river and into the back of beyond. There were lots of signs of civilisation on the march for Frank to see as a little boy: the town's isolation had been relieved in the year of his birth by the establishment of a twice-weekly mail service between Wentworth and Wilcannia; in 1888, its water supply was constructed, and a splendid Customs House was built to mark Wentworth's importance as a border station negotiating the free-trade policies of the colony of Victoria and the strong protective tariffs of New South Wales; in 1887 the Wentworth District Hospital arose, although, in one of those bizarre instances of ad-hocery that mark the tumbling-up of frontier towns, it did so on the east bank of the Darling, rather than on the one where all the people lived:

> Patients and doctors were rowed to and from the town in boats manned by wardsmen. Ringing of a bell on either side of the river would summon the boat.[18]

By 1890, the town had seventeen hotels, and its first tennis-court. There was sufficient civic confidence for Wentworth to nominate itself as the natural capital for the newly federated Australia that was envisioned at a number of congresses and conferences through the next decade. It was (very roughly) halfway between the great competitors for that honour, Melbourne and Sydney, and offered itself as a happy compromise as well as a boom town. In the end, the founding fathers of the commonwealth weren't persuaded. But the fact that the case could be made, barely thirty years after William and Elizabeth had come to live at the river junction where there were three shops and a pub, was a sign of just how much Wentworth had changed, and how respectable it had become.

However, though there was money to be made, in trade or on the wharves, by the second half of the 1890s the development of Wentworth had begun to lose that heady momentum. The expansion of the railways was threatening to subvert Wentworth's privileged location at the confluence of the rivers; the sudden drop in the price of wool hit the town hard, and

18 *100 Years of Wentworth 1859–1959*, centenary souvenir volume collated and written by David J. Tulloch, no publication details, p.11.

frustrations came to a head in 1894 when striking shearers came to town and burned the steamer *Rodney*. The rude awakening from its dreams of becoming Australia's capital city at the same time came to Wentworth as 'a bitter blow'[19]. The town may have started to feel too small for a young man with big plans; even if the financial prospects had still been attractive, a town so anxious to be seen as worthy wasn't necessarily the right place for a lad who was slick with a deck of cards. Moreover, his grandmother had died there in 1885, his grandfather William in 1887; the story as he told it had his father William as an itinerant labourer, and did not include Angelina at all. It doesn't sound as though the young Frank had too many emotional ties to the town of his birth.

There are good reasons to be sceptical about this version of the story, though, especially given the absence of any evidence to confirm it. The notion of an adolescent 'starting' or 'running' Biograph Pictures anywhere requires a generous suspension of disbelief, and the claim that he did it in one of the wildest and most isolated parts of the country calls for a lot more. Moreover, the west coast of Tasmania is far from the most obvious place for young Frank Thring from Wentworth to go to seek his fortune; Adelaide, just down the river, and Melbourne, the burgeoning city that lay due south, en route to Tasmania, offered rich pickings of a much more accessible kind. And the fact that when Frank next enters the public record in 1904 his occupation is listed as 'bootmaker' surely required that a couple of his teenage years had been spent settled somewhere while he completed an apprenticeship.

Still, it could all have been true. Stranger things have happened in frontier communities, and clever boys might have been, then as now, rather better at mastering new technologies than their elders. While the west coast of Tasmania was a long way from Wentworth and most other civilised places, it was a great place for someone who didn't want to be found to lose himself, and with the discoveries of rich deposits of silver and gold through the 1890s it offered all the seductions of an El Dorado. Besides, apprenticeships didn't necessarily pose much of a problem for a young man as accomplished in the arts of deception as Frank. Papers could be organised, if they were really needed, with a bit of ingenuity, and Frank was never one to confuse certification with fact.

The second implied account of his first twenty years has at least the supporting evidence of an official certificate – though this, on the precedents

19 ibid, p.12.

created by all the others that document the lives of the Thrings, may be a good reason to take no notice of it. It is the last public record relating to this Frank:

> Death in District of Melbourne
> 1 July 1936 "St Andrew's" Presbyterian Hospital, Grey Street, East Melbourne, City of Melbourne, County of Bourke
> Usual Residence: "Rylands" Toorak Road, Toorak, City of Prahran
> Francis William THRING, company director, male, aged 53 years
> Carcinoma of the oesophagus; haemorrhage; myocardial failure
> Indefinite period of last illness
> Seen by Dr A M HILL on 1 July 1936
> Father: Francis William THRING, no occupation
> Mother: Laura THRING, maiden name MCKENZIE
> Informant: H R SLEIGH, Authorised Agent
> Buried: Burwood Cemetery, 2 July 1936
> Undertaker: Gordon Stuart SLEIGH acting for A A SLEIGH Pty Ltd. Certified by H R SLEIGH
> Minister: Charles J W WOOD
> Born: Wentworth, NSW
> 25 years in Victoria; 28 years in South Australia and Tasmania
> Married:
> First at age about 26 year at Gawler SA to Grace Margaret WIGHT, deceased.
> Issue: Viola, 25 years
> Second at age 38 years at South Yarra to Olive KREITMAYOR
> Issue: Francis William, 10 years

There is the usual collection of inaccuracies. Poor Angelina McDonald appears once again as Laura McKenzie. Frank's father William Francis has become again the Francis William that he was christened, and, after passing through a range of public occupations in previous certificates from 'labourer' to 'sawyer' to 'maltster' to 'gentleman', is now recorded as having had 'no occupation' at all. Frank's age at his marriage to Grace is recorded as 'about 26' instead of twenty-two, and Grace is awarded a second name, Margaret, that she never had.

It's a reasonable presumption that the source of the details given to the informant, one of the Sleigh undertakers, was Frank's widow Olive. Although her own maiden name is mis-spelt, the details relating to the twenty-five years in which she has known Frank (the same twenty-five that he is recorded as spending in Victoria) are all accurate. She is vague about his age at first marriage, possibly because she is working back to some notionally plausible date before Lola's birth in 1911, and bestows 'Margaret' on Grace, perhaps from her knowledge of the name of Grace's mother, perhaps partly by some associative extension of her own more exotic Marguerite.

But what is material to the unravelling of the story of Frank's youth is the information about the years before the twenty-five spent in Victoria: '28 years in South Australia and Tasmania' – which is to say, the rest of the fifty-three years of his life. Since Frank spent no time in either state, apart from a couple of fleeting visits to Gawler, after he arrived in Melbourne in 1911, this suggests that the infant Frank (presumably with William and Angelina) must have headed down the Murray into South Australia soon after his birth. That was the version that Frank had given her, obviously; it led her, as informant in the registration of their son Frank's birth in 1926, to give her husband's birth-place wrongly as Adelaide, though this was not a mistake that she repeated on the death certificate a decade later. Wentworth, on this account, is a paragraph, not a chapter, in his story.

There is no further evidence either way; if William (and, for some of the time, Angelina) lived in South Australia through this period, they were not listed in any of the records. Though William was earning his living as a maltster by the time he married Leonora in 1902 (a trade he would obviously have picked up from his own father William, the former publican of Middleton), there is no sign of his doing it there or anywhere else before that year.

So instead of the runaway solitary who left New South Wales for Tasmania at about fourteen and then resurfaced inexplicably in South Australia at twenty-one, it's possible that we are looking at a boy whose youth was much less dramatic. This young Frank grows up in outer suburban Adelaide, dutifully studying his indentures as a bootmaker until he marries a girl who worked as a dress-maker just a couple of streets away. His time in Tasmania, on this reading, is confined to the period that he spent there verifiably from 1909 with his wife Grace; that young man in his late twenties who acted as business manager for The World's Pictures in Zeehan is a more plausible approximation to the pioneer 'running Biograph Pictures in Tasmania' than the remarkably precocious adolescent who is the hero of Frank's customary version of the narrative.

There's a third possibility, too, which conflates the two stories. It restores the intrepid teenager in Tasmania, but lets him take his journey there in 1897 rather more conveniently from Adelaide. It takes him back there, perhaps on a boat laden with rich materials for the new metal-processing works at Port Kembla, to rejoin his family at some point early in the new century – possibly, we might speculate, because of the illness and/or death of his mother Angelina, who otherwise steps out of the recorded history immediately after giving him birth. It has him pulling up roots again and heading back to Tasmania with his bride, which is perhaps less characteristic of the young man who came home to his trade than the compulsive wanderer who spent his childhood in Wentworth. But it's plausible enough. It still allows a total of '28 years in South Australia and Tasmania', even if it is the product of a different sum. It's a good enough story to have told Olive. And it might even be true.

Frank, though, preferred to tell the Wentworth version. And whichever of the stories was true, the Wentworth one matters because it was the one that he wanted people to believe. The mythology of the self-made man gains enormously from a seriously deprived childhood, but Frank's self-conception as a successful one-man band added vast distances and implied emotional neglect to evident economic disadvantage. A man had to be heroic to undertake a journey like that.

In the process of making and living that myth, Frank effectively wrote William and Angelina out of his story, whatever role in it they had actually played. He dismissed them even more comprehensively, if less luridly, than his son would do decades later in relation to Frank himself and Olive.

By one route or another, Frank arrived on Boxing Day 1904 at the altar of St Andrew's Presbyterian Church in Gawler, a bustling little town in the Barossa Valley, about twenty-five miles from Adelaide. It was a few weeks after his twenty-second birthday, but perhaps out of some consideration for the fact that his bride was a little older than he, or perhaps to add a little more maturity to his claims as a suitor, he declared himself on Boxing Day 1904 as twenty-seven.

> Marriage in the District of Barossa, book 221, page 1271
> 26 December 1904
> Francis William Thring, 27, bachelor, bootmaker, Lyndoch Road, Gawler

Father: William Francis Thring
Grace Wight, 29, Spinster, dressmaker, Edith Street, Gawler
Father: William Wight
St Andrew's Presbyterian Church, Gawler

Grace lived a few hundred yards from Frank's bootmaker's shop, just around the corner in Edith Street, where she ran a little dressmaking and millinery business from her parents' home. At twenty-nine, she must have felt in some danger of confirmed spinsterhood when Frank Thring loomed into her life.

Grace was the youngest of five children, and the only one still at Edith Street; her three brothers and her sister were all married, with families of their own. Frank appeared in her town in 1902, and for a youth of nineteen made quite a splash. He was an outsider, a bit of a rolling stone with a big presence and big aspirations, and he could do conjuring tricks. Grace, living in the cottage where she had always lived and making hats and frocks for the good matrons of Gawler, would have found him a most unusual man.

Gawler's new cobbler's assistant first made his mark in August that year as a debater, appearing as the closing speaker for the St Andrews Literary Society against Tarlee in its unsuccessful attempt to prove that 'the sword has greater influence than the pen'.[20] That was in the week that his father, almost certainly without Frank's knowledge, married his second wife, Leonora Comley, in the Registrar-General's office in Adelaide. But it was with the local theatre group that Frank could really strut his stuff, and in March of the following year, a few months after his twentieth birthday, 'F. Thring' was not only a prominent member of the cast in the Gawler Theatrical Club's production of *Outcasts of London*, but was also credited as its Business Manager. The leading lady in that show was Miss G. Wight, who seems to have been Gawler's favourite ingénue: she had starred in the company's two seasons of *London by Night* in 1901 and 1902. Somebody clearly thought Grace had a flair for dialect; she and 'F. Thring' were featured in the Club's season of *The Lancashire Lass* in September 1903.

By the middle of the following year, when the highlight of the anniversary concert of the St Andrews Presbyterian Church (apart from 'a dance by a number of children') was 'the humorous finale by Miss Wight and Mr Thring', it seems clear that Grace and Frank were, in one sense or another,

20 *Advertiser*, 27 August 1902, p.7.

an item.[21] Frank supplied a conjuring performance for that occasion, and was still playing his tricks in 1905, the first year of his marriage, when he 'gave an exhibition of juggling and ventriloquism' as part of the Theatrical Club's tour to Tarlee.[22] But Grace evidently decided to make her walk down the aisle the last of her public performances in Gawler.

They settled into the Wights' family home together, sharing the bedroom that she had slept in as a child, while they looked for a place of their own. When they found one late in 1905, it was conveniently close, just around the corner in Murray Road. For some husbands, it might have been all a little too cosy. It almost certainly was for Frank, whose conception of himself and his future had even less room for extended happy families than for the predictabilities of a life devoted to other people's shoes.

Within a few days of the move to their own place in November 1905, the Thrings were the victims of a robbery. A tin box containing nearly twenty-one pounds was stolen from their new home.[23] It must have felt like a very unpropitious start to fully independent life together – and to Frank's career as a suburban businessman, since he had in the same week become manager of the shop in Lyndoch Street in which he had worked for three years, and the tin box probably contained the week's takings.

Two weeks later, Gawler's local newspaper, the *Bunyip*, carried an advertisement that proclaimed that, in his resilience and cheek as much as in the quality of his workmanship, F.W. Thring was no ordinary bootmaker:

> Our boots are neat
> They fit the feet,
> And wear they will forever.
> For hall and street,
> They can't be beat.
> They're made of solid leather.
>
> No paper used,
> No faith abused
> With F.B.C. the brand,
> Our standards high,
> We're set to fly
> And by it we will stand.

21 *Advertiser*, 1 June 1904, p.7.
22 *Advertiser*, 14 October 1905, p.12.
23 *Advertiser*, 15 November 1905, p.9.

So come along
And join the throng
That hurries to our store.
Just come and see
And then you'll be
Our friend for evermore.

The F.B.C.
The big store,
Murray Street.

F.W. Thring – Manager.[24]

Frank Thring the poet had probably gone about as far as he could go. But Frank Thring, showman, entrepreneur, self-promoter, was only just beginning.

In the following year, Frank and Grace moved to Hindmarsh, an inner suburb of Adelaide, where they lived behind another bootmaker's shop that Frank managed in Milner Street. Perhaps the campaign in the *Bunyip* was not as successful as they'd hoped; perhaps even 'the big store' in the Wights' home town was a little too small for comfort.

They stayed in Hindmarsh for a year, or perhaps two; by 1907, though, they were no longer on the electoral roll for Hindmarsh, or indeed anywhere else in the state. When Frank and Grace next appear together on the public record in August 1909, it is in a very different context, and a long way from home. Suddenly, Frank was in Zeehan, a frontier mining town on the west coast of Tasmania, the kind of place in which legend had it he had worked for Biograph a decade before. This time, though, we know he was there.

What happened between the bootmaker's shop in Hindmarsh and the wild west of Tasmania is unknown. The fact that Frank and Grace were no longer registered to vote in South Australia is not conclusive evidence that they were somewhere else, since they don't appear on the record for any other state in 1907/8 either; when certificates of births, marriages and deaths could still be so haphazard and negotiable, electoral rolls are approximate at best. The likeliest scenario is that they were on the road, in South Australia, northern Victoria and western New South Wales; somehow or other,

24 Gawler '*Bunyip*', 1 December 1905. Quoted in Margaret Blacker, *Things About Thrings*, p.109.

anyway, Frank not only gathered the credentials to be appointed business manager for World's Pictures in Tasmania in 1909, but a claim to renown as a conjuror and elocutionist.

By the time he reached Zeehan, Frank had a credible enough reputation (or perhaps sufficient barefaced cheek) in the role of 'The Great Dexter' or 'Dexter the Mystic' to persuade the *Zeehan and Dundas Herald* that he had 'gained many encomiums as a conjurer, both in South Australia and Victoria',[25] and, moreover, that:

> Mr F.W. Thring, it has to be said, is an adept at this art. Mr Thring has appeared in many of the leading variety theatres in Victoria and South Australia, where he is well-known under his professional nom-de-plume of "Dexter the Mystic."[26]

The same paper had earlier carried a testament to Frank's status as an actor, as it eagerly anticipated his monologue from *Caged*:

> Mr Thring has already given residents of Zeehan a taste of his quality as an elocutionist, and as the piece he will recite on Sunday is that with which he has won competitions on the mainland, and in Launceston, a very enjoyable item may be anticipated.[27]

It might have been true, or it could have been a convenient fiction. The mainland was not so far away, but a lot of things struggled to cross Bass Strait. Neither boats nor truth could be assured a smooth passage.

Frank Thring's first recorded appearance in Tasmania is noted in the *Zeehan and Dundas Herald* on 31 July 1909, when the forthcoming season of 'The World's Pictures Co' at the Gaiety Theatre in Zeehan is declared 'THE FINEST EXHIBITION OF MOVING PHOTOGRAPHY SEEN IN TASMANIA'.[28] The source of this grand claim is one 'F. Dexter', the company's Business Manager; Frank apparently flirted with employing for his commercial activities the name he had used for his conjuring act.

The advertisement was a declaration of war. Royal Bio Pictures had for some time enjoyed a monopoly in Zeehan, with their regular Friday and Saturday showings at the Theatre Royal. The Royal Bio fare was a miscellany

25 *Zeehan and Dundas Herald*, 20 August 1909, p.2.
26 *Zeehan and Dundas Herald*, 19 August 1909, p.2.
27 *Zeehan and Dundas Herald*, 14 August 1909, p.2.
28 *Zeehan and Dundas Herald*, 31 July 1909, p.1.

of short dramatic pieces, newsreels and tourist novelties; Herr Holm at the keyboard, and the vocal talents of Zeehan's foremost teacher of singing, Mrs Leo Cronly, added their lustre to the proceedings. The evenings at the Theatre Royal had all the advantages of comfortable familiarity and local connections. It was a tough challenge for any outsider, especially one from the mainland.

Frank Thring's first move was to emphasise the sophistication of the equipment he had brought from the 'big smoke'.

> It is promised that the World's Pictures will be the biggest, brightest and best pictures that have ever been exhibited on the West Coast. The irritating flicker, which has always been a drawback in picture entertainments, will be noticeable only by its absence, all films being shown by the very latest pattern of bioscope, which projects pictures with great brilliance and steadiness.[29]

The day before the season opened on Thursday 5th, Thring raised the bid:

> By a special apparatus attached to the machine, the World's Picture Co. claim to be able to show a larger picture than any before seen in Zeehan. The advantages of this are readily apparent. The details of the picture are more vividly brought out, facial expression being shown with a perfection impossible in a smaller picture.
>
> The entertainment promises to be one of the best of its kind seen here, and as much interest is being manipulated, a full house should result on Thursday evening next.[30]

The implication, of course, was that Royal Bio, without the 'special apparatus', was a backyard operation, doomed to the old-fashioned 'irritating flicker'. Frank was sufficiently confident of the attraction of his product to charge a shilling for admission, and two shillings for the front seats; his rivals at the Theatre Royal charged just sixpence for any seat in the house. He took the program, now featuring the film adaptation of Scott's *The Bride of Lammermoor*, to the Metropole at Queenstown, twenty-one miles away, on the Saturday night, with the same price of admission.

---

29 *Zeehan and Dundas Herald*, 2 August 1909, p.2.

30 *Zeehan and Dundas Herald*, 4 August 1909, p.2.

Although the strategically placed 'news' reports in the following week noted the 'large and appreciative' audiences that had attended the screenings of the new arrival, it was impossible to disguise the fact that the established operators at the Theatre Royal, with their 'full houses', had won the first round.[31] Frank had to come up with something, and he did. His competitors had Herr Holm and Mrs Leo Cronly to supplement the offerings on celluloid; he added the vocalists Master Harold Scott and Mr W. Lovett, a recital of *Caged* performed by the noted elocutionist F.W. Thring, a conjuring act 'Magical Moments' performed by the noted illusionist F.W. Thring, and a comedy sketch, 'An Act of Piracy', performed by the noted comedians F.W. Thring and Mrs Thring. He dropped the price for tickets to the gallery from two shillings to one and six. And he added a Sunday night extravaganza, billed oddly as a 'rational entertainment', that featured all of the above and a number of films for a modest donation: 'It is expected that Patrons of the Gallery will contribute not less than Sixpence'.[32]

The Royal Bio people were threatened. They countered with their own Sunday evening at the Theatre Royal, where 'In addition to usual entertainment a Splendid Lot of Views of the Gordon River will be shown'.[33] Frank raised this modest bid with a new comedy act, 'Only Amateurs', starring those irrepressible Thrings, and then for the following Sunday produced his trump card, Mrs Leo Cronly, now performing exclusively for World's Pictures. His advertisement taunted his opponents with the triumphant 'We Lead – Others Follow'.[34]

The Royal Bio responded next day with the claim 'We Originate – Others Imitate!'[35] But despite the exclamation mark, it lacked conviction. Frank now declared his Sunday concert, proudly if still puzzlingly, a 'GRAND RATIONAL CONCERT – for the People', and clinched the local connection with the proclamation 'Last but not least, the Zeehan Military Band have been secured to play appropriate music in connection with the performance, as well as previous to the performance'.[36] Victory, too, had been secured, for the second round at least. In his first two weeks in Zeehan, Frank had established World's Pictures as the biggest show in

31 *Zeehan and Dundas Herald*, 10 August 1909, p.4.
32 *Zeehan and Dundas Herald*, 14 August 1909, p.1.
33 ibid.
34 *Zeehan and Dundas Herald*, 20 August 1909, p.1.
35 *Zeehan and Dundas Herald*, 21 August 1909, p.2.
36 ibid.

town. The Royal Bio incumbents had lost the battle for the numbers and for Mrs Cronly, and seemed to have conceded on the matter of picture quality, too.

And Grace was with him on the bill, the Great Dexter's right-hand woman, ready in those early days to primp and flatter and cajole, or to vanish altogether, should the script require it. She was prepared to play the straight-woman in the Thring comic duo, as well, just as she had when she and Frank had charmed the congregation in the church concert at Gawler five years before. Certainly, for Grace, if not for Frank, the title 'Only Amateurs' was a perfect choice. Zeehan was a long way from Edith Street. But that, presumably, was part of its attraction.

The west coast of Tasmania had been tamed a little by the time Frank Thring arrived in Zeehan with a wife, a bioscope, a suitcase full of film and little else, but the west was still wild. It was always violent in its weather, with an average rainfall of three metres each year. The locals liked to say that it only rained twice in those parts – once for six months and once for five; they exaggerated a little, but with feeling. And the towns down the west coast were still rough and tough and makeshift in their living conditions and their culture. The mining settlements had mushroomed along the coast, filled with men who wanted to get rich quick; in 1891 the correspondent of the *Australasian* had been appalled by what he found in Zeehan:

> Houses, tents, gunyahs and habitations of every describable and indescribable condition have been run up … the bars are crowded day and night … the insanitary condition of the place even now demands the urgent attention of the government.[37]

By 1894 there were thirty-five hundred miners in the region, and by the turn of the century that number had doubled. Men outnumbered women by more than two to one. As Lloyd Robson observed, it was a savage irony that 'El Dorado appeared in the most inhospitable part of the country'.[38]

If Frank had indeed made the journey there that he claimed to have made a decade before, he was a game man to be going back. But he had, on his own account, survived and even prospered there, and in 1909 there was still

37 *Australasian*, 24 January 1891.
38 Lloyd Robson, *A Short History of Tasmania*, Oxford University Press Australia, 1997, p.61.

serious money to be made for a man who knew how to get it: the carnival circuit was still potentially a goldmine in itself. What is strange, though, given all that he claimed to know, was that he took Grace there.

A number of people would have felt at the time that it was no place to take a lady, especially one who had seen little of the world beyond a millinery in Gawler. The world of the travelling picture show and the carnival could be a sweaty and seedy one, especially in places where respectable women were a novelty and men were desperate. Grace was thirty-four now, an age at which a woman of her generation who had married unusually late might be contemplating having a child, and making a home somewhere. But here she was, in Zeehan and Queenstown and Strahan and Dundas and Tullah of all places, living out of a suitcase and prepared to act like a showgirl.

Perhaps Grace was too timid to challenge Frank's relentless ambition, or fearful of how life might look, especially to him, if it shrank again to the domestic scale that measured ordinary people's lives. Perhaps the reason why she followed him to Zeehan, to virtually the end of the continent and the alphabet, was simply that she loved him.

By the time Grace went with Frank on the Tasmanian mining circuit, things had certainly improved a little. Every town that he took her to had its marks of civilisation: a tennis court, a cricket club, a brass band. When Frank took his travelling picture show to Tullah, the venue was the Academy of Music (although it was better known on most days as the one-room local school, where Joseph Lyons – later to become Premier of Tasmania, and then Prime Minister of Australia – had been Tullah's first school-master, a couple of years before the Thrings descended on the town).

But while some things were safer and more sanitary, others were a constant reminder to Grace that this was the wilderness. Moving between the towns was tough at best, and sometimes terrifying. There was no highway to the mining centres of the south-west. Travel between Zeehan and Tullah, for instance, was dependent on the little steam engine named 'Puppy' which from 1902 was Tullah's only link with the outside world; it cut through dense forest to join the Emu Bay Railway at Fernal Siding, which then pushed along sixty kilometres of mountainous track through eucalypts and native pine to Zeehan.

The journey from Strahan to Queenstown was even more hair-raising. The train from Regatta Point ran on a track overhung with branches, with thick rain forest on one side and the King River, already sluggish and sickly yellow from the effects of mining, on the other; after negotiating the tiny settlements of Lowanna, Teepookana and the evocatively named Dubbil

Barril, it reached Rivadeena Saddle, where a rack-and-pinion system only just enabled it to crawl up the 1:16 gradient. This was real pioneering. Frank and Grace traveled in an open carriage, trying to protect reels of film, projection equipment and themselves from whatever the forest and the climate might have in store for them.

Then there was Queenstown itself, already a surreal moonscape with bare, ravaged hills and rivers and creeks the colour of vomit. The locals played football on a ground without grass, and covered entirely with pyrites. And they drank as though there was no tomorrow. To survive in Queenstown, you needed, in every way, an unnaturally thick skin. For Grace, who had barely seen anything of life outside Gawler, this was surely the landscape of nightmare.

Frank's own feelings in this period are, as at almost every moment of his recorded or unrecorded life, impossible to gauge. But there were good reasons for him to be quite happy. He was doing something that he liked to do, for a start; he seemed to have a genuine talent for sleights of hand and creating illusions. He was learning some important skills, too, as he came to understand more about what films could do, and became more familiar with the mechanical business of showing them. Most of all, Frank was combining his talents in the timeless arts of deception and the new technology of cinema and finding, in that process, his true vocation. He was an operator – entrepreneurial, clever, daring, opportunistic, ambitious, and not too scrupulous; business was a game, and there, in a succession of little towns in a remote part of the country where the rules were few and the stakes were small, Frank proved that he could play it very well.

It was probably not by any means the future of which he dreamed – there was a limit to the amount of time an ambitious young man could spend playing tricks in Zeehan. But it was preparing him for something, and a shrewd player like Frank must have been reassured by that, even when the crowds were small and suspicious of his magic. Film was the medium of a brave new world, and just the job for a man who had come, like it, apparently out of nowhere.

Frank learned, too, that you could never rest on your laurels. Suddenly, in the third week, the opposition at the Theatre Royal risked another sortie, replacing the deserter Mrs Cronly with 'ILLUSTRATED SONGS BY MISS ALMA SMITH, Zeehan's favourite', promoting Herr Holm to the rank of Professor, doubling the size of its regular advertisement, and presenting in the boldest of fonts its price of admission, '6d', drawing attention to the fact that the Thring operation was so much more expensive.

Frank called their bluff, dropping his own price of entry in Zeehan (though not in Queenstown, Strahan, Dundas or Tullah, where there were so far no competitors) to sixpence, represented in a font that was bold enough to rival the banner of the paper itself. He instituted, too, a limerick competition, which anyone could enter with an accompanying ticket stub from one of the sessions at the Gaiety; multiple entries were permissible – if they were accompanied by the requisite number of stubs. Two guineas was the prize for the person who could most cleverly complete the promotional limerick composed by the man who had penned those unforgettable lines about boots for the *Bunyip*. Evidently he had lost none of his way with words:

> Steadiest, brightest, flickerless, too,
> Food for the brain, a pleasure to view;
> In public esteem
> By their merit supreme ...[39]

Sadly, no record of the winning fifth line has survived. But the challenge to the rhymesters of Zeehan did what it had to do. Frank Thring and World's Pictures scored a third round knockout over Royal Bio.

The triumph was unmistakably marked when Frank graciously hosted at the Gaiety the farewell concert for Miss Alma Smith, as she set off for the bright lights of Melbourne, balanced of course by a program of the latest offerings from World's Pictures and some songs from Master Scott.[40] At the same time the regular Sunday evenings at the Gaiety were reconstituted; they were no longer the rather abrasively secular 'rational concerts', but now proudly 'national concerts',[41] and deeply embedded in the local culture. As an example, World's Pictures generously offered children who had taken part in the Zeehan Hospital Ball a complimentary ticket to one of its evening shows.[42] No doubt it occurred to its Business Manager, now firmly Thring rather than Dexter, that this might encourage – or even require – a useful component of paying parents.

Grace's return to the stage was short-lived. With the combined forces of Mrs Cronly, Master Scott and Miss Smith now in the World's Pictures camp, Frank no longer needed to draw on the unpaid contribution of his wife. By the end of that first month, her name had disappeared from the bill, though

39 *Zeehan and Dundas Herald*, 31 August 1909, p.1.
40 *Zeehan and Dundas Herald*, 15 September 1909, p.2.
41 *Zeehan and Dundas Herald*, 6 September 1909, p.2.
42 *Zeehan and Dundas Herald*, 28 August 1909, p.1.

Frank's continued to appear, and reviews marvelled at how his sleight-of-hand had 'his audience thoroughly mystified with his deft manipulation of billiard balls, handkerchiefs and other articles'.[43]

A consistent feature of the Thring strategy in the battle with Royal Bio was the focus on a single main feature; it was a policy that became increasingly prominent in his Tasmanian programs, and that anticipated the future of the cinema industry. Implicitly, it shifted the emphasis on film as a novelty, a version of miscellaneous variety entertainment, to film as a way of telling a developed story. On the day of his opening in Zeehan, Royal Bio was offering a wide range of short films:

> My Lady's Revenge (a Sensational Dramatic Picture), Historic Cortege of the Jubilee of the Emperor Francis Joseph, Manners and Customs in Burmah, The Great Italian Earthquake (Second Series, First Time in Tasmania), The Witch's Secret, The Nervous Kitchenmaid, The Old Mashers.[44]

Thring's first program reflected a much stronger commitment to entertainment and to powerful narrative, and was concerned to distinguish the genres to which each offering belonged:

> TROOPER'S BRIDE
> TROOPER'S BRIDE
> A Sensational Drama, Pourtrayed [sic] by America's Best Actors and Actresses.
> THE WITCH OF SEVILLE
> THE WITCH OF SEVILLE
> The Magnificent Dramatic Picture,
> BRIDE OF LAMMERMOOR
> Unequalled for Dramatic Intensity and Perfection of Pourtrayal [sic]. A story that reaches every heart and touches the springs of human feeling.
> HUMOROUS FILMS that are laughter compelling, including
> STRANGE INHERITANCE
> HOW KIDS GET EVEN
> CURE FOR BASHFULNESS

43 *Zeehan and Dundas Herald*, 21 August 1909, p.2.
44 *Zeehan and Dundas Herald*, 3 August 1909, p.1.

> BACHELOR'S PARTY
> "A little nonsense now and then is relished by the wisest men." These Films are calculated to drive dull care away at first glance, and make you merry. Come and Have a Laugh.
> A TRIP THROUGH THE BEAUTY SPOTS OF THE WORLD,
> Showing other scenes, other customs, other sports, than what we are accustomed to, vividly pourtraying [sic] the humor, pathos, interest and beauty of this world in which we live.[45]

It was a much more appetising menu than that offered down the road at the Theatre Royal.

The bills of fare at the subsequent World's Pictures showings were similarly varied, and spruiked with similar enthusiasm. More and more, though, the emphasis was on the main course and its literary credentials, such as *The Gold Seekers* ('which only three weeks ago was the Star Film at West's Pictures, Melbourne. Sublime in its conception, magnificent in its construction – a Picture that will live in the memory of every spectator and enhance our reputation for presenting the Latest and Best Films');[46] *Dr Jekyll and Mr Hyde* ('A Pictorial Dramatisation of Robert Louis Stevenson's Splendid Story … Prior to this Picture an explanatory synopsis of the plot will be given, enabling those who have not read the book to follow the weird and thrilling situations with ease from the commencement');[47] and *King Lear* ('A Magnificent Film from the American Vitagraph Company. Educational, Interesting, Entertaining').[48] It was the way of the future, and on the west coast of Tasmania only Frank Thring was blazing that particular trail.

The game, however, was constantly changing, and in his time in Tasmania he had to be constantly on his toes. With the defeat of the local contender, Royal Bio, Thring reduced the element of live local entertainment in his programs, and joined his wife in retirement from the stage (though Dexter reappeared for 'Fifteen Mystical Minutes' on the program at the Pontifex Hall in Strahan on September 28).[49] But at the end of September a new threat emerged, in the form of the touring World's Picture Company, a well-

45 *Zeehan and Dundas Herald*, 3 August 1909, p.1.
46 *Zeehan and Dundas Herald*, 11 September 1909, p.1.
47 *Zeehan and Dundas Herald*, 18 September 1909, p.1.
48 *Zeehan and Dundas Herald*, 29 September 1909, p.1.
49 *Zeehan and Dundas Herald*, 28 September 1909, p.1.

established and well-endowed operation that some people, not surprisingly, confused with Thring's The World's Picture Company.

Whether the remarkable similarity of name was coincidental, or, if not, who was copying whom, was never established. Given the differences in scale between the two companies, it's unlikely that the big operators from the mainland were exploiting the name of the Johnny-come-lately outfit that had suddenly appeared under the management of the Great Dexter in the wilds of Tasmania. But, whatever the legalities, the new contest produced another skirmish in the advertising columns of the *Zeehan and Dundas Herald*.

The battle began with the arrival of Thring's new opponent in Strahan two days after his own program had shown there. This World's Picture Company advertised nine thousand feet of film, including newsreel footage of the local galloper Bribery winning the Grand National Steeplechase in Melbourne. It asserted, no doubt gallingly for Frank Thring, that its offerings showed 'ABSOLUTELY NO FLICKER'.[50] The proprietors of the new arrival, Messrs Hogg and Semoff, opened hostilities with a Public Notice:

> We, the ORIGINAL WORLD'S PICTURE COMPANY, wish to inform the public in general that we have NO CONNECTION WHATEVER WITH THE ZEEHAN ORGANISATION trading as the World's Picture Company. We show 9000 Feet of Film every night, not 3000 Feet.[51]

Thring responded next morning with a salvo of his own:

> THE WORLD'S PICTURE CO. which have been established in Zeehan for the past two months do not, nor would not, claim any connection with the World's Picture Co. now showing in Queenstown (as the latter would lead the public to suppose, in view of an advertisement appearing in these columns yesterday). We succeed in the merits of our entertainment alone; not by the title we assume … We show 6000 Feet Film per night, not 3000 Feet as alleged. We would not attempt to project 9000 Feet, because by so doing the Pictures would be passed through the Machine with such rapidity that they would not be shown to the best advantage. It is our motto to Project Pictures Artistically and

50 *Zeehan and Dundas Herald*, 29 September 1909, p.2.
51 *Zeehan and Dundas Herald*, 30 September 1909, p.4.

> Naturally … THE LEADING AND PERMANENT 'WORLD'S PICTURES'.[52]

They were fighting words. Hogg and Semoff, naturally, published their reply next day:

> Mr Thring states that 9000 Feet of Film could not be screened nightly to the best advantage. This may be the fault of Cheap, or Common, Machines, but as we have the Latest and Best Machine that is on the market, we have no difficulty in putting this quantity before the Public, which we do at each and every show. As Mr Thring says, let the Public judge for themselves.[53]

Mr Thring abandoned the argument about equipment, and settled down to a duel fought with adjectives. His World's Picture Company was, in the days that followed, presented variously as 'the Popular'[54] and 'the Permanent'[55] variety of the species. The enemy in turn claimed to be 'the Original',[56] whereupon Thring declared his company 'UNEXCELLED AND UNEQUALLED', citing 'The People's Verdict – The Best of All'.[57] When his company visited Waratah in the wake of its rival, Thring asserted in the *Burnie Advocate* that this was 'the Genuine' World's Pictures, with 'no connection with any company of the same name'.[58]

The battle faded as the invader moved further along the coast. Increasingly, though, Thring's World's Picture Company was distinguished from the self-proclaimed 'original' not by its Zeehan association but by the name of its manager. If it could claim to have achieved 'permanence' in a two-month run, then surely it was not too much to cite the man in charge for that period as a personal guarantor of quality. Phrases like 'Under the direction of Mr F.W. Thring'[59] and 'Under the expert operation of Mr F.W. Thring'[60] recur in the reports of the company's programs. As the weather started to improve with the summer, other organisations appeared on the west coast

52 *Zeehan and Dundas Herald*, 1 October 1909, p.1.
53 *Zeehan and Dundas Herald*, 2 October 1909, p.4.
54 *Zeehan and Dundas Herald*, 5 October 1909, p.1.
55 *Zeehan and Dundas Herald*, 6 October 1909, p.4.
56 *Zeehan and Dundas Herald*, 9 October 1909, p.1.
57 *Zeehan and Dundas Herald*, 11 October 1909, p.4.
58 *Burnie Advocate*, 20 October 1909, p.3.
59 *Zeehan and Dundas Herald*, 20 October 1909, p.4.
60 *Zeehan and Dundas Herald*, 3 November, 1909, p.4.

with films to show – companies like Acme, and Paris, and Pathe Freres; but none advertised their wares with quite the vigour and impudence of Thring's version of World's Pictures, and none mentioned at all the individual who put them on.

Frank had quickly acquired a reputation for astuteness, and it was soon enhanced by his extension of operations in Queenstown. The Masonic Hall there was reconstituted as the World's Picture Palace, with his installation of electricity and refurbishment of its façade; its official opening stole a further march on the competition by some strategic consultation with the civic elders:

> The recent resolution passed by the Council provided that only one bioscope entertainment would be supplied with current on Saturday nights. Mr Thring put in an early application for the current on that night, and announces that the World's Pictures will be shown by electric light.[61]

Things did not always go so pleasantly to plan. The next edition of the *Zeehan and Dundas Herald* carried a report of an accident at the Palace, just before the Grand Opening, which testified to the precariousness of the travelling cinema business, especially for a man who liked to run the whole show himself:

> While erecting the screen at the World's Picture entertainment on Saturday, Mr F.W. Thring fell from the ceiling of the Masonic Hall to the floor, the ladder on which he was standing slipping under him. He struck the boards face downwards, and Mr J.H.Keogh, who was near by, and who at once went to Mr Thring's assistance, found him dazed and bleeding. He assisted him to a chair, and after a little while Mr Thring recovered sufficiently to operate his machine, though it was apparent he had suffered a severe shock.[62]

The report, while showing the requisite sympathetic concern, conveyed the subtext that you couldn't keep a good man down.

In a number of ways, Frank Thring's time in Tasmania anticipated the tone and tenor of his much higher-profile career two decades later. The

---

61 *Zeehan and Dundas Herald*, 5 November 1909, p.4.
62 *Zeehan and Dundas Herald*, 8 November 1909, p.3.

determined promotion of his product and himself, the rhetorical flair in that cause, the relish for a fight and the cavalier approach to protocol, all were hallmarks of the man who set out to make the history of Australian film and theatre his own. Frank was an adventurer, and in Tasmania, as in most other places in the years to come, he won the game. He emerged from his time on the frontier with an evident sense of where he was going, and with new skills and a new reputation to help him get there.

And then something happened that changed everything – something probably unplanned, and, for Frank at least, possibly quite unwelcome. Grace became pregnant, and a not particularly promising stage career was ended at a single stroke.

Life on the road, moving from one theatre or Mechanics' Hall or fairground to another, was no life for a woman in her condition – especially when the road was rough, and ran through 'the most inhospitable part of the country'. Moreover, when a woman was pregnant for the first time in her mid-thirties as Grace was, people talked darkly about 'complications'. She needed to be somewhere safer, and more secure. She needed to go home. The only reasonable course of action was to take her back to Edith Street, where she could have her baby in the bosom of an over-protective family, snug in her own little bed.

Frank, meanwhile, would return to Melbourne, to make his – their – way. That was the plan, and it seemed sensible enough; Adelaide was a small stage for a man of his abilities, and with his interests in the very newest in entertainment. Grace and the child would join him in Melbourne in due course, and they would make their home there. All it would need was a spot of luck, and everything would fall into place.

An observer would have pointed out to the prospective new father that it might have been more sensible still to have stayed with his wife and her family, for a while at least. His father-in-law William Wight, the train driver and father of five, no doubt pointed it out, since Frank's plan to seek his fortune in a city nearly two days' journey from his wife and infant child must have looked to him very much like negligence. But there were a number of reasons why Frank preferred his own strategy, as well as his desire to be in a place that more closely approximated his size.

Gawler was, of course, one of those reasons; he had made it very clear already that Edith Street held no charm for him. And the bourgeois domesticity that it represented was surely a factor, too, wherever it might be; Frank had never shown an inclination for the role of suburban man, and the thought of the three of them, Grace and baby and father makes three, may have turned any prospective family home into a Gawler in his mind. Frank was used to doing things his way, if not alone, and while Grace the supporting act had been able to adjust to that, Grace the mother, with babies to feed and change and cosset, could not, however hard she tried.

There was another reason to keep him out of South Australia, too. His father William had settled comfortably in Norwood with his second wife, the widow Leonora Comley, in 1902. He had left his own place, where he had been working as a maltster, to move into hers, where he appears not to have been working at all. Getting away from his father and a stepmother he had barely met would have been a persuasive argument for Frank leaving Adelaide altogether in 1907, and it was a good reason to not go back there several years later. Sometimes it was best simply to draw the curtain on an unhappy Act, and move to a new scene unencumbered.

Then, in 1911, he had just the stroke of good fortune that he needed – a position at Kreitmayer's Wax Museum in the middle of Melbourne, where he was entrusted with developing the diversification of a declining waxworks into something that resembled a cinema. So Frank went to Melbourne, Grace had her baby in Gawler, and eventually the two of them joined him in the rooms that he rented in the middle of Melbourne, at 51 Bourke Street. To that extent, then, things went according to plan. And Grace's pregnancy, that seemed to have come so inconveniently at the time, marked the beginning of the next phase in Frank's brilliant career. In Melbourne he found a number of the things that he wanted very much – fame and fortune came to him quite easily in the end. The things that he achieved from the time he started work with the Kreitmayers in 1911 were things that he could only have dreamed of when Dexter the Mystic was playing his parlour tricks in one scruffy little fairground after another.

They christened their daughter Viola, which had impeccable Shakespearean credentials. To her father, though, she was immediately and always Lola, perhaps in homage to the popular stage that was closer to the world he knew, and the life that he led.

Birth, District of Barossa, Book 864, page 411
22 May 1911 at Edith Street, Gawler

Viola Margaret, female
Father: William Francis THRING, aged 32, born Wentworth, NSW
Mother: Grace THRING formerly WIGHT, aged 34, born Edith Street, Gawler SA
Year of Marriage 1905
Rank or Profession of father: Manager of Boot Shop, Bourke Street, Melbourne
Registered: G THRING, mother, Melbourne on 23 June 1911

This time the informant was Grace, who should have known better about a few of the details. The year of her marriage was 1904, not 1905; her age at the birth of her only child was thirty-five and eight months, not thirty-four; her husband's age then was twenty-eight, not thirty-two. The first two, at least, she might have been expected to get right.

Grace registered the birth in Melbourne, where she had brought her month-old daughter to join Frank in his new rooms in Bourke Street; perhaps it was vagueness about what on earth Frank was actually doing at Kreitmayer's, or some sensitivity about the respectability of his 'rank or profession' that persuaded her to describe him as still a bootmaker. The plan was presumably for Grace and the baby to stay with him at the Waxworks. But motherhood had come at a more than usual cost to Grace; she seems to have been sick almost from the beginning of her pregnancy, and she never really got better. The young woman who had travelled the film and carnival circuit like a trouper, living in a succession of dubious hotels in raucous mining towns, was, all of a sudden, a semi-invalid. She needed help with little Lola, and Frank was neither prepared to supply it himself nor yet able to pay someone else to do it. The experiment in family life at Bourke Street was a disaster, though it was revived a couple of times over the next three years, and the flat remained Grace's nominal home. But mother and child spent most of those years back in Edith Street, where the Wights could play nursemaid to both of them.

In every other respect, the cards had fallen perfectly for Frank in Melbourne. He had a job that was fascinating in itself and developing in all the ways he might have dreamed of; he had a boss who was canny but quite old, and who trusted his judgement completely; he had a boss's daughter who was sometimes demanding and difficult, but was obviously keen on him. Frank was on a roll, and while there was unfinished business of several kinds over the border in South Australia, it seems to have been far enough away to have not concerned him unduly. All that he did and did not do suggests that he had effectively closed the curtains on another scene, and was, once again, starting afresh as though there was almost no yesterday at all.

From 1915 Grace's official residence was Edith Street, Gawler, and she seems not to have attempted the journey to Melbourne again. She developed tuberculosis late in 1919, and moved into a nursing home at Dulwich, which she never left.

Lola spent almost all of her first ten years in Adelaide, and did not join her father in Melbourne until January 1921, when her mother died. Three months after that, Frank married Olive Kreitmayer.

TRAVELLING FROM STRAHAN TO MELBOURNE

S.S. Lubella, 5 January 1911

It was a balls-up, whatever way you looked at it.

He'd sailed this Strait, sailed, as a matter of fact in this very boat, before. And for the first time the crossing made him feel sick. Not sick the way the other people hanging over the rail were sick, or the way poor bloody Grace was, blurting her guts out down in the cabin. But sick none the less. Sick at heart, as the poets would say. Sick with anxiety about the future and regrets about the past, and sick of being poor and unknown, and of making things up as he went along. It was no way to live.

He had a dependant. Well, a dependant and a half, if you counted the prospective kid. Dependants normally needed your income, or your arm, or your love, but Grace needed all those and more. Women were supposed to bloom in pregnancy. Not Grace, though. She was doing it hard, poor little bugger, her face the colour of putty, her hair that was once so neat and so pretty, lank and lustreless. She looked like a ghost, and the smell of vomit hung around her like a cloud.

It wasn't her fault, but he couldn't stand to be with her in that lousy little cupboard they called a cabin. Some berth. Some birth, too. Somehow she'd slipped up. A baby hadn't been part of his plans, or theirs, as far as he knew. Better out here on the deck, even in the wind and the spray and drizzle, and the chorus of retching on every side.

So, Frank. Nearly thirty, and what have you got to show for it? Well, you've managed to be big in Zeehan, my boy. But a bloke doesn't have to be all that big to be big in Zeehan. In the end, it's neck and neck on the scale of importance with the bloody Isle of Wights.

He'd have to take her back there, obviously, but there was nothing she or they could do to make him stay. She'd go along with whatever he wanted anyway; she always had. One thing about little Gracie, she was loyal to a fault. A real trouper. Well, she loved him, didn't she. But she was also scared of losing him. That was always in the air, something they both knew but never said. It gave him power, and that was a useful thing to have: it made most decisions much easier.

He loved her too, of course, not much doubt about that. She was his wife after all, soon to be the mother of his child. Sometimes, though, he wished she wasn't quite so predictably bloody compliant, not quite so contented with always playing in support. Sometimes, when people clung to you, you got this almost irresistible urge to shake them off.

Might risk a beer in the lounge after all. The financial situation was, you'd have to say, less than flush. Zeehan had worked out passably in the end, but there were those other one-horse towns that made Zeehan look like London. They had been a disaster. He hadn't told Grace, of course, she had enough on her plate. Anyway it was his problem, and he was the only one who could solve it. It was a frustrating game. You could take a lousy Masonic Hall and call it the World's Picture Palace or some bloody thing, but there was no point if you couldn't make a quid. Turned out Dexter couldn't make a silk purse out of a sow's ear after all, let alone put some cash in it.

But a man was entitled to a cleansing ale. There was more than enough time to worry about stock-taking. Tomorrow, in Melbourne, was another day. And Grace would be all right. She'd be happy enough back in Gawler; she'd never known any other home, after all. It wasn't his, though, never could be. Nothing wrong with nice people; they made the world go round, and you couldn't do a show if they weren't there . But Christ, they could be boring.

Edith Street. Such an orderly little world. Margaret's special tea cake and old Bill's platitudes, and an antimacassar on every armrest. It'd be a bloody tough macassar that managed to infiltrate that couch.

They'd like nothing better than to get him back there, stitching and patching up soles, and putting on protectors. Not because they cared about him that much, of course, but because they wanted her to come home – and because they wanted him to fail. Old Bill still looked at him with suspicion. You could tell Bill Wight tomorrow that Frank Thring was a crook or a polygamist or Jack the bloody Ripper and he'd nod his shiny dome in that sanctimonious way and say, yep, yep, doesn't surprise me, yep, always thought there was something fishy about that bloke. Yep, nothing could ever surprise Bill the Wise. Monosyllables were easy to rhyme; antimacassars were another matter.

They wanted him brought to heel and broken. Which made it, sadly, out of the question to lean on them for a loan.

Funny to think of the kid. In six months or so it'd be a person. What would it be like – small and sweet and Presbyterian like its mother, or large and discontented like its Dad?

A little Thring. Contradiction in terms, really.

It'd better be a boy – a Frank or a William, or both, like the rest of the tribe. Pity help any girl who was stuck with the Thring inheritance. All he'd ever been bequeathed was a pair of bloody big feet, a pair of bloody big ears, a bloody big nose, and a body too big for most purposes.

It was a lousy dowry for a daughter; she'd be on his hands all her life. No, much better a son. Sons could look after themselves.

Chapter Three

THE OPERATOR

Sometimes, some men can be very lucky.

Frank Thring arrived in Melbourne in early 1911, having deposited his pregnant wife with his in-laws in Gawler, and found an advertisement for a job at Kreitmayer's Waxworks that he could have written himself. Nothing in Frank's background particularly prepared him for working with effigies, and the general sense that the waxworks were a bizarre relic of a bygone era might have suggested to most people that it was not a job with potential. On the other hand, the fact that Kreitmayer's had seen the writing on the screen, and had begun already to change the emphasis of the business from static figures to moving pictures, was of real interest to a man with his ambitions.

The waxworks in Bourke Street had been a going concern in the centre of the city – indeed, 'as much a part of the city as Bourke Street itself'[63] – for more than half a century when Frank joined the firm, but it had been through a number of names and addresses, and a number of shifts in emphasis, too. Its first incarnation was as Mrs Lee's Waxworks in 1857, where 'Madame Lee', a rope and ballet dancer, and her 'petite family' of dancing juveniles, performed 'drawing room entertainments' for her visitors after they had completed their tour of the British royal family and sundry military heroes.[64] The waxworks would never be so decorous again.

In the following year the business was taken over by a wax modeller, Ellen Williams, and reopened in larger quarters as Mrs Williams' Wax Exhibition. This time it included a room devoted to 'Notorious Malefactors', in which a number of especially vicious murderers were lovingly recreated. They were

63 'Mr Max Kreitmayer', *Table Talk*, 18 December 1889, p.3.

64 Mimi Colligan, 'Waxworks shows and some of their proprietors in Australia, 1850s-1910s', *Australasian Drama Studies* 34, April 1999, p.87. Much of the following discussion of the background to the Kreitmayer enterprise is drawn from this article.

displayed for the most respectable of reasons, of course. Mrs Williams attached a suitably moralistic message to each of her killers ('This frightful murder should be attributed to the action of excessive drinking upon a mind naturally vindictive'), and laid claim to an educative purpose; her domestic partner and later husband, the phrenologist 'Professor' Philemon Sohier, was able to add his analysis of the criminal bumps that might explain such atrocities. But the crowds who came along to Mrs Williams' Wax Exhibition are likely to have been keener for a taste of delicious revulsion than a moral or phrenological lesson. That appeal to sensationalism, the sense that there was a touch of something disreputably, even dangerously, carnivalesque about the Waxworks, was part of its character when Frank Thring joined the firm, fresh from the Tasmanian picture-show circuit.

The Waxworks had another change of name when Mrs Williams and the 'Professor' married in 1859; Madame Sohier's Wax Exhibition lent a dash of the exotic, and a touch of Tussaud, to the business. In 1863 the Sohiers added a new partner, Maximilian Kreitmayer, as well. Kreitmayer had arrived in Melbourne in 1856, one of the hordes lured by the gold rush. He was a medical wax modeller, born in Munich and trained in Glasgow and London, and after a couple of years of notably unrewarding adventures on the northern diggings from Gympie to Palmer, Kreitmayer returned to Melbourne, and to a version of the career he was trained for. At first, he stayed just on the right side of respectability; he set up an anatomical display at the Polytechnic Hall with Dr L.L. Smith. It was a museum specialising in models that represented the effects of sexually transmitted diseases on the male and female reproductive organs; Max Kreitmayer lectured to exclusively male audiences on the perils that might lie in store for both sexes, while his wife Eliza talked to women about the threats to misbehaving or unlucky members of her own. This initiative was rewarding enough for the Kreitmayers to buy half of the Sohier Waxworks, and then, in 1869, the whole business. The Museum's blend of science and prurience made it a natural enough progression for Max. He proclaimed the legitimacy of the business, despite its new 'foreign' name, by staging its Grand Opening on May 24, Queen Victoria's birthday.

For the next four decades, Kreitmayer's Wax Museum was a Melbourne landmark. Though it remained in Bourke Street, the major commercial thoroughfare that ran from Spencer Street Railway Station to the south to Parliament House in Spring Street at its top end, the Waxworks changed its address several times, each time to premises larger and more stylish than the last. Its final home was 202 Bourke Street, on the west side of the block between Swanston and Russell Streets, in prime retail territory. Max Kreitmayer had, eventually, done rather well.

The exhibits retained throughout a mixture of the great and supposedly good on the one hand, and the salacious and bizarre on the other. The figures of the Royal Family were always closest to the entrance, and set a suitably serious and respectful tone for a visit; but the catalogue of human depravity and deformity that followed it was the aspect of the Waxworks that got people talking, and that provided a ready remedy whenever business became slack.

> Mr Kreitmayer, in spite of his loyalty, owns a liking for his criminals, before even his kings and queens, as the former are a more potent attraction with the public, with whom he always keeps faith.[65]

There were always new rapes and murders to supplement the graphic tableaux of crime scenes toward the back of the display, and there too could be found the live acts that Kreitmayer increasingly favoured as a source of novelty: exhibits like Abomah 'the Amazonian Giantess', nearly eight feet tall and the daughter of black slaves from South Carolina, Chang, 'the Chinese Giant', Jo-Jo, the 'Dog-Faced Youth' who had toured with P.T. Barnum, and Fat Fred and Stout Sarah, the most bloated children in the world. When exotic imports were not at hand, Kreitmayer offered local variants, like the 'Pig-Faced Boy', Annie 'the Aboriginal Giantess', and the 'Giant Family' of exceptionally fat people from Gippsland. He astutely enhanced his return on these investments in the living by reproducing each of them in wax.

The public's fascination with the extraordinary tended to focus on the freakish, but it could embrace the seemingly superhuman too. John Lee, 'the man they could not hang', was suspended from his noose several times daily, while 'Sacco, the man they could not starve' proved a major hit in one of the Waxworks' last seasons:

> Sacco Homar, who hailed from Eastern Europe, claimed to be the world's No. 1 fasting man, and threw out a challenge to all comers. A Scotchman took up the challenge ... and he started favourite for the competition. The Caledonian, however, was much over-rated, and after a three weeks' fast he "threw in the towel" and went back to his porridge.

---

65 *Table Talk*, 18 December 1889, p.3

> Meanwhile, Sacco, the Starving Slav, enclosed in a glass room, was feeling in the pink of condition on his spa water and cigarette diet. He fasted for six weeks, and so kept the title.[66]

Kreitmayer's guaranteed an unforgettable visit. When Jane and Nellie Rowe, the daughters of a prosperous Catholic family, made the obligatory Grand Tour 'home' to London, they wrote back about how let down they felt with the famous Madame Tussaud's; twelve-year-old Nellie thought the Chamber of Horrors at the Melbourne Waxworks 'far superior', while her eighteen-year-old sister, finding that the Tussaud Chamber was 'only busts of Murderers', was 'greatly disappointed, they are not nearly such fun as the Melbourne ones'.[67]

The Waxworks could be shocking, even scandalous, but it was evidently sufficiently a part of the Melbourne establishment in the mid-1870s for a couple of convent girls not only to know it well, but to show that they did so in letters to the family at home. The *Age* would periodically shake its head at the Waxworks' exploitation of the unfortunate, and the deplorable taste of the public in paying to gawk at them, as it did over another remarkable faster in 1891:

> Today we treat our insane with a certain amount of consideration, we hang our condemned in private, but as often as a simpleton essays a feat likely to end fatally, the shillings of the mob are at his disposal.[68]

But the flurries of editorial disapproval had little effect on the takings of the Waxworks, and none at all on the pleasures of its patrons.

Max Kreitmayer's life in many ways reflected the delicate balance that was struck by his business. There were several rapid changes of fortune, including a bankruptcy in 1889, and there were three Mrs Kreitmayers to give the gossips food for thought. The German with the strange occupation and the suspicious continental charm was a natural subject for speculation, and there was plenty of that about the legitimacy of his two marriages and the five children that they produced. The first Mrs Kreitmayer, whom he

66 Ron Testro, Junior, 'Thrills and Chills in the Waxworks. A Famous Bourke Street Show was a Melbourne Institution for More Than 50 Years', *Argus Weekend Magazine*, 10 June 1939, p.3.

67 Quoted in Colligan, p.97 from T.F.Pagliaro, 'An Australian Family Abroad: The Rowe Family Letters, 1874–74', Monash University M.A. Thesis, 1981.

68 *Age*, 3 January 1891.

had married a few days before sailing from England in 1856, disappeared suddenly without trace, and by the time the second one died in 1879 three of the five children had vanished as well. There was no doubt or mystery about the third relationship, though. Five years later, Max married the third Mrs Kreitmayer, Harriett Watts, from 'Rylands' in Somerset, lately of Launceston, a woman twenty years his junior, who would become the mother of Max's sixth and seventh 'official' children, Olive Marguerite Cecilia (born in 1886) and another Maximilian (Jack), born three years later. The marriage certificate whimsically declared Max, whimsically enough, a bachelor.

Despite his colourful romantic history, his exotic background, his curious vocation and his slightly disreputable business, Max Kreitmayer was accepted, in due course, as a very solid citizen. A study of 'Our Local Men of the Times' in 1889 noted his benign and sober influence on local government since his entrance into political life as a Collingwood councillor in 1887; though a Liberal-Protectionist, an ardent pro-Federationist, and a devout Roman Catholic, his role is defined in terms of a wise and gentle pragmatism.[69] Max's election as Mayor of Collingwood in 1893 confirmed that he had won respectability, rather against the odds. Even after his bankruptcy in 1899, Max remained on the right committees, kept the right friends, and managed a rapid, if modest, financial recovery. Insolvency was the kind of misfortune that could befall any chap who dabbled in the volatile commercial world that was Marvellous Melbourne in the 1890s.

Max died in 1906, and so never met Frank Thring, but the two of them would have found much in common. Frank sought a similar delicate balance; though his dreams were bigger, it was always important to him that he should achieve wealth and position and respect, without necessarily being bound by the procedural niceties that often attended them. And for him, as apparently for Max, show business was never just a business. It was an adventure-ride in itself, a continual battle with the unpredictabilities of the game, and a constant quest to draw from the audience its laughter, wonder and acclaim, as well as the price of admission.

So Frank Thring's engagement at Kreitmayer's Waxworks in 1911 could be seen as a marriage made in heaven – even if he hadn't in due course taken the boss's daughter as his bride.

---

69 *Our Local Men of the Times. Biographical Sketches of the Prominent Citizens of Collingwood and Fitzroy*, Melbourne, J.M. Tait, 1889, pp.17–18.

The catalogue issued for the 1912 Kreitmayer's Waxworks Exhibition, the first year in which Frank Thring was in charge of the business, and its swansong, suggests something of the way the old show was winding down inexorably to its death. There was still plenty to see – two hundred and thirty exhibits are listed there. But only two of them had been updated since Max Kreitmayer's death six years earlier, the effigies of Edward VII and George V near the main entry. Just two new displays had been introduced in those years, in a museum that had always prided itself on being up with the latest in atrocities: the notorious Doctor Crippen, who had been executed in November 1910, and his typist 'companion', Ethel Le Neve, who had been acquitted of complicity in his crimes. It was the minimal acknowledgement of the passage of time.

On Max's death, his wife Harriett had formally taken over the management of the business. Harriett was regarded as a competent businesswoman, shrewd and unsentimental in her judgements; she had a valuable assistant in her daughter Olive, now twenty, and a young woman who did not allow a lack of experience to prevent her from holding and expressing strong opinions. But it was a difficult challenge. Not only had the Waxworks lost some of their old attraction, but Max's financial disaster in 1899 meant that there hadn't been much to bequeath in 1906. After his liabilities were met, there was only one hundred and thirty-five pounds left in the estate, leaving forty-five pounds each for his daughters and nothing at all for his sons. Astutely, Max had registered the family property in his wife's name, presumably to guard against future insolvencies, so there were some assets to fall back on. But there was not much margin for error.

Harriett employed several managers to keep the operation going, but it was hardly enough. There is a hint of desperation in the advertisement placed in the Melbourne dailies in September 1909:

> The Management of "the Waxworks" having secured the services of a first-class artist, can now undertake Cleaning, Colouring, Dressing the Hair, and generally renovating wax-heads, hands etc, at a moderate price. Reductions made for a number of heads.[70]

70 Draft advertisement, F.W. Thring Collection, Performing Arts Museum, Melbourne, 1995.116.257.

It is hard to imagine that many readers were moved by the chance for bulk refurbishment of their waxen heads. The Kreitmayers did not repeat the advertisement. By 1910, Harriett had come to the conclusion that the Waxworks had had its day, and that the moving pictures were the entertainment of the future. In June 1910 the Museum was formally renamed the Alexandra Hall, and 'The Royal Pictures' opened with a newsreel of Edward VII's funeral.[71] The *Bulletin* published a lament for the demise of Kreitmayer's: 'Now it has gone to the Pictures business and changed its name, as though ashamed of its interesting past'.[72]

Harriett and Olive knew little about the Waxworks, and nothing about the cinema business; the managers that they had installed to preside over the exhibits knew about wax, but hardly anything about celluloid. Hence the advertisement that Frank Thring saw early in 1911; hence his appointment, as a man who offered just what they were seeking. Harriett and Olive both got a little more from the transaction than they had bargained for – Harriett gained a trusted manager and eventual son-in-law who proved to have a knack for spending her money spectacularly but profitably, while Olive gained a husband and, through him, an empire of sorts.

That final exhibition in 1912 was representative of the kind of show that Max Kreitmayer had made, and at the same time an anticipation of the kind of showman that his son-in-law was about to become. Visitors began, as they always had, by paying their respects to the Royal Family, and then proceeded along an avenue lined with distinguished statesmen and militarists, and the odd Pope; the robes of Pius X had been lovingly sown by the sisters at the Abbotsford Convent.[73] There was some attempt, in the associated commentaries, to inform, but it was fairly perfunctory, and omitted any details that were less than sensational. Thus the note accompanying Abraham Lincoln's effigy summed up his life in a way that made it clear what the Waxworks found interesting about him:

> This great and good man was shot on April 14, 1865, by John Wilkes Booth, a young actor, at Ford's Theatre, Washington, on the benefit of Miss Laura Keene. Born in Harding County, Kentucky, Feb 12,

71 Colligan, *Australasian Drama Studies* 34 p.104.
72 *Bulletin*, 7 July 1910, quoted in Colligan p.104.
73 'Famous Bourke St Waxworks', *Australasian Post*, 5 January 1950, p.11.

> 1809. His career was indeed a complex one, ranging from "Log Cabin to White House."[74]

Frank Thring, in preparing that guide to the final exhibition, was drawing on catalogues past; but the style is very reminiscent of his promotion of filmed history in the multiple bills at the Zeehan Gaiety, and it reflects an assured sense of just how much the public might care to know, and of how complexities might get in the way of a ripping yarn and a good night out.

The 1912 tour passed by a couple of distinguished actors (Bernhardt and Irving) and a couple of lurid Biblical moments (John the Baptist's head on a platter, and Solomon poised to split an infant down the middle) to reach, in the mid-forties of the catalogue, the section headed 'Freaks'. Abomah the Giantess was there now as a wax dummy, alongside Chang. Just down the hall was a miscellaneous sequence including Esau, the Bearded Boy; his mother Madame Ghio, the Bearded Woman; the not very obviously notable Clara Snell ('one of a family of 14. Born at Bunyip'); General and Mrs Mite ('the smallest couple in the world'); General Tom Thumb ('A man who derives his greatness from his littleness'); Commodore Nutt ('A clever comic actor and singer, and good billiard player'); Mr and Mrs Chauncey Morlan ('the heaviest married couple in the world. Weight: Mr Morlan, 748 lbs; Mrs Morlan 454 lbs'); and finally Crippen and Miss Le Neve. The disparateness of the display suggests either that somebody was not thinking very well about the coherence of the collection, or that somebody had decided that it really didn't matter any more.

The Crippen tableaux from early 1911 were tacked on to the Freaks in the 'Large Hall' as exhibits 54 and 55; the Chamber of Horrors, a separate room, began at exhibit 113, and the items there ran through almost a hundred representations of murderers, their victims, and the scenes of their crimes, before ending in an assortment of fiendish torture devices. The missing attractions from 56 to 112 had given place to the stage area at the back of the main auditorium, where live performances and selected short films alternated through the afternoons and evenings. Given the emphases of Kreitmayer shows of the past, and of recent Thring programs, it's probable that the effigies that had been consigned to the basement were assorted dignitaries who were too worthy to provide a lively plot.

74 'Kreitmayer's Waxworks Exhibition. The Oldest Exhibition in the Southern Hemisphere', catalogue not dated but either 1911 or 1912, State Library of Victoria.

The murderers in the Chamber were presented with the kind of appalled moral sensitivity that ensured that the visitor would savour, and be outraged by, every word. And a lot more words were lavished on the criminals than on the famous men who stood by the Bourke Street entrance. Every grisly detail was disclosed, though always prefaced by a statement of general revulsion that such depravity could possibly be. Remarkably, the author of the catalogue managed to repeat the sentiment again and again without ever quite repeating himself: 'this inhuman monster', 'this notorious individual', 'one of the most revolting tragedies ever heard of', 'one of the most diabolical murders ever committed in the world', 'one of the most horrible crimes perpetrated in Australia'[75] – the parade of human vileness was so shocking and relentless that no-one, surely, could bear to look away.

The violence was an obvious selling-point. The other, less explicit, drawcard was sex. The tableaux in the back half of the Chamber were almost all concerned with it – with adulteries, infanticides, rapes, and with the deceptive deadliness of the female of the species. Elizabeth Scott, hanged at twenty-three for cold-bloodedly organising the murder of her husband by her nineteen-year-old lover, was notable for a beauty that Max Kreitmayer had lovingly recreated:

> When she was brought out for execution, an exclamation of surprise broke from the bystanders that one so young and of so amiable an aspect should have been the prime mover in so horrible a deed. She alone preserved an air of the most perfect unconcern.[76]

Mrs Needle, who 'poisoned her husband and children', was similarly 'very prepossessing and stylish in appearance'.[77] The 'Gatton Tragedy', in which the young and attractive Murphy sisters were the victims of an unknown killer, was depicted in a series of tableaux; the catalogue and caption noted that 'The post mortem disclosed that the girls had been brutally outraged prior to death'.[78]

There was a touch of titillation in almost every exhibit, even in the Instruments of Torture at the far end of the Chamber. These purported to be 'The Remains of the Inquisition'; among the vast array of devices for twisting, tearing, searing and disembowelling, implements like the Tarantella ('to tear

---

75 Catalogue, Kreitmayer Waxworks Exhibition 1912, passim.
76 Catalogue, Kreitmayer Waxworks Exhibition 1912, items 127/8, p.8.
77 Catalogue, Kreitmayer Waxworks Exhibition 1912, item 132, p.9.
78 Catalogue, Kreitmayer Waxworks Exhibition 1912, items 182/3/4/5/6, p.12.

women's breasts from their bodies') and the Iron Virgin added the frisson of an appeal to sexual prurience.[79]

The catalogue reflects the principle that in order to attract the general public, you can't go far wrong by appealing to a bit of sex and violence. The slow decline of the Waxworks in the years preceding the 1912 exhibition, and its demise a few months later, confirmed that the movies did these things better. When the Waxworks closed in 1913, Harriett Kreitmayer had a little money to invest, and was persuaded to purchase a number of shares in motion picture companies – twenty-five one-pound shares in the Empire Picture Theatre Company Ltd in August 1913, another three hundred and seventy-five shares in Brunswick Theatres Ltd in October that year, and a further one hundred in Brunswick Theatres in April 1914, all of which paid off very nicely.[80] In the unlikely event that those investments were not prompted by Frank Thring, the remarkably clever young man who had wound up the waxworks so efficiently and knew so much about the possibilities of film, they would at least have had his vigorous approval. His career was now quite clearly defined, and moving very fast.

There is no doubt that Frank Thring had charmed his new employer: ten years after their first meeting, and riding the wave of financial fortune that Harriett's money had made possible, Frank bought a substantial residence in Toorak for Olive and his mother-in-law, and named it 'Rylands' in honour of the house in Somersetshire that had been Harriett's family home.

He had also charmed his employer's daughter, whose influence in all these developments was no doubt significant, too. Olive Kreitmayer was twenty-five when she first met Frank, a young woman with no career apart from the informal advisory role that she played in relation to the family business, and rather less bothered by potential suitors than a supposed heiress of marriageable age might have expected to be. Even as a girl, Olive had been, as observers in those circles would delicately say, 'big-boned'. She was no beauty, though the photographs of her as a young woman all suggest a physical bearing that promised an imposing presence.

---

79 Catalogue, Kreitmayer Waxworks Exhibition 1912, items 208, 225, pp.13,14.

80 Share documents held in F.W. Thring Collection, Performing Arts Museum, Melbourne 1995.116.249–51.

The photograph of Olive with Max and her brother Jack, taken in 1900 when she was fourteen and Jack was eleven, is a revealing one. There is a placid, pleasant quality to Olive's expression here which makes it the most attractive picture of her that has survived, and she has not yet 'bloomed' into the substantial figure that she presents in school photographs a few years later. But even at fourteen Olive has a matronly air. It is there in the large and elaborate hat that she wears, and the carefully coiffed hair on which it sits; it is there in the dark jacket and the high ruffled collar of her blouse, and perhaps even in the casual assurance with which her left hand rests on the shoulder of the patriarch sitting sternly in the centre of the composition. Jack is formally dressed for the occasion too, but appears indisputably as a boy of his age, young enough even to be allowed to smile.[81]

Max was deeply attached to his third family, and in particular, it seems, to his daughter. Certainly from the age of about twelve she was his regular companion on a number of holiday cruises in the Pacific, while Jack and his mother stayed home. In 1901 he and Olive were travelling with their old family friends, the Smiths, whose connection with the Kreitmayers went back to the business in anatomical models that Max had established at the Polytechnic Hall on his return to Melbourne forty years before. The letter that Max wrote to Jack from Thursday Island to mark his son's twelfth birthday is revealing, both for the paternal warmth that pushes against all the protocols of cultural reserve, and for the moral anxiety that Max, whose respectability had been hard-won, felt about any potential lapses in the behaviour of his offspring:

> My dear, dear Boy,
>
> I wish you many happy returns on your birthday, I am very sorry I cannot do so personally, and hope you will have many of them and happy ones too. We are having a very pleasant trip and wish you could be with us, only I should not like you to be associated with Leo Smith as he is not very desirable to be with as he seems to me the rudest boy I ever came across and you know the old proverb about bad manners corrupting good ones, whatever will become of him. We have a young scientist on board who is going to write a book of the different habits and manners of nations and natives, he would be pleased of telling you some of his adventures as I know you are such a good listener and take

81 Photograph held in F.W. Thring Collection, Performing Arts Museum, Melbourne, 1995.116.224–5.

> a lot of interest in him. He is giving lots of information to Olive and Louise.
>
> I trust you will pay all your attentions to your lessons so that I shall have some pleasure awaiting me on my return, do not be too daring as you have recently experienced what can happen.

The letter, after the reminder 'Don't forget Church Sundays', sends heartfelt 'love and kisses, my dear Boy' before closing formally with 'Ever affectionately, M.L. Kreitmayer'.[82]

What young Jack made of all this is an interesting subject for speculation. It's unlikely to have been much comfort that he was being spared the pernicious influence of Leo Smith when it brought home so pointedly that other families thought it appropriate to take a boy of his age on a luxury cruise; doubtful, too, that Jack found in the claims of 'lessons' and 'Church Sundays' very persuasive reasons for having been left behind, especially when they appeared to be no obstacle in the case of his sister. Nor would there have been much pleasure in the fact that Olive was hearing all those exotic things that would have been of particular interest to him. He may not even have noticed, though any adult reader would find it unmistakable, how much his father loved him.

Jack was not included in the extended trip that his father took in the following year to Japan, either. But Olive was, and was taken out of school for a term in order to do so:

> After mid-winter Olive Kreitmayer will return as a boarder; she has had a very enjoyable trip to Japan with her father.
>
> Lately she paid a visit to the convent which she evidently did not forget in her travels, for she brought the nuns a present of two handsome jardinieres and a Japanese tortoise-shell boat called "Sampan."[83]

Over the years, Olive brought back many exotic gifts from her travels to the nuns of Genazzano F.C.J. College. Jack was not a member of the touring party on any of them. In the year of his father's death, disregarding all wise counsels about doing nothing 'too daring', Jack headed north for Queensland,

---

82 Letter dated 2 February 1901, from the S.S.Taiyuan. F.W. Thring Collection, Performing Arts Museum, Melbourne, 1995.116.333.

83 *The Genazzano,* 1902.

and effectively went into smoke. He was moving around a lot, jackarooing they said; the next decisive contact that he had with his mother came twenty years later, as the Thrings were about to take up occupancy at 'Rylands'. The contact was initiated by Jack's children in Western Australia, where he was living as a farmer, having changed his name by deed-poll to Jack Watts. Taking his mother's former surname was presumably in part a response to the awkwardness of carrying a name like Kreitmayer through the years of the First World War. It was not a good time to flaunt a German ancestry; another branch of the family became subtly Anglicised to Creightmore for the same reason, and Harriett in 1916 formally reaffirmed her British citizenship in case it might be assumed that she was bound by her late husband's nationality. But perhaps Jack didn't feel a strong sense of family connection, anyway; the anxiety that comes through his father's devotion may have been prompted by the sense that Jack was always a bit of a renegade.

By contrast, Olive seems to have been ever the dutiful daughter. She and her brother were very different, and no doubt each to some extent exaggerated their difference in the way that siblings are inclined to do. Olive was the one who was her father's beloved companion, who was kind to the nuns and was a 'good scout' to her schoolfriends, who stayed close to her mother after Max's death, who took an active interest in the family business. Olive was the one, until she married, who kept the family name.

Genazzano, the convent that Olive attended as a boarder, was a school that reflected two important things about the Kreitmayers – their Catholicism and their wealth. Both, by the time their daughter arrived at the appropriate age, were rock solid. Genazzano was the most conservative and socially prestigious of Melbourne's Catholic schools for girls. Apparently, it suited Olive perfectly. She does not appear in any of the lists for academic prizes, though she was given an honourable mention for Drill and Calisthenics in 1901, and in 1903, her last year at the school, Olive was awarded the Medal of the Blessed Virgin as a mark of her kindness, dedication, and service to the school.

The general impression, apart from conspicuous virtue, is of Olive as a big well-meaning presence; she looms large in the back row of the Old Girls' victorious Catte team for 1907, a formidable group of glowering young women bearing bats, and was celebrated in verse for probably the only time in her life:

> How my heart gave a leap of tremulous joy
> When fair Olive, of stately dimensions,

> Stood first for her Cross, and got it at once
> By a hit of most wondrous pretensions.[84]

As an Old Girl, 'fair Olive, of stately dimensions' was exemplary. She was a determined contributor to the Catte team for a number of years, her dedication signalled in 1912 by the fact that 'she not only played, but practised in advance, that she might further the interests of her side';[85] she was there again in the back row of the team photograph, head and shoulders above the rest, the large head slightly downcast as it had been five years before as though resenting the blank stare of the camera. She was a regular contributor to the Fancy Goods Stall at the annual School Fete, providing in 1906 'dainty needlework, silver spoons and a tea cosy' for sale,[86] and in 1910 contributing 'a handsome offering of beautiful dolls for the bazaar'; the school magazine singled her out in that year for a special vote of thanks:

> Olive Kreitmayer has always been generous in her donations towards the garden fete. Olive is very faithful, and never forgets her friends at Genazzano; neither will they forget her.[87]

And she maintained a regular contact with the nuns at the convent, never failing during her times overseas (several weeks in the South Sea Islands in 1913, several months in Japan in 1917, and 'a most delightful trip to America' in 1920)[88] to send cards and letters to them. Those gestures, too, were deeply appreciated:

> Dearest Olive,
>
> Rev. Mother asked me to write you a little card of thanks for her for your kind remembrance of her and all at Genazzano at Xmas and to convey to you her best wishes for the New Year – I hope you got the 'Genazzano' & that you liked it. We are at present at Woodend, nine Mothers and four sisters, having a beautifully cool day after two or three days of very great heat.
>
> Remember me to your Mother & with love & all good wishes,

84 *The Genazzano*, 1908.
85 *The Genazzano*, 1912.
86 *The Genazzano*, 1906.
87 *The Genazzano*, 1910.
88 *The Genazzano*, 1920.

> Yours, dear Olive,
>
> very sincerely always,
>
> M. Spillane FCJ.[89]

Olive continued to make regular appearances in the Old Girls' section of the magazine until a particularly momentous year, after which she did not appear again:

> Olive Kreitmayer (Mrs F.W. Thring). Olive was married on 25th April, 1921. What do you think? Olive was the first Genazzano girl to welcome Reverend Mother-General, having met the latter on the "Niagara" on her way from Honolulu. We were sorry she could not be present at the reception, but hope to see her soon.[90]

The interpolated 'What do you think?' referred of course to Olive's great good fortune in running into the Reverend Mother-General on her honeymoon, not to her amazing luck in finding a husband. But some of her old schoolfriends, recalling those 'stately dimensions' and the fact that she was almost thirty-five, might have been forgiven for misreading.

Olive was not as saintly as the good sisters liked to think; very few could have been. As she made herself at home in the role of society wife and mother, hostess, philanthropist and a dangerous lady to cross, she showed more and more of the tough and cheerfully coarse humour that a girl from Abbotsford might find it useful to acquire, and of the imperiousness that her privileged position in the family had encouraged her to develop. Olive could be loud and unreasonable when she chose or after a couple of sherries, and, though her son would later liken her to Lady Bracknell, her Bracknellisms were mostly not suited to an audience of Canon Chasubles and Miss Prisms. Her niece Minty Creightmore found her wonderfully shocking at times, and remembers an occasion when her brother John had made a clay sculpture at school, and was required to present it to his aunt. John was nervous about doing so, partly because it wasn't very good, but mostly because it had a flaw; 'I'm sorry, Auntie Ol', he confessed, 'I'm afraid it's got a crack in its bottom'. Olive instantly made it all right – 'Good heavens, John, we've all got one of

89 Postcard, n.d., held in F.W. Thring Collection, Performing Arts Museum, Melbourne, 1995.116.371.

90 *The Genazzano*, 1922.

those!'[91] She became more formidable with the years, but she was mostly good-natured, and often kind. While her generosity to the Fancy Goods Stall may have been partly for self-gratifying effect it was also, probably, a reflection of genuine charity.

And there was the matter of her relationship with Mr Thring, the young man who was engaged by her mother to run, dissolve and redirect the family business in 1911. He was married, and the father of a new daughter, when Olive first met him. When Grace Thring brought little Lola to Melbourne to join Frank in the second half that year, Olive would have met them both. Grace, the suburban girl from Gawler, preoccupied with the baby and unused to the ways of wealthy people in big cities, would have been a fish out of water in those early days in Melbourne. That, as much as her poor health, might have been the explanation for her decision, or Frank's, that she would be better off back with her parents. Over the next few years Grace and Lola spent no more than a few months in Melbourne; Frank alternated between the family-sized hotel apartment in Bourke Street and later the rented house in Kew that he lived in when his wife and child were in town, and the rooms above the Assembly Hall, or in other Kreitmayer-owned properties nearby in Bourke Street, when they were not. How, and how early, and how far, the relationship with Olive developed during those years is something about which there is no evidence at all. He wasn't with her, certainly, on those voyages to the South Sea Islands, and Japan, and America. But he was, clearly, very much in the picture. The rather precipitous wedding, just three months after Grace's death, encourages a clear inference that something was always waiting to happen between them; the fact that throughout the decade between there was no suggestion of any other romantic interest in Olive's life provides another. How much Olive diverged from the path of saintliness that she seemed forever to be treading in the pages of *The Genazzano* is anybody's guess, but even if one chooses the more charitable but less likely interpretation that no 'sin' was committed, it is probable that it was very thoroughly contemplated, and imagined, for a long time before it was possible for Frank and Olive to marry. Frank's commitment to Grace was clearly over, and a provisional commitment to Olive clearly established, through much of those ten years, and, given the pattern of Grace's movements, probably earlier in the decade rather than later.

91 Interview with Minty Lalanne (formerly Minty Creightmore), 24 January 2005.

So Olive was no angel, and thankfully so – for her husband, probably for their son despite their dysfunctional dealings, and certainly for their biographer. Still, she was an odd match for Frank. The conspicuous Catholicism was one aspect of that, as was the social milieu of balls and charity lunches; Frank had never shown the slightest religious inclination, and, though he liked money, was hardly the kind of man to hanker for the circuit of repetitive chat. Grace looked like an odd match for Frank, too, but more in retrospect than she had at the time. And Olive was nothing like Grace. Olive was a handful.

The absence of information about what was going on between them from 1911 till 1921 is so complete that it seems almost wilful. But nor is there any real evidence of the substance of their feeling for each other after their marriage, either. They appeared together in public, and travelled, and bought things, and entertained, and had a child together – there was nothing to suggest any failing in their love for each other, though they spent much of their time in separate worlds, Frank busy being an entrepreneur, Olive a hostess or guest at most of the significant parties around town.

During the early 1930s, Frank sent Olive several handsome studio portraits of himself, each of them with a scrawled personal message. It's not clear in what sequence or circumstances they were sent, but the annotations cover an intriguing range of implied feelings; there is the brief, even pointedly perfunctory 'To Olive from Frank', the cheerfully matey 'Best Love 'Ol' F.W.T'., and the rhetorically romantic 'Ever Thine Frank'.[92] Is any one more genuine and revealing than the others? Did he 'mean', or even think about, any of them? Did Olive find any of them more touching, or disappointing, than any other? Are the messages indicative of the subtle oscillations of feeling in any marriage, or do they just reflect the fact that people don't always give much thought to what they write on these occasions?

It was, of course, a handy connection for Frank to make in 1911, and to confirm at the altar in 1921. He was a man who had most things he needed in order to achieve his dreams, except for seeding capital. The link with the Kreitmayers fixed all that at a stroke. It was the sort of thing that people can sometimes whisper about, and Olive, whether or not she ever wondered if Frank had married her for her money, must at least have been sensitive to the possibility that others might view it as a marriage of convenience. As for his perspective, the only thing we can be fairly

---

92 Photographs, n.d., held in F.W. Thring Collection, Performing Arts Museum, Melbourne, 1995.116.272–4.

certain about is that Frank would have seen it as a much less inconvenient marriage than the one that he was already in.

The Waxworks effectively ceased to exist some time late in 1913 or early in 1914, though a number of the effigies remained to provide a forlorn avenue for patrons hurrying past to visit the moving picture show in the back half of the building. The rest of them were taken to Harriett's new house in High Street, Prahran, and left to gather dust in several sheds in its back yard. Frank, now thirty, once again just a projectionist, and working in a building limited by poor equipment and the ghosts of a past life, needed more. His mother-in-law's investments helped secure shifts with the Brunswick and Empire circuits, but Frank's ambitions did not include a career as a hired hand. Somehow, extraordinarily, with whatever balance of the familiar mix of cleverness with luck and pluck, the Great Dexter transformed himself by the beginning of 1915 into the General Manager of Electric Theatres Ltd.

It was a turbulent time in Australian film, when a man had to be in just the right place at just the right time. Frank, on the face of it, was a critical twelve months or so out; he was heavily involved with wax dummies while the country's cinema industry went through the most remarkable two years in its history, and was free to engage in it at precisely the point that many people declared its darkest days, between 1913 and 1915. But, as an exhibitor, he caught and rode the backwash of the first wave in Australian cinema; it would be another decade before he would find his way into the business of building picture-theatres, and two decades before he ushered in the second golden-age of Australian film-making.

In the first decade of the century, the burgeoning cinema business had been characterised by the travelling picture show. In halls and theatres and mechanics institutes, at fairgrounds and beaches and parks, touring projectionists like Frank Thring put together programs with something for all the family, rarely staying in the same place for more than a couple of shows. But by the end of the decade, two powerful new elements were transforming that landscape.

One was the development of the purpose-built cinema in the cities and larger country towns, and with it the rise of a small group of big-spending, high profile exhibitors – men like the Scotsman, T.J. West, who by 1907 was confident enough in the new medium to take out leases on the Sydney Glaciarium and the Melbourne Olympia, and by 1910 controlled fourteen permanent cinemas throughout Australia, playing to an estimated nightly audience of twenty thousand;[93] the Englishman Cozens Spencer, who built theatres in four capital cities, and at his Sydney cinema (rented improbably from the Methodist Church) boasted to have, in his wife Senora Spencer, 'the only female operator [projectionist] in Australia'; and the American J.D. Williams, who established Australia's first continuous cinema at the Colonial Theatre in Sydney in 1909, and in 1912 opened the most spectacular of the new cinemas, The Crystal Palace, described by the *Bulletin* as 'a symphony in dark green with pictures painted on the walls, and framed heavily in old gold'.[94] These were not simply large venues for exhibition, but a key ingredient in the magic of the event. The *Lone Hand* noted how enticing these new wonderlands were:

> The theatres are all placed where there is a large and increasing foot passing traffic. The gay exterior, the light and the music, all attract the people. The splendid vestibule, with marble steps, marble ticketboxes, splendid doors, and the vast marble staircases, with railings of burnished brass, make an alluring bait. And when all this splendour is available for sixpence and threepence the places are naturally rushed. It's worth a shilling an hour just to sit there and rest, but when the world's best photoplays are laid on the value received for the money becomes overwhelming.[95]

It was a fashion that would not go away. Later, in fierce competition with his great rival, Stuart Doyle, Frank would raise the stakes in the creation of grand and opulent picture palaces to another level, on a scale that has not been matched in Australia since. During that pre-war boom, though, Frank Thring was showing films in much less glamorous circumstances at the back of the Waxworks Museum, while Doyle was a very junior part of the Williams organisation. But both men learned their lessons well.

93 Graham Shirley and Brian Adams, *Australian Cinema: The First Eighty Years* (1983) revised edition Sydney, Angus & Robertson in association with Currency Press, 1989, p.22.

94 *Bulletin*, 27 June 1912, quoted in Shirley and Adams, p.23.

95 *Lone Hand*, 1 March 1912, quoted in Shirley and Adams, p.23.

The other major development in Australian cinema at the end of that first decade was the explosion in films made by and about Australians. It was a much more fleeting development, as it has tended to be in the several golden ages in Australian film-making that have happened since. While the *Lone Hand* correspondent revelled in having seen 'the world's best photoplays', there was plenty of evidence in 1911 and 1912 that the public not only wanted to see local work, but that Australian films might be able to take their place among the world's best, too.

> The number of local features released in 1911 and 1912 reached a level unequalled until 1975, a peak year in the much later revival. The year 1911 saw the most prolific output, with no less than fifty-two narrative fiction films making their appearance.[96]

In part this explosion was simply a reflection of the demand for product. The proliferation of cinemas, their necessarily rapid turnover of programs and the popular appetite for 'the pictures' put a lot of pressure on the market for importation, and there were, for a time, clear advantages in the cost and predictability of supply in drawing on local material. A number of the major exhibitors, including West and Spencer, set up very active production arms. But there were signs, too, of a genuine interest in local subjects. Initially, the field was dominated by films set in colonial times, following in the footsteps of Australia's first features, *The Story of the Kelly Gang* (1906), *Eureka Stockade* (1907), *Robbery Under Arms* (1907) and *For the Term of his Natural Life* (1908). There was a particular vogue for the bushranger story, ushered in by Cozens Spencer (*The Life and Adventures of John Vane, the Notorious Australian Bushranger* in 1910, and *Captain Starlight*, *Captain Moonlite* and *Captain Midnight, the Bush King*, all in 1911), and the actor/director John Gavin (*Thunderbolt* and *Moonlight, the Bushranger* for the exhibitor H.A.Forsythe in 1910, followed by *Ben Hall and his Gang*, *Frank Gardiner, King of the Road*, and *Keane of Kalgoorlie* in 1911). So popular did the bushranger film become, in fact, that the New South Wales Police Department, fearing that it might have an evil influence on impressionable audiences, banned the subject in films altogether in 1912. It was the first of several cruel blows to the industry over the next year.[97]

96 Shirley and Adams, p.24.

97 The ban remained in force until 1940. It did not apply to the theatre, perhaps because audiences there were not only smaller but assumed to be more discriminating. In consequence, the bushranger became a popular figure in the commercial theatre.

There were signs in 1912 that the bushranger as a subject, and indeed the whole genre of the bush epic, was running out of steam, anyway. John Gavin, who had specialised in playing charismatic outback villains, made no secret of his feeling that the market was saturated. He had been contracted to a make another series of them by the Australian Photo-Play Company, newly floated by Stanley Crick and Herbert Finlay, for whom Gavin had made four previous films of that kind, but resigned after making only one. It seemed for a while that he might have misread the market; in the halcyon days of 1911, Australian Photo-Play was the busiest of all the production houses, churning out twenty features with more or less interchangeable characters and plots. But in late 1912, the company, having over-committed its capital to simultaneous projects, was bankrupt. Its remnants were sold to the international distributor, Gaumont, which had no intention of filming anything in Australia. Australian Life-Biograph, the third busiest of the film-makers in 1911, and Amalgamated Pictures, the fifth, both ceased production in November of that year, when they merged with West's Pictures and Spencer's Pictures (the second and sixth most active production companies in 1911) to form the General Film Company of Australasia. In January 1913 the new conglomerate was enlarged to include the Greater J.D. Williams Amusement Company, and the infamous 'Combine', Union Theatres and Australasian Films, was born.

The 'Combine' retained some interest in making films, but at a much reduced rate, and it established an immediate stranglehold on distribution. Lincoln-Cass Films, the one remaining major player in the 1911 boom, lasted until late 1913, when its Managing Director H. Dean Stewart announced its closure as a result of 'the pernicious system of Australasian Films Ltd, in binding the showmen to take their full program from them'.[98] There were obvious advantages for the new bedfellows in terms of economies of scale, though Cozens Spencer resigned from the new superpower in protest:

> Picture production has been killed. Today it is as dead as the proverbial doornail. Can you believe that this is the only place in the world where pictures are not being made? Such is, indeed, the case. Australia has become the dumping-ground for all the producers in the world, when it could profitably be taking its place side by side with other picture-

98 Shirley and Adams, *Australian Cinema,* p.42.

> producing countries, and providing work in Australia for thousands of its people.[99]

Certainly the priorities of the Combine lay in efficient distribution, and though supplies of European films dried up with the outbreak of a world war, the consequence was an increase in the dominance of the American product rather than an encouragement to the local one.

Through all this turmoil, the audience continued to grow. It had to, in order to populate those palaces. In 1912 Melbourne alone had twenty-five cinemas, with a combined audience capacity of fifty thousand; by the following year, sixty-five thousand people were attending city and suburban cinemas in Melbourne on a Saturday night.[100] And with the rapid increase in the size of the audience came, of course, a broadening of its composition and character. J.D. Williams, when he turned his attention to film after a short and disastrous career selling novelty walking sticks, felt that West and Spencer had missed the democratic potential of the cinema. And he was right. They had begun with a model of an evening's entertainment that was drawn without much reflection from the relatively privileged audience for the stage. It was reflected in their schedules, with evening performances at eight and two matinees each week, and in their prices: they began by charging from one to three shillings for a seat (another shilling if it was a reservation), up to twelve times the price of a ticket in an American cinema.[101] Williams, who had seen the drawing power of the nickelodeons back home in West Virginia, ran continuous sessions from eleven in the morning till eleven at night, and charged adults threepence and children a penny. He was more interested in the volume of sales than the return for each sale, and therefore in widening his audience base. Williams publicised his theatres as picture shows 'for the masses', but his strategy had much less to do with a discounting broadside than with a careful identification of neglected markets. His cinemas targeted women and children in particular. They offered special matinees and an assurance that the Colonial was 'a ladies' rendezvous', with female ushers, ladies' retiring rooms, and a child-minding area, so that mothers of young children could not only watch a movie undisturbed but have a free (if very

---

99 *Theatre*, 1 February 1914, quoted in Shirley and Adams, p.33.

100 Shirley and Adams, p.23.

101 Diane Collins, *Hollywood Down Under. Australians at the Movies: 1896 to the Present Day*, North Ryde, Angus & Robertson, 1987, p.7.

short) holiday from them.[102] In 1910 Williams was the only one doing this, but others were soon compelled to follow suit, and to keep their prices down. The democratisation of the cinema was perhaps inherent in the form, but it was certainly hastened by some shrewd marketing and by the imperatives of bricks and mortar.

Frank Thring had learned very quickly in his Tasmanian adventure that an exhibitor needed to do much more than simply put on the show, and that building an audience involved catering for a variety of needs. He was designing programs specifically for the women and children of Zeehan even before Williams introduced the practice in Sydney. And though Frank's admission prices at the Gaiety in 1909 had been based on the 'going rate' that West and Spencer had established on the mainland, he moved within weeks to a policy similar to that which Williams introduced in the following year. But there were other things that he learned as a keenly interested observer in the roller-coaster years from 1911 to 1915 that had a decisive influence on the rest of his career.

One of those things related to repertoire. While making Australian films probably was not high on Frank's agenda at this point, the evidence that the appeal of mythical and historical tales of the outback tended to fade quite quickly clearly affected the subjects of the films made by Efftee Studios twenty years later. The nationalist agenda of Frank Thring's company was explicit, yet Australia's most obvious source of culturally distinctive material was never tapped. All his completed features were urban or suburban in their focus. Efftee's city stories, like *The Sentimental Bloke* and the George Wallace films, focussed on the larrikin, who was in these depictions a comic/sentimental figure; drama was something that happened in domestic spaces that were not unlike the living-rooms in imported films about the perils of relationships, and usually quite similar to the realist sets of the proscenium stage. In that first wave before the war, films like *The Silent Witness* (1912), directed by Franklyn Barrett for West's Pictures, and *The Silence of Dean Maitland* (1914), a major hit for the Fraser Brothers directed by Raymond Longford, showed the advantages of filming proven theatre scripts in controllable interiors. The Efftee policy of integrating projects for theatre and cinema may well have had its origins in Frank Thring's observation of what came closest to a safe bet in the risky business of film finance.

Lesson number two concerned distribution. Part of the cause of the ludicrous over-production in 1911–12 lay in the attempts by individual

102 Collins, *Hollywood Down Under*, p.23.

exhibitors to create their own programs; inevitably, in the process, they reduced the profitable potential of any of their films. The attractions of a distributor, a middle-man who would ensure the widest possible exposure for the producer while at the same time relieving the exhibitor of some of the pressures of sustaining a rapidly changing repertoire, were obvious. Pathe Freres had established an outlet for its release of features from France in 1909, and soon after sold its operation to T.J. West. But the precedent was established. When the Combine began what some independent film-makers would see as its reign of terror in 1913, a key element in its agenda was to eliminate the middle-man by appropriating his function. Having allowed the role to develop by default, the prime movers in Australian film recognised its possibilities as a source of almost guaranteed profit.

But what if you had a commitment to making not only a name and a lot of money, but films by and for Australians? It was the conundrum that faced Frank Thring for the next two decades, because he came to want to do all of those things, very much. The economics of distribution were brilliantly clear, as long as the product came from somewhere else. If Australian films were to be competitive in that market, the answer was obvious. They needed to be given either subsidy, which would reduce their costs, or protection through import duties, which would reduce their disadvantages. They might even, in a country that was huge and sparsely populated, need both. For a brief period, during the 1914–18 war, the cinema industry in Australia had the second; the Labour government under Andrew Fisher was either principled or impressionable enough to impose a tariff on films from other countries. J.D. Williams noted approvingly that protection had worked to consolidate the industry in America, and would surely do so here:

> Now, when Australia is in imminent danger of being literally swamped with millions of feet of cheap film from abroad, this tariff will prove not only a beneficial measure but an absolute necessity.[103]

At the end of the war, though, the duty was substantially reduced in response to pressure from the importers. And the opening that it had provided for the making of local films was largely wasted.

> The combine might have decided that this was the time to use its distribution and exhibition power to gain a secure niche for

103 *Theatre*, 1 April 1915, quoted in Shirley and Adams, *Australian Cinema*, p.34.

> Australian films in the Australian market, but it did not. Three Australasian features were released in 1915, two of them endorsed by the Department of Defence, but for a decade after that the combine determined to stick with what it knew best, distributing and exhibiting films from abroad.[104]

The field was left to Hollywood, and, once conceded, it proved mighty difficult to reclaim. The only possible strategy, as Frank Thring would argue before countless government committees and boards of enquiry and Royal Commissions from 1930, was the restoration of protective tariffs and quotas. He had some luck in that respect, but the debate was always skewed by the knowledge that these things had been tried before, and that they had been so little used and so lightly abandoned.

The third major lesson to be drawn from the volatile world of Australian film between 1911, when Frank Thring took over projection duties at the Waxworks, and 1915, when he became the General Manager of Electric Theatres, concerned the path to power. The 'Combine' had changed the rules. By 1915, it was apparent that no individual or fledgling company could succeed without appropriating and capitalising on the structures of established rivals. Electric Theatres had a couple of solid assets, but it could hardly be expected to compete with the much bigger and richer players in the game. Its only chance for growth, and arguably its best hope for survival, lay in building alliances. That might mean taking over a slightly larger operation, which wasn't out of the question in a youthful industry sustained by a fairly rough and ready frontier economy; the more practical course, though, was acquisition by such a company, and then transformation of the host body. This was the Thring recipe for corporate success. It rested for its effectiveness on the superior energy and determination of the junior partner, but that never seemed to be particularly a problem to Frank. He had effectively taken over Kreitmayer's after a short period as employee. He established Electric Theatres after an even briefer period as a casual hand. He prepared it for absorption by J.C. Williamson Films, the cinema arm of Australia's largest theatrical producers, and capitalised on that transaction by rising within a few months in 1918 to become, at the age of thirty-five, Managing Director of that company, and one of the two or three most

104 William D. Routt, 'Our reflections in a window: Australian silent cinema (c.1896–1930)', in James Sabine (ed.), *A Century of Australian Cinema*, Port Melbourne, William Heinemann Australia, 1995, p.55.

powerful distributors in the country. He retained his position as Managing Director of Electric, and two years later brokered a further expansionary partnership between Williamson's and Electric and the 'Combine', Union Theatres and Australasian Film. He became a director of both Associated Theatres and Hoyts Pictures; by 1923 he was Managing Director of the former, by 1926 Managing Director of the latter. Frank had a finger in every pie. In the process he became a very wealthy man, and adopted a style of living that made him look even wealthier.

His first move had been to rename the cinema at the Waxworks. In May 1911 it ceased to be 'The Royal Pictures', with their touch of homage to Max's monarchism, and became the 'Star'. At first the place hardly lived up to the razzle-dazzle that its new name seemed to promise, but by the time the last of the wax dummies had wended its way to Windsor, the Star at 202 Bourke Street had expanded to accommodate an audience of twelve hundred. Harriett was persuaded to take an option on a block of land across the road at number 243. These two properties were the only recorded assets of Electric Theatres Proprietary Limited when it was formed in 1914. Among the shareholders of the new company were Francis W. Thring and Harriett Kreitmayer, who owned nineteen and fifteen per cent of the shares respectively.[105] By the time the war was over, a new cinema, the Paramount, had been built at 243 Bourke Street, and Electric, in conjunction with Williamson's, had acquired two other cinemas in the same street, the Strand at 210 and the Empire in the block between Russell and Exhibition Streets at 151. The Empire opened in 1916 with the phrase 'The World's Pictures' emblazoned on its façade, which would have brought the man who was driving Electric Theatres particular satisfaction, given the skirmishes over that phrase when he had been just another travelling showman in Tasmania.

It was an astonishing rise for the young man who had landed in Melbourne after a stint in the Tasmanian wild, with a pregnant wife, a presumptuous curriculum vitae, and very little else. A number of men got rich quickly in those heady times in cinema, and some of them managed not to lose it all; the Frank Thring story has an ironic parallel in the story of his arch-rival Stuart Doyle, who had begun his career like Frank as a sideshow conjuror and at about the same time raced up the ladder from junior employee in the Williams organisation in 1911 to General Manager of the Union Theatres

105 Bernie Halperin, 'How the Talkies Changed Bourke Street', *Cinema Record*, journal of The Cinema and Theatre Historical Society Inc., Issue 48, Edition 3, 2005, p.26.

wing of the 'Combine' in 1918, and Managing Director of the company by 1920. But the rise and rise of Stuart Doyle began and remained within the major organisation in the industry; that of Frank Thring was a move from periphery to centre, through a series of business deals in which the smaller fish offered itself to be devoured by a larger one, and proceeded to take control of the predator.

The Thring story is distinctive, too, for its shadowiness. Tracking Frank Thring through his thirties is in one sense much easier than tracing his movements through his late teens and twenties; he was now, as he would remain, a very visible man. But while joining the dots is a relatively easy task for Frank's biographer, reading their connections is not. The murky share exchanges and wheelings and dealings that took him to the top of his industry in less than a decade are in their way as mysterious as the movements of the boy from Wentworth who pops up from time to time playing magic tricks in three states, and just occasionally plying his respectable trade as a bootmaker. Frank was naturally an accomplished businessman, and smart enough to cover his tracks when that was in his interests, as, usually, it was.

Through this period of intense entrepreneurialism, where competitive practices merged so easily into collusive ones, and allies and enemies regularly changed roles, Frank made no friends. He had a wide circle of pleasant connections, business acquaintances, and people with whom he exchanged dinner invitations. But none of them got very close. The warmest and most significant of his professional relationships was certainly that with George Tallis, the theatre manager who in 1913, on the death of James Cassius Williamson, had risen to become head of the 'Firm'; Tallis was thirteen years Frank's senior, and had the requisite wealth and experience to act as a mentor. In 1916 Tallis overcame the objections of some members of the Williamson board, who had 'heard bad reports of Thring',[106] to install him as the head of J.C. Williamson Films, funded with Tallis' personal capital;

106 Michael and Joan Tallis, *The Silent Showman: Sir George Tallis, the man behind the world's largest entertainment of the 1920s*, revised edition, Kent Town, Wakefield Press, 2006, p.139.

in the same year, he supported Frank in the acquisition of the Paramount in Bourke Street. He introduced his protégé to the commercial advantages of playing golf, first at Riversdale, and later at Peninsula, not far from 'Beleura', the Tallis mansion at Mornington. He was Frank's companion on his trip to England and America from March to September 1927. George Tallis had an impeccable business reputation and manners to match, and from 1922 he had a knighthood; he was a very useful person to call your friend. But a man as secretive and strategic in his dealings as Frank Thring was not suited to forming strong attachments.

The connections that made him vulnerable were the family ones that had been around for quite a while but had effectively been left behind in Adelaide – Grace his wife, Lola his daughter, and William his father. They all stayed considerately in the background in the decade in which Frank was shaping his brilliant career. But the three of them became quite intrusive through 1920 and the early days of 1921, just when he was sealing the deals that ensured that hardly a film could be shown in the country that did not have, at some point in the process of its distribution, Frank Thring's fingerprints on it.

Whether their being out of sight had quite put his unfashionable little family out of Frank's mind is a subject that the absence of any surviving letters or other kinds of evidence leaves us quite free to speculate about. The odds are that, for much of that period, his wife, daughter and father had the status of distant relatives; he had more than enough on his plate in Melbourne without worrying about them. As he began making money at a startling rate, he presumably sent some of it over the border; in the face of the feelings of love, or guilt, or obligation that he might reasonably be expected to have felt in the circumstances, a man like Frank would have found regular donations a sufficient and even generous way of meeting his responsibilities. But nothing of this is known. All that we do know is that William, Grace and Lola stayed conveniently out of Victoria, and out of Frank's hair, until late in 1919. But then, when they did re-enter his stage, they did it in ways that could not possibly be ignored.

Grace's perpetual state of illness became quite suddenly worse. She had been a semi-invalid in her parents' home for almost ten years, apparently trying not to be a bother and mostly succeeding in being just a dependant who needed to be kept out of draughts and comfortable. Now, though, the persistent cough and the weakness had a name, tuberculosis; she needed permanent care, and so Grace made the move from Edith Street late in 1919 to the nursing home in Swift Avenue, Dulwich, in which she died on 22 January 1921.

William was dying, too. In 1919, at sixty, he had treatment for a heart condition in Hindmarsh, where he lived alone; Leonora's death, and the departure of her children (her youngest, Mary, was now thirty) had left him quite isolated, and Frank seems to have brought him to Melbourne, and presumably paid his dues at the Stuart Hotel, 195 Bourke Street, while he saw people who knew about hearts. Cruelly, quite unpredictably, what killed William Thring had nothing directly to do with his well-established 'dicky ticker'. William became suddenly ill with acute stomach pains that barely allowed the time for diagnosis as appendicitis before his death from peritonitis on 27 March 1920.

These two very significant deaths within a ten-month period, and the illnesses that preceded them about six months before that, must have rather spoiled the party for Frank as he strode confidently from takeover to takeover and from triumph to triumph. But the most problematic of his emotional ties to Adelaide was very much alive, and suddenly insistent on his attention.

Viola was nine when her mother died, ten months after her paternal grandfather, whom she very likely never met. Suddenly, in early 1921, Lola was the sole survivor from the first thirty years of his life. Amid all the brokering of deals and trading of commitments, in the wake of the remarkable string of victories that promised to take him to the prizes he really wanted, the question of what to do about a little girl in Gawler became suddenly paramount.

It was one of those watershed moments in a life that define what a person has been, and determine what a person might become. Frank had become very good at making decisions, partly because there was nothing to consider in any of them but his own advantage. But now there was a daughter, whose interests could not be ignored. And now the matter of what constituted Frank's advantage was not quite as clear as it had been. This time the negotiations involved a substantial investment of love, and that tended to make for pre-emptive contracts.

So Frank did what he probably had to do.

TRAVELLING FROM MELBOURNE TO ADELAIDE

Melbourne-Adelaide Express, 25 January 1921

Going back to Gawler. Something he thought he'd never do. And yet he'd known for a while that Grace was dying, and that would always mean the long trip back to the world of her childhood. She'd been sliding away for years – it'd got to the point where she wasn't even in his life as a source of guilt. She'd slipped right out of the frame. The little mate who'd been around the traps with him in Zeehan, and Strahan, and all points west, had been dead for years anyway. She'd been replaced by a creature with skin of paper and the scent of old violets who had nothing to laugh at, nothing to say, nothing to do.

A bit of his life had curled up and died with her. No one else he knew had been part of that, and while he'd always been careful when leaving a room about closing the doors and leaving no traces, it left an emptiness. People were tending to die on him lately. They left a space, and a small pain.

He'd managed to avoid going back when he'd organised the old bloke to Melbourne less than a year ago. Virtuous son takes responsibility for dear old Dad. Callous husband and father avoids seeing sick wife and neglected daughter. Well, you can't please everyone.

The third whisky. Service'd smartened up, anyway, since his last pilgrimage. A toast to Gracie, then, poor faded little Wight rose that she'd become. It hadn't been much of a life for her, when you did the sums. The best bits for her were the ones he'd quite successfully erased. All downhill from there for her, everything on the up for him. Funny the way things worked. Here's to you, kid.

The kid – the real kid – was another matter, of course. Big problems, small parcels. He'd never been keen on the idea of Lola growing up in the bosom of the Wights, but as long as her mother had been vaguely still around, there'd been no alternative. Now there was.

It could hardly have happened at a worse time, what with the business with Olive, and Harriett, and the pot of gold they were staring in the face, to mangle a metaphor. But it'd happened, and a man had to do something. Apart from anything else, Lola was about to become the person who'd hung around in his life the longest. Not known him, because she couldn't, but attached to him, because she had to be. That entitles her to a bit of consideration, surely, Frank my boy. To a better future than crocheting with Margaret, or pottering in the broad beans with Bill, anyway. Plus she's a pretty enough kid, all Thrings considered.

Nothing quite like a Havana with a Glenfiddich malt. Nice contrast to the time he made this trip, what was it, ten years ago, when Lola was just a bloody big bump. And now Gracie was dying. Memory was a mystery; now it felt like they'd never really known each other. But, in another sense, they certainly had; they'd made love, for Christ's sake, not that often mind you, but sometimes, if he remembered correctly, there'd been a need, a fierceness about it, wherever that'd come from. They'd made Lola. Inconceivably. Where had it gone, then, that Grace seemed now so much a part of somebody else's life, so remote from his own, like some fading bloody maiden aunt you visited dutifully and wearily, whose letters, rarer now, shorter too, in their spidery copperplate, were an unspoken reproach for all the ways you'd let her down. Was it that he wanted it over, then, once and for all? Didn't she matter? Had he really come so far?

Sometimes he wondered whether there was something wrong with him. Other people didn't forget to feel as he did. Wives, daughters, fathers, mothers, slipping and sliding out of the picture; other people seemed to grieve and pine and generally get knocked about, and he – well, he just kept rolling along.

A man could have a couple of single malts and work himself into a melancholy, but he couldn't make it last; the thoughts kept pushing you, out of that moment and into another that had bugger all to do with it. Were the others just pretending, then, when they wallowed in their mourning misery and made people like him feel guilty that their emotions seemed to lie on them so lightly?

It was bloody unfair, actually. Every time he started to doubt himself, it offended his sense of justice. Grace had accused him of it, in that timid devious way of hers, saying that he thought all the time of himself and never enough of others; she'd cut all that out, thank Christ, in the last few years, though those limp little missives about how tired she was or how poorly she'd slept or how much she'd been coughing lately were saturated with it. And it was bloody unfair. People like Grace spent their lives feeling sorry for themselves because they had nothing better to do. Just slip on this sackcloth and roll in those ashes, my dear.

And then they attacked him because he couldn't despair. He felt, all right. He cared. He just didn't make an epic production of it, that's all.

What he did feel now, and bloody strongly, was the irony. If there was some divinity shaping our ends, the bloke was quite a prankster. No wonder we had such bloody rough-hewn ends. Just when you thought you had the game by the throat, life raised its ugly head and kicked you in the privates.

One year ago exactly, things'd been travelling nicely on course. All the various dependants were getting on with it, in their own dependent ways – Leonora was keeping the prodigal dad more or less out of trouble, Lola was being cared for with the best of Presbyterian parsimony by the Wights, and Grace was in the gentle hands of the good nurses of Dulwich. And he, of course, was paying for the lot of 'em, though there frankly didn't seem much acknowledgement of that.

And then the cards had collapsed, one after another. Leonora died, so he'd had to bring his father back to Melbourne. His father had died, so he'd had to – well, bury him. Now Grace was going to die, and there was the problem of Lola. All in one bloody year. It was either lousy luck or hubris.

And they looked at him as though he was a man who couldn't feel. Who couldn't feel love. Well, bugger them. He would bring his little girl home. All right, he should've done it years ago, but it was bloody tricky. There was Olive, for a start. She wanted a kid, but a kid of her own; she could tolerate one that was only his, but for her it could never be the real thing, and the thought that she mightn't like Lola made him feel fear, in a way that nothing, not even failure, ever had before. It was like ice, a shard of ice, in the heart; the pain was there, always, especially when he dared to think things were going well. Children, Christ; they could get at you without even trying. All they needed to do was look, or hold out their arms. He'd hardly been a father, truth to tell.

But now Lola needed his love, and he felt her need with a poignancy that came from his sense that it might just be too late. Perhaps this was to be the tragedy that made his life significant after all.

He'd thought it for the best, when he'd left them in Gawler, and perhaps even now he could make it up to her. Poor little Lola. He would show her what he was really like. She loved him already, you could tell by the letters and the drawings she sent him, but she would come to know him better now, and he would show her how much he loved her, and she would know it. 1920'd been a hell of a year, but 1921 was going to be a happy new one. He could feel it.

Chapter Four

THE GENERAL MANAGER

Sometimes, luck can choose the worst possible moments to run out on a man.

For Frank, by 1920 the Managing Director of Electric Theatres and J.C. Williamson Films, and a powerful member of the boards of Hoyts and Greater Union, it was a particularly unfortunate time for funerals. Perhaps to a man who had moved around as self-sufficiently and opportunistically as Frank had done, the deaths of a father and a wife meant less than they did to most other men. But there was sadness, certainly, and some unmistakable symbolism. The implications of Grace's death, particularly, were substantial. There was Lola, for a start. And there was Olive, whom he was now free to marry.

Still, whatever was to be done about his obligations to the living, Frank made a reasonable fist of his obligations to the dead. Having set his father up in the Swanston Family Hotel in the summer of 1919, he sent him off in style in the autumn of 1920. It was a small funeral, necessarily; William Francis Thring's few connections were in Adelaide. But Frank arranged a suitably respectable Presbyterian service, and buried his father in a double plot in the Presbyterian section of Burwood Cemetery in a gesture that was only explained at Frank's own death in 1936, when he stipulated that he should be interred at his father's side. The Presbyterianism was a touch accidental; his father had been baptised and first married as a Catholic, and had become an Anglican for his second marriage to Leonora. But perhaps those labels were as irrelevant to the father as they were to the son.

Grace was farewelled in an even smaller service, in the home town that she had hardly ever left. Frank made the dreaded crossing to pay his respects, and to open some difficult conversations with little Lola and her grandparents. Perhaps there were some, the Wights at least, who felt that he might have made it more often.

After all the obsequies were decently done, though, it must surely have occurred to this practical man that his luck was actually not so bad. Several things in Frank's life had been left messy and unresolved through the decade in which he had made his first serious push for fame. The deaths of his father and first wife drew a line under the life of the boy from Wentworth who had become a bootmaker, and cleared the way for Frank Thring, buccaneer businessman, to stride boldly toward his destiny. Frank would have been aware that it was not the kind of thought you were supposed to have, let alone express, around funerals. But he would have reflected, too, that only fools denied the obvious, especially when things were falling so nicely into place for them.

Lola was another matter. For a man who kept reinventing himself as Frank did, a motherless daughter represented a very long loose thread. She had been living her childhood four hundred and fifty miles away without any of it impinging on her father's life too much, but suddenly that had changed. Decisions had to be made. Lola could stay with her grandparents, who had been *in loco parentis* all her life; but if she did, that was a recognition, and indeed a public declaration, that her relationship with Frank was, and was likely to remain, marginal in her life. It would be a massive concession to the Wights, too – not only of power and influence, but of moral advantage. There were compelling reasons, therefore, to bring Lola to live with her father in Melbourne.

There was one fly in the ointment, though. Frank was free now to marry Olive. What was she, childless spinster become blushing bride, to do with this nine-year-old she had barely met? Less urgent, presumably, but similarly tricky for Frank as newly remarried man, was the question of how Lola was to deal with this domineering stranger who was to be her new mother. Just thirteen weeks after her mother's funeral, young Lola had to dress up again for her father's wedding. It's not likely that the relationship between stepmother and stepdaughter occupied much conversational space in this hectic period; it was not Frank's way to spend much time on these emotional complexities, and neither the woman nor the girl could feel sufficiently secure about his absolute love to push her luck. So probably no one behaved badly.

The problem, as any amateur Freudian might have observed, was that suppressed resentments tend to find ways of making themselves destructively known. For most of the time in which they knew each other, Olive and Lola kept their distance; their dealings were rarely if ever warm, and occasionally cold to the point almost of estrangement.

The process of connecting his past life with his new one would have involved Frank in a number of tricky conversations through the spring of 1920 and the summer of 1921. There were items of unfinished business to be resolved, and old compromises to be renegotiated. Frank's dealings with his daughter and his future wife, and even his former in-laws, were just a dress rehearsal for the challenges that were to face his new ostensibly blended family after Anzac Day 1921, when Frank and Olive were married.

The marriage certificate completed by the newlyweds that day is very revealing about how they saw their past and their future, and about how they would like others to see them.[107]

> Certificate of Marriage in the State of Victoria 1921/1801
> 25 April 1921, at Christ Church, South Yarra.
> Denomination: Church of England
> Francis William THRING, manager, 38 years
> Queensland Hotel, Bourke St, Melbourne
> Widower (June 22nd, 1920)
> Father: Francis William THRING, gentleman
> Mother's maiden name: Laura MCKENZIE
> and
> Olive KREITMAYER, no occupation, 34 years
> 123 High Street, Prahran
> Spinster
> Father: Maximilian Ludwig KREITMAYER, gentleman
> Mother's maiden name: Harriett Mary WATTS
> Minister: Rev. Leonard TOWNSEND

Partly the document marks a declaration of the couple's social status, some of it pretended, some of it real. Both Frank's illegitimate father, the sawyer who became a maltster, and Olive's legitimate one who spent so much of his life in an industry that was never quite respectable, are now recognised

107 A copy of the certificate is held in the F.W. Thring Collection, Performing Arts Museum, Melbourne, 1995.116.256.

as 'gentlemen', right at the top of the pecking order. The choice of Christ Church in South Yarra for the ceremony, just near the mansion in Toorak that the happy couple was about to move into, and sharing the highly desirable postcode of S.E.1 that in Melbourne was synonymous with 'class', was similarly significant. And even the form of service had its implications in terms of social advantage. Frank, born a Roman Catholic and first married as a Presbyterian, and Olive, educated in a very exclusive convent and conscientiously Catholic till now, were suddenly Anglicans. There are all sorts of reasons why this may have been so, ranging from Road to Damascus conversions to careless coincidence; but the likeliest explanation is that, in Melbourne at this time, the Church of England was the religious home of political and commercial influence, and the best place to be for anyone who aspired to it.

For Frank these religious labels seem always to have been disposable; fifteen years later, at his burial by his father's side, he became a Presbyterian again. But for Olive, this was a very big decision. All of her history was against it. The Genazzano girl who had always been so dutiful, not only in her observances but in her little acts of thoughtfulness for the nuns, was doing something that many of her friends and family would have regarded as shocking, even scandalous. To wed 'outside the Church' meant, quite simply, that the marriage was unrecognised – not only by the Church, but by God. To marry a non-Catholic was awkward enough; it was not permissible in the church itself, but was still legitimate if the sacrament was celebrated by a priest in the vestry, and if the couple pledged to bring up their children in the Catholic faith. To marry in an Anglican church was to burn a lot of bridges. Olive did so, and Harriett her mother supported her, not only by attending the ceremony but by signing as a witness. Olive's choice meant a permanent break with the world of Genazzano, and with the friends she had made there.

Frank brought to his marriage certificate his customary freedom with the facts. This was the first of several documents in which he recorded his mother not as Angelina McDonald, but as the mythical Laura McKenzie. It was a most peculiar thing to do. It is difficult to put down to absent-mindedness, even if his mother's name is the sort of thing that a son is likely to be absent-minded about; the fact that Frank had named his mother correctly on his father's death certificate on March 20 of the preceding year makes that explanation even less plausible. Whatever the motive, it seems that Frank made a conscious decision to write Angelina out of his story. Perhaps it was her Catholicism, or her lack of education, or her servant status, that made her an undesirable connection. Perhaps Frank simply wanted a new start, with a kind of genetic blank sheet. Perhaps he was being mischievous or subversive, just for fun; perhaps he had a psychological aversion to telling the truth. The fictional Laura, wife of a gentleman, could be represented as whatever kind of mother he wanted her to be. The irony was that Angelina, who was real and had actually given birth to him, was every bit as unknown and negotiable a figure in his past as the person he invented to replace her.

The big lie, of course, was about the date on which he had become a widower. Grace had died not ten months before on June 20th, but three months before on January 22nd. That was the kind of thing that a man was not likely to misremember. Someone was being fooled or placated in this calculated tampering with the facts. Possibly it was an attempt to save the Reverend Townsend from troublesome thoughts. It is hard to think of any other people who needed to be protected from the truth. Olive certainly knew when Grace had died, and had been confronted with its consequences for her, in the form of a child who had never been a part of her plans; her complicity in the deception may have been with half an eye to the history, and perhaps to the judgement of the child of her own whom she hoped to have one day.

For the people who knew them, then, Frank's marriage to Olive was a controversial affair. Those who were aware of the actual date of Grace's death would have been struck by the hastiness of the arrangements; to set up a stylish South Yarra wedding with a service at the fashionable and popular Christ Church, Frank and Olive must have begun preparations while the telegram from Gawler was still on the table. And those who recalled Olive's dedication to the faith of her father, like the nuns and Old Girls of Genazzano, would have been astonished at how quickly and irrevocably it was jettisoned in her rush to the altar.

They would have been perplexed by the fact that, surely, it didn't need to be like that. Frank and Olive had been, in one sense or another, lovers for a decade; a few more months, for the sake of propriety, wouldn't have been an unreasonable concession to make. And since Frank had never shown any sign of having a religious bone in his body, a token commitment to his fiancée's church wouldn't have been an unusual accommodation, either. Frank chose not to do any of these things, and the only acknowledgement of the claims of respectability was made in a false statement in a legal document.

For two people who in some respects cared a lot about how they were perceived socially, Frank and Olive made their marriage a declaration of independence. It was the start of a new life, as citizens of Toorak and notable members of the Melbourne establishment. Old commitments and constraints were cast aside. All that, of course, highlighted the one major item of unfinished business in Frank's life.

The question was what was to be done about Lola. The answer was the obvious one for a man committed, in principle, to his role as a father, who was managing these matters in the context of a formidable new wife and substantial new wealth. Lola was brought to Melbourne, but dispatched almost immediately to boarding school, firstly to a small private college where she finished her primary education, and then to St Catherine's, an exclusive Anglican girls' school in Heyington Place, Toorak, where she spent not only her school terms, but large parts of her school holidays as well. During her time at St Catherine's from 1923 until 1928 she was living just a couple of blocks away from 'Rylands', the mansion on the corner of Toorak Road and Orrong Road that Frank had bought for his wife after their marriage in 1921, and named after the childhood home of his mother-in-law Harriett. It was handy enough to encourage regular visits, but for the most part they kept a tactful distance, as though still in different cities.

For Lola it must all have been very strange, and, at least at first, very painful. In Gawler, presumably, she had been the adored centre of a cosy little family; her mother and her grandparents had very little else in their lives on which to lavish their care and attention. That was the world she had known since infancy, and it was small and safe. Then she was suddenly transplanted from Edith Street to live among strangers; there is no record of her returning to see her childhood friends or the Wights at any point in the next twenty years. In Toorak things could hardly be more different. Far from being at the centre, she seemed barely at the margin of her new family, with a father with whom she had spent so little time, a stepmother who probably would have preferred that Lola had never been born at all, and their quite separate existence in their big house with the old lady she didn't know and, in due course, their new full-time adorable baby. She must often, in those early years, have felt surplus to requirements.

Frank would have found it uncomfortable, too. He was under a lot of pressure. The speed with which he remarried must have complicated things enormously for his dealings with his nine-year-old daughter, who had very little time to grieve over the loss of her mother before she was required to welcome a stepmother. Did he try to explain it to her? Probably not. Children were adaptable creatures, in Frank's very limited experience; he himself had

had to be resilient to the point of insensitivity. Young Lola was included in the wedding – of course, and was welcomed into the new family – of course. But she couldn't live with Frank and Olive – of course; so the best boarding arrangements that money could buy would be hers – of course.

Yet there was a sense that she was the sole connection to his past, and while that probably wasn't something that a determinedly unsentimental man would dwell on for very long, it was something that might make a man who was conscious of being destined for importance pause for thought. And, rather inconveniently, Lola reminded Frank of himself. She was very tall for her age, and at the time she came to Melbourne she was as gawky as a colt. But though she would never be a beauty, she had enough of Grace's genes to offset the heavy Thring inheritance. Moreover, Lola seemed surprisingly astute. Frank discovered suddenly a daughter with an interest in performance, and even in some of the things that he cared about. That recognition, and the fact that he had not only missed out on knowing Lola through the preceding decade but could not afford to let her get too close now, must have added a poignant irony to the new situation. It would take another decade, and the gambling of everything he had made and done, before he would be able to create the circumstances in which they could work creatively, side by side, and have their own time together.

So there he was, with a child who was absolutely dependent on him, and a woman who loved him and whose family connections had facilitated every entrepreneurial move that he had made. Whichever way you chose to look at it, there was some kind of choice to be made. Frank took the option that was most immediately importunate, and the one that would have been hardest to deny. History would have the option of seeing him as simply a serial opportunist, but history was probably wrong. The more likely diagnosis is that Frank was torn, inescapably and excruciatingly, between emotional demands that could never be reconciled. It was, for him, the best of times, and the worst of times. He had to choose, somehow, between his daughter and his second wife. Both of them would have been watching every move, interpreting every nuance, to see which way he would turn.

The child and the woman were, inevitably and probably permanently, locked in a tussle for his love, or at least for the small victories that came with subtle signals that one or the other of them had his primary attention. Both of them needed him – not only his public acknowledgement and his financial support, which was easy enough, but his almost-unconditional love. That was much trickier.

The new parameters of Lola's life were established almost immediately. Her father and her new step-mother headed off on the *Niagara* on a honeymoon cruise around the Pacific immediately after their wedding, and left Lola to celebrate her tenth birthday less than a month later with her new schoolmates in her new school. Over the next few years, it became the habitual pattern; Frank was very busy in Melbourne when he wasn't travelling somewhere else with Olive or without her, and Lola became quite accustomed to being left behind.

St. Catherine's seems to have been good to Lola. She made the boarding school her home, as in the circumstances it had to be. Its joint Principals, the Misses Ruth Langley and Flora Templeton, were warmly parental in a rather faded-Edwardian way, challenging their pupils to follow 'the line of service', and 'to make life lovely for those they live amongst':

> Miss Templeton and I have always striven to make friends with our girls – we have always met them half-way. They have entry to our rooms when they desire, and though sometimes it has been to report themselves, we think they have left us feeling they have received understanding, and though their faults were not condoned or made less, they were encouraged to try harder to please the Mistress whom they had offended.[108]

Lola, inexplicably nicknamed 'Tops', was popular with her peers and made a number of friends who remained close to her throughout her life. It helped that the school was not too large (there were just a dozen girls in Lola's leaving class of 1928, and only forty-two in the entire boarding house in her first year there), and that she entered enthusiastically into just about every aspect of the school's life. Her height made her very handy at inner goal for the school's netball team, and she was a regular member of its baseball and tennis teams, too; she was a prefect in 1927 and 1928, on the Editorial Committee for the School Magazine in 1927, on the Sports Committee in 1928. She dabbled in theatre, appearing in the productions by Miss Nellie Veitch's elocution class in 1923 (as Rose Bud in *Little Blue Bell* and *Will o' the Wisp*) and 1924 (as Peggy in a scene from *Cranford*), and

108 Annual Report, *St Catherine's Magazine*, August 1928, p.5.

returning to play the villain in the school production of *Monsieur Beaucaire* in her final year. And although she sadly failed to pull off the Award for the Least Troublesome Girl that Mrs Llewellyn had thoughtfully donated, Lola managed to complete her Leaving certificate without disasters. It was a much more committed and solid school record than that of any other major player in the stories of her father and half-brother, which were variously forgettable or (in the case of the younger Frank) appalling.

A couple of her smaller achievements at school would have particularly pleased her father. Lola appeared with two other girls as Mack Sennett's Bathing Beauties at a fancy-dress function in 1925, bringing what the school magazine called 'a touch of the movie world' rather daringly to an occasion otherwise marked by safer choices; the winning entry (Mary and her little lamb), the hordes of Japanese and Chinese ladies, and Maisie Cowper, who 'looked very sweet as a fluffy little duck', were more genteel, and much more comprehensively costumed.[109] And there was another hint of chips taken from old blocks when Lola won a prize for poetry (the competition was for four lines of verse about school life written against the clock) with a piece entitled 'An Impromptu Poem':

> There was a great commotion at a School in Toorak,
> When Miss Monks took all the powder, and wouldn't give it back;
> And now the girls are rather careful, when they go down to tea,
> And should you look around the rooms, no powder would you see.[110]

The epic tale was a bit limited in its scope, but there was a flair for doggerel, and a cheerful indifference to scansion, that the bootmaker-poet from the 'Bunyip' must have been proud to recognise as rather like his own.

So there are plenty of signs that Lola thrived after being abruptly transplanted to Melbourne. She was busy, she was cheerful, and before too long she may even have been quite happy. It is tempting to read quite a lot into her school photographs through her time at St Catherine's; Lola was in the school's first teams in netball and basketball for five years, from her fourteenth year to her eighteenth, and the formal groups of girls identically arranged and dressed encourage some comparisons. At fourteen Lola sits at the end of the front row, the junior member of the side and about the same size as her team-mates; her hair is done in two ribboned plaits that

109 *St Catherine's Magazine*, June 1925, p.21.
110 *St Catherine's Magazine*, May 1927, p.9.

just reach her shoulders. At fifteen, though, she has the position that she retains for each subsequent photograph, centre of the back row, the tallest girl in the picture by a head; the plaits by 1928 have almost reached her waist. Some things became habitual. But some things changed for the camera, too. The expression on her face in the early years is anxious and self-conscious, but in the last two years there's a wry smile and an air of composure that suggests a girl who is much more comfortable about who and where she is. The Thring family photographs from those two years are also revealing. Some of them show her with her father and Olive, three very tall figures, usually smiling in a restrained and patient way, occasionally grouped around a plump and scowling infant who was the latest Francis William Thring; but some of them show her with her friends, Nan and Pat and various others, and in those the girl with the extraordinary plaits is always laughing or smiling as she and her friends – metaphorically at least – let their hair down.[111]

So Lola came through it all pretty well, all things considered. She clearly had some version of her father's capacity for surviving and getting on with things, but in her case it was not at the cost of friendships. Her later life contained more than its share of bad luck and unhappiness, but a lot of that had to do with tragic events along the way rather than the legacy of a peculiar childhood. Some of her choices, from the long perspective of an outsider that turns most elements of a life into dramatic ironies, might suggest a woman trying to replace the father she had hardly had and prematurely lost; but who can be sure about these things?

Though she kept her close friends from St Catherine's, Lola didn't spend much time on nostalgia after her final Speech Night. A girl who had been as intensely involved in school teams and activities might normally have been expected to plunge into the activities of the Old Girls' Association, but Lola was a conspicuous absentee from its doings. This girl, to whom school sport had been such a continual and consuming commitment, never raised a bat or threw a ball at a basket in competition again in her life. Like her father, she closed the door on that place in her life, as she entered the next. Part of the reason for that clearly lay in a new connection with her father. The de facto family of Blair House at 'St. Caths' had been critical in the years after her mother's death and Frank's remarriage, but a number of things changed in the Thring household that made it easier for her to find a place there. The arrival of Frank junior in May 1926 when she had just turned fifteen was

111 Private photographs held by the Wilson family, into which Lola's daughter Jo married.

one of them. Lola had a new blood relative. The gap in age was big enough for her to play at a vaguely maternal interest in the baby, and to have no obvious points of focus for sibling rivalry; in different circumstances, the age difference might still have permitted some fears about displacement, but Lola was thoroughly used to that.

Frank's birth brought her closer to the centre of her family. Quite apart from her own pleasure in becoming a big sister, there were the implications for her in the ways her father and stepmother subsequently lived their lives. Frank was less inclined to lightly plan trips interstate and overseas. When he needed to take them, Lola was able to lend a hand to the beleaguered new mother. For Olive, having a child of her own seems to have eased or distracted some of those tensions and resentments that had from the beginning made for an awkward relationship with her step-daughter. The feeling between them would never be particularly warm, but with a chubby infant to coo over together Lola and Olive were probably as close at this period as they were ever able to be.

Frank took some strong decisions domestically, too, which confirmed the new state of affairs at Rylands. He had been away when Lola had played the dastardly Duke of Winterset in *Monsieur Beaucaire*, and had never had the time to watch her play netball. But now the interesting young woman that his daughter had become would have a much more acknowledged place in his feelings and his calendar. Olive's besottedness with the infant Frank cleared some space at his side, which Lola was able to fill. First, she came home. Rylands would henceforth not be a place that she visited in term holidays, but the place she lived in. Secondly, he arranged an extended journey abroad with his daughter, to mark the end of her schooldays and her new status.

When the Thrings had gone to America with their new baby in 1927, Lola had, naturally, stayed at school. But when Frank was contemplating a business trip to America for 1929, it was both a poor time to travel with his cantankerous toddler son and an excellent one to do so with his daughter. It was the ideal eighteenth birthday present for her, especially when Frank extended it to allow some time for touring in England and France. So in early April father and daughter set off together, and were gone for almost four months. It was a decisive shift in their relationship.

From this point until Frank's sudden death seven years later, Lola was much more actively a part of her father's career than Olive. They shared time on film-sets, at auditions, and in planning for a glorious tomorrow. He came to rely on her absolute support and her occasional challenges to his ways of thinking; she, having reclaimed a point of ease and intimacy with him at last, threw herself into his affairs with delight and enthusiasm. No wonder there was little time or thought for basketball or the Old Girls' Association. When they returned from Marseilles at the end of July 1929, Frank gave her a job, too, on the Hoyts payroll, and her first salary; but Lola's new vocation was clearly a labour of love.

The plaits went, too. Lola now sported a bob that was fashionable as well as functional, and looked every considerable inch the smart young woman around town. But she showed little interest in the social round that put a number of her contemporaries at 'St Caths' regularly into the social and gossip pages, and there were no signs or rumours of romance. The only left arm on which she was photographed during this period was that of her father, and a concerned or cruel observer might justly have said that Lola's devotion to her father was certainly unusual, probably excessive, and perhaps quite damaging to her chances of forming independent relationships with other men. Olive would have thought so, undoubtedly, and it is hard to believe that a woman as wilful and forthright as she would not have made her feelings known to her husband at least, loudly and clearly and possibly often. But, whatever the complicated causes and the eventual cost, it could now be said with reasonable confidence for the first time that Lola Thring was happy.

Frank, meanwhile, was about to make another major move in determining the future of Australian film. Part of his focus on that American trip was genuinely on his daughter; but part of it was on an audacious scheme that he had in mind, one that, if he did manage to bring it off, would turn the whole industry upside down.

He did bring it off, and when he did the world of Australian cinema was, for good and ill, changed forever.

The birth in 1926 of Frank Thring the baby had been a crucial element in the development of that new, stronger connection between father and daughter. Olive must been starting to wonder whether she would ever have a child. Frank had bought Rylands for her and her mother, and they had moved there after the wedding. But there were three empty bedrooms to testify that things don't always work out as planned; one of them Lola occupied now and then during the holidays, but the other two were of no use at all. And then, at last, she had a son. She had to be very careful early in her pregnancy, and again near the end; she settled into the little private hospital in Kooyong Road where they could keep an eye on things. This was a particularly precious child; she would never have another, and what would her life be about without one?

The birth, in the end, was straightforward enough, and she agreed that he should bear his father's name, and the name that his father's father had been given at the obscure beginnings of the dynasty.

> Birth in the District of Armadale
> 11 May 1926 at 51 Kooyong Road, Armadale, County of Bourke
> Usual Residence: Rylands, 534 Toorak Road, Toorak
> Francis William, female
> Father: Francis William THRING, managing Director,
> aged 43, born Adelaide SA
> Mother: Olive Mary THRING formerly KREITMAYER, aged 39,
> born Abbotsford
> Married 25 April 1921 at South Yarra
> Informant: Olive Mary THRING, mother, Rylands, 534
> Toorak Road, Toorak

Among all the unreliable documents that chart the Thring genealogy, this one has both the fewest inaccuracies and the most bizarre. It was not surprising, given the vagueness of Frank's stories about his former life, that in the confusion of the moment Olive got her husband's birth-place wrong. There was something quite definite about her re-naming of herself, though; 'Mary' was either a pious or nondescript replacement for the exotic 'Marguerite', and confirmed the removal of the last traces of her cosmopolitan heritage, while 'Cecilia' vanished altogether.

But the real oddity here, of course, is the declaration of the sex of the baby, and that presumably was not the kind of mistake that even a flustered new mother would make. It was presumably just a slip of a clerk's pen, but it was a remarkable error that young Frank himself, who must surely have seen it at some point in his adult life, would have found delicious. When he was a little boy, there were people who mused, when they noticed his fondness for playing dress-ups with his mother's wardrobe, that he really should have been born a girl, and that his half-sister Lola, his father's right-hand woman and inheritor of much of Frank senior's acumen and organisational skill, should have been the son of the family. When he was a bigger boy, they taunted him at school for being different, and mocked his queer manners and his sexuality. When he was a man, the discovery that he had been registered legally as a girl would have given him the perfect cue to celebrate the fact that his interest in males defined him as respectably heterosexual after all.

The latest Francis William Thring was an extraordinarily indulged baby. The domestic staff at Rylands, which already included a housekeeper and a chauffeur domiciled above the stable, plus a part-time gardener and several occasional maids, was augmented by a full-time Nanny, who moved into the room in the main house beside little Frank's nursery so that she could monitor his well-being at all times of the day and night. Nanny and Olive lived their lives around him, Harriett and the housekeeper were always hovering around somewhere, and even Lola, when she was at home, seemed always to be wanting to help. Five women, ranging in age from fifteen to seventy-six, were almost constantly at his beck and call. From Olive's point of view, this was natural and appropriate; she got on much more cheerfully with her mother and step-daughter now that they all seemed to agree that the comfort of baby Frank was the most important matter in the world.

From the perspective of Frank senior, life at Rylands in the second half of the decade was at last proceeding just as it should in a well-managed family. He was still away a lot, but had less reason at such times to have reservations about leaving Olive and Lola behind; the baby gave Olive not only something to do but a welcome distraction, and Lola was now able to feel much more a part of things. He could play the benevolent patriarch, either surrounded by his dependent womenfolk or from afar, just as he chose.

Everything at last was running according to plan. Once again Frank's life seemed sustained by good fortune on all sides, and all the while the money kept rolling in. The purchase of Rylands had marked his arrival as a man of substance in Melbourne, a man to invite to important functions who could buy most things that he wanted, a man not to be ignored. The expensive decoration of Rylands, alongside the regular trips abroad and the dabbling in art, charted the way in which Frank Thring's substance conspicuously grew from that point.

He had had none of the advantages of the Taits and the Tallises and the other sons of well-known, well-heeled families with whom he was dealing. He was the son of a sawyer, though nobody was allowed to know it. They knew him as that chap who had been just a projectionist, the hustler who had dealt himself into playing with the big boys. He had started behind all of them, not only the silver-spoon brigade but people like Stuart Doyle who had climbed their way up somebody else's ladder. He had come to Melbourne with nothing in his wallet; worse than that, he had come with a sick wife and a baby, and nothing in his wallet. At thirty-five, he ran two companies; at forty, he ran three, and had an address in Toorak; at forty-five, he ran four, and was a very rich man with an infant son who bore his name. Some day, it would now have occurred to him, young Frank would take the baton from him, and in time his son after him. A Thring dynasty, all of it created in just fifteen years. He was part of the main game; he may have bent the rules a little to get there, but now he had a seat at their table, and they were all looking sideways at him. Against all the odds, Frank could look at all he had, and say that he had made it.

Now he wore his power like a well-tailored suit. In the past, it had been something that he had had to assert against obstacles that had sometimes made him push too hard. But it was second nature to him now. How comfortable he felt in the role may be gauged from an exchange of letters in 1923, when Frank was faced with a protest from one of his performers. Signor Kost, who conducted the orchestra at all the Electric Theatres venues, was no ordinary employee. He led an orchestra of twenty-eight, and, in the miscellaneous variety bill that Frank had developed in Tasmania and that retained an important role in his film programs at all his city venues, Signor Kost's Concert Orchestra was always a prominent feature. In June 1923, though, Frank's penchant for an eclectic program that included a few audience-indulging laughs seemed to have come back to bite him. He suggested, or allowed, a comic song that parodied the Italian approach to war to be performed at the Empire. Signor Kost, who found suggestions of army-issue running-shoes repugnant, wrote to Frank on the following morning in defence of his countrymen. Kost's passion is obvious, and his difficulties with English syntax and spelling add to the impression of outrage that could barely be controlled. Frank, who spoke no other language than the one he had to, probably found the malapropisms amusing, though he scrupulously didn't acknowledge them when he replied the next day.

> Dear Mr Thring,
>
> Mr. Cowen informed me tonight that you gave order to Mr. Dampier to sing the burlesque impersonification of an Italian people.
>
> As for us Italians this song sounds very much offensive, especially at the present times in which our Country is affected by such tremendous

> misfortune and hundreds of thousands of our countrymen are homeless and deprived of all theyr means of existence, my heart is acking and cannot bear anything which sounds as ridicule to my people.
>
> Whith great sorrow, therefore, I am conveing to you with this letter, my resignation as Musical Director of your Theatres, asking you to accept my notice from Friday next.
>
> With kind regards,
>
> Yours Sincerely,
>
> E.Kost[112]

It was a relatively minor issue, one that a General Manager might comfortably have handled with a placatory response. Frank chose to play it very differently.

> Dear Signor,
>
> I am in receipt of your letter advising us of your resignation. We regret that you have seen fit to take this step, but it is impossible for us to allow the orchestra to dictate what we shall submit to the public.
>
> I think you are supersensitive in taking notice of songs sung from the stage referring to Italians, inasmuch as every other Nation has humorous and character songs sung about them without taking it seriously. However, I suppose this point is only one of several grievances that probably you have, and as it is useless for you to remain under possible unharmonious conditions, we have nothing, of course, to do but to accept your resignation.
>
> Sincerely yours,
>
> F.W. Thring[113]

Among all the professions of sincerity and kind regards, the message in Frank Thring's reply was clear. You were either with him or against him. Signor Kost learned that day that he was not indispensable. He had played his strongest card, and the Great Dexter had trumped him, because in the

112 The exchange of letters is held in the unclassified Frank Thring papers, Performing Arts Museum, Melbourne.

113 ibid.

end only one person's commitment was crucial to the Thring empire and that was the commitment of the man himself. To Signor Kost's consternation, perhaps, his ultimatum carried no weight at all; Mr Thring may have needed the Signor's talent and his string section, but not nearly as much as the Signor Kost Concert Orchestra needed him. There were very few other opportunities in Melbourne for a large orchestra to work regularly several nights every week, and Frank knew it. Signor Kost would have been left with a fair bit of explaining to do when his musicians turned up for their six o'clock call.

Frank chose not to give him an inch, or even a pretext to continue the correspondence. Perhaps the seemingly casual supposition that 'this point is only one of several grievances that probably you have' indicates that this disagreement is the last straw, or that Frank had decided that it might be a good time to bid a fond farewell to Kost and all his associated expenses. But the style reflects the confidence of a man who needs nobody and knows it. This knowledge, for Frank, when backed by the tangible assets of money and influence, was power.

The showdown with Kost was one of those difficult things that a smart man handled immediately; the seemingly impossible took a little longer. Belief in himself carried Frank Thring a long way, even when more of the money and influence seemed to be lined up on the other side. This was the case in his war with Stuart Doyle and Union Theatres for the hearts and minds of the paying public, and for the most impressive and abiding architectural symbols of their visions for the future of Australian film.

Frank Thring's rivalry with Stuart Doyle had a number of dimensions in addition to their business competition as the men in charge of Australia's two major groups of film companies. One of them had to do with the remarkable parallels between the two careers, which probably helped each man to understand and distrust the other rather more shrewdly than the people who sat with them on boards. Doyle was five years and one day Frank's junior; born in the inner Sydney suburb of Leichhardt, and growing up in Blackheath, to the north of the Blue Mountains, Doyle was a New South Welshman all his life, whereas Frank did little in that state other than being born on its border.

But when Frank Thring was touring the regions of South Australia and Victoria as the Great Dexter in 1906–7, Stuart Doyle was playing the fairgrounds all over New South Wales, practising the fine art of deception under the name of Frank Stuart. In 1909, when Frank travelled to Tasmania for his first documented stint as a motion-picture man, Doyle moved to Sydney to work for the J.D. Williams Amusement Company. With the amalgamation of four companies in 1913 to form the Combine, he moved as quickly up the corporate ladder as Frank Thring, in his less conventional way, was climbing it in Melbourne; from the position of Business Manager he quickly rose to become Joint Managing Director, and by 1929, when Frank Thring was running the show at Hoyts Pictures, Electric Theatres, J.C. Williamson Film and Associated Theatres, Doyle was Managing Director of Union Theatres and Australasian Films, and could claim twice as many directorships as his Melbourne rival.

Like Thring, Doyle was a largely self-made man whose pursuit of wealth and status was founded partly on his business acumen and drive, partly on a happy knack for being in the right spot at the right time, and partly on an advantageous marriage. The year after Frank Thring formed his decisive connection with the Kreitmayers in general and with Olive in particular, Stuart Doyle married a grazier's daughter, and stepped effortlessly into the world of the Sydney establishment. It took Frank another decade to move into the most prestigious part of town, but Doyle made his journey to a house on Sydney Harbour quite speedily; he joined the Royal Prince Alfred Yacht Club, became Commodore of the Royal Motor Yacht Club of New South Wales, and must have marvelled, sometimes, as Frank must have, at how far he had come from the carnival circuit, and how easily and quickly he had got there. Doyle was, genuinely, a very skilful sailor. Frank, who never sailed and rarely swam, took up golf, unconvincingly; for him, the value of the game would always depend on how one played the nineteenth hole, where there were potentially useful friends to be made.

Stuart Doyle and Frank Thring found that a man could belong to any club that he wanted to, providing that he had money and knew the right people, and had the right sort of wife. But you could never cover your traces completely. In the way that the two of them played the game, there would always be a marked trace of the rough-and-tumble world in which they had cut their theatrical teeth, as well as a suitably hidden tinge of the skills in sleight-of-hand that they had developed along the road.

They had a lot in common, then, and that was a promising basis for a contest. And their personal rivalry was fed by, and fed in turn, the routine cultural antagonism between Australia's two major cities. In part, of course, the animosity between Sydney and Melbourne was simply a myth, taking the form mostly of banter, and rooted in the simplest of stereotypes: Sydney, home of entrepreneurial daring and big punters, and the place where the first convicts had come, where the arts were bright and brassy, and where the sun sparkling on the harbour could make everyone feel like a hedonist; and Melbourne, home of blue-chip commerce, where the arts were inventive and the morality was appropriately Victorian, where the insecurity fostered by having four seasons in a day made everyone serious and philosophical, and the only river in town flowed upside-down. But it was, and remains, a myth with clear political implications to do with investment resources and access to influence over governments. Through the 1920s, the delicate balance of power was subtly beginning to shift north, from Melbourne, which until 1927 was the interim national capital, to Sydney, which had a more immediate relationship with Canberra.

The battle between Doyle and Thring became increasingly a matter of monuments. It wasn't surprising, in terms of psychological patterns, that two men whose careers had been assembled like a house of cards chose to proclaim their triumph in bricks and mortar, or more accurately in marble. The great attraction of buildings as signs of a man's success was that anyone could see them, and that they lasted a long time; they were especially visible, of course, if they were particularly big. Stuart Doyle announced an ambitious program to modernise cinemas in the Union Theatres chain in 1921; Frank Thring, who had already dabbled in the building of new cinemas in the process of launching Electric Theatres, raised the stakes in March 1923, when he committed Electric to spending half a million pounds on constructing new theatres. In part these declarations of spectacular intent had more to do with self-promotion and window-dressing than a genuinely expansionary program; it was easy enough to defer or diffuse the real costs by the traditional tactic of blaming delays on the tradesmen. By 1925 neither of the great competitors had done much to put their plans into action at all. But that was about to change dramatically.

Doyle in 1925 had committed Union Theatres and Australasian Films to a cautious revival of their interest in making local films; the result was *Painted Daughters* (1925), a piece of froth-and-bubble promoted as 'a glorious whirl of perfect girl', with 'one hundred Australian beauties in the cast'.[114] The move was significant in two ways in shaping Frank Thring's career.

114 Routt, in Sabine, *A Century of Australian Cinema*, p.60.

One of those consequences would not become clear until 1930, when Efftee was created. *Painted Daughters* was made to be undistinguishable from the current Hollywood product; though it was marketed locally as 'Made in Australia – for Australia – by Australians', its script and its Hollywood director F. Stuart-Whyte made sure that the film had nothing specifically to do with Australia at all. Frank Thring not only stole the nationalistic slogan for his Efftee repertoire five years later, but very determinedly set out to capture the niche market that Doyle, prudently perhaps, had not been prepared to trust after all.

The second consequence of Doyle's shift in direction was immediate. The need to make space in its programs for its own product had the effect of loosening Union Theatres' hold on its position as Australia's primary distributor. The opening was narrow but it was there, and Frank Thring moved quickly to exploit it. He formed an alliance with Hoyts Pictures, the third major player in the market-place. Hoyts was a Melbourne company too. It had begun life in 1909, in a rented hall where Arthur Russell, a dentist and (surprise, surprise) a magician, showed films as a hobby. The business had taken off in those heady days for the magic picture show; Russell gave up his practice and his conjuring, and formed a company that was rumoured to be named after a circus that he had worked for in England. By 1925, Russell was out of the picture; George Griffiths was the new head of the company, and was open to a strategic partnership with Frank Thring's multiple interests. The variety magazine *Everyones* reported in October 1925 that the deal was already done:

> Mr G.F. Griffiths (Hoyts) and Mr F.W. Thring (Associated Theatres) have just completed the amalgamation of interests involving no less than 64 picture theatres in Melbourne and its suburbs, says our Southern representative.
>
> The object of the amalgamation is, we understand, to control the purchase and distribution of films and supplies for all suburban theatres, and also to negotiate with the small showmen with a view to preserving their interests.[115]

But it took more than a year for all the agreements to be signed, and to incorporate the J.C. Williamson branch of the Thring empire. *Everyones*

115 *Everyones*, 29 October 1925, p.16.

announced the news under a banner headline that simply cited the capital value of the new entity (three-and-a-half million pounds); the focus was absolutely on the scale of the new operation:

> The amalgamation brings under practically one banner eighty theatres operating in the capital cities and metropolitan areas in Victoria, New South Wales, and west Australia, and by the end of the coming year will also be operating in other cities in the Commonwealth.
>
> This move brings unto [sic] being by far the largest picture exhibiting organisation in Australasia, insofar as the number of theatres which will be controlled is concerned.
>
> In the City of Melbourne the new company will carry on its business or be otherwise represented, by virtue of its share-holdings, in every picture house except one.[116]

The gauntlet was thus thrown down to Doyle. The vast majority of the cinemas involved in the deal were in Melbourne, but the press release made it clear that this was not a limitation that was going to last much longer. Like the Thring companies, Hoyts had made a number of post-war forays into other capitals. It had been difficult to gain a foothold in Sydney, however, where in 1921 Union Theatres controlled eighty per cent of city and suburban cinemas. The pooling of resources in 1926, following closely on Union Theatres' dalliance with movie-making, changed the landscape profoundly. By the end of the decade, the reconstituted Hoyts not only was the major distributor in the country, but had gained an edge in the Sydney market as well.

The merger between the Hoyts and Thring circuits was controversial, and the rumblings weren't confined to Doyle's offices in Sydney. It looked like one of those moves towards monopoly that in Australian film had always squeezed out the small player; the reference in the *Everyones* article to the sole surviving independent operator in Melbourne was ominous. Frank Thring, having been promptly installed as Managing Director of 'by far the largest picture distributing organisation in Australasia', issued a statement early in 1928 that sought to smooth ruffled feathers which *Everyones* ran as its main feature:

116 *Everyones*, 24 November 1924, p.10.

> At the outset may we point out that that the impression which has gained currency that the company is a combine and as such may be detrimental to other exhibitors, is entirely erroneous. Hoyts Theatres Limited, in fact, may be likened to a co-operative amalgamation of corresponding interests formed not only for mutual protection but for the assistance of all those associated in the ever-growing business of moving picture presentation.
>
> The company aims for the firm establishment of its business on a sound financial and economic basis, and at the same time the proper protection of those independent exhibitors who now are or may, from time to time, be associated with us.[117]

It wasn't entirely convincing. The distinction between 'a combine' and 'a co-operative amalgamation of corresponding interests' was not as self-evident as its author appeared to assume. Nor was the reassurance that the new Hoyts simply sought its own financial advantage, and posed no threat to any exhibitor 'associated with us', of much comfort to its few remaining competitors. The message was clearly that independent operators would have nothing to worry about, providing they were safely 'associated'. Frank presented the new Hoyts as a defensive alliance against enemies from overseas, and a pragmatic consolidation of resources; it was thus a product of simple common-sense and normal commercial evolution:

> A merger such as this is the natural outcome of a growing business which for self-protection must adopt the proper means of safeguarding its future against the possibility of foreign competition, and the economic waste which must always result from unnecessary overhead, and the more serious burdens arising from unproductive capital, expenditure.[118]

Stuart Doyle, however, would have known exactly what it was about. The real adversary was not a hypothetical one from across the seas, but the Union Theatres corporation on the other side of the border, and the pooling of resources was no budgetary rationalisation but the creation of an industrial war-chest.

---

117 'Hoyt's Theatres Ltd. – F.W. Thring in Explanation', *Everyones*, 5 January 1927, p.3.
118 ibid.

Everything Frank said in the rest of his article to placate the fears aroused by his new company had the effect of confirming how threatening it really was, to the point where it is impossible to believe that this wasn't his purpose all the time. When he proclaimed that 'we give our assurance that our financial resources will not be used in any way to unreasonably hamper or depreciate the business of others', he left enough doubt about what might be construed as 'reasonable' hampering and depreciation to make any rival uneasy. When he disclaimed any attempt to 'endanger' Sydney independent exhibitors providing they took no action that might 'put any theatre or theatres actually against us by alliance or other method', he left them no alternative to war but appeasement. At the end of the article, the tone shifted from forceful reassurance to genial good-will to all men:

> We trust that the foregoing may be of some little interest to our contemporaries in the business, and we take this opportunity of wishing all a very bright and prosperous New Year.[119]

Again, the subtext was unmistakable. The effect of the disarming Season's Greetings was to remind 'all' of Hoyts' opposition of what a very tough year they were in for, and of the challenges to their prosperity it would bring. Frank's benediction reminded his readers that one of the pleasures of power was the freedom it gave to be playful sometimes about serious things, like livelihoods and other people's lives.

The Hoyts merger changed Frank's life in a number of ways. He had been busy and rich before it, and had been away from home a good deal; from 1926, the year in which his son was born and his theatrical empire roughly doubled in size, Frank was probably busier, certainly richer, and travelled much more. His business trips before then were almost all interstate, a week or two at a time. His only known venture overseas was the honeymoon cruise on the 'Niagara' in 1921, the first time he had been out of Australia in his life. But from 1926, Frank went to America or Europe or both in almost every year, for periods of three or four months at a time.

119 'Hoyt's Theatres Ltd. – F.W. Thring in Explanation', *Everyones*, 5 January 1927, p.3.

It was a pattern that had clear implications for his relationships with Olive, Lola and Frank junior. Frank went, ostensibly, because he needed to be talking distribution with the overseas studios, because he needed to observe the ways in which the big players in other countries did things, because he needed to see the latest in theatre design on the grand scale, because he needed to select the furnishings and the art-works that would make a night at one of the Hoyts' Regent Cinemas that he built a journey into Aladdin's cave. But he went, mostly, because he wanted to. Though he often came home with new deals and connections, and was always accompanied by a vast array of classical pots and sculptures, and bolts of expensive cloth, there were other people in his new giant conglomerate who might have attended to these things. Frank clearly enjoyed the style and status, and the very conspicuous wealth, that was proclaimed in these ventures onto the international stage. In particular, he seems to have taken with great relish to the role for which he was least qualified, that of a patron and authority in the arts. The foyers of his cinemas, and the rooms at Rylands, were filled with beautiful things that were a testimony to the fact that money could buy not only power and influence, but cultivation and, in every sense, class.

And so in 1927 began the public contest between Hoyts and Union Theatres, but more accurately between Thring and Doyle, to create the most sumptuous picture palace in the land. One of Frank's first moves, on acquiring a budget to play with that more closely approximated his aspirations, was to announce a splurge on new cinemas, as he had several years before; but this time the emphasis was on quality rather than quantity, and this time the places were built, quickly and spectacularly, according to plan. They were the Regents, and one them appeared in each of the five mainland capitals in Australia over the next four years, and in several of the more prosperous suburbs and provincial towns.

The Regents were named after one of the picture palaces built by the New Yorker Samuel 'Roxy' Rothapfel, who had pioneered a style of cinema architecture that sought a grandeur more magical and marvellous than the classical sobriety of other kinds of public building. Rothapfel believed in 'dynamically "escapist" cinemas, refuges from office enterprise or the homemaking treadmill, which would rest eyes, soothe senses, ease pain, and provide edification in the process. This deeply affected Australian proprietors'.[120] One of those most deeply affected was Frank Thring. The

120 Conrad Hamann, 'Heralds of free enterprise: Australian cinemas and their architecture from the 1900s to the 1940s', in James Sabine (ed.), *A Century of Australian Cinema*,

Rothapfel connection couldn't be too widely advertised, given that at the time Frank was at least publicly wielding the cudgel against the pernicious invasiveness of American ideas; but the name 'Regent' managed to combine a discreet acknowledgement of influence with an apparent invocation of Empire and King that sounded safe as well as special.

The first of them was built a year before the Hoyts merger in Toorak Road, South Yarra, a pleasant ten-minute stroll from Rylands. It was a relatively modest prototype for the magnificence of the cinemas that shared its name. For Frank Thring it was an experiment in targeted marketing. The movies, as everyone kept saying, were a democratic form; this was entertainment for the masses, and the burgeoning prosperity of the industry depended absolutely on the accessibility of the places and the product. But what if the affluent patrons of Toorak, Olive and her sherry circle, for example, wanted something a little more salubrious than the middle-class audiences in Malvern, or the working-class ones in Richmond and Collingwood, were happy with? The South Yarra Regent was like other suburban cinemas in scale, but more comfortably appointed, and certainly more lavishly decorated, than any of the other theatres in the Frank Thring chain. The notion that a cinema might borrow something of the ambience of an art gallery and a private club, and even a hint of the drawing-room in a stately home, worked well in South Yarra. It was adapted and magnified, beyond any visitor's sense of the familiar, in the five capital city Regents that appeared in the second half of the decade.

The Perth Regent was the first of them, rising spectacularly from the ruins of the old Queen's Hall in William Street in September 1927. The program for its Grand Opening on September 10 hails it as 'A Temple of Thespis', a 'noble edifice' offered as 'a rendezvous de luxe for the residents of the capital city of the Golden West'; it emphasises, though, that this temple is not only massive but magical, a quintessential Roxy Rothapfel dream-palace. That quality is there in the two-thousand seat auditorium:

> The principal colour combination is formed of a neatly interwoven combination of mauve, cyclamen and gold, giving a charm of beauty and brightness, and an artistic magnificence unparalleled in theatre construction in the Antipodes. In its scheme of almost bewildering

Port Melbourne, Willliam Heinemann Australia, p.94.

> enchantment, also, will be discovered new and bizarre harmonies in the bewitchery of light and iridescence ...[121]

It is there, too, in the foyer:

> Unquestionably original in design and attaining a standard of artistry and comfort beyond compare, it is difficult to lure one from its charming surroundings. Beautiful crystal glass chandeliers – they are fitted at intervals throughout – illuminated pillars, and bevelled glass mirrors stretching the length and breadth of the spacious foyer, throw their dazzling reflections before the eye; a fascinating and fairy-like scene ...

It is there in the open-air promenade under a thousand stars, and even in the control room, where 'the patent dimming machine, the first of its kind in Australia', creates wondrously shifting patterns of illumination. This is a journey into an imaginary world, whatever the story that might be played on the screen when the lights eventually go down.

The Perth program made a feature of the comfort of the Regent's seating, too ('it can be said without fear of contradiction that a degree of comfort is assured that is not be met with in any other part of the Commonwealth'); it drew on the South Yarra experiment by making things even more incomparably comfortable for those patrons who could afford to pay a little more ('several hundred chairs in the circle are of lounge design'). The perfect conjunction of art, enchantment and a well-cushioned bottom became a familiar refrain with each successive Regent, though with a steady increase in hyperbole.

The Adelaide Regent followed in 1928, described glowingly as 'the crown of a queen', and later in that year the ultimate challenge to Doyle, the Sydney version. Designed like its Adelaide namesake by Cedric Ballantyne, the latter offered art works and furnishings from 'London, New York, Paris, Berlin and Rome'; it promised the attendance of young men called 'cadets', and of usherettes who were 'typical of Australian beauty, cultured, intellectual, each with personality and charm'.[122] Both theatres offered the continually changing play of light that the audiences in Perth could

121 Souvenir program, copy held in Performing Arts Collection, His Majesty's Theatre, Perth.

122 Hamann, in Sabine, *A Century of Australian Cinema*, p.94–5.

marvel at – but the display was bigger, better, more beautiful than anything previously dreamt of in the Antipodes. So, at least, it said in the programs.

Stuart Doyle was by this time well-advanced on his counter attack. In 1928 he opened the Capitol Theatre in Sydney in April, and soon after matched the Thring bid in Perth and raised it, with the Perth Ambassadors; in 1929, the year in which Thring unveiled the finest Regent of them all in Melbourne, Stuart Doyle ventured onto his opponent's home turf to open the State, the largest theatre in the country. And Doyle added another element to the game. He introduced to Australia the concept of the atmospheric cinema, the latest trend in American theatre design, and the products were spectacular:

> … the Sydney Capitol was Australia's first fully atmospheric cinema. The right side of the auditorium represented an Italian palace with a flirtation balcony similar to one in the Doges' Palace in Venice. The left side of the auditorium featured a piazza with a Grecian garden and peacock walk, by way of distinction. Flowering vines drooped toward the orchestra pit and, for added realism, stuffed pigeons rested on roofs and cypress trees. Moving stars and clouds also passed and repassed across the ceiling and the Southern Cross was poised patriotically above the proscenium.[123]

Pigeons and peacocks were prominent in Perth, too; the ones in the artificial garden at the Ambassadors were specially imported from South Africa. Like Thring, Doyle made the selection of artefacts a personal responsibility, almost a matter of honour. The publicity brochure for the opening of the Sydney State assured the reader that Stuart Doyle had 'personally supervised every detail' of this new triumph, and had 'twice travelled the world in search of novelties and ideas'.[124] Frank Thring had made the trip to the Old World twice more, as it happened, and his claim to 'personal supervision' had been a continual, and reasonably accurate, assertion throughout his career. It was an unusually presidential strategy for the conduct of a very complicated commercial duel. Doyle's move to emulate that kind of personal guarantee both confirmed the irritating effectiveness of the tactic as Frank had been practising it so far, and gave Frank a compelling reason to keep travelling on boats.

123 Collins, *Hollywood Down Under*, p.122.
124 Shirley and Adams, *Australian Cinema*, p.79.

The counter-blast was evident everywhere, even in the toilets. The State in Sydney provided a variety of experiences to ensure that going to the bathroom was yet another journey to a rich and fabulous world:

> The Ladies at stalls level had the Pompadour Room, allowing patrons to ablute in *ancien regime* surroundings. Its circle counterpart (for the matinee customers) was the Butterfly Room, and the balcony, presumably for young moderns, had a Futurist Room, in striking pentagonal patterns suggesting German expressionism or English vorticism. Stalls gentlemen could find the Pioneers' Room in an odd 'squatters' Tudor' with Enfield muskets crossed significantly over a fifteenth-century fireplace. Above came the Empire Builders' Room, lined with portraits of men of military daring or mining or agricultural enterprise. Above them came the College Room, with crests of Sydney's great public schools edifying balcony lads. Everything was summarised over the basins.[125]

The Doyle cinemas had a good deal in common with the contemporary theme-park, except that each one had a multiplicity of themes. And, above all in every sense, they had skies. The ceilings, brilliantly painted and lit to 'recreate' the galaxy, were a signature effect that reached its apotheosis in the wondrous starlit roof of the Melbourne State.

The Regents had themes, too. The Brisbane Regent took its audiences through a Gothic chapel; the Melbourne Regent's foyer with its Agincourt mural ushered its visitors into the ambience of a mediaeval court. But the Frank Thring approach was even more eclectic than Stuart Doyle's. The signature effect of the Regent Theatres was primarily in its classical decoration, Greek and Roman, and that was a direct reflection both of Frank Thring's genuine enthusiasm for the adventures in knowledge that wealth had made possible for him, and his conception, as a highly aspirational man, of what others might find most tasteful.

The encroachments into other states, especially Stuart Doyle's state, were all no doubt dear to Frank's heart. But the Melbourne Regent was, in the end, the one that mattered most. This was now his city. It had always been Olive's. If there was a place in which it was important for Frank spectacularly to make his mark, it was Melbourne, and it was the home of the last and finest of the Regents.

125 Hamann, in Sabine, *A Century of Australian Cinema*, p.98.

The theatre opened on March 15, 1929. It was built in Collins Street, one block south of the former Kreitmayer's Waxworks, where Frank Thring had made his modest start with nothing in his pocket eighteen years before. It cost three hundred and sixty thousand pounds, and seated 3,250. Both its size and its capacity were exceeded in Australia only by the State Theatre, which Stuart Doyle opened on the corner of Flinders and Russell Streets a few months later.

The program for the opening night of the Melbourne Regent probably set some records for self-importance, too. A brief prologue, surrounded by portraits of the five directors of Hoyts, Frank Thring, George Tallis, George Griffiths, John Tait and Frank Challingsworth, made it clear that these men, heroes all, had rescued the cinema in Australia from tawdriness and futility:

> To five men the Regent Theatre represents the realisation of dreams. Years ago they saw in motion pictures a potent force trammelled by disrespect. Few shared their vision, until the great chain of Hoyts Theatres Ltd. stretched throughout Australia – substance of steel and stone built on the stuff of dreams.[126]

Doyle, when he read this, was unlikely to have been impressed. He would have felt even less so, when he read, after the staple, and by now almost perfunctory, description of the 'Salle de Reception' ('Broad stairs lead into a Gothic court; deep carpets underfoot; high overhead, arched ceilings, with heraldic emblazonment'), a provocative statement that declared the Regent loftily beyond crass superlatives, and even modish 'atmospherics':

> In all its dignity, the Regent takes pride in no finer achievement than this: While fortunes have been spent, it leaves the impression not of cost, but of culture.[127]

It was Melbourne's last thrust in its battle with Sydney, Thring's in his battle with Doyle. And it was a very powerful card. The implication that there were some competitions one would never want to enter, and moreover would be appalled to win, was the last refuge of the defiantly underfunded. The tactic was unlikely to win the war, but guaranteed to get under the skin of the enemy.

---

126 Souvenir program for the opening of the Melbourne Regent, held by Frank Van Straten.
127 ibid.

The new Regent catered lavishly for the Europhile, as all the Regents had done, with its 'exquisite Louis XIV furnishings' surrounded by 'the works of Italy's greatest modern painters'. But the Melbourne version was not just a place to admire. It catered for the Very Important Person in every conceivable way:

> Luxury – luxury to the utmost degree of service! A telephone call? Just mention the number to a Regent Cadet, and the instrument is plugged into the wall beside us. Expecting a message? The Professional Service Bureau will bring it. [128]

Frank had borrowed Doyle's idea of the helpful Cadet and turned the Regal Promenade into a very superior business club; the program noted that, and then turned it to democratic advantage – 'yet it admits us all to membership'. It was a clever, if by now rather familiar, marketing ploy.

The program that opening night was identical in its range to the four Regent openings that had preceded it, and represented the traditionally eclectic Thring bill at its finest moment. It began with the Overture from *The Desert Song*, played by the Regent Grand Concert Orchestra, under Ernest Mitchell; Signor Kost, if he was still in Melbourne, must have felt a tinge of resentment, and quite possibly regret. 'The Regent's Welcome' was next, followed by the first film of the evening, a Regent News presentation of 'The World's Events'. Stanley Wallace at the Wurlitzer organ then appeared, to accompany a 'glorified scenic setting' that depicted the marriage of Miss Regent to Mister Melbourne, which sounds about as excruciating a symbolic ritual as can be imagined. A 'Screen Color[sic]-Gem' entitled 'The Love Charm', a vaudeville act called 'Cheerie-Ho!', and a dance sequence with The Regent Beauty Ballet choreographed by Maurice Diamond completed the first half. Patrons were invited to tour the theatre during the intermission, with the ever-obliging Regent Cadets on hand to answer any questions, before settling down to the feature film that occupied the second half, *The Two Lovers*, starring Ronald Colman and Vilma Banky. It was quite a night, and the *Herald* had no hesitation in declaring it 'The greatest theatrical event in the world for 1929'.[129] Frank, flanked by Olive and Lola, watched the proceedings with pride. It was his show, his theatre, his town. Doyle could do what he liked with his

---

128 ibid.

129 *Herald*, 16 March 1929, p.3.

Sydney money and his privileged pals from the Yacht Club. This was one battlefield on which, surely, he could never win.

In the short term, by all the relevant measures, Doyle won, and Frank came in an honourable second. It was not the position that he wanted, or could be contented with. Frank was not disposed to be runner-up in anything. But Doyle out-built, and possibly out-imagined him; that was clear, and quantifiable. There were Regent Theatres in every mainland capital, each more beautiful and opulent than the last, but Doyle built the biggest of the palaces (the State in Melbourne) and, by most estimates, the best (the State in Sydney).

The contest between Thring and Doyle was, at its most dispiritingly personal moments, a stereotypical 'my foyer is bigger than yours' competition. At another level, though, the inspirationally nationalist one, it was a fascinating duel that left behind it a profound inheritance. Stuart Doyle and Frank Thring spent a decade locked in a struggle to see which of them could build the more glorious monument, to the cinema, to his country, and to himself. The citizens won, in the end, which was a very good result; the edifices outlived the men who imagined them, and a few have even remained important to the performing arts in their cities in the next millennium.

The States and the Regents were temples to the magic of the movies, and to their capacity to touch and to brighten the lives of the millions of ordinary people who saw them, almost every day of every year. Most of the films shown in this golden age in cinema-construction were from Hollywood, and the dreams and fantasies that they fed were in a sense not only imported but imposed. But they had an importance in the emotional lives of most Australians, and in their sense of connectedness with the rest of the world, that made 'going to town' to see the pictures in one of the great houses a pilgrimage heavily laden with symbolism. Donald Horne remembered the cinemas as 'the true cathedrals' of his childhood,[130] and Conrad Hamann has drawn attention to the religious iconography in their architecture and rituals:

> Not only did the cinemas challenge the churches; they even took on elements of liturgy. Communion found its counterpart in 'God save the King', for which all but the most determined republicans stood up in a custom that lasted to the end of the 1960s. Hymns were supplanted by community singing and the following of bouncing silver balls.

130 Collins, *Hollywood Down Under*, p.120.

> Recessional and other music was played on organs, the crystalline and luminous encrustations of which began to rival the greatest of church lofts. People dressed up. As if conscious of this, the managers and cinema chains began to proclaim both the solace and edification cinemas offered.[131]

Doyle and Thring were at some level aware of the cultural obligations, as well as the marketing opportunities, that lay in the cultivation of awe. And so the contention between them involved something more than ego, though it was undoubtedly very much concerned with that. In their determination to leave spectacular legacies to their own community, there was a messianic sense of mission, as well as a resounding clash of horns between the two biggest bulls in the paddock.

It was a wonderful duel while it lasted. Perhaps there was still some scope in the finances and imaginations of the two men for it to run a little longer; the State in Melbourne, with its spectacular canopy of stars, suggested that, for Doyle at least, the sky was the limit. But the exercise in one-upmanship ended abruptly in 1929, when the stakes were at their highest. Frank Thring decided then to change the rules of the game completely, and it took another twelve months or so before the spectators, and even Stuart Doyle, would fully understand what he was doing, and why.

Perhaps he lost interest in the contest, especially when Doyle seemed able to counter every move. Perhaps Frank's accountants persuaded him that pouring so much investment into infrastructure left Hoyts and its affiliates dangerously short of available capital for other kinds of initiative. Perhaps there were simply other things that were more important to him to do. The events that followed suggest that the explanation lay in a combination of all of the above.

Although he and Doyle had made it very conspicuously a two-man war, and though the result clearly mattered to both of them, there was always a touch of bluff and bravado about the whole performance. As far as the public was concerned, Thring and Doyle were mighty opposites, locked in a

131 Hamann, in Sabine, *A Century of Australian Cinema*, p.89.

metaphorical fight to the death, and mostly that was the way the two men liked to see it. But they were both too shrewd to allow anything they did to be quite as simple as it seemed.

For a good deal of the decade in which their relationship was so fiercely competitive, their affairs were carefully structured to make it subtly collusive at the same time. It suited both of them to keep others out of the market, particularly as long as there was a tacit understanding that the territory was divided into two empires, in which Doyle allowed Thring to rule Melbourne as long as Thring allowed Doyle to rule Sydney. But the layers of complicity went deeper than that. They were at least partly exposed in the Royal Commission into the industry of 1927, though the complexity of the arrangements and the obfuscation of the testimonies ensured that the suspicions of anti-competitive practice could never be proved. John Tulloch notes the difficulty of tracking the connections between Union Theatres and J.C. Williamson, and through them the intertwined interests of those dedicated adversaries, Union Theatres and Hoyts.[132] Union/Australasian, managed by Doyle, and Williamson/Electric, managed by Thring, had announced an 'amalgamation of interests' in 1920; when the Hoyts merger with Williamson/Electric went through in 1926, Frank Thring, now director of all three, thus clearly had an established business relationship with Union Theatres and had been working closely with William Gibson, who headed Union Theatres' Melbourne office, in the month preceding the announcement of the Hoyts deal.

Gibson's evidence to the 1927 Commission was a smokescreen, so evasive and self-contradictory that if the Commissioners had a sense of humour they would have been very inclined to laugh:

> At the Royal Commission, W.A. Gibson of U.T.-A.F. was asked to explain his firm's connection with J.C. Williamson. He replied "I am J.C. Williamson Films." The following day he said he was not J.C. Williamson Ltd. but J.C. Williamson Films Ltd. Asked to explain, he said "The J.C. Williamson Films Ltd. was a separate organisation created by J.C. Williamson Ltd. and Mr Thring … but we have nothing to do with J.C. Williamson Ltd." It is not surprising that the commissioners found his explanations "pretty difficult to follow." When they pressed the matter further by asking him whether Union Theatres

132 John Tulloch, *Legends on the Screen: The Australian Narrative Cinema 1919–1929*, Sydney, Currency Press, 1981, p.425n.

> and Hoyts were connected, Gibson said "No. They are in opposition to each other." When the commissioners suggested that "there have been directors from each organisation sitting on a certain board ... interested in suburban shows," Gibson replied, "Not from Hoyts, but from J.C. Williamson Ltd., Electric Theatres and Associated Theatres ... J.C. Williamson Ltd. and Associated Theatres came together. Never at any time were Hoyts' directors connected with the organisation with which I am associated."[133]

Frank Thring, of course, was 'connected' with every one of the organisations that Gibson mentioned. He had been on the board of all of them. Tulloch points out that two of the directors of J.C. Williamson Ltd., Theodore Fink and F.J. Smith, were also board members of companies under the Union Theatres umbrella.

A key element in the commissioners' deliberations was the nature of the connection between Hoyts, Electric and J.C. Williamson, since the questionable understandings between Hoyts and Union Theatres had all been directed through the conduit provided by Frank Thring's first two companies. It was at this point that another stratum of the subtext of Frank's extended article for *Everyones* was exposed, although not quite clearly enough to be incriminating. His statement then that the company was not 'a combine', but 'a co-operative amalgamation of corresponding interests', was critical; what read in the New Year as a protestation of innocence, a reassurance that this seemingly predatory coalition was really just a loose and benign get-together of a group of like-minded chaps, became later in the year the evidence that cleared Hoyts and Union Theatres of impropriety. 'Cleared' in this michievously muddied context is, in every sense, an ironic word.

In trying to excavate Frank's motives and strategies through the layers of his clever disguise, it is probably, again, reasonable to look at the effects of his actions and infer from them his intentions. The short-term effects of the blandly conciliatory *Everyones* article had been to induce paranoia in everybody else in the industry, and in January that had pretty clearly been Frank's aim. Its longer term effects were to bamboozle anyone who might become too curious; quite possibly, that had occurred to him as a useful outcome, too, and so it proved.

Frank had learned in the hard school of Zeehan the possibilities for profit that were opened up by Romeo's sophomoric question, 'What's in a name?'

133 ibid.

'The World's Picture Company' had proved to be a very different kind of beast from 'the World's Picture Company', depending on whether you used a capital 'T', or whether your 'Ltd' was 'Pty' for the occasion, or 'Inc'. Now 'J.C. Williamson' proved to have a myriad of identities, depending on whether you called it 'J.C. Williamson Ltd', or 'J.C. Williamson Pty Ltd', or 'J.C. Williamson Film', or 'J.C. Williamson Films', or 'J.C. Williamson Film Pty Ltd', or anything else that you cared to write on a business register. Frank had never been notably pedantic about records of births, marriages and deaths, and could hardly have been expected to be too scrupulous about more ephemeral and worldly things like companies.

When the moment came, though, to give evidence before the Commission, Frank was able to support Gibson's very equivocal testimony quite unequivocally. He was asked whether, as the Managing Director of Hoyts and of their partners in the 'co-operative amalgamation of corresponding interests' Electric Theatres and J.C. Williamson whatever-you-chose-to-call-it, he had any investment in Union Theatres. He replied, boldly and, as it happened, truthfully, 'No'. It was a decisive moment. The fact that he had sold his shares in Union Theatres that morning, and was able to buy them back just before close of trading that afternoon, was not revealed in the hearing. From Frank's perspective, it's likely that there was a moral as well as pragmatic dimension to this exchange. People who failed to ask what they wanted to find out didn't deserve to be told what they needed to know.

What all of this meant, in relation to the most publicised commercial arm-wrestle in the country, is that Frank at least recognised it as a sham. It was an enjoyable sham, even a worthwhile sham, but it wasn't the kind of sport on which you could waste a lifetime. Everything that he had done so far had somehow involved the art of illusion. In some areas, like the card-tricks, or the magic lantern shows, or the imaginative approaches to commerce, this had been clear to any intelligent observer who looked closely enough. In others, like his marriages, and perhaps even his golfing friendships, the strategies and the layers of pretence were much harder to pick. Perhaps sometimes those things even deceived the Great Dexter himself. But when it came to business, Frank not only knew the game, but knew that it would be won by the man who recognised the moment when he had to make his move.

So there was, potentially, a sound basis in self-knowledge and a profoundly compromised investment portfolio to provide Frank with reasons to look for the meaning in his life that might constitute its next chapter. Having a child, for most people, and perhaps especially for a person as emotionally unencumbered as Frank had tried to be, is an experience that challenges, and usually rearranges, the priorities that drive their lives. But for Frank the full consequences of these things had been diffused or deferred. There was always something really important happening at the time. Lola was born in 1911, the year in which he had taken over the helm at Kreitmayer's; she had come back into his life, disconcertingly, in 1921, just as he was taking Electric and Williamson's into a particularly tricky partnership; Frank, the son to whom he would one day entrust everything he had made, was born in 1926, the year in which he had brokered the deal with Hoyts that through a series of internecine connections involved everyone who had a financial, or even sentimental, interest in the Australian film industry. The year 1929, when he found time for a delightful trip away with his daughter, was a good one in which to take an emotional inventory.

It was a terrible year, of course, in which to be taking the biggest financial gamble he would ever take. The Wall Street crash in October of that year might have persuaded a wise capitalist to put his money under the mattress. Frank elected to put it all on the line. He floated a new company when companies everywhere were going under, and set out to make some films.

TRAVELLING FROM MARSEILLES TO ADELAIDE

S.S. Narkunda, 23 July 1929

Homeward bound. And a lot to be pleased about. Going home being one of them, naturally. It'd be good to get back amongst it, and see the little bloke, and Ol of course. But this whole thing had gone well. Couldn't have gone better, really. The business with Fox still had some sorting out to go, but it'd come a long way, from a whim, an idea too crazy to happen, to have a show of actually coming to fruition. And if it did, they'd be choking over their port and cigars at the Melbourne Club. Not to mention Doyle at the Royal Bloody Sydney Yacht Club. Not such jolly bloody boating weather up on your poop deck today, eh, Commodore? Better batten down the hatches, mate. Could be a bit of a storm coming up on the old port bow.

And Lola. It'd been good to do it all with her. That couldn't have gone better, either. The kid had certainly come up trumps. He'd been sceptical about St Catherine's. Sometimes it seemed that the Maiden Aunts who ran the joint thought education was all about hats and gloves, and charging an arm and a leg for it. But they must've done something right, because Lola had a way of looking at things, a kind of eagerness, that made all the tourist stuff somehow brighter. And fresh. He'd done the Louvre and all the recommended cathedrals and charming accidental villages with Olive two years ago, and it'd been well worth it, of course, partly because you knew it was meant to be. But Lola loved it, genuinely loved it all. Like that girl in the Shakespeare, suddenly gazing at the Brave New World. She was worldstruck. And she was pretty cluey, too, young Lola, about art and history and so on. It caught you by surprise, and, once you got used to the notion that your daughter might actually be able to teach you something, it was, there was no doubt about it, it was bloody good. So let's raise a Glenfiddich to the saintly spinsters of St Cath's. Good on you, girls. Ladies, sorry. Nice work. Cheap at half the price. And a toast to Twentieth Century Fox. May you continue to think that all of us down under are idiots, you patronising bastards.

The one problem with having a whisky by the pool was that you were supposed to drink it in your bloody togs. Well, he was keeping his shirt and pants on, thanks very much, and a couple of dozen of his fellow-loungers, if they'd had a bit of consideration for others, would've done the same. Not all of them. Amazing what some girls could get away with in public these days, and a bloke can't be shot for looking. Presumably that's what they want you to do. But he was forty-six, and a man'd been in a pretty good paddock. Keep your shirt on, Thring. What they can't see won't hurt 'em.

Lola wasn't one of the swimsuit brigade, which was a good thing on the whole. She was down on the lower deck, demolishing some poor sap at deck tennis. God knows where the sporting talent came from, but it was plain for all to see whose daughter she was. Tall, poor kid, your proverbial beanpole; she'd have to find herself a ruckman. But clever. Very tall and very clever, like her Dad.

The bar service was the one good thing about the pool on the Narkunda. Indian chaps, anxious to please. And not too heavy-handed with the soda. Wonderfully trained.

So, another toast. To the mysterious East; may it be ever obliging. And, while we're about it, to Lola. Best and most favoured of daughters, daughter with so much to forgive, who has already given so much. Kept on saying thank you when they visited yet another wonder; St Cath's obviously spent a lot of time on the p's and q's. She was the generous one, not him.

He'd wasted time. No, that wasn't it. He'd wrung everything out of time, he was a bloody successful man, for God's sake. A lot of people, including her, needed that; Olive, and little Frank, and hundreds of people he knew and didn't know, they all depended on his making good. Hanging off his coat-tails, a dirty great army of them. But he'd wasted chances, with her, things he probably didn't have the time to enjoy, but in another life might've been part of. That was what sometimes slipped a scalpel right under your heart, and it hurt like hell.

Well, she'd be part of it from here on. She wasn't going to miss out on any of it, not any more, and he wasn't going to waste the chance to be part of her life either. Olive wouldn't be thrilled, but stiff cheddar. No more conversations in which 'Your Daughter' would be talked about as a problem, an inconvenience like some dotty relative, or a shameful mistake, or a bloody congenital flaw. When he got home, that was all going to change. Bugger it. A man was apparently meant to feel embarrassed and defensive because he had a daughter. Well, hard though it may be for some people to imagine, life did not begin with Olive. And Lola is no ordinary kid. Lola is a daughter to be proud of. With all due deference Ol, it is not possible to pretend that our child, much as I care about him, means more to me than she does.

To Olive. May she bloom and be happy, and get off my back. May she come to see that she's got nothing to fear from either of them: not from this wonderful young woman who will live with us in our home, or from her mother, who as far as I can remember meant less than Olive thinks she meant and who is besides, poor desperately sad little Gracie, absolutely and unarguably and miserably dead. Funny. It can still hurt, when you try to remember. Just a little bit.

Perhaps one for the road. Channel, I suppose. Yeah, just a dash of soda. We've come a long way on this cruise. A toast to the future, then. Happy families, peace and prosperity, and a bloody long life. And the new company, of course. Thring's, perhaps, no ambiguity about that. Thring Films. Shit. Try saying that with a mouthful of nuts. Viola Productions would be a nice touch, and she'd like it, but, sadly, a touch musical for the purpose, not to say foreign, so probably not, I'm afraid, love. And Dexter Films would be apposite, but only one bastard in the world would know what the hell it meant. Ah, what's in a name, Romeo? Greater Olive Incorporated. Olive Unlimited. No. Thring and Son? Or Thring and Son and Daughter.

> *Thring and Son and Daughter,*
> *They refused to be just an importer.*
> *They made films of their own,*
> *Which made Doyle moan,*
> *And Olive said they just shouldn't oughter.*

It'd be the gamble of his life. Not only all his money on the line, but his name, and all he'd done and dreamed of doing. Some of them would see it as a sell-out, giving the Yanks a foot in the door so that they could flood the place with their stuff and no Australian could get a look in. They'd think what they bloody wanted to, whatever he did. The Fox people thought that was exactly what they were buying, of course. Majority distribution, instant and on the cheap. The country cousin wanders down Sunset Boulevard with a wad of shares in his pocket, wondering if someone might be interested in buying them. Show the man some movie stars, buy him a beer, give him a hot dog, fix him a martini, make the cretin feel at home right here in the centre of the universe. Hey, Frankie baby, come on, loosen up, relax and enjoy. We're your buddies, sweetheart, we'll take those Hoyts shares off your hands. And then you know what, dumb-ass? We'll screw your two-bit fucking industry for good. Like taking candy from a baby.

If he failed, that was the price. If it came off, though, Br'er Fox had outsmarted himself, and Br'er Rabbit would be laughing all the way to the bank. So would Australia; Fox might just have agreed to a deal that bankrolled an independent Australian film industry, for Christ's sake. The screwer, permanently screwed. Let's see who's really the bunny round here. Welcome to our humble colonial version of the briar patch, buddy boys.

Sure, why not? Keep the whiskies coming, Ahmed, plenty more to celebrate. Another toast. How about the West Australian sun, or the sparkling pool, or the gorgeous golden girls beside it? All in good time. No, this one's to you, Uncle Remus. Here's mud in your eye, and skin off your nose.

Chapter Five

THE SPECULATOR

Nothing in Frank Thring's career to this point would have suggested that he wanted to make films. He liked the technology, obviously, and he liked the strange, showy, volatile, dangerous world that grew up around it. He liked the kind of people that it attracted, too, though most of them were his sworn opponents; but they were mavericks as he was, and with enemies like them a man didn't need to bother much with friends. Most of all, of course, he liked the wheeling and dealing, and the startling amounts of money that it could generate. All that was very clear, in everything he had done since he had travelled to the backblocks of Tasmania to show some movies and play a few tricks in 1909.

Frank's involvement in the game had always involved exhibition and distribution, though, and there had never been any indication that it mattered much to him where the product came from. His interest in local performers had been confined to the vaudeville acts which he had always included in his repertoire. But suddenly, out of the blue, Frank Thring in 1930 abandoned all of his interests, personal and financial, in exhibiting, and with it all of the guaranteed income and much of the guaranteed status that was entailed in his role as the nearest thing Melbourne had to a movie mogul. With the establishment of Efftee Films, following Frank's sale of all his holdings in Hoyts, he set out in a completely new direction. The road he had been travelling was one that he was helping to clear and to chart as he forced his way along it; it was sometimes tough going, but it was the only route to the prize. The Efftee track led into the absolutely unknown; Frank's accountants would have seen it as leading straight to the edge of a precipice.

And yet he did it. It must have looked, to his golfing partners and his fellow board members and Stuart Doyle, and possibly to his wife, as though Thring had taken leave of his senses. But there were several pragmatic considerations, as well as a couple of emotional ones and a leap of faith, behind the founding of Efftee.

The seeds were planted in the previous year, when Frank and Lola took their first and only holiday together overseas. They left at the beginning of April, a fortnight after the spectacular opening of the Melbourne Regent. The itinerary as planned was a practical blend of business and pleasure: after a few days in San Francisco, they would head for Hollywood, where Frank would attend to a solid schedule of industry meetings; then to London, where there were more connections to be followed up but where the balance would shift toward sightseeing; then to Paris and a selection of charming villages in Provence before their departure for home from Marseilles on the Narkunda at the end of June. The time in England and France was primarily for Lola, a version of the debutante's Grand Tour; Frank wanted to show her the legendary places she had read about, and to be there to share some of her excitement when she saw them. But there was usually a Hoyts interest to pursue, whether it was an exercise in networking or a purchase of some new treasure to grace the foyer of a Regent. Frank needed to be able to find a secondary commercial reason for this adventure with his daughter, partly because he was temperamentally disinclined to any single agenda, and partly because it was important to persuade Olive, left at home holding the baby, that it was a journey that he had to make.

It went wonderfully. Lola not only showed all the appropriate delight in sampling the splendours of Europe, but took an unexpectedly avid interest in all that her father did on the American leg of the tour as well. Her time in Hollywood wasn't simply about spotting the stars, though any bright young thing having her eighteenth birthday in Tinseltown would naturally engage in a bit of that. Lola wanted to know how it was done, the whole process from go to whoa. This made her an unusually contented companion on all those days when he had to talk to industry people at the studios and on sets.

Lola's enthusiasm for the business of film production was undoubtedly one of the elements in her father's decision to take his great gamble in 1930. It probably wasn't a primary motive; Frank was still a businessman, every waking minute, and he had not made a fortune and an intimidating reputation by indulging whims, sentimental or otherwise. A number of good reasons for making the break with Hoyts emerged during 1929, and all the others were based on sound budgetary calculations. Most of them, though, were even stronger arguments for getting out of the industry altogether. That Frank saw the dangers, and chose not only to stay in film, but even more perilously to make films of his own, was an act of defiance of purely commercial logic. No doubt he genuinely believed that fortune favours the brave; but he would also have been conscious that fools rush in, and that most gamblers lose. Among all the impulses, quixotic or egotistical or romantic or nationalistic, that lay behind the founding of Efftee, Frank's realisation that Lola shared some of his passion for the industry and could share many of his ideas was, at least, an added attraction in his plans.

Three things, other than that momentous journey overseas, occurred in 1929 to force a decision of some kind. The first of them was the coming of sound. Al Jolson's voice had been heard on film when Warner Brothers' *The Jazz Singer* opened on 6 October 1927; he spoke just sixty-one words, but they were extraordinarily influential. It was more than a year before the first of the talkies played at Union's Lyceum Theatre in Sydney on 29 December 1928, by which time its continuing popularity in the States had demonstrated that this was no passing fad. Hoyts opened *The Red Dance* at the Sydney Regent on the same night, just to confirm that the old rivalry was alive and well. But *The Red Dance* was a silent movie with sound-on-film musical accompaniment; *The Jazz Singer*, although working with the older Vitaphone sound-on-disc technology, had the advantage of the human voice. Doyle had won another round.

Both did exceptional business, each grossing a record four thousand pounds in their first six days.[134] The *Sydney Morning Herald* estimated that by January 4, thirty thousand had seen *The Jazz Singer* at the Lyceum, and thirty-five thousand had been to *The Red Dance* at the Regent, which led it to some editorial musing:

> Are the "talkies" just a craze, or have they come to stay? Judging by the attitude of the audience inside the theatres, one is bound to admit that the "talkies" will switch the motion picture industry onto an entirely new road.[135]

Songs and music on film were an obviously attractive development; dialogue was another matter. Harry Warner, the accountant brother of the Warner family, acknowledged the attraction of what he called 'canned vaudeville', but remained sceptical as to whether there was anything else

---

134 Shirley and Adams, p.103.
135 *Sydney Morning Herald*, 4 January 1929, quoted ibid.

that audiences would bother listening to, asking scornfully 'Who the heck wants to hear actors talk?' But the audiences were voting very differently with their feet. The Sydney Prince Edward was wired for sound in January, and in February *The Jazz Singer* and *The Red Dance* opened in Melbourne. Thring and Hoyts gained, or at least claimed, a small victory when *Mother Knows Best*, starring Madge Bellamy, Louise Dresser and Barry Norton, followed at the Sydney Regent. Billed in large letters as 'THE FIRST REAL TALKING DRAMA' and in much smaller ones as 'A heart-stirring romance of love-starved youth', it was pretty clear what the film's primary attraction was perceived to be. The advertisement proudly proclaimed that the actors 'ALL SPEAK', on a night of 'TALKIES SUPREME' that offers a smorgasbord of other sounds and voices: 'The KING speaks from our screen', while the comedian Chic Sale ('as funny to hear as to see'), the 'first talkie dancer' Ruby Keeler ('Her twinkling feet will tap their way to your heart'), and the singers Raquel Meller and Bonelli ('Every note and every tone is perfectly reproduced') are all featured in supporting short films. A large injunction at the bottom of the advertisement, 'ATTEND MATINEES. AVOID NIGHT CROWDS', was a classic Thring marketing manoeuvre: at one stroke he managed to declare the season a smash hit, build his matinee houses, appear to have only his audience's comfort and well-being at heart, and, most of all of course, create exactly the sort of hysteria that he was claiming to be at pains to avoid.

The triumph of the talkies had a number of implications for a man like Frank Thring as he pondered what to do next. The audiences came in droves, and the industry could surely never have looked healthier. That was something to gladden the heart of any exhibitor. But there were some conspicuous negatives, too. If silent film was now to be seen as a thing of the past, there was an urgent need for supplies of the state-of-the-art product that the people were clamouring to see; there were no local studios to help to meet that demand, and there was an inevitable lag, both in the generation of talkies from Hollywood (or, a little later, England) and in the channels of distribution that might get them all the way to cinemas in Australia. Moreover, the theatres that had run silent movies would become as anachronistic as the genre itself if they were not quickly converted to allow provision for sound. And that was a costly business. Hoyts, for instance, ran over a hundred cinemas; wiring them for sound, especially at the shamelessly exorbitant rates charged by the monopolistic American company Western Electric, entailed a capital outlay that turned black figures into red virtually overnight.[136] That problem was exacerbated by the arm-wrestle between Doyle and Thring, which had left in each city over-sized and over-embellished picture palaces that were an acoustic nightmare. The costly complications of installing sound into theatres like the States and the Regents offered another very good reason for Frank, seemingly the perpetual runner-up in that competition, to call a halt to it immediately.

The sense that his building of imperial monuments had gone about as far as it could go, compounded then by the massive risks of over-capitalisation that were entailed in the coming of sound movies, gave Frank Thring plenty of food for thought when he contemplated it all from afar in the middle of 1929.

In the course of his discussions with the American studios, several things must have crossed and recrossed his mind. One of them would have been that things were only going to become tougher for Hoyts in the foreseeable future, and that this might be an appropriate moment to bow out. Another would have been that a company like Fox Studios might be very receptive to the idea of a majority share-holding in a company like Hoyts at such a time, and that their keenness to eliminate the middle-man in the distribution process might incline them to pay a very good price to a man who had a parcel of shares that was just the size that they needed. Another might have been what he really wanted to do with his life. It was possible that he could go no further at Hoyts than he had already, and that the future would not be about expansion and pastures new at all, but about strategic defence and simply more of the same. A career that had always seemed to be heading ever upwards on a very fast escalator might now be simply marking time, on something much more like a treadmill.

And it was not just about the career, of course. Coming to know his daughter through the northern hemisphere summer of 1929 was a process that also reminded him of everything that he had neglected and missed out on, in chasing whatever it was he had been chasing since he and Grace had headed off to Zeehan, two decades before. Perhaps it even occurred to him that his escalator might really have been a treadmill all the time.

---

136 Shirley and Adams, p.104. Western Electric refused outright purchase, and instead charged an installation fee of ten thousand pounds, plus an obligatory weekly service charge, for a contractual minimum of ten years. This situation was only improved when the Australian Raycophone and Auditone equipment was judged to be of sufficient quality, after which it was able, from 1930, to offer a cheaper alternative, and (with some substantial tariff protection), some healthy competition, to the American predator.

A man of forty-six who for the first time in many years is not quite sure what to do next is quite likely to ask himself some searching existential questions. Not that he was ready to take a back seat, and call for his pipe and slippers. Frank Thring, on all the evidence, was too much the compulsive achiever to sit down for long, let alone to stop moving altogether. That was the reason for his vigorous resumption of his managerial duties when he got back to Australia, driving the installation of sound in cinemas large and small all over the place; nobody, certainly not Stuart Doyle or Frank's old cronies Griffith and Tait, and probably not Olive either, would have guessed the contingencies for which he was preparing while he and Lola were seeing the world together. It was also, no doubt, the basis for the crazy idea that kept returning to him as the one way out for an Australian cinema that in the age of the talkies seemed irrevocably bound to the men in Hollywood who controlled the product: to meet the local demand for motion pictures with sound by making them.

The third major development to influence Frank's plans came later in 1929, though its consequences weren't really felt in Australia until well into the following year. The Wall Street crash on 'Black Thursday', 24 October 1929, had obvious consequences for patterns of investment in Hollywood films, though initially, as the Depression cast its shadow wider and more darkly over the lives of ordinary families, its impact on movie audiences was less dramatic than might have been predicted. Celluloid dreams offered a precious counter-balance to tough reality, and a ticket to the movies was still, for a time, an affordable indulgence to people who were otherwise doing it hard. That changed, of course, and with a correspondingly devastating impact on attendances, whereas the effect of the stock market collapse on the financing of films was almost immediate. Frank, viewing the whole debacle from the seemingly safe distance of Melbourne, would have been very aware that the impending decline in Hollywood production intensified the argument for an Australian making movies of his own.

Wall Street, initially, was characterised as America's problem. For Australia, at the bottom of the earth, and with no essential economic links to the wider world beyond its residual umbilical tie to Britain, it seemed yet another of those big stories that were played out in the cities that really mattered. But in time it came to be recognised as a graphic first lesson in the evolving phenomenon of a global economy. The disaster for American capitalism was a catalyst for the Great Depression that followed, but it was as much symptom as cause. Earlier in 1929, Stanley Bruce, the Australian

Prime Minister, had warned of the impending crisis in terms that invoked the film industry as a modern manifestation of Nero on the fiddle:

> We are facing more economic troubles now than ever before in Australia's history; tens of thousands of men and women are suffering through unemployment; and it is increasingly hard to obtain money for industry. Surely, then, it is rather dreadful to see great queues of people waiting outside cinema palaces that have cost hundreds of thousands to build.[137]

It was not a good time, apparently, to be asking the government for subsidy, or protective tariffs, or really for anything at all.

By 1930, the Depression in Australia was beginning to bite, and over the next three years things became progressively worse. By 1932, the rate of unemployment had risen to almost one in three. Frank astutely sold his holdings in Hoyts to Fox in September 1930, and from a purely commercial point of view, he couldn't have bailed out at a better time.

> By mid-1931, film returns across Australia were at their lowest for five years. After earning a profit of £80,000 in 1929–30, Hoyts Theatres Ltd lost £18,500 in the second half of 1930. Union Theatres Ltd and its associated companies suffered even more heavily.
>
> Early 1931 saw a £44,000 plunge in the profits of Amalgamated Pictures and J.D. Williams and in the first half of the year, Union Theatres and Australasian Films together lost £48,012. From May 1931, Union Theatres began to reduce salaries and retrench staff, the orchestras of the Sydney Capitol and the Melbourne State were dismissed, and male ushers at the former were replaced by women on lower wages.[138]

The film industry was not going to curl up and die without a fight, and it was always capable of exerting an influence beyond its sphere. The fall of the conservative Bruce/Page government in October 1929, a week after the New York stock exchange spun out of control, was in part attributable to the political power of the film industry lobby, and in particular to the machinations of Stuart Doyle. Bruce proposed a five per cent levy on all amusement receipts and 'a tax of 12.5 per cent upon the payments made to persons outside the Commonwealth by film importers for non-British

---

137 Shirley and Adams, p.108.
138 ibid.

films'. It was a death sentence for Australian exhibitors, and Doyle fought it like a tiger. He won, too, at first; the Labor Party under James Scullin was returned, and briefly local investors' confidence in the film industry was revived. Then the new government announced its own tax arrangements: thirty per cent tax on all overseas remittances, film import duty up from threepence to fourpence per foot, with a further levy of 2.5 per cent to be imposed on the profits of each film. Even Doyle had to admit defeat.

> In early October 1931, after Union Theatres had reported a loss of £100,000, the E.S.&A. Bank announced it would force the company's reconstruction. When it went into liquidation Stuart Doyle formed a new company, Greater Union Theatres Ltd, to purchase the assets for £400,000, the amount of the overdraft ...[139]

By that time, of course, the game had changed significantly. Hoyts, now effectively an arm of American Fox, had no tax obligations under Australian law. And Frank Thring, once the driving force of Hoyts, was no longer a participant in the debate. He had been strangely silent even in the cut-and-thrust of the political campaign trail of late 1929, though he had every reason to make a lot of noise. Frank was not usually quiet about things that affected his sense of well-being and his finances. Perhaps, even then, he had made up his mind about what he was going to do next.

For a man too smart to ignore his accountants but too intelligent to let them determine his life, this was one of those forks in the road where no choice was clearly the right one, and no choice was clearly wrong.

There were three options. Frank could stay, like Stuart Doyle, in a game that he knew well but that he knew he had to lose. He could throw in his cards and spend the next decade or two or perhaps even three in metaphorically smelling the daisies, which meant knowing his wife and his children a little better, and becoming acquainted with the garden at Rylands. Or he could set up Efftee, and change the game entirely.

The 'arguments for' the last of the three options were a mixed bunch:

> (1) There was a shortage of imported film. This was partly because nobody wanted anymore to watch actors they couldn't hear, a taste which made all old stock redundant; it was partly because in straitened

139 Shirley and Adams, p.108.

circumstances the last thing a shrewd American investor would want to do was to gamble on a movie, especially when most people were struggling to pay for their next meal.

(2) He could afford to do it, if he cashed in his Hoyts shares, used all his liquidity, and mortgaged everything he owned. Perhaps that wasn't a very conclusive 'argument for', after all.

(3) Lola would like it. She might even make it a career.

(4) It would be, in principle, a good thing to make films by, for, and about Australians, and with Australian accents.

(5) It was the daring option. Sometimes, there was a moment, a chance to make a difference to the society from which one came. There wasn't another person in Australia who would dare to start up a company to make local films in the middle of a depression, especially when that entailed building an industry in sophisticated sound technology from square one. What a compelling reason, then, to be the man who did it.

(6) If it really succeeded, he would make a fortune, and become indisputably the most important figure in the Australian film industry.

The 'arguments against' were fewer, but powerful:

(1) Olive would take a lot of convincing.

(2) It was a terrible time to invest in anything, and there was a good chance he could lose the lot.

(3) Australia represented a very small market. Its population in 1930 was 6.4 million, less than five per cent of the US figure of 123.2 million, and hardly bigger than that of the state of Texas. And there was no distribution deal to offset costs by taking its films anywhere else.

(4) If the move failed, Twentieth-Century Fox would have the chance they sought to dominate the market in Australia. The sale of the Hoyts holdings didn't just open the door to let the fox among the chickens; it gave him the keys to the hen-house, to live there as long and as gluttonously as he wanted.

In the end, the ayes had it. The bolder option won out, as with Frank it was probably always going to do, and Melbourne became the home to a brand new film company dedicated to making talkies with an Australian accent.

Of course, a shrewd speculator would never take a leap in the dark without some idea of what he might land on. And Frank's speculations were always shrewd. Part of the deal with Fox involved Frank's retention of a seat on the board of Hoyts, and a guarantee of distribution through Hoyts cinemas for films under the Efftee banner. The executives at Fox probably found this an easy concession to make, given the prize they were being presented with.

Frank's revelation of the sale of his shares in Hoyts was accompanied by his announcement of the birth of a company yet unnamed that was going to transform the motion-picture industry in Australia.

> "I have taken this step sincerely, feeling that the association of a powerful production company with Hoyts is immensely desirable," said Mr. Thring, "and that it is in the interests of shareholders ..."
>
> "For some time it has been my desire to embark on production of Australian pictures, but the work of actively directing some hundred theatres that constitute Hoyts' circuit has prevented me from being able to devote to production the time and personal attention essential for success. I shall now be free to give the whole of my time to the establishment of a comprehensive organisation for this purpose, and I am confident of success.
>
> The Fox Film Corporation has given me every assurance of its support, and the Hoyts circuit of theatres will be open to exhibit the product ... I have great hopes that this step will provide considerable work for actors and people connected with the stage, who have been so severely hit by the present conditions."[140]

It wasn't altogether clear what the 'assurance of its support' from Fox was worth, let alone that the move was 'immensely desirable' from the perspective of Hoyts' shareholders. What was clear was that film in Australia would be very different from this day on.

140 *Sydney Morning Herald*, 3 September 1930, p.5.

Frank also exploited some connections, naturally enough. He needed a trusted lieutenant, so Tom Holt, who had spent several years in London as Williamson's representative, was persuaded to come home to the position of General Manager of the new company. He needed a reservoir of reliable acting talent, so through his old mates at Williamson's he enlisted the support of Gregan McMahon's Melbourne Repertory Company, a group of more than respectable amateurs which had a long association with 'JCW'; McMahon would provide assistance on the directorial and casting side, and his stable of actors would be the core of an inexpensive supporting cast. He needed technical expertise, and the prevailing drought in Australian film-making made it fairly simple to secure the best cameraman in the business, Arthur Higgins, and the gifted sound engineer Alan Mill.

He needed equipment, too, and in October 1930 dispatched Higgins and Mill to Hollywood to investigate the startling new technologies that Frank had found so impressive, if mysterious, when he and Lola had looked at them in 1929. When they chose the state-of-the-art RCA Victor sound system, Tom Holt followed with a cheque-book, and in February 1931 the three of them returned with equipment that had cost twenty-five thousand pounds. Meanwhile, Frank had successfully lobbied the Minister for Customs, Frank M. Forde, to reduce the customary and prohibitive sixty per cent tariff on imported sound gear to just ten per cent, for reasons that were never quite clear.[141] The Minister was pressed in Federal Parliament to explain his move, but after asserting the employment potential of the film industry and noting that 'a sub-committee of cabinet' had been unanimous in supporting a one-off concession, seemed to rely on the vaguely tautologous argument that Mr Thring deserved special treatment because he was a special case:

> Mr. Thring's project is the first definite move to establish talking picture production in Australia on a large scale, and he is not doing it with shareholders' money, but is risking private capital.[142]

There is no record of what the Opposition made of the idea that the law should only apply to capitalists when profits went to people other than themselves. Anyway, the variation was made. Frank Forde continued to be

141 The sixty per cent tariff was designed to protect the Australian sound reproduction company, Raycophone, against competition from overseas.

142 *Parliamentary Debates. House of Representatives Hansard*, 12–13 March 1931.

shamelessly cultivated as a good friend of Efftee, with an open invitation to look in on shooting and mingle with the stars, and was, of course, a splendid choice for the honour of formally opening Efftee Studios on June 2, 1931.

Frank also needed a home for the new enterprise, and here he had the advantage not only of one of his substantial networks, but of a timely accident. In the small hours of Friday 25 October 1929, the day after 'Black Thursday', when the American financial system imploded, another disaster occurred in Melbourne. Alongside the headline in the *Argus* that shouted 'NEW YORK "BEARS" CAUSE COLLAPSE. WORST WEEK IN HISTORY. WILD SCENES ON 'CHANGE' was another equally large: 'FIRE AT HIS MAJESTY'S. THEATRE TO BE REBUILT. DAMAGE ESTIMATED AT £60,000'. 'The Maj' in Exhibition Street, a beautiful building with a rich history as one of the homes of J.C. Williamson,[143] was seriously damaged by a fire that swept through its circle and stalls. The façade was barely touched, but the theatre's interior was gutted.

'The Firm' announced immediately that the theatre would be rebuilt and refurbished as soon as possible, and even more sumptuously than before.

> His Majesty's Theatre ... will be rebuilt as a modern theatre, with the newest systems of lighting, ventilation, and decoration. It will not be available for productions for at least six months. In making this announcement yesterday, Mr Frank S. Tait, a director of J.C. Williamson Ltd., said that the seating accommodation would not be increased, but the appearance of both the exterior and interior of the new theatre would be much more ornamental that that of the old theatre, which was erected in 1887.[144]

But, as the full implications of the stock market crash became known and painfully felt, restoring a theatre became suddenly a less urgent priority. His Majesty's stood for several months as a desolate reminder of the bleakness of the times, until Frank Thring, a man who knew the company well, and still assiduously played golf with Tait, George Tallis and other members of its board, came up with a bright idea for a leasing arrangement that would relieve Williamson's of any anxiety about the cost of restoration, and any guilt about deferring it. He needed a large empty shell to provide a home

143 The theatre had begun life as the Alexandra in 1886. When Williamson's took over its lease in 1900 it was renamed Her Majesty's; it became His Majesty's in 1924, and was again re-gendered on the accession of Elizabeth II.

144 *Argus*, 26 October 1929, p.19.

for Efftee Films, and His Majesty's had just the right kind of prominence to suit a grand idea.

It was a perfect solution in other ways. Apart from installing some highly expensive machinery on a stage that was to become a sound-stage for domestic interiors, there wasn't a great deal to be done to the rest of the wreck. Frank had signed the comedian Pat Hanna for a piece of First World War buffoonery called *Diggers*; the devastated stalls became part of the debris of the battlefield, while the sludge in the ruined orchestra pit was just right for a muddy trench. And it stayed that way. Two years later, when Hanna's sequel, *Diggers in Blighty*, was being filmed in the stalls, Bill Kerr, then the child-star Wee Willie Kerr, was filming *Harmony Row* with George Wallace on the stage, and has a vivid memory of 'sand and shit and trenches all over the place'.[145] Frank was always good at making the most of what fate delivered.

A new company needed a striking logo, and Frank moved immediately to do what he had done when the upstart World's Best Pictures had needed a promotional limerick: he set up a competition. The prize was five guineas, and in the event it was split between five contestants who proposed the emblem of a koala for the new All-Australian company. Frank could have come up with a koala himself, just as he was more than capable of a rhyme for 'view' and 'too' in Zeehan twenty years before, but when you could combine creative consultancy and advertising in a way that provided both for almost nothing, it would be a pity to deprive the public of their pleasure.

The Efftee koala, a fair facsimile of Norman Lindsay's Bunyip Bluegum, looks quizzically at the viewer as he munches on a sprig of eucalyptus. The publicity shot in which he was first revealed to the public carried this caption:

> The trade-mark that, it is hoped, will eventually become the hall-mark of Efftee Film Productions throughout the world. The native bear is photographed in his natural surroundings and natural movement.

The bear, though certainly 'in his natural surroundings' up a gum-tree, is framed on a vaguely heraldic disc, studded with what appear to be jewels and set in a bed of what might be half an acanthus wreath. But there's no doubt which country he comes from, and if the Efftee scroll below proclaims this the work of one man, the emblem boldly asserts his nationalism.

By December 1930, though not an inch of film had been shot, Efftee had all the appearance of a juggernaut. In its end-of-year report on the state

145 Bill Kerr, interview with the author, 4 August 2004.

of Australian film, the film weekly *Everyones* saw just one bright light in the general gloom. Under the bold headline 'Thring's Project Only hope for Australian Production 1931' it observed:

> Australian production fell to its lowest ebb during 1930. To a large degree the advent of talking pictures, finding Australia unequipped with recording plants, can be blamed for that ... That section of the industry that has lived precariously on production looks to F.W. Thring to steer the business to prosperity. His project is blessed by sound finance, and sound show-sense.
>
> Resigning from the managing directorship of Hoyts Theatres Ltd. when Fox bought control of the company last September, Mr Thring immediately put into effect production plans which he had been harbouring for years. He lost no time about it. Within a few weeks he had taken over His Majesty's Theatre, Melbourne, as his studio; sent a cameraman and sound expert to Hollywood; engaged Tom Holt as his general manager and dispatched him to America to purchase recording equipment, as well as to bring back dramatic and comedy directors. By January, it is expected, the complete plant will be in operation.[146]

In the event, the starting date was in February. But it was still very impressive. The sense that Thring had hit the ground running was everywhere, and was a key element in Efftee's attempt to promote both an air of excitement and the style and status of the man whose initials it carried. Frank's sense of mission bordered on the messianic, and that was a mantle that *Everyones*, and the interests it represented, were happy to bestow. The newspaper treatment of Frank throughout the early days of Efftee was so laudatory that it might have been written by the man himself – as sometimes, no doubt, it was. Frank liked to involve himself directly in the process of turning press releases into news items, and his name, whether on a modest bootmaker's shop in Gawler, a film night in a draughty hall in the wilds of Tasmania, or on a company whose koala emblem would be recognised 'throughout the world', was readily offered as a guarantee of quality.

Later in the year, the press release accompanying the first batch of Efftee releases included a panegyric that should have brought a blush to his cheek:

146 *Everyones*, 10 December 1930, p.18.

> **A Dream That Came True**
>
> As romantic as the history of Barnum and Bailey or any of the great showmen is the life story of Frank W. Thring, the driving force behind Efftee Films.
>
> From a modest beginning in a small entertainment in Bourke Street, Melbourne, he was a power in the building of the mighty chain of Hoyts Theatres throughout Australia. These modern theatres are among the best in the world and will stand as lifelong monuments to the far-seeing qualities of this man.
>
> When he relinquished his interests in Hoyts Theatres Ltd. he saw the fulfillment of his dream in sight – the establishment in Australia of the production of motion pictures.
>
> With the launching of this new Australian industry his faith still remained in his native country, and, selecting several Australians, he sent them overseas to gain the most up-to-date knowledge, method, and technique for the production of the motion picture.
>
> The prestige of Mr. Thring gained for them entry to the foremost producing companies in Hollywood – world head-quarters in the production of motion pictures.
>
> Efftee Films is Mr. Thring's own personal venture and he has directed the whole of the productions so far completed by the company.
>
> Men that know "F.T." assert that this idealist will eventually build to his lifelong memory the firm establishment of the production of the talking picture in Australia.[147]

Much of it was the familiar stuff of the new Thring mythology: the self-made man from nowhere, the decisive man in a hurry, the man who makes monuments, the ardent nationalist who none the less draws on the best from overseas, the man whose signature counts for everything. But now there were some new elements – the global power that could open any door, the visionary imagination, the prospective legacy to a grateful nation. This Frank Thring was not just a very big man. He was a colossus.

Frank quite possibly wrote it. At the very least, he approved the piece for publication. It reveals an extraordinary sense of his own importance and

147 *Everyones*, 28 October 1931, p.14.

his destiny; and, like all Frank's advertisements for himself, it reflects an assumption that speaking things made them so, as it often did for him.

The creation of the F.T. persona was more clearly a strategy for fame and power than his son's outrageous role-playing, but it was equally in its way a seemingly instinctive way of trying to make the world do what he wanted.

The formal launch for Efftee's premiere season took place in July 1931, but filming on at least four planned projects had begun in March. The plan was to release first a double bill of the wartime comedy *Diggers* and the horror film *The Haunted Barn*, closely followed by *A Co-Respondent's Course*, a comedy of marital misunderstanding.[148] That plan was changed when the Chief Censor refused to allow *The Haunted Barn* to be shown to audiences under the age of sixteen, on the grounds that the ghostly wailing of the wind in the film would be too frightening to children; Thring accordingly replaced it for Efftee's initial program with *A Co-Respondent's Course*, which, with its plot of multiple infidelities, more obviously warranted a restricted rating. But that issue (and that film), and the rest of the political shenanigans of Efftee's extraordinary first year, were nowhere in evidence on that gala evening in July, when Frank introduced his new company to the world.

In the film that recorded the Efftee launch, F.T. the man appears before a plush curtain in full evening dress, with white waistcoat and bow tie. He has filled out considerably since his last appearance on film in a 1925 Australasian newsreel, formulaically chatting with W.A. Gibson on the deck of the *Ormonde* as it docks in Melbourne after their (triumphant, of course) visits to America, England and 'the Continent' 'to secure the world's best pictures for Australian theatres'.[149] Frank is now a man of visible substance, and his speechmaking manner builds on that impression; the Australian vowels are overlaid with an exaggerated cultivation, the right hand remains stiffly by his side while the left is advanced in a gesture of slightly strained informality, and the air is one of confident command.

148 The projects were initially titled *The Co-Respondent's Course*, *Dinkum Diggers* and *The Body in the Barn*.

149 Archival footage from the National Film and Sound Archive, Canberra, released in the compilation *Efftee's Australia*, research by Chris Long, 1989.

The speech itself, though, is a surprisingly modest one: the Efftee initiative is not a magnificent invention but the 'inevitable' culmination of a process, the 'opportunity' to make it happen has not been seized or created but generously 'given', and its destiny lies entirely in the hands of his audience:

> Ladies and gentlemen. It was inevitable that, sooner or later, a serious attempt would be made to produce talking pictures in Australia, on a scale and of such a quality that they would bear favourable comparison with similar products from overseas. It has been my great privilege to have been given this opportunity of making this initial attempt – with what success, you will be able to judge for yourselves this evening.[150]

The Australian-ness of the new enterprise at every level is something of which Frank declares himself 'exceedingly proud', and it remains relentlessly the focus of his introduction of the stars of the forthcoming films. Donalda Warne (*A Co-Respondent's Course*), elegant in evening gown, is 'a Sydney girl, and typical of the land she lives in'; Cecil Scott (*Diggers*, *The Sentimental Bloke*), wreathed in pipe smoke and sporting a bush hat, is 'another good Australian'; Pat Hanna (*Diggers*), 'who is full of droll tales from behind the lines when our boys fought in France', leans nonchalantly on his diminutive partner George Moon, 'his cobber in trouble'; and Ray Fisher (Doreen in *The Sentimental Bloke*), a curly-haired girl-next-door in a tartan frock, responds with suitably modest simper to Thring's ponderous compliment, 'I think you will all be prepared to [*pause*] dip your lid to Miss Fisher'.

Frank ended with the same strategic humility with which he began.

> This, ladies and gentlemen, is but a beginning. If you are prepared to say it is a good beginning, we shall be well rewarded, and encouraged to go on, to try and produce better and better pictures in the future. I thank you.

Having spent much of his life boosting his projects and his persona, the sub-text is that on this night, in this august company and at this stage of his career, neither the boy from Wentworth nor the venture that bears his name is in any need of promotion or special pleading.

As the July launch made clear, Efftee was to be no show-by-show proposition. It was a production house, with some films completed, others

150 'Frank Thring Introduces the Stars', speech launching the first Efftee season, ibid.

in progress, and yet more contracted and scheduled. And, given the situation with *The Haunted Barn* and the Censor, it was just as well that it was so. The projects were shot in parallel; Donalda Warne was not only playing Nellie, the mischievous party-girl who is the major source of male confusion in *A Co-Respondent's Course*, but was at the same time appearing as Joan, a pretty ingénue but also an escaped lunatic, in *The Haunted Barn*; another Sydney nineteen-year-old, Patricia Minchin, was filming *A Co-Respondent's Course* on the sound-stage at His Majesty's in the role of Nellie's friend May, while concurrently appearing in a Nurse's uniform for *Diggers* in the devastated stalls.[151] Frank liked to bring the repertory model to film; it saved a lot of time and money if one could ensure that actors weren't at a loose end between takes. George Moon, in addition to his major role as Pat Hanna's mate Joe in *A Co-Respondent's Course*, also bobbed up as a hapless private detective in *Diggers*, as did Ed Warrington, who was at the same time playing Fatty down in the 'trenches'. Cecil Scott, while preparing for *The Sentimental Bloke*, was contracted to keep his hand in as Bluey, another of the lovable larrikins in *Diggers*. As Frank developed the theatrical arm of Efftee, the policy of parallel engagements became almost the norm.

That policy was even more marked on the production side. Arthur Higgins was credited for 'Photography' on all the Efftee features except for *His Royal Highness*; Dan Bloomberg, the American sound expert, worked simultaneously on *Diggers*, *The Haunted Barn* and *A Co-Respondent's Course,* and was replaced on all Thring's later films by Alan Mill; W.R. Coleman was acknowledged variously for 'Art Direction' or 'Settings' on all but two Efftee productions. And two people were part of every film: Frank Thring, and his daughter Lola.

Frank was billed as 'Producer' on all the Efftee Films, and as 'Director' on all but three: E.A Dietrich-Derrick is named as Director for *A Co-Respondent's Course,* and Pat Hanna for the *Diggers* sequel, *Diggers in Blighty*; for *The Haunted Barn*, that role is awkwardly divided between Dietrich-Derrick (Camera Direction) and Gregan McMahon (Dialogue Direction). Frank nominally directed all the other features that he produced: *Diggers* (1931), *The Sentimental Bloke* and *His Royal Highness* (1932), *Harmony Row* (1933), and *A Ticket in Tatts*, *Clara Gibbings* and *Streets of London* (1934).

151 Minchin's cameo was not included in the final cut of *Diggers*; in an interview in October 1978 with Chris Long and Graham Shirley she recalled it as 'just something to do with thermometers and getting into bed and being a little bit naughty, not very, but just a tiny little bit flirtatious with this funny long thing in the bed [Pat Hanna]'.

What precisely this meant is a matter of conjecture, and probably varied quite a lot. On *Diggers*, for instance, there were good reasons to defer to his star. Pat Hanna had written the script, based on sketches that he had produced for his wartime touring concert party 'The Diggers', and his was the marquee name on which Efftee's initial sales depended. Hanna was an established star of vaudeville; he was well-placed to do with the film whatever he wanted, and some of the time he did. Frank found it difficult to play second fiddle, though, and he and Hanna managed to disagree a good deal. In particular they argued about the sequence of the routines, and that was an argument Frank won. But in most directorial matters, Bert Nicholas, Higgins' assistant on camera, judged that Pat Hanna had prevailed; Hanna 'saw to it that he was in nearly every shot' of the film, and insisted on the scenic model shots that Frank Thring thought unnecessary but which had been essential 'to tie things together'.[152] For *Diggers in Blighty*, there was no argument as to who was directing; Pat Hanna had leased the Efftee Studios for the purpose, and Frank Thring was mercifully out of the country for most of the shoot.

Given Frank's self-referential and hands-on conception of the producer's role, it's likely that he had quite a lot to do with the other two projects for which he received no attribution. After all, the mansions, the cars and the furnishings were mostly his own – not to mention the money. And Frank thought he knew quite a lot about performing, and what audiences liked.

Dietrich-Derrick had been hired by Tom Holt on the recommendation of his Hollywood contacts. No-one knew exactly what he had done to earn the appointment, but Thelma Scott, one of McMahon's protégés who made her film debut in *The Haunted Barn*, found him at least dressed for the part:

> He looked like some Hollywood director, you know. He had riding boots on, and dark glasses, and [*laughter*] carried everything but a whip. And I just assumed that he'd had Hollywood experience. But I didn't know.[153]

Patricia Minchin was even more sceptical about his credentials:

> Derrick Dietrich or Dietrich Derrick or whatever his wretched name was – he was a silly little fellow … He ran about like a little mouse, you

152 Bert Nicholas, interview with Graeme Shirley and Chris Long, 23 November 1978. Transcript in the possession of Chris Long.

153 Thelma Scott, interview with Graham Shirley and Chris Long, 28 November 1978. Transcript in the possession of Chris Long.

> know, or a little person flipping and flopping about, and all the time we thought he didn't know what he was doing … We [she and Donalda Warne] didn't like him because he used to keep – approaching us … He was the naughty one who kept asking us to get undressed! I have no idea [where he came from] – Dietrich-Derrick sounds like a very got-up name to my mind, it doesn't sound real, and I think he was posing, I always did think so … [154]

Bert Nicholas had the impression that Dietrich-Derrick knew what he was about, though he thought him 'a bit of a ratbag'; 'I don't know where he came from, but they should've sent him back'.[155]

Frank Thring, too, was clearly not convinced. He was always on the set, watching, and finding ways of making his feelings known:

> He never said very, very much. He used to whistle, if he was annoyed about anything. He never scolded, or … He was a very quiet man. But if something went wrong and he had to wait a long time, say, you'd hear this little [*whistles tune*] … and you always knew he was getting *very* irritated – either with camera hold-up, or electrician hold-up, or a sound hold-up.
>
> You heard F.T. whistling, you knew he was getting very irritated. But not saying a word. He was a very patient man.[156]

He was prepared to say a word or two to his Director, though:

> Well, I think that Dietrich-Derrick had to work in with Mr Thring. Whatever Mr Thring wanted, Dietrich-Derrick had to give him. So if Mr Thring wanted a re-take, Dietrich would have to take it.[157]

Dietrich-Derrick, one way or another, had a good deal to take. With a producer whose word was law and whose whistling was terrifying, and a co-director whose background was entirely in theatre of the more earnest kind, his position on *The Haunted Barn* could never be comfortable. And Frank Thring was whistling through *A Co-Respondent's Course* as well. Dietrich-

154 Patricia Minchin interview.
155 Bert Nicholas interview.
156 Thelma Scott interview.
157 Thelma Scott interview.

Derrick made no more films with Efftee, and the grand plans for McMahon's continuing involvement with the studio were conspicuously unfulfilled.

The power relationships were similarly complex on the films for which Frank Thring is named as Director. He had always liked to append the phrase 'under the personal supervision of F.W. Thring' to his projects, and that probably is a fair representation of his approach to directing. Nothing could happen that he did not like, but creative ideas and approaches to acting and spatial awareness and technical skills – these were matters that he knew little about, though he would always have an opinion on the results that they produced. And there were people around him who knew rather more about these things than he did. Arthur Higgins was a fine cinematographer, and a man giving personal supervision to the composition of a scene would be a fool not to trust his practised eye; George Wallace was, like Pat Hanna, a big enough comic talent to organise himself and the show around him; smart and seasoned actors like Cecil Scott, or Tal Odell who had been a hit as Ginger Mick in the stage version of *The Sentimental Bloke* twelve years before, or the formidable English comedienne Ada Reeve, or her fellow-countryman Frank Harvey not only knew their craft and would take care that their camera angles were right, but might even teach fresh young things like Donalda Warne and Patricia Minchin a thing or two in the process. Moreover, on the Efftee periphery were other assets to draw on that were barely unacknowledged. Raymond Longford, Australia's most distinguished director of silent films, was contracted in early 1931 for a remake of *Robbery Under Arms*, but in the light of the censorship problems of *The Haunted Barn* Frank thought it prudent first to postpone and then, two years later, to abort the project. In the interim Longford hung around the studio, working on *His Royal Highness*, *The Sentimental Bloke* and *Harmony Row* as an uncredited 'associate', and on *Diggers in Blighty* as Associate Director and bit-player; there was nowhere else at the time, for anyone who wanted to do nothing but make films, to go.

How Frank's 'personal supervision' operated, then, with or without a directorial credit, varied from project to project. Lola's work as editor, though, was in every respect a constant. The strange thing was that she turned out to be good at her job. It might have begun as a sinecure, a father's gesture to a girl with no career and no obvious skills in anything, but at least some dexterity with a pair of scissors. But Lola was clever enough to learn on the job from old pros like Arthur Higgins, and smart young ones like Bert Nicholas, and not to mind if they sometimes showed her what to do by actually doing it: Bert felt that she'd been 'pushed into editing', and that Arthur Higgins did a lot of work in the cutting-room for which he was never rewarded, but Lola earned her stripes, and their respect, surprisingly quickly.[158]

Editing was not a high-profile occupation for the daughter of F.T., but she seems to have preferred things that way. There must have been talk around the studio about the blatant nepotism, talk that she would have tried hard not to hear; in a work-place where everyone else except her father had claims to be an expert at what they were doing, Lola's complete lack of training was all too noticeable. So there were good reasons to keep her head down. It helped that she liked the job, and that most of her interactions were with celluloid, and Lola went to some lengths to keep it that way. At the Sydney opening of *A Co-Respondent's Course* and *Diggers*, *Everyones* noted the unsuccessful attempt by the Federal Treasurer, Edward ('Red Ted') Theodore to avoid attention, by slipping out just before interval and delaying his return until the lights were safely down, in the course of reporting on another social triumph – and an even more reluctant centre of attention:

> There was a distinct change of demeanour at the Hotel Australia afterwards when, in the private reception room, Tom Holt, general manager of Efftee, summoned 30 or 40 film folk and newspaper bloques [*sic*] to supper.
>
> In this limited company, Mr. Theodore had no hesitation in rising to extend his best wishes to the Australian production enterprise. Stanley S. Crick uttered a ditto; Donalda Warne, one of Efftee's contract stars, was introduced; and then a whisper suggested that a second talented young lady should speak her piece. This was Miss Lola Thring, daughter of F.W.T., who is responsible for the cutting and editing of the Efftee productions.
>
> Panicky moment for Lola! Sliding from her chair, Lola vanished into the ante-room as a haven of refuge from rhetoric; and even next day she was still unnerved by her narrow escape.[159]

Lola's horror of public acknowledgement, or (heaven forbid) of speaking her piece, might have been prompted by a reflex maiden modesty that Donalda

158 Thelma Scott interview.

159 'Treasurer Theodore Shuns the Spotlight', *Everyones*, 18 November 1931, p.7. Stanley Crick was Managing Director of Fox Films.

Warne, at nineteen a year her junior, could not afford to feel; perhaps the Misses Langley and Templeton at St Catherine's had inculcated the virtues of demureness a bit too thoroughly. Or perhaps it was embarrassment at being on Daddy's payroll. Probably it was a combination of both. But perhaps her hasty exit from the spotlight was yet another indication that the person whose good opinion of her was most important was in the room, and she knew that she had it already. That person at this point in her life was her father, though the man she was to marry was in the room on that evening, too; it had taken most of her young lifetime for Lola to catch her father's attention, and no man could match the power of his approval for at least as long as he lived.

Filming *A Co-Respondent's Course* was quite a family affair. Frank and Lola did not miss a moment. Olive was quite often on the set, bringing little gifts of food to the crew, and volunteering helpful suggestions about direction.[160] And little Frank spent a lot of time at His Majesty's, playing with Pattie Hanna, Pat's four-year-old daughter; Pattie's recollection of their games, shaped of course by the seventy-four years that had passed since she had played them, was that Frankie, a year her senior, was 'completely spoilt' and 'a real cry-baby'.[161] Later, he plagued his big sister while she tried to work in the editing suite: sound recordist Alan Stuart remembered the boss's son all too vividly:

> Yeah. School cap stuck in his pocket … Fat kid. He was kicking the film on the cutting-room floor![162]

Dietrich-Derrick, whatever his actual credentials and experience, must have wondered how he'd ended up in this antipodean amateur hour.

'Rylands' was in the film, too, and Frank's green Packard, and various Thring holiday haunts at fashionable Portsea, to confirm the sense of a home

160 Bert Nicholas interview.
161 Pattie Hanna, conversation with Mimi Colligan, Chris Long, Betty Hanner and the author, 3 April 2005.
162 R. Alan Stuart, interview with Chris Long and Graham Shirley, March 1978.

away from home. And homeliness is evident, too, in much of the method, and in some of the quaint casting of minor roles. The publicity people made much of the fact that Miss Noel Clapp, daughter of the Victorian Railways Commissioner and a 'well-known Melbourne society girl',[163] was making her screen debut in a minor role; the press release enthused that 'her titian hair and expressive features ideally fit her for screen work', but failed to note that this would only be so in films with scenes set on Flinders Street Station, and requiring her father's generous co-operation in loaning the odd train. Frank Thring might have had his limitations as a director, but he knew a thing or two about the politics of casting.

Donalda Warne starred as Nellie, the 'little devil' with whom James Lord (John D'Arcy) the stuffy solicitor has fallen in love. She is variously described as a vamp, a girl who likes to live dangerously, and a modern woman defiant of convention; in fact, she's a sweet but silly juvenile tease, and enjoys making James worry about things that he really has no reason to worry about at all:

> NELLIE: You kiss so nicely. Much nicer than any other boy I know.
>
> LORD: Now I don't care for that kind of joke, Nellie. It's not funny.
>
> NELLIE: Kisses aren't jokes. If they were, I'd be one of the world's greatest humorists.
>
> LORD: Nellie!
>
> NELLIE: Poor old Jim. I do make you jealous, don't I?

Nellie has come to his office to tell James that she is going away for a week with her friend May (Patricia Minchin) to Portsea, where there are 'lots of nice boys'. She tells him, rather unnecessarily, that she is hardly taking any clothes – just her pyjamas and her daring new bathing suit ('You ought to see it – but you must have good eyes if you can!') – which gives James further food for confusing thought.

Nellie gets the dates wrong, and goes down a day early; when James finds out, he immediately assumes that she's up to no good. His fears are reinforced when his client Rouse bursts in, convinced that his wife has left him because of their argument over the toast that morning, and has run off with Dane, a man he is sure has been trying to seduce her for years.

---

163 Press release for *A Co-Respondent's Course*, National Film and Sound Archive.

ROUSE: Mark you, she knew Dane before ever I met her. And these premarital associations have a habit of recurring. Oh, I've had experience of these women. They're all the same.

LORD: Perhaps.

The language of this exchange is characteristic. The 'upper class' romance-plot people speak with a high-falutin vocabulary, and an accent to match. It's only among the 'lower class' characters – sundry servants and porters, and the three bumbling private-eyes who set out for Portsea to catch Mrs Rouse *in flagrante* – that a genuinely Australian accent can be heard. Even the porter calling 'All aboard!' at Flinders Street Station has a touch of the toff – not surprisingly, since the role is played by (though not formally credited to) Frank Thring. It would have been a long time since Frank had caught the train to Frankston.

The screenplay, by Monty Grover, editor of the Melbourne tabloid the *Sun*, flirts with the possibility of becoming the daring comedy of modern manners that it pretends to be, but there is not much to cause a sensitive censor many qualms. Nellie appears fetchingly in her swimsuit, and indeed marries James in it, but, while the camera fawns on her, she is by most standards respectable enough. And although she is no blushing maid, Nellie is, when she has given her heart and her word, absolutely a one-guy gal; much of the early Portsea action shows her dealing kindly but firmly with one eligible pursuer after another ('Somebody got ahead of you').[164] Similarly, though Mrs Rouse might have had enough of her husband's toast, she shows no consequent interest in tasting another man's. She has been waiting for him at their friends' house in Portsea, we're told, 'fretting her heart out'. The film is not about women's frailty, or even about how the liberated New Woman complicates the Holy Estate. It is about the foolish madness of jealousy, in a world where it seems every woman is scrupulously faithful and every man pathologically possessive.

The script aims for a little more titillation than the final cut, which was edited with one eye to a censor who could take offence at a howling wind. The decision to have three private eyes on the case, which seems an extravagant choice for Sleath's Detective Agency and for Grover's script, let alone for Thring's budget, is explained when each of them takes his salacious turn at

164 *A Co-Respondent's Course*, draft screenplay RIS034934, National Film and Sound Archive, p.11. Dialogue quoted in the text that is not attributed to this source is taken directly from the soundtrack of the film.

bursting in on the three supposedly guilty couples (who turn out, of course, to be the reconciled Mr and Mrs Rouse and Mr and Mrs Dane, and the newly married James and Nellie Lord). First Hall (Ed Warrington) lets himself into the Dane suite, where the bed is rumpled but empty; he takes a long look around the bathroom door before it is slammed shut by the disconcerted Mrs Dane, smirks contentedly when she cries out (rather unnecessarily) that 'I haven't anything on', and doesn't quite avert his eyes when he leans in to hand her a kimono. Then Ratchet (Oliver Peacock) disturbs the Rouses, but leaves with a similar smirk when Rouse, in unbuttoned striped pyjamas, lets him know his services are most definitely no longer required. Finally Maloney (George Moon) blunders in on the honeymooners, who respond with admirable restraint when he asks what he should do with Rouse's divorce papers:

> LORD: I don't know. We don't want them, do we Nellie?
>
> NELLIE: Not just yet, anyhow.
>
> LORD: You just put them in the fire and forget them.
>
> MALONEY: I will that. Sorry I disturbed you, Mr Lord. Sorry I woke you up Mrs Rouse – Mrs Lord.
>
> NELLIE: Oh! You didn't wake me. Did he, Jimmy?

Maloney's 'Good night' is accompanied by George Moon's most knowing wink. The censor was comfortable with the mildly risque when the subjects were decently married and had at least one foot on the floor, as long as the wind was not blowing too passionately.

Much of *A Co-Respondent's Course* is heavy going. The lack of action in many of its dialogue scenes is exacerbated by the static single-take camera work, and by an excessive concern with circumstantial realism that produces 'book-ends' of extended hellos and goodbyes in many scenes, and excruciatingly prolonged telephone calls in which phone numbers are always carefully enunciated and there are long pauses while the caller listens patiently to someone whom we cannot see or hear. And a lot of the conversation is stagey and stilted.

Still, there are two forces at work that not only mitigate those faults, but give the film at least a period charm. The rhetorical excesses in the script that sound so dated have less to do with Monty Grover's limitations, in the end, than with those of his male characters. To a man, the husbands strike melodramatic poses that reflect the absurdity of their fears about the fidelity of their women; thus Rouse, after '*He casts himself into a chair, the picture of misery*',[165] on being asked by James Lord what seems to be wrong:

> ROUSE: Wrong, wrong ... You ask what's wrong when a man's whole life's ruined ... when all he's worked for and slaved for falls to pieces like a pack of cards.
>
> LORD: Your finances are all right.
>
> ROUSE: Finances! Damn finances! Lord, I loved my wife; I love her still, in spite of everything.

Lord has a fair line in histrionic despair, too. When he rings from a pub and learns that Nellie has only just arrived in Portsea, '*he hangs up the receiver in a dazed way, totters to the bar and gulps down his drink*'.[166] The Barman fails to notice that the world has suddenly gone dark:

> BARMAN: Do you happen to know a good thing for the Metropolitan?
>
> LORD: To hell with everything!
>
> BARMAN: Must be a long price. Never heard him mentioned.

Barmen, and women like May and Nellie, have a grasp on reality that throws into relief the preposterousness of these men who think they are the central characters in a tragedy. By the time Lord declares his intention to kill himself, the ironic principle has been absolutely established:

> LORD: No dinner for me. No more dinners in this life.
>
> MAY: What on earth's the matter now?
>
> LORD: The matter is that I know all now. I know that I have been tricked, deceived, probably held up to ridicule.
>
> MAY: Are you talking about Nellie?
>
> LORD: I am. Poor fool that I am ... She's a false, faithless woman, but I love her in spite of it all. Tell her that when I'm gone.
>
> MAY: Gone where?

165 *A Co-Respondent's Course*, draft screenplay, p.6.
166 ibid, p.27.

> LORD: Where I'm going now – into the great eternity. I'm off to seek the forgetfulness of death in the shark's mouth, or from the top of the highest cliff I can find.[167]

Of course, he changes his mind about jumping when he reaches the edge of London Bridge – seconds before Nellie, in that fashionably revealing bathing costume, rushes up to drag him back from the brink. In *A Co-Respondent's Course* as in marriage, there's no room for tragic heroes.

The other element that enlivens the film is its use of exterior locations and, more generally, its frequent reliance on visual language. Sometimes the latter moments are scripted, like Rouse's desperate attempt to fall asleep ('Three thousand eight hundred and seventy one, three hundred and seventy two – Damn them, they're too fast for me'), which is to be accompanied by an inset of sheep jumping a hurdle.[168] Mostly, though, they reflect directorial decisions; thus another of Rouse's moments of misery, when his car is bogged and he begins his trudge to Portsea, is enhanced by an unscripted cut-away to a kookaburra chortling at his misfortune. The broader location work was Dietrich-Derrick's initiative, according to Bert Nicholas;[169] quite apart from the historical interest of these scenes of old Portsea, they are integrated with the scripted action with a confidence that suggests that Dietrich-Derrick, for all his mysterious past, must have spent some of it making movies.

Patricia Minchin, who went from a couple of small amateur parts with the Bankers' Operatic Society into a major role in virtually Australia's first talkie feature, found filming *A Co-Respondent's Course* 'a lot of fun':

> Dear old Frank Thring was like a lovely big old father. The whole atmosphere was very nice. When he was about it was absolutely lovely. When he wasn't about his – was he called director or producer? – um … Dietrich … Derrick? was quite another kettle of fish. It was fun because we laughed behind his back ... And we didn't do that when Mr Thring was there.[170]

But she found the whole operation in retrospect a shambles. The significant exception was Arthur Higgins, who 'was the one who seemed to know what

167 *A Co-Respondent's Course*, draft screenplay, p.36.
168 ibid, p.20. Sadly, the sheep insert was omitted from the final version of the film.
169 Bert Nicholas interview.
170 Patricia Minchin interview.

he was doing, when the scene was to be shot'. She recalled Higgins trying patiently to stop the cast 'madly over-acting', but nonetheless 'We were all, I thought, fairly frightful'. The actors had no idea about the technicalities of film-making, and nobody but Higgins made any effort to teach them:

> 'What's that?' someone would say, when someone came out with the clacker [*sic*] you know … 'What's that for?' We didn't hear anything! Mostly what we heard was 'Take your clothes off!' … I didn't learn anything at all, not one single thing![171]

And the environment in which the film was shot proved a serious challenge even to the professional skills of Higgins and Dan Bloomberg:

> This great huge barn of His Majesty's Theatre, totally empty except for flaps, and all sorts of different bits of wood, and wire, and invariably when we'd got the shot we thought was perfect there'd be the most appalling noise of wood falling over, someone had jumped on something, or there'd be a great squeak ... We were such amateurs, you know, in those days – everyone was! Of course, they quickly found that the boom picked up everything.[172]

It's surprising, given the degree to which some were learning by doing and the rest simply making it up as they went along, that Efftee's first film achieved what it did. As Jack Murray, an assistant sound recordist on the project, observed with some surprise when he saw the film for the first time nearly fifty years after shooting it, 'It wasn't too bad, was it?'[173]

It looked like a sure thing. Pat Hanna had established his 'Diggers Concert Party' in his role as recreational and entertainment officer with the New Zealand contingent during the post-war occupation of France; the company had travelled to Britain and America before coming home to a further

171 ibid.
172 ibid.
173 Quoted by Chris Long in the Patricia Minchin interview.

eleven years on the road throughout New Zealand and Australia. Hanna at the same time established a parallel career as a popular recording artist – his wheedling vicar declaiming 'The Gospel According to Cricket' and 'the Gospel according to Racing' are among the legendary acts of Australian comedy. He and 'his cobber in trouble' George Moon were much-loved variety performers, and they came with established scripts and routines that promised to exempt Efftee from all the messiness that came with finding writers and casting performers. Making *Diggers* seemed so much simpler than the painful trials-and-errors of *A Co-Respondent's Course.*

Frank Thring, as producer and titular director, learned quite quickly that nothing in film-making is ever simple, and that managing to obviate some of the usual problems simply creates space for new and different ones. Pat Hanna knew what had worked on the vaudeville circuit, and had no desire to be told what to do by a man who had no experience of directing anything bigger than a card-trick. Nor was he keen to have his jokes appropriated by another hand; Thring and Eric Donaldson have subsidiary writing credits on the film, which reflect their often vain attempts to adapt Hanna's sketch comedy to a structure that resembled a coherent film narrative. The fact that its star was very good at his job was at once the great strength of *Diggers* and its major difficulty. The directorial issue was mostly resolved by Frank's capitulation; except when the budget was at issue, where the man whose initials gave the company its name waved his producer's hat and claimed the right of veto, most scenes were shot as Pat wanted them. The script issue was mostly not resolved at all.

Diggers is still an engaging film, and, though some of the routines are protracted, the unaffected good-heartedness of the comic style pulls them through. The structure, though, is always a problem. The plot consists essentially of the forced merger of three of the most popular routines in Hanna's touring show: the Hospital scene, in which Chic and Joe (respectively Pat Hanna and George Moon) are reunited in a ward in London, and try unsuccessfully to fool the medicos into sending them home and to gain their revenge on Fatty (Ed Warrington), who has pinched Joe's girl and half his pay; the Rum scene, in which the two old mates, abetted by Bluey (Cecil Scott) unsuccessfully try to sneak some rum from the Pommy bastards who always seem to get in the way of a bloke having a bit of fun at the Front; and the Mademoiselle from Armentieres sequence, which is a poignant coda that reminds us that war is more than a campaign to 'put one over' authority, that some diggers die very young, and that some girls are left waiting forever. The radical shifts in locale and (especially) tone present quite a challenge to the writer who tries to integrate them in a story without curtains or intervals.

The structure was the major point of conflict between the nominal director and his star. Hanna wanted to begin with the Rum episode, segue into a little schmaltz at Armentieres, and come home hilariously in the hospital; it was his habit, and his nature, to leave his audiences laughing. Frank wanted, and got, his sentimental closure. Whatever concessions might be won in moment-by-moment matters, in the end, as Alan Stuart put it, 'There was always God upstairs'.[174]

Eric Donaldson, who was primarily charged with the responsibility for disguising the narrative seams, came impressively close to bringing off the impossible. Not that the framing device, an Old Soldiers' reunion some twelve years after the war, is itself particularly brilliant; the move into the first routine, when Chic and Joe spot Fatty at the bar and Joe says portentously 'What a mess he got us into. Do you remember?' is not so much a cue for a flashback as a warning siren. What makes the story nearly work is the conflation of time, through the juxtaposition of the visual event with either voice-over or song, which can produce some startling results. In that 'first act' of *Diggers*, for example, we are taken under Joe's narration back to the hospital, where Chic, now clearly if inexplicably confined to his bed, transports us under another voice-over to a time earlier in the war when Joe 'did his block' over the 'ginger-headed tabby in London' who duped him into signing over half his pay ('Look, orderly, I'll give yer an idea of what a silly coot he is!'), before we return to the hospital and find that Fatty in the next bed is the beneficiary of that arrangement. It's the kind of cleverness that could make a post-modernist's day, or even career; it is certainly a skilful attempt to solve the insoluble.

The narrative is held together, too, by the knowledge that our lads, in their continual quest to cheat or defeat imperial authority wherever it raises its snooty nose, are doomed inevitably to fail; however ingenious Chic and Joe are in their efforts to fake the disability that might have them sent home, or to steal the rum that might make the fields of France feel more like a Saturday night in Paddo, we know it will always end in their being sent back into the mud and slush of the front line. Their humour depends on the fact that men like them never get the girl, or the cushy job; they stand for an underclass that, while it will never be promoted, will always be able to laugh hard and long at the affectations of those who are.

174 R. Alan Stuart interview.

The counterpoint between image and sound-track works surprisingly well to find the complexity of tone that Hanna sought in his stage shows, too. While in his revues the balance was characteristically, as it is in the film, heavily skewed toward comedy, there was always room for a reminder, as in the 'Mademoiselle' sequence, that war was about much more than a couple of mates on a trip away. *Diggers* opens with the returned soldiers standing with heads bowed, remembering fallen comrades, then cuts through clouds of cigarette smoke to the raucous laughter and clinking of glasses to which those memories have thoroughly entitled them. It ends with the song 'Mademoiselle from Armentieres', done rousingly at first as it is juxpaposed with glimpses of the lads as they march out of the village to another battle, and then poignantly, as we see 'the little French girl with eyes of brown' first watching at the window, and then sobbing into the slouch hat of the lover who will never come back. The tone shifts abruptly again for the final twenty seconds of the film, as Chic, back at the reunion, grabs a piece of fruit and scores a direct hit on Fatty Jones, in a more triumphant kind of remembrance of things past.

Diggers is driven, though, by the three things that made Hanna's concert parties a hit: the rapport between Chic, long and lean as the proverbial pull-through, and Joe, his little mate, as they battle authority in all its forms; George Moon's genius for physical comedy; and, above all, a delight in verbal gags built on the intrinsic slipperiness of language, especially as used by Chic and Joe. Some of that joy is expressed through one-liners imported straight from the music-hall – Chic's 'I don't drink rum. I'm a totalisator!' for example, which instantly defines him as a clown, a liar and a betting man; or their greeting to their mate Bluey (Cecil Scott) when they come across him driving a broken-down cart, 'It might be a hansom cab, but it's a very ugly driver', where the line draws for its humour simultaneously on mock-heroic inflation, a playful pun, and affection for the butt of the joke. Elsewhere the verbal humour builds more slowly from character and situation, as when Fatty makes a cumbersome pass at the nurse:

FATTY: I say, Nurse. Do us a favour.

NURSE: What's that?

FATTY: Give us a cuddle.

NURSE: You'll have to wait till ten o'clock for that. [*Pause*]

The orderly comes on duty then. He does all the dirty work.

The writing there gives Ed Warrington, who has a very eloquent face, plenty of time to savour his improbable success before plunging him first into confusion and then into despair. Hanna's sense of timing, in a line or in a comic sequence, rarely misses a beat.

Technically, too, *Diggers* is often impressive. The camera follows Hanna, or Hanna and Moon, religiously, but even in the tightest of two-shots it finds opportunities to move. The interior sequences are not as wooden as those in *A Co-Respondent's Course*. And the trench scenes are so cleverly lit that no audience could ever suspect that it was really looking at an orchestra-pit. Even Bill Coleman's mock-ups of French villages have their charm, although the street outside the inn where the Mademoiselle waits (in both senses) sometimes looks as though it's only a couple of metres wide.

The shot widens to enter the street in the last verse of the song, when a small boy in a Legionnaire's hat topped with a huge cockade ambles across the street, holding hands with an even smaller girl in a massive bonnet; they turn back from the door of the house opposite the inn, and skip back to the camera, with huge smiles on their faces. Who they are, what they are doing, and why they are there is a mystery that is never explained; perhaps they are the children that the Mademoiselle (Eugenie Pescott, wife of the sound engineer Dan Bloomberg) will never have with her lost lover – certainly that moment precipitates her tears over his slouch hat. The only other evident justification for their presence is that they are very cute.

The real reason for the children's presence is clear, though, when the viewer recognises who they are. Frankie Thring and Pattie Hanna, such reluctant playmates through the long days in which their parents were making movies, are given their moment in the spotlight, and make *Diggers*, for a moment, a family affair as, in a different way, *A Co-Respondent's Course* had been. It marked the first small steps in two substantial performance careers, and they look as though they are enjoying it hugely. Pattie, who thought Thring Junior such a sook, must have found it a challenge to hold hands with that awful boy, and the feeling was probably reciprocated. But they have both, apparently, learned already how handy it can be to act.

Despite the teething problems and the demarcation disputes, *Diggers* came up trumps. Some of that cobbers-together whimsicality has worn a little thin from the perspective of another century, but the audiences of ex-diggers and their families seem not to have felt that at all. The film's popularity, especially when it moved to the outer-suburban and rural circuit, was sufficient to indulge Frank in his belief that Efftee might even make a profit. And it encouraged Hanna to produce two sequels in 1933 that were funded largely from his own resources, *Diggers in Blighty* (shot at Efftee's Wattle Path Studios under its nominal banner) and *Waltzing Matilda* (filmed in Queensland for Pat Hanna Productions). It was a good thing, probably, that Frank Thring, director, had done so little to direct it.

He had still less to do with the making of *The Haunted Barn*, the film that opened a fortnight after Efftee's initial double bill, and had been scheduled to share the company's premiere with *Diggers*. That film already had one director too many. Not that a surfeit of directors or the absence of a credit would have been an obstacle to Frank; certainly, as Thelma Scott recalled, Frank whistled his anxiety quite a lot on the set of *The Haunted Barn*, at least as much as he did with every other film his company made.

The third feature in Efftee's opening season gave him a lot of reasons for whistling. There was the script, for a start. T.A. Swain had been invited to adapt his short story, for no obviously compelling reason. Swain had no experience in writing for film, and the decision to engage him represented a view that was probably a general one, but seems certainly to have been held by Frank Thring, that any wordsmith worth his salt could write a screenplay. When the Efftee initiative had been first made public, Frank had announced the appointment of two 'literary advisers' – the poet C.J. Dennis and the novelist and painter Norman Lindsay. Dennis' *The Sentimental Bloke* was planned to appear in the second Efftee season, while Lindsay's adaptation of his novel *Redheap* was at one stage contemplated for its first. Neither had any experience of writing for the cinema. Indeed, though *The Sentimental Bloke* had been adapted for the silent screen in a celebrated production by Raymond Longford and Lottie Lyell, Longford expressed his gratitude for the fact that Dennis 'offered no suggestions or interfered with the making of the film whatsoever'.[175] Lindsay had had no involvement with the screen at any time; he was relieved when the project was aborted, and none of his works would be adapted to film until *Age of Consent* in 1969, the year of his death, a film that featured Frank Thring's only son. Frank had a remarkable capacity to enlist for Efftee the best creative people in the country – providing they had no real knowledge of the medium at all.

Moreover, Swain had written a very strange short story. Ina Bertrand's summary would be hard to better:

175 Raymond Longford, letter to H.L.White, 23 March 1958, Longford Papers, National Film and Sound Archive, quoted in Philip Butterss, 'A 'careful little housewife': C.J. Dennis and masculinity in The Sentimental Blokes', *Screening the Past* at www.latrobe.edu.au/screeningthepast/firstrelease.

> Mr Moon intends to spend the night in a barn hoping to see the ghost of the bushranger Sturdy who died there when betrayed to the police by his friend Rogan. Already in the barn are two tramps, one of whom is dumb, who have sheltered from the rain, and a strange wild-looking man who repeatedly threatens their lives. They are joined by Ralph and Joan, a young couple eloping and fearful of reprisals from Joan's father. Rose enters with a gun and then leaves after demanding that no-one leaves till dawn, and later a man burst [*sic*] in with the news that lunatics have escaped from the local asylum and 10 pounds per head is offered for their capture. While all are asleep a body appears on the floor which all (particularly Mr Moon) are convinced is Sturdy's ghost when it mysteriously disappears again. In the morning Rose, Sturdy and Rogan confront each other and Sturdy explains he was not seeking to kill Rogan but to get his permission to marry Rose (who is Sturdy's sister) and thereby end the family feud. Rogan admits to being the body, having fallen from the loft while hiding from Sturdy. Dr Glass arrives to claim Ralph and Joan who are the lunatics, and Mr Moon's two friends arrive and explain that they hired an actor to act wildly and provide the exciting ghost that Moon had hoped to find. The two tramps are left by themselves with momentary dreams of wealth till they open Ralph's wallet and find it is stuffed with newspaper.[176]

All this happens in a barn, in a little over forty minutes. If readers find the plot hard to follow after the first sentence, it's impossible to imagine what viewers made of it. The proliferation of detail is only part of the problem – the absurdity of the motivation (who is asking whose permission for what, and why?), and the way in which the attractive ingénues whose love is the only recognisable human feeling in the place are suddenly revealed as crazy, turns the whole thing into something between farce and surrealist dream.

Then, to direct this dog's breakfast, Frank employed two men who could never have worked productively together. In the white corner was Gregan McMahon, nearly sixty, a serious director of experimental and literary theatre, whose particular skills lay in teasing out the intellectual subtleties of a playscript and working intensely with actors to discover authentic patterns of feeling. In the red was E.A. (nobody ever found out what his initials stood for) Dietrich-Derrick, youngish, from somewhere in Europe via the States,

176 Ina Bertrand, *Australian Film Studies 7*, p.19.

a possible charlatan whose focus as a director was on external action and persuading young actresses to take off their clothes. It might have been an inspired pairing of opposites, or simply a bad idea. The fact that it resulted in disaster suggests that it was the latter all along.

Finally, just when it seemed absurdity had gone as far as it could go and the film was apparently safely in the can, Professor Osborne, the State Censor, took a hand, and banned it from general release because of the sound of its wind. It was probably one of the biggest favours anyone had ever done for Frank Thring in a career that he liked to think had been all his own work. At a stroke it saved him from opening his company with a folly, and gave him publicity that benefited both *The Haunted Barn* and the Efftee enterprise.

Frank waited until *A Co-Respondent's Course* and *Diggers* had enjoyed a suitably supportive reception before he played his trump card. Under the startling headline 'CENSORSHIP MAY FORCE THRING TO PRODUCE IN LONDON', less than three weeks after Efftee's triumphant launch, *Everyones* ran another of those heavily editorialised news articles that sounded as though they came straight from the pen of Frank Thring:

> Official pin-pricks and censorship may compel F.W. Thring to abandon his Australian talkie enterprise and choose London as his preferred production headquarters.
>
> Having completed four features, he finds that two of them have been banned by the Victorian censors from exhibition before children between the ages of 6 and 16, the latest being "The Haunted Barn", to which the censor has attached the conditional clause on the ground that the wailing of the wind in the sound effects of this mystery burlesque may frighten children. The industry as a whole regards that as an amazing and ridiculous ground for a ban.
>
> "It is practically impossible to go on under the present circumstances," Mr Thring told "Everyones." He has already invested upwards of £50,000 in the establishment of his sound studios and the production of four features and a number of shorts. If he is to be harried by officialdom he will toss that investment overboard and go elsewhere to produce.[177]

177 *Everyones*, 25 November 1931, p.7.

The asperity of tone in the opening phrase 'Official pin-pricks' and the closing reference to being 'harried' and tossing investments overboard seems to come unmediated from the horse's mouth. And the notion that 'the industry as a whole' could feel any common emotion, given that a large proportion of it certainly wanted Efftee to fail and would always have a terrible tendency to *schadenfreude*, was an obvious fiction. Frank was flexing some new-found muscles. Of course he wanted *The Haunted Barn* to be released for general exhibition; there were compelling financial reasons for that to happen. But mostly, Efftee's battle with the censor was about personal power, and Frank needed to take this chance to put 'officialdom' permanently in its place.

He won the game, of course. The threat was a completely empty one, but extravagant enough to apply pressure where it was needed. In the 'Stop Press' column of the same edition, *Everyones* carried a wire report from Melbourne:

> Professor Osborne has upheld the appeal lodged by Efftee Films against the banning of "The Haunted Barn" before children between the ages of 6 and 16, and has ratified its release for general exhibition.[178]

No doubt children flocked to see this controversial new film with its terrifying sound-effects, which was partly the aim of the exercise. What they made of it, with its dead bushrangers who come to life and its lovers who turn out to be lunatics and the rest of its Gothic whimsies, is – again – unimaginable. All one can hope is that they were excited by the wind.

Through all the intensities that came with that frenetic first year of Efftee, there was something else that made Frank inclined to whistle. Donalda Warne was its particular focus, but Donalda was just one of a number of attractive girls who had suddenly come into his life: she and Patricia Minchin, both aged nineteen, were promoted as 'the Greta Garbo and Norma Shearer of Australia';[179] Thelma Scott and Coral Brown (later Browne), aged eighteen,

178 ibid, p.24.

179 *Table Talk*, 23 April 1931, p.3. The faces of the two new stars appeared together on the cover of the magazine, in a partly explicit competition between blonde and brunette.

stepped from the periphery of Gregan McMahon's amateur company into major roles in Efftee films and plays. They were all surprisingly young, completely inexperienced in film, and stunningly pretty.

This was quite a novelty for Frank. He had been married at twenty-two to a woman seven years his senior, who but for him would probably never have got out of Gawler, who had been increasingly inclined to be ill, and who for most their marriage had lived with her parents in another state. Through that period Frank had been a young man playing old, attempting to convince the world that he was a businessman, his focus absolutely on the next step in his brilliant career. Then at thirty-nine there had been another wedding, to a woman of thirty-six who had in some ways been matronly since her teens. His focus had remained the same, as the steps became bigger and bolder; Olive would never fade conveniently into the background, but much of their married life had been spent in parallel rather than together, and probably that came to suit both of them, well enough. A man approaching fifty, with a keen sense of the pathos of his own mortality and of all that he has missed in his life, finding himself suddenly in all the hectic glamour of film-making, and surrounded by a bevy of beautiful young actresses: anyone who knew anything about movies would have recognised it at once as a scenario in which a man might make a terrible fool of himself.

Their youth was central to their appeal. Frank chose these ingénues, rather than other attractive women who had a bit more experience of life and acting, because they matched the image of unspoilt charm that he believed in and wanted to promote as 'typically Australian'. Donalda was introduced first among the 'stars' at the Efftee launch in mid-1931 as 'a Sydney girl', and a girl she was. So was Patricia, and Thelma, and Coral. The men who played opposite them were not teenagers, though; the male romantic leads, John D'Arcy, John Maitland (*The Haunted Barn*) and Cecil Scott were all thirty or more, and while handsomeness was obligatory, their experience in film was a crucial factor in their casting.

They lit up his studio, the Efftee girls, and among all the good business reasons that Frank found for his constant presence at rehearsals and shooting added another still more delightful. Frank Thring the son liked to tell stories of his father's predilection for endearing young charms, and claimed that there had been an affair with Coral Browne at least. No-one else has told this story. And Frank junior is a very unreliable witness: not only was he five or six years old at the time, but his predilection for salacious gossip, for the spectacular lie, and for representing his father as a satanic force all provide grounds for caution. The gossip of the time presented Coral as an unusually 'advanced' young lady, who had had a relationship with McMahon when she was a seventeen-year-old schoolgirl, and who had never been reluctant to do whatever was necessary to get what she wanted – but that might be unfair, too. The casting couch has traditionally been a way not only for ambitious young women and unscrupulous old men to fulfil their aspirations, but for all those who missed out to vent their resentment by spreading scurrilous rumours.

Donalda was the first of the Efftee ingénues, and Frank was very fond of her, whatever that may have meant at the time. It would have been obvious to him, as it was to everybody else on the studio floor, that Dietrich-Derrick was quite taken with her, too, and there was certainly no mistaking his intentions. He was at her side encouraging her to show a little more flesh in *A Co-Respondent's Course*, and there again for *The Haunted Barn*, giving her the benefit of his continental experience in building the character of a deranged young lover. Donalda and Patricia Minchin used to giggle about his roaming hands and his obvious innuendos, but Patricia was not there for the filming of *The Haunted Barn*. And she had her own suspicions about the way her friend's career was progressing.

> I didn't think she could ever act. I thought she was an appalling actress, even worse than I was … but I think that Dietrich liked her, you see. She may have been a little more accommodating than I was, I don't know![180]

Both comments were probably unfair. Donalda Warne has a naturalness in *A Co-Respondent's Course* that makes Patricia Minchin's over-elocuted May look a very forced performance. And her 'I don't know' is a genuine admission of what can never be known, as well as a mischievous disavowal of what Patricia has just said. But all this was in the air as Frank Thring watched and whistled, while the opportunistic man from nowhere with the improbable name practised his craft with Frank's favourite juvenile lead.

Frank's solicitude for Donalda Warne may have been prompted by paternal protectiveness, or avuncular affection, or just possibly by a delicious reminder of the half-forgotten sweetness of desire. Patricia Minchin, with her memories of 'Dear old Frank Thring … like a lovely big old father', was very clear about where Frank stood in the world of eligible men. But that was not the way Frank at forty-nine would have seen himself; he would not have

---

180 Patricia Minchin interview.

been ready to be anybody's 'dear old' anything. Whatever it was that Frank felt, he felt it strongly. The immediate aftermath of the play-within-the-play on the set of *The Haunted Barn* was that Frank dismissed his director. There were no announcements, no explanations. E.A. Dietrich-Derrick, sometime (perhaps) Hollywood director, disappeared into an obscurity as complete as the one from which he had emerged.

The second apparent consequence came a few months later, when Donalda Warne suddenly left the country. In the interim she had been very busy. She made one more film that summer for Efftee, *His Royal Highness*, to which Frank Thring had appointed himself director. She did two plays, too, in rapid succession: she starred in Noel Coward's *Bitter Sweet* for J.C. Williamson in March and April 1932, with another Efftee alumnus in Cecil Scott, and in the following month she and Scott appeared in *Turn to the Right* at the Theatre Royal, which also featured Tal Odell from *The Sentimental Bloke*. Then in August the *Sydney Morning Herald* carried a small notice in its 'Personal' column:

> Miss Donalda Warne, formerly a member of the cast of "Bitter Sweet," and her mother are sailing by the *Comorin* to London.[181]

Donalda didn't stay around for the opening of *His Royal Highness* in late October; it's unlikely that she ever saw a print of the film. Was she running eagerly toward a dream of stardom on the West End stage? Or was she running away from a prominence in Australian film and theatre that she no longer wanted to have? Whatever the hopes or fears that took her to London, it was effectively the end of her career. She appeared once more on the stage, as a member of the chorus of the Kern and Hammerstein musical *Music in the Air* at London's Haymarket in early 1933. After that, Donalda Warne, a few months short of her twenty-first birthday, disappears altogether from the record. Nobody heard from her. Her erstwhile best friend, Patricia Minchin, always wished that she had: 'I've always wondered what happened to Donalda. She just – disappeared'.[182]

Donalda Warne's brief and precocious reign as Australia's Greta Garbo lasted less than a year. With any luck, she did what most girls of her age in 1933 aspired to do if they had no plans to become film-stars – found herself a good husband, and lived happily ever after. Perhaps.

181 *Sydney Morning Herald*, 10 August 1932, p.7.
182 Patricia Minchin interview.

At the end of Efftee's first year, the most glamorous of his life, Frank Thring could look back with a lot of satisfaction. A few things – loose ends with a leading lady or two, problems with a shyster director and a pernickety censor – had made life unnecessarily complicated. But Efftee had established its position as a serious player in cinema – perhaps the only one in the country. It included among its assets a flexible and well-resourced studio space at His Majesty's, and it had produced four films, three of which had been released. *The Sentimental Bloke* was edited and ready to go, and *His Royal Highness* had been scripted as far as George Wallace, a comic presence even more bankable than Pat Hanna, ever bothered with such things. And it had begun to put together an impressive series of short films – some of them documentaries, some vaudeville acts – to support the features. Frank's experience in cobbling together programs in his time in Tasmania was decisive in the way Efftee's programs were constructed: thus *Diggers* and *A Co-Respondent's Course*, and then *Diggers* and *The Haunted Barn* ran with a miscellany of four or five films, ranging in length and subject from a George Wallace routine running to seven minutes to J.C.W'.s Grand Opera Orchestra presenting a three minute snatch of Bizet's *Carmen*. The bill of fare reflected Frank's conviction that, in order to maximise the size of his audience, he needed to offer something for all the family; the sense that *The Haunted Barn* was sufficiently spooky to attract children was surely behind its selection for the initial program, and prompted his sabre-rattling when it seemed that the censor might keep them out of the theatre.

It had implications for the length of the features, of course. *Diggers*, as the nominal main feature, came in at fifty-eight minutes; *A Co-Respondent's Course* and *The Haunted Barn* ran for less than three-quarters of an hour. That had repercussions for the imaginative scope of all three films, and in turn perhaps for their status and longevity. It was probably a mistake. Certainly the Efftee films that followed were longer: *The Sentimental Bloke* (released March 1932) came in at ninety-two minutes, *His Royal Highness* (October 1932) at ninety, *Diggers in Blighty* (February 1933) at eighty-two, *Harmony Row* (February 1933) at seventy-eight, *A Ticket in Tatts* (January 1934) at ninety-one, and *Clara Gibbings* (October 1934) at eighty-eight.[183] Frank had

183 These times are as listed in the first authoritative Efftee filmography, published in Chris Long, 'The Efftee Legacy', *Cinema Papers*, December 1982, p.521. All the Efftee

always liked the idea of combining film with live variety, and the early Efftee programs were an approximation of the ones he had carted around Zeehan and Dundas and all points west; but twenty years had passed since Frank had last had a go at cobbling a program together, and times had changed. He adapted, of course, but a man of his acumen should have sensed the public taste a little earlier. Nobody could have known, of course, how narrow Efftee's window of opportunity was.

But that misreading of the market had its benefits. The eclectic mix of short films generated in those early months of frenetic activity stand now as, arguably, Efftee's most significant bequest. Certainly, as a matter of historical record, those early travelogues of Melbourne and Ballarat, and the archival footage of so many of the great entertainers, is a priceless national treasure. They were made well, by people who understood the state of their craft; and they were made with a passionate belief in the importance of their subjects. Frank's insistence in that otherwise uncharacteristically modest speech on Australian themes, Australian images, Australian voices wasn't always evident in his feature-films, which were sometimes excessively influenced by the accents and conventions of the Anglophile repertory theatre. It was fundamental, however, to the Efftee shorts.

In the company's first year, alongside its five completed features, Efftee produced more than fifty short films.[184] Chris Long has described the studio's first three years as 'the most active period of sound film production in Melbourne's history'.[185] The shorts came from everywhere. George Wallace's comic routine on that first program was the screen-test he had made when he first came down from Queensland to explore the possibilities of adapting his stage act to the talkies; Frank Thring saw it, liked it, and added to it the Efftee koala.[186] George is inimitably there in his stage persona, with the check shirt, the undersize hat and the oversize ears and eyebrows, the odd mixture of shrewdness and gormlessness, and the stumbling diction of a bloke who has had one or two too many – just as he looked and sounded

---

features were cut by several minutes at least for their English release.

184 Of the fifty-one short films, thirty-one were acts in the 'Efftee Entertainers' series, eleven were made by Noel Monkman in partnership with F.W. Thring under the 'Australian Educational Films' banner, five were miscellaneous news shorts, three were Efftee documentaries in the 'Cities of the Empire' series, and one was the two-reel one-act play, *Oh, What a Night!*, featuring George Wallace. See Chris Long, 'The Efftee Legacy'.

185 ibid.

186 This short film is one of nine appearing on the VHS video *Efftee Entertainers*, collected by Chris Long for the National Film and Sound Archive in 1989. Most of the acts referred to in this discussion are part of that compilation.

in his three feature films for Efftee. In his audition he promises to sing a song called 'My girl works in the bottle-works and the boys say she's a corker', but gets distracted by the prospect of performing the 'Dance of the Wombat' (inspired by 'the Russian ballerina Palmolive'[187]); then he loses the thread again, sings a song ('Donovan's Store'), tells a story, and finally does an impressive tap-dance routine with occasional brilliant pratfalls, ostensibly dramatising a white leghorn's discovery of its first-ever egg. This is variety, in every sense. George's other short film for Efftee, *Oh, What a Night!*, is based on a vaudeville sketch, but is much more closely scripted; his character, Tom, who has come home drunk again to his long-suffering wife (Maida Jones), has barely passed out on the bed when a burglar breaks in:

> WIFE: There's a man in the house!
>
> TOM: I know. It's me.
>
> WIFE: No, I meant a real man.

In the kerfuffle that follows, Tom manages to knock out both his fearsome neighbour Mrs Malone and a policeman (the massive John Dobbie, as a startlingly camp constable); the thief gets away, naturally. The piece has a shape, a plot, strong characters and some expert Keystone Cops slapstick, and is a small gem of Australian film comedy.

In the Efftee Entertainers shorts Jack O'Hagan sang five of his songs, the beautiful Kathleen Goodall gave flawlessly arch performances of 'Widows are Wonderful', 'Little Mr Baggy Breeches' and 'Little Mary Fawcett', The Sundowners Harmony Quartette did some whimsical barber-shopping, and Will Cade and the Regent Theatre Orchestra played selections from *Desert Song*. Sixteen dancing violinists leapt bizarrely from beneath the lead violinist's hooped skirt in 'Melody and Terpsichore', the impressionist Minnie Love mimicked Gracie Fields and Maurice Chevalier, and Melbourne's Chinese Orchestra performed traditional pieces inscrutably. The English music-hall madam Ada Reeve hammed her way through 'I Never Forget I'm a Lady', and later starred in a one-act comedy about reversed gender-roles, *In the Future* (1933). Frank Thring, with his customary skill in making the most of whatever and whoever was at hand, drew not only on his Hoyts and J.C. Williamson connections, but on the people whom he had already contracted for Efftee features: not only Wallace, but people like Marshall

187 George meant Pavlova, of course.

Crosby (singing 'Somewhere South of Shanghai'), Byrl Walkley and Thelma Scott (who found herself seconded to an ingénue role in the Ada Reeve one-acter) were either pressed into service above-and-beyond or given a chance to record a favourite party-piece.

Frank did some moonlighting himself. Not only was the chairman of the company and its executive producer credited as director on three of these short features and all three travelogues, he also narrated one of the latter (that on Ballarat) and three of Noel Monkman's 'Marvelogues' about the quirkiness of Australian fauna. Frank's is the cultivated voice-over on *People of the Ponds* (dealing with microscopic life in the rock pool of an extinct Queensland volcano), the self-explanatory *Catching Crocodiles*, and *Nature's Little Jokes*, a miscellany of Queensland's animal oddities. Monkman, a brilliant naturalist and cameraman, went into partnership with Efftee as 'Australian Educational Films', and made for it six 'Marvelogues' and, in early 1932, five films shot on the Great Barrier Reef.[188]

It was an extraordinary achievement. Of course, it was parochial. It never pretended to be anything else. And it was paternalistic, even if Frank would have preferred that it didn't look that way. But no-one had done anything like it in Australia before, and, in terms of productivity, no-one has come close to matching it since. That first year of Efftee Films, for all its homeliness, made a statement – about the culture it came from, about an uncomplicated nationalism, about what might one day be possible. It was also the most spectacular, heady and disruptive year of Frank's Thring life.

---

188 These were *Ocean Oddities*, *Coral and its Creatures*, *Secrets of the Sea*, *Strange Sea Shells* and *Birds of the Barrier Reef*. All were scripted, directed and photographed by Monkman. Frank Thring supplied the voice-over for the first film in this series, too.

TRAVELLING FROM MELBOURNE TO LONDON

S.S. Cathay, 3 October 1932

Strange, going away by yourself for six months. Not that by yourself was that much of a novelty, he was used to that. But overseas was different.

Lola had been with him for the last one. And Olive the one before, of course, and the baby. On this ship, actually. But that trip with Lola, that'd been one of those golden, out-of-the-box times. He'd known it then, known it well, but sometimes you only fully understood these things when they were gone, and you and the world had shifted. When you're discovering your daughter and having the biggest dreams you've ever had, everything glows.

Three years, a bit more. Fair bit of water had passed under the boat since then. You could say that again, but don't.

Six months. It was a hell of a long time. He'd said he needed it, to make the contacts, do the deals. Maybe longer. But probably he didn't. Three or four'd do. So why had he set it up like this? Long enough to get bloody fed up with anyone's company, but especially your own. Half a year, for Christ's sake. His son would be growing and changing, and he wouldn't even know.

He'd had to do it, though. Had to make a space. He was doing it for Efftee, too bloody right he was, and without distribution deals outside Australia the whole thing was going to stay a tuppenny-ha'penny operation in some backyard in the colonies. And he'd do the deals, and he'd take the next step, whatever that was.

But he was getting away from Efftee too, and the whole bloody menagerie. Including the one at home, actually; women everywhere, fussing about, trying to make themselves indispensable. You could have too much of that.

Sometimes Efftee made him feel sick with fear. He couldn't tell anybody that, and wouldn't if he could. But it was bloody frightening. It was him, all him, but it was not him, too. He'd made it, in his own image you could say. Now it had a life of its own, and sometimes it seemed to have taken over his.

Starting it was the easy bit, he saw that now. Starting it was an adventure. Keeping it going, keeping it growing – that was the tough part. And bloody hard work. When the joy goes, and you've got to find more ideas to replace the ones that'd seemed to find you, that's when you get scared; scared you won't have any ideas as good as those, that you won't feel the joy again.

The Yanks reckon that's when the tough get going. Got a cliché for everything, those blokes.

He'd done it. He'd actually bloody done it. That was the extraordinary thing. When you wake up and find hundreds of other people living your fantasies, that's when you know you've done it. And that was just the people you knew. Thousands, millions maybe, would know your name. Efftee, that's Frank Thring. Son of a sawyer. From Wentworth, for Christ's sake. Some people get an inside run, but Frank Thring, he came from a bastard of a barrier, and was lucky to get into the race at all. And here he was, on his way to London, with tea-chests stacked with films that would've never been made if he hadn't said they would be.

Jack Daniels? Sure, why not? You had to admit it, the Septics knew a bit about whisky. Some of their ideas weren't so bad when you gave them a try.

Thing was, this time he had to be away, for a lot of reasons, and six months was about as long as you could say without serious questions being asked. Questions like all the ones in Co-Respondent's Course that tried so hard to be frivolous. Questions like, why are you really leaving? Questions like, are you happiest at home with us, or when you're on your own? Questions like, is there Someone Else? Questions like, what the hell do you think you're doing with your life?

Questions. He hated 'em. A lot of people wasted a lot of time asking questions, and trying to work out answers. He'd always preferred to deal in certainties, and statements. Till now.

It might've been because of the fear. Or maybe it was the other. A Bit Of The Other, that's what they called it, wasn't it? He could have it easily, if that was all he wanted, any bloke with a cheque-book could. And he knew plenty of 'happily married men' who did, a couple of late business meetings every week.

But that wasn't what the other was to him. It was beauty, that was a big part of it. And a little bit of wildness. And, God help us, romance. Romance. Shit. It was everything he'd missed, in the end.

Which made it sad. Life was, probably. But other people seemed to've had more chance not to be left with regrets, at least.

Every time beauty and wildness and God-help-us-romance had ridden by him, he'd been looking the other way. Being busy, or just keeping moving. He hadn't seen it. Till he was nearly fifty, for Christ's sake. What an irony, what a brilliant bloody cosmic prank. Self-pity was part of the joke, of course. Everywhere you looked, the prankster had got there before you.

Donalda would be in London. She'd left forty-eight days ago, precisely. Arrived, what, last Tuesday. He would try to see her. No obligations, just one colonial paying his respects to another. Make sure she was all right, after giving that greasy little Kraut the flick. To have a girl like that on your arm, publicly, proudly, that'd be something. Not everything, just more than he'd known. Living, as he'd lived, a career and not a life.

No. The Scots, it had to be said, have got it all over the Yanks when it comes to whisky. As they do, presumably, with kilts. So a wee dram of Glenfiddich, thank you kindly. A couple. While we practise.

Good evening, Mrs Warne. Frank Thring. Not sure if you remember me but of course you do you stupid cow, the immensely rich but scrupulously trustworthy man who plans to take your daughter out for dinner, and I promise nothing more, though given my age you'd hardly need that reassurance would you, pardon my devastatingly attractive self-deprecating Australian sense of humour. And yes, while it's true that you and I are of an age and it may seem strange that I should be asking your daughter to accompany me rather than your eminently eligible self, especially given the absence of the mysterious Mister Warne whoever he might be when he's at home if he ever was, unfortunately a great biological unfairness has made you a person of no interest to me whatsoever.

While I have some reason to hope. Only to hope.

It'd take more than two Glenfiddichs to do it. Christ. Fear can make a man feel like a boy. Perhaps that's where he always lives, in the end. Where he's always most alone. That would be the joke, then.

Chapter Six

THE IMPRESARIO

Frank Thring left Melbourne for London at the end of September 1932. That was nothing unusual in itself. In the fifteen years since he joined J.C. Williamson's, Frank had made six such journeys; he had spent effectively two of those years in foreign cities, and another eighteen months sailing to and from them. And this one had a more defined purpose than his previous fact-finding and sight-seeing junkets. This time, Frank was a travelling salesman, carrying five Efftee features and more than twenty short films in his luggage. It would have been more remarkable had he delayed his seventh excursion any longer.

Yet several things about it didn't quite add up. It was a very long leave of absence, for a start, by far the longest time he had spent away from Melbourne; six months was the original plan, but it turned out to be eight, and at a critical time in the development of Efftee. The timing of his departure was odd, too. Frank left two days before *His Royal Highness* had its premiere at the Regent in Brisbane, before the final cut of *Harmony Row*, which he was ostensibly directing, and in the middle of negotiations for another film with George Wallace. Efftee Studios were busy enough, but with *Diggers in Blighty* and *Waltzing Matilda*, the sequels to *Diggers* that Pat Hanna was producing almost wholly independently.[189] Nothing much was moving while Efftee waited for its founder to return, and that was something he showed surprisingly little haste to do. On previous trips, there had been at least a couple of destinations, usually the UK as well as Hollywood. This time, he was bound for London, and nowhere else. And on those earlier trips, Frank had always had company: Olive on three of them, and business connections like Gibson and Tallis, as well as his daughter. This time, he was going alone.

189 While *Diggers in Blighty* shared a double bill with *Harmony Row, Waltzing Matilda* had no part in any Efftee program.

Olive must have thought it a most peculiar plan. But then perhaps she knew more about what was going through her husband's head than she let on. Perhaps Olive understood completely – or perhaps, if she didn't, she was disinclined to ask, in case she found out more than she preferred to know. Frank's pattern of work took him away from 'Rylands' a lot, even when it wasn't to the other end of the world, and, though separateness was not necessarily a sign of separation, the Thring marriage was obviously running by a very idiosyncratic set of rules. His General Manager must have thought it a strange plan, too. Tom Holt was left 'minding the store' at a difficult time, when it might have been more logical, given his long-established contacts in London, for him to have been the man who headed off with the films to sell; moreover, Tom would have had a realistic sense of what work was entailed, and of how long it might be reasonably expected to take. Given that, by Christmas 1932, Frank had achieved all that he had set out to do and more, Tom Holt might well have wondered why it was that he did not come back until May 24.

The press followed Frank's adventures abroad closely at first. *Everyones* on November 9 reported his safe landing at Southampton, where he gave a press conference expressing his confidence in gaining a satisfactory release for Efftee product, and where Frank was told by Tom Holt over the wireless telephone of the success of *His Royal Highness* in Melbourne.[190] On December 7, it announced that all of Efftee's output had been successfully sold for the United Kingdom, in a deal that would assure the future of the company;[191] on December 28, it quoted cables confirming that Universal would distribute all Efftee productions throughout the UK, giving Frank Thring a blanket contract for films yet unmade.[192] The mission, then, had been accomplished, and spectacularly well.

But Frank stayed on, and though *Everyones* did its best to keep his name in the news from time to time, there was nothing of substance to report. Frank gave a statement to the effect that 'success for Australian-made films in England is no longer in doubt'[193] in early January, and in early February forecast even closer co-operation in the future.[194] Then there was an eerie silence until he took up the cudgels on landing at Fremantle on May 16, to assert the necessity of strict quota regulations in Australia to give producing companies security in the home market.[195]

190 *Everyones*, 9 November 1932, p.3.
191 *Everyones*, 7 December 1932, p.3. See also Melbourne *Argus*, 6 December 1932, p.7.
192 *Everyones*, 28 December 1932, p.3.
193 Everyones, 4 January 1933, p.5.
194 *Everyones*, 8 February 1933, p.3.
195 *Everyones*, 17 May 1933, p.3.

It was a long time for a workaholic to be away from the office, especially when he was on his own and had no interest in being a tourist. There were connections to be reinforced, of course, and no doubt a lot of whiskies and cigars were consumed for the greater good. But Frank would surely have wanted more return on his precious time than that. And for a man as accustomed to being lord of all he surveyed, including a host of dependents and sycophants, London offered little in the way of power and adulation. If anything, it provided a constant reminder of how much, from the centre of the Empire, a colonial corporation could look like a corner-store in Gawler.

Two other factors may have played a role in Frank's extended absence. One might simply have been the pleasure of his own company. Frank was accustomed to doing things on his own, and life had taught him early a self-sufficiency that was hard to distinguish from self-enclosure. It was evident not only in his carefully maintained emotional reserve, but in a habitual secrecy designed to drive business competitors and biographers to drink. After a couple of years in which his life had been over-crowded with creative people and other suppliants, Frank might have felt that there was a lot to be said for the simplicity that can come with solitude. If it brought relief as well from the social calendar of a gregarious wife, and from all the tensions of domesticity and parenthood, then so much the better.

The other may have been the young lady who had borne the weight of expectation (not to mention the resentment and suspicion) that came with having been 'personally selected by Mr Thring' for stardom.[196] Donalda Warne had left Australia seven weeks earlier than Frank, her reasons for going to London as mysterious as his for staying there longer than he needed to. They were both conspicuous absentees from the first screening of *His Royal Highness*. Frank was in London for his fiftieth birthday – and for Donalda's twenty-first, too, which she celebrated a few days before he, at last, came home. There is no evidence to support mischievous hypotheses about an older man's obsession with a beautiful girl, but such things have been known to happen. And if such an idea had not occurred to Olive, or to Tom Holt (who was at the time dealing with not unrelated feelings of his own), then neither was nearly as shrewd as everyone believed them to be.

---

196 The notion that Frank Thring and Efftee had 'discovered' Donalda Warne was always, at best, an exaggeration of the facts. Donalda was billed for the June 1928 production of Ben Travers' *Rookery Nook* at Melbourne's Comedy Theatre as 'J.C.W.'s latest discovery', and was described in an article in the *Age* as having been 'discovered' in the chorus line of *The Girl Friend* in Sydney. She had celebrated her sixteenth birthday during the run of the latter show.

Frank came back at the end of May, and said nothing publicly of what had kept him in London for an additional four months after he had completed his business there. He never saw Donalda Warne, or London, again.

Meanwhile, back in Melbourne, people waited to find out what was going to happen next. *The Sentimental Bloke* and the two George Wallace films had built on the steady gains of *Diggers* to suggest not only that Efftee Studios might have a genuine future, but that it had found its signature kind of film. Frank's success in convincing the British that George Wallace was just the kind of comic genius that they (occasionally) unearthed in the North Country corroborated both those impressions. Yet it was not until the boss had resumed the reins that Tom Holt felt free to articulate the company's hopes and plans for the future:

> "Four full programs a year!"
>
> That is the schedule that Efftee has set itself – as I discovered when I questioned Mr Tom Holt, manager of Efftee, in regard to the future plans of the studio.
>
> "That will entail eight feature pictures, newsreels and shorts ... In regard to the material for feature pictures, it is the intention of Efftee to continue with comedies. Not only do we find that audiences display a preference for this type of film, but we consider comedy the natural forte of the Australian artist."[197]

Alf Daff, the Victorian manager for Universal, with whom Frank had brokered his English distribution deal, was similarly bullish about the prospects. He predicted 'a big talkie boom here in Australia' over the next two years, and saw 'every prospect of Melbourne becoming the "Hollywood" of Australia';[198] the key to that success lay precisely in the rough-hewn comedy that George Wallace and Efftee did so well:

197 'Talkies that Only Australia Can Make', *Table Talk*, 24 August 1933, p.19.
198 'Present and Future of Australian Talkies', *Table Talk*, 17 August 1933, p.9.

> "George Wallace is proving particularly popular in England, not in the West End, perhaps, but certainly in the North of England," Mr Daff told me. "Mr Thring is not worrying about a West End public, however, for in his productions he is catering for the masses and not for a limited few."[199]

Frank Thring was now positioned as the champion of democratic sentiment, and comedy for and of the people was to be his stock-in-trade. That hadn't always been the way he had defined either his public role or his preferred repertoire. *A Co-Respondent's Course* was about the affluent at play; *The Haunted Barn* had sprung from a conviction that quirky literary texts might somehow make a kind of art. But things had begun to change with *The Sentimental Bloke*, and the Wallace films confirmed the new direction.

The Sentimental Bloke was a particularly important project to Frank. He liked C. J. Dennis' poem,[200] for a start, and came to feel a protective affection for its author. And it was to be Efftee's first try at a piece of quintessentially Australian popular literature, and accordingly something of a status symbol. Moreover, it would be a Melbourne film, located (as Dennis had set his poem) in the culture of the larrikin pushes of Melbourne's 'Little Lon' (Little Lonsdale Street). The Raymond Longford – Lottie Lyell silent film made thirteen years earlier had transported the Bloke and his disreputable mates to Sydney, and dropped them in the slums of Wolloomooloo; when Bill took Doreen to the beach, instead of taking the light-rail to St Kilda, he travelled on the Manly ferry. Restoring the action to its original home would strike a blow for authenticity, not to mention civic pride. Finally, the fact that the Longford film had broken records at the box-office, and was much admired for its artistry, was both an opportunity and a challenge; if Efftee managed to pull it off, the Frank Thring version would define all the things that talking pictures could do that silent movies could not. There was always a risk of odious comparisons, of course, but a man who was wary of risk would hardly have taken a punt on Efftee.

This time the gamble failed. Efftee's *The Sentimental Bloke* was not a disaster, at the box-office or with the critics.[201] But it was not any of the things that Frank had wanted it to be – the great film, the spectacular hit, the rich

---

199 'Present and Future of Australian Talkies', *Table Talk*, 17 August 1933, p.9.

200 *The Songs of a Sentimental Bloke* was published in 1915, and quickly became, as it remains, Australia's highest-selling volume of poetry.

201 Frank Thring declared in his appearance before the NSW Film Enquiry that he lost five thousand pounds on *The Sentimental Bloke*; since he rarely gave information of a financial nature without some ulterior motive, this may have been a rhetorical exaggeration. The detail was duly highlighted in the report in *Everyones*, 10 January 1934, p.5.

expression of a distinctive national myth. It was a moderately entertaining movie that reflected a nice eye for the iconography of Melbourne, and that did nothing that its predecessor had not done better – other than allowing its characters to be heard. The silent *Bloke* is still revered as perhaps the finest film made in Australia in the first quarter of the twentieth century; the *Bloke* that talked has fallen further and further from favour with the years:

> Even if the freewheeling Longford version of 1919 had not existed to allow present-day comparison, Thring's *Sentimental Bloke* would still seem static and cloyingly moralistic ... On balance, it seems to be a fair indication of Thring's abilities as a director and is characterised by static camerawork and frequently stolid performances.[202]

It looks like an open-and-shut case for the prosecution of the directorial dead hand.

But while the film's limitations are clear enough, the responsibility for them is probably more complex than the standard historical estimate has allowed. The 'static camerawork' is the work of the same Arthur Higgins whose genius had enlivened Raymond Longford's *The Sentimental Bloke* in 1919. The 'cloyingly moralistic' plot is largely the work of C.J. Dennis, who refused to be involved with the earlier film but had perhaps too much influence over this one. And the variously 'static' and 'stolid' direction in the Efftee version, while owing a good deal to the customary 'personal supervision of F.W. Thring', may have been primarily attributable to Longford, the man who directed its silent precursor.

Longford received no credit for the 1932 film. However, he was on the Efftee payroll, and almost always on the set. Higgins' assistant Jack Murray remembered him as a 'quiet chap' who 'didn't interfere with Frank Thring's direction because Frank was the boss and that was it ... ';[203] but he and Arthur Higgins, in their own quiet ways, shaped the whole film:

> Arthur was practically the director... Thring was in name only, really, but of course he was the boss and that was the end of it ... But basically it was directed by Arthur and Raymond Longford, they knew the subject, they'd been through it before.[204]

---

202 Shirley and Adams, *Australian Cinema*, p.114.
203 Jack Murray, interview with Graham Shirley and Chris Long, April 1989.
204 ibid.

Alan Stuart also remembered Ray Longford as 'always around', wearing 'a dodgy toupee ... [that] didn't sit too hot' and frequently having 'a word on the side' with the actors.[205] For Jack Murray, the presence of Longford and Higgins helped guarantee the superiority of the 'talkie' version:

> It was practically a replica, only with sound. And locations were better – see, they had those locations down in Little Bourke Street ... It was a better production generally.[206]

His view of the quality of the two *Blokes* is a minority one. Indeed, no one else has dared to suggest that the Efftee film is 'a better production generally', and for a surfeit of good reasons.

Some key choices in the later version do replicate those taken by Longford and Lyell in 1919. Both films begin in the middle of a two-up game rudely interrupted by the police, rather than with the state of wistful melancholia ('yearnin' fer – I dunno wot') in which the poem first places Bill; both end with Bill and Doreen on the farm, with land and a baby and everything they could ever have wanted. Both add to Dennis' romance-plot a scene in which Bill prepares to meet Doreen's mother by studying *Etiquette for Australians*. There are familiar camera-angles in the crowd-scenes, especially at the two-up school and the pickle-factory where Doreen works. It may not be precisely 'a replica', but a lot of the time the Efftee film is at the very least a faithful translation. Perhaps Thring was backing someone else's proven winner; perhaps Higgins and Longford, having already been on a good thing, were sticking to it.

The real differences between the film made by Longford and Lottie Lyell and the one ostensibly directed by Frank Thring were all to do with choices made long before the cameras began to roll. They concerned the shape of the narrative, the casting of the two central roles, and the place of Dennis' original verse.

Longford had kept the loose romance structure of the poem; the story was focussed on Bill (the Kid) and Doreen, and others (Bill's mate Ginger Mick, his rival the 'stror 'at coot', and Doreen's mum and Uncle Jim) are either transient or (finally) peripheral in their lives. The Efftee version adds something like a detective-plot. Uncle Jim is being conned by some city slickers over his discovery of gold in his orchard; protecting him takes up

205 R. Alan Stuart, interview with Graham Shirley and Chris Long.
206 ibid.

two-thirds of the film, and justifies the 'stoush' that breaks Bill's promise to Doreen to keep out of trouble, and nearly ends their romance. But the villains are easily dissuaded, the cache of gold turns out to come from the dentures lost by Uncle Jim's dopey hired hand, and life goes happily on. In the process, though, a number of minor characters manage to become quite intrusive – Uncle Jim (Keith Desmond), Arty the frustrated thespian from the pickle-factory (Athol Tier) and, especially, Ginger Mick (Tal Ordell) are given lots of room to show their comic talents, and to put the lovers somewhat in the shade. Mick is never far away, getting the Bloke into hot water, getting him out of it with Doreen, and even turning up as a swagman in their rural idyll at the end. Dennis' screenplay loses the focus of his poem, and the film sometimes seems like another anthology of Efftee's Entertainers.

Frank Thring, who liked his comedians, was no doubt happy with the changes. Though Tal Ordell at fifty-two might struggle to pass as a larrikin lad, he was a smart and recognisable actor, and a marketable name. Though Athol Tier as Arty was almost completely irrelevant to the plot, he had made some popular shorts for Efftee. And though Keith Desmond threatened in the middle of the shoot to shave off his beard if Thring didn't add another pound to his pay-cheque, Frank found the threat amusing, and chose to indulge him; that was not his customary response to people who challenged him, as Signor Kost had discovered a decade before. Someone needed to tighten things up, but since it was hard to tell whether *The Sentimental Bloke* was being directed by everyone or no-one, it was not at all clear who that should be.

The casting of Bill (the Kid) and Doreen imposed a model of conventional romance on Dennis' unlikely lovers. Arthur Tauchert and Lottie Lyell, who had played the roles in the silent version of *The Bloke*, were wonderfully convincing: Tauchert, with his crumpled face and dumpy frame, captured the awkward self-protectiveness of the sentimental bloke who was hiding beneath that rough exterior; Lyell, as the working-class girl with genteel aspirations, was sometimes tough and sometimes tender, and always vulnerable, to Bill and to the world.

Ray Fisher finds Doreen's sweetness, but there is no hint of pickle-factory earthiness about her; she has a carefully cultivated accent more appropriate to one of Lola's friends from St Cath's, and her attempts to pull the Bloke into line reflect her solidly suburban attitudes. Her Doreen has a natural gentility beyond her station. She lives in a modest inner-suburban terrace, with a neat picket-fence, and her mother is a monument to propriety. She forgives Bill his shameful week behind bars in the interests of bourgeois aspiration ('It's not what you were that matters to me; it's what you're going to be!'), and even brings to her marriage a kind of dowry – the fruit-farm that Uncle Jim bestows on the happy couple.

Cecil Scott, conventionally tall, dark and handsome, makes a very different kind of Bloke. Tauchert's Bill scrubs up well enough in his wedding suit, with his straggling hair stuck down, but it takes a special effort, and it could never last; when Cecil Scott puts on his Sunday best, he looks completely at his ease. Scott could be cast as the leading man in almost any movie one could imagine; Tauchert, with a face only a mother or a Doreen could love, need not bother to apply. The distinction is one of predisposition, too. Cecil Scott's Bill embraces his bright future as a breadwinner ('I can work. Work like blazes!'), and we know that he is on the straight-and-narrow for good; Tauchert's Bill will do his best, but he'll fail, early and often. For Jack Murray, Cecil Scott was the only thing wrong with Efftee's *Bloke*:

> They couldn't get a proper Sentimental Bloke. The best they could do was Cecil Scott ... Frank Thring went around second-hand shops to get old clothes for him. And of course to make him more masculine – Cecil was rather slim – they padded up the shoulders, and that sort of thing. Cecil wasn't a bad sort of an actor, but nowhere near Tauchert. He wasn't rough enough.[207]

The sentimentality of Cecil Scott's Bloke comes as no surprise, and he is from the beginning quite defensive about his masculinity. Ginger Mick is fond of mocking him about it: when Bill wants to quit the two-up while he's ahead, Mick calls him 'a careful little housewife'; when he suggests that he and Mick could meet in the Botanical Gardens where he hopes to catch sight of Doreen among the flowers, his mate farewells him with 'In the Gardens, Gertie. I'll be there'.[208] There was never any need to make Arthur Tauchert look 'more masculine'. And nobody would ever dare to call him Gertie.

The screenplay, like the casting, turned the Bloke and his 'bit o' fluff' into a much more conventional romantic couple. The relationship between the dialogue of the talkie version and the larrikin vernacular of the poem was always going to be a problem; short of doing the whole film in voice-over, it was hard to imagine how it could avoid sacrificing some of the charm and

207 Jack Murray interview.
208 These examples are drawn from Philip Butterss' 'A "careful little housewife"'.

integrity of the original. The only words on the screen in Longford's film were direct quotations from the poem, and its strength lay in the way the visual images supported lines that were already widely known and much-loved. Ninety per cent of the language in Frank Thring's reworking is new; stanzas from Dennis' poem appear from time to time, embellished with the Hal Gye illustrations of cherubs behaving badly that had adorned the published text, to add moments of interior monologue and remind us of what we might have read. But it's an uneasy compromise.

One of the most famous episodes from the poem, when Bill takes Doreen to the theatre, encapsulates the problem of adaptation. Doreen has persuaded the Bloke to take her to *Romeo and Juliet*; the show and the crowd are 'real bon ton', and Bill feels like a fish out of water until the romantic stuff gives way to a good old-fashioned donnybrook. The silent version quotes his enthusiastic response in its entirety:

> A tug named Tyball (cousin to the skirt)
> Sprags 'em an' makes a start to sling off dirt.
> Nex' minnit there's a reel ole ding-dong go—
> 'Arf round or so.
> Mick Curio, 'e gets it in the neck,
> 'Ar rats!' 'e sez, an' passes in 'is check.
> Quite natchril, Romeo gits wet as 'ell.
> 'It's me or you!' 'e 'owls, an' wiv a yell,
> Plunks Tyball through the gizzard wiv 'is sword,
> 'Ow I ongcored! 'Put in the boot!' I sez. 'Put in the boot!'
> ''Ush!' sez Doreen … 'Shame!' sez some silly coot.[209]

The camera cuts back and forth between the doublet-and-hose action on stage and the couple holding hands in the stalls; when the Bloke starts barracking, it stays squarely on him, and on Doreen's startled attempt to restrain him.

The Efftee version moves into dialogue at the climactic moment; Bill shouts 'Put in the boot!' and in a general flurry both Doreen and the man behind him try to push him back into his seat. The punch-line in the verse disappears in a moment of chaotic slapstick. Perhaps it had to; there's a limit to how much a talkie can present its dialogue as printed text. But when the

209 C.J. Dennis, *The Songs of a Sentimental Bloke*, Sydney and Melbourne, Angus and Robertson, 1917, p.62.

quirky pleasures of that text are the main reasons for making the film, the writer (even when he is also the poet) is, like poor old Mick Curio, on a hiding to nothing. The main interest in Efftee's *The Sentimental Bloke* when the 'ding-gong go' threatens to spread into the audience is probably in that affluent couple sitting behind Bill and Doreen. The 'silly coot' in the tuxedo who this time doesn't get to say 'Shame!' is Frank Thring, making another of his cameo appearances; the lady on his right with the magnificently bejewelled bust is Olive Thring, in her first and final screen appearance.

The Sentimental Bloke was Efftee's most expensive film, and, partly for that reason, perhaps its most disappointing. Frank would not have expected too much from its international sales when he took the studio's current offerings to London in 1932; he would have anticipated that the idiom of Little Lon could not travel far before it became completely unintelligible. And he would have known something of the sad fate of the silent version in America, which was saddled with the multiply misleading title, *The Sentimental Bloke: The Story of a Tough Guy*, deposited in a vault, and forgotten. This film he made for his fellow-Australians, and the fact that it did not come to mean as much to them as he had hoped must have been one of the great regrets of the Efftee adventure.

The Sentimental Bloke, however, had a significance in national terms that could not have been known at the time. It was the beginning of the career of perhaps the most recognisable actor that Australia has produced, Frank Thring junior, though he didn't quite take the screen by storm:

> Audiences will see me in the magic moment when the Bloke picks up Doreen in the Fitzroy Gardens. I didn't have a speaking part, I was rather on the young side, but I was the little boy rolling around on the lawn in the background. On that day, a star was born in the Fitzroy Gardens.[210]

Diggers, released four months earlier, formally marked Frank's film debut, but the scene in *'The Bloke'* had been shot before it. That day may well have been at the forefront of Olive Thring's plans for a glorious future. But her husband's dreams about *The Sentimental Bloke* were larger still. Hers were realised; his were disappointed, as they were probably bound to be.

---

210 Geoffrey Hutton, 'The Frank Mr Thring', *Australian*, 26 November 1981, p.16. In fact, the little boy on the picnic rug with his nursemaid rolled just once, to play with his toys, as Doreen passed briskly by. And he is hardly 'in the background'; young Frank is very much front and centre, as first Doreen and then Bill pass behind him on the path.

Frank wanted too much from a film that seemed to represent everything that Efftee was about: literary but popular, rather daring but tried and true, and Australian to the bone. In the end, evidently, none of that was enough. But the George Wallace films were a different matter. Wallace's comedy played well, whether at home or away. And it offered Efftee's only real route to a viable, perhaps even brilliant, future. The popularity of *His Royal Highness* and *Harmony Row* with English audiences (especially, as Alf Daff had enthusiastically noted, 'those in the North') promised to make George Wallace's name as well-known abroad as it was in Australia. It also looked like a timely trump card in another game that Frank was playing on a local front, with his old rival Stuart Doyle. Greater Union, taking its lead from the Efftee initiative, had decided to re-enter feature film production, under its newsreel banner Cinesound, and once again Melbourne was playing Sydney in what was probably destined to be a winner-takes-all competition.

The first round had involved a race between *The Sentimental Bloke* and another remake of a Raymond Longford silent classic, Cinesound's *On Our Selection*:

> "The Sentimental Bloke" and "On Our Selection," regarded as the two most valuable pieces of talkie property, will go into production simultaneously during the first week of August …
>
> From that day-and-date start, there is lively speculation as to which picture will be through earliest, and win the big blast of newspaper publicity the first out will naturally attract.
>
> Working in Melbourne, F.W. Thring has specified no time limit on "The Sentimental Bloke," but it seems probable that he will go all out to beat "On Our Selection" to the public post.[211]

Efftee won that race comfortably, by three months. But *On Our Selection*, directed by Ken G. Hall and starring Bert Bailey and Fred MacDonald, who had become synonymous with the roles of Dad and Dave on stage, was by common consent the better film, and its takings were eight times Doyle's original investment.[212] That gave the points clearly to the Sydney contender. It was a scenario that Frank Thring would have found gallingly familiar.

211 *Everyones*, July 1931, p.9.

212 Gayne Dexter, reviewing the balance sheets of Australian talkies at the end of 1934, ranked *On Our Selection* first with gross Australian box office returns of £48,000, and *The Sentimental Bloke* third (after Cinesound's *The Squatter's Daughter*) with £22,000. This compared well with *His Royal Highness* (£20,000), *Harmony Row* and *A Ticket in*

George Wallace was signed to a very generous contract. He was installed immediately as the star of the studio, his name appearing above the title in all three of his films for Efftee. He started on a salary of one hundred pounds a week, with a provision for bonuses and increments unheard of in Australian film. For a man of Wallace's unsophisticated tastes and egalitarian instincts, it was more than he wanted, and Bert Nicholas recalled the scenes every Friday night outside His Majesty's, when George emerged with his pay-packet:

> … it was the period after the Depression, and there'd be a line-up there of thirty, forty actors and actresses. George would come along you know – two shillings here and two shillings there, a couple of pound to you, and Arthur [Higgins] and I stood and watched that many times … and I'd say what's the difference, and he'd say, well, you know the ones that got a fiver, there've got a wife and family and two kids or three kids, the other one, he's just going to cross to the pub. And he was going along paying out, paying out …[213]

Wallace got on well with Frank Thring. Both men liked a laugh and a whisky, and preferably plenty of both, and each was aware that he might not be able to do without the other. Only once did they come into conflict, when Thring allowed Wallace to take time out from his Efftee contract for a stage tour of New Zealand between the filming of *Harmony Row* and *A Ticket in Tatts*. Wallace, who was being paid one hundred and twenty pounds per week to perform on the other side of the Tasman, was grateful for his employer's kindness, until he found out that Frank Thring was being paid one hundred and eighty pounds per week to allow him to appear.[214] Frank's charity always tended to have its own very tangible reward.

Tatts (both £18,000), but these were less costly films. Dexter's figures are estimates, and he admits the difficulty of unlocking the secrets of Efftee's finances in particular, but they are probably close to the mark, and certainly an accurate reflection of industry perceptions ('Counting the CASH in Australian Films', *Everyones*, 12 December 1934, p.19.

213 Interview with Bert Nicholas.

214 ibid.

George Wallace's Efftee films followed a strikingly similar pattern, though in each the setting made the most of its distinctive local colour. In all of them George appeared exactly in the character he played in the Efftee audition that the company's resourceful founder had immediately packaged under the Efftee Entertainers label. It's the role of the little Aussie battler, much more innocent and good-natured than his great comic contemporary Roy Rene (Mo), that Ken G. Hall said made George Wallace 'the people's comic':

> He was the put-upon little man, honest as the sun, who, no matter what the circumstances, could never put a foot right. The heart and soul of the Chaplin figure.[215]

George even wore his trademark saggy check shirt, though for the Betonia scenes in *His Royal Highness* it was topped by an unbuttoned braided jacket, for most of *Harmony Row* it was replaced by a hopelessly ill-fitting policeman's uniform, and for *A Ticket in Tatts* he briefly donned a dinner-suit and moustache to act as a waiter. He found at least one opportunity to fall on his left ear in all three films – and to fall as well for a pretty girl who, understandably enough, was less than bowled over by his charm. But gormlessness had its own reward. In two of his three films with Efftee, George not only defeated his persecutors, but also got the girl, which for a man with George's looks and propensity for taking a tumble was quite a strike-rate. The exception was *His Royal Highness*, in which his triumph was only in dreams; but there was some comic satisfaction even in that.

His Royal Highness (or *His Loyal Highness*, as it was known in England in deference to the imagined sensitivities of George V), the first of the three, was also the most complex of them. George plays Tommy Dodds, a cheerful bumbler down on his luck, who manages to get a job backstage in a theatre that allows him to be a little closer to Miss Molly, the actress he adores from afar. He is, of course, a spectacularly incompetent stagehand, and nearly knocks himself out several times against the genuine hazards backstage at His Majesty's, before he is laid low by the nasty piece of work whose sacking had given Tommy his chance. He dreams a wonderful dream, in which he is no longer the most precariously employed rouseabout in Australia, but heir to the throne of Betonia. Tommy graciously accepts the bequest, and for a

215 Ken G. Hall, quoted in *The George Wallace Story*, ABC Television feature, directed by Don Percy, written by Jim Murphy, and narrated by Bill Kerr (1999). Hall would later direct Wallace for Cinesound in *Let George Do It* (1938) and *Gone to the Dogs* (1939).

while has an absolute ball – he inducts his prune-faced stewards into the rituals of the poker school, teaches his geriatric Prime Minister to (almost) roller-skate, and finds that his subjects are mostly willing to see his blunders as moments of inspiration, not yet quite understood. Then his scheme for exposing the villains who are conspiring to replace him is so successful that it also reveals the true heir to the throne, and another bump on the head restores him to the theatre. He comes to just in time to see Miss Molly leaving on the arm of her beau. In every sense, poor old Tommy has come back to earth with a bump.

Like all the Wallace films for Efftee, the plot frequently pauses for one of George's routines; in the most extended, the rest of the crew philosophically gets on with cleaning the theatre while he sings 'My Girl's Got It', tells a studiously aimless story about a girl he knew back home, and shows some fancy tap-steps and falls – all of it straight to camera. The roller-skating lessons are a hilarious diversion, though the star was not always amused:

> Mr Thring said, "Now, I want you to do a skating sequence, and I want you to do a lot of falls in it." He got a huge slab of concrete made, and I had to skate on it so they'd get the noise of the wheels, but what he forgot was, I had to fall on it.
>
> After the first day I was just a mangled heap of bruises, and he said, "There's a bottle of liniment there, you'd better take it home and rub yourself," and I said, "You'd better fill the bath up, I'll have to get in it."[216]

It was the one time in the film that George was not doing something he had done, on the vaudeville stage, hundreds of times before.

What made *His Royal Highness* the most complex of the three films had little to do with the way George played the loveable larrikin. It came from the film's claim to be 'the first Australian film musical', and with the culture-clash between the world of operetta and romantic melodrama and the world of Tommy Dodds.[217] In the high-falutin courtly world of Betonia, people speak with English accents, sing with fruity vibrato, and always take themselves extremely seriously; in Tommy's world, a bloke from the bush looks, speaks and sings like a bloke should, and most moments are so unmanageable that in the end you've just got to laugh.

216 George Wallace, recorded reminiscences, *The George Wallace Story*.

217 The credits for the songs in *His Royal Highness* are shared by George Wallace and Alaric Hewitt; the latter wrote the music for the pastiche-operetta sequences in the film.

It's the counterpoint between those two worlds, as well as George's virtuosity, that drives the film. Strictly, it's not really a musical – the score consists basically of just four songs: Tommy's early solo, two full chorus numbers ('Your Majesty', which farewells him from Melbourne, and 'Long Live the King of Betonia', which welcomes him to his new kingdom), and a wonderfully incongruous duet between the conspirators Torano (Lou Vernon), who wants to kill the king, and Yoiben (Byrl Walkley), who plans to become Torano's queen. They sing quite stylishly, in a floridly comic-operatic way, about their schemes and their mutual distrust. But the effect is parodic: if Torano's co-respondent's moustache and Yoiben's matronly malevolence have not already defined them as papier-mache characters from a theatre where all the soldiers are chocolate ones, the affectation of the vocal style makes it unmistakable.

The sense of satiric play extends to the only significant dance-sequence in the film. The Royal Ballet of Betonia consists of six heavily built blondes in oversize ballet-skirts; the comedy in their performance is enhanced by its studious seriousness, and by the fact that they are nearly competent. No-one draws attention to their chubbiness, not even George, and the cinematography pays them the compliment of two crane-shots a la Busby Berkley, which makes a pretty if not quite symmetrical pattern out of those large, round shapes. It's a clever but gentle spoof, in keeping with the amiable tone of the piece.

Everybody in Betonia plays straight man to George, even his massive mate John Dobbie, who as head of the Army in Tommy's dream tries in vain to persuade him to sense. Even the Amazonian Yoiben is reduced to speechless indignation in his presence; Tommy's kindness is as disconcerting as his absurdity, as his Chancellor Alfram (the inevitable Marshall Crosby) finds when he suggests what to do with Yoiben:

> ALFRAM: I would advise the guillotine without further parley.
>
> TOMMY: Oh you're a bloodthirsty old thing, you are! The gelatine! It'd spoil all her neck. She'd have nowhere to put her beads!

As Babette, a winsome Betonian maiden, Donalda Warne plays her scenes with George as though she has no idea what he might do next; it works well as a kind of comic foil, and it was probably an exact reflection of what she was feeling in her last role with Efftee.

Much of *His Royal Highness*, most of *Harmony Row*, and some of *A Ticket in Tatts*, had its source not only in George's music-hall act but in what chanced to come into his head at the time. It made him a difficult actor to direct, which made it just as well that Frank Thring's trust in his headliner and the paternalistic distance of his 'personal supervision' were so deeply entrenched. And it made him a tricky man to share a scene with, since the script, to the extent that it existed, was understood to be always negotiable. Certainly Bill Kerr, then the ten-year-old child-star Wee Willie Kerr, never saw anything resembling a script in his work for *Harmony Row*:

> We didn't rehearse, we talked. He'd tell me what to do, and then they said, let's shoot it.[218]

Thelma Scott received a similar lesson:

> ... I was used to the theatre. Learning your lines ... So naturally, I thought, I must have a script. So I waited around. Because there was quite a big cast in *Harmony Row*. I mean, George was flying around all over the place ... So eventually it was coming near the time. I was told I would have to be in that little doorway, all ready for His Nibs' appearance. So I dashed up, and I said, 'Look Mr Wallace, I haven't got a script'. He said, 'What do you want a script for, darling? You don't want a script. Just improvise it'. 'But,' I said, 'What am I going to say?' He said, 'Don't worry, honey. You go inside. When I knock on the door, you open the door, and you say, "Good morning, Constable", and I say, "Good morning, madam", and then I'll say a lot of things, and you just answer. And we'll take it from there. If it doesn't come out right, we'll do it again.'[219]

It was all about George. His fellow-actors knew it, he knew it, and Frank Thring knew it. Extraordinarily, no one seemed to resent it at all.

Part of that tolerance of the Wallace ego and unpredictability had to do with his status and public appeal; the success of the film, the reputations and livelihood of the company, and the profitability of the studio, rested squarely on his round shoulders. But partly, too, it was a reflection of his off-stage personality. George liked the girls, enjoyed a smoke, and loved a drink, and the parties during and after the shoot were legendary; most

218 Bill Kerr in *The George Wallace Story.*

219 Thelma Scott, interview with Graham Shirley and Chris Long.

importantly, he was every bit as good-natured as his persona on stage and screen – just a good deal smarter. Making a film in such circumstances could have been a nightmare, but everyone who made a film with George Wallace seems to have recalled the experience with pleasure, and with genuine affection. Wee Willie was left with vivid memories of his kindness in the filming of *Harmony Row* – and of one of George's other strong character traits:

> How was George with the ladies? Oh boy. He was a killer. Well, I remember one instance. George had gone home to have a rest because he was a bit crook. And Harry Kitchener, the manager, gave me a letter, said take this over to Mr Wallace, deliver it. I said, oh yes, he gave me a zac, off I trotted ... I walked in, and there's George in bed with a beautiful lady. One of the ladies in the show. And I said, 'Excuse me, Mrs Wallace, but I've got a message for your husband'. And they both fell out of bed laughing![220]

Wallace's dealings with Willie may have been softened by some sentimental associations of his own. He might, perhaps, have thought of his own son, who just a few years before had toured with him as Wee Georgie Wallace.[221] That son, George Leonard Wallace, may have been in his mind, too, when he named the boy in *Harmony Row* Leonard in his script, or more correctly his loose scenario, for the film. It might explain the intensity of the emotion in the curious scene in which George, the most hopeless cop on the beat, thinks that young Leonard has been fatally shot in saving his life.

Harmony Row was virtually a collection of vaudeville sketches, yoked together by George's attempt to prove himself as a policeman on one of the roughest streets in town. It's the least interesting of the three Wallace films for Efftee, largely because of the perfunctoriness of the narrative links; once again, George is smitten by a girl named Molly (he was in certain ways a man of very regular habits), but between the moment of love at first sight and the point where he improbably wins her, nothing about their relationship develops at all.

---

220 Bill Kerr in the *The George Wallace Story*.

221 George Wallace Junior (1918–1968) followed in his father's footsteps as a multi-talented vaudevillian. Though he never became the household name that George Senior had been, he had a significant career on the Tivoli circuit, and later in Brisbane television variety.

The two sequences that remain in the memory have little or no connection with Wallace revues of the past. One is the superbly choreographed boxing match in which George takes on the fearsome Slogger Lee (John Dobbie), and for a long time manages to do a lot of damage to sundry audience members while not laying a glove on Slogger. But at last his shimmies and pratfalls bamboozle Goliath, and bring him to his knees. George goes home a hero, with the adoring Molly suddenly on his arm, and virtue, or at least genial good-nature, is triumphant.

The other is the death scene with Wee Willie. We know, as everyone but George does, that this is a set-up engineered by George's boss, the Sergeant (the inevitable Marshall Crosby, again); we are invited to laugh at him as the victim of a practical joke. But the scene is played with a strange conviction, and a Dickensian sentiment and fascination with the poignancy of child-death for which Tommy, at least, is an absolute sucker. It seems to have strayed in from some other film.

> LENNY: Don't leave me Cop. I think I'm gonna die.
>
> TOMMY: Come on, sonny, snap out of it. You're not gonna die, you're all right. Come on.
>
> LENNY: You know, it must be great to have a home. And a mum and dad. And sit round the warm fire and have your Daddy tell yer stories. Gee, you're a great feller, Cop.
>
> *(Long pause)*
>
> LENNY: Don't leave me, Cop. I feel so lonely. Hold me, Cop. I'm tired …
>
> *(His eyes close, and his head falls back.* TOMMY *lowers him very gently to the ground)*

But while George is blinking back the wave of proto-parental tears, the little lad picks his pocket and sneaks away. Next, we hear Lenny's indignant complaint that all he got was a lousy watch and chain, and the laughter of all those who were in on the hoax. George has no lines in response, and no action in particular; we simply register the pathos of his discovery of how vulnerable you become, when you are foolish enough to feel.

Frank Thring was still, nominally, the director of *Harmony Row*, but George Wallace was running the show. Frank still had cause for some anxious whistling, but about budgetary matters rather than creative choices or pretty leading ladies. He attended shooting less than he had in the frenetic second half of 1931, and sometimes he was late for afternoon calls as a result of a long lunch. His employees noticed the change. Some thought he was drinking too much, but tended to put it down to the need to wheel and deal at the powerful men's tables. As ever, you could never be quite sure what the man was thinking and feeling, and he made sure that it stayed that way.

Bill Kerr remembered little from him of a directorial kind, but would never forget his solicitude at a particularly uncomfortable time:

> There was this scene where I had to lie across George's lap while he stitched up the seat of my shorts. And everyone knew it had to be one take – Mr Thring had been getting very twitchy about wasting film. Trouble was, George stuck the needle right into my backside. Again and again, every stitch. I wanted to yell out, or cry, but I knew I couldn't, or it'd bugger up the scene and we'd have to start it again. So we did it in one take, and everyone was happy, but the pain was killing me. Nobody noticed except old man Thring. He said, 'Why, Willie, what's the trouble?', and I just broke down and said, 'I'm really sorry, Mr Thring, but I think Mr Wallace has sewn my pants to my bum!' And he said, 'Well, we'd better do something about that, hadn't we?' and he got a pair of nail scissors from his daughter, and put me over his knee, and unpicked the stitches one by one. He was a kind man, Mr Thring. A really kind man.[222]

Frank was a more prominent contributor to the process of making *A Ticket in Tatts*, refreshed, or galvanised, or perhaps in some way liberated, by his extended business trip to London.

After the sketch-based meanderings of *Harmony Row*, the third of the Wallace films for Efftee has something closer to a conventionally shaped plot. Presumably Jock McLeod, credited with George Wallace as co-writer, was a restraining influence on his collaborator's anarchic talent. The film has an over-arching narrative, driven by two sustained romance-plots, in both of which a persistent male lover pursues an apparently unresponsive girl. In the relationship that runs the plot, Brian (Frank Harvey) promises Dorothy (Thelma Scott) that if the horse owned by her father (the inevitable Marshall Crosby, once more) beats his in the

222 Bill Kerr, interview with the author, 4 August 2004.

Melbourne Cup, he will never bother her with his repeated proposals again; her forfeit, should Hotspur be beaten, is to marry him. In the comic sub-plot, George pursues Marjorie (Joyce Turner), Dorothy's maid, from one humiliation to another. Both relationships hinge on the result of 'the race that stops a nation'.

Dorothy bets her future on Hotspur beating Surefoot at a time when her future seems a matter of tedious indifference to her. When she meets Harvey Walls the dashing novelist (Campbell Copelin), the game changes, and she tries to persuade Brian to release her from their agreement. He confirms his inconceivability as a lover by refusing to call it off; rather than telling him where to put his wager, Dorothy accepts that she must go through with this absurdity, because, as she sagely observes with a sigh to Walls, 'a bet's a bet'.

Now and then the plot marks time while George does his free-wheeling comic thing. He loses his first job at the grocer's shop after a series of extraordinary accidents with eggs and wrapping-paper, and is inducted into his second at the stables via some extended horsing-around with the other hands. He manages to get a third job for a night, as a waiter at the Cup Eve extravaganza where the crooks who want to 'nobble' Hotspur are conspiring, and finds that the job requires him to entertain; George not only sings, tap-dances and falls on his left ear, but conducts the Phenomenal Philharmonic Phanatics in some musical mayhem. He shares the bill with a string of Efftee Entertainers, including the Regent Theatre Ballet, General Judge and Nick Morton the sobbing tenor. It's a ten minute interlude in the racing-and-romance action, and a monument to Frank Thring's fondness for variety and for getting his pound of flesh from Efftee's contracted performers. It also threatens to derail the film.

But generally the narrative rattles along, even if the emotional stakes are probably not as high for the audience as Jock McLeod intended that they should be. Hotspur wins the cup, naturally, despite the efforts of a crooked jockey to hold him back. When the horse hears George's familiar piercing whistle, he flies home to nose out Surefoot on the line. Margery embraces George, Dorothy is free to accept Walls' proposal, and all but the undeserving are sure to be happy ever after.

A Ticket in Tatts reveals a new sureness in the handling of external locations. Where the street-scenes in *Harmony Row* have a distinctly canvas-and-cardboard quality, these are actual exteriors, beautifully shot and cleverly integrated with the emotional action. The racecourse scenes were filmed at Flemington on Melbourne Cup Day 1933, Hall Mark's year, and provide great historical footage; the feeling of actuality is enhanced by a commentary by Eric Welch and cameo appearances by two Melbourne jockeys and the prominent bookie Alby Sluice. The scenes at the stables, and of George playing the fool in a grocer's shop, were shot on location at Kilsyth. Jack Murray's recollection of the company excursion to Kilsyth is another reminder of the Happy Families atmosphere that defined so many of Efftee's activities:

> And Frank Thring says, 'Better go down, and get some beer', and they had a party. Everything was a party in those days, when we went on location.[223]

There was still a wonderful spirit of amateurism, underneath a welcome development in professionalism, at Efftee.

Some of that pleasure in making a film, in embarking on a shared adventure, finds its way into all three of George Wallace's films for Frank Thring; it dovetails nicely with the cheerful spontaneity of their star's approach to the business of making people laugh:

> The grocer's shop, well, that was hilarious, because he had everything to play with – the sugar, the salt, the pepper, he used to sneeze all over the place … And he'd make dough, and then he'd make scones, and he'd throw them, you know, he'd throw them at the stagehands, you know, everybody standing on stage would get hit with a scone![224]

For Wallace, who had grown up with a live audience, there was potentially a dangerous and unnerving remoteness about film; he overcame it by working off whoever was on set, in front of the camera or behind it. When the crew get covered in flour and are still laughing, you know the comedy is working. The heart and the humour touched tens of thousands of strangers, too, and ensured that the George Wallace vehicles were Efftee's golden days.

They proved a very hard act to follow.

---

223 Jack Murray in *The George Wallace Story*.
224 Iris Shand in *The Georce Wallace Story*.

Whatever important matters had so inexplicably detained him in London in the early months of 1933, Frank returned to Melbourne with all the energy and drive, and the apparently ruthless ambition, that was synonymous with his name. At a welcome-home dinner in May, on the night after his return, attended by 'prominent men in the public life of Melbourne, and the film industry',[225] Frank's old foe the State Censor was among those to heap praise on the conquering hero:

> Professor Osborne referred to the magnificent material offering in Australia, both historically and from the point of view of scenic beauty, to be exploited by film producers. The man best able to exploit that material was unquestionably Mr. Thring.

Frank and the Professor were, for once, marvellously at one:

> I may add that my visit to England demonstrated clearly that there is a wide field for Australian films in England, particularly for films depicting our out-door life, and idealising the work of the early pioneers, and also for films featuring the Australian brand of comedy.
>
> To that extent I have returned full of encouragement for the future of the talking picture industry here, and confident that given security of distribution in the home market, the future of our films is assured.

The reference to 'security of distribution' was, of course, another salvo in the quota wars. A captive audience of Very Important People, including the Premier and Chief Secretary, was an opportunity too good to resist.

Two weeks later, Frank proclaimed that Efftee had begun 'a search for suitable material for Australian scenarios'.[226] One week after that, he revealed that Efftee had bought the rights to William Hatfield's novel, *Sheepmates*.[227] A fortnight later, he announced that he had bought the Wattle Path Dance Palais in St Kilda, and that Efftee would be transferring all its operations there; at the same time, he outlined an ambitious new theatrical program in parallel to the company's work in film, for which he had taken a lease on the Garrick Theatre in South Melbourne.[228] After another two weeks, he unveiled a national

225 'Quota Depends on Prices and Quality: Tribute to Thring', *Everyones*, 24 May 1933, p.29.
226 *Everyones*, 7 June 1933, p.23
227 *Everyones*, 14 June 1933, p.9.
228 *Everyones*, 28 June 1933,p.25.

competition for the best Australian play, with a prize of two hundred and fifty pounds.[229] The judges were to be Gregan McMahon, Bernard Cronin, and the warmly supportive Professor Osborne. The irrepressible Mr Thring was, in every sense and very conspicuously, back in town.

The purchase of Wattle Path, and the move there from the rented shell of His Majesty's, was a major investment in continuity. The burnt-out theatre had always looked like temporary accommodation: to make it viable as a sound-stage, there were 'miles and miles of thick heavy felt hanging everywhere', and unpainted sheets of cheap caneite had been hastily nailed to its walls.[230] 'The Maj' had the great attraction of a very recognisable name and façade, but Efftee's new premises were almost as well-known. The Wattle Path Palais, 'one of the world's largest dance halls',[231] was a St Kilda landmark, built on the crown of the Esplanade overlooking the beach.[232] At the peak of its popularity, it had packed in five thousand revellers. But it had proved a costly business, and had never recovered from the depths of the Depression. When it had first opened for dancing a decade before, the building had cost eighty-three thousand pounds; Frank Thring, ever with an eye to a bargain, picked it up for twenty-three thousand.[233]

Frank explained his plans for the Garrick in terms of its usefulness to his core business in film, 'as a try-out spot for plays with motion picture possibilities, and as a training ground for players deemed to have screen personality'.[234] Gregan McMahon was to have responsibility for direction and casting, and for spotting potential stars. Frank was clinging stubbornly to what others were starting to see as an outmoded assumption, that there was a necessary nexus between good theatre and good film. It was the kind of thinking that had led him to appoint Norman Lindsay and C.J. Dennis as arbiters in a medium in which they had no experience; it was always a powerful element in his choice of Efftee's repertoire, and it probably lay behind some of the ponderous and unimaginative direction of the interior scenes in Efftee features. Men like Longford, and Charles Chauvel and Ken G. Hall, worked from the premise that the language of film was unique, and that the skills needed to use it well were completely distinctive.

229 *Argus*, 12 July 1933, p.7.
230 R. Alan Stuart interview with Graham Shirley and Chris Long.
231 'Famous Dance Hall As Studio', *Table Talk*, 29 June 1933, p.5
232 The site is now occupied by the Novotel hotel and apartments.
233 'Thring Makes Big Production Move: New Studio & Theatre', *Everyones*, 28 June 1933, p.25.
234 ibid.

But the Garrick was also Frank Thring's attempt to create something like a full-time studio ensemble:

> In the past he has been compelled, in casting Efftee productions, to depend upon a few artists who happened to be in Melbourne, and had to fit in his production plans accordingly.
>
> But in forming his own company for stage productions at the Garrick, he hopes to establish a permanent supply of suitable acting talent for the Efftee Film productions.[235]

In some ways it was simply a formalisation of Frank's familiar habit of squeezing all he could from the money spent on his actors. But there was a bigger, and riskier, agenda than that. Frank acknowledged that it was 'an experiment';[236] what he didn't admit was that it was a huge gamble. Diversification in a fragile market was in itself a dangerous game.

A key element in the strategy was implicit in the reference to 'actors who happened to be in Melbourne'. Doyle and Greater Union had re-commenced production through Cinesound, in unspoken acknowledgement of Efftee's unlikely success. Frank's plan to establish a stable of actors in Melbourne was, in part, a pre-emptive strike against the old enemy in Sydney.

Efftee staged four plays at the Garrick, and all reflected the sense that the theatre was 'a try-out spot' for possible cinema projects. The first of them, Aimee and Philip Stuart's comedy *Clara Gibbings* in August 1933, duly found its way a little more than a year later to Melbourne's Mayfair Cinema as the twelfth and last film shot at Efftee Studios. The last of the four, *Streets of London*, was produced for the screen, though never released. And the other two, Patrick Hamilton's *Rope* and Christa Winsloe's *Children in Uniform*, certainly had film potential. *Rope*, an unsettling piece about a plan to commit the perfect murder, was loosely based on Leopold and Loeb's infamous crime; fifteen years later, with a screenplay adaptation by Arthur Laurents, it became a film for Warner Brothers, directed by Alfred Hitchcock and starring James Stewart in the role played by Frank Harvey in the Efftee production. *Children in Uniform*, an all-female play dealing with hectic relationships in an oppressive school for girls, had already been adapted for the screen in Germany, in 1931. It would be filmed again in

---

235 'Thring Makes Big Production Move: New Studio & Theatre', *Everyones*, 28 June 1933, p.25.

236 ibid.

1958, with Romy Schneider playing the part that twenty-year-old Coral Brown (who had not yet affected the final 'e' in her surname) performed at the Garrick.

The fact that the domestic comedy and the fruity melodrama came through Efftee's 'try-out' process, and not the two powerful plays that made it to the screen in Hollywood and Europe, is quite suggestive of the company's priorities, and Frank Thring's sense of the tastes of his audience. It indicated a preference for the comfortably comic over the disturbingly dramatic, obviously. It reflected, too, an understandable wariness about the implicit sexual politics that made both plays, and the films that were based on them, controversial. The homoeroticism underlying the conspiracy of the two killers in *Rope*, and the lesbian passions that simmered through *Children in Uniform*, were probably not likely to appeal to the broad family audience that Frank thought crucial to Efftee's survival. These things made the choice of the two plays for the first and final season at the Garrick quite a bold one; it also indicated the clear distinction, in Frank's mind as well as in the wider community's perception, between the two audiences – the popular one for film, the peripheral more 'sophisticated' one for theatre.

There was one other dimension to the Garrick initiative, but possibly even Frank was unaware of it at the time. It might even explain why the experiment, though successful enough, was so short-lived. Though in every statement about this new focus for his company Frank had been at pains to insist that it was both related and subordinate to Efftee Films, there was something about the theatre, and its live audience, that appealed to the old showman in him. The problem with the Garrick was not that it failed as a 'try-out spot', but that that was all it was. It was, after all, Gregan McMahon's kind of theatre, not Frank Thring's. In McMahon's world, challenging plays that hardly anybody wanted to see were almost an absolute good; the fact that people might be affronted, or stayed away in droves, could even be a badge of honour. In Frank's, there was little point in doing things that audiences didn't like.

The reasons behind the dalliance with theatre that produced Efftee's first venture into that territory in June were more clearly evident in August, when Frank made the announcement that was the death-knell for its flirtation with the Garrick. Melbourne's *Argus* carried the news under the banner headline 'PRINCESS THEATRE. BOUGHT BY EFFTEE FILMS'.[237]

---

237 *Argus*, 4 August 1933, p.7.

> Mr. F.W. Thring, managing director of Efftee Film productions, said last evening that he had completed negotiations for the purchase from Ben and John Fuller theatres Ltd. of the Princess Theatre, Spring Street. The transaction involved the freehold of the block upon which the theatre stands, together with the whole building, including shop frontages and the storeroom at the rear. Mr. Thring will take possession of the theatre about the middle of next month, and he will at once commence the production of musical plays there.[238]

The Princess was three times the size of the Garrick, and had a much more imposing profile. It was opposite the Treasury Gardens in Spring Street, a block north-east of His Majesty's, which it rivalled in High Victorian opulence. All the signs suggested that Frank Thring had found the business of making talking pictures very profitable. That wasn't precisely the case, but appearances were important to Frank; he had always believed that if you looked like a tycoon, there was every chance that you might become one. He was investing not just in real estate and an industry, but in a reputation.

Frank's move into musicals would have been encouraged, no doubt, by his success in selling *His Royal Highness* in England. But it surely began with *The Jazz Singer*, and the realisation that, of all the theatrical genres, the musical was the one that silent movies could never do. The implications of that perception would have been clear from what was happening in Hollywood. Busby Berkeley produced *Roman Scandals* for MGM in early 1933 before Warner Brothers poached him for two other hits in the same year, *42nd Street* and *Gold Diggers of 1933*. MGM in 1933 countered with *Going Hollywood* and *Too Much Harmony*, featuring its new star Bing Crosby; Warner Brothers struck back with *Footlight Parade*, starring James Cagney, Joan Blondell and Dick Powell, and Al Jolson's comeback movie, *Hallelujah I'm a Bum*. Fred Astaire and Ginger Rogers in the same year made the first of their movies together, *Flying Down to Rio*, for RKO, and there was a stream of dance movies like *Bundle of Blues*, *Dancing Lady* and *Symphony in Black* (featuring Snake Hips Tucker). People seemed to be making film musicals everywhere, except in Australia.

An argument about potential profit was always a persuasive one for Frank. But there was more to his sudden enthusiasm for the musical than that. It was also a form that offered the immediate gratification of applause, and that

238 *Argus*, 4 August 1933, p.7.

was something that Frank had always liked about live audiences; you could tell that they loved you, in the theatre, on the night.

It was different with film: you made them months in advance, and tweaked them and cut them, and when finally they were released it wouldn't matter if a director was on the other side of the world. The show was all celluloid, and the projector rolled on regardless, whether the people cheered or booed, or indeed whether anyone was there at all.

Moreover, as a form, the musical held some unique attractions for a man with a sense of national mission. The great musicals were all about communities: whatever conflicts might divide them, 'the people' could still sing together, in harmony or in unison, with what felt like a single voice. Anyone who wanted to arouse and shape a national consciousness needed someone to write a decent tune for it. Frank saw very clearly the powerful arguments, to do with patriotism and profit, for musical theatre about Australia. And he saw, too, that local cinemas were being saturated with the songs, and behind them the myths, of Hollywood.

Frank articulated his feelings on the matter in early 1934. In the midst of a good deal of uncertainty about whether or not he might be able to secure a quota law that required a percentage of Australian films in the program of every exhibitor in the country, he was invited as guest of honour at the ANA (Australian Natives Association) dinner on 26 January 1934, the 146th anniversary of the arrival of Governor Phillip at Port Jackson, the day now annually celebrated as Australia Day.

Frank had just come back from the New South Wales government's enquiry into the case for a quota, where he had argued, cajoled and threatened, in the interests of achieving the thing that he thought essential to the survival of the industry, and his own company. He was to propose the toast of 'The Day We Celebrate', and predictably enough he used the occasion to repeat some arguments that he had put before Commissioner Marks, very forcibly, in Sydney a couple of weeks before: arguments about the growth of the motion picture industry as a major contributor to the national economy, and about the need to lend support to local enterprise.

But then he switched his emphasis to the kind of Australia that he believed in, and each generation's obligation to the next to pass on the values that were at once part of its British heritage, and part of its distinctive Australian-ness:

> I also submit an even greater reason than the purely economic one as to why we should now recognise it as a national obligation to take a hand in the production of an adequate supply of worthy motion pictures on

> our own soil. The immense influence of motion pictures was increased tenfold with the introduction of talking apparatus, and today all children are consciously or unconsciously being influenced for the rest of their lives by the type of pictures placed before them …
>
> Our forefathers strove at great sacrifice to keep Australia white, and with that great racial ideal to instill a love of country, pride of race and respect for the great history of the British Empire. Purity of speech and a wholesome love of clean comedy, untainted drama, and manly adventure were among the best traditions handed on to us with this heritage. Are we, therefore, going to stand idly by and watch the sure and rapid dissipation and demoralisation of those splendid ideals? Or are we going to stir ourselves into action, and do something worth while as Australian adults of this generation for which the children of the coming generation will eternally be grateful to us?[239]

The audience of the ANA would have lapped it up, but from the perspective of another century its language is inevitably uncomfortable. The fact that few people at that time in the nation's history would have felt that, or understood why it was so, makes it one of those Grand Statements that need to be taken with a little tolerance, and some understanding of its cultural context.

For Frank, this was a risky thing to say; not because it was an unpopular sentiment at the time, or because it was naïve or jingoistic or racist or any of the things that it seems to be more than seventy years on, but because it was acutely personal. He was not accustomed to wearing his heart on his sleeve; that habit not only made you vulnerable in general, but got in the way of whatever card you had strategically placed inside it. But on this occasion, Frank said what he believed in. Of course it looks embarrassing now, in its insistence on racial purity (the need 'to keep Australia white'), on the importance of Australia's colonial heritage (the need to have 'respect for the great British Empire'), and on a quite conservative morality (the need to satisfy 'a wholesome love of clean comedy'). Something about it, though, makes it too urgent an appeal to be dismissed with a superior chuckle. It is passion, of course, and a kind of selflessness. This is a man who, in this moment at least, cares less about the political support he might be able to enlist and the profits he could make than an idea of the collective good. That makes it moving, and even impressive.

239 *Everyones*, 31 January 1934, p.3.

Films could do it, musicals could do it, and just possibly filmed musicals could do it better than anything else. What Frank needed now was a musical by, for and about Australians. It was a tall order. The repertoire at the Garrick consisted mostly of plays from overseas, and every one of them found its subject in another culture. The Efftee national competition for playwrights was based on two assumptions – that Australians were capable of writing first-class scripts, and that they weren't, in the current climate, doing so. The odds of coming up with an Australian musical, fully written and scored, that could fill the bill, seemed astronomical.

Frank Thring had always ridden his luck, and once again it paid off. He found the show he was after; more accurately, it found him. Its name was *Collits' Inn.*

By the time *Collits' Inn* came into Frank Thring's life in July 1933, it had been through a couple of incarnations. The first was in early 1932, when a Sydney singing teacher, Miss Rosenwax, had funded a competition for an original operetta or musical play; Mrs Varney Monk persuaded her next-door neighbour in Mosman, Stuart Gurr, to collaborate on an entry as her librettist. The starting-point for the plot was a romantic tale she had heard, set in the actual Collits' Inn that was still a popular roadside tavern for travellers in the Blue Mountains. *Collits' Inn* won second prize, but Miss Rosenwax thought it more suited to a small production than the not-so-lucky winner, *The Island of Pines*, which immediately sank without trace. *Collits' Inn* was staged for five performances at the Savoy Theatre in Sydney in December 1932, revived with some revisions by Miss Rosenwax in March 1933 at the Mosman Town Hall, and then recorded by the ABC for radio broadcast.

Several things happened almost simultaneously in late June. Frank Thring, as one of the stream of initiatives that he launched after his coming home from London, announced a quest for new Australian scripts. Varney Monk saw the item, and thought it might be worth asking him to look at *Collits' Inn.* A musician friend, Howard Carr, happened to be going to Melbourne, and undertook to take a script down with him. He managed to get an appointment with Frank Thring, who after a cursory look at the script asked Varney Monk to come to Melbourne and play through some of the score for him; he undertook to provide the venue and the musicians, and everything was organised within three days:

> The way Mr Thring heard the music of Collits' Inn was that I took a good girl to Melbourne with a good voice and she sang it with a good band and I have never seen Mr Thring look so pleased since. [240]

Frank organised a three-person panel for the audition, consisting of Lola, Olive and himself. When it ended, 'Mr Thring walked alone over to me and said he'd take it'.[241]

A week later, the songs were broadcast on Melbourne's ABC station, 3LO, and the production planned for the end of the year was given some handy preliminary exposure. Decision-making in the theatre is almost always a ponderous process; Efftee's acquisition of *Collits' Inn* is a wonderful story of serendipity, as well as a powerful argument for the advantages of the entrepreneurial one-man band.

The musical was scheduled to open just before Christmas. It was already July. Frank moved very fast to secure the Australian soprano Gladys Moncrieff for the role of Mary Collits, the girl who is torn between two lovers – Captain Lake, the English Redcoat, and Bob Keane the bushranger. 'Our Glad' at forty-one was strictly too old for the part, not to mention at least a stone too heavy; but she was adored by audiences, and a guaranteed drawcard. He enlisted three other big names for the production: Robert Chisholm came home after six years on Broadway to play the dashing Captain; Claude Flemming, who had been working on the London stage, was to double as Keane and the show's director; and George Wallace was cast as Dandy Dick, the comic rouseabout at the Inn. The sense that Thring was sparing no expense in staging the show was not only accurate, but part of the promotional build-up to the premiere on 23 December.

It turned out to be one of those very rare landmark moments in theatre: Spring Street blocked by cars and cabs, filled with people coming to see 'Australia's First Musical Comedy' and with many more who had come just to gaze at the glamorous first-nighters. Radio station 3KZ provided live

---

240 Varney Monk, letter to C.B. Cochran, 28 August 1935, National Film and Sound Archive. The 'good girl with a good voice' was Philippa Alston, who had played a minor role in the Savoy production.

241 Letter from Varney Monk, 1958, quoted in John West, 'Introduction' to *Collits' Inn*, Sydney, Currency Press, 1990, p.xi.

coverage of their arrival, and stayed to broadcast the entire first act. And all this excitement over an Australian show with an all-Australian cast. Nothing like it had happened before. Frank, sitting with Olive and Varney Monk in the 'royal box' above the stage at the Princess, must have felt like a king: this was what it had all been about, then, the struggle and the scheming and the refusal to despair. It was certainly the most triumphant night of his life.

There were the obligatory opening night curtain calls and standing ovations, and at the end of the evening Olive Thring bestowed on Gladys a giant flag of Australia made of flowers, and on each of the leading men a floral basket filled with fruit and bottles of champagne. Then Frank Thring was persuaded to take a bow, and once again the audience was on its feet. There was nothing quite like rapturous applause to convince a man that he had done well. All the things that a year before had made Frank doubt, the thoughts that had taunted him in London of a life that he might have led, a life that he knew, nearly knew, was no longer possible for him, were suddenly gone. Possibly not gone for good, admittedly; thoughts like that were never finally laid to rest. But for now, this would surely do. Perhaps it might even prove to be enough.

The reviews on Boxing Day were excellent, as they were bound to be. In a sense, the show was a hit almost before it had opened; even the Sydney press became caught up in Melbourne's anticipation, declaring that 'next Saturday will be a 'first night' memorable in Australian drama'.[242] A Grand Gala occasion, billed as the '*Collits' Inn* Party', had been held at Menzies Hotel a week before the opening, with Frank and Olive, Varney Monk, and the stars of the show as guests of honour. An invitation to that party would have been the only rival to *Collits' Inn* as the hottest ticket in town. Nobody with that kind of ticket would ever declare it time wasted.

Collits' Inn gave them, the people in the stalls and the circle as well as the initially anxious trio in the box, a lot to be excited about. The star performers more than paid their way, although Claude Flemming, even more than 'Our Glad', was carrying more than weight-for-age. The songs were good – 'Stay while the stars are shining', the romantic duet between Mary and Lake, and the rousing finale 'Australia', which made all but the most devout monarchists in the house flirt with the idea that it might be our new national anthem, were always sure to bring the people to their feet. George Wallace was terrific, even if he threatened to take over the show.

242 *Sydney Morning Herald*, 18 December 1933, p.5.

And there were two breathtaking things in *Collits' Inn*, the like of which no one had ever seen before. There was a revolving stage, a 'first' for Australian theatre that signalled Frank Thring's typical readiness to spare no expense.[243] The revolve not only made blackouts largely a thing of the past but became a powerful image of the momentum of the plot; it made the scene-changes almost as engrossing as the scenes. Then there was an Aboriginal corroboree at the opening of Act Two; some people said it wasn't authentic, but for most of the audience it was just the way you imagined they'd do that kind of thing. It seemed symbolically to complete the way the show represented what was distinctive about Australia's past.

The revolve really was something of a wonder.[244] And the corroboree was well-intentioned. It had its beginnings when Varney Monk happened to run into Queen Rosie, the last surviving full-blooded member of the Illawarra tribe, in a toyshop in Kiama; some big moments in musical theatre have possibly had stranger origins. She transcribed what seemed to be a 7/4 rhythm as Rosie danced it for her, and later built on it a melody of sorts that became the second-act opener; Harry Jacobs, Efftee's musical director, polished the music, Jennie Brenan, Efftee's choreographer, added a few fancy steps, and the ladies of the Efftee ballet were kitted out in hand-painted tights and extravagant head-dresses. What relation it might have had to the traditional ceremonies of the Illawarra people is a very doubtful matter, but it was probably as well that few if any tribal elders were in the stalls.

Amid the euphoria of the response to its opening, a few reviewers noted some tiny flaws in the book of *Collits' Inn*. In retrospect those flaws seem much bigger. The structure struggles to hold together its three major components, the love-triangle, the historical material that surrounds the building of a road through the Blue Mountains, and the knockabout humour of Dandy Dick and his pals. The love-story drives the plot, but since Mary falls in love with Lake within a minute of meeting him, there is never much prospect of her choosing the bushranger who adores her; she feels enough for Bob Keane to save him from the soldiers who are led by the man she loves, but that gives Bob only a temporary reprieve. He dies, and Lake is summoned home to England. The final act shows Mary three

243 J.C. Williamson's claimed to have used one previously, but even if they had been able to substantiate their claim, it's likely that this cavil would have been drowned out in the hyperbole that surrounded *Collits' Inn*.

244 The press marvelled at its scale (a diameter of 35 feet, and a capacity to move a load of eleven tons), and almost every reviewer commented on the way it accelerated the action.

years later, sitting sadly at her spinet in a kind of stupour; but then Lake miraculously appears, recalls her to life and love, and the entire company celebrates with a hearty chorus of 'Australia'. The politics of road-making, which in truth have never been compelling, are mercifully put aside for the last half of the show.

The comedy often threatens to take over the show. In Gurr's original conception, Dandy Dick and his skirmishes with Sally the barmaid are a quaint diversion in a corner of the plot, but George Wallace was not made to play in a corner. Quite apart from his capacity to steal scenes and milk every moment, casting George on a salary of a hundred a week was a strong argument for enlarging Dandy's scripted role. A couple of extra scenes were added here, a couple of funny songs there; George wrote them himself, in collaboration with Jock McLeod. Then of course when one signed George Wallace to a show, one also had to find a place for the inevitable Marshall Crosby and George's long, lugubrious sidekick John Dobbie. Crosby slotted in easily as Pierce Collits the publican, but a new character had to be created for Dobbie. Thus Toby, the slow-thinking barman, was born, and with him a comic romantic triangle to balance the melodramatically emotional one.

In the end, Dandy Dick had more stage time and almost as many songs as Mary Collits – and that is a calculation of his share of the scripted action that takes no account of George's fondness for following his inspiration of the moment. The version of *Collits' Inn* that played the Princess had come a long way from the one that had charmed Miss Rosenwax; in the end, the inflation of the comedy was probably a good thing, but it certainly left the show looking lopsided. Varney Monk frequently expressed her faltering hope that one day her show might be played as it had been meant to be.

The intersection of the worlds of earthy comedy and operetta works in *Collits' Inn* very much as it did in *His Royal Highness*. Their collision is fraught with misunderstanding, as when Dandy tells Mary that 'I've got something wrong with me and I don't know what it is – so I must be in love', and she (although she has never been in love, of course) agrees to give him some advice on how girls like to be wooed:

> MARY: … Every girl likes to be swept off her feet. A girl dreams of a lover who will catch her in his arms and carry her away with him.
>
> DANDY: I couldn't carry her away.
>
> MARY: I mean – metaphorically speaking.

> DANDY: [*nonplussed*] Meta – meta – meta – beg your pardon Mistress Mary, but I didn't quite catch that last word.
>
> MARY: I said, 'metaphorically speaking'.
>
> DANDY: Oh, no, no. She's not a girl like that. In fact, she's rather on the quiet side.
>
> MARY: No, I mean talk to her – say nice things to her …
>
> DANDY: But what'll I say? What would you say?
>
> MARY: I'd start with, 'Ah, my beloved'.
>
> DANDY: If I said that, she'd swipe me.

He agrees to try the pretty compliments that Mary teaches him ('her hair as beautiful as the windblown grass, her lips like twin rubies', etc etc); but when Dandy puts it into practice ('that sweet little nose, like the finest ruby, your hair like the flyblown grass'), Sally is strangely unimpressed. Even if he got them right, she would probably tell him not to come the raw prawn. Needless to say, such blandishments come very smoothly from the lips of Lake, and Mary finally gets her wish to be metaphorically carried away.

Most of the reviews were anxious to acknowledge both the quality of the show and the courage of the man who staged it. The Melbourne *Truth* was representative:

> To say that we were surprised at Collits' Inn is to put it mildly. We were amazed not only at the gameness of Frank Thring but the sheer achievement of this all-Australian musical play … We want … to pay tribute to Frank Thring for being so game as to put on a show like Collits' Inn.

The applause kept coming. Not surprisingly, Frank Thring, who just a few months before the premiere of *Collits' Inn* was defining his theatre productions as 'try-outs' and 'forcing-houses' for potential feature films, suddenly found life as a stage impresario very gratifying.

It would certainly have seemed a great deal simpler than trying to make films, when you had to contend not only with the commercial opposition (Stuart Doyle, and his Sydney entourage and networks), but with the Victorian State Government, the New South Wales State Government, and a lot of other people who would prefer you simply to go away. It still wasn't a simple either/or; *Collits' Inn* remained on the drawing-board as an Efftee Films project, of course, and some time early in 1934 at Wattle Path a number of the songs were recorded on soundtrack. In theory, the plan remained the same, and the theatre initiatives were subordinate to the ones for film. But it didn't feel like that in the aftermath of a standing ovation.

Collits' Inn played over one hundred performances at the Princess before closing on April 9, reopening for its Sydney season at the New Tivoli on June 22; it came back to the Princess for a three-week return season on 13 October. It did well at the box-office everywhere, though the bigger capacity of the New Tivoli restricted its Sydney run to six weeks. Frank spent Christmas 1933 and New Year 1934 not basking in the triumph of his opening or in the sun down at Portsea, but at his desk, negotiating deals to make the most of the success of his first stage musical. He arranged, by a series of telegrams to the London theatre entrepreneur C.B. Cochran, to bring out the French star Alice Delysia in two of her West End hits, *Mother of Pearl* and *Her Past*. He arranged, in a number of telephone calls to the Adelaide composer Dudley Glass, to revive *The Beloved Vagabond*, which had played successfully in London. He arranged, over a dinner with Varney Monk, for a commissioned sequel to *Collits' Inn*, which she thought of as a possible collaboration with the librettist Edmund Barclay; this was *The Cedar Tree*, which opened on the Saturday before Christmas, the anniversary of the premiere of *Collits' Inn*.

The stars of *The Beloved Vagabond* and *The Cedar Tree* were to be the principals of *Collits' Inn* – Gladys Moncrieff in the winsome soprano role, Robert Chisholm as the handsome baritone, and George Wallace as his customary self; they would feature Marshall Crosby and John Dobbie of course, and would, like *Collits' Inn*, be 'produced by Claude Flemming under the Personal Direction of F.W. Thring'. In the event, George was unable to appear in *The Cedar Tree*, and the veteran comedian Albert Frith came out of retirement to replace him as the Flying Pieman.

One of the most striking things about Frank's grand flirtation with the theatre was the way that he worked his high-profile stars. He had developed over the previous three years a quite distinctive employment strategy. Its premise was that there was no particular reason why actors should not work as hard as other people; probably, Frank found it hard to understand why, since he devoted every waking hour to Efftee, anybody else should have a problem about doing the same.

When it came to hiring performers like George Wallace, and then Robert Chisholm and 'Our Glad', Frank not only paid generous wages, but offered the rarest of experiences for an actor, security. Twelve-month contracts must have sounded like the stuff of dreams. Then, of course, they found out what being signed up with Frank Thring really meant. It meant being ready to jump on board with whatever wild scheme he had come up with this week; it meant committing to shows that he didn't even know he wanted to do yet; it meant being prepared to drop everything and head to Sydney if it was decreed that the show was to go there; it meant rehearsing a new script by day while you played another one at night; it meant riding the roller-coaster with him, as though you were a part of his most peculiar family; it meant wondering why you'd ever agreed to step on this artistic treadmill, and then trying to imagine what more worthwhile projects you could ever have found than this odd amalgam of egoism and nationalism. It probably meant that you'd accepted some ancient bond of fealty, in the guise of a new, rational and considerate industrial model.

For a performer with a viable international career like Gladys Moncrieff, it offered a strong economic inducement to stay home. But her schedule for 1934 was, by any theatrical standards, extraordinary. On April 15, six nights after *Collits' Inn* closed, she opened in *The Beloved Vagabond*, which ran until 16 June. Six days later she began the Sydney season of *Collits' Inn*. It finished on August 18, and six nights later at the New Tivoli she was playing *The Beloved Vagabond*. That tour ended on October 10; this time she had a break of three weeks rather than the customary six days, before the first night at the Princess of the pirate musical, *Jolly Roger*, though it would have been a break filled with intensive rehearsal. That 'naughtycal comic-opera' ran until December 15. Then, on December 22, came the premiere of *The Cedar Tree*, and a two-month run, followed by a transfer to the Sydney Criterion.

Frank expected a lot of his actors, and they never 'rested', but no-one in his stable seems ever to have protested that he or she was exploited. Perhaps that was because they understood that hard work was part of the game, when the goal was the invention of an Australian sound picture industry, or an Australian musical theatre tradition. You could do without a lot, for a while, if you believed that the sacrifice was worthwhile, and that was as true for Frank as it was for the people he carried with him on the Efftee juggernaut.

It was always different for him, though, and not just because he was Efftee. Each of the people he worked with had one kind of talent to put on the table; to the extent that they thought about options for the rest of their lives, most of them probably had two – a road that they were on, and another that they imagined might be better. Through the 1930s, Frank had almost always had many options; sometimes, it seemed, a new one every week. In early 1933, in London, there was a possibility of doing and being something different, of beginning all over again. There had been a brief period, in mid-1933, when the options appeared to have run out. Post-London, it must have looked as though there was nothing he could do but, in every sense, to go back; he tried hard to resume things, but really he was thrashing about, trying to see the next step forward. At the end of 1933, though, he had Australia's first unquestioned hit musical, and he saw and, for a while, followed a road that might take him to the thing he sought – not just wealth, not just power, but significance.

But by the middle of 1934, that was giving up on him, too. All the shows performed reasonably in that year, but in terms of both box office and impact they seemed subject to a law of diminishing returns. The two vehicles for 'the divine Delysia' proved popular enough, but after *Collits' Inn* had set such high expectations, the other initiatives seemed increasingly disappointing. In the program for *Collits' Inn*, Frank Thring had hailed 'a new era in Australian stage productions':

> In the past Australians have had to rest content with seeing reproductions of musical plays which have been established successes abroad. For such a musical and artistic community as undoubtedly exists here, this was proof of the lack of enterprise on the part of Australian theatrical managements.[245]

He claimed to have 'several other Australian musical comedies under consideration', and foreshadowed 'a permanent policy of Australian musical comedies at the Princess Theatre'. But it was much more easily said than done. The only Australian musical 'under consideration' was *The Cedar Tree*. *The Beloved Vagabond*, set in seventeenth-century France, could be called 'an Australian musical' only on the tenuous grounds that its expatriate composer, Dudley Glass, had been born in Adelaide. Shows like *Mother of Pearl* and *Jolly Roger* were precisely 'reproductions of … established successes abroad'. Australian managements were guilty of a 'lack of enterprise', but they could also claim with some justification to be hamstrung by a lack of good scripts. So when *The Cedar Tree* finally came to the stage, it showed a number of symptoms of having been pushed too quickly into production.

245 Program for *Collits' Inn*, Priness Theatre, December 1933.

It played just two months at the Princess, and less than a fortnight when it transferred to the Criterion in Sydney. The script carefully followed the *Collits' Inn* template: a romantic colonial setting (the 1840s, in a picturesque timber-town in the Hawkesbury region); a striking and innovative ballet interlude (child dancers prettily frolicking as koalas and bush birds); a generous slice of knockabout comedy; and, of course, a great love that seems doomed but finally conquers all.

The critical response to *The Cedar Tree* was warm, but the familiarity of its recipe for success gave it an air of predictability. The Sydney *Sun* observed that it 'runs on time-honoured lines to a foregone conclusion, but is otherwise pleasant enough',[246] while the Melbourne *Herald* made the obvious comparison, and unfavourably:

> For one thing, the resemblance in period and costume (and cast?) is too great, and the verve and gusto of that happily successful initial production are lacking.[247]

Perhaps there had been 'several other Australian musical comedies under consideration', but Frank Thring was watching the dissolution of another dream. His second all-Australian stage-show was destined to be his last.

Sydney, the market that had given him so much trouble in film, was a significant part of his problems again. The run of *Collits' Inn* there was undermined – Frank would have preferred the verb 'sabotaged' – by the appearance, improbably, of J.C. Williamson's first-ever Australian musical, *Blue Mountain Melody*, just down the road at the Theatre Royal. 'The Firm' had summarily rejected *Collits' Inn* when Varney Monk had offered it to them early in 1933, but the show's success in Melbourne prompted them to commission a very similar kind of work, with music by Charles Zwar and book by Jim Bancks, the creator of the comic-strip character Ginger Meggs. The romantic leads were Australian musical theatre's favourite couple, Cyril Ritchard and Madge Elliott, while Gus Bluett was featured as Dynamite Danny, a role strangely reminiscent of Dandy Dick. It was a shameless attempt to catch a wave of popularity, and, had it not had a predictable effect on his takings, Frank might have felt some ironic pleasure in such a clear case of the sincerest form of flattery. But Frank Thring was not amused.

---

246 *Sun*, 18 March 1935, p.4.
247 *Herald*, 27 December 1934, p.11.

Nor could he take much satisfaction from the opposition's lack of success. *Blue Mountain Melody* persuaded J.C.W. that they had been right all along in having no truck with new work, especially new work by and about Australians. It was twenty-two years before they did another one, and the irony of that choice, too, may have tickled his fancy, if he had been around to be tickled – the show was Albert Arlen's musical version of *The Sentimental Bloke*. But if Williamson's, with all its heavy weaponry in the theatrical market-place, could not stage a successful Australian show, what were the implications for Efftee, driven by one man's money and passion? Frank was beginning to see the answer to that question, though it would take him some time to accept it, and a little longer to act on it.

TRAVELLING FROM MELBOURNE TO SYDNEY

Melbourne-Sydney Express, 8 January 1934

Almost eleven. Not much point trying to get some shut-eye, so the only thing left to do was drink. And that was, he knew, not one of his better ideas.

Three whiskies and a man felt at peace with his world, four and he felt like he owned it. He knew those feelings well. But you had to be careful, and he was trying to be. Not because Olive told him he was making an exhibition of himself, or a fool. Not because it worried him particularly that he was drinking more and more and taking more risks. Those were reasons, those sensations, to have another one. And not because his doctor told him he needed to ease up, or because he'd had some vaguely awkward, or was that awkwardly vague, afternoon meetings in the last couple of years, though that had encouraged him to flirt with the absurdity of New Year's resolutions a week ago; resolutions that, yes, of course, he'd immediately, and rather spectacularly, blown at the Mateers that night. These things happened, sorry Ol.

No, the main argument for counting your glasses was none of the above. Truth was, the false bonhomie of the third, and the delusive power of the fourth, were the best times of the day, at whatever hour they came. The problem was, three and four led you to five and then six, and that was when the world turned dark and bleak and a man felt so alone sometimes that anything, a cough, a fart, the clink of a glass, seemed to echo, all the way down your years, and leave you alone in your universe again. That was the argument for counting, and he could never say that to Olive, or his daughter, or his son when he became old enough, or anyone.

Three and four to five and six also made you maudlin. Nothing to be gained from that.

No, better just to roll your eyes at your companions in the parlour car at the absurdities of a bloody railway system that got every one out of bed at Wodonga, and out on the platform at Albury at midnight. Some clown had decreed that the tracks in New South Wales would be five-foot-three, while the Victorian trains would be, what, six-and-a-half inches narrower. That just about summed it up, the whole catastrophe. The Grand Folly of Federation, played out by children in pyjamas, and adults who kept themselves awake by having one glass too many.

He was about to walk straight into it, of course. The interstate rivalry schemozzle. Tomorrow morning, in a bit under ten hours, when Marks was going to ask him about comparative quota rules between the states. What's the difference, Mr Marks? Six and a half inches, that's what. That's the difference between me and Stuart Doyle, in the end. Six and a half bloody inches. My God, what a man. No wonder they'd made him a Commodore.

This was going to be it, though. It, absolutely It. That's what they didn't know. Marks, and Doyle, and all the people who went to the flicks, all the mums and dads and the kids in pyjamas who were getting ready to waste an hour of their lives just changing trains. Francis William Thring was crossing the Murray, the bloody Rubicon, and there'd be no going back.

You never really lost if you took a stand. Especially when there mightn't be a lot to lose. He'd started to think that, lately. There might be more films to make. But Sheepmates, though – what a cock-up, sorry ladies, that was. A cock-up on a colossal scale, like the railway gauge, and the stupid things a man managed to do with his life. There were plenty of other things he could do – theatre, radio, who knows what else. He could come up with plenty of things to keep him off the streets. You needed options, if only so people might think you had alternatives.

Truth was, he'd done it, and didn't know what to do with it. Truth was, he could see the stairs, but had no idea why he was keeping on climbing them. Truth was, he'd trade it now, for a boot-shop in Gawler and a beautiful girl. Well, almost.

It was hard to know what the truth was. Only good thing about that was that, if you didn't know when you were telling it, others'd have a bugger of a job finding out. So he could make whatever threats he wanted. To close Wattle Path, get out of film altogether, didn't matter. When you don't care any more, you're free. He felt that a lot, these days. Especially after glass number six. You could do and give up anything, after glass number six.

No, he'd save six till after Albury, when they were rattling along on Doyle's turf, and his startlingly expansive gauge. Then he could think about Coral again, and Donalda, and a life other men have led. And then there'd be seven. And he'd sink, as he always sank, under the rim of the world he knew, and he'd long for a world in which he would still be rich but everything else would be changed.

But in the morning, at ten, he'd be bloody sharp as a tack. That was what they didn't reckon on, these private school boys with their silver spoons, and these Sydney shysters with their yachts and their harbour views and their bloody five foot three gauges. He knew them, he knew the game, and he knew himself, pretty much.

Five could wait, too, for half an hour or so. He wasn't that desperate. That should impress Olive. Though it wasn't clear that it's any of her bloody affair. He'd keep his end of the contract, as long as she kept hers.

He'd keep them all. He'd keep Miss Kreitmayer, in the manner to which she'd become accustomed. He'd keep Lola, in the class the Old Girls had sentenced her to live in. And he'd keep little Frankie, in a world that he'd believe was going to come running when he whistled.

He could tell them about another world, a world they'd hardly recognise, it was so dark, so deep, so uncertain. But they wouldn't understand. They never would. No reason why anyone should, really.

Wodonga. Time to be out with the unopened bags into the sticky air of a stinking hot night. In Wodonga. O what a glamorous life it is. But in the morning, who knows? You might change the bloody world.

Chapter Seven

THE LEGACY

The final act of Frank Thring's life is almost as puzzling as the first, but for very different reasons. The riddle of his early life in Wentworth and beyond begins in a lack of information, in documents that lie and histories that are lost; it is compounded by the way Frank suppressed or fictionalised his story, and by the way he played the role of a man of mystery. Working out what he did and where he went in those first two decades is as reliant on inference as imagining what he might have been thinking and feeling.

There is no shortage of facts about his last years; we know exactly where he was, and what deals he was striking, for virtually all of that time. Frank Thring's life was a matter of public importance, carefully charted by the press, closely monitored by anxious rivals and dependants, and followed with interest by thousands of people he had never met, but for whom the Thring name had become as familiar as names like Hoyts or Williamson's, or even MGM The name was hardly ever out of the papers, even on those days when it appeared only under 'Entertainment' in the classifieds section. What is missing from the account of Frank's not-so-grand finale is precisely the element that, amid all the murkiness of his early career, was never in doubt for a moment: the goal, the over-arching motive, the master-plan.

Frank Thring had spent most of his first fifty years chasing wealth and power. Whatever his personal empire at the time, whether it was a boot-shop or a picture-show or a chain of luxury theatres or a film company that bore his name, his aim was to make it bigger. Expansion was an absolute virtue, and Frank gave no hint at any time of what for him might be, hypothetically, big enough. The agenda for Efftee, certainly, was about much more than unremitting acquisitiveness; it was a defiantly nationalist project, for a start, and while it could hardly be described as a philanthropic gesture there was a genuine conviction that it was for the public good. And all his initiatives had expressed a strong desire for creative fulfilment, even when the art was only the game of politics. There was nothing secret about any of these ambitions. They were expected of a man of substance, and Frank Thring declared them in everything he said and did.

There had been, of course, that odd six months of inertia just when Efftee's fortunes had appeared to be relentlessly on a roll, when not much had been happening at the studio at all. But Frank on his return at the end of May 1933 looked like a man determined to make up for lost time. The Efftee juggernaut was back, moving faster than ever before: moving to consolidate, with the purchase of a splendid new studio at Wattle Path, moving to diversify with the acquisition of the Garrick and then of the Princess and the theatre programs that culminated at the end of that year in the genuine triumph of *Collits' Inn*, and moving to enhance the fame of F.T. himself.

The public perception of Frank would have been of a man who knew just where he was heading. The flurries of activity, first in 'straight' theatre from overseas and then in relation to Australia's first major musical, were part of a strategy that served the interests of the company's cinema arm; providing raw material and sustained employment for Efftee's contracted actors, as Frank Thring had said, and providing also some insurance for him in his continuing wars over the quota issue. A man who seemed to shift his focus from screen to stage so seamlessly was in a good position to put pressure on the film establishment, on the basis that it needed Frank Thring more than he needed it. Anyone who had ever followed his brilliant career would have known that The Great Dexter had always had something up his sleeve. The fact there seemed to be a new Efftee project every week confirmed that the old operator was not only back in the game, but at the very top of his form.

A year later, when only one more film (*A Ticket in Tatts*, the last of the Efftee features to be shot at His Majesty's) had been made, the existence of a grand plan was much less clear. Two other films were in process at Wattle Path, *Clara Gibbings* and *The Streets of London*, but both were modest tales of Old England shot in stagy interiors, and a long way from the kind of thing that Efftee had defined as its core business.

On the theatrical front, the reasoning behind the Efftee program was similarly hard to follow. *Collits' Inn* and *The Cedar Tree* made perfect sense: they were Australian, they were original, and their stories and locations had plenty of screen potential. But the Delysia vehicles, A.P. Herbert's *Mother of Pearl* in July 1934 and *Her Past* in September, were the kind of fare that

J.C. Williamson had been providing for decades. With *Jolly Roger*, billed a 'naughtycal comic opera' fresh from London's Savoy, Frank Thring seemed to have moved about as far from his professed priority – the making of films by, for and about Australians – as it was possible to do. But there was further to travel still. The two seasons of *Peter Pan* for the Christmases of 1934 and 1935, and the three shows featuring George Wallace that played at the Princess with increasingly disastrous results during 1935 (*Crazy Nights Revue*, *S.S. Sunshine*, and *The Oojah Bird*), suggested that Efftee Attractions had become the kind of commercial production house that runs by the principle that nobody ever went broke by underestimating the taste of the audience. Lots of people have, of course, and its handful of stage shows in 1935 did nothing for Efftee apart from keeping its star attraction on the production line.

Wattle Path, which when its purchase was triumphantly announced in June 1933 had seemed the most tangible of statements that Efftee was not only flourishing but was here to stay, quickly became an expensive pawn in a very volatile game. The Efftee operation finally moved there just before Christmas, but the New Year had barely begun before Frank was talking about shutting it down for good unless the New South Wales Film Enquiry saw sense on the need for quotas:

> Production operations at Efftee studios, St Kilda, will be suspended next month. That announcement by F.W. Thring sent a breeze through the trade, and grew into a storm when it reached the public and the N.S.W. Film Enquiry.[248]

Frank argued that 'the insecurity created by the present Film Enquiry' made it impossible to continue, and helpfully calculated the cost in employment terms if he was forced to carry out his threat; seven films in a one year 'would support 10 families, at an average of £5 per week, who, in turn, would keep others in employment'. The ultimatum was clear. But 'next month' nothing happened; the report of the Commissioner had not been handed down, and Frank was busy lobbying the Victorian Chief Secretary Mr McFarlane for a five per cent quota in his own state. The Melbourne *Argus* reported on 28 March that the Chief Secretary was doubtful that Australian producers could fill even that modest quota, and had therefore rejected the proposal. That decided the matter; a fortnight

248 *Everyones*, 14 February 1934, p.5.

later, the *Argus* reported the closure of Wattle Path.[249] Frank Thring had done what nobody had thought he could afford or dare to do.

The quota wars were the occasion and, apparently, the immediate cause of all this cultivated instability. When Frank first made the threat to close the studio, it had barely opened for business; the move seemed transparently a bluff, and the fact that it had so little immediate effect suggests that other people thought they saw through it straight away. Wattle Path had involved a massive investment in real estate and equipment, and it would have seemed inconceivable that a businessman as canny as Frank Thring could so lightly throw it all away. That it wasn't just an idle threat became apparent two months later, when the removalists were summoned to take away all the stuff that they had deposited there some one hundred and fifty days before. Within the week, the Wattle Path Studio was back on the market. The only certainty in the situation was that nobody in Melbourne would be silly enough to think of buying it to make movies. After all, no-one in town had ever shown any inclination to do such a thing, other than the vendor.

When all the posturing was done and Wattle Path had begun its bright new era as the St Moritz Skating Palace, there was time to reflect on the nature of the games that had been played over the quota issue. The general view was that Frank Thring's noble, if possibly quixotic, enterprise had been stymied by petty bureaucrats; that was the view promulgated by *Everyones* magazine, and certainly by the man himself. Having been frustrated in one crusade he would transfer his boldness and his capital to live theatre, and then they'd be sorry. The story may have been more complicated than that, however. The power of Frank's threat to close Efftee rested on the premise that it was the last thing in the world that he wanted to do; paradoxically, the same assumption encouraged others to call his bluff. But what if getting out of Wattle Path, even getting out of film-making altogether, was something that at least part of him was quite keen to do? What if the intransigence of the politicians gave him a righteously indignant pretext for making a grand exit from a world for which he had lost his appetite?

Wattle Path had promised to be Efftee's crowning glory, but it made a quite meagre contribution to the output and reputation of the studio. During its tenancy at His Majesty's, the studio had made nine features and begun two others, and Chris Long's definitive filmography lists seventy-

249 *Argus*, 11 April 1934, p.3.

nine shorts from that period.[250] At Wattle Path, *Clara Gibbings* and *The Street of London*, and some interior scenes from the Charles Chauvel epic *Heritage* which rented the space, were all that there was to show.

That comparison appears to confirm the pernicious way in which his frustrations over winning quota concessions had slowed down a man who had always been in a hurry; however, the drop in production was not quite as sudden and dramatic as it might appear. Efftee Film Productions had been slowing down progressively for some time, long before Commissioner Marks and his Film Enquiry began its tortuous task. Efftee's peak period had been the fifteen months or so at His Majesty's between the first studio takes for *A Co-Respondent's Course* in mid-1931 and Frank Thring's departure for England in late September 1932; seven of the nine features that were shot there, and forty-seven of those sixty-nine shorts, were made at that time. Its activities dropped off sharply not only during his six-month absence, which was understandable enough, but also during the six months that followed, prior to its departure for Wattle Path. The latter period produced one film, half-a-dozen theatre seasons at the Garrick and the Princess, at least as many negotiations for projects that were never begun, and countless submissions on the subject of quotas.

The Efftee juggernaut was running out of steam. But almost certainly it didn't feel like that at the time, either to Frank, whose days probably seemed shorter and more crowded than they had ever been, or to the interested public, who would have assumed with a wink and a nudge that that Thring bloke was always up to something. After the disposal of Wattle Path in 1934, a small item in *Everyones* in September conceded the fact that, although Frank Thring was very busy, not much was actually happening, and reassured readers, under the headline 'When Efftee Starts Again', that this was only a temporary lull:

> Present quietude of Efftee productions is only the calm preceding a storm of activity. On the company's schedule for next year are "Collits' Inn", "Sheepmates" and "Desert Saga", with a couple of George Wallace comedies as well ... Efftee should be able to throw its weight about quite a lot.[251]

---

250 This includes ten shorts released under the 'Non-Stop Variety' label, which were compilations of assorted acts from the 'Efftee Entertainers' series re-packaged for the English market.

251 *Everyones*, 5 September 1934, p.11.

None of those projects came to fruition, and some of them were at best a gleam in an old showman's eye. But there were always schemes. There were schemes everywhere. They made it hard for anyone to imagine that Efftee Films might be dead, and that Frank Thring, who had set out to rewrite the story of Australian cinema, and who had shown every sign so far of doing so, might actually, crucially, have lost the plot.

All that energy could easily be mistaken for momentum. But there was something oddly desperate about all the acquisition and disposal of property, all the projects begun and abandoned. It was not unusual for Frank Thring to behave unpredictably; that was a habit that had always worked well for him in the past, in establishing that he was a man who moved in mysterious ways. But his behaviour after he came home from England was increasingly, often inexplicably, erratic.

The rolling of the dice in relation to Wattle Path is the most obvious instance. It looked like a clever ploy at the start, the kind of brinkmanship that a powerful man might engage in when he is confident of out-staring his opponent. But it was never likely to win the game in which it was produced. As it happened, Commissioner Marks came to a conclusion very close to the one that Frank had been arguing for, but it had nothing to do with coercion from south of the border.

In July 1934, Marks finally handed down his report, recommending a five-year quota for Australian pictures in all programs, commencing with a requirement of four per cent for exhibitors and five per cent for distributors; he also urged uniformity of quota legislation in all states, which offered some hope of breaking the deadlock in Frank's negotiations with Victoria's sceptical Chief Secretary. By the end of the year the New South Wales quota was enshrined in law. It was a remarkable irony. The attempt to pressure Marks into supporting Frank's demands achieved nothing, other than further retarding a cumbersome process. And by the time Marks came to the conclusion he wanted, Frank Thring had no studio to make films in.

There were further ironies to come. When the bill was put before the New South Wales parliament in October, Frank again started issuing ultimatums to the Victorian government, declaring that he would move Efftee to Sydney unless it followed suit;[252] when the bill was belatedly passed in April of the following year, Frank repeated the threat.[253] It was ineffective on both occasions, partly because he had played the identical card before, and partly because with the sale of Wattle Path he had already thrown in his trump. By that point, it was no longer evident what Frank was putting on the table – or what he imagined he might do if the gambit was successful.

The whole affair came to look less and less like the actions of a hard-nosed businessman who refuses to compromise, and more and more like those of a boy who, when the game seems to be running against him, grabs his bat and heads for home. It was a dimension of the wholly personal power that he was accustomed to wielding, of course, and of his history of getting his own way. A company run by a benevolent despot has all sorts of advantages, but when the boss starts to govern recklessly, and decisions are determined by whim or pique, the company is unlikely to last very long. There was no Board of Directors to run the business at Efftee, such as Stuart Doyle had at Cinesound; there was no-one, really, except occasionally Lola or Olive, with whom Frank could discuss policies and tactics, and no-one who could tell him when he was behaving impulsively or stupidly. He had never needed such a person before, but he certainly could have done with one now.

Frank had always presented himself as a man in control of his emotions. His passion for the schemes he devised was always there, of course; there were much less troublesome ways of making a fortune if wealth and power in themselves had been all that mattered to him. But it had been kept in check, behind a mask of shrewdness and solidity. Frank had always been a maverick in conservative clothing; his pragmatism and his self-containment ensured that people rarely saw the vulnerability of the man beneath.

They were seeing it, if they cared to look without preconceptions, more and more in the period following that strangely protracted visit to London. That excursion in itself, and the way in which at least one of Efftee's beautiful girls seemed to have derailed his hitherto well-organised life, was one of the signs that something had shifted. Far from hiding his feelings, Frank Thring was living on the edge of them, and that came increasingly to affect the way he did business, as well as the way he lived.

The other indication that some carefully constructed walls were crumbling was his drinking. Frank had always been fond of a glass, and a lot of his cleverest deals had been driven through over leisurely meals in golf clubs, gentlemen's

---

252 *Argus*, 14 November 1934, p.7.
253 *Argus*, 1 May 1935, p.5.

clubs, and whatever places rich men decided to call their office. That was how the world was run, and before he went to London nobody had found anything particularly unusual or excessive in Frank's way of doing things.

After he came back to Melbourne, though, it was quickly a problem. The lunches were longer, and everyone noticed. Bert Nicholas, as the most junior member of the crew, was given the job that nobody wanted – bringing back the boss:

> G.S: On the subject of his drinking, was he – I don't know whether you know this, but was he drinking because he was ill?
>
> B.N.: Oh no, he was a good whisky drinker, oh yes. Because he – again, of course, he was the big business man, he was the Managing Director, he was this and – he was producing, he was directing. So that we might be stuck, we were going to knock off one o'clock, back two o'clock, he wasn't there ... [S]ometimes I was the poor mug. And Arthur would say, "Go on, Bert, up to the Occidental and see what's happened", and I'd be pushed off to the Occidental Hotel, this is half past two, three o'clock, everyone's sitting around waiting, and of course we had fellows like Frank Harvey and Campbell Copelin, he was a bit of ratbag, even George Wallace, George'd say, "What's happening?" you know, "Bert, come on." I was the poor assistant![254]

There were some advantages, after all, in the fact that Efftee was doing less and less. Not only did it mean that Frank's lunches could last longer, but Bert and the rest of the company were spared the embarrassment of dealing with them.

But the problem grew, as these things are inclined to do. In early 1934, while Commissioner Marks was pondering what to do about Frank Thring's latest histrionics, the Efftee crew set out for the interior, for location work in the Flinders Ranges on *Sheepmates*, the adaptation of William Hatfield's novel. They were to film several of the broad-horizon action sequences, but most of the shooting was devoted to building a bank of images of that extraordinary desert landscape to be drawn on as the plot allowed. It was inhospitable country, especially for a group of men who were used to making their living indoors, were encumbered by a mass of machinery, and had no idea of what to expect of the outback.

254 Bert Nicholas interview.

The expedition was an all-male affair, as indeed was the film. Its advance publicity made that a strong selling-point. Under the odd but certainly attention-grabbing headline, 'Sheepmates, Sexless Drama of Outback, Heads Efftee's Production Programme', the Melbourne *Sun* made it clear what was most definitely not going to be happening on location:

> Sheepmates is a notable experiment in Australian film making. There is no sex interest in the story, and not one woman character in the cast.[255]

Frank Thring was again the notional director of the film, but there was no expectation, let alone any need, for him to be a member of the party. However, he insisted on coming, in his luxury Packard. Ernest the chauffeur was mercifully relieved of his usual driving duties, and his employer took the wheel. And so the convoy headed out for the middle of the wide, brown land – three trucks and a couple of trailers, crammed with a dozen men and a heap of equipment, trailing a limousine driven by a man in a three-piece suit.

The trip was an unmitigated disaster. This was partly a consequence of the naivety and poor preparation of all concerned, but it was also in large measure due to the seeming disintegration of Frank Thring's life. No-one knew what was troubling him, but for Bert Nicholas it seemed like a kind of madness, and it turned a difficult trip into a journey into hell. There was a desperation about 'Daddy Thring' for a start, a disregard for danger that bordered on self-destructiveness:

> When he came to a fence of course he'd go, fences never worried him, and he'd take the bush, trees – oh, you've got no idea – in the big Packard, and I'd roar up behind him, and open the gate and get out of the road and go through and shut the gate and chase him again. Of course we eventually found him in the creek bed …

This, of course, was why he had been determined to come: the chance to get away from it all, and especially from his wife and family, and to indulge in living dangerously with a bunch of blokes in the desert. His carelessness about his life and general welfare extended to his approaches to matters like meals, where all that Frank seemed to have on his menu was whisky:

255 *Sun*, 15 July 1933, p.29.

> We'd stop for lunch, he wouldn't have anything to eat. Because I had some stuff, but he said, "No," so he had a drink and he said, "No, I'll go on," and we found him in another creek bed, and we limped into Broken Hill and he'd smashed all the lamps on one side and the car was, oh ...

Bert thought the way his boss was hitting the bottle was 'pathetic', but there was nothing anyone could do about it, other than some judicious damage control. The climax of the adventure occurred when Frank headed off in his Packard with the cook from the pub at Narrilgo. He was adamant that he would carry all the food. This looked like a very bad idea, but nobody argued with Frank Thring when he was adamant. Almost immediately the battered Packard disappeared into the tracts of sand, leaving the crew with nothing to eat and no idea where he had gone. Night fell, and fortuitously Bert and Arthur Higgins spotted a flare against the dark sky; 'I said, bloody Thring, he must have struck camp that way'. In the morning they set out to look for him, and found the car, bogged in the sand. But there was no sign of the men who had travelled in it.

> It was hot, damn hot, believe me ... I got the Ford, and said, "Right, I'll take that up, he must be out that direction further," Arthur and a couple of others with me, and away we went looking for him. We'd gone about three mile when we found him – the two of them walking. Thring was a big man, we eventually found out they'd walked five mile in the heat. They were exhausted ... he'd just about had it, as for this other bloody fool [the cook], he'd taken them right past the camp ... What happened to the car, they'd lost themselves ... backed down a hill ... and backed into a bloody tree stump. They didn't have their axe with them, and when they went to start the car it wouldn't bloody well start because he'd [the cook] put the case on top of the battery and a bit of wire had got across the back and shorted the bloody battery. Well of course, if you can imagine, Daddy Thring can't start the bloody car ... old Daddy Thring could've cut his bloody throat, he said we've got all the food ... he said, "I realised you had no bloody food and therefore we had to get back to somebody, you know," and he said "We couldn't just sit there, we had to go and walk ... "

It was nearly the curtain to Frank's final act. The impression left by Bert Nicholas' horror story is that Frank might not have cared if it had been.

Suddenly, Frank Thring had become a danger to himself and to others. London, as Frank Thring Junior would have good reason to say a quarter of a century later, had a lot to answer for. But whatever had happened there, and whatever hazardous thoughts were swirling about his brain in consequence, there were soon plenty of good reasons at home for a man to feel at the end of his tether.

The permutations of the quota debate obviously provided one of them, whether they are seen as symptom, cause or consequence of the unravelling of Frank's state of mind. He had been trying to make some inroads into the walls of complacency on that issue from the inception of Efftee, but they seemed to be made of rubber. It didn't help that Stuart Doyle, with his seemingly impregnable Sydney power-base, was fighting on the other side; while Cinesound was now in the business of making Australian films, riding the wave that Efftee had created, its intimate connection with Greater Union and all the associated networks of distribution and exhibition meant that it was doing quite nicely, thank you. Cinesound had nothing particularly to gain from a quota, but for its competitors, as Frank Thring often argued, it was the one hope of long-term survival. Efftee was a one-man operation fed by one man's private capital; there were excellent reasons why its rivals might seize any chance to exploit that obvious vulnerability.

It especially didn't help that Hoyts, with whom Frank thought he had a rock-solid agreement dating back to his spectacular deal with Fox in 1930, had cemented its own connections with Greater Union. Hoyts hadn't quite reneged on a contract, but they had found a way to honour it in the most perfunctory, even mischievous, way. Frank's first bit of sabre-rattling about the closure of Wattle Path drew an outraged response from Charles Munro, Hoyts' Managing Director, who 'countered hotly that houses were always ready to release Efftee films'[256] – but it was a question of which houses. When *A Ticket in Tatts* could only find a home for its premiere on 6 January 1934 at a suburban theatre in Fairfield rather than at one of the city venues that had presented all of the other Efftee films, it was clear that a number of forces were conspiring to destroy it, by slow strangulation.

It was an insult as well as a form of sabotage, and when Frank caught the train a few days later to make his representations to Commissioner Marks, he must still have been seething at the ignominy and injustice of it all.

256 *Everyones*, 14 February 1934, p.5.

Throughout his career he had been quite comfortable with being a solo act, but now, all of a sudden, he was more than usually friendless. When Efftee had begun, it seemed that Frank Thring had friends at court everywhere. By 1934, they were remarkably hard to find. It was no wonder that he behaved so petulantly at and around the Enquiry. The combination of impotence with outrage produced plenty of sound and fury, but it was never likely to beget justice, change, or a brave new world.

The success of *Collits' Inn* was a brilliantly bright spot in the Efftee landscape, of course. It had appeared so suddenly, so improbably, from the periphery of all his plans. But it, too, created its own problems. The Melbourne season had been an unqualified hit, and the Sydney one had survived its venture into shark-infested waters. Filming it, though, was another matter. Musicals were big-cast affairs, and the sound had to be very good – better than it had been on Efftee's first tentative steps into that world in *His Royal Highness*. And stars like George Wallace, Gladys Moncrieff and Robert Chisholm were expensive. The budget would make Efftee's costliest film so far, *The Sentimental Bloke*, look about the size of *Clara Gibbings* and *The Streets of London*, the two humble offerings made at Wattle Path while its owner had his mind on bigger things.

Moreover, the successors to *Collits' Inn* had been disappointing. If this was Frank Thring's new career, and Efftee's new *raison d'etre*, it looked and must have felt like a step on to a much smaller stage. Becoming a provincial Antipodean version of the West End impresario C.B. Cochran had never been part of Frank's scenario for his life, but suddenly destiny seemed to be driving him in that direction. He had always acted in the past as though he expected to drive it.

And finally there were those two modest films made at Wattle Path in 1934. Frank's disengagement from them was palpable. Nominally he directed both, but in practice Frank Harvey, who is credited as Associate Director and adaptor of Aimee and Philip Stuart's stage play on *Clara Gibbings*, and who played the lead in Dion Boucicault's period melodrama *The Streets of London*, literally called the shots. Frank Thring, preoccupied with his plays and his politicking, and possibly with the meaning of his life, was on the set only some of the time, mostly unpredictably.

Clara Gibbings is clearly the better film of the two, and Frank, who thought the English musical comedy star Dorothy Brunton far too old for the leading role, was too quickly dismissive of it. It is a measure of how little he had to do with it that he found fault with its casting, of course; previously, on any project that carried his name, he not only attended all auditions but exercised the decisive vote. Dorothy Brunton was certainly in her mid-forties, but with a good deal of help from Arthur Higgins' sympathetic camera angles and innovative soft gauze screen, she makes a perfectly passable young woman with marriage on her mind. Campbell Copelin, as wickedly devil-may-care as ever, is a completely convincing object for her affections, in the role of Elliot Carr, cricketer, gentleman and bon vivant. When Clara, a no-nonsense barmaid, finds that she is miraculously an heiress, she is able to pursue her infatuation with him. But Elliot has a lot to learn from her salt-of-the-earth integrity before they can be together, as it seems at the end they will; to seal his love for her, and his disdain for wealth and the entire English class-system, Elliot books two tickets on a ship to Australia, and we are to assume that this will probably make everything all right in the end. It's a pleasant if fairly fatuous social comedy, and its preoccupation with the niceties of class defines it as thoroughly English, removed from anything to do with Australia and Australians by much more than a long sea voyage. But it's stylishly done, even if any opportunity for a glimpse of a wider world (a cricket match, or a journey, or anything at all without a roof) is resolutely resisted, as the sets and the blocking from its production at the Garrick the year before are faithfully replicated. *Clara Gibbings* looks like a run-of-the-mill British B-picture, and that is at once a badge of proficiency and a mark of its remoteness from everything that Efftee stood for.

The Streets of London makes no secret of its theatrical origins; indeed, it makes the notion of public performance a frame, by periodically recalling us to the sounds and silhouettes of a live audience. The cinema audience was warmly invited to boo, hiss and cheer with the one that they were watching while it watched. Thring (ostensibly), via Harvey, is playing with the conventions of the melodrama, and the fact that the film makes no attempt to disguise them allows and legitimises its almost unmediated translation from stage to screen. But it is still hard to avoid, let alone answer, the question that must surely have struck Frank Thring as he watched its rushes: why was it made?

That question would have recurred more insistently when *The Streets of London* was offered for general release. Nobody took it up. More gallingly still, it was assessed as having failed to meet the 'quality' standards required by the new quota legislation. Of all the ironies in Frank Thring's last year as a film-maker, that must have been the most bitter. The final Efftee offering, denied release by the laws he had fought so hard to get; the final Efftee offering, vindicating so completely the Victorian Chief

Secretary's cautious philistinism. Mr McFarlane had dared to doubt whether Australian film-makers could make enough good films to meet a quota. Now Frank Thring, who had treated his reservations with the contempt that they deserved, had produced the first film to fall short of the standard – the first film to be deemed unworthy even of being seen by the public. Frank could attribute that decision to all kinds of political malice and skulduggery, and almost certainly did. But the fact of its rejection remained, a public embarrassment and a personal affront, and the most inglorious of swan-songs for Efftee – not to mention for F.T. himself.

Making films had ceased to be much fun for Frank, and not just because of uninspiring scripts and the difficulties of distribution. Shooting the first of them, *A Co-Respondent's Course*, had been a kind of picnic, where the Efftee team had sallied forth to Portsea in a version of the family outing; the back seat of Olive's green Marmion was dragged out to accommodate Alan Mill's barely portable sound-desk, while Frank's blue Packard was heavily loaded with beer for the end of the day. The equipment was state-of-the-art, but the tone of proceedings was all cheerful amateurism.

The two Wattle Path films were all interiors, and the shoot could never have been mistaken for a party. Frank as director was somewhat superfluous to requirements in a room filled with old hands like Frank Harvey, Dorothy Brunton, Harold Meade and even the scapegrace Campbell Copelin; none of them would have been made anxious by the ominous sound of whistling. The young people who had been learning on the job in the early Efftee projects, especially the delightful young girls like Donalda Warne, were nowhere to be seen on the sets of *Clara Gibbings* and *The Streets of London*. A lot of the joy had left with them.

The experienced hands came with strong opinions, which could be irritating enough. But they also came with baggage. Part of Campbell Copelin's attraction on screen, apart from perfect features and a sense that he really couldn't believe that he was being paid just to look seductive, was a self-destructiveness that could be terrifying. Thelma Scott had been warned about it; when she and Copelin rehearsed their tender scene riding side-by-side by a river in *A Ticket in Tatts*, she hadn't been surprised, though she had been very scared, by the fact that he tried to shepherd her into the water, just for the hell of it. [257] When Campbell decided that he would like to fly, it was time for everyone to run for cover:

> Noted for his many somewhat risky escapades, Campbell Copelin … suddenly decided to see the opening of the Sydney harbour Bridge … Copelin removed (unauthorised) an Aero Club Moth plane VH-UKM from the club's hangars, Essendon, Victoria, and a few minutes later the machine was a tangled wreck on the Sandridge Golf Links, Port Melbourne, with the unfortunate pilot in bad shape.[258]

Frank was finding that living with actors every day, though it might look wonderfully unpredictable, could also be tediously difficult.

Frank's growing disaffection can be measured partly by what he no longer bothered to do for his films. It was not just the active directing; he had never had many illusions about his talents in that area, and had prudently surrounded himself with people who knew more than he did. It was also in marketing the movies, which was something upon which he had always prided himself.

When Frank had gone to England with reels of *His Royal Highness*, he took with him pages filled with ingenious advertising gimmicks. It might well have been the world's first promotional pack. The ideas were offered to independent proprietors as well as to the owners of cinema chains, and all of them were unmistakably his own. The boot-making rhymester of Gawler, the man who conceived the great limerick competition in Zeehan, the quirky creator of hundreds of novelties, games and outrageous puff pieces, was doing again what he most liked to do. So there are odd bits of trivia that might appeal to the local press – like the claim that Efftee had built 'the largest table in Australia' for George to skate on, or the fact that Frank Tarrant's father had been a fine cricketer for Middlesex. There are suggestions for contests, like The Town's Gloomiest Man (nominate your grumpy neighbour for tickets to the show that will bring a smile to his face) and Your Happiest Moment (describe it in a hundred words or less and you might win another one). There are novelty give-aways, like George Wallace masks or safety pins with message attached ('KEEP THIS PIN FOR SAFETY when you see GEORGE WALLACE in 'HIS

257 Thelma Scott interview.
258 'Actor's Unfortunate Accident', *Film Weekly*, 24 March 1932, p.14.

ROYAL HIGHNESS' An Efftee Films Production'). There are suggested formats for advertising links with local tradespeople – grocers, tailors, pastrycooks, and even dentists ('Laugh in comfort when you see George Wallace in 'His Royal Highness' by getting your teeth from [insert name of dentist]').[259]

It was clearly a humorous labour of love, and indicative of an investment in the film that was much more than financial. After his return from London, though, Frank took no more initiatives of this kind. The game had changed in a number of ways, but one of them was that Efftee was clearly no longer a game. Though Wattle Path was gone, there were still, periodically over the next couple of years, schemes for films that might yet be made: *Collits' Inn* was on the drawing-board for more than two years, and thirty-five minutes of its soundtrack was recorded; *Sheepmates* was still around, though Frank's dissatisfaction with the footage that he had seen – and possibly some residual embarrassment – had persuaded him to shelve the project; and a fourth George Wallace vehicle, *A-Sweepin' the Deep*, was not only scripted but widely publicised.[260] He commissioned Noel Monkman to prepare a screenplay based on his book *Typhoon Treasure*, and secured the rights to Rolf Boldrewood's *Robbery Under Arms* with a view to developing a stage musical (to be written by Frank Harvey and Dudley Glass) that would have a subsequent life on screen. It was clear that, at least some of the time, Frank still had hopes for Efftee, with or without a studio and a permanent company.

But a lot of his other choices raised doubts about where the company was heading, and whether its owner had any better idea than anyone else as to where that might be.

Frank still had the Princess, in which he had planned first to develop scripts and actors with feature-film potential, and then changed his priorities to large-scale commercial stage productions. In 1935 he gave it two new identities, as the home for radio station 3XY, which began broadcasting on September 8, and as the proposed venue for regular programs of film; after dabbling in most conceivable kinds of performance-making, he was about to turn the clock back, it seemed, and resume life as a film-exhibitor. How this was to happen, given the virtual monopoly exercised by his old enemies at Greater Union and his more recent ones at

259 Thring Papers, National Film and Sound Archive, folder 38 (*His Royal Highness*).

260 A report in *Everyones*, 13 February 1935, stated that shooting would begin in just six weeks.

Hoyts, was anybody's guess.[261] Perhaps Frank was just hoping to ruffle a few feathers; the new policy was never implemented, so we can never know the truth.

At the same time, he declared his intention of making good his threat to move the Efftee operation to Sydney. In February 1936, that plan gained some substance, with the announcement that Frank Thring and Noel Monkman were about to open a new partnership in film production, and that Thring had accepted the position of chairman of directors at Mastercraft Film Corporation.[262] It looked like a move away from the creative side of things, and back to the world of business chicanery where most people felt he belonged. Frank, though, insisted that running Mastercraft was no obstacle to making films for Efftee:

> Apart from his interest in Mastercraft, Mr Thring, as head of the Efftee organisation, will personally produce two independent productions each year, using the Mastercraft studios.
>
> The first will probably be 'Collit's [sic] Inn', with 'Shipmates' optional. He has decided that all scripts should go to Hollywood for final treatment. Three are already there, and two are on the water on the way back to Australia.[263]

How far the new arrangement promised a genuine resuscitation of Efftee Films at Mastercraft's new studios at Lane Cove, how any such initiative might be reconciled with the continuation of Efftee Attractions, Thring's new radio station, and the new seasons of Hollywood features at the Princess, was not clear. Nor was it clear where the new chairman of directors was to reside. Was this to be Frank Thring's farewell to Melbourne, and, if so, who was to run his diverse interests there? If it was to be Tom Holt, the likeliest candidate, what did that mean for the administrative structure of the new film studio that was promising to take the fight to Doyle on his own turf?

---

261 The plan was outlined in *Everyones*, 10 July 1935, which anticipated unspecified 'deals with US distributors' (p.21).

262 *Everyones*, 12 February 1936, p.3. The new company was presumably formed with the immediate purpose of producing *Typhoon Treasure*, whatever might have been envisaged thereafter. Mastercraft Film Corporation had been founded by Raymond Longford in October 1934, in anticipation of the successful passing of the New South Wales Quota Bill.

263 *Everyones*, 12 February 1936, p.8.

That was one set of questions prompted by Frank's sudden attraction to the joys of the Harbour City, and they kept the tongues wagging in the film industry through the early months of 1936. There was another set, though, at least as intriguing, that no-one was asking in public. Frank had always prided himself on being hard to predict and impossible to read in his business dealings, but suddenly the entire structure of his life seemed up for grabs. If he was living and filming in Sydney, what were the implications for his family?

Olive had spent all her life in Melbourne, apart from cruises to foreign parts with her father or her husband. She was at the centre of a number of lively sherry circles; there were friends, and fetes, and charity groups to consider. It was hardly conceivable that Olive would leave Rylands, let alone Melbourne, to live among strangers in a city that she'd barely seen. There was little Frankie, nine-years-old now and enrolled with boys from suitably good families at Wadhurst, the preparatory school for Melbourne Grammar. And then there was Lola. At twenty-four she was old enough to fend for herself most of the time, but she was still unmarried with no immediate prospects; her only paid employment so far had been as editor of her father's films. Were they all to follow him to Sydney? Did Frank think about what his latest scheme might mean for any of them? Did he bother to discuss it with any of them before he signed the contract with Mastercraft, and fired off his latest press release to *Everyones*? Those conundrums are all variants, really, on the two questions that are prompted by every move he made after coming back from London in 1934. What was he thinking, and what did he really want?

Frank's early death left most of those issues unresolved. The rhythms of his life suggested that being on his own was a kind of pleasure in itself, and that his need to be away from his wife and children (for business reasons, naturally) was something that they all understood. Whether anything had changed substantially is anyone's guess. There were signs, of course, in his solitary eight months in 1932–3; while most of Australia seemed to be preoccupied with Bradman's attempts to cope with Bodyline, Frank was in London, trying to find out how much of the rest of his life was set in stone. There were other signs in his journey into the interior, or possibly the heart of darkness, in the Flinders Ranges.

But when Frank organised his trip to London in March 1936, he included his wife and his son and heir in the plan. Perhaps he thought he owed it to Olive after the last time; certainly, she would have thought he did. Perhaps he thought it important for his son. The only other time little

Frank had been overseas he was barely more than a bundle, and he was old enough now to appreciate the experience: not the European experience, of course, which had been so important to Lola, but the Hollywood experience, which any kid could understand. It was to be a shorter stay, too, just five weeks or so – the shortest he had ever made to the other hemisphere. There was only so long you could stay in Los Angeles, after all, before you became hysterical or one of its longer-term residents; but the schedule was also a tacit acknowledgement that his previous absence from home had been longer than anyone could satisfactorily explain. It suited them all, anyway. Olive would not miss too many meetings and cocktail parties, and young Frank, who seemed to need a lot of amusing, surely couldn't become too bored in that time.

What it meant, both personally and professionally, was, as Frank would always have wanted it to be, too deep and devious to be known. The intricacies of his dealings with Olive were long established; he would keep her in the manner to which she had become accustomed, and she would rule his home and entertain his guests in style. His behaviour suggests that there was nothing about his feelings for her that could ever be compelling enough to influence the grand plans for Efftee, and that was something that she seems to have understood completely. Whether he would wake up at her side on any given morning may well have been, by now at least, a matter of indifference to them both.

His son was another matter. It had always been easiest, in the end, to see little Frankie as Olive's boy. It was obviously liberating, in some ways. It allowed him to leave all the arrangements about his son to her, in the absolute certainty that she loved him; it freed him to concentrate on defending the right of his daughter to be in their lives, in the absolute certainty that Olive could never love her. And so he had been rather a distant father to his son, as men of his wealth and importance mostly were, and were expected to be. Nobody questioned it; privileged boys were brought up by women – mothers, nurses, nannies. It was the way that people of a certain class were expected to grow up. A man like Frank was the last person to question it, when so many people believed in it, and it suited him so well.

Two things, though, were clear. Young Frank Thring was a very different boy at nine years old in Toorak than his father had been at that age in Wentworth (or elsewhere), and that was – almost certainly – a good thing. Privilege was preferable to deprivation. But Frank Thring junior's knowledge of his father was quite possibly as slight as Frank Thring senior's had been of William, or Frank, or whatever he chose to call himself depending on where he was. The death of Frank's own father in 1920 had appeared to be much more symbolically important to him than it had any right to be; hence the arrangement about the dual funeral plot. He had done that in acknowledgement that it was all too late, and that there was nothing to be done to retrieve a kind of closeness. In 1936, he had a chance to take his son into the more glamorous end of the world he lived in, and he had to take it. That meant, of course, that Olive would have to come, too. But perhaps he felt that he owed her at least that for all he had done, and had failed to do.

Frank had tried, in the months before they left, to make some other reparations. A couple of years earlier, while they were filming *The Sentimental Bloke*, he had helped out C.J. Dennis with what amounted to a donation to genius. Dennis had been having difficulties meeting the costs of maintaining 'Arden', the property he and his wife owned at Toolangi, thirty miles north-east of Melbourne; until the appearance of Efftee, he had rarely known the pleasure of a regular salary. Frank was attracted by the notion of a rural retreat, for the rest of his family at least. Almost every other resident of Toorak seemed to own a holiday house. So he offered to take over the payments. Frank acquired the leasehold, on the basis that Dennis and his wife could come and go (or, in her case, stay) as they pleased, provided that the Thrings could spend a few weeks there, on the rare occasions that weeks were available. The Thring family went there every winter – at least the Olive/Lola/Frank junior end of it; Olive's niece Minty Lalanne remembered playing there very happily, some ten years later, so the arrangement developed the non-negotiability of a tradition.

Frank himself was not often of the party, but he saw enough to know that he liked it, at least in small doses. Arden offered serenity, and rare photographs of a happy family for the album. They spent a week or so there in January 1936, all four of them together. How they managed the unusual proximity, how spontaneous were those smiles for the camera, none of the four is still around to tell us. But there is no doubt about the symbolic importance of the occasion. The patriarchal figure trying hard to relax in an open-necked shirt certainly knew it; and he knew the things he had done and not done, the things he had thought and perhaps still did, for which he wanted to make some recompense.

Those were the kinds of thought that must have been running through Frank's head as he contemplated yet another voyage. There were plenty of other things on the agenda: reciprocal casting and distribution deals for a possible revival of Efftee Films, irresistible inducements to American studios to bypass the Doyle axis and provide product for the Princess, negotiations about shares in *Typhoon Treasure*, and possibly *Collits' Inn*. More than enough to keep him busy while Frankie star-gazed and Olive shopped. So many things to begin.

They left on Wednesday March 4, and came back on Thursday June 17. It proved a very eventful couple of months.

The trip was successful, in most of the measurable ways. Frank came back with something like the quid pro quo he had been seeking: American leads in Australian films in exchange for guaranteed opportunities for Australian actors in Hollywood, and reciprocal understandings about exhibition; a genuine interest (in-principle only at this stage, of course) in the Monkman film, and even in *Collits' Inn*; and the promise of a continued conversation with contacts old and new.

There was no sign of a firm distribution agreement to support the hypothetical programs of movies at the Princess, but in the end that was probably a primarily mischievous objective, and might already have fulfilled its function in the consternation it had caused. There was no sign either of the two unnamed Americans (one director, one star) whom he had undertaken to bring back with him, in order to start work on the first project at Mastercraft.[264] He had in mind a kind of production line, which would involve him in regular commuting across the Pacific:

> For the first year Mr Thring plans to engage three stars and three directors. One of each of them will come back with him, finish their jobs and return, so that the next unit arrives here immediately after the first unit has finished. This will eliminate waste of time as well as the heavy cost of having more than one American star and director here at the same time ... Mr Thring figures that the three weeks' journey from Hollywood to Sydney will give the star and director a chance

264 'Mr. Thring's Plans. Help from Hollywood', *Sydney Morning Herald*, 29 February 1936, p.8. Frank had foreshadowed in that article a schedule of six films for the coming year, each involving a different director and star.

> to familiarise themselves with the story, and thus be in a position to commence work immediately upon arrival here.[265]

But though he might not have had the people to start 'immediately', he did come back with agreements about an American distribution of the films shot in Australia with their Hollywood marquee-names, and on the principle of creative exchange. It was an encouraging new beginning, and just might have put the Australian film industry on a firmer foundation than it had ever had before.

Frank came back with oesophagal cancer, too. It had begun as a sore throat soon after their arrival in San Francisco. But perhaps it had begun much earlier than that, and Frank, as a busy man, had not had time to notice. The American doctors ran their customary tests, and suddenly Frank's illness was no longer an annoying glitch in the itinerary. It was a death sentence.

Frank Thring was fifty-three. It felt, as of course it was, unnecessarily young. And it was, as it is so often, desperately unfair. Frank woke up one morning believing himself to be in the third act of his story, and found himself by that evening in the fifth. He was still considering whether he was married to the right woman, still making up for the years apart from his daughter, just beginning to sort out his responsibilities to his son. He still believed that his best days lay before him.

He had a few weeks, in the end, to distinguish between reality and fantasy, the present and the possibility. His wife and his son were watching, which must have made it even harder.

Frank junior enjoyed it all enormously, right up until the departure for Melbourne.[266] Hollywood turned out to be just like the movies, and a great place to have a tenth birthday party; any boy his age, especially a very spoilt and often obnoxious one, was likely to complain when it was time to come home. But what made it worse were the two things that spoiled the whole return voyage on the *Mariposa*: his father's inexplicable illness and awful appearance, which not only cast a pall over everything but meant that his mother, for the first time in his life, was preoccupied with something other than her son's happiness; and his own accident, a few days out of San Francisco, when he had fallen down the stairs and broken his left arm. He would have registered the great unfairness that his father's problem seemed to be taken more seriously than his own.

---

265 *Everyones*, 4 March 1936, p.5.

266 Frank's recollections, fifty-six years later, are quoted in the following chapter.

Moreover, as they neared Melbourne, Olive told him that he would be expected to represent his father when they docked at Station Pier, greeting any welcoming dignitaries and answering questions from the press. Young Frank was a very precocious child, but it is unlikely that he thought it a particularly good idea, or that he responded very sweetly when it was first put to him.

Still, he was his father's son. Playing the role you had to play, irrespective of your feelings, was second nature, though there was probably quite a lot of nurture in it as well. So, when the photographer asked him to pose for a hearty handshake, there he is, costumed in his Wadhurst cap and blazer, smiling dutifully while his right hand does what it is still fortunately able to do:

> The top picture shows Frank Thring, son of 3XY's Managing Director, shaking hands with Stan Thomas, Publicity Officer, while Roy Steyne, Production Manager, looks on. Mr Thring unfortunately contracted a severe illness in America and had to go straight from the boat to hospital. Frank himself had his troubles, suffering a broken arm.[267]

Frank senior was whisked away to the Epworth Hospital in an ambulance, with Olive, of course, by his side. He was transferred then to St Andrew's Hospital in Lansdowne Place, East Melbourne. A fortnight later, he was dead.

Frank Thring left a lot of unfinished business, only some of it to do with the ideas about film and theatre that drove his life. The obituaries were fulsome. He would have wished that some of the space had been granted to him while he was still around to make the most of it.

Everyones, under the headline 'A BRILLIANT LEADER PASSES', was the best of the eulogies. Given that Frank had written most of its articles about him, there was a certain fitness in that:

267 *Radio Times Radioprogram*, 24 June 1936, p.4.

> The late Mr Thring was a pioneer exuding the true spirit of great leadership; big in stature and in outlook, his was the lot to guide the destinies of many sections during a long and brilliant career
>
> On the scroll of Australian film history the name of Thring will be forever indited. He made money and enjoyed the sweetest fruits of success, but not without learning to take defeat and suffer the bitterness which is the lot of the trail-beater. Unselfishly, he fought the clean fight, and while others would have given up many times he never lost sight of the goal ahead.[268]

Even Frank would have blushed a little at 'fought the clean fight'. But people rarely spoke ill of the dead, or told the truth about them.

A lot of things died with him. Some would say that one of them was a sustainable film industry in Australia. Some would say that a certain way of thinking about that grand delusion – a slightly crazy, but probably brilliant way, a way so uncompromising that it probably never had any hope of success – went, too. Others might focus on the delusion itself, in which case Frank's premature death was the one sure thing in a narrative that hinged on eventual failure – like those other heroic Australian losers, Les Darcy and Phar Lap, his moments of triumph only had enduring meaning because they were so brief.

The scheme for six films a year at Mastercraft died with Frank. So did the uncompleted business left over from Efftee, *Sheepmates* and *Collits' Inn*, Australia's first major movie musical. So did the theatre seasons at the Princess that he'd begun, and the showings of feature-films there that he had threatened to introduce. So did the plans for taking *Collits' Inn* the stage musical to London; he had begun those negotiations with C.B. Cochran in the course of securing the incomparable Delysia for Melbourne, and George Wallace had understood the talks to have come so far that he had his suitcase ready:

> We were all ready to go to London. For Cochran. Gladdy Moncrieff, meself, and some of the others. And we'd sold practically everything. But Mr Thring … he got very ill. So we just – stayed in Australia.[269]

A lot of people's lives were changed when Frank's so unexpectedly ended.

268 *Everyones*, 1 July 1936, p.3.
269 George Wallace, recorded reminiscences, *The George Wallace Story*.

And what of the effect of his death on the three people who might have been thought closest to him? What people do when a husband or a father dies might not have much to do with the strength of their feelings, of course. Olive, for instance, was never going to play the role of the grieving widow for long. She liked other people's society too much to withdraw into mourning, and she had never been partial to black. So her life, after the great disruption, quickly resumed its pattern, and she never stopped wearing chartreuse. As Frank's primary beneficiary, she inherited a convoluted portfolio of investments and company responsibilities. Olive moved immediately to shut down all the projects that Frank had left unfinished; she retained the Princess, though, for the time being, as a house for hire, and she decided to keep 3XY, appointing Tom Holt to manage it for her. Life at Rylands rolled on, in the way that it always had when Frank had been on one of those frequent long trips away.

Frank junior went back to school, after bereavement and a broken arm ceased to be persuasive reasons to stay at home. The emotional effects of his father's death are the subject of the next chapter, and in some ways the entire second half, of this book; but if it did affect him as deeply as it seems, he wasn't showing it in his responses at the age of ten. Perhaps it was a space in his life that was only felt in retrospect. After all, it wasn't as if his father had been a prominent presence in his world; it was useful to have a father who was rich and famous, certainly, but there were precious few shared experiences to be missed. Frank became the little man of the house. From the moment he figuratively stepped into his father's shoes on the wharf at Station Pier, he was established as his father's replacement; his mother enlisted him as co-host and consort in all the activities of her crowded social calendar, and he became officially, as he had always been in practice, the absolute centre of her affections. That possibly meant that he became a more indulged and insufferable child after his father died than he had been before, but that's as hard to imagine as it is to gauge.

The person on whom Frank Thring's death had the most dramatic and verifiable impact was Lola. She had always been on the periphery of life at Rylands, though her father insisted, when he was around, on her rights as the daughter of the house. But her relationship with Olive had never been better than cordial, and sometimes much worse; her relationship with her half-brother had been warm while he was able to be cuddled, but twenty-four-year-old big sisters had little relevance to the life of a truculent ten-year-old, especially one as spoilt as little Frankie. Frank's will, drawn up on June 22, five days after his admission to hospital and at a time when he could no longer speak and barely sign his name, reflects his anxiety to protect his daughter – in particular, perhaps, from her stepmother.

He had some reason to be concerned. The first bequest is a lifetime annuity for Lola of five hundred and twenty pounds per year. After an appropriate deduction for the trust fund that would fund it, the rest of his estate devolves to Olive. In the event of his wife pre-deceasing him, which at that moment looked a purely academic provision, the estate would be divided simply into equal shares for his two children. The point of including it, beyond the legal formality, was presumably to suggest strongly to Olive how she might draw up her own will. When she did so, two years later, an early provision acknowledged 'an undertaking given by me to my late husband on the Twenty-second day of June One thousand nine hundred and thirty-six' to leave all her shares in his continuing theatre companies in two equal parts to Lola and Frank. But her own preferences were clear in what followed, with 'all the rest and residue of my property and effects whatsoever and wherever situate' to pass to 'my son the said Francis William Thring'. Rylands, all of Frank senior's other investments, his stake in Arden and the Princess Theatre, even the panel-beaten blue Packard, were to pass exclusively to her precious boy.

Probably it would not have come as much of a surprise to Lola when, on Olive's death in 1953, she discovered where she stood in her stepmother's sense of the family. She would have been aware, at least, that it was not the way her father had meant things to be, which might have provided some comfort as well as confirmation of a grievance. After the first of July 1936, Lola knew her place in the pecking order, and it seemed to suit everybody quite well if her dealings with Olive and her little half-brother were kept to a minimum.

The most immediate repercussion of her father's death was marked by two modest announcements in the press later in that year. The first was an engagement notice in September:

> Lola, only daughter of the late Mr and Mrs F.W. Thring of Melbourne, to Thomas James Holt, of South Yarra.[270]

To most people who knew Lola, it was a bolt from the blue. Tom Holt was a widower, just a few years younger than her father. His two sons Harold and Cliff were a couple of years older than their stepmother-to-

270 *Argus*, 30 September 1936, p.16.

be. Harold, the elder, had been elected to the House of Representatives in the preceding year, and thirty years later became Prime Minister of Australia. Cliff was already a prominent labour organiser in the theatre industry. It was quite a formidable instant family for a young woman to acquire, especially one as reserved and inexperienced in the ways of the world as Lola Thring. But the marriage duly took place, just six weeks later, and the *Argus* reported on the subdued festivities under the heading 'Quiet Wedding':

> The marriage of Mr Thomas James Holt and Miss Lola Thring was quietly celebrated yesterday evening at St Matthew's Church, Prahran … the bride, who is the daughter of the late Mr and Mrs F.W. Thring, wore a charming frock and full-length cape of white chiffon and a coronet of white velvet violets on her hair. She carried a pearl bag adorned with a spray of gardenias.
>
> After the ceremony the bride's stepmother, Mrs F.W. Thring, invited a few close friends to extend their congratulations to the couple at Rylands, her home in Toorak Road, Toorak. Among those present were the bride's brother, Frank, and the bridegroom's sons, Mr. Holt, M.H.R., and Mr. Clifford Holt.[271]

It was the least Olive could do. All in all, it probably wasn't the kind of wedding that Lola had imagined, or that her father might have envisaged for her. Most of her school-friends from St Caths had managed to be married over the preceding couple of years; Lola is mentioned in the extensive guest-lists at several of them, and as a bridesmaid at another two, and without exception those weddings were very slap-up affairs. Perhaps the fact that the groom was a widower, and more than twice her age, made a 'Quiet Wedding' seem more appropriate; the fact that her father had died just a few months before, too, might have been a reason to not do things too loudly. Given Lola's horror of making a spectacle of herself, it might even have been the wedding that she really wanted.

Tom was, like his Prime Minister son, a handsome man with a relish for the good things in life, especially young women, and Lola certainly wasn't chaining herself to an ancient ruin. But he was, as everyone would have duly noted when the shock announcement was made, old enough to

271 *Argus*, 17 November 1936, p.3.

be her father. It's hard to resist the hypothesis that that fact was important in the first bold decision Lola had ever had to make. The space that her father left in her life was a chasm. With his death she had lost not only a father who was clearly loved, a man she barely saw for the first ten years of her life but with whom she had come to share a great deal; she had also, effectively, lost her home and her family. Rylands now was Olive's home, not hers, and her only meaningful link to anyone there was the man who had gone. It would be understandable for her to try, in some way, to replace him, and to find a new home and family somewhere else. Tom Holt was not only a quite attractive man of her father's generation; he was Frank's friend, indeed his right-hand man. Most of the world her father built had been demolished at a stroke, but with Tom Holt she could keep some active memory of it alive.

Among all those damaged in the fall-out from Frank Thring's death, his daughter wore the most obvious scars. Her life with Tom in their modest bungalow in Waiora Road, Caulfield, seems to have been a contented one; in 1941, she had a child of her own, a daughter named Frances.

But Lola seemed to be always living in the shadow of other people's deaths. Tom Holt died in 1945, leaving Lola a widow at the age of thirty-four, with a little girl who hadn't yet started school. Frances followed her mother to St Catherine's, and completed her schooling there, but at eighteen she became suddenly very ill with leukemia, and in the following year she died. Cancer haunted Lola; it killed her at the age of fifty-eight in 1970, and her only other child, Jo, the daughter of her second marriage to Philip Portus, was to die in her late thirties, a victim of breast cancer like her mother. Some people seem to have all the luck, and that probably means that some people only get a little of it at best. Lola seemed always to have less than her share, and especially in matters of inheritance.

Frank predicted some of that unfairness, and tried from beyond the grave to mitigate it. He had caused some of it himself, of course, and it was one of the things, when he sat down with the extra glass of whisky that it wasn't wise to have, that made him sad. He wouldn't have predicted that she would rush into marriage with his old friend, and probably would have disapproved if he had; he was too susceptible to the attractions of young women himself to be very tolerant of other men's predilections of that kind, especially when they involved his daughter.

If there was one thing his life might have taught him, it was that the attempt to control – children, audiences, politicians, even sometimes oneself – can't ever work, in the end. Without thinking that events can be shaped, of course, a man like Frank Thring might never have done, or built, or been anything – that was the paradox. When Frank was unable to speak or to write in those excruciating last three weeks of his life, he was still able, some of the time, to think. That paradox was probably not such a bad place to start.

TRAVELLING FROM SAN FRANCISCO TO MELBOURNE

S.S. Mariposa, 15 June 1936

7.10 p.m.

He'd never had much time for doctors. Especially when they told you that you didn't have much time. The fool Olive had dragged him along to in Los Angeles was a particularly fine example of the species, and not just because of the diagnosis. You paid a lot these days for a bow-tie, a bad moustache, and a bedside manner.

Unfortunately, even cretins sometimes got things right. Hard to imagine what cancer meant, precisely; it was an idea more than a disease, a concept, a canker, a something from nowhere. But something was bloody wrong, that was certain, because he'd never felt as crook as this. At first, he'd assumed it was just some wog he'd picked up from the Yanks, the only thing they'd let him have for nothing in the whole time he'd been there. One of those wogs they reckon are always going around. But this was a bloody stubborn wog, and it showed no inclination to go anywhere.

There was a lot he had to think about, plans and provisions and God knows what, the kind of things a man should probably be thinking about when he was fifty-three but never did, because fifty-three was ridiculous. Ridiculous. Jesus Christ, even his Dad'd shambled his way to sixty. He should be thinking about those things, but it was hard to concentrate.

At the beginning it was just the cough, the scratchy throat, the hoarseness; now there was this bloody great football in there, though you could hardly see anything, and it hurt like hell.

There was the pain, and there was the panic. He'd hardly ever known fear, not the pure primitive kind that made you feel as though you'd shrunk to nothing, not for a long time anyway.

Now he'd listen to his heart, and the bloody thing would start hammering away so hard that you'd think it would blow a fuse, and the more he tried to think of something else the louder it got, echoing down every byway of his body. He'd try to control it, breathing as evenly as he could with the pain, till it seemed he had slowed his pulse to a standstill. Then the panic came again, and the thundering.

There were more bloody tablets on the table beside him than they kept in Ford's the Chemist. Pills to make him numb, pills to help him sleep, pills to do whatever it was they did. The painkillers hurt the most, of course. Dirty great big bastards, with sharp edges that seemed to rip all the way down. You'd want to scream, if it didn't hurt so much to make a sound. Food was out of the question, of course; strained fruit, pap for babies, that was the only course on his menu, and as Olive brought the spoon to his mouth and clucked and fussed and cajoled him to open wide, he realised that was what he'd become. A muling, puking, helpless infant. Here comes the choo-choo, into the tunnel. She was in her element, of course. Mothering. They love it. Get a man on his back, hardly able to move or speak, and they can play nursemaid to their heart's content. That's my good little boy.

He'd tried to speak to his son, a couple of nights ago. He'd been feeling better then than he was now, which wasn't saying much. But it was still bloody tough to walk down the corridor to Frankie's room. He just felt he had to, that there were things he needed to say, and if he left them for another night he might never get another chance. So he'd dragged himself there like some damned geriatric, and opened the door, and there was his son, tucked up snug as a bug in a rug.

The boy had looked terrified. He looked at his father, and he was terrified.

He'd wondered at first whether he really looked that bad – touch of the ghost of old Hamlet, perhaps. Then he realised that the boy didn't expect to see him there because he didn't do this kind of thing – unless, of course, the boy was in trouble, and what he saw in Frankie's eyes at that moment was fear. That'd made him feel sad, so desperately sad, that he couldn't stay there any longer. It'd been a mistake to have gone at all. Nothing to say, nothing to do. So he'd mumbled something about that filthy bloody blanket that the boy should have thrown away years ago, and closed the door.

He still wasn't sure what it was he'd gone there to say. Well, obviously, that he loved him, it would've been that, in some shape or form. He loved his son, that was a given. But there were other things, or perhaps just other ways of saying it. Perhaps he wanted to tell him to grow up to be brave and good, to look after his mother, to be a man. Perhaps he wanted to leave him some wise maxims: about being neither a borrower or a lender, unless the interest rates were favourable, or about always remembering to call employees by their Christian names, or about never marrying a virgin or a gold-digger … There were many things he'd learned that could save a lad a lot of time and trouble if he knew them in advance. Perhaps he wanted to warn the boy about his mother, about the dangers of being smothered, the risks of becoming a sook. The world could be hard on mummy's boys.

But he'd said nothing, except about the rug. And so he was condemned, it seemed, to be an irrelevance in his son's life, as he had been in his daughter's. As he lurched his way back to his cabin, walking like a drunk though he hadn't had a drop because he was doped to the bloody eyeballs with other palliatives, he decided he'd lost them both – never had them perhaps. Lola, and young Frank. Nothing to show but a stack of squandered opportunities. A man had every right to feel sorry for himself.

7.35 p.m.

The morphine took half an hour to kick in.

He knew when it was happening, because the things that were central to your days and nights, like the crease in the sheet or the lump in the pillow or the coarseness of the blanket, became suddenly smoothed and softened, and far away.

He longed for those moments in-between, when the pain stopped and the thoughts stopped. He swam in those moments, floated on the surface of the regrets that swamped him. He missed the pain for as long as he could recall it, because that was living, living proof of it, and he knew through the haze that the morphine was a way of not really living at all; he needed the hurting, because in amongst it were things that he knew he needed to think about, to deal with and organise and make right. But floating beyond it was irresistible, as the drug moved through him, making nothing matter, nothing matter at all.

Olive had been somewhere there. She came in, didn't she? To tuck him in, plump up the pillows? He might have imagined it, but he was certain it'd been her. On her way to the captain's table, where the better people broke their bread, as was only fitting for the daughter of a man who made dummies out of wax. One of nature's aristocrats, Ol.

She'd been there. Yeah, she had. He could tell because of the breasts. A man couldn't dream those. Big buggers, coming at you like a tidal wave. Or a continental shelf. If a continental shelf moved, which was probably a bloody disconcerting thing to happen. Boom and bust, that's Ollie. More front than Myer's in every respect. Morphine made everything slip and slide, metaphors especially.

But she'd gone, in a dress too tight with a laugh too loud, to be with her people. Big people, substantial people. Massive bloody people, who'd been to Grammar and given balls and bequests, and put their names on buildings.

Never mind the quality, feel the width. She was spending his money, distributing his favours, telling others what he thought when she'd never known, never ever known. How could she? Wonderful woman, Ollie, but somehow … somehow it was hard to find the girl in the woman. Fifty years old, finally grown into her age. Sad, really. Little Gracie, big Ollie, and that was it. All those beautiful girls, stunning girls, Coral and Donalda and all the eager starlets with their shining eyes, and for him it'd come down to little Gracie and big Ollie, and that was it.

Which was all beside the point in the present circumstances. The killer wasn't just the cancer, it was what the cancer made you see. Which was why you needed the bloody pills. You spent a whole life searching for ways to feel, and you finished up longing to be numb. That must be what they call maturity.

She'd be back soon, of course. To make sure the invalid was all right. To show that she was doing all she could. To look after things. Nothing like a sick husband to supply Ollie Kreitmayer with the meaning of life. For other people, with morphine or without it, it was a hell of a lot harder to find.

8.05 p.m.

Nothing to be done. Too bad. Sorry Ol.

Let you down badly. Some things a man can't do.

See? Nothing up my sleeve. Little Grace. Dying with little grace. She liked the rabbit. Always a kid, really.

But aren't we all, my son, aren't we all?

Two pillows. She insisted. Plump, plump, plump Ollie plumping pillows, to make you nice and comfy, at an angle no neck was made to go. Too many pillows, blankets. Too many pillows, too many pills.

Water, water all around and nothing else to bloody drink. No wonder a bloke felt crook. Give the man a cigar for Christ's sake. Hey, mister, watch out. Bang. Things that go bang in the night. Bump.

It's all right, darling. Plump. Nothing to be afraid of. Though nothing to be done.

Nothing to fear, Daddy's here. Now you see him, now you don't.

My darling boy. Mummy's little darling. Lola, Lola, Lola, what are we going to do with you, little long-lost Lola, poor little lost girl. Crying in the wilderness. No home. Nowhere to go. Nothing to be done.

Only the pain, and the waves, and the waiting. Not waving, waiting. Waning and waving.

Well, all right, drowning, bugger it. Crossing the bar.

No ice for me, thanks mate.

Frank and Olive with baby Frank, 1926

Courtesy of the Performing Arts Collection, Melbourne

Olive and Lola with small Frank, 1930

Courtesy of the Performing Arts Collection, Melbourne

Portrait for Olive, inscribed 'Ever thine Frank' c.1930

Courtesy of the Performing Arts Collection, Melbourne

Olive c.1930

Courtesy of the Performing Arts Collection, Melbourne

Thring at Efftee launch 1931

Photograph from private collection of Chris Long

Efftee trademark

Photograph from private collection of Chris Long

Frank Thring and Arthur Higgins filming *A Co-Respondent's Course*, 1931

Courtesy of the Performing Arts Collection, Melbourne

Wedding scene from *A Co-Respondent's Course*, 1931,
with Donalda Warne and John D'Arcy

Photograph from private collection of Chris Long

Filming *Diggers* in the burnt-out stalls of His Majesty's Theatre, 1931

Photograph from private collection of Chris Long

Scene from *Diggers*, with Pat Hanna, George Moon and Eugenie Pescott, 1931

Photograph from private collection of Chris Long

Scene from *Diggers*, with small Frank Thring and Pattie Hanna

Courtesy of the Performing Arts Collection, Melbourne

Frank Thring and Arthur Higgins filming *A Ticket in Tatts*, 1933

Photograph from private collection of Chris Long

No 2
No 2

Previous page, top: Frank Thring (leaning on fence) on location at Kallista filming
A Ticket in Tatts, 1933
Photograph from private collection of Chris Long

Previous page, bottom: Filming *A Ticket in Tatts* on location at Flemington, from a temporary tower in the middle of the race-course, 1933
Photograph from private collection of Chris Long

Above: Scene from *Harmony Row*, with George Wallace, 'Wee Willie' Kerr and an uncredited FrankThring junior
Photograph from private collection of Chris Long

Scene from *Collits' Inn* at the Princes,
with Gladys Moncrieff and Robert Chisholm
Photograph from private collection of Chris Long

Scene from *Collits' Inn* at the Princess
with George Wallace as Dandy Dick incurring the wrath of the Redcoats
Photograph from private collection of Chris Long

Group scene from *Collits' Inn*,
with John Dobbie (striped top) and Marshall Crosby at Pierce Collits

Photograph from private collection of Chris Long

Arrival of Efftee convoy at Nockatunga Station for location shoot of 'Sheepmates', headed by Thring Packard

Photograph from private collection of Chris Long

Frank Thring washing at Cooper's Creek camp

Courtesy of the Performing Arts Collection, Melbourne

Frank Thring bearing firewood at Cooper's Creek camp

Courtesy of the Performing Arts Collection, Melbourne

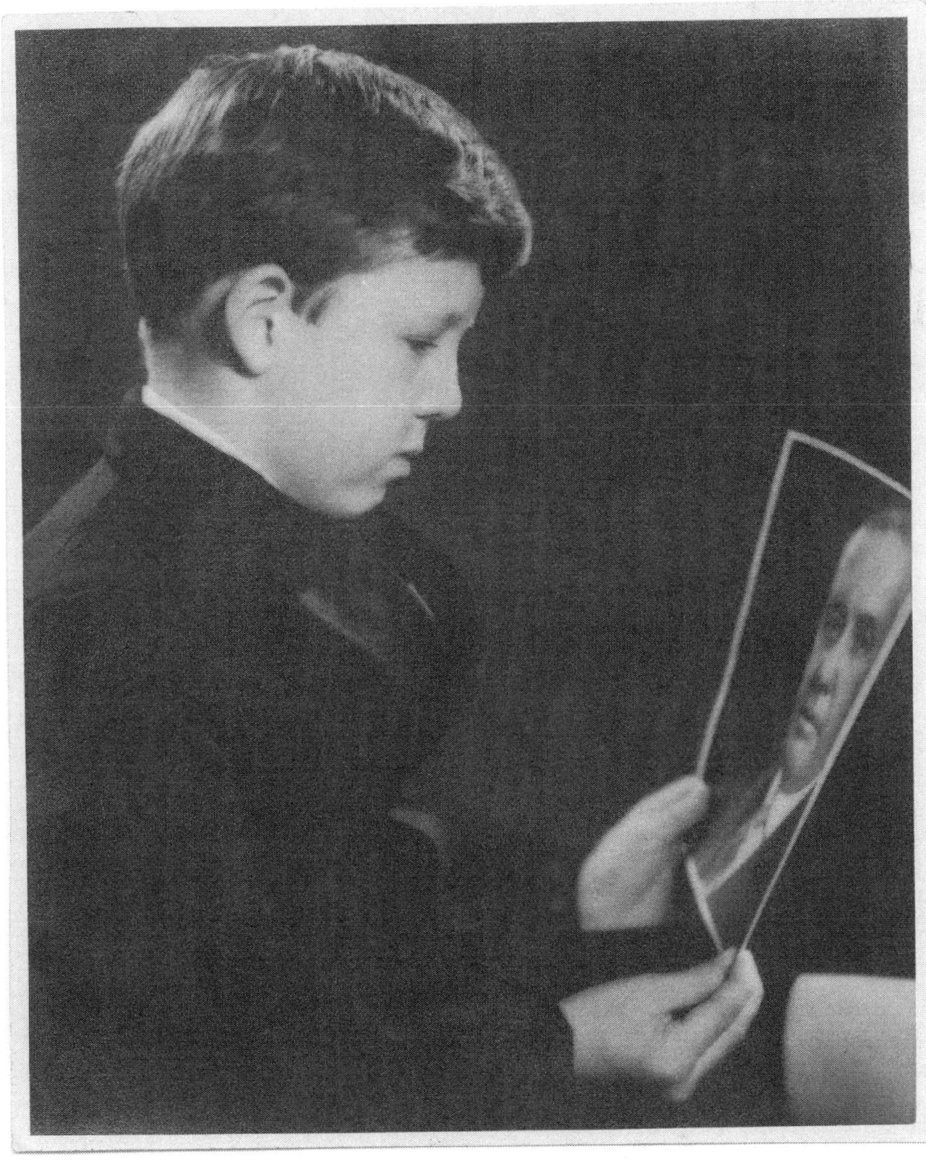

Frank at ten looking at photo of his father, 1937

Courtesy of the Performing Arts Collection, Melbourne

Frank with Olive, c.1940

Courtesy of the Performing Arts Collection, Melbourne

Photograph given by Frank to Joan Cunliffe, 1945,
inscribed 'To Flowergirl from Pansyboy'

Courtesy of Joan Thring

Frank as Hal in *Hal's Belles*, 1946

Courtesy of the Performing Arts Collection, Melbourne

Frank as Herod in *Salome* at the Arrow Theatre, 1952, with June Brunell as Salome

Courtesy of the Performing Arts Collection, Melbourne

Frank in *Othello* at the Arrow Theatre, 1952, with Zoe Caldwell as Desdemona

Courtesy of the Performing Arts Collection, Melbourne

Frank as Herod in *Salome* at St Martins,
London, 1954, with Agnes Bernelle as Salome
Courtesy of the Performing Arts Collection, Melbourne

Frank and Joan, wedding at Holy Trinity, Stratford, 21 November 1955
Courtesy of the Performing Arts Collection, Melbourne

Frank as Saturninus in *Titus Andronicus*,
Shakespeare memorial Theatre, Stratford, 1955
Courtesy of the Performing Arts Collection, Melbourne

Frank as Sir Lancelot Spratt in *Doctor in the House*, London, 1956, with Philip Gilbert, Sonya Cordeau, Edward Woodward and Alan White
Courtesy of the Performing Arts Collection, Melbourne

Frank as King Aella in *The Vikings*, 1958

Courtesy of the Performing Arts Collection, Melbourne

Frank with Charlton Heston, on the set of *Ben Hur*, 1959

Courtesy of the Performing Arts Collection, Melbourne

Frank as Herod in *King of Kings*, 1961, with Brigid Bazlen as Salome

Courtesy of the Performing Arts Collection, Melbourne

Frank unusually active in *El Cid*, 1961

Courtesy of the Performing Arts Collection, Melbourne

Frank as Ahab in *Moby Dick – Rehearsed*, 1959, with Mary Hardy as the Boy

UTRC production, courtesy of the Performing Arts Collection, Melbourne

Frank on *In Melbourne Tonight*, 1964,
with Tonia Berne, host Noel Ferrier and Robert Helpmann

Courtesy of the Performing Arts Collection, Melbourne and GTV

Frank with Mary Hardy, c.1966, photograph by David Parker

Courtesy of the Performing Arts Collection, Melbourne

Frank in front of 'Ham Reduced' sign. Photograph by David Parker

Courtesy of the Performing Arts Collection, Melbourne

Frank in his bathroom at 'Rylands'

Courtesy of the Performing Arts Collection, Melbourne

Frank as King of Moomba, 1982

Courtesy of the Performing Arts Collection, Melbourne

Frank as Mother Superior in *The Nuns*, 1976,
with Edward Hepple and Stephen Oldfield

Courtesy of the Performing Arts Collection, Melbourne and Melbourne Theatre Company

Portrait of Frank by David Parker, c.1984

Courtesy of the Performing Arts Collection, Melbourne

Frank as Lord Hawke in *Bodyline*, ABC-TV mini-series, 1984

Courtesy of the Performing Arts Collection, Melbourne and ABC Television

Frank as Whiteside in *The Man Who Came to Dinner*,
Queensland Theatre Company, 1979, with strategic script-tray
Courtesy of the Performing Arts Collection, Melbourne

Frank learning the didjeridoo, c.1987

PART TWO

FRANK THE SON

TRAVELLING FROM SAN FRANCISCO TO MELBOURNE II

S.S. *Mariposa*, 15 June 1936
5.45 p.m.

It was hard, being the only ten-year-old on board. The only one above steerage, anyway. Harder still, when your arm was in a sling, and blowing your nose or doing a pee involved some kind of gymnastics.

And yet it still might have been all right. At home, a broken arm would get you attention and an audience, for sure. But here he was, leaning over the sliprails of the Mariposa, staring at the seaweed somewhere in the middle of the Pacific, and nobody cared. No one asked him what was wrong, or fussed around trying to help, or even begged him to be careful. Nobody was thinking about him at all.

It wouldn't have been so bad, except for his father. Something strange'd happened to his father in Hollywood, and although she said everything would be better when they got home, she was lying. Thought she could fool him like he was still a little kid. Mothers were so stupid.

His father had hardly left the cabin since they'd sailed. He'd come up to sit in the sun on the upper deck on the first two mornings, but since then he'd stayed in bed. This was a relief. Everybody had stared at his father on those mornings, because he looked so ridiculous. The dressing-gown was embarrassing in itself, but the scarf round the bottom half of his face made him look like some bad guy in a worse movie.

Frank had been so ashamed the second day that he'd bolted. Straight down the stairs, arse over tit, till he bounced off the metal lockers at the bottom, felt the pain in his arm, and knew there was nothing to do but cry.

She was certainly lying. She was really worried, you could tell. Normally, when she was just a bit worried, which was most of the time, she'd bluster and boom and generally make a stupid idiot of herself. But she was quiet now. She hardly ever raised her voice, and she never laughed. He'd done everything he could to distract her, busting his arm, standing too close to the edge of the pool, moping. None of it worked. At least, not for long.

As for his dad, he was pretty quiet, too, behind his stupid scarf. Down in the mouth, you might say, but perhaps best not to. On the second night, perhaps, after the Incident of the Arm, he'd come in to say good night. He'd hung around for a while by the door, after asking 'How's the arm?', which must have been one of the stupidest, most ridiculous questions ever asked, because it was broken, obviously, and therefore, as any dumb bum could see, just a bit below its best. But he'd said 'OK', because what else would you say. And still his father had hung around, half in the corridor, looking dumb, like a man who wanted to say something.

In the end, he'd said almost nothing at all. He sort of lurched into the room, finally, and messed around trying to straighten the sheets, and then he said, 'You're getting too old for that, Frankie'. And for a terrible, agonising moment, Frank had no idea what he meant.

But then he knew. It was all about Eidy again. So he dragged her right under the blankets where she couldn't be seen, and stared at the old man in the scarf, and said nothing at all.

He was going to go on about it, he could tell; he loved giving those stupid lectures about growing up and being a man, my son, about once a month on average, and all you could do really was nod, and think of something else, and wait for it to be over.

But then his father looked at him, for four, five, six seconds, just stared at him. Maybe he'd even smiled, but how could you tell whether he was underneath the stupid scarf, and what he was thinking. Frank wondered, even, whether this could be leading up to a kiss.

But the panic passed. His dad moved slowly to the door, was briefly silhouetted in the weird white light from the passage, and gently closed it.

Frank stared into the water. So much of it, so many days to go. The Mariposa was a boring boat, filled with boring people, and he couldn't wait to get home.

7.50 p.m

She hadn't even hung around at dinner. She broadcast to anyone who might be listening that she was just going to check on her husband, and left him to eat with the awful family from Box Hill South, wherever that was. You'd think if they could afford the Mariposa they'd find a place somewhere decent.

They asked him whether he liked school, and if he played footy. He told them, and that shut them up.

But then she'd come back, while he was still on the ice-cream, and though she'd made an effort and fixed her make-up and all that you could see she was upset. Everyone could, even the Box Hill South people. She was putting on a show, and making a lousy job of it. Adults could be so pathetic.

And then she'd told him, so everyone could hear, that he'd need to be a big boy now, Mummy's special little man, and make Daddy very proud of him. He thought he was going to be sick. Puke all over the tablecloth, and the floral arrangement, and Mummy's very best shantung.

Why she had to talk like this in front of people, even people like that, he'd never know. Maybe it was so he couldn't say no, or maybe she just didn't know any better. Mothers. Bloody bloody mothers.

So there it was. What she'd meant, with all her little-manning, was that she wanted him to talk to the press when they landed on Tuesday. Daddy would have to go to hospital so they could make him well again, and Mummy would have to go with him, so Frankie was going to have to be a real grown-up and talk to the men who'd be there to ask questions. Diddums diddums doodle-diddle-ums. So cute it was disgusting.

He'd said yes, of course. Not because he wanted to, or because he wanted to please her or him, or impress Box Hill South, or anything like that. Because he couldn't give a flying fish-hook. And that meant he wasn't scared. He wasn't scared of anything.

He'd said yes, and he'd left her to have a Pimms with those people, and he'd gone down the stairs quite carefully, and he'd come back to Eidy.

Here, with her, he was safe.

Chapter Eight

THE SUCCESSION

Frank the son could hardly have designed a better arrangement, in theory. Rich father, conveniently out of the picture before he was likely to become interested in the choices he was making, or, even worse, to think he needed to do something about changing them. Rich mother, irretrievably widowed, unfailingly indulgent. Big house, a stage for any fantasy. Big sister, affectionate enough, but fifteen years older and rarely on the premises, so no competition. Doting Nanny, devoted to keeping him happy. Efficient accountants, dedicated to taking care of any bill he cared to run up. Unusual and well-known name, redolent of risk and razzamatazz. It should have been like Christmas every day of the year.

It wasn't, and, given a retrospective wish, Frank would probably not have chosen the circumstances of his childhood at all. He would have retained the doting Nanny and the understanding accountants, no doubt, but the rest of the script would have been rewritten. With his childhood safely behind him, he talked about his father and, especially, his mother so scathingly that he made the whole thing sound like a species of hell. Frank on his own account was the poor little rich boy, doomed to realise every whim. Fortunately, apparently, very few of us have to endure the horrors of a dream run.

Why, then, didn't it work? Of course, almost every prince and princess, every media heir and heiress, appears to find a sure-fire route to unhappiness, so young Frank, born to be the Black Prince of Toorak, was never quite as uniquely cursed as he thought he was. But that is hardly an explanation, or any compensation. The notion that wealth and privilege are somehow in inverse relation to contentment is probably a quite effective opiate of the people who don't have them. Frank, in the midst of all the bright bounty of Santa's sack that he was born with, was prevented from enjoying it to the full by the two things that most immediately defined him as a person: his intelligence and his sexuality. The former might have made it difficult for him to be contented at any time; the latter, in the age and culture into which he was born, made it impossible.

Neither of those inconveniences in his situation emerged significantly to blight Frank's first ten years, when his father was, intermittently, on the premises. As an infant universally adored, it is unlikely that he found life unduly grim. Some things were missing that might have come with the rough-and-tumble of school. The lack of contact with other children of his age was a cost, but Frank seems to have come to the conclusion early that other people were more trouble than they were worth, anyway. Learning to share things – possessions, insecurities, attention – is the kind of process that looks valuable only in adult hindsight, and it is hard to see how it could ever have much appeal at the time. Frank, surrounded by women who apparently lived to pamper him and a father who could buy just about anything, may not have thought his lack of playmates a deficit at all.

So there are grounds for thinking that Frank's early childhood was quite a lot happier than he subsequently claimed it to be. The trouble with early memories is that they tend to slip away, to be rediscovered perhaps in the senility that Frank died too soon to experience; certainly the things about his early life that he recalled most readily and vividly in later interviews were adolescent experiences, and those were typically at best bizarre, at worst excruciating. He did remember one incident from early childhood in a spectacularly drunken conversation on radio with Philip Brady and Bruce Mansfield in 1992. It referred to a promotional stunt for one of the wildlife features that his father's company produced in 1931, in which Frank junior was photographed with a snake for the evening newspapers. Despite a little incoherence caused by the lateness of the hour, it was a quintessential Thring anecdote; startling, loaded with a potent verb (Frank the child was enveloped, perhaps, but never 'whipped'), and closed off by an even more startling challenge to emotional orthodoxy:

> FT: He [my father] didn't like to see anything not used. He'd wander around, he'd employ a staff [sic], but he wouldn't have anyone who couldn't act … He once had me whipped by a snake in the foyer of the Regent Theatre.
>
> PB: Was he a part of Efftee Broadcasting?
>
> FT: Well, you'd better dig him up and ask.[272]

272 Frank Thring, radio interview with Philip Brady and Bruce Mansfield, 'Remember When', 3AW, 15 February 1992.

The signal given in this exchange, and in others like it, was that Frank was a man who didn't like talking about his father, and didn't like him, in about equal measures.

But while his father was alive, he ensured that young Frank's life was colourful and lively, at least. There were two trips overseas, for a start, though he was too young when the first of them happened to remember it at all. And his father's determination that everything should be 'used' to its maximum led to Frank junior's debut on film, when he even consented to hold Pattie Hanna's hand for their brief cameo in the closing moments of *Diggers*. It led to other appearances, in *The Sentimental Bloke* and *Harmony Row*, in the taxing role of little boy in the park. Young Frank liked being around the studio, where he could not only enter a world of spectacle and make-believe but, as the spoilt son of Mr Thring, get away with just about anything. Bill Kerr, as Wee Willy Kerr the child-star of *Harmony Row*, played with him a little, though he found Master Thring rather awkward and boring, as children a couple years younger often seem to be; he remembered Frankie staying very close to his mother, who was often a conspicuous presence on the set.[273] He always, in one way or another, stayed very close to his mother, even when he couldn't stand the sight of her. Hanging around the filming at His Majesty's and Wattle Path gave him a chance to be at least in the world his father lived in, and perhaps even a glimpse of what staying quite close to his father might mean.

When his father foreshadowed the trip to America in 1936, Frank must have been ecstatic. He hadn't yet learned to be bored with celebrity, and he was already well and truly sick of school. Hollywood was laid out before him as a playground, day after shining day, while his father wheeled and dealed. It promised to be the most exciting year of his life.

Little Frank was taken around all the studios, and introduced to some of the stars that he found, as he later recalled, 'lying about the place'.[274] What else, in sixty-year-old Frank's disenchanted retrospect, did stars do? But it was quite a treat for a ten-year-old, and it was clearly intended to do

273 Bill Kerr, interview with the author, 4 August 2004.
274 Frank Thring, Brady and Mansfield interview.

more than keep him expensively amused. There was a general sense that the boy, given his delight in putting on costumes and make-up, just might become an actor. Olive nursed that ambition for him in its most specific form; there was no reason, surely, why all this time and energy and money and power that her husband directed to Australian film should not have a tangible spin-off for the most important child in the world. The boy himself showed little interest in the prospect, but everyone else seemed to think it an excellent idea.

So his parents ensured that he met Shirley Temple, the curly-haired poppet who might one day be his American anima, and the reigning sweetheart of Hollywood film. He was able to meet Boris Karloff too, and any other big name that took his fancy. Fifty years later he would say, with lofty disdain, 'I hated them. It was terribly boring'.[275] But Frank said that at a time of his life when almost everything was boring, even things that once he had rather liked. Professions of luxurious hatred came much more easily then than professions of affection, and even Frank could feel that his over-statements needed some qualification: 'It was hysterical. That dreadful Boris Karloff, and that idiot Shirley Temple. In fact she was a monster, and he was quite nice'. Later in the same interview, he could even drum up some sympathy for Shirley Temple – a child who achieved wealth and celebrity so early could hardly help being spoilt, he conceded, and it must have been hard to have to deal with some of the consequences of fame: 'You're the world's top box office star at ten years of age and here you are meeting this vile boy dragged all the way from Australia to meet you ...'[276]

Everything changed with his father's illness. Frank senior saw doctors in Los Angeles, and was effectively an invalid on the journey home. Almost certainly the ten-year-old wasn't told how sick his father was, let alone how hopeless the prognosis was. Most families would have stopped short of the truth, and Frank's family was one that had always gone to some lengths to avoid it. But he must have been aware that it was serious. The hurried plans for their return, Olive's preoccupation, and all the painfully false conversations that adults fall into in front of children whom they think are too young to understand, would all have indicated how concerned other people were.

Then, when the *Mariposa* landed at Station Pier, there were two more very loud alarms. The first was the ambulance waiting on the dock, and

275 ibid.
276 ibid.

the haste with which his father and mother were bundled into it. The second was the fact that ten-year-old Frank, resplendent in the uniform of Melbourne Grammar's Junior School, his arm in a sling because of a rash moment on the ship's stairs, was left to face the press. There they all were, as expected: a large group of Melbourne's journalists hoping that they might be able to turn a half-interesting piece on the future of Australia's film industry into a page-one revelation that F.W. Thring was critically ill. Somebody had to deal with them. The details of the actual exchange have not survived, but the general sense that the boy had handled his first press conference with style is implicit in all the reports, especially, of course, those of Frank himself. It's an extraordinary scene to imagine. It was an extraordinary thing to do to a child.

The decision was Olive's, presumably. Leaving the ten-year-old alone on the wharf was not quite as negligent, in practical terms, as it sounds: Nanny was, as ever, at hand, and Ernest the chauffeur would have been there with the Rolls, so Frank would find his way safely back to Rylands. But expecting the boy whose father was dying to step so soon into his patrimony is revealing of the way Olive saw her son, and of the role that she would have him play from that point on. The press conference given by the small boy with the sling is a bizarre image in itself. The psychological assumptions that lay behind the decision to put him there, and its emotional implications for the child himself, make the moment stranger still. While young Frank was obliged to talk about things he could not know about, he was effectively disabled from expressing the things that he actually felt.

Performing an adult was, for Frank, probably not such an onerous task. He was a precocious child, apparently supremely confident, and obviously very different from other boys of his age; this had something, at least, to do with the fact that he didn't know any of them. He had been around articulate, powerful adults all his life, and was accustomed to wielding power himself – over the servants, and over all the females in the house. No wonder he made such a good fist of the role at Port Melbourne that day. But he was, after all, a child, who depended more heavily on the reassuring maternal presence of his Nanny than a genuinely mature ten-year-old would, and whose father was frighteningly sick. The only way to sustain the quality of his performance was to deny what he was, and to detach himself from the troublesome feelings that were attached to it.

His father died ten days later. The succession was clear, just as it was anticipated on a grey winter morning on Station Pier: Frank Thring is dead; long live Frank Thring. An actor's career had begun.

Frank never spoke about his reaction to his father's death. Apart from the scrupulous care he took in selecting the few bits of his private life that he felt suitable for general consumption, there was something else operating to censor any comments about his parents. In all the interviews in which he told his story, Frank senior and Olive are mentioned only in passing, and are invariably dismissed with savage humour. He was gentler with his father than with his mother, as well as generally less forthcoming. Frank senior's personal qualities were referred to in one of those conversations only, the boozy one with Philip Brady and Bruce Mansfield, in which Frank's guard was a little lower than usual, though he would never let it slip very far. That was the interview in which he described his father as 'a strange ruthless man, slightly evil', and gave him for the first time a mythic dimension as 'my father, Simon Legree'.[277] The tone was not dismissive, though; there was a touch of fascination, even perverse affection, in that comment. Frank, who spent fifty years of his life cultivating a satanic persona, and would have been well satisfied with being described in just that way himself, could well be suspected of following in his father's hoofprints.

The references to Olive similarly mythologise her as a powerful figure with a touch of the demonic: Frank calls her variously the Boadicea of Bourke Street, the Antipodean answer to Lady Bracknell, the Volumnia of Toorak, the Lady Macbeth of Toorak Road – primally female, certainly, but with not a loving and nurturing bone in her body:

> She was the sort of … Lucretia Borgia of Toorak. Because you see my father died when I was in Hollywood with Shirley Temple, at the age of ten, so that got rid of him. And Mum just took over the whole Frank Thring empire, 3XY, the Princess Theatre, you name it, she got it. Well, I managed, with some effort, to get rid of her, and I took it over.[278]

He characterises getting rid of Olive as a process that not only took a little longer, but was a triumph over oppression. His father had prematurely

277 ibid.
278 Frank Thring, radio interview with Bill Howie, 'Thanks for the Memories', 3AW, 12 November 1989.

stepped aside; his mother had to be defeated. Of course, speaking about his parents so callously was part of Frank's performance as the junior Simon Legree; it was a calculated flippancy, designed to shock, and offered strategically in a morning radio interview when Frank was more or less sober. It would be quite possible to argue that this outrageousness is no more than a mannerism, and even that it might be a hard shell, worn to hide and protect tender feelings underneath. In relation to Olive, though, there are good grounds for believing that Frank meant every word. He may not have murdered her, precisely. But he felt nothing recognisable as love for her, and removing Olive metaphorically was a powerful impulse and, eventually, a crucial act of liberation.

When he did refer to his mother, it was always in connection with money.

> When his mother died, she left Thring the Toorak house and contents and a large sum of money ... Was he close to his mother? 'Very close over the money ... However, I got it'.[279]

The House of Thring sounded, in all Frank's reminiscences, very like the House of Borgia. It was a favourite joke, but also very much part of his psychic furniture. When Frank took over the actual house, Rylands, he had its interior painted entirely in black, and it remained black throughout until it was demolished when he left it, thirty years later.

Those signs of hostility towards his mother would have been less apparent, if they were there at all, in Frank's early adolescence. But most of the foundations for it were laid in the next few years after his father's death. Some of them may have formed that day on the pier, when she took his father away from him, and he never came back; part of Olive's fault consisted in being the one who didn't die. And something else happened, something irrevocable, some time in his early teenage years, that ruined that relationship completely.

Frank recalled the way in which his mother immediately employed him as a surrogate for her dead husband with his usual darkly self-parodic humour. But, like that first press conference on the pier, it presents an extraordinary picture. Frank the pint-sized escort at cocktail parties, Frank the child-host at lavish Rylands dinners, Frank in school uniform with cocktail and canapé in hand, Frank diminutive in penguin suit with bowtie and starched shirt beside his mother, the stately galleon in full sail. The smart set of Toorak

279 Peter Wilmoth, 'The Agony of Being Frank', *Sunday Age*, 19 June 1994, p.3.

presumably became accustomed in time to the odd couple, but it must have been something of a shock.

Olive, who was in some ways so protective and in all things so indulgent, would have seen nothing of the exploitative dimension of all this, or of its potential to harm her son. For her the whole arrangement would have been a testament to the unusual depth of the bond between them, a token of her trust and her social encouragement of the boy, and a recognition of how extraordinarily grown-up he was. The fact that it was driven by her needs, and not at all by his, was clear to other people, but inconceivable to her. Little Frank, clutching his adult sherry as he was inducted into all the adult gossip, was not only pretending to be something that he was not, but forfeiting his childhood.

> One led a different life ... When school finished, I never went through all that dreadful sports and cadets, and the gibberish that they are. The Rolls Royce would pick me up, I would have a change of clothes in the back seat, and get out of that ghastly navy blue uniform, and change crouched on the floor while the chauffeur drove me to a cocktail party.[280]

It started at the private prep-school to which his mother sent him in the year after Frank senior's death. Glamorgan, a cosy enough playground for the sons of the establishment run by its founder, Miss Isobel McComas, was the feeder-school for Melbourne Grammar, one of the city's elite private schools, with which it shared the 'ghastly navy blue'. Frank duly moved on to 'Grammar' in 1939.

The Rolls-Royce was part of the package. If Olive was to send her precious son out into the world, he would travel there safely and in style. Ernest, the family chauffeur, would ferry little Frank to school each morning, and be there at the school gates at 3.30 to take him home to Rylands; unless, as was often the case, there was an engagement elsewhere. Partly, obviously, the whole ritual was an expression of maternal anxieties – not for her boy the vulgar contingencies of the streets. Partly, also, it was a declaration, of class and of difference. Frank, who was different enough already, had no need for any further advertisement of the fact.

Each day that the Rolls set off along Toorak Road for school, it would pass the other boys as they waited at the tram-stops. Often, there would be teachers there as well; Olive, who was anxious that her son should be suitably

280 Interview with Bill Howie, 12 November 1989.

valued by the staff, had instructed Ernest to pick up any that were reduced to public transport, and accordingly three of the Melbourne Grammar staff would be chauffered to school most mornings with little Frank. The only days that they would miss out were those when Frank decided not to go. These days came reasonably often, and much more frequently with the passing of time as the adult Frank recalled and mythologised his schooldays:

> I couldn't bear it. I just refused to go, so I hardly ever went there. They never taught me anything that was of the slightest use ... I think I might have taught them a thing or two.[281]

It must have been excruciating for him. It is hard to imagine that Frank would have fitted in at any school, but for him Melbourne Grammar was no better than Borstal. 'Grammar' had its clear notions of what a young man should be like, and what kind of education would best prepare him to be the leader of men that Old Grammarians were cut out to be. The school produced Prime Ministers like Bruce and Fraser, Governors-General like Lord Casey, captains of industry, fellows of real substance. It was a heavily masculine culture, where the sport and cadets that Frank regarded as 'gibberish' provided a critical training in toughness, self-reliance, team spirit, and the capacity to command.

Frank had no interest in any of it. He survived by making sure that his contempt for all the other boys always exceeded theirs for him. If they despised him for his manner and his indulgent mummy and his lack of enthusiasm for games or girls, his response was to exaggerate how little he had in common with any of them; in his final year, he took to wearing a voluminous black cloak over his school uniform. The son of Simon Legree could surely have nothing to fear from the abuse of children.

The impression that Frank liked to create was that nothing and no-one could get to him. His performances among adults as precociously urbane cocktail guest and to children of his own age as witheringly vicious outsider were, it seemed, equally convincing and effective. The Toorak matrons were duly charmed, the other kids successfully repelled. He seemed really to be a man in the body of a child, a preternaturally knowing creature whose power and poise rested in his indifference to the fears and longings that made normal mortals vulnerable. There were no cracks in the public mask, but

281 Keith Dunstan, 'Frank Thring' in *Ratbags*, Sydney, Golden press, 1979, p.129.

there were small signs, for the few able to see them, that the little boy who had lost his father and had no friend was still there somewhere underneath.

Nanny and Margaret the housekeeper had some glimpses, certainly; they might have called him 'Mister Frank' from the age of twelve, but according to Joan Thring (*nee* Cunliffe) they both saw a sadness that others, including probably his mother, could not see.[282] Nanny was the only person whom he would allow to cuddle him, and she retained that place in his life even when he grew big enough to dwarf almost everyone he met. And she knew of the existence of Eidy, the faded and worn child's rug that Frank took to bed and slept with every night until at least his late twenties; Margaret knew too, since she would have to slip it into the wash surreptitiously so that Eidy was always soft and warm and ready for the next night. His security blanket was one tangible sign of the persistence in private of the childhood needs that Frank denied in his every public action.

Frank told the story of the trams and the teachers often, and most of his interviewers were happy to leave it as just another anecdote from a most peculiar childhood. One of them, though, Bill Howie, in a radio interview on 3AK, pushed things a little further. Noting that schoolboys tend not to be very sensitive and supportive to classmates who are different, Howie wondered what it must have been like for an odd little boy who came to school in a Rolls with his teachers:

> BH: God, some of your days must have been unbearable.
>
> FT: Not when you're as vicious as I am.[283]

It was the classic, half-revealing, self-protective Thring answer. But the interviewer's persistence drew a response that loosened some of his subject's defences, as well as his syntax:

> One has to shake off the shackles. I don't know, I suppose I was some strange exotic creature in the middle of all this … thing. I mean, I couldn't understand Melbourne Grammar … But I never understood any … you see … the people were … I mean the only other thing that Melbourne Grammar has contributed to Australian culture is Barry Humphries. You can't fit people into slots …[284]

---

282 Joan Thring, interview with the author, Kensington, 14 December 2004.
283 Bill Howie interview, 12 November 1989.
284 ibid.

It was a rare moment, quickly closed off as soon as Frank realised the territory he had waded into: rare not only for the genuine reflectiveness, but for the glimpse of what it felt like to be different. In most of his reminiscences about 'silly Melbourne Grammar', Frank adopted a stance that was wonderfully superior; he alone was interesting, everyone else was boring. This time, though, he admitted the possibility of a different way of seeing, in which it was not he who was too difficult to understand, but them. It was they who were mysterious, all those other boys who found their way unerringly into one slot or another, while he could not. It was generous, probably, to allow the satirist Barry Humphries to share with him the title of Grammar's most distinguished Old Boy (although Frank might have been granting him only second place). But even Humphries would not have paid for it so dearly; he shared Frank's acerbic non-conformism and high camp manner, and would certainly have fancied a black cape, but his family could never have sent their son to school in a Rolls-Royce. What makes Frank's remarks so poignant is their revelation of a deeply frustrated effort to understand the people that the slots were made for, and the glimpse of hurtful years spent in trying to do so.

The 'shackles' that Frank referred to were not old school ties, but family ones. It was his mother, after all, with her sense of what was proper and fitting, who sent him to Melbourne Grammar. It was one of a number of ways in which her influence over his life was conspicuous in every day that he lived it; his father's was much less obvious, though probably finally the more powerful for that, and for the fact that the tie had in one sense been broken so early. Melbourne Grammar was Olive's choice, and Olive's fault. Frank dismissed it as 'silly', but it was not merely silly, it was a daily nightmare, and one of a growing list of things for which Frank would never forgive her.

Frank's dysfunctional childhood became a permanent part of the Thring myth, and even those who knew him much later in his life saw Olive's perverse understanding of mothering as a kind of disability. The actor John McCallum felt that it explained a lot about the way Frank went on to manufacture his life.

> He had a very difficult time with his mother. Used to dress him up as Little Lord Fauntleroy with those great wide collars. Going to school

> in the chauffeur-driven Rolls Royce. Must have been hell for him at school. [285]

Joan Cunliffe, who moved in with the Thrings when she was seventeen, a year younger than Frank, and ten years later briefly became Frank's wife, saw the process at first-hand:

> Olive was a wonderful person, such a strong, gutsy woman. But she was a terrible mother, so destructive. When his father died, she turned Frank into a replacement – he was only twelve or so, and yet he had to escort her to parties, be the host at dinner. She treated him like her boyfriend or something. He had to behave like an adult, and he was just a child. She never allowed him to grow up like other people. [286]

Blaming everything on the mother is a time-honoured ritual, and mostly profoundly unfair. But Olive just might be one of those mothers to whom it is not so unfair at all.

It was a strange and lonely childhood. In all the stories of his childhood told about and by (mostly by) Frank, there is no mention of a friend. In fact, only one story entered the Thring canon that involved Frank and another child, and a very famous one he was. Little Bobby Helpmann, the boy from Mount Gambier, who was destined to become, as an actor, a dancer and a choreographer, one of Australia's most distinguished cultural exports to the old world, crops up a number of times in other people's fond memories of what Frank told them about his childhood. The two little boys, according to the tale, had in common not only a prestigious Toorak address but rampantly ambitious mothers and exquisitely feminine tastes. So when Mrs Helpmann popped in for a cup of tea with her friend Mrs Thring in the sitting room at Rylands, their sons would be sent upstairs to play. And play they did, in Olive's bedroom, trying on her satins and furs, and puckering up in the mirror plastered in her make-up. Fred Parslow had the story from Frank, and delighted in the picture of Olive Thring and Mary Helpmann sitting there over the tea-tray, marvelling as they passed the sugar at how well the youngsters seemed to hit it off, and how quietly they were playing together.[287] It sounded like the foundation of a beautiful friendship, as well

---

285 John McCallum, interview with the author, Bayview, 22 August 2004.
286 Joan Thring interview, December 2004.
287 Frederick Parslow, interview with the author, 16 September 2004.

as a wonderfully subversive conspiracy between two little boys who had no intention of growing up 'straight'.

However, it simply wasn't true. Not any part of it. Frank and Robert Helpmann became friends, certainly. Later on they did find a lot in common, and there was warmth as well as some wariness between them; on Frank's several trips to London, Helpmann opened a lot of doors for him – he was a well-established star as well as a resident of London, and it is likely that Frank's friendships with the Oliviers and with Noel Coward came primarily through that connection.

But those daring little ventures in cross-dressing never happened. Robert Helpmann was born in 1909, seventeen years before Frank. The Toorak that little Robert moved to was certainly an exclusive suburb – but of Adelaide, not Melbourne. He did come to live in Melbourne, to study dance with the famous Anna Pavlova, but in 1923, three years before Frank was born. On Frank's first birthday, Helpmann at eighteen was already playing the lead in J.C. Williamson's season of *The New Moon*. And then Helpmann went to England, in 1932, when Frank turned six. He didn't return to Australia until 1955, when Frank was heading the other way to London, Olive had been dead for more than two years, and her satins and furs had presumably been dispersed through charity shops among a number of ladies of similar stateliness.

The story was an invention, from beginning to end. This is a pity, since biographies try to deal in true stories and gain a lot of liveliness from good anecdotes that really happened. But it is still a tale worth telling, because it represents the way in which Frank saw himself as a fictional subject, and because it allows a glimpse into his motives for doing so.

Sometimes, the stories that Frank told about himself – especially the more improbable ones – were true. Sometimes they were partly true, and just needed a little tweaking in the performance to add the requisite colour and movement to the narrative of his life. Sometimes they began with Frank confiding in someone else, and just grew – perhaps it was a case of Chinese Whispers operating on an already hectic personal life, or the encouragement that he seemed to give to others to play as he did with the intimate details of his past. Sometimes they were myths, like those that surrounded his marriage, that were contradicted by the facts. Sometimes, as in the Helpmann story, they are not only demonstrably false, but impossible; so inconceivable, in fact, that the funny story itself is subsumed within a wider funny story, where the joke is that anyone could actually believe it.

Frank would have liked the story about playing dress-ups with Bobby to be true, naturally; partly because he liked confirmation that his was an interesting life, but, more importantly, because he had never shared a secret with anyone. So much of his childhood was spent by himself, and in pretending. Bad lies tend to be born of desperation, rather than carefree invention.

Bobby Helpmann played the lead in another of Frank's supposed reminiscences. This one was about the distinctiveness of The Voice. Depending on when and where Frank told the story, it was either a blessing or a pathological problem; those who might have defined it as a disability could have included Helpmann, in what might have been an audition or a private audience that may conceivably have happened in 1946 or 1954 or not at all. But that devastating critique of Frank's undershot jaw was also attributed to a Drama teacher at Melbourne Grammar, a speech therapist in London, and one conservative director or another at the Little, or at Melbourne Repertory Theatre. It might have been a comment by somebody else altogether; it might, of course, have come from a diagnosis from the man himself. Frank created his mythology from the rich materials of his self-consciousness, and the things that he thought and that others might or might not have said were always as important to it as what might or might not have happened. The diagnosis – that with those peculiar consonants he could never become an actor – allegedly left him feeling 'suicidal', but it could well have been his own assessment, his own fear. Significantly, Frank didn't talk about any of this until he was sufficiently established in his career to present it both as a grand irony, and a triumph over adversity; presumably he felt free, then, to turn his insecurity into a joke.

Peter Cooke, who knew Frank much later but knew him well, and didn't need to believe Frank in order to like him, said this about his stories:

> It was rubbish. Fantasy, all of it. The thing was not to ask yourself whether these things were true, or half-true, or completely made up, but to try to work out why he was telling you, and what that really meant.[288]

It wasn't all rubbish, not all of it. But fantasy was a critical ingredient in Frank's sense of himself and his world. Trying to work out what it really meant is the process of uncovering his life.

---

288 Peter Cooke, interview with the author, 24 August 2004.

One of Frank's favourite anecdotes from this period of his life concerned his abortive drama debut at school. It was a safe story, in which the emotional costs were comparatively low and the joke was on the mundane experience of 'the master':

> I auditioned for the school play. So we're all up there in the middle of this dreadful Memorial Hall thing and the master – you would hardly call him a teacher – said, 'Now, ... we want you all to stand up and pretend you're hanging on to a strap in a tram which is swaying back and forth'. So everybody got up, and did this idiotic thing ... And he said, 'Well, Thring, you're not any good, you're absolutely hopeless. You'll never make a career'. And I said, 'Well, I hate to tell you, but I've never been on a tram. So I don't know what I'm doing'.[289]

Frank saw the trams every day, of course; they rumbled and clanged down Toorak Road on the other side of the high wall at Rylands. But actually to take a tram was unthinkable. It was an attitude he had absorbed from his mother. Toorak was synonymous in Melbourne with gracious living and indifference to cost, and its postcode, the legendary SE2, added a small fortune to any property in itself. The suburbs that lay to the south or the east were like another country; did human beings really live at the other end of that tramline?

> When my father built the house the Toorak tram finished at Orrong Road. This was the Styx and out there beyond Glenferrie Road was practically sheep pastures.[290]

Orrong Road was a couple of blocks away, Glenferrie just two more. Those areas were thoroughly, and prosperously, settled when young Frank put on the despised navy-blue. But imaginatively the universe according to Toorak was unchanged, and he inherited it. The notion that one might fall off the edge of the earth at Camberwell, just a couple of miles further east, was one that Frank never quite discarded.

So the strap-hanging story was most immediately a joke against ordinariness, and the deserts of suburbia, and silly Drama teachers – especially the one in question, since as one of the three teachers who regularly came to school in the Thring family Rolls, he should have known better.

---

289 Bill Howie interview, 12 November 1989.
290 Dunstan, *Ratbags*, p.128.

But even here the joke was finally on Frank. It was as though the boy was permanently a visitor in an alien land, in which all the signs, all the values and assumptions, were unintelligible. As in so many of his stories, Frank's assertion of a secure individuality sounds more like an admission of the ways in which he would always be vulnerable.

He wasn't chosen for the school play. In fact, Frank managed to pass through Melbourne Grammar without distinguishing himself in any way in anything. That, in itself, was quite a rare achievement. He did manage to fail the examination for the Intermediate Certificate, however, which was a little unusual. Students who did that at an expensive private school in those times either stayed on to repeat it for years as senior men in sporting teams, or left to run one of their father's businesses somewhere. Frank did neither. At the end of 1941, he left to take an unfashionable third option, at Taylor's Coaching College, an institution in the city that had a reputation for managing to push recalcitrant students over the line and into a qualification. He would work in the evenings and at week-ends at 3XY, the radio station his father had bought, and during the day he would go to Taylor's and do whatever people did to get their Intermediate.

> I failed what was called in those days the Intermediate Certificate ninety-seven times, and I said this is just absurd, I can't waste time piddling around with this, I'll go to work.[291]

As Frank presented it, the decision was entirely his, and he had but to speak and it was so. It seems a little odd that Olive was, for once, compliant – especially when going to Taylor's was such a lower-middle-class thing to do. She was the kind of mother who would insist on paying whatever had to be paid at Grammar until the tiresome people saw sense, and gave her son the certificate that mattered to them so much. There would be some embarrassment for her, at least, in telling her friends over cocktails that her only child preferred this dreary place to finishing with their sons, boys of his own kind, at Grammar. Moreover, if Frank refused to go back there, Olive would see no reason for his going instead to this place called a Coaching College. If he was to be an actor, an Intermediate Certificate was a particularly unnecessary piece of paper – as indeed it was if he chose to

291 Bill Howie interview, 12 November 1989. This is one of the more restrained versions of the story; as Frank told it to Steve Cossar on 'City Extra' in Sydney in 1980, after failing 'for the nine hundredth time', he informed 'what was left of my parents' of his decision to go to Taylors and to 3XY.

do as he then showed every sign of doing, and spent his life on the cocktail circuit courtesy of his father's shrewd investments.

But Olive agreed, or at least capitulated. Frank went to Taylor's, where he duly failed his Intermediate again at the end of 1942. His great discovery in that year, when his days seemed suddenly so spacious, was the back bar of the Australia Hotel, which was conveniently close to Taylor's on Flinders Lane. They served brandies there all day, and a pleasure that till then had had to wait until after school was suddenly much more available. There was another attraction there, too. The back bar was a notable meeting-place for homosexuals, where men in search of a partner, or men who thought they wanted no more than a sympathetic friend, or men who thought they were simply attracted by the ambience, could gather in reasonable safety. The times being as they were, a great deal remained covert, but most of the Australia's clientele found what they sought. What precisely Frank was after at this point in his life is uncertain, but probably he found it too.

Frank's relationship with his mother in these years was visibly more difficult, and when Joan Cunliffe saw it in 1945, she was both shocked by it and perplexed as to what could have brought them to such a point:

> It was just appalling. Something must have happened between them. I don't know what, and I never dared to ask. But they never spoke. It was terrible. She was devoted to him, but he would behave as though she wasn't there. Perhaps it was something at school, I don't know. But there was nothing to be done about it. Often, when we'd come home after seeing a film, and we'd be sitting in the kitchen talking, Olive would get out of bed and come down to us. As soon as she entered the room, Frank would walk out. Not a word to either of us ... It was tragic. She was so proud of him. I remember when he was in that play of Ray Lawler's [*Hal's Belles*], and after the show Ray saw this huge stately woman bearing down on him, and he braced himself for congratulations, and all she could say was, 'Isn't it amazing? He's only nineteen. Who'd believe it? Nineteen! It's extraordinary' – and so on. Not a word to the author. It was always all about Frank. It always was.[292]

The hostility that Joan saw was all on Frank's side, so if it was in fact precipitated by something that he had done, either at school or in his year in the bar behind Taylor's, the problem lay with his mother's response to it.

292 Joan Thring interview, 14 December 2004.

Whatever it was, by the time Joan knew the family it seemed not to affect Olive's devotion to her son; but, if she was right in her surmise, it had been a betrayal on Olive's part for which he could never forgive her. It might have been no more, perhaps, than a moment of courageous self-disclosure, in which she had failed him, by her disapproval, anger or incomprehension. Sons were not homosexual in the best of families. There were many things about the way that Olive had shaped his life that Frank had good reason to resent, but this additional wrong that was not to be discussed could not be expiated by any amount of love or indulgence.

Frank started work, in a fashion, at 3XY in 1942, and in the following year he became, in name at least, a full-time actor and announcer at the station:

> Because one didn't know what to do ... silly Melbourne Grammar. So I just went into this radio station as a sound-effects boy ... It was fortunate that I owned the radio station ... I fired revolvers, and poured water out of decanters, and did strange steps up gravel paths ... [293]

It was exaggerating matters a little to claim that he 'owned the radio station'; his father had bequeathed it all to Olive. But perhaps her compliance could be sufficiently taken for granted for her son to see his mother's ownership as just a technicality.

The 3XY studio was still in the Princess Theatre building, where Frank Thring senior had established it, and where he had had some of his most memorable triumphs. When his son strolled languidly into 'his' radio station, he was literally retracing steps that his father had taken, and that Frank junior at the age of nine had taken when he walked in there with his Dad in 1935. It was the first of a number of occasions when choices about the direction of his life, or the accidental circumstances that determined it, occurred in his father's shadow.

In 1943, at the age of seventeen, Frank began a regular program on Saturday afternoons between twelve and two in the afternoon, when Melburnians were by convention in their gardens or going to the football. The first half of

293 Bill Howie interview, 12 November 1989.

the session was dedicated to short works, with a weekly spot for a 'Famous Personality' and a smaller one reserved for 'Australian Artists'; its second half, which acquired a surprising following, consisted of 'Classics by Request'. He invited listeners to choose their favourites, and when they failed to respond he would invent names to attach to whatever he fancied playing that day. Frank's choices were more adventurous than those of his actual correspondents – in an interview, he later described his own musical tastes as 'completely – I don't know what the word is … I embrace anything, if you'll pardon the expression, as long as it's worthwhile …'[294]

Sometimes his choice would be determined by a different kind of taste. He was increasingly bored by the format and repertoire, and increasingly inclined to take a bottle of brandy or gin with him to make the time pass more agreeably. A long symphony was always a chance for a glass or three, and Joan Cunliffe, who met him at this time while she was working as a telephonist at 3XY, was a regular and rather anxious listener:

> We had a regular Saturday night date, and met each other at the corner of the State Theatre. I'd stand there I remember, like a little lost soul, but having listened to him all Saturday afternoon – I used to be glued to the radio listening to him – I could hear that he was getting rather inebriated. Because Frank had a low threshold of boredom, and he got really fed up with this deal, it was two hours long, and in between the records he was wine-tasting. So sometimes I was met by an inebriated Thring, and sometimes I was met by his elderly childhood nanny, who stayed on at Rylands until she died, and then I'd have to go home with my tail between my legs, often, because he hadn't turned up, he wasn't feeling well, and I remember my sister being told firmly by my mother not to tease me, or I'd be upset.[295]

Somehow the program lasted, which was more than could be said for his excursion into broadcasting an after-school children's show in September 1944. It was called 'The 3XY Pals' Session', and ran from five till five-thirty from Monday to Friday. Frank shared the program with 'Connie' (Zell Manners) and 'Auntie Dot' (Dot Mendoza at the keyboard). As Uncle Frank, he offered a variation on his Simon Legree persona that his young

294 ibid.
295 Joan Thring, interview with Clive Starke and Frank Van Straten, 3LO 'Nostalgia Show', commemorative program on Frank Thring, 5 March 1995.

listeners probably found deliciously scary. But he was mostly an endearingly wicked uncle: he popped up in drag with Nance Martell as the Ugly Sisters in 3XY's Christmas panto Cinderella later in the year, and as the avuncular narrator of 'Santa Comes to Earth', in which Santa's efforts to find someone in Melbourne who still believed in the true Christmas spirit ended triumphantly, if improbably, in his discovery of a kindly parking inspector. And he gave the weekly prizes for best riddle – a cricket bat for the lucky boy, a tennis racquet for the lucky girl – with a commendable show of enthusiasm.

Still, the combination of boredom and brandy could lead a man like Frank into perilous waters. Joan listened to the 'Pals', as she did to 'Classics by Request', with less personal investment but with even greater horror:

> He used to say the most awful things when he was drunk, he didn't care what he said, and I don't know how on earth he got away with it. He'd say in this sinister voice, 'Now children, have you got a pussy? I want you to look underneath your pussy if you have one, and see what you can find'. You couldn't do that now, it was unbelievable. No one ever said a thing.[296]

All the same, the management was listening, and in due course thought it prudent to give Uncle Frank an indefinite rest.

Frank's career as an announcer was not entirely disastrous, and his debut as a radio actor in 1944 won immediate notice. He had shown no particular desire for life as an actor until this moment, and, like a lot of the decisions that shaped his career, it happened by accident. For once it was determined by somebody else's bad habits:

> One day, an actor in one of our programs showed up drunk – as is their wont – and I volunteered to do his part. Since I owned the radio station, no one dared to object. My performance that day was so effective that a local newspaper bestowed on me The Best Radio Performance Of The Week Award. That essentially was the beginning of my acting career.[297]

The story sounded improbable, but for once nothing was exaggerated. The role was a suitably sinister one, 'one of those Vincent Price, out-of-the-grave

296 Joan Thring interview, 14 December 2004.
297 Interview with Steve Cossar, 2BL, 1980.

parts',[298] and it ushered in a number of others of the same kind. The *Listener-In* for July 1–7, 1944, announced with some breathlessness the premiere of a new series of weekly plays on Monday nights at nine, entitled 'Strange Library', sponsored by the makers of the breakfast cereal 'Vita-Brits'. These 'eerie stories with a hint of the supernatural' were the work of Arthur Collins, and featured 'a young aspirant to radio acting honours in Frank Thring, son of the founder of the station, the late F. T. Thring. Frank has a good radio voice, sound diction and a sense of the value of pause to provide dramatic emphasis'.[299] The review of the premiere, 'Lady Without a Soul', a week later, presumably by the same anonymous critic, found all expectations triumphantly (if predictably) met:

> Listeners with a penchant for plays dealing with the macabre and uncanny should make an early date with 'Strange Library', which had its premiere at 3XY last Monday evening. …Reminiscent of the horror stories of Edgar Allan Poe, the drama was well acted by a cast in which Robert Burnard as the artist, Madge Aubrey as Lola and Frank Thring as the mysterious Mr Brown were outstanding figures. Frank Thring brought excellent diction and a sense of character and dramatic emphasis to his first important role.[300]

Frank was away. Suddenly, he had something that looked almost like a career. The horror genre was popular, and he brought to it a sardonic humour that made the tone a little more complex and, perhaps, widened the potential audience. He tried his hand at writing in the genre, too, and later in 1944 produced a script of his own, 'Devil's Holiday', in which Frank played the lead role of Lucifer, the genial host. Its style is neatly encapsulated in the play's opening moments:

> T.T. OPENING CHORDS.
>
> A/CER (CUE) 'Devil's Holiday'
>
> TT COMPLETE THE OPENING MUSICAL FIGURE THEN FADE AND HOLD.

---

298 Interview with Steve Cossar, 2BL, 1980.

299 *The Listener-In*, July 1–7, 1944, Frank Thring scrapbook, Performing Arts Museum, Melbourne, p.2.

300 *Listener-In*, July 8–14, 1944, Frank Thring scrapbook, Performing Arts Museum, Melbourne p.2.

> A/CER (CUE) Lucifer takes a vacation on earth and meets – a client!
>
> TT THEME
>
> A/CER (CUE) Ssh! Quiet! Here he comes – now.
>
> TT FADE IN ELEVATOR RISING TO STOP. DOOR CLANGS.
>
> LUCIFER (CHUCKLES) Good evening friends! Badness me, I nearly omitted the 'r' and called you fiends. Of course you're not – (CHUCKLE) – not yet, anyway. Do you know I feel quite at home on this earthly talent quest of mine. What with inflation, black markets, spy fever, war fever, atom bombs and cement at forty pounds a ton, I feel we should transfer my establishment up here holus bolus and give my guests some real discomfort. Still I suppose if you can put up with this you can put up with anything. Some people even go out of their way to come to us. Take for instance what's going to happen within a few minutes in the twenty-seventh floor penthouse of an apartment building on Riverside in New York.
>
> Tonight, a certain person will be – er – (CHUCKLES) – going down in my lift. Which one? See if you can guess. Perhaps there'll be more than one. If that happened I would be a lucky devil, wouldn't I?[301]

It is Frank's satanic persona in full flight, with a fair dash of bad jokes left over from his scurrilous career as Uncle Frank.

In his first year in radio, Frank had made, by happy if ironic accident, a move from a career in production, such as his father might have chosen, to the acting career that his mother had always had in mind for him. A stint reading Lucifer or the mysterious Mr Brown was still some way short of a conquest of the Australian stage, but it was not necessarily as ludicrously far as it might seem at first glance. The opportunities for Australian actors and writers were perennially limited, and in 1944 were further constrained by a world war. The choices for Australian audiences were similarly narrow, and television did not arrive in Australia to widen them until 1956, the year of the Melbourne Olympics. Till then, as Frank recalled in conversation with Keith Dunstan, radio drama was the staple domestic entertainment, and radio plays and series provided significant employment for people committed to a theatrical career.

301 Typed manuscript in Frank Thring papers, Performing Arts Museum, Melbourne. Final page has note 'Typed: Jean Hanger 18:7:51'.

> Like the pictures, radio was big then. It was all radio serials and they were so important you had to choose your nights. When *One Man's Family* or *Coronets of England* was on you just had to stay home to listen in. And these shows were all done live in the studio. We didn't have the convenience of tapes. If you wanted to record there was a bloody great disc about four feet wide.[302]

The *Listener-In*, a weekly magazine devoted to the doings of Melbourne's radio performers both in front of the microphone and away from it, often ran studio photographs of the stars at work, with the 'bloody great disc' squarely in view to confirm the impressive technology of the process.

Rather paradoxically, then, the radio actor enjoyed a high degree of visibility, which was very useful between stage engagements. Frank found his way into the spotlight with ease, as a little item of hot news headlined 'Getting the Bird' shows:

> Frank Thring was in for a surprise when he opened a parcel that arrived at his home one day last week. It contained three dead chickens. The gift was anonymous and Frank is wondering who chose this unusual way of giving the bird. Obviously intended to arrive alive, the birds had been killed by the hot day and the confined space. Not so funny – for the chickens.[303]

To receive a three-chicken salute, whether as a thoughtful gift or an insult, was a sign that someone out there was listening. But as Frank probably observed, it was a paltry matter; the fact that it was thought worthy of a newspaper report suggested that some people were actually interested. This was stardom, Melbourne style, in 1944. It could be a very small world.

At the same time, Frank took a regular spot in 'Youth Parade', a weekly playhouse for young actors and younger listeners that followed the 'Pals' program on Friday evenings. He also made a significant mark over several weeks in 'Robin Snood and his Merrie Men', inevitably as the villainous Sheriff foiled again and again by Jon Ewart as the charismatic Snood. But while Thring the actor had taken wing, a report in the *Listener-In* later in the year suggested that his propensity to become easily bored was already a problem:

---

302 Dunstan, *Ratbags*, p.130.

303 *Listener-In*, undated, Frank Thring scrapbook, Performing Arts Museum, Melbourne p.6.

> Frank Thring, spreading his wings in XY's productions, has come to the conclusion that he's been 'typed' already in his new found career. He's had role after role in broadcast and recorded productions and all have been of the sinister type.
>
> In fact, Frank's six feet something of height is slowly acquiring a sinister hunch and he almost slinks around the many rabbit warren passages which is the 3XY studios.[304]

Relief, however, was on the way, from two unlikely sources: from the stage, in which Frank had thus far shown no interest at all, in the form of the Melbourne Repertory Theatre; and from the Australian government, which, startlingly, conscripted him into the Royal Australian Air Force on his nineteenth birthday.

The Melbourne Repertory Theatre was looking for someone to play Henry VIII in *Hal's Belles*, a new work by the young playwright Ray Lawler, who a decade later would change the direction of Australian theatre with his classic play *Summer of the Seventeenth Doll*. At a grim time for Australian writers and performers, Melbourne companies like the Repertory, established by Gregan McMahon in Middle Park, and the Little Theatre in South Yarra under its indomitable co-founder, manager and director, Irene Mitchell, were among the few forums in which they could strut their stuff. It was prestigious amateur work, reasonably adventurous, and provided a place where theatre people might genuinely learn their craft. The Melbourne Repertory wanted a big man with a big presence for the lead role, and someone suggested the nineteen-year-old who was playing whatever devils were going at 3XY – especially as, by a neat coincidence, he had recently been cutting a dash in a lunchtime fashion show at the Myer Emporium, squiring the models as just the character they were after:

> Now I'd just been appearing as Henry VIII in a dreadful sort of wartime pageant in the Myer Mural Hall. Because you see, one was six feet and

304 *ibid.*, p.7.

> one had the beard and the red hair, in the days when one had hair … and somebody said, well, Frank Thring's looking magnificent going up and down the catwalk with six Toorak socialites and an executioner at the Myer Mural Hall raising money for war bonds or whatever the hell we were doing.[305]

The cause was in fact a fund for 'Totally and Permanently Incapacited' ex-servicemen. It was one of Olive's fundraisers, which added a touch of irony to an occasion that was bizarre enough in itself, let alone in its freakish significance for her son and the producers of *Hal's Belles*. Frank's memories of the event forty years on were a little cloudy: in the same show he was also camping it up as Louis XV, with Miss Sunday Wenham as his Pompadour, with a beardless chin to which the 'Brevettes' gossip columnist for the *Listener-In* delighted in drawing attention:

> We secondarily refer to expectations aroused by the promised Friday arvo Myer Mural Hall debut of hairless boy Frankie Thring in the role of heavily bearded Henry, which will necessitate his coping with six temporary wives … as pretty a harem as ever a fledgling boy had at his disposal.[306]

The people at Melbourne Repertory must have felt some qualms about his youth, and at the stories that were already circulating about his habits. But Frank was offered, and accepted, the role. He had already devoted quite a lot of his life to playing roles much older than his years, and he was unlikely to resist any opportunity to slip into king-size doublet and hose. As he would have said – and indeed almost certainly did say – he always had a weakness for a bit of ruff.

It was not quite a triumph, though, whatever Olive in her post-show euphoria may have believed. It was an important production for launching two of the major careers in Australian theatre, Lawler's and Thring's, but neither saw it as very auspicious in itself. Lawler later suppressed and destroyed the script, and Frank would later refer to his stage debut in 'some awful thing by Ray Lawler'.[307] He kept the reviews in his scrapbook, though they were not

305 Interview with Steve Cossar, 'City Extra', 2BL,1980.

306 *Listener-In*, undated article on 'The Cavalcade of Famous Lovers', Myer Mural Hall 10–17 August 1945, Frank Thring scrapbook, Performing Arts Museum, Melbourne, p.82.

307 Interview with Steve Cossar, 'City Extra', 2BL,1980.

quite as he would have wished, especially the one that hailed the 'memorable performance' of 'Harry Thring'.[308] Still, *Hal's Belles* did neither the actor nor the playwright any harm. Frank Thring was now established as a likely leading man for companies like the Melbourne Repertory and the Little, which put him right on the edge of a profession.

His call to military service in the twilight months of the war was a minor irritant to the budding actor, though almost certainly a greater one to the Air Force. Olive was appalled that her son was supposedly going into battle, and immediately began exerting what influence she could to put a stop to the nonsense. She was somehow able to defer his departure until *Hal's Belles* closed in mid-October. But even she could not prevent the government having its way, and Frank was duly enlisted.

> It was a brilliant example of the idiocy of government. I mean, the war was almost over. I spent the first night at the Melbourne Cricket Ground and they packed me off to Shepparton. I won a lot of money at poker in the train on the way.[309]

Joan, with whom he was having a friendship based on movie matinees that was looking increasingly and surprisingly like a youthful romance, was called to farewell him at Spencer Street railway station as he set out for the dangers of the training camp at Shepparton, a Victorian country town around one hundred kilometres north of Melbourne:

> He rather liked the dressing-up. He asked me to come and see him off at Spencer Street, and to wear a hat – for some reason, he thought the hat was very important. In those days we wore these digger hats with the upturned brim. When I look at the photo I think it looks frightful.[310]

Frank liked the sentiment in the situation, and costumed it accordingly. Joan Bennett and Celia Johnson and all those other stoic sweethearts in war romances always farewelled their young men under a significant hat, and evidently Frank felt it only fair that, like him in his handsome new uniform, Joan should dress for the part.

---

308 Unattributed and undated review, Frank Thring scrapbbok, Performing Arts Museum, Melbourne, p.84.

309 Dunstan, *Ratbags*, p.130.

310 Joan Thring interview 14 December 2004

The right hat was a crucial consideration, and had determined Frank's decision about which sector of the services he should adorn. The little RAAF cap was much nicer than anything the Army or Navy could offer, and one of the first things Frank did on taking possession of his uniform was to arrange a studio sitting with a photographer. There he is at nineteen, then, with the cap perched fetchingly at an improbable angle, the collar of his greatcoat turned up against the elements. There is not a hint of the heaviness of feature that later made him such a natural in all the variations on King Herod that he went on to play in the next two decades. In fact this young man with the slightly delicate long, smooth face, the full lips that decline to smile, the dreamily distracted eyes, is a revelation; he could play a romantic lead if he wanted, one of those magnificent boys in their flying machines doomed to die heroically in some foreign field. The inscription to Joan on the photograph disturbs the stereotype a little – 'To Flower-Girl from Pansy-Boy'.[311]

Cameras can tell very pretty lies. His couple of months in the Air Force were a travesty, and fortunately ended before he could do significant harm to himself or others. The Rolls came up from Melbourne every second day on a regular errand of mercy with supplies, and Frank settled into full-time subversion of the war effort:

> Frankly I rather liked the idea of Thring the sharp-shooting tail gunner, but when I got to the camp I saw … really … it wasn't me. The food wasn't quite that to which I was accustomed. So I devised all the various methods I could [to] bludge and languish in the sick bay. They put me in a hut with seven others and most of the time I just refused to get up. In the evening I would wait for the others to return and I would have whisky, champagne, delicious food, all sent up from Melbourne, like anchovies and caviar, and we would have a marvellous party.[312]

When inspections were made of Hut AC2, Aircraftsman Thring, if he wasn't already in the sick bay, would hide in the lavatory. His aim was to persuade the Air Force that he did not exist. If half of Frank's stories of his time on active service were true, the Air Force must certainly have wished that it was so. The farce came to an end when Olive's rich and powerful friends arranged his discharge on medical grounds. It was established that Frank had a hammer-toe that prevented him from marching. A man could

311 Inscription on photograph given by Joan Thring to the author.
312 Dunstan, *Ratbags*, p.130.

hardly fly if he couldn't march. So Frank left Shepparton quite unscathed by the war, and a terrible line of jokes about rear-gunners mercifully came, as Frank no doubt observed on his return to Melbourne, to an appropriate end.

He came back to town just in time for a return season of *Hal's Belles*, which was picked up by Gertrude Johnson of the National Theatre for a Christmas season at Eastern Hill, just opposite St Patrick's Cathedral. There was nothing to stop him resuming exactly where he had left off three months before. Joan was there under an appropriate hat to welcome the hero home, a career on the amateur stage beckoned, and a fatted calf was always on offer at Rylands. But while the interruption had been a minor one, it was quite decisive. He had, in some degree, freed himself from his 'shackles': a combination of his dissoluteness and his absence had largely exempted Frank from some of those youthful responsibilities as Olive's consort, and he had no need anymore to pretend that her friends were his own. And he had spent long enough going about his father's business at 3XY.

The first of the independent steps seemed quite a small one. He involved himself enthusiastically in amateur theatre in Melbourne, to a degree that looked dangerously like a commitment to a career. This in itself probably would have surprised nobody; a young man with a considerable fortune and a tendency to be easily bored needs a hobby, and a young man with Frank's predilection for dressing-up and showing-off was always likely to be drawn to the theatre. The possibility that Frank's interests might, for once, have been serious, however, is supported by the choice he made as to where to pursue them. Frank didn't continue with either of the companies that had given him his chance in *Hal's Belles*, although they offered the longest traditions and the most glamorous foyers in the local amateur scene. He chose the Little Theatre in South Yarra, a company that had plausible pretensions to serious, and even radical, practice.

Melbourne Repertory and the National were worthy institutions, but there was something about their attitudes as well as their clientele that would be forever middle-aged. The Little was more youthful and adventurous, and a number of its actors moved between its seasons and those of the Melbourne University Drama Club. Irene Mitchell, its resident director, and Brett Randall, its administrator, were respected theatre people, and determinedly unconventional in choice of repertoire and approach. Its facilities were poor: its home was 'a dreadful 120-seated church hall', in which 'you were lucky if you could find a door that opened so that that you could get on the set'.[313] But

313 Bill Howie interview, 12 November 1989.

even that was a sort of warranty of lofty aims. The Little was the company with which he was most likely to learn something.

The small step was a decisive one, but there was a larger one in prospect behind it. The Little Theatre, though delightful in its way, was, for a big man, very small. And so, in a way, was Melbourne. Casting off shackles was a difficult thing to do in a city where the ghost of a famous father or the looming presence of a very conspicuous mother seemed to be waiting around every corner.

For eighteen months, there was plenty to distract him. He appeared briefly in Melbourne Repertory's next show, Perry Frame's *No Other Heaven*, in March, before embarking on an unbroken series of productions for the Little. There were six of them, all of them wonderfully varied in style, and each adding to Frank's standing in local theatre.

In June there was Shaw's *The Simpleton of the Unexpected Isles*, in which he played 'the imperturbable priest Pra';[314] in August, *Acacia Avenue* by Denis and Mabel Constanduros, in which he proved surprisingly ready and able to blend into an ensemble; in October, *Enduring as the Camphor Tree*, an oriental tale written by the Australian playwright, Russell Oakes, a lieutenant in the Army's Medical Corps, in which Frank appeared as 'the abominable Lord Ku';[315] in December, another Australian work, Sumner Locke Elliott's *Invisible Circus*, a satire on the radio industry, in which he played the tycoon J.B. Olliphant; in March, he was one of a number of Little Theatre luminaries who anonymously donated their talents to a spectacular production in the Melbourne Town Hall of Dorothy L. Sayers' Passion Play *The Just Vengeance*;[316] in April, he played the lead, Joris Kuiper, in Jan de Hartog's drama *Skipper Next to God*; in June, he was a villain again, as 'the sinister Prus' in Karel Capek's *The Macropulos Secret*.[317]

Frank's appearance in Sumner Locke Elliott's satire *Invisible Circus* was notable for two reasons. The play was a smart, contemporary treatment of life

314 Frank Thring scrapbook, Performing Arts Museum, Melbourne, p.42.

315 Unattributed and undated review of *Under the Camphor Tree*, Frank Thring scrapbook, Performing Arts Museum, Melbourne, p.44. The reviewer noted that 'Mrs F.W. Thring was there to see her son in the villain's part – and very good he was'.

316 The production was under the auspices of the Methodist Young People's Department, which was a most unlikely patron for a man of Frank Thring's habits.

317 Frank Thring scrapbook, Performing Arts Museum, Melbourne, p.65.

in radio drama, a subject that Frank knew a little about. 'Brevettes' reflected with a little acerbity on an actor of whom perhaps too much was being seen, in every sense:

> … the inescapable Frankie Thring, who if he continues to land fat parts with this outfit, is going to begin kidding himself that he's a rival for Charles Laughton at any drop of the handkerchief.[318]

Whether Frank drew for this role on some special knowledge, real or imagined, of his father, is not clear; the script gives Olliphant no redeeming virtues, and most of those who knew F.T. granted him either a fair share of those or, at the very least, complexity. But Frank, certainly, would have been conscious of the irony.

The Sumner Locke Elliott connection came to have greater significance for Frank a couple of years later, in relation to Elliott's much more distinguished play *Rusty Bugles,* which appeared at Sydney's Independent in late 1948. Frank wasn't in the right town at the right time; Doris Fitton's celebrated and controversial production was already playing, or being banned, at just the time that Frank came home to Melbourne after his first excursion to London. When the production was taken over for a commercial – and now fully professional – tour in 1949, however, the cards fell perfectly for Frank to take over the role of the least likeable character in the play, Sergeant Brooks. It was to prove another moment of serendipity, to add to the timely tipsiness of another actor that started his career in radio drama, and the fashion fundraiser at Myer's that led to *Hal's Belles.*

The six major roles that he played for the Little in 1946–7 were strikingly diverse. But some things were constant. Irene Mitchell, whose eclectic interests were directly reflected in the repertoire, was always director. Frank was continually playing men at least a generation older than himself, all of them domineering types, and most of them vicious. And he, and the company, won favourable notices in all six from a press that seemed always determined to look on the bright side.

There was a touch of the exotic about almost all of them that fed the image of cultural openness that the Little was keen to cultivate, and that must have delighted Frank with his interest in, and flair for, that kind of thing. The newspapers liked it, too, and they liked to link it especially with

318 *Listener-In*, undated review, Frank Thring scrapbook, Performing Arts Museum, Melbourne, p.52.

the young man who had already become through his work in radio very visible in the social scene that surrounded, supported and inflated the egos of local performers.

Frank had come a long way in a short time on the local theatre circuit for a young man without actor-training or an Intermediate Certificate. The question that faced him now was where to go next. He had no evident talent for anything else, so it was clear that, wherever it was, it would involve the theatre. But the step into the professional arena was a big one for Frank, not only because of his lack of formal credentials or relevant connections, but because it would mean turning a delightful hobby into a regular job, and Frank's temperament and habits were not particularly suited to regularity.

While rehearsing the role of 'the sinister Prus' in *The Macropulos Secret*, Frank had celebrated his twenty-first birthday. But he had been behaving in some respects like an adult, and had had the key to the door at Rylands, for years. The symbolic moment called for a decisive act. The problem was to find what might be worth doing.

At twenty-one, Frank did what hordes of other young Australians, with or without artistic ambitions, have done when faced with the panic of becoming an adult. He went overseas, to fumble his way through some version of the Grand Tour of Europe, with a typical focus on England, the place that Australians were still quaintly inclined to call the mother-country. For him it was easier than it was for most others; his mother's customary generosity with his father's fortune could still open almost any door. He went for a while, and came back for a while. Then he went again for a while, and came back for a while again. So it continued, really, for more than a decade. During that period Frank achieved quite a lot as an actor, and seemed several times on the edge of an international fame that he perversely refused to grasp. But the dominant impression is of a man looking for something that he couldn't find.

That wasn't the public story, of course. That story was about an outrageously confident young man eager to embrace the theatrical destiny that surely awaited him. He was too big a fish for this colonial pool. Frank announced his plans to conquer London in May. Not for the first time, and certainly not for the last, the article was rather less specific about its subject's achievements than those of his father:

> Frank, who had his 21st birthday during the run of the play [*Skipper Next to God*], and had a party at his home to celebrate the occasion, plans to study with the Royal Academy of Dramatic Art as a preliminary to embarking on a career on the London stage. He has inherited a flair for the theatre from his father, the late F. W. Thring, who prior to founding Station 3XY, presented many attractions in Melbourne, including the first production here of 'Children in Uniform'. He also introduced Australian audiences to that delightful artist Alice Delysia, who appeared at the Princes Theatre under his direction in 'Mother of Pearl'.
>
> Young Frank Thring, in addition to marked talent for acting as revealed in the several good roles he has played for the Little and National theatre groups, has also ambitions as a producer.[319]

Frank had not thought to alert RADA to the privilege they were about to enjoy, and indeed seems to have had no contact at all with the Academy before or during his London visit. The notion that some 'study' (something for which Frank had never shown any inclination) might be necessary before 'embarking on a career on the London stage' was an unusually modest gesture, but it confirmed how little he had actually thought about it.

A couple of days before Frank's departure, the *Argus* ran an editorial on the way Australia's brightest and best were forced to take their talents out of the country, if they were to find a more fitting stage.

> The passenger list on the 'Stratheden', when she leaves this week for London, will contain the names of a number of artists prominent in different fields of Australia's entertainment world. They include from Melbourne: Robert Chisholm, Les Raphael, Alan Christie, and Frank Thring. Their departure serves to emphasise once again, that in the show business at any rate, Australia is no land of opportunity.
>
> The three last-named travellers are all going overseas to seek the "break" which has not come their way here. Alan Christie has retired into oblivion after a number of appearances as juvenile lead in musical

319 *Listener-In*, undated article, Frank Thring scrapbook, Performing Arts Museum, Melbourne, p.63.

> comedy, and Frank Thring, who has attracted attention as a repertory actor, has ambitions to follow in the footsteps of his father, the late F.W. Thring, as stage producer and entrepreneur.
>
> … And so another of her talented sons is lost to Australia … [as each of them] goes to join the ranks of his numerous predecessors who found in London and New York, the encouragement and opportunity denied them in their own country.[320]

It was an old complaint. The fact that Robert Chisholm, the dashing Captain Lake of *Collits' Inn* thirteen years before, was of the company seemed to confirm that it was not a problem peculiar to young men in a hurry.

The *Stratheden* had more theatricals on deck than most theatres: Brett Randall, the co-founder and Director of Melbourne's Little Theatre, was one of a number who might fairly have felt a bit miffed at being left off the editor's list.[321] But while his explicit agenda was according to stereotype, Frank was very vague about when, where and how it was to be achieved. He gave the impression to the *Listener-In* that he was going to London for the foreseeable future, but in fact Frank had no idea how long he might stay, and must have had some awareness of the complex feelings about his home that would always bring him back. Apart from a general aspiration 'to follow in his father's footsteps', it's not clear that Frank knew what he was looking for at all.

The permanent characteristic of that searching was his solitariness, and it was the critical fact that Frank must have confronted whenever he thought that he might as well go overseas, and then that, after a while, he might as well go home. His relationship with his mother, on Joan's account, was irreparably distant and disastrous. Even Olive's victory over the armed services in winning him a discharge did nothing to change those horrible, cruel, cavernous silences at home. Rylands retained all the infuriating

---

320 *Argus*, 'The Editor's Box', 10 August 1947, Frank Thring scrapbook, Performing Arts Museum, Melbourne, p.67. London was sometimes the artistic El Dorado that ambitious young colonials hoped to find, but at least as often it proved an unmanageably large and anonymous place that swallowed outsiders. For Allan Christie and the musician Les Raphael the latter was the case, though Raphael re-established a successful career in Australia in the late 1950s and 1960s.

321 The first edition of the *Newsletter*, published by The Melbourne Little Theatre in August 1947, has Randall's imminent departure as its lead item; in smaller font on the second page, the fact that Frank Thring would also be sailing on the *Stratheden* provides the fifth brief paragraph in its 'People … ' column. Frank is reported to be 'contemplating a dramatic course at the Old Vic'.

elements of the matriarchy, and it had turned colder still: Nanny, always the warm and welcoming breast, ever giving while demanding so little of him, was sick now, and dying. There was Joan, of course. In one sense or another, there would always be Joan. But in those years, at least, Joan could hardly hold him.

The relationship with Joan that had started when they were not much more than a couple of mischievous kids at 3XY had already passed through several permutations. She was an interesting, unrealised mixture, this rather quiet, well-brought-up girl from the suburbs, who happened to be also strikingly pretty, and to nurse a vague hankering to be a fashion model one day. She started work at the 3XY switchboard, and immediately encountered Frank. She had never met anyone remotely like him before. This was not surprising, since few people had:

> He used to pester me, when I had my little switchboard room, which was the side entrance of the Princess Theatre, and of course people came in to see radio shows, so I had to greet all these people, and he was not supposed to be there, of course, so he used to hide under my desk, which had a cover all around it, and he couldn't be seen, and so while I was trying to have a proper conversation he'd be tickling me … He was a prankster, childhood jokes he liked playing, really rather frightening ones a lot of the time. He made me play truant, too, I used to make up stories about suddenly having a violent stomach ache or something, and we used to go to the movies.[322]

Frank was a thoroughly bad influence, and the nice seventeen-year-old girl from West Preston had never really met one of those before. The demonic persona that the 3XY audiences, adult and child, had found so deliciously unsettling, was part of that appeal. He was, by all accounts, wonderfully disreputable and talented, too. And there was the sense as well that Frank knew things, about art and the world and life, that were hardly dreamed of in her West Preston philosophy:

> He taught me a lot. We went to a lot of plays and films, and we'd go to Florentino's for lunch, or the Windsor Bar for brandy crusters. I just adored him. But he was terrible, even then.[323]

---

322 Joan Thring, 3LO interview, 5 March 1995.
323 ibid.

It was a very odd romance, for all sorts of reasons. Moreover, there were quite a lot of those Saturdays when Joan was dressed up for an evening out and Frank had become a little too bored during the afternoon, and she and Nanny would go home on their respective trams, for a cup of tea and an early night.

An attractive girl could arguably have done better, and, normally, would certainly have required that she should be taken less for granted. But one of the reasons why Frank came to trust and depend on Joan was that she seemed to understand him, and yet, extraordinarily, still liked him. She placed no demands on him, as almost everybody else tried to do. She never disapproved; Joan was always, in those years, sufficiently intrigued by what was different about Frank not to try to change him. Joan was a younger, lovelier version of his Nanny, and even when he drank far too much or behaved disgracefully, he knew that she would never despise him.

He tested her, and even seemed to try to drive her away, but Joan stayed.

> He loved hiding in cupboards and leaping out to terrify you. There was one day when I came home from working at the Melbourne Reporting Branch, and he'd been at home all day; he was in a play at night, but had nothing else to do. Suddenly he just appeared on the stairs as Frankenstein's monster, hideously deformed and covered in boils. I knew it was him, but it was terrifying seeing him like that. I had to run out of the house … He loved frightening the bejesus out of me.[324]

Joan's loyalty and resilience made possible the nearest thing to a romance that Frank would ever know. She talked about it in an interview with Clive Stark fifty years later, when she briefly came back to Melbourne for a memorial service in Frank's honour:

> JT: *Kings Row* we were besotted by, we saw that about five times, and we used to go rowing, Frank used to row me down the river in a boat …
>
> CS: It sounds very romantic.
>
> JT: It was romantic, he was very romantic. Nobody understands Frank!
>
> CS: I'm trying to picture you in a sort of a picture hat lying back under the willows …
>
> JT: No, it wasn't that romantic. I think I had to help with the rowing.[325]

---

324 Joan Thring interview 14 December 2004.
325 Joan Thring 3LO interview 5 March 1995.

But it wasn't enough to keep him in Melbourne in 1947, or on a number of other occasions. Nor was it enough to sustain their marriage beyond a year. It would prove the basis for a life-long friendship, but for Frank the relationship was less the culmination of all that he could expect of love than a reminder of a kind of love that he could never have.

Joan followed Frank down a number of the roads he took, and finally across the world into a Stratford wedding. She was one of the behind-the-scenes belles in *Hal's Belles* in late 1945, and her living arrangements at Rylands had their origin when she was persuaded to stay over after rehearsals rather than attempt the long journey out to West Preston late at night. She stayed, on and off, for eight years. She performed in plays that Frank acted in at the Little Theatre and prompted in plays that he directed at the Arrow. She lived with his mother at Rylands, a friend and confidante and sometimes almost a daughter, whether Frank happened to be there or not. She mediated between Olive and Frank without ever asking the terrible questions, and comforted each of them when the other became more than usually intolerable.

In the end, though, she wanted more from Frank than he could give, and, after his father and his Nanny and his mother had deserted him and died, Joan let him go, as it would always have been apparent to everybody but the two of them that she would have to.

TRAVELLING FROM FREMANTLE TO LONDON

S.S. Stratheden, 9 August 1947

For the first time he could remember, he was clear. Frank leaned back in the deckchair on the first-class deck of the Stratheden, testing it first to be certain that it hadn't been designed for a person of more compact or Asian persuasion (everything these days seemed to be made in Hong Kong), and closed his eyes.

It was a tad alarming, this freedom. For one thing, he couldn't help feeling that he was expected, at last, to put his money where his mouth was, or some equally disagreeable gymnastic manoeuvre. Well, it was her money, of course; but having it, without her, without her for the first time being there to watch and to approve or more likely disapprove, or even without her to tell him for the umpteenth time how much she loved him .... Well, anyway, it was legally, at least, her money, and it laid out before him a disconcertingly broad vista of opportunities, while at the same time depriving him of someone, anyone, other than himself to blame.

People's expectations were their own problem, but he couldn't deny that he'd fed them a little. As one does. He had contacts in London, as he'd blithely been saying for months. But what he hadn't told them was that his contacts were his expatriate cousins Kreitmayer, or whatever they were calling themselves this week, and while John was a decent doctor, and an almost excessively decent man, he was hardly an entrée to jolly old RADA, or the Old Vic, or any of the other places Frank had told people he might grace.

Truth was, his planning hadn't extended far beyond the escape from Melbourne and Mother and all the other things that had so brilliantly and completely fucked up his life. Anyway, there'd be plenty of time to call in on RADA or the venerable Vic when he got there. This was a time to enjoy just being away.

He hadn't escaped altogether, of course. Apparently one never could. Brett Randall was on board, holding court night after night to a bunch of budding actors even younger than Frank. Less than budding, in truth, though rather beautiful, some of them. Brett had been surprised, well, appalled, that none of them actually knew who he was. Fuckwit. Still, one's connection with Brett could be useful, providing it didn't turn into a leash. Frank had joined them at the hilariously shrill Table Fifty a couple of times, and said several things he probably shouldn't have. Well, more than probably. Poor old Brett was never much chop at irony. Still, it was all in fun, wasn't it. Fun of a sort. Well, fuck it, not that much fun at all, in the end. There was a lot to be said for being alone in a deck-chair, even if one was not at one's best in bathers.

Melbourne was snapping at his heels in other ways as well. A postcard from dear Mama had been lying in wait for him in Perth. He hadn't even left the country, for Christ's sake. Fortunately the notorious irregularities of the post relieved him of any need to acknowledge it. Postcard? What postcard?

And there, on the boat, was the family from some god-forsaken suburban hole in the outer suburbs that'd taken a fancy to him. The mother suffered from a chronic case of the Mrs Bennetts, and had lined him up as a suitable catch for her pretty pulsating Pussy, or Poppy, was it? Penny. Pennies from heaven, but the mother's from hell.

Poor Penny. One noticed little about her but the freckles, and of course the inordinate height. Which presumably made him such an attractive option. They thought, poor eager darlings, that courtesy meant Country Matters. He'd eventually been disgracefully rude to them, but evidently not rude enough. They thought he was just pretending, and laughed like drains.

The brother was attractive, if a little lugubrious. Nice eyes. One wondered whether he shared the family fancy; once or twice there'd been a look, or a gesture, or a verbal nuance, which suggested that young Simon, unlike the feverishly fecund sister, might not be the marrying kind. Funny how you could always tell. Frank had looked for him by the pool, but so far in vain. Which might, after all, have been just as well. Mrs Bennett's eagle eye was on him. A ship was a small world, and one could get into tricky situations if one was not very good – or very careful.

There'd be plenty of pale and interesting young men in England – well, plenty of pale ones, certainly. Mothers he could do without. He'd had more than his fair share of mothers. And lovers – they could wait, too, for a little while. He was warm, on a ship, miles from Melbourne, and life was not too bad at all. 'Mother, give me the sun', he murmured, and then opened his eyes to check that no-one was close enough to hear.

No, nobody was listening. But Simon, a towel over his shoulder, was sauntering, in rather perfunctory black togs, towards the pool.

Frank turned to smile at him, as if surprised.

Chapter Nine

HE THAT PLAYS THE THRING …

In some ways, it was so predictable, the whole going-overseas, rites-of-passage thing. Frank, the determined non-conformist, set out on the obligatory trip to the Old World with all the stereotypical hope that it might add up to more than the New one.

Money was no obstacle to a Thring, but getting to England and back was still a major disincentive. Five to six weeks at sea was the standard in 1947, and even in the mid-1950s when Frank took two more return voyages, the journey took a month. To head off to the other end of the world, one needed to want very badly to be there, or at least to want very badly to leave home. For Frank, who headed off and returned three times in the next decade of his life, with no particular plan in mind, no-one in particular to see, and almost certainly a deep scepticism as to why he was bothering at all, it is likely to have been the latter that was the most powerful motive. Whatever it was that he wanted from Australia at that stage of his life, it appeared unlikely to be able to give it. Instead, it offered him more of the same; more of the conservative insularity of the culture, more of the bitter silences at Rylands, more of the sense that there was no compelling reason to do anything.

Frank's previous trips overseas had been as a child, completely controlled by where his father had to be and who his father had to see. This time the visit was open-ended and effectively anonymous. He knew no-one in London, or in any of the other great cities that he idly thought he might visit. It must have been in some ways a relief, but also a searching test of how much he enjoyed his own company. The fact that it turned out to be a briefer trip than Frank had envisaged might in itself answer some of the questions. Sometimes, when he referred to it a few decades later, he talked about it as a time when he was away 'for a couple of years'.[326] All up,

326 Steve Cossar interview, 1980.

though, it was about eleven months, spanning the last months of 1947 and most of 1948.

Frank managed a couple of brief forays to Paris, but otherwise his plans for a version of the rich young gentleman's Grand Tour were abandoned, and he spent almost his time in London. The way in which he referred to the experience suggests that it didn't provide quite the epiphany that is normally on the itinerary of the Tour:

> I just sort of choofed around to see all the performances and the operas and the ballets that one was deprived of in Australia, but I didn't attempt to work. I simply went to look.[327]

Even when he tried to give the experience a more sober benefit, in discussion with Keith Dunstan, it didn't sound completely convincing:

> That was an education. It was a case of sorting myself out. I didn't really know what I wanted to do, but I suppose I had acting in mind. It was bred into me.[328]

The genetic predisposition wasn't as obvious as that implies, and nor was the sorting out so easily concluded. But it is true that when he returned in the autumn of 1948, certain things about his immediate future seemed to be fixed. He would never again be expected to charm the ladies at Olive's bridge-parties, and he would henceforth call himself 'an actor'.

Frank's first venture abroad began unpropitiously when he was detained by Customs officials on arrival at Southampton.[329] The problem had nothing to do with Frank's exotic tastes in drinks or baubles or young men; for once he could not be accused of doing anything illicit at all. The problem was a mysterious blanket, small and obviously well-used, that was found in one

327 ibid.

328 Dunstan, *Ratbags*, p.131.

329 This story, and the details that follow of Frank's otherwise rather shadowy stay in London in 1947–8, were offered by Frank's cousin Minty Lalanne (formerly Minty Creightmore) in a conversation with the author, 24 January 2005.

of his suitcases. Eidy, his night-time comforter, had accompanied him on the voyage – naturally. Whether the issue was simply one of incongruity or a potential threat to public health, or the absence of the child that might have been expected to be attached to it, the rug was a matter for urgent investigation. It must have posed quite a challenge to Frank's well-practised savoir-faire, and his determination never to be embarrassed, to explain Eidy to the professional sceptics in Immigration.

His cousins the Creightmores, who had gone back to England at the end of the war to live at Brackley in Northamptonshire, provided Frank with a crucial introduction to a strange land. John Creightmore, deputed by Olive to find her son some respectable lodgings, fulfilled his commission to the letter. He arranged for Frank to have rooms with a formidably good woman in Hampstead. The connection with Miss Cavendish and her impeccably respectable house might have been expected to provide a scene for comic embarrassments to rival the Eidy incident, but in fact it worked out wonderfully well.[330] Miss Cavendish, like most ladies of advanced years who found themselves part of Frank's story, adored him; Frank, as he tended to do with all women other than Olive who mothered him, responded with warmth and considerateness, and was, seemingly, on his best behaviour.

Part of the attraction for Frank may have stemmed from the stereotypically theatrical qualities of his new home. His cousin Minty, when she visited him in Hampstead, found herself in a 'time-warp', complete with shilling-in-the-slot gas heating and a clientele, apart from Frank, that seemed to have been left over from another century.[331] Everything in the Cavendish house was Victorian – the furnishings, the plumbing, the menu, the smells, the guests and rules and rituals. Frank found it enchanting.

But it was also the first time Frank had really been away from his mother, and paradoxically, at least from the perspective of his fourteen-year-old cousin, the first time he had felt at home. Frank handed over his food coupons to Miss Cavendish, and she would provide him with a good plain meal every night at the same table at exactly the same time; Frank, Minty Creightmore concluded, 'enjoyed anything that smacked of a family atmosphere because he'd never had it at home'. He spent Christmas with the Creightmores in Brackley, and they all marvelled from the window at his childlike pleasure in the first fall of snow:

330 Minty Lalanne in conversation with the author, 24 January 2005..
331 ibid.

> He was terribly excited. He walked up and down with an umbrella, singing and jumping up and down. We thought he was mad.[332]

He showered the family with gifts, especially Minty's mother. Again, he revelled in finding a family to be part of, and though he continually made them laugh the Creightmores found it sad that he seemed to have 'missed out' on finding one genuinely his own.

The glimpses that we have of Frank on this first venture overseas, from Minty's memories or from Joan Thring's, of the 'enticing' letters that he sent to her back in Melbourne, are happy ones, though it's not clear that he was doing very much. There are no signs, certainly, of any of the professional or social initiatives that a Grand Tourist might have been expected to make, especially one as apparently shameless as Frank Thring. He wrote to Joan (and she dutifully read to Olive, who naturally received no letters from her son at all) about the shows that he had been to, the bars and restaurants that he had visited, the rich and famous that he had seen and occasionally even met. But there was much more observation of life on the big stage than participation in it. There were no performance activities at all – apart from the usual ones, of course, outside the theatre. Nor is there any sign of any of the relationships with young men, even casual ones, that Frank, twelve thousand miles from his mother, might have been expected enthusiastically to pursue. That is not to say that they didn't happen, of course; he was careful about such confidences, even with Joan, and even in London the homosexual world was a wary and secretive scene. But there were no connections made during Frank's stay there in 1947–8 that were renewed when he came back in 1954 with the aim of making headlines and influential friends. Miss Cavendish, of course, ran a very tight ship.

Not that Frank had particularly changed his personality in response to the quiet gentility of his new surroundings; Minty remembered him landing on post-war London like a 'bombshell'. But he evidently tempered at least some of his habits. It would not be the last time that there was more style than substance in Frank's high-campery.

---

332 ibid.

On returning from England, Frank picked up some modestly paid acting work with the touring Anew McMaster company, 'selected from Stratford-Upon-Avon', and headed by the eponymous Irish actor/director. His professional debut was not a spectacular one: Frank was cast among the extras playing 'Courtesans, Soldiers and Coolies' to McMaster's Othello; though he would probably have been delighted to play a courtesan, it's likely that Frank appeared in one or both of the other categories. He fared a little better in the company's next production, playing Vincentio of Pisa, Lucentio's father, in *The Taming of the Shrew*.[333]

The McMaster connection, and a previous one with the work of Sumner Locke Elliott forged during the run of *The Invisible Circus* in the summer of 1946–7, paid off much more handsomely when Frank stepped into the role of the repellent Sergeant Brooks in Elliott's *Rusty Bugles*. The role of a crass, coarse and distinctly Aussie bully like Brooks, 'a very *butch* sergeant',[334] was not an obvious one for an exotic theatrical bloom like Frank Thring, but it seems to have worked out remarkably well. It gave him the chance to show that he could play something other than 'those Vincent Price, out-of-the-grave parts' at which he had become such a dab hand on radio, and that suited his delivery and demeanour. It also enabled him to have a fleeting association with the history of Australian writing for the stage, in one of its most significant chapters. *Rusty Bugles* was certainly the most distinguished new Australian play of the decade, and until Lawler's *Summer of the Seventeenth Doll* appeared in the mid-1950s Elliott's play was widely regarded as the one that set the standard in terms of both critical reception and box-office receipts.

Elliott had previously been known as a comic and satiric playwright, but *Rusty Bugles*, though generously laced with rough humour, was a thoroughly serious analysis of the attitudes and forms of interaction of Australian men. The focus was entirely on a group of sixteen assorted blokes condemned to share close quarters in an Ordnance Depot in the Far North, through a war in which, for them, hardly anything ever happened. Frank's adventures in the Air Force at Shepparton may have informed his strong performance in the role. Or possibly – perhaps preferably – it may not.

Rusty Bugles had run into serious problems with the censor in its premiere amateur season at the Independent in Sydney. The problem was 'bad language' – never on an Australian stage had so many bloodies consorted with so many

333 The character does not appear till Act Four, Scene Five, and speaks a total of thirty-eight unremarkable lines.

334 Dunstan, *Ratbags*, p.131.

buggers. It had been briefly banned, and then allowed to resume its season after Doris Fitton, its director, agreed to modify the script. The controversy, not to mention the quality of the play, made it an attractive option to the entrepreneurs Garnet Carroll of Fuller's Theatres and Kenn Brodziak of Aztec Services. Surprisingly, given the track record of previous contenders for the title of 'the great Australian play', it had a substantial run, starting in Sydney, but beginning for Frank at the Kings Theatre in Melbourne, some fifty metres from his father's old stamping-ground at Kreitmayer's Waxworks. The play went to Adelaide and Perth, stopping at Kalgoorlie along the way, before returning to Sydney's Tatler Theatre via Brisbane. Frank left the show after Perth to join another Brodziak production in Melbourne, Stanley Lupino's *The Love Racket*, starring the popular English comedian Arthur Askey.

Frank's decision to leave the *Rusty Bugles* tour was more timely than he could possibly have foreseen. The run at the Tatler ended prematurely, and with a whimper. The entrepreneur Royston Darling, who had joined the consortium, announced in the press that the Sydney season was not the money-spinner he had anticipated, and that he planned to withdraw his investment. From there the production spiraled down into disaster. Darling's announcement was made public on a Monday. Then, on Tuesday, Carroll and Brodziak called the cast together, gave each of them a week's salary in lieu of notice, and closed the show. On the same day, Darling was in Sydney's Central Court, charged with failing to remit income tax for the company over a six-month period; in an adjacent court, Robert Rankin, one of the cast who was unable to make the meeting at the Tatler, was being convicted of obscene exposure in a public lavatory in the Domain. And there was more to come – on the Wednesday of that week, another cast member, John Craig, was remanded for trial on a charge of indecently assaulting a naval rating. It was quite a week.

> The final curtain was rung down on 'Rusty Bugles' on Thursday when Mr Robert Porter, representing Ben and John Fuller Theatres Pty. Ltd., arrived with five stage hands and two lorries at the stage door of the Tatler to take possession of furnishings owned by the company.
>
> 'Rusty Bugles' had blown.[335]

---

335 Article in the *Daily Telegraph*, undated, Frank Thring scrapbook, Performing Arts Museum, Melbourne, p.28.

All things considered, Frank, who came to develop a taste for collecting sailors himself, was well out of the whole schemozzle.

Frank Thring was not, in style or in personal inclination, particularly suited to be part of a ruggedly Australian theatre, based as it was on a notion of cultural distinctiveness that was narrowly focused on the values and rituals of mateship. But he had been in the right place at the right time to be able to claim a connection with original Australian work that his father would have loved to have had. For Frank as an actor, the most immediate spin-off was a place in the Brodziak stable. *Rusty Bugles* provided his entrée to a commercially gilt-edged season in *The Love Racket,* which opened at the Melbourne Tivoli two nights before Christmas 1949, and that part led in turn to the role of the Bishop of Lax in Philip King's farce *See How They Run*, one of the most cleverly crafted pieces of theatrical fairy-floss ever written. In both these roles he was playing a pompous and venerable Pom, which suited the elaborate grandeur of his presence and his diction. Frank's stage persona turned banality into something like wit, and Brodziak, who had discovered an actor who offered a dash of West End theatricality for an Australian salary, must have been delighted.

The Love Racket was promoted as 'the gayest and happiest of musicals';[336] the graphic in its newspaper advertisements featured a pretty blond girl leap-frogging a young man, who is enjoying the chance to take a peek up her diaphanous gown as she does so. It was promoted as a shamelessly popular show, and it was, breaking all records in its nineteen weeks at the Tivoli, and touring nationally for another seven months.

The show was indicative of the way in which Frank had already graduated to the memorable cameo. His role as The Visitor was too small to get his face into the program, but still won him a warm review and, apparently, an even warmer reception:

> Frank Thring was Monty Woolley to the life ... Frank Thring's grandiloquence seemed temporarily to overpower an audience used to the lighter things of life, but his impersonation of portentous eccentricity won him an extended ovation.[337]

The only thing that now stood between Frank Thring and a comfortable career as the Antipodean Woolley or Wolfit or W.C. Fields was Frank's inconvenient tendency to be bored.

---

336 Frank Thring scrapbook, Performing Arts Museum, Melbourne, p.14.
337 ibid.

Actors are, by grand tradition, poor. Peter Finch, another Australian actor whose story winds in and out of the Thring story through the 1950s, once remarked about his choice of a vocation:

> If I was going to be broke I decided I might as well be with actors as anyone else. They were cheerful idiots and seemed to take it better.[338]

Frank would have agreed thoroughly with Finch's estimate of the intelligence of most actors; but no matter what he chose to do with his life, no matter how perversely or disastrously he chose, Frank knew that he would never be broke. An actor with guaranteed finances is a rarity, and potentially a problem:

> All these shows [*Rusty Bugles, The Love Racket, See How They Run*] were incredibly successful – three shows in five years and I was never out of work. There was talk of the last show going to New Zealand and I said to Kenn Brodziak 'For Christ sake, I can't stand this. I'm going out of my mind'.[339]

It was the first of a number of indications in Frank's career that the scenario that is supposedly every actor's dream – a long-running hit – was for him a nightmare; his habit of becoming almost immediately bored laid the foundations for a career full of diversion, but perhaps also for a discontented life. For a while he managed to keep those feelings at bay by working on two projects at once. Frank may never have needed to earn some money in the day-time, but now at least he was being paid at a modest professional rate to rehearse in office-hours. His evenings and weekends, during the rehearsal period, were often free, however, and, in marked contrast to his old habits, he chose to spend most of them in working, too. During the run of *The Love Racket* he indulged his fascination with design by creating twenty-five spectacular masks for Melbourne University Dramatic Club's production of Ibsen's *Peer Gynt* at its Union Theatre. And in the early days of *See How They Run*, he travelled to Bendigo to give a demonstration of theatrical makeup in the Town Hall as part of the 'Cover Girl for Victoria' competition. It was an odd, as well as very generous, thing to do; presumably, the photographer

---

338 Elaine Dundy, *Finch, Bloody Finch: A Life of Peter Finch*, New York, Holt, Rinehart and Winston, 1980, p.128.

339 Dunstan, *Ratbags*, p.131.

Athol Shmith and his soon-to-be-wife Bambi Tuckwell, roped him into it.[340] But Frank would have done it for love – not so much of the Bendigonians or his friends, but of the arts of cosmetics and costumes in themselves. He gave a much longer presentation than was strictly called for, delighting the locals with his elaborate faces and fingernails for Huyssens in *Shipwreck*, Henry VIII, a Chinaman, and Frankenstein's monster – the role in which he had once enjoyed terrifying Joan Cunliffe on the stairs at Rylands.

There were acting projects, too. The company at the Little Theatre was still producing interesting work, and Frank was able to combine his professional schedule with Brodziak with the amateur pattern of rehearsal after-hours. Between *The Love Racket* and *See How They Run*, he appeared in two seasons at the Little, in Douglas Stewart's epic verse play *Shipwreck*, which opened a few days after Christmas in 1950, and, immediately after it, the George S. Kaufman and Moss Hart comedy *The Man Who Came to Dinner.* In *Shipwreck* he was back to playing one of his stocks in trade, insidious evil; a reviewer found Huyssen, Frank's character, 'as deeply dyed a melodramatic villain as anyone could wish for, blood and all'.[341]

In *The Man Who Came to Dinner* he was in another of his comfort zones, playing comic bombast in the lead role of Sheridan Whiteside, the first of five occasions on which he was to play the part. In lots of ways, the role was made for him – the self-dramatising domestic tyrant was a character he regularly played at home, and the mixture of pomposity and wit was an approximate match for his own. Furthermore, the background to the role – Whiteside was a devastating theatre critic and controversial radio broadcaster – fitted Frank like a very large glove.

> The star of the evening was Frank Thring, running the gamut of emotion from the caustic to the coarse. It is a moot point whether this play was tailor-made for Mr Thring, or vice-versa; but as a one-man extravaganza neither could be bettered.[342]

The fact that the role was written for a Grand Old Ham, and Frank at twenty-two could best be described as a grandiose young one, was the only question-mark about the casting. The critics couldn't help noticing it, but

340 Frank Thring scrapbook, Performing Arts Museum, Melbourne, p.40–41.

341 Frank Murphy, *Advocate*, 11 January 1951, Frank Thring scrapbook, Performing Arts Museum, Melbourne, p.38.

342 'Diamond-Studded Kitchen Sink', review by 'Daisy Ashford', unattributed and undated, Frank Thring scrapbook, Performing Arts Museum, Melbourne, p.39.

the local audience loved it; for the man who could bluster his way through Henry VIII at nineteen, the next step seemed naturally into the slippers of Monte Woolley. *The Love Racket* took the challenge one stage further:

> David Martin rang and said, 'We're doing *Love Racket* and Askey won't accept a particular member of the cast. Can you do it?' I said, 'What's the part?' 'It's a seventy-five-year-old eccentric'. I said, 'Oh, that's me. I'm twenty-two!'[343]

Frank had already played a number of men old enough to be his father. Now he seemed to have graduated to the generation before him.

There was a down-side to all this, which would recur over the next decade as Frank attempted to build his career at home and abroad. He was never the obvious choice for a handsome prince, despite those slim, arresting, beardless youths that look sensitively at us from his photographs in this period. But he who in youth plays the King, over and over, obviously restricts his chances to come to those mature roles when he knows enough to play them properly. Actors like Charles Laughton, Robert Morley and Monte Woolley grew into those roles at a suitable time in their lives. Doing the full Monte at twenty-two encouraged a notion of acting that was all about pretending, and could be hard to distinguish from showing off.

At the Little, Frank was delighting in the chance to be outrageous, and while his parallel career as a paid actor necessarily cramped his style, he felt free to give the amateurs all the benefit of his pleasure in practical jokes. He had been decidedly unimpressed by the down-at-heel costuming and décor, and insisted on providing some 'decent stuff' more appropriate to the social world of the play: his mother's genuine mink coat for Joan Harris, a young actress making her debut at the Little Theatre who was playing the ingénue, and a range of Rylands valuables for the set. At one point in *The Man Who Came to Dinner*, Joan Harris had to snatch a book from the top of the piano and hurl it at Frank, who would – usually – catch it.

Early in the season, Joan was initiated into the perilous business of the theatre, at least when it was theatre with Thring.[344] She grabbed the book and found that 'someone' had nailed it to the lid. Thinking quite quickly for a panic-stricken person, she seized the nearest thing and threw that at him instead. It happened to be one of his father's prize purchases, a precious blue

343 Frank Van Straten, *Tivoli*, Lothian Books, South Melbourne, 2003, p.185.
344 Joan Harris, interview with the author, 16 September 2004.

Ming dog. He caught it, with an extra degree of urgency. He stared at her through an even-longer-than-usual Thring pause, and the show went on.

He made no comment backstage, other than a low and incoherent rumble when she caught his eye, but the next night when she reached apprehensively for the book, and found it to her great relief unsecured, it opened suddenly in mid-air and released a cascade of confetti. Somehow, again, the scripted action resumed. Joan Harris inferred that honour was now satisfied for Frank, and she felt that she had passed a test. That didn't preclude another small challenge later in the run, though, when a whoopee cushion appeared mysteriously on the sofa, to add to one of Joan's romantic swoons an unmistakable fart.

Joan Harris became, with her husband Fred Parslow, one of Frank's closest friends, and when recalling her first experience of acting with him she was anxious to protest his absolute professionalism in other respects; Frank was always early at rehearsal, right on time for performance calls, and diligent in knowing his lines even if he sometimes liked to vary them.[345] But a selective discipline, especially one that only applies to one's own performance, is arguably not much of a discipline at all, and Frank's playfulness in the amateur arena says more about his level of maturity than it does for his new commitment to his vocation. He didn't play tricks on his fellow-actors when he played Oedipus or Othello, and that suggests that his readiness to do so was determined not by the status of the company but by that of the play. *The Man Who Came to Dinner* is a neatly crafted piece, but only one rung above *See How They Run* on the scale of theatrical confectionery. However, to decide that Frank took his art seriously when he thought it mattered is not a particularly powerful argument for the defence.

The fake book filled with confetti is inventive in its way. The whoopee cushion, though, is another matter. For the biographer, it offers a rare and wonderful glimpse of the child within the man. As Sheridan Whiteside, Frank Thring the actor was playing a man more than twice as old as he was himself; getting a laugh from the sound of a fart in a love scene might suggest that the person playing Frank Thring the actor was a boy less than half his age. In one sense, it is good to know that the boy was still alive and well, given that a very curious childhood had seemed so thoroughly to suppress him. From another point of view, it is the first of a number of signs in Frank of something like arrested development. The boy forced into a form of false consciousness from the age of ten insisted on reappearing,

345 Joan Harris, interview with the author, 16 September 2004.

in moments of childlike egocentricity or of infantile rage at a world that refused to conform to his will. Some of those moments were part of his outrageous persona, when Frank's disdain for the rules and euphemisms that guided most other people's behaviour made him seem such a deliciously iconoclastic figure. Some of them were the things that made him seem startlingly vulnerable and human, under that massive, highly polished carapace of arrogance and wit.

There was no place for a whoopee cushion on the Brodziak stage, though *The Love Racket* and *See How They Run* might both have given one a happy home. Nor was there any chance to run amateur and professional careers in parallel when the Brodziak shows went on the road. The agony of the minor hit on a seemingly endless tour demanded more drastic treatment than an occasional amateur production on the side. Accordingly, Frank threw off the episcopal robes of the Bishop of Lax, and the laughs and the livelihood that came with them, and came back to something like square one – which for the heir to the Thring name and fortune, of course, was already well ahead of the starting-point for most other people. He decided, in perhaps the first genuine initiative of his adult life, to start a theatre company.

It was the kind of idea that Olive might well have had for her son, but there is no evidence to suggest this time that it was hers – and there is plenty of evidence, of course, that if it had been, he would automatically not have done it. However, Olive signed the cheques, so the plan certainly required her approval; she would have been pleased to see him taking command as his father would have done, and she would certainly have endorsed any arrangement in which Frank guaranteed himself all the best roles.

> I decided to open an amateur theatre and do the plays I wanted to do. This dubious venture was backed by my mother, the Antipodean answer to Lady Bracknell, who, under threat of suicide and, on occasion, murder, forked out miniscule sums that kept the Company in mink and rubies but did not stretch as far as paying their salaries.[346]

346 Geoffrey Hutton, *It Won't Last a Week! The First Twenty Years of the Melbourne Theatre Company*, Melbourne, Sun Books, 1975, p.vii.

Olive's 'miniscule sums' in fact paid for the theatre, the rights, the sets, the publicity, and all the mysterious costs incurred as 'consumables' and 'contingencies'. She paid nothing at all for minks or rubies, but loaned them instead, free of charge from her impressive wardrobe. There are probably sons who might think her contribution quite generous. Frank was not one of them.

Frank took over the Arrow Theatre in Armstrong Street, Middle Park in October 1951. It was to be amateur, in that the actors would not be paid, but determinedly not amateurish. The Thring finances guaranteed a certain level of production quality, at least in what immediately met the eye. The new company was to be radical in its ambitions, and collaborative in its practice. A number of its members had been stalwarts of the Little Theatre, and indeed continued to be; good amateurs hungry for decent roles went wherever the best plays happened to be.

> I used to design sets, sew rubies on the costumes, check the lighting. That's why one is slightly intolerant now when one is rung at one in the morning – needing help … I can still paint a set. The trouble was we made no money at all. I would spend a week's takings on one costume.[347]

The fact that he was engaged creatively across so many areas of responsibility and skill was part of the attraction for Frank of the collaborative repertory model; one may be peeved when one is rung at home at one, but anyone with a feeling for the stage takes masochistic pleasure in those nights when, at one, one is still in the theatre, painting.

The repertoire, the best of the classics and the most acclaimed work from contemporary Europe, was radical from Frank's perspective, in that it determinedly avoided the bourgeois popularism that he saw as the dominant force in Australian theatre. From another point of view, though, it was quite conservative. The list of twenty-two Arrow plays – Sophocles' *Oedipus Rex*, Shakespeare's *Othello,* Jonson's *Volpone*, Sheridan's *The Critic*, Anouilh's *Point of Departure* and *Ring Around the Moon*, Coward's *Present Laughter*, Wilde's *Salome* and *The Importance of Being Earnest*, Fry's *A Phoenix Too Frequent* and *Venus Observed*, Wilder's *Our Town*, Somerset Maugham's *The Letter*, Mordaunt Shairp's *The Green Bay Tree*, Lorca's *The House of Bernarda Alba*, Kaufman and Hart's *The Man Who Came to Dinner* and *You Can't Take It With You*, the thrillers *Rope* and *Murder Without Crime*, the fantasy *Beauty and the*

347 Dunstan, *Ratbags*, p.131.

Beast, the melodrama *Maria Maren or The Murder in the Old Red Barn*, and the Arrow's sole Australian play, Ralph Peterson's *The Square Ring* – looks more like a marriage between suburban repertory and a university Drama syllabus than the work of an innovative company, even in the early 1950s.

That it was almost all proven work is one source of that impression; the absence, with a single exception, of anything Australian, in content or even in playing style, is another. It wasn't, then, a repertoire that would have appealed particularly to his father. Frank senior would pardon the choice of one or two of those titles, as the recognisable kinds of names that could pay for the real stuff to be staged – the work that nobody else would ever do; he himself had staged the thriller *Rope* twenty years before. He would have cautiously approved the gamble with *The Square Ring*, especially when it moved to the Princess. He would have to find the Arrow's performance record – twenty-two plays in less than three years – satisfactory from a productivity point of view; how many amateur companies have managed to keep up a rate of seven new productions a year? But F.T. would have looked in vain for the creative risk that would make it all worthwhile, and for anything much that spoke to or for Australians.

It was almost as though his son was reacting against the father's models of an unapologetic Australian-ness. Perhaps, though, Frank junior was simply defining himself against the nationalist flirtations of the Little Theatre, with their sometimes awkward attempts to animate the early work of Ray Lawler and Sumner Locke Elliott. More prosaically still, perhaps he was just choosing the plays that fitted his voice and his mannerisms, which seemed always so much at odds with the society he lived in. Whatever his motives, Frank Thring the son was acting on two of the cardinal principles that lay behind his father's Efftee enterprise: if a thing is worth doing, you'd best do it yourself, and if you don't like the temperature, take over the kitchen.

The Arrow was just a couple of miles from the Garrick in South Melbourne, where his father had staged several seasons of the Efftee Players. Perhaps if the building in Aikman Street had been available, Frank might have chosen it for old times' sake, but it was now an industrial site. Certainly the press coverage of the Arrow initiative saw it very much in terms of a young man embracing his patrimony, though the powerful maternal presence was rarely out of the picture:

> Frank Thring, son of the late entrepreneur and early film-maker, has taken one more step towards emulating his father's career ... Many of you will remember his father, who pioneered some of our first

> talking pictures. The letters F.T., over the proscenium at the Princess, commemorate his association with that theatre.
>
> One thing I can tell you for certain about both these productions [*Salome* at the opening of the Arrow, and Frank's return in *Enduring is the Camphor Tree* at the Little Theatre]. Mrs Olive Thring, Frank's mother – most inveterate of all Melbourne first-nighters – will be right in the front row.
>
> And, if I know her, she won't hesitate to criticise if she thinks it necessary![348]

As it was, Frank took over the home of Melbourne Repertory, where less than six years before he had made his stage debut in *Hal's Belles*. He marked the occasion, as he did with Rylands some years later when erasing all memories of Olive, by spending the first four weeks of his tenancy repainting the place. On this occasion, however, the décor was not to be all black, but unapologetically vibrant:

> Under the direction of Frank Thring jun., son of the late Frank Thring, who was well-known as producer and founder of Efftee Films, the Arrow opened with an effective production of Oscar Wilde's "Salome". Thring carried off acting honours as Herod.
>
> Of the new theatre, the social editress of a Melbourne daily wrote: "the Arrow Theatre should become a rendezvous for our brighter young and not-so-young people. Those who attended the opening found the scheme of decoration – deep blue and chartreuse – effective and stimulating."
>
> Mrs. Olive Thring, mother of the director, wore a deep blue taffeta gown with chartreuse accents, in exactly the tones of the Arrow décor.[349]

Having parents so conspicuously present, either posthumously or vividly in the flesh, might understandably have been a little frustrating to an actor keen to read more about his own 'honours'. But perhaps it was so customary that he saw it as par for his chosen course. Or perhaps it was just one more small resentment to add to the heap.

348 Frank Doherty, 'Thring Following in Father's Footsteps', *Argus*, n.d., Frank Thring scrapbook, Performing Arts Museum, Melbourne, p.76.

349 Undated clipping, Frank Thring scrapbook, Performing Arts Museum, Melbourne, p.78.

In fact, there was a third colour in the new foyer, a spectacular shocking pink. Olive was wise not to have taken her identification quite that far. It confirmed a dash of flamboyance at the Arrow. The critic for the *Port Phillip Gazette*, 'J.W.K.', found the colour scheme 'rather alarming', but symptomatic of the 'new lease of life' that had been given to the old place.[350] The Arrow's repertoire might not have been very different from that of the Melbourne Repertory Theatre, but the ambience was determinedly so. No more earnest forays into high culture by Melbourne's upper middle class, no more grey perms and respectable suits; that was the message. This was a young company, its resident director just twenty-five, its attitudes as daring as its décor.

The choice of *Salome* confirmed those bold intentions, and just in case the opening night audience was unaware that to spend an evening at the Arrow was to live dangerously, a pre-show announcement warned them of what was in store. Minty Lalanne recalled it with the vividness that tends to mark mortifying adolescent experiences with aunts:

> We sat with Olive and her party in the front row and I remember my embarrassment when the presenter announced we were to see vice at its lowest and sin at its worst and Olive, obviously delighted, boomed out audibly "That'll be good!"[351]

Frank Doherty had been spot-on in his prediction about Olive's accustomed prominence. Frank Thring, waiting in the wings to give his all in a major role, no doubt wished he could have her head on a platter.

Barry Humphries visited the Arrow often as a schoolboy bohemian, especially on Sunday evenings when Kevin McBeath, its 'Musical Supervisor', put on jazz nights where the performers and the audience wore turtle-neck sweaters and flaunted their contempt for conformity.

> ... there, once a month, flocked the highbrows and *poseurs*, the precious, the pretty and the pretentious ... When the New Music Society met, the small theatre was thronged with long-haired youths in suede shoes and corduroy trousers smoking Turkish cigarettes with the wrong fingers. 'Window-dressers!' someone whispered, grinning. There were

350 *Port Phillip Gazette*, volume 1, number 1, Winter 1952, p.33. J.W.K. was the by-line of James W. Kern.

351 Minty Lalanne, email to the author, 30 January 2005.

> beards too, and women who, in the age of the perm, wore very long straight hair, sandals and not much make-up. And there was a loud babble of foreign tongues. It all felt, well, continental.[352]

With the seeming defiance of cultural convention at the Arrow came a frisson of sexual possibility, of a fairly unspecified kind. Theatrical people have always been inclined to relaxed approaches to such matters, or have been assumed to be so; but the image of radically disaffected chic that was cultivated by the Arrow shaded into the camp aesthetic that Noel Coward had celebrated in 'Green Carnations':

> Pretty boys, witty boys, too, too, too
> Lazy to fight stagnation.
> Haughty boys, naughty boys, all we do
> Is to pursue sensation.
> The portals of society are always opened wide,
> The world our eccentricity condones;
> A note of quaint variety we're certain to provide,
> We dress in very decorative tones.
> Faded boys, jaded boys, womankind's
> Gift to a bulldog nation -
> In order to distinguish us from less enlightened minds
> We all wear a green carnation.[353]

For Coward, who preferred to be seen as heterosexual with a mischievous twist, this was about as close as one came to candour. Frank Thring, who was less squeamish, or perhaps simply had less reputation to risk, would have had no problem at all in presenting his theatre as a garden of all the conceivable earthly delights. That was part of the fascination to Humphries, too; he had already been lectured by the Reverend Hone, the Principal of Melbourne Grammar, about showing dangerous signs of becoming a 'pansy'. Frank, as an Old Boy of the school, would have had a number of things to say about that.

A lot of it, of course, was window-dressing. There was nothing in the Arrow repertoire that would have been surprising in a Little Theatre or Melbourne Repertory season, and a good many of the heads in the foyer at

352 Barry Humphries, *More Please. An Autobiography*, London, Viking, 1992, p.104.
353 Noel Coward, 'Green Carnations', from *Bitter Sweet* (1929).

interval were grey. There was no hint of revolutionary zeal anywhere – the company was unapologetically a rich young man's plaything, funded by his despised but ever-indulgent mother. There was nothing in the program to alarm or offend Olive either, at least as long as her son was playing the lead.

For Frank, the big roles – Oedipus Rex in *Oedipus Rex*, Othello in *Othello*, the man who came to dinner in *The Man Who Came to Dinner*, and three or four others that fell just short of eponymous – were one of the attractions of working for himself and not for Kenn Brodziak. Another powerful benefit was the repertory model itself, with seasons just long enough to develop a character, but not long enough to become sick of it. Great roles, lots of plays, designing, directing and sewing on sequins, and the constant goad of personal accountability; it was the perfect counterblast to boredom.

Othello was by general consent the Arrow's particular triumph. Staged cheekily a couple of months before the Shakespeare Memorial Theatre's visit to Melbourne with the same play and Anthony Quayle heading a distinguished cast, it insisted on comparisons that could not always be to its advantage – but, in retrospect, sometimes were:

> The Moor was Frank Thring, and in the first part of the play, the time of the reasonable, calm Othello, the honors lay with Mr Quayle. But in the second part, the period of the Moor's searing anguish and soul torment, Mr Thring played with a savage intensity that was, at times, terrifying.[354]

H.A. Standish was similarly impressed:

> Frank Thring's Othello is the best thing he has done. He is completely and impressively in control of his conception of the part. It seems to be personality, rather than acting, that achieves such tragic conviction.[355]

It was an interesting distinction. Most people were inclined to see Frank, even in his best performances, as too much himself; but the self on show was the self that he was practised in performing, and the line between acting and being, telling and showing, became blurred in that process. Just possibly, as Othello, Frank found a way of acting that reflected a 'personality' that his persona was designed to conceal.

354 J.W.K., *Port Phillip Gazette*, volume 1, number 4, Spring 1953, p.41.
355 H.A.Standish, 'Othello triumph', *Sun*, undated, Frank Thring scrapbook, Performing Arts Museum, Melbourne, p.89.

That review goes on to assess the performances of Alex Scott as Iago ('too jumpy throughout … and yet a thoughtful and impressive portrayal'), and of Zoe Caldwell as Desdemona ('an example of good casting, despite the limitations of her speaking (and singing) voice'). It's a reminder of the calibre of the actors that Frank gathered around him at the Arrow. Other notables like Bunny Brook, Frank Gatliff, Michael Duffield, June Brunell, Sheila Florance, Wyn Roberts, Moira Carleton and Robert Gardiner found opportunities at the Arrow that, in some cases, laid the foundations for highly successful careers in the theatre.

The mainstays of the Arrow also provided the core of Melbourne's first professional theatre company, the Union Theatre Repertory, which had its birth in 1953, the year of the Arrow's demise. Some time early in that year, Frank met an Englishman who had just been appointed to manage the Union Theatre at the University of Melbourne. John Sumner had come to Melbourne with the Royal Navy in 1944, and liked the look of the place. When he applied for the job with the Student Union eight years later, he proposed to the Vice-Chancellor, Sir George Paton, that the University should establish a professional company, sharing the Union fifty-fifty with the student societies; the University had the venue, Melbourne seemed to have plenty of talented actors who spent their days 'selling underwear or doing radio',[356] and all it needed was the funding. The University Council was reluctant to come to the party. Then Sumner met Frank Thring:

> It wasn't at the Arrow. The National Theatre had a reception at the Princess, to announce that they were going to do *St Joan*. June Brunell would play Joan, and it was Anne Frazer's debut as a designer.
>
> In the course of the evening this extraordinary person made himself known. You would have thought it a reception for him – but he was just one of the guests …[357]

The flamboyance wasn't particularly to Sumner's taste, but the enthusiasm of his new acquaintance for Sumner's plans for a repertory Company at the Union certainly was. Sumner remembers Frank saying loftily, 'Well, if you can get the theatre, I'll get the money!',[358] after a suggestion that Sumner

356 John Sumner, interview with the author, 11 January 2005.
357 ibid.
358 ibid.

might find it more salubrious to work for the Arrow was politely declined.[359] Frank recalled the occasion slightly differently.

> As memory serves, Sumner made a proposition to me that involved me closing the Arrow and moving the artists, myself and Ron Field to the Union ... where we would actually be paid for acting. I hesitated, and, after a three second pause, accepted. A 500 seater theatre, money, a competent production unit (which mine never was), the backing of the University of Melbourne ... a struggling actor should be so lucky.
>
> Out of the blue, or possibly considering out of the red, the Volumnia of Toorak struck again. The actual words were I think . . 'Why should this dreadful Englishman come along and take over all you've built up'. There was no redress. I had to go and tell Sumner (who, to add to the horror, was living next door to me) that I couldn't honour our agreement.[360]

Olive again bore the blame, which was handy. Her 'actual words' were not so surprising, though, given that she had put significant funds, not to mention her clothing and jewellery, into a theatre company on the basis that it belonged to her son. She had never pretended to any missionary zeal for Australian theatre in general, though she had a string of other charities as long as her pearls. Olive's particular project was her son, and anything that didn't have his name all over it was unlikely to engage her.

This is one of those moments in which Frank's account of Olive's views and the embarrassment they caused him rings true enough. His depiction of his own feelings about it, though, is not quite so convincing. The move from visionary artistic director to employee was one that surely might have been expected to detain him for more than three seconds. At the Arrow, the name of Frank W. Thring was everywhere, and Frank enjoyed wonderful roles. The 'dreadful Englishman' would run the show at the Union Repertory, and he would decide who played what. And the economic argument was not for him as compelling as his reminiscences suggest. Every one of Frank's company at the Arrow could fit the description of 'a struggling actor', but not him. Frank would surely need a better argument to trade in 'all that he had built up' in the previous two years, however modest it was.

359 John Sumner, *Recollections at Play. A Life in Australian Theatre*, Melbourne University Press, 1993, p.20.

360 Geoffrey Hutton, *It Won't Last a Week!*, p.vii.

Moreover, the timing of it all was a little strange. The painful conversation with John Sumner happened at the end of 1952, after which there was such bitterness, according to Frank, that 'we didn't speak to each other for three years'. This is nearly true, though Frank was in England for at least two of those years, which made speaking more difficult. From Sumner's point of view there was a coolness between them – after feeling 'devastated'[361] when the offer was withdrawn he felt let down, certainly, and began exploring other options, including abandoning the idea of a professional company altogether. He didn't feel a need to speak to Frank Thring about anything on the revised agenda.[362]

Frank, however, should really have spoken to him. A few months after Frank's discussions with Sumner, Olive was dead. The money was Frank's, to invest in Sumner's company or not. He seems to have chosen not.

At the same time, the Arrow was being wound up. Its perennial problem, as Frank presented it in the farewell program for the double bill of *The Critic* and *Oedipus Rex*, was the lack of an audience. A lot of theatre initiatives in Australia, before and since, have known what that was like. It was a consideration that might have been taken into account earlier, had the accounting been less of a family matter. In principle, there was no reason why the Arrow should not have gone on for some years, just as it was, with a group of mostly very talented amateurs giving all that they had in creativity and time to help realise the destiny of the young man who ran the show. Frank had the style, the name, the profile and the serious money, and some of his fellow-actors at the Arrow might fairly have resented that; there were some extraordinarily talented people in the company. Frank called the shots, however; there was no genuine committee. When he decided it was time to drop the curtain, it fell. It is likely that his decision had more to do with his mother's death, and the need to close a chapter in his own life, than with any nasty surprises in the Arrow's accounts. The balance-sheet had, from the beginning, been entirely predictable.

The company, taking the interim identity of The Arrow Associate Company, signalled that it was not as ready to close the chapter as its restless

361 John Sumner, *Recollections at Play*, p.22.
362 John Sumner interview, 11 January 2005.

and capricious founder. It limped through two Thring-less and uninspired productions – one of the melodrama *Sweeney Todd*, the other of Terence Rattigan's *Playbill* (comprising the one-acters *The Browning Version* and *Harlequinade*) – before accepting the inevitability of its fate in early 1954.

Frank was clear that it was time to say good-bye. He designed an unusually lavish program for the Arrow's farewell season in 1953. It featured, when you turned the first page, two selective pictures of the group, both taken by the photographer Helmut Newton. One was of 'The Leading Ladies of the Arrow', and featured seven of those ladies gathered languidly or defiantly around a bed; Bambi Shmith lounged at centre, in a composition that affirmed the power of women – every one of them was challenging the camera, but in a coolly provocative rather than confronting way. 'The Leading Men of the Arrow' did their lounging in an alley-way beside the theatre, some smiling enigmatically but most wanting to make it clear that they were artists and bohemians, and couldn't give a stuff whether the viewer liked it or not. Frank, front left, looks surly, but his sunglasses tell you instantly that of course this is because he is highly intelligent, and so has no reason to smile. The stark location, and the fact that most of 'The Leading Men' seemed to be suffering, was a sure sign that this company compromised for no-one, and took seriously the current existential questions.

Frank's farewell to the loyal Arrow audience was appreciative of their discrimination, while it also professed a real generosity for all those people in Melbourne who had never heard of the Arrow, and probably wouldn't have gone to a place like that if you'd paid them. His reflections on the experience followed a photo of himself – brooding, but charmingly – that, in an apparently self-deprecating gesture toward democracy, took up less than a quarter of an otherwise blank page; the caption, just as his father would have required, was 'Frank W. Thring'. There was no explicit reference to the Francis W. Thring whose photograph had adorned the Efftee Players' programs twenty years before, but for those who knew their history the father was part of the myth of heroic failure that his son was in the process of writing.

The next page told them the sad news that the company was folding. The readers would have (or some of them, at least, should have) had a strong sense of the way in which father and son had tried to bring culture to people who could never really appreciate it.

> The comments of the Press would lead one to believe that the standard of acting and production has been consistently high. If therefore the Arrow has failed to draw an audience, the blame must be laid at the

> door of Melbourne's public. These poor people have however been so scathingly denounced by the Press that in the end even I began to feel sorry for them.
>
> Their constant denunciation has however had little effect and so before the Arrow curtain is rung down for the last time I would like not to write of the empty houses and the diminishing bank balance, but of the successes we have enjoyed together.[363]

And so he does, generously and at length, in what follows. For Frank the diminishing bank balance was hardly a consideration. The absence of an audience, however, was obvious enough, and Frank's need for one, and for its approbation, was fundamental to the Arrow enterprise. He chose, then, to 'forget the bad moments and remember the good ones'.

> I hope that you will find similar moments in our two plays tonight and that you feel as I do, that the Arrow, short-lived as it was, cannot be called a failure.[364]

It was a relatively defensive assertion, but it is interesting for its finality and its sense of history. It was important to Frank that if the Arrow had to go down it would go down gloriously. Like his father, he had done what he could. Although Frank sought to accentuate the positive in that last Arrow program, it left an unmistakable impression that the war was unwinnable.

Frank would have felt grimly vindicated in his view of the unresponsive philistinism of the community before which he had been casting his pearls by one of the reviews of that farewell double bill.

> I find Sophocles a prize bore as a playwright, and I have no doubt that Rex Oedipus is staged occasionally simply because some important actor – in this case Frank Thring – wants the large opportunity of playing the King. Mr Thring does the job wonderfully well and, considering the limitations of the Arrow stage, there is poetry in some of the movements.

363 Souvenir Program for the final presentation at the Arrow, November 1953.
364 ibid.

> Nevertheless, when I began to consider the characters of some of the dressed-up savages and the revolting story, such as it is, I could not help wondering how it would play as entertainment if the tempo were stepped up and Groucho Marx or George Wallace played Rex.[365]

Sadly, no record remains of Frank's remarks on reading this analysis.

There were implications for Sumner's initiative at the university, of course. If the Arrow could not succeed with the best actors in Melbourne, including and especially Frank Thring, how could the Union succeed with the same aims, same actors, and with no Frank Thring? The plans to wind up the Arrow thus did nothing to clear the field for its professional successor; they declared the whole contest at an end.

The other death in the Thring family, eight months before that of the Arrow, was Olive's. She had been ill for some months, and in hospital for most of that time. Frank went to visit her, occasionally with flowers, but there was to be no rapprochement. There was nothing that he wanted to say to her, and she had long ago learned to censor what she talked about with him. They must have been horrendous, those visiting hours with their cavernous silences in the glare and sterility of the ward.

At the time of Olive's last illness, Joan had moved out of Rylands to share a house in Hawthorn with a bunch of cheerful theatricals. She had heard Olive was sick, and was anxious to know how she was; at the same time, she knew enough about what was unsayable in the Thring family to feel reluctant to ring Frank and ask. Then, one morning, she literally bumped into him. Of all places, they met on a tram – if only Frank's Drama teacher from Melbourne Grammar had been there. She was on her way to work, he off to perform his filial duty. Joan asked him, tentatively, how Olive was. 'Oh, she's all right', he growled.[366] The warnings were unmistakable, and she didn't pursue the subject. A couple of weeks later, he rang her. They talked about a few inconsequential things before Frank apparently remembered the reason for his call. 'Oh, by the way', he said, 'she's dead'. Joan, who

365 Darrell Symmons, 'On the Stage', *Sun*, Weekend Magazine, 21 November 1953, p.46.
366 Joan Thring, interview, December 2004.

had always been fond of Olive and had been moved by Olive's fondness in return, mumbled something inadequate, as people do on these occasions. Frank brusquely changed the subject.[367] There was no place for routine expressions of sympathy, even ones that were deeply meant; they were ludicrously misplaced. Frank did not say a word about what he was feeling. The impression he gave was that he felt nothing.

He said relatively little about her thereafter, apart from those lurid invocations of Medea and Lady Macbeth and other metaphorical man-eaters. People on the whole sensed that he would prefer not to talk about his mother, and those radio interviewers who were unaware that they were entering dangerous territory tended to be placated by one of his grimly comic characterisations of her. The comedy lay in the fact that the listener probably put all this down to the naughtiness of that Frank Thring, who never had a nice word to say about anybody; in their innocence, they would assume that no son could ever really feel such hostility or cold indifference to his dear old mum, and that this was another case of Frank pretending to be mean. But the inescapable truth seems to be that he felt, for once, as he said he did. Of course it must have been more complicated than common-or-garden hatred; a mother, especially one that a son has lived with for almost all of twenty-seven years, is enmeshed in his history, quite apart from whatever the two of them create of the usual Freudian baggage. Frank's mother had been unusually closely involved in all the key decisions and developments in his life, and supportive in every one of them that we know about. So whatever it was that he went through that brought him to be indifferent to her death, or even to be relieved or glad, must have been momentous.

Some twenty years later, Fred Parslow had the gall to ask him about it.[368] He had been to Rylands a number of times, and had always been struck by the handsome portrait of Olive that hung in the hall. It was of Olive at forty-five perhaps, a big woman in her best blue. Everything about the picture – its size, her jewels, the comfortable expression that tells the viewer that she is the kind of woman who expects to be painted – signifies power and influence. The eyes, though, are soft and kind. For Joan Thring this was the Olive that she knew, and after Frank's death the portrait came to London, to take pride of place in Joan's Kensington apartment. To other people, who knew the stories at second hand, it was a surprisingly benign Olive, with not a hint of Lucretia Borgia anywhere.

367 Joan Thring, interview, December 2004.
368 Frederick Parslow interview, 16 September 2004.

Fred Parslow certainly found it so, and the fact that whenever he visited Rylands there were fresh white flowers on the small table beneath it suggested that there must have been somebody who missed her. So he asked Frank what these mixed signals meant. Having always said that he and his mother didn't get on, did the little domestic shrine express Frank's mixed feelings about his mother, perhaps? Or had there been some mellowing with the years, that had led him to forgive what she had done or not done to him, or at least to conclude that things were more complex than they had seemed at the time? Frank took a moment, and then closed the subject for good. 'I'm glad she's dead', he said, 'I hated the cunt'.

The savagery would be shocking in any circumstances. For once there seemed to be no intervening persona, no calculation of effect. The one thing certain is that, whatever the perceived betrayal, it was a very big one. Almost as certainly, it had a significant effect on how Frank saw the world beyond his mother, and on the ways he chose to live in it.

It was, about as graphically as such things can be, an end to a chapter. His mother was dead, and his company had been, much more eloquently and sensitively, buried as well. John Sumner was very effectively building a company at the university that involved a number of the Arrow's actors, and Frank had no part in the process; he and Sumner were managing to avoid each other with surprising success. There were all sorts of reasons why it might be awkward to be in Melbourne. The one thing that might at least ameliorate it, his curious relationship with Joan Cunliffe, would work just as well, or so it seemed, from the other side of the world. It had done so, more or less, eight years before.

So Frank decided, again, to go to London. This time, though, it was not just to 'choof around', but to have, at last, a serious shot at a career in the theatre. By early 1954, the Thring estate had devolved to Frank; Lola had her smaller share, of course, but nothing now could bring her in from the periphery of Frank's life, and she was of no relevance to any choice that he now had to make. He would, as he liked to put it, 'take' four Arrow productions, and run them in London. By taking the shows, Frank did not mean the kind of thing that others would mean by the phrase – taking actors and sets and production teams. He meant taking himself, and the costumes that Joan's mother Edith had made for *Salome*.

Two other Arrow people would be part of the project. Fred Farley, now back in England after the last season of *The Critic* and *Oedipus Rex* in Middle Park, was crucial both for his talents and his London contacts. Barry Gordon, already established at the 'Q' Theatre in Kew, provided an effective means to a suitable venue. But it was really, as Joan Thring said about Olive Thring's life, all about Frank.

The 1954 campaign had its moments of glory, but both the battle-plan and the victories were less grandiose than Frank, in an interview with Keith Dunstan, liked to recall:

> Mr Thring certainly did not plan to go to London to hang around stage doors looking for bit parts. He decided to start from the top and put on his own plays at his own theatre with Thring in the starring roles.
>
> He rented the Q Theatre, which was appropriately enough in Kew, not the centre of things but always considered a good try-out theatre for shows on their way to the West End. He planned to put on four plays 'all marvellous for myself' and he took from Melbourne all the costumes for Salome.[369]

It was primarily Frank's initiative, no doubt, and it was financially underpinned by a fair slice of his inheritance. But the season of shows was organised by Fred Farley, and advertised as 'Mr Frederick Farley's season of Australian plays'. It opened not with one of Frank's 'marvellous' roles but a modest little comedy by Alex Atkinson, reviewed in *Theatre World* without ever being actually named, and featuring an Irishman, Patrick McGoohan, who the anonymous reviewer conceded 'almost made the whole thing worth while'.[370] The rental of the Q Theatre was for just eight weeks, which hardly made it 'his own theatre'. For a grand strategy, it was heavily dependent on good luck. *Salome* did make a splash, but almost by accident.

Frank remembered it like this:

> We opened with *Salome*. That only runs for an hour and there had to be another before it – *The Respectable Prostitutes* [sic] by Jean Paul Sartre. The Q doesn't normally get the big time critics from London, but we did get the celebrated Harold Hobson from the *Sunday Times*. Huh, he wasn't

369 Keith Dunstan, *Ratbags*, p.132.
370 *Theatre World*, volume XLX, number 354, July 1954, p.8.

> faintly interested in me or *Salome*, he was keen to see the Sartre play. Hobson had something wrong with his legs. He could hobble along only on steel sticks. He had to be driven everywhere. This night something went wrong with his car arrangements and he didn't get to the theatre until the Sartre play was over, so he had to put up with *Salome*.
>
> His story in the Sunday Times came out under the heading WHO IS THIS MAN. He reported how his car didn't turn up, how he had to sit, reluctantly through Salome. Then, he said, 'Suddenly this six foot two monstrosity came on the stage and went through all the performance of hysteria, paranoia, bloodlust and homosexuality. Who is this man? Why haven't we heard of him in the West End?'[371]

This story, too, was a mixture of truth and creative embellishment. Hobson's review, under the much less compelling headline, 'Roaming Round', actually said this, after two paragraphs reflecting on *Salome* as 'one of the great, if corroded, moments of the English theatre':

> Herod is played by Mr Frank Thring. Who is this actor? I do not remember ever having heard of him. There seems to be some injustice here. It is amazing that actors who have voices like the whining of helicopters and actors who have no voices at all should get long engagements in the West End, whilst Mr Thring is giving a performance as eloquent, as throbbing with passion and perversity and terror as this out in the suburbs.[372]

Hobson's puzzled 'Who is this actor?' had a slightly different weight from the astonished 'WHO IS THIS MAN?' that Frank preferred to recall, but it was still a wonderful notice for an unknown performer from a senior critic. He made no reference at all to car problems and arrivals after interval, though perhaps the fact that the performance of *The Respectable Prostitute* is described blandly as 'also comparatively sure' and that Hobson mentions only its final moments might suggest that he got there rather late:

> Though the irony of the ending was missed, it may be said to have triumphed over an audience inclined to think that any play with a bedroom scene in it must be a farce.[373]

371 Dunstan, *Ratbags,* p.132.
372 Harold Hobson, *Sunday Times*, 20 June 1954, p.11.
373 ibid.

The only other review of *Salome* at the 'Q' was in *Theatre World*, which noted dutifully that 'Frank Thring (director and founder of the Arrow Theatre) made an impressive Herod and Agnes Bernelle a seductive and imperious Salome'.[374] But Hobson's review was the one that counted, anyway, and Farley moved quickly to capitalise on it by striking a deal with St Martin's Theatre.

Frank moved quickly too, placing an article with Frank Doherty in the *Argus* at home (headlined 'Gambler Thring Hits the Bulls-eye')[375], and giving a remarkably similar interview in London to the 'Evening Standard Show Reporter':

> The baritone voice on the telephone said: 'I look rather like Cesare Borgia; I have a Mongolian beard and a taste for heavily embroidered waistcoats. You can't possibly miss me'.
>
> This self-portrait was for my benefit. It was to help me recognise actor Frank Thring at a film premiere.
>
> Thring, 28-year-old, wealthy, self-sponsored actor from Australia, is determined to be recognised. And not only in cinema foyers.
>
> In Australia he owns a radio station and four cinemas. But business bores him.
>
> He would much sooner earn fame in the London theatre than wealth in the Australian bush.
>
> The idea of knocking on agents' doors did not appeal to him. He is an independent fellow. So he set about promoting himself in a more congenial way.
>
> He took over the 'Q' Theatre for a season … Today Thring has reason to believe that the gamble has paid off. He will open at St Martin's theatre on July 20 in Oscar Wilde's Salome, playing Herod.[376]

Frank was marketing a personality. His tactics in conquering London were as distinctive as his waist-coats; some people hoped for success, he commanded it. In so doing, as Frank told the story, he won it.

---

374 *Theatre World*, July 1954, p.8.
375 *Argus*, 15 July 1954, p.8.
376 *Evening Standard*, 18 July 1954, p.2.

> We played only a week at the Q then switched to St Martin's in London all on the strength of Hobson's review ... Our Salome went so well I even did the jewel speech on BBC television and Harold Hobson actually introduced me on the show. We never got around to doing the other shows and I decided to come back to Australia. Wouldn't you know the word got around everywhere, 'Ahh, he's come back home. Must have been a terrible flop'. That infuriated me.[377]

The West End season of *Salome* became in Frank's reminiscences a bigger hit with each passing year, and the unfair inferences of his countrymen, who were always so quick to cut down tall poppies, never ceased to rankle:

> I didn't like London. I didn't want to spend my life playing Herod ... so I just came back. And everyone in Australia said – typical – oh, he must have been a dreadful flop in London, who would come back here if he was a success in the West End ... [378]

Again, the myth was founded in fact, but creatively edited and embroidered. They only played a week at the 'Q' because a week was all they were ever booked for there. The transfer was certainly made, and the London season received some good reviews; the cameo appearance on the BBC occurred, too, and gave it excellent publicity. But the notion that Frank was 'a success in the West End', given that the run of *Salome* at St Martins consisted of just twelve performances, was open to debate, at least. In fact, the company did 'get around' to one of the other original Arrow productions at the 'Q'. Mordaunt Shairp's *The Green Bay Tree* played for a couple of nights before it came to a premature close; the anonymous critique in the *Times* was tepid, although it did single out one of the cast, in the role of 'the fastidious Mr Dulcimer':

> He is impersonated by Mr Frank Thring, an actor who, though he is too young for the part, has uncommon resources – a compelling bass voice, a sureness of subtle timing, and a smouldering dignity in his frequent mute asides to the audience. His diverting character sketch does much to redeem the evening.[379]

---

377 Dunstan, *Ratbags*, p.132.
378 Bill Howie interview, 12 November 1989.
379 *Times*, July 14 1954, p.11.

This was one of the four roles, 'all marvellous for myself', that didn't quite hit the mark, and Frank accordingly dropped it from the story of his triumphal march.

Salome on the West End was reviewed by all the major critics. Hobson was again the most enthusiastic of them, and there was no sign of the interest in *The Respectable Prostitute* that a month before had taken him all the way to Kew:

> In Wilde's 'Salome' at the St Martins (Sartre's 'Respectable Prostitute' is also in the bill) Mr Frank Thring's Herod is a splendidly full-blooded, full-throated, full-hearted and full-bodied performance. It is splendid on a ten-league canvas, and playgoers should run miles to see it. Miss Agnes Bernelle's Salome also rises surely to Wilde's sensational climax, which like Beachy Head is terrific even if a bit steep.[380]

A month later and in a city venue, *Theatre World* was much more animated than it had been after the Q Theatre production. The reviewer liked the production now, and complimented Frank on delivering a performance that was more than sound and fury, though it wasn't clear in what way:

> Frank Thring was able to frame this pinchbeck Nero with undeniable histrionic magnificence and his turgid sentences, sonorously launched, were somehow weighted with meaning.[381]

The thumbs-up from the critics was not unanimous. Darlington in the *Daily Telegraph* merely noted that the Dance of the Seven Veils 'excited me considerably less that [sic] it did Frank Throng's Herod, who went into paroxysms over it',[382] while Ivor Brown, similarly cool about the play, commented drily that 'Frank Thring, evidently not afraid of being chargeable with out-Heroding Herod, mixes his own thunder with the blood in a grand manner'.[383] Kenneth Hurren, declaring the double bill a 'noxious notion', found the climax of Salome a 'disgustingly emetic' culmination of 'the fetid atmosphere of the entire work'. He described the Thring approach to

---

380 Harold Hobson, 'Murder?', *Sunday Times*, 25 July 1954, p.11.
381 *Theatre World*, volume XLX, number 356, September 1954, p.7.
382 W.A.Darlington, *Daily Telegraph*, 21 July 1954, p.8.
383 Ivor Brown, 'Grim Tales', *Observer*, 25 July 1954, p. 11.

Herod as 'that excessively florid style usually associated with the storming of barns'.[384] It was hardly a triumphal critical chorus.

Still, although the St Martin's season was short, it bore some resemblance to the flying start Frank had been seeking, and the 'success in the West End' that he subsequently claimed. This was what he had come for. He had the money, the costumes and the lines for a couple of other productions, and Hobson was not the only theatregoer in London who was keenly interested in what he would do next. So Frank made his next move, the one that he had made before and would make again when stardom seemed to beckon him. He went home to Melbourne.

Why did he come back? It might just be a very Australian kind of question. Englishmen naturally go home after scoring successes overseas, and so do Americans; Frenchmen go home, too, on the rare occasions they go away. Australians, though, often don't. Melba stayed away between farewells, and a host of others from Keith Michell to Kylie Minogue have chosen to make their homes where the big games are being played. Helpmann went to London to dance in 1932, and didn't come home for twenty-three years. The fact that Frank, having apparently won the chance he came for, should consider his business finished, is extraordinary.

He had been writing regularly to Joan Cunliffe about the compliments he was getting, the parties he was attending, the people he was meeting. She envied him all of it; for a court reporter stuck in Melbourne in mid-winter, his letters beamed light into grey days. The glamour of the life that Frank was leading, that he seemed to have been born to lead, seemed impossibly distant to her. When he told her, matter-of-factly, that he had booked his ticket home, he gave no explanation. The one that for her explained it best, many years later as Joan Thring and in the context of several other perplexing departures, was the big-fish-in-a-small-pond one. She felt, too, that under all that affected cosmopolitanism Frank was a 'home-body'; it was easier, certainly, to look big in Melbourne, but it was also possible to feel comfortably small.

There are other possible reasons for the decision. Two were the ones he gave: that he 'didn't like London', and that he had no desire 'to spend my life playing Herod'. The first is undermined somewhat by the evidence that he had seemed to be having such a good time, and by the fact that he was back again within nine months. The second becomes less persuasive in the context of the short West End run (the Farley/Thring *Salome* in England had played

384 Kenneth A. Hurren, 'Not the Girls for Me', *What's On in London*, 30 July 1954, p.4.

fewer than twenty performances) and the fact that nobody was asking Frank to play Herod any more at all.

Another was the possibility that he came back for Joan. It's an unlikely grand-passion scenario perhaps, but he did invite her to go to England with him in the following year, and she was, clearly, very important to him. Quite apart from his genuine feeling for her, she was someone to share it with, a still point in a turning world – and, as she observed acerbically herself, she was at the very least 'a good cover'.[385] On the whole, though, the prospect of Joan's companionship looks more like a reassuring argument in favour of going again to London than a powerful motive for being in Melbourne. But how can we read at such distance emotions that often the people feeling them could not recognise or understand?

Several other potential influences might have to be taken into account: mundane ones like the last rites in the resolution of Olive's estate; unnerving ones, like a fear of what might come after the role that he knew and the small adulation that he had imagined; more deeply psychological ones, like the sense that he needed to return to the place and the task that his father had bequeathed him. All of those things might be powerful reasons to return to Rylands. Furthermore, Frank's capacity to offend people, and occasionally to get into serious scrapes, can never be ruled out as an overwhelming argument for moving as far as possible from London. Who knows what kind of mischief he might have made there.

In the absence of compelling evidence for any one explanation in particular, probably a number of those possible motives played a part. Complexity might be the last refuge of the confused biographer, but it's also a fair bet that most brilliantly simple explanations for the things that people choose, or feel they have no choice not to do, leave something out. None of these possible reasons for Frank's coming home would strike an observer as very good on their own, but together, for a man who had not looked at all beyond the first hurdle, they were enough.

There was nothing to entice him back theatrically in Melbourne, certainly. In his absence John Sumner had steered the Union Theatre Repertory Theatre

385 Joan Thring, interview with the author, 10 January 2005.

Company through its second precarious season. But though Frank might have liked to be part of that, his relationship with Sumner and a number of associated issues not unrelated to the Thring ego seemed to rule out his connection with the only interesting professional theatre in Melbourne.

The Little soldiered on at St Martin's in South Yarra, but the arrival of paid repertory in the city had forced a rearrangement that seemed to render a return to its stage unthinkable. In time Frank did come back to the Little, but at this point it would have looked an odd move for an actor who wanted it known that he had conquered the West End. So Frank, after cooling his heels for a couple of months, did what a frustrated and floundering big fish might predictably do in such a clichéd situation. First he became a theatre critic, in order to confirm the burning of all the bridges that had already been very badly damaged. Then, when his position became quite untenable, he pursued any contacts that he could think of elsewhere.

He also did what Frank would now habitually do whenever he was at a loose end. He partied hard, and drank, rather like a big fish in fact. Frank and Joan had for years moved, mostly together, in the more stylish of Melbourne's social circles. They were a striking couple – Frank ever-reliably outrageous, Joan now attracting some attention as a fashion-plate. Frank could be terrible, of course, but as long as there was only one person like him in the room a party could stay on the fun side of disaster. Joan was still bemused by some of the things she saw, but growing in confidence. She recalled those days as 'completely wild', and in early 1954 they seem to have been getting wilder still. A party at Rylands in January got out of hand, and Joan recalled Frank sheltering foetal under the table, clutching a precious glass vase till the tumult and the shouting diminished to normal.[386] Twice within a week the police came to the house. On the first occasion, Frank and Joan were having a lively argument on the footpath at six in the morning, on their way back from a long dinner hosted by their Toorak neighbours, Peta Dulier and Jimsie Ross. Joan's diary for February 28th read 'Peta's dinner. Jimsie. 6 am police'.[387] What happened could have been tragic, but quickly turned to farce. Frank pushed her; she stumbled back into the road just as a car turned the corner; Frank grabbed her to pull her back, and in doing it tore the smart new dress that Mrs Cunliffe had made almost completely off her; the car was a police car. After some explanations the policemen adjourned with them into Rylands, where Joan put on some clothes and

386 ibid.
387 Joan Thring, personal diary for 1955.

cooked them all bacon and eggs, and then went to work at eight, leaving Frank entertaining the pride of the force. The following Saturday night the police were back. It was another of those seemingly endless progressive dinners, where the conversation turned ugly by dessert, and one of the guests threw a punch at Frank; it missed, but Joan, intervening, managed to land a useful blow on the man herself, which did nothing for his temper.[388] Her diary for March 5 is typically cryptic: 'Progressive dinner. Brawl. Police'.[389] This time it was she who called the police station, and Frank gave a hand with the eggs.

It was all fun in the end, of course, good for a laugh and an anecdote. But when events that don't seem fun at the time keep happening with exactly the same people, a town can seem uncomfortably small. Something similar was happening with Frank's new career as a theatre critic.

Frank's role as guest reviewer for the *Argus* was short-lived, but notorious. It lasted for a couple of months, but some of the enemies he made – and he made very few friends – lasted a lifetime. Nothing quite like it had ever happened in the cosy world of Melbourne theatre; there had been negative reviews, of course, but they had been presented more in sorrow than in anger, and tried generally to be careful. In Melbourne, after all, critics were always running into their victims. Frank managed to alienate almost everyone in his first two weeks.

Much of it can be explained away as the response of a man who felt, in most important ways, still an expatriate; he had surely done Melbourne a favour by coming back, and a lot of its citizens seemed to be appallingly unappreciative of the fact. A lot of it was simply the whim of a writer with a chip on his shoulder and a big persona, a hide toughened in the crucible at Melbourne Grammar, and a flair for putting people down and sending them up that he had been working at since he was a small boy. Some of it was quite brave, taking on the local theatre establishment and exposing its complacent vanities, its portentousness, its narrowness. It was a thankless task, but it could be argued that someone urgently needed to do it; and Frank, for all sorts of reasons worthy and unworthy, took to it with gusto.

It began early in the new year, on the recommendation of the resident critic at the *Argus*, Frank Doherty, who had always been a kindly reviewer to the Arrow and to almost everyone else, and who was taking leave. The replacement Frank quickly established himself as a hanging judge. He

388 Joan Thring interview 10 January 2005.
389 Joan Thring personal diary for 1955.

announced his arrival with a critique of the Tivoli's current revue, *La Vie Parisienne*, featuring Jean Sablon, 'The Voice of Paris', that registered profound distaste for the show and the kind of burlesque, à la the *Folies Bergere*, that 'the Tiv' was accustomed to presenting:

> There is really very little one can say about Mr Sablon except that unlike children, he should be heard and not seen ... There is, of course, the inevitable presentation of living pictures, which in this case appears to be not so much Old Masters as Old Mistresses. The management must tell their nudes to suntan all over or not at all, as a pair of white bosoms protruding between a brown neck and a pink stomach is hardly likely to excite anyone under ninety. The producers have tried to be terribly naughty and terribly French, and breasts are bared at every conceivable opportunity. The result is as naughty as *Boy's Own Annual* and as French as ravioli.[390]

On the following evening, he reviewed an amateur *Antony and Cleopatra*, and reported only that 'Last night Cleopatra barged up the Nile and sank'.[391] Ten days later he went back to the Tivoli, and dispatched its new offering with minimum effort, maximum style:

> THE THEATRE: The Tivoli.
>
> THE SHOW: Jack and Jill.
>
> THE CAST: Roy Barbour, Nina Cooke, John Bluthal, Ivor Bromley.
>
> THE CRITIC: The End.[392]

The variety show *Coloured Rhapsody* three weeks later was dismissed just as acerbically, though at greater length. The show contained 'five of the worst-dressed, most unoriginal dance routines it has ever been by [sic] misfortune to witness'. But there was, unfortunately, more.

> ... adding insult to this almost insufferable injury is the nerve-shattering voice of Irene Bevans, which has much the same effect as a nail on a piece of tin.

---

390 *Argus*, 7 January 1955.
391 *Argus*, 8 January 1955.
392 *Argus*, 18 January 1955.

Then there was its headline act, Britain's 'Heart-Throb' David Hughes:

> Like the H-bomb, Mr Hughes is one of the menaces of modern civilisation. With the nauseating charm of a precocious child he alternately bellows and moans through a mass of sickly sentimentality culminating in a terrifying example of commercialised religion.[393]

Hughes was an easy target. He was only passing through, and presumably a lot of the readers of the *Argus* would find it good sport to cut an over-rated interloper down to size. But when Frank attacked the National Theatre, with its mission to elevate the nation to an appreciation of what cultural capital was all about, he effectively ended his career as a theatre critic. The National was largely amateur, but it was serious, and anybody who was Anybody knew that its productions were things to see and things to be seen at. Frank's critique was devastating. Despite the arrogance of the review, its off-hand citation of international credentials, its indifference to what it might do to the feelings and livelihoods of all the people that it didn't bother to mention, it was probably in the interests of Australian theatre. But those of us who weren't there can only imagine what we might have felt had we been on the receiving end:

> Last night in its grim graveyard of the taxpayer's money, the Australian National Theatre Movement inaugurated its Shakespeare Festival with a diabolical performance of Twelfth Night.
>
> This presentation (one hesitates to use the word production since the imaginative and guiding hand of a producer was at no point evident) plumbed the depths of incompetent amateurism.
>
> To list the players would be sheer cruelty as they have been handicapped not only on the production side, but also by the most appalling stage management it has been my misfortune to see, either here or abroad.
>
> Lights flashed on and off, scenery quivered, and a rather tired cypress tree, which for some reason had been leaning against the sky, fell over with such monotonous regularity that eventually one thought it must be part of the plot.[394]

393 *Argus*, 16 February 1955.
394 *Argus*, 24 February 1955.

Letters were exchanged, phone calls were made, and there was much wailing and gnashing of teeth. But the real climax was still a couple of weeks away. On the evening of March 9, Frank Thring and his guest, Joan Cunliffe, took their complementary seats for the National's next production, *The Merchant of Venice*. They were in the stalls at the Princess, where a lot of Thring memories were in the air. A few minutes before the curtain was due to rise, Gertrude Johnson, the National's distinguished director, asked them to leave the theatre. Voices rose, ushers gathered, people whispered and pointed, and they left; Frank couldn't make an inconspicuous exit if he tried, and it is a safe bet that he wasn't trying that night. Joan's diary just says, cryptically, 'Merchant. Thrown out of theatre'.[395] The two of them spent the evening laughing long into the night about it at a nearby pub. But suddenly and incredibly, on the next morning theatre in Melbourne was front-page news.

The third Shakespeare in the National season opened the following week. It was the Moomba festival, and on a balmy March evening *A Midsummer Night's Dream* was performed outdoors in the Fitzroy Gardens. The critic from the *Age* was not on the guest-list for the evening, but Frank managed to see the performance none the less. He claimed that he watched it from a tree, but Frank's body and his views on what constituted reasonable physical effort make that incredible. He is more likely to have found cover in an unusually large bush.

Another critic might have been more circumspect about a declaration of war on the National, which had rich and influential friends. To Frank the size of the enemy added to the pleasure of cutting it down, and he clearly had a lot of fun in a situation in which most other people were becoming very upset. He was a difficult opponent, because he couldn't be shamed, and because as long as the role he was playing was a public one his self-confidence was boundless. If his bravado was ever inclined to falter, as of course it was not, there were two handy weapons to add to the power of his words. One was that his vitriolic reviews were a boon to the sales of the *Argus*, and that readers, if they weren't in the productions, loved them; they touched a vein of *schadenfreude* and ghoulishness that always sells newspapers. Nor was everyone terrified by the prospect of becoming Thring's next target, either. The *Argus* ran a page three feature about responses to its terrifying critic, under the headline 'They Want Thring to Tear Them to Pieces', which suggested that there was a long queue of all-too-willing victims. The Ferntree Gully Reps sent an invitation saying 'Request please,

395 Joan Thring personal diary, entry for 9 March 1955.

your presence. Guaranteed no throw-outs Wednesday, Thursday next'; the secretary of Caulfield Repertory Players wrote, 'Dear Cruel Mr Thring. Just write something, we don't care a hang what's said'.[396] The principle that there was no such thing as bad publicity was overlaid with a sense that a deliciously negative review from Frank Thring might even be preferable to a forgettably sympathetic one. Miss Johnson and the National Theatre, understandably, did not agree.

Two days later the letters to the editor in the *Argus* were all about Frank. Princess Margaret's romance with Peter Townsend claimed the front page, but there was no doubt about what was being talked about in Melbourne. Under the headline 'Mr Thring is a Big Bully!', one of the correspondents, Miss H. O'Brien, a near-neighbour of Frank's in fashionable South Yarra, would have epitomised for him all his stereotypes about carping Melburnians, and reminded him of all the excellent reasons not to have come home:

> If he was so brilliant and much sought-after, why, oh why, did he have to come back here. The sooner he goes overseas again the better for Australia. A shave wouldn't go astray, either; if he can't afford blades I'll send him some.[397]

Frank's stint as a reviewer was almost at an end, anyway. Frank Doherty was back from his holidays, and Frank Thring, whose diary was starting to look alarmingly free from engagements, was scheduled to appear at the Little Theatre again, in Irene Mitchell's production of *The Prisoner*. There was a lot of talk, most if it from Frank himself, about the imminent opportunity for reprisals. A return to the Little provided a neat closure to a role as evil genius and Big Bully that, for all its pleasures, not even Frank could keep playing for long.

The other thing that added to his armoury was a telegram that he had recently received from Anthony Quayle at the Shakespeare Memorial Theatre in Stratford, in response to a speculative one that Frank had sent several days before:

> ... the reception here infuriated me so much that I sent a cable to now unfortunately the late Sir Anthony Quayle saying 'Anything going Butch?' ... and I got a cable back saying 'Will you join Oliviers and self

396 *Argus*, 12 March 1955.
397 *Argus*, 15 March 1955.

> in Peter Brook production of Titus Andronicus? Well I had it published in all the papers – in three inch type – saying 'Oliviers send for Thring'. And I went. And I did it.[398]

The telegram arrived on February 12. A few days later he savaged the National's *Twelfth Night*. Presumably it was easier to be defiant when you knew that you were leaving town quite soon; and not only going away for a bit, but indefinitely, and to do a production of Shakespeare that was a far, far better thing than the National had ever done.

It was a nice little token of his theatrical credentials, too. Frank's summons was revealed in the *Argus* on the day he eviscerated *Colored Rhapsody* and David Hughes. The page three article 'Frank Thring to co-star with Oliviers' reported that 'the controversial guest critic of the *Argus*' had said he was 'thrilled and delighted with the highest post you can aspire to in the theatre'.[399] It quoted Quayle's telegram in full, including the sentence 'You will be superb'.

For decades, Frank kept the cable at hand, to show to anybody who might need to be reminded of their place. He just happened to have it with him when he dropped in most unexpectedly to see John Sumner, with whom relations were still strained; he left it carelessly on a coffee-table at Rylands in case his visitors might be interested in such trivial things, just as years later he absent-mindedly left another telegram there, one inviting him to play a major role in the movie *El Cid*.[400] In relation to passing nods of approval from famous people, as in most other matters, Frank believed that if you'd got it, you should flaunt it.

As Frank presented it, he had had only to speak, and it came to pass; Quayle and the Shakespeare Memorial Theatre were suitably honoured to secure his services. The truth was a little different. They were relieved, certainly, but Frank was not the company's first choice for the role. Ruth Ellis, in her column 'Peeps Behind the Scenes' for the *Stratford-upon-Avon Herald*, reported on February 18 that Brewster Mason, who was to play Saturninus, had injured his foot, and would not be able to appear in the forthcoming season at Stratford.[401]

---

398 Bill Howie interview 12 November 1989. In a rare reversal of Frank's tendency to increasingly exaggerate his stories, the headlines had shrunk to three inches from the four he remembered in Keith Dunstan's *Ratbags* (p.132). The font was certainly larger than one inch.

399 The *Argus*, 16 February 1955.

400 Phillip Adams, 'Frankly sssspeaking', *Sydney Morning Herald*, Weekend Review, January 21–22 1995, p.21.

401 *Stratford-upon-Avon Herald*, 18 February 1955.

There was no mention of a replacement until three weeks later, when at last she revealed that Frank Thring would step into the role that Mason had hobbled out of.[402] It was an extraordinary stroke of luck, matching and recalling those that had begun his career as a radio and stage actor.

Frank's foot problem had saved him from a war; now Brewster Mason's took him back to London. The gods were smiling, it seemed. Retrospectively, though, given what they had in store, Frank might well have thought they were laughing at him.

402 *Stratford-upon-Avon Herald,* 11 March 1955.

TRAVELLING FROM MELBOURNE TO LONDON

S.S. *Arcadia*, 15 June 1955

Arcadia. Well, it fell some way short of paradise, but it was good. Bloody good. Better, in most respects, than boats one had been on in the past. He leaned on the rail and gazed at the horizon, in what he hoped was a fair facsimile of a man lost in thought.

He had, after all, a friend in Arcady. Well, in a fashion. Flowergirl was down in her cabin, dead to the world. It'd been a lively night in the saloon bar, continuing into a lively dawn. She'd done well, though, Joanie. You could never say the girl lacked staying power. She'd managed to stay somewhere in his life for nearly a decade, apart from anything else, and you needed a forgiving heart and an iron fucking constitution for that.

It made this a very different kind of voyage, having her with him. In performing to other people he caught himself often performing for her, and though by now she had to know most of his tricks she still seemed to find them diverting. She was an audience within an audience, someone with an eye for the art and not just the spectacle. But she was, of course, at other times, someone for whom it was impossible not to perform. He couldn't ever be quite honest, perhaps, not completely; perhaps one never could be, with anybody.

He could be nearly honest, nearly all the time, with her, and that was a lot to be able to say of a friendship, or whatever the fuck it was they shared.

He liked showing her things. It was as though her excitement at being on a boat, at seeing exotic places, at sitting at the captain's table, at doing and saying deliciously terrible things with delightfully awful people, recreated his own, the first time.

The pleasures of innocence, or was that an oxymoron? Of course, all that was his own indulgent fantasy. He couldn't remember the first time, and he couldn't remember ever being as young as Joan seemed. Innocence wasn't really a Thring thing. He'd always known too much – apart from those times, early mornings after sleepless nights, mouth dry from too much brandy, when he could move himself to tears at how little he really knew about anything important.

He was glad she'd said 'Yes' when he asked her to come. Glad, too, that she'd said 'No!' when he'd proposed, though it might've been kinder if she'd hesitated for just a moment.

Things were better as they were. People would've laughed at them. Their friends, for a start, who already knew too fucking much. Strangers he had known, like the men in the Australia bar and the boys on balmy weekends at Portsea. And strangers he'd never meet, thank Christ, like the solid citizens who called him a poofter when they thought he couldn't hear. Well, fuck 'em all, every last one of them. Which, not to miss a cue, he would if he could. The pretty ones, anyway.

There was no reason ever to go back to Melbourne, if he didn't want to. Perhaps, for the first time, he didn't. How strange that, when she'd been alive, he'd always wanted to go home, though dreading seeing her again – the massive figure in chartreuse or menopausal blue with her smothering mothering insufferable concern, all the intrusions of her voice, her scent, her intended touch. So much of her, so much too much.

But now that she was dead, and he had Rylands and the freedom to do whatever he wanted with whoever he wanted to do it to, there seemed no reason to be there at all. London had always felt like the start of a new chapter, of course, and then something had happened, or not happened, to make it turn out to be more of the same.

He had a telegram from Tony Quayle in his pocket, however, that told him that this time was different. And he had Sleeping Beauty downstairs, to keep his eye on the prize; she didn't need to bear his children to make him feel the confidence of a father, of his father, of a man who knew what to do because he had others, as well as himself, to do things for.

Et in Arcadia ego. Well, fuck it. There always had to be a little ego. Not to mention a bit of fucking id.

Chapter Ten

THESE FOOLISH THRINGS

Two things distinguished the journey to London in 1955 from Frank's earlier expeditions: he had a companion, and he had a clear sense of purpose. The presence of Joan, his favourite listener, was a good thing in itself, and while in some ways it cramped his style, it also kept him to some extent in line. It was one thing to proclaim, as he had done before, that he intended to take London by storm, and another to be in some sense accountable to somebody each evening for how much notice London was actually taking.

They sailed from Melbourne in the 'Arcadia' at noon on Saturday 4 June. On the 8th they docked in Perth, and their itinerary took them on through the other more exotic ports on the standard Suez run: on the 15th to Colombo, on the 17th to Bombay, on the 22nd to Aden, on the 25th to Cairo, and finally on July 3rd to London, where they were met by Fred Farley and Robert Helpmann.

Joan had never been out of Australia before, and that imposed another kind of responsibility on Frank. She was an innocent abroad, and Frank, who always showed some fondness for the roles of protector and pedagogue on the rare occasions that he was encouraged to play them, seemed to enjoy her reliance on him. Joan had been apprehensive about the trip, amid all the excitement, from the time they started to talk about it:

> Well, first of all, Frank went twice to London, ahead of me, and each time I waved him off. And then I used to get wonderful, wonderful letters from him all the time, describing who was sitting at the next table at the Caprice, and things like that ... Anyway, when we went to England, he wanted me to go, and I said, well, having wanted to go for years I then became very nervous, and I said I'd only go if you promise

> to send me home if I hate it, and he said, OK, and of course I didn't hate it, I loved it.[403]

Joan never came back to Australia, except for brief visits. She made London her home for the rest of her life, which must have been inconceivable in her early days there. For the first year, the more they became established in England, the more she felt as though she was swimming out of her depth.

They moved straight into a place in Battersea, in a house owned by the English actor Peter Cushing, who had swapped houses with Frank while he was on tour in Melbourne. Soon there were dinner parties with Bobby Helpmann, now entrenched as distinguished expatriate, and with Noel Coward, where the wines and the wit were intimidatingly good; there were weekends at Notley Abbey, where Laurence Olivier and Vivien Leigh played at being more aristocratic than the aristocrats. There were evenings at the theatre, where people who were apparently very clever all seemed to know each other intimately, and to look over your shoulder while they talked to you to see who else was in the room. Almost everybody she met seemed to be famous, even when she had never heard of them. It was a daunting challenge.

> Well, for me it was rather frightening, because I was a little Australian mouse, frightened to speak. The first weekend I went to Notley I was absolutely terrified. When in fact everybody was just like – humans … and Vivien, who could eat people alive, and did in front of me, was always absolutely sweet to me, really nice to me … I was one of those innocents abroad. Anyway, I changed somewhat, over the years.[404]

She passed some of the tests, at least. There was usually a role, at parties and in photographs, for an attractive ingénue.

> He [Frank] was always very proud of me. He liked showing me off. People used to say that I looked like Jean Simmons, and when we'd go out they'd come up to me and I'd get embarrassed and say, 'No, I'm not Jean Simmons, sorry', and Frank would say 'You don't have to tell them, you silly bitch'.[405]

---

403 Joan Thring interviewed by Frank Van Straten and Clive Stark, 3LO Nostalgia Show, Melbourne, 5 March 1995.

404 ibid.

405 Joan Thring, interview with the author, London, 15 December 2004.

Frank had a reputation for his way with words, but, as in that exchange, it wasn't always apparent. Perhaps it was just that the sepulchral tone and the affectation turned everything he said into parody, or perhaps he really was pathologically incapable of speaking lovingly. But the way that he looked after Joan in this period – and, for the most part, the way he talked about her long after they were together – suggests that he felt at least some of the tenderness that he didn't express.

While Joan often thought of herself as treading water desperately in a very deep pool, Frank stroked his way through it in style, and with apparently no effort at all. He was in his element. Whether it was a bit of Wildean thrust and parry with Noel Coward, or swanning with the nobs on the lawns at Notley, he took to it as to the manor born. Coming to the Q Theatre a year before, Frank had greeted the actors of the *Salome* company at their first rehearsal as though he owned the place – as, in a sense, he did. Now, arriving for his first rehearsal of *Titus Andronicus* at Stratford with some of the greatest actors of the age, his entry was exactly the same. Trader Faulkner recalled how the new arrival came into the room and filled it:

> This extraordinary, flamboyant creature, swept in. His arms were spread wide, he called us all 'darling'. He was like a giant sunflower.[406]

Several months later, after Frank had revelled in the triumph of *Titus* and improbably become a married man, John Gielgud, in a letter to Vivien Leigh, noted with a touch of irony how conspicuous this very theatrical young man had become in their social world. There was just a hint, perhaps, of a pursed lip at how little he had done to earn it:

> I see you married off the many-splendoured Thring, and now he is going to terrify the children as Hook![407]

Surely Frank could not have scripted it better. The first of his two years with Joan in London, surrounded by Larry and Viv and Noel and a host of other people who had swiftly become his very best friends, was in many ways the best period of his life, filled with achievement and with the promise of better things still.

406 Trader Faulkner, interview with the author, London, 26 January 2005. Faulkner, a fellow-Australian expatriate, was appearing in *Titus Andronicus* unobtrusively as Third Goth.

407 25 November 1955. *Geilgud's Letters*, ed. Richard Mangan, London, Weidenfeld and Nicolson, 2004, p.189

It was, from a number of points of view, a great time for them to be in London. The city was slowly emerging from the pall of the war and the grim constraints of post-war rationing, and Australian finances, for once, enabled the visitor to live there quite well. The mid-1950s were a time of renewal in the theatre, too. All the established giants – Olivier, Gielgud, Richardson, Redgrave, Quayle and men of that ilk – still prowled the Shakespearean stage. But two revolutions in particular, marked by the appearance of Osborne's *Look Back in Anger* and Beckett's *Waiting for Godot*, occurred in that period that permanently changed the shape of English theatre. Osborne's play redrew its parameters of class, while still testing the relationship between politics in contemporary Britain and the issues of personal meaning that Jimmy Porter keeps bumping into. Beckett's carried those existential matters to another level, challenging every received assumption about the ways in which language worked and life should be lived.

Kitchen-sink realism and absurdism came to the West End, and Frank and Joan were in the audiences for the first seasons of both. Frank enjoyed Osborne's savage 'comedy' of disaffection, though it had no roles for him – it suited his off-stage style, and the role of intellectual rebel without a cause had been one he had been playing just a few months ago, in those restless last months in Melbourne. He liked *Godot* even better; there was a remorseless dark humour to relish there, too, and as an actor he would have loved those pauses that plumbed eternity. At the end of his career, one of the few regrets that Frank expressed was that he had never had the chance to do a Beckett play.

But even the less iconoclastic London theatre seemed in a state of exuberant revival. On the next three nights after their arrival, Frank and Joan saw three plays: on Monday night it was *Tiger at the Gate*, with Michael Redgrave, on Tuesday *Salome* the opera at Covent Garden, and on Wednesday Orson Welles as Captain Ahab in *Moby Dick – Rehearsed*. Exciting theatre all of it, the Welles play in particular so affecting that Frank pursued him for a copy of the script, and four years later persuaded John Sumner to direct it in Melbourne, with Frank giving one of his best performances as Ahab. The classical stage was, in its way, being revivified, too; suddenly England was producing directors to match its great actors, and Frank, by a combination of good luck and good salesmanship, had fallen into a production where he would be working not only with 'the Oliviers' and Quayle, but Peter Brook.

It was, as well, an especially good time to be an Australian in London. Australians are by and large accustomed to feeling that their country is some distance off the map when they visit the great capitals of Europe, and unless a news item feeds a paranoia about sharks or snakes the English press is normally inclined to ignore what is happening at the other end of the world. In the mid-1950s, though, Australia was regularly in the news. The Petrov affair, a spy drama in Canberra featuring a photogenic woman and a cast of sinister Russian secret agents with guns and grimaces, ran for weeks in all the British papers. Australian sports stars were everywhere, it seemed: the swimmers' achievements at the Empire Games in 1954 were a small foretaste of their triumphs in 1956, when Melbourne hosted the Olympics; a young Melbourne golfer, Peter Thomson, had emerged from obscurity to win serial British Opens; in tennis, the dominance of Sedgman and McGregor was immediately followed by the triumphs at Wimbledon and in the Davis Cup of Hoad and Rosewall; the Australian cricketers, led by their fast bowlers Lindwall and Miller, dispatched Len Hutton's English tourists to reclaim the Ashes. The newspapers and magazines were reflecting Australia's vigorous push in post-war immigration, with sunlit scenes of beaches and barbecues enticing many thousands of Britons each year to make a fresh start 'down under'. And then there was conspicuous wealth; even trivial matters seemed fascinating to the English press when they seemed to demonstrate what a lucky country Australia was. The *Daily Telegraph*, on the day Frank Thring's *Salome* opened at St Martin's in 1954, ran an article headed 'AUSTRALIAN GIRL HAS 10,000 DANCE AT STOLL. THEATRE CONVERTED'. It reported a coming-out party in London for Miss Barbara Stanley-Smith, 18, of Sydney, given by her father, a mining magnate who was too busy to attend. The foyer of the Stoll Theatre was transformed for the occasion into a bower of roses, and the auditorium into an 'azure-blue pavilion':

> Miss Stanley-Smith, who was wearing a full-length evening dress of pink lace, said to me 'I wanted really to have my dance at the Ritz, but it didn't prove large enough; Hutchinson House, off Oxford Street, was big enough, but they wouldn't allow my flowers, so I decided on the Stoll'.[408]

When rich schoolgirls from Sydney found the Ritz inadequate to their needs, it fed an impression that the Empire was striking back. In all sorts of areas, these brash unfairly blessed colonials were riding rough-shod over the sensitivities of staid old London.

---

408 *Daily Telegraph*, July 20, 1954, p.7.

Some of that impudence was evident among the actors, artists and writers who were following the well-worn path to England in the mid-1950s. The myth of expatriatism in Australia has at its core an assumption of a deep insecurity in the colonial country. The term that A.A. Phillips coined for the phenomenon in this period, 'the cultural cringe', implies both a self-consciousness about the marginality or shoddiness of Australian cultural life, and a need for authentication and acceptance by the colonial parent. It has become a catchphrase in the endless debate about an Australian national identity, and has made a transition from academic lexicon to common parlance rather like that of Freud's Oedipal Complex, to which it is not unrelated. There is an important partial truth in Phillips' hypothesis: Australians still like to be assured that their cultural exports are vindicated by acknowledgement overseas, and they still sometimes make wryly self-reflexive remarks disparaging their own culture. But these matters are complex; there is a good deal of robust defiance to counterbalance the rueful irony, and often a rather embarrassing self-congratulatory nationalism to offset what sounds like modesty. The circumstances of Frank Thring's assaults on London in 1954 and 1955, and the situation into which he stepped on both occasions, reflect just that complexity.

In Frank's account of his approach to making a name in London, he regularly defined himself against the ways in which others tried to do it. Instead of waiting passively in the corridors of casting-agents, or auditioning for bit-parts, the legend ran, Frank's intention was to stride in and simply take over the place. There was, certainly, something novel in his approach; very few aspiring Australian actors could match Frank for money or for gall. But the abjectness and tentativeness suggested by 'the cultural cringe' wasn't really borne out by the ways those other actors approached the task, either. The element of Australian expatriatism in the 1950s that Arthur Phillips' concept doesn't acknowledge is the sense of confident expectation that many of them, in their own ways, seemed to share. These weren't, on the whole, country bumpkins coming to town to be taught their manners, or suppliants hoping for a few crumbs from the rich man's tables. If they were naïve, it was in their lack of concern for the real difficulties and dangers that might be involved in diving so recklessly into the big pool. Frank was an extreme case, certainly. But he was not wholly unrepresentative in his determination to ask not what he could learn from London, but what London could learn from him.

Some of them were there already, and enjoying disproportionate success. There was Helpmann, of course, though he had made the trek so early he seemed to belong to another generation. But at the Shakespeare Memorial Theatre in Frank's season there, there was already a strong Australian presence. Leo McKern and Keith Michell were already prominent in the company. The Peter Brook production of *Titus* included not only Frank Thring but four other Australians, Ron Haddrick, Kevin Miles, Trader Faulkner and Nancye Stewart. In film, Peter Finch had joined Errol Flynn as a leading man much in demand. A little later, Barry Humphries landed on London, with an expectation very similar to Frank's that he would immediately become its queen. It looks a remarkably upright and even arrogant way to cringe.

Frank, then, came at a propitious time for Australian actors in London. Moreover, having had the good fortune to be invited, and to be able to afford to come, he could not have been luckier in the production that brought him back in 1955.

The whole season at the Stratford Memorial Theatre generated an extraordinary amount of public interest. The fact that the Oliviers were sharing the stage at Stratford for the first time, with a star-studded company in support, caused unprecedented demand for tickets to the season, and it duly broke all records for the company. It was news even in New York, where *Variety* announced an 'Olivier-Leigh Advance Stampede at Stratford'.[409] There was particular interest in *Titus Andronicus*, partly because of the involvement of Brook as director, but mostly because the play came with the irresistible attraction of being mad, bad, and dangerous to know. *Titus* had not been performed professionally since the mid-nineteenth century. It was, as all the papers delighted in describing it, a shocker, its plot directed by atrocities more than by character, its people driven and diminished by a world that had become a chamber of horrors.

But Peter Brook's production was greeted, mostly, as a masterpiece. It had a powerful and convincing ensemble quality, plus, paradoxically, one of the performances of the decade in Olivier's Titus; it was, by general consent, the jewel in the crown of a stellar season. Nearly two decades later, Robert Speaight remembered it as 'perhaps the greatest Shakespearean

409 *Variety*, 9 March 1955.

production of our time'.[410] When, in 1957, the production was selected for revival as Britain's key contribution to a succession of European arts festivals, it confirmed the fact that reputations are often to be made on supposedly unproduceable plays. Frank was there for the triumphant revival, too. Having fluked the role, he was very much a man in the right place at the right time; professionally, he seemed suddenly to be leading a charmed life.

The serious critics in the broadsheets hailed the production as a major achievement, while the tabloids were fascinated with its gruesomeness. Queasy theatre-goers were quizzed, week after week, on their reactions to the violence; the *Daily Mode* noted with concern that 'several dowagers drank whisky neat at the interval',[411] while the *Birmingham Post* reported, under the headline 'Isn't Shakespeare a Shocker?', that twenty-two patrons required medical help at one performance, prompting the man in charge of the Stratford St John Ambulance Brigade, Mr Sid Lively, who had already doubled his troops, to worry that they might not be able to cope.[412] The Shakespeare Memorial Theatre was for once regularly in the news; the publicity was free, and priceless.

Though some found its depths of depravity unbearable, *Titus* was a hit from the start. J.C. Trewin recalled the euphoria on opening night:

> Curtain-fall that August evening brought the longest, loudest cheer in Stratford memory. One heard people, normally decorous, shouting at the pitch of their voices, hardly knowing that they did so, and denying it afterwards; a critic said it could have been the scene at a Cup Final.[413]

The opening-night party beside the Avon was appropriately an extravaganza, and the *Evening Standard* in listing all the luminaries noted particularly the caperings under the midnight moon of 'Mr Noel Coward, in tropical evening-dress'.[414]

Inevitably, the main focus of the reviews was on another masterly performance by Olivier. The ever-quotable Kenneth Tynan in the *Observer* had a sense of the historical importance of the moment:

---

410 Robert Speaight, *Shakespeare on the Stage*, London, Collins, 1973.
411 *Daily Mail*, 24 October 1955.
412 *Birmingham Post*, 22 October 1955.
413 J.C. Trewin, *Peter Brook. A Biography*, London, Macdonald, 1971, p.82.
414 *Evening Standard*, 17 August 1955.

> This is a performance which ushers us into the presence of one who is, pound for pound, the greatest actor alive. As usual, he raises our hair with the risks he takes ... [His final cries are] dredged from an ocean-bed of fatigue. One recognised, though one had never heard it before, the noise made in its last extremity by the cornered human soul.[415]

The *Times* gave it a strong vote of approval, too, noting the 'magnificent performances' of Olivier and Quayle, and finding Frank Thring 'a lusty if somewhat Mongolian Saturninus';[416] Frank had called attention to the 'Mongolian beard' that he had cultivated for Herod in his self-promoting interview a year earlier, and would have appreciated its being noticed.

Even those who could not fully enjoy the production acknowledged the craft of its director and stars, and referred all blame to Shakespeare. Noel Coward did so (relatively) privately in his diary:

> Peter Brook had done a stupendously good production, really most impressive and extremely clever in avoiding pitfalls. Larry was wonderful although, at moments, a little funny ... It is a very, very silly play with some good moments.[417]

Darlington in the *Daily Telegraph* found the play 'revolting', and was unusual among the reviewers in not being particularly taken with the headline performers:

> His [Olivier's] outbursts of rage and hate and near-madness are nothing more than theatrical tirades and do not give a really fine actor a chance to [sic] his best. Lavinia is not much of a part for Vivien Leigh, either.[418]

But he, too, found things to admire in the performance, awarding 'the real acting honours' to Anthony Quayle as Aaron the Moor and Maxine Audley as Temora, since below the super-stars 'the players can indulge in an orgy of straightforward villainy. Frank Thring is also impressive as Saturninus'.

---

415 Kenneth Tynan, 'Chamber of Horrors', *Observer*, 21 July 1955, p.11.

416 'Special Correspondent', *Times*, 17 August 1955, p.2.

417 Entry for Friday 19 August, 1955. Graham Payn and Sheridan Morley (eds), *The Noel Coward Diaries*, London, Weidenfeld and Nicolson, 1982, p.279–80.

418 W.A. Darlington, *Daily Telegraph*, 17 August 1955, p.8.

Most of the other reviewers were complimentary about Frank's Saturninus, too. Derek Granger found him 'sleekly evil',[419] and the critic thought him 'every lecherous inch a Roman emperor'.[420] J.C.T. (Trewin), marvelling at the 'surprising felicities' of the production, noted prophetically that 'Frank Thring has here a first sketch of a potentially Neronic voluptuary'.[421] Geoffrey Tarran settled for 'Frank Thring is in every way excellent',[422] while Rosemary Anne Sisson liked his 'good, plain, convincing Saturninus',[423] despite her incongruous choice of adjectives.

Frank did his brand of villainy again over Christmas 1955, in *Peter Pan* at the Scala Theatre. Professionally, at least, he was on a roll, and his last performances as Saturninus merged seamlessly with first rehearsals for the Barrie play. Peggy Cummins, the film star playing the Principal Boy, was the name in large letters, but in the traditional double, Mr Darling and Captain Hook, Frank had most of the good lines. The audiences loved it, as they almost always do.

Frank was unusually well-behaved, given the opportunities in the script for large slices of ham. Peggy Cummins remembered that he could be mischievous in the sword fights, and that sometimes 'that hook was used a lot more than it ought to have been, on and off the stage'.[424] But compared to his pranks at the Little Theatre at home, Frank's performances at the Scala were the epitome of discipline. Perhaps it was the residual influence of Brook; perhaps it was the insistence of Peggy Cummins, on whose reputation and marketability the show depended, that her Hook should run a tight ship. Whatever the constraint, two shows a night for six nights a week, Frank flounced absolutely on cue, and saved his playfulness for the hapless children in the stalls.

The 'serious' theatre critics rarely bothered with the deluge of school holiday shows, and *Peter Pan* received just half a dozen reviews. Harold Hobson merely noted in passing that 'Peggy Cummins is a great attraction', which seems a sure sign that he hadn't seen it.[425] Cecil Wilson in the *Daily Mail* quite liked it, and was the first to make a theatrical comparison with the Thring persona that was to become quite common: 'Frank Thring's Captain Hook has the urgent unction of a Charles Laughton expecting the Bounty

419 Derek Granger, *Financial Times*, 17 August 1955.
420 F.G.B., *Plays and Players*, September 1955.
421 J.C.T., *Birmingham Post*, 17 August 1955.
422 Geoffrey Tarran, *Morning Advertiser*, 24 August 1955.
423 Rosemary Anne Sisson, *Stratford-upon-Avon Herald*, 19 August 1955.
424 Peggy Cummins, interview with the author, London, 24 January 2005.
425 Harold Hobson, *Sunday Times*, 25 December 1955, p.8.

to mutiny any moment';[426] though the concept of 'urgent unction' is elusive, the connection with Laughton seems complimentary enough.

John Gale's notice in the *Observer*, though, was euphoric. He found the show, frighteningly, 'enough to make an analyst burst',[427] and was much taken by the Thring performance:

> Frank Thring is a fine and unctuous Mr Darling (Darling is *amazing*), and he is so good a Captain Hook, fierce, sad and witty, that he deserves not to be eaten.

The *Times* review was positive, too, observing that 'Captain Hook, with his slight but sinister lisp, will leave on younger playgoers an impression that will take a lot of forgetting'.[428] Frank would have been flattered to have been thought the stuff of nightmares, and who would be silly enough now to think that a minor speech impediment would hamper an actor's career?

A few of the reviews recognised qualities in Frank's performance that went beyond 'straightforward villainy'. Gale's adjectives, 'fierce, sad and witty', implied it: Anthony Cookman in the *Tatler*, after approving his 'stealthily malevolent Hook', similarly suggested that there was more to the Thring malevolence than was evident on a first impression:

> He is extremely good in his way – a slightly decadent way, as though James Hook rather fancied himself as the reincarnation of a French king, proudly tossing his full black wig and lisping horrible threats with blood-curdling glances which have a hint of inner misgiving.[429]

Those *Peter Pan* reviews were the first to attempt to define Frank Thring's stage persona. Since the one that was so obtrusive on stage was similar to that which was very visible in the foyer, those comments have some interest, too, as responses to the man. The implication of a 'slightly decadent' sexuality, reinforced by the high-camp accessories, the lisp and the leer, is offset by a vulnerability that in the end has not much to do with any 'rulings' by the author; the sense that 'at heart he is really not all that bad', and that he feels an 'inner misgiving', is part of the complexity of the performer, not the character. The performative quality was so evident in almost all Frank's

---

426 Cecil Wilson, *Daily Mail*, 23 December 1955.
427 John Gale, *Observer*, 25 December 1955, p.5.
428 *Times*, 24 December 1955, p.2.
429 Anthony Cookman, *Tatler and Bystander*, 25 January 1956, p.138.

appearances, on and off the stage, that it exposed something of the naked self that it was so elaborately designed to disguise.

It was partly that quality that in 1955 made him, by and large, a very popular member of both the *Titus* and *Peter Pan* companies – that, and the fact that he was reliably an amusing companion. Although he was capable of spectacular bitchery, the sense that his malice was part of a ludicrously overblown act softened it, and made Frank forgiveable. Now and then he could be genuinely cruel, and in the company of the intimidatingly waspish Alan Webb (who played Marcus Andronicus in the Brook production) the routine disparagement could become more vicious.[430] But mostly it seemed harmless enough, heavily mediated by self-parody and by a sense of generosity not only of scale but of intention. The implication that nothing he said was to be taken too seriously was greatly assisted by the fact that, from the time he arrived in London in the middle of the year, he had been in a splendidly sunny mood. So his role in the company, and within the Olivier circle when the court convened at Notley Abbey, became that of the jester. The 'giant sunflower' who had beamed on that first rehearsal at Stratford continued, mostly, to make people feel happier than they were.

He was forgiven and indulged, not only for his posturing and the outrageous things he said, but for other lapses as well. Trader Faulkner recalled the day that Frank broke one of the production's cardinal rules:

> If there was one thing that Peter Brook could not, well, brook, it was lateness. Nobody would ever dare not being on time. But one day Thring wasn't there, and Brook is asking where the hell is he, and nobody knew. Then suddenly he burst in, red in the face and sweating all over the place. He'd been running across the fields. He'd taken the train up from London, and it went straight through Stratford, it was an express. So he just pulled the communication cord, stopped the train, jumped off it, and he's standing there panting, 'But it's all right, darlings, here I am'. Well, what could you say?[431]

Rosemary Anne Sisson, in her theatrical gossip column for the local Stratford paper, told another tale from the final dress rehearsal for *Titus*:

430 Trader Faulkner interview 26 January 2005.
431 ibid.

> Sir Laurence Olivier, giving it all he'd got, was just finishing the speech in which Titus reveals that the meal he has just served the Emperor and Tamora consists of the bones of her murdered sons. Frank Thring, however, as the Emperor, absently munching and smoothing his new finery, had evidently lost sight of the action in the play for the moment, and the voice of the producer was suddenly heard plaintively from the stalls. 'Frank, don't go on eating that stuff. It's not very nice, you know!'[432]

He had stepped comfortably into the role of acerbic clown, the kind of fellow-actor that people remember with a smile and an anecdote. His presence was disarming, and it assured the security of his place within the group. In something like the way that Minty Lalanne described his time with the severe Miss Cavendish in 1947, Frank was creating around him a surrogate family. As the joker in the Stratford family, or as paterfamilias in *Peter Pan*, he was at home.

All things considered, 1955 should have been an excellent Christmas for him. Straight from a landmark production at Stratford to popularity in the West End, with a rather fetching little wedding in between; he could hardly have scripted it better. A quarter of a century later, in a Sydney radio interview with Steve Cossar, it was a day right there at the beginning, in the *Titus* season in the spring of 1955, that he nominated as the high point of his career:

> The most exciting moment was indeed the Stratford season, when one is sitting in this beautiful theatre by the side of the Avon, with swans gliding up and down the river, and you're sitting there quivering in a superb dressing-room – rather better than this studio, I might add – and you suddenly hear the stage manager say, you know, 'Three minutes. Will you come on stage please, Sir Laurence, Miss Leigh, Mr Thring, and I thought, Oh God. We've got there at last, baby.[433]

There were a lot of good roles to come, but for uncomplicated joy in achievement and satisfaction it's not surprising that Frank might need to look back so far.

---

432 *Stratford-upon-Avon Herald*, 14 December 1956.
433 Interview with Steve Cossar, Sydney, 1980.

Then, in the new year, came the tour that followed the London season of *Peter Pan*. It was a remorseless program, twelve cities in eleven weeks, starting in Southport, then on to Brighton and Morecambe, Dundee, Aberdeen, Edinburgh, Glasgow, Liverpool, Sheffield, Leeds, Manchester and Newcastle. Frank got back on April 8. Joan, who had been in London all this time, threw a small party to celebrate his return; it was the party discussed later in this chapter, where everything went disastrously wrong.

Frank had disliked the Brodziak tours in Australia, and taking *Peter Pan* on the road in an English and Scottish winter, never quite unpacking his suitcase in hotel rooms with eccentric heating, and striking the set every week to head for another town, must have confirmed every bad impression. He was still behaving unusually well, however, though Peggy Cummins recalled him often complaining ritualistically about 'this interminable bloody tour'. He and she embarked on a diet together, which, if that fact was not strange enough in itself, inconceivably restricted him to a single glass of wine each night.[434] Frank's social life was confined to the weekend touring that Peggy's husband Derek organised for them when he drove up every Friday evening from London. However, his phone calls to Joan, back at their house at Westgate Terrace, were, surprisingly, cheerful enough. There were enough grisly experiences to transmute into jokes, and he was genuinely excited to report from Brighton that he had walked on water (the shallows had frozen over just enough to help him to perform a miracle).

By the time he made his next appearance in London, things were rolling along less merrily. It was almost two months before he began rehearsing another play, and while few people could be unemployed as stylishly as Frank, it left a lot of time to agonise about the way in which his marriage to Joan was unravelling. The honeymoon was, in every sense, over, and the experience of his next show was blighted by that knowledge from troubled beginning to excruciating end.

Doctor in the House opened on July 30, 1956. Ted Willis' adaptation of Richard Gordon's bestseller about scapegrace medical students was a romp in three acts. Unlike the novel and film that preceded it, the play was restricted by its realistic box-set; all the action was squeezed into the students' lodgings, and the hospital locations were a serious loss. Still, the jokes still worked well enough, and the role of Sir Lancelot Spratt, played in the film version by James Robertson Justice, fitted Frank like a pair of

434 Peggy Cummins interview, 24 January 2005.

surgical gloves. In his prefatory note to the published play, Richard Bird, its first director, set out the specifications for the part:

> In this kind of broad comedy it is quite legitimate to cast to type and, if you have anything approaching a real-life Sir Lancelot among your members, the part will play itself. When he is on the stage he should dominate; choose, if possible, a tall prosperous-looking man and give him a beard. It must be quite obvious from his appearance and bearing that he is a success at his job and he should have a deep, penetrating voice as he spends most of his time topping the laughs.[435]

Frank had the size, the voice and the presence. And he brought his own beard. It was all too easy.

Sir Lancelot has four big scenes, one in each of the first two acts, and two in the third. While he is on stage he has by far the lion's share of the lines, almost all of them roared; the role is written to provide maximum impact for relatively limited effort. Each time he comes in shouting, and three times the stage directions require that he 'sweeps out'. Only once does he not do so, and that is the joke that closes Act Two, in which Sir Lancelot is for once the straight man.

> SIR LANCELOT: … Fortunately, after a certain period, the chemicals in the blood stream form a clot and stop it. Now, this interval is known scientifically as the bleeding-time. (*To* SIMON, *who is whispering to* JOHN) You, boy, what's the bleeding-time? (*Slapping* SIMON'S *arm*)
>
> SIMON: (*Coming to with a start and looking at his watch*) Half-past six, sir.
>
> (SIR LANCELOT *turns away in disgust while* JOHN *and* TONY *tell* SIMON *what a clot he is*)

A contemptuous slow burn as the curtain fell came naturally to Frank, and for once it was completely in character.

After a week warming up in front of the holiday-makers at Brighton, the production followed the Crazy Gang group into the Victoria Palace, and this helped arouse expectations that it be would light and lively, as it was.

---

435 Ted Willis, *Doctor in the House: a Comedy in Three Acts*, from the novel by Richard Gordon, London, Samuel French, 1957, p.6.

But while the association was probably good for promotional purposes, it encouraged in the critics a tendency to patronisingly, if not damningly, faint praise. Richard Buckle in the *Observer* gave the show a cursory paragraph, a post-script to a Chekhov review:

> *Doctor in the House* is an unpretentious farce which may not disappoint – unless you wander into the Victoria Palace expecting the Crazy Gang.[436]

The lukewarm reviews didn't deter the audiences, though, and the production ran respectably, ten shows a week, for nearly five months. It had some unexpected help from some University College medical students, who picketed the theatre with placards reading 'Doc Strike', 'We Are Not Amused', and 'Our Landladies Are Pure'.[437] The show finally closed on December 15, to be replaced, inevitably, by the Crazy Gang. Their Christmas show was called *These Foolish Kings*.

As Lancelot Spratt, Frank had his first experience of a long run in professional theatre. This was, relatively speaking, success. He had known stardom on the Melbourne scale; now he had a taste of what it meant in the West End. It meant doing shows for five months that were enjoyable for one, tolerable for two, and grimly repetitive thereafter. For most working actors, what he found at the Victoria Palace, and in the long touring season of earlier in that year, was a glimpse of heaven; for Frank, who never really needed a livelihood, it was a form of purgatory, and would always be so. By the end of the run, as the dismal winter afternoons were closing in and Frank fulminated his way through Spratt for the one hundred and fiftieth or one hundred and sixtieth time, his mind very much on other matters, it had become a form of hell.

Christmas 1956 was a much less happy one than Christmas 1955. Mercifully, though, *Doctor in the House* was over. On the face of it, it had been a satisfactory year for the Thring career. There were perhaps a few warning signs, though nothing very alarming. The relative success of *Doctor in the House* had raised, much more directly than the Brodziak productions at home, the question of what, for Frank, was to constitute success; he had a great fondness for adulation, but did he really want to go through long seasons of theatrical fairy-floss to get it? Did he have the patience, or the discipline, to stick at it, or was he by nature and nurture a dilettante? There was also

---

436 Richard Buckle, 'Going to Moscow', *Observer*, 5 August 1956, p.6.
437 *Daily Express*, 31 July 1956.

the matter of the kinds of roles that he was getting, big ones though they were. Playing the Hook/Mr Darling double at twenty-nine and Sir Lancelot soon after his thirtieth birthday was at once a remarkable achievement and a slightly ominous one. The photograph of Frank during the 'operation' scene in *Doctor in the House* is instructive; there is Frank at centre, just thirty but looking forty-five, flanked on his right by Philip Gilbert who was five years his junior, and on his left by Edward Woodward aged twenty-six and Alan White as Grimsdyke, who was a year older than Frank. Spratt looks every minute of a generation older than all of them. Frank had always been clever with make-up, of course, but the receding hairline, the heavy features and build, are part of the man himself.

Frank had aged quite disconcertingly from the languid, insouciant figure who had lounged in that very alternative-theatre alley beside the Arrow in 1953. Just as at the Little Theatre, where he had gone straight into roles that would normally be a couple of decades away, and now on grounds that were less negotiable, there was some danger that he was pre-empting a career that still had some way to grow. For the moment, though, there seemed no shortage in London of corpulent middle-aged tyrants to play. The 'young Australian actor' was travelling like an old pro, and it looked as though there were even better things to come.

The things that were on his mind long before the Crazy Gang came to his rescue, though, were more pressing than creative opportunities, casting agents, even confirmation from his public. They concerned how he was to live from this time on, and the choices, which were in the end not his to make, were irrevocable.

For the first time in Frank's life, the world had conformed to his fiction. The scene, London; the time, 1955–6. The appreciative audiences, the celebrity friends, the obliging casting agents, and, for a time, the adoring wife – all of them were actually there. This was the life Frank was built for.

The unreality of much of it was what made it come so easily to him. Someone like Joan, keenly aware of who she was and where she came from and conscious of suddenly having to pretend to be someone rather different, was naturally going to find it all difficult. Someone like Frank, who had been pretending triumphantly since childhood, was always going to be much more comfortable in an environment in which his family background and the complexities of his culture were of no interest or importance to anybody. In Australia, it was those things that were often tricky to negotiate, and that sometimes caught him out. In England, it could be all performance, and that was always Frank's preferred milieu.

The fact that Joan was there, though, was an important counter-balance. He did not have to put on a show with her, or, if he did, it was a different kind of show, that assumed as its context all the curious history that they had shared. Frank's life had never before moved in such a conventional rhythm, where the public and the private seemed so happily complementary, and it never did again.

There were a few crises, but once negotiated they were the kinds of things that couples survive together, and turn into shared anecdote:

> He had learnt to drive a car just before we left for England, and we bought a car, and he had to drive down to Stratford-on-Avon to go to rehearsals, and every weekend I joined him, and it wasn't long before we were spending weekends at Notley Abbey with Larry and Vivien, and a number of other people, and one day he was driving down to rehearsal and he smashed the car up, ran into a brick wall in Banbury, ... and he got to the nearest phone, rang me up, and said to me go and take driving lessons straight away, you know, and I said what's happened, and he said well, I've crashed the car. So after we went through it all I said, well, how did you do that, there's a road turning left there, why didn't you turn left or right or anything, and he said, I couldn't, I was paralysed, so I just took my hands off the wheel and screamed.[438]

Joan took over the driving, fortunately, and Frank's brush with death in Banbury became an event that defined their relationship: girls from West Preston might sometimes struggle with repartee, but they can always be relied on to take the wheel when drama-queens from Toorak become hysterical about handling the routine business of life.

All of this suggested that Frank was, astonishingly, in something like a partnership with the woman who at various points in his previous life had been playmate, little sister, confidante, alibi, trophy, and best friend.

438 Joan Thring interviewed by Frank Van Straten and Clive Stark, 3LO Nostalgia Show, Melbourne, 5 March 1995.

The notion that if one had to marry, one could hardly do better than Joan, was in the air when they first talked about the shared adventure. Olive had always wanted it, of course, which for Frank was an excellent reason for not doing it. But with Olive safely dead, and Frank about to head overseas with a young woman in an arrangement that boring people would probably find compromising, it suddenly seemed not such a bad idea after all. Frank may have found Joan's initial reaction a touch disconcerting:

> He proposed to me before we left, but I said, 'Don't be silly!' But then when we were in England, and doing everything together, Vivien Leigh said 'Why don't you two get married?', and we thought, well, why not? So we were pushed into it, in a way. [439]

Encouragement from that corner would have weighed heavily with both of them. To Joan, who had laughed at the earlier proposal, it offered the approval of one of her few friends in England, someone who had noticed her from the start, a patroness. To Frank, it was the blessing of a star; in a world of stellar couples, it seemed almost perverse not to couple. For both of them, the fact that Vivien seemed able to sustain a strong, passionate relationship with a man who also fancied men was a sign of what was possible.

Vivien Leigh's judgement, especially at that point in her life but at most others too, could be relied on to be seriously awry. She herself was in some degree recuperating from a long and scandalous relationship with the Australian actor Peter Finch, and her marriage to Laurence Olivier was failing by the day. It was a perfect time, in Vivien's brilliant, sad, unworkable view of the world, for everyone to play Happy Families.

The parties on the lawn at the Oliviers' splendidly renovated thirteenth-century abbey should have sounded some warnings. On the surface, things could hardly have been more delightful. Yet there was Vivien, alternating between being a marvellous hostess and sobbing inconsolably in the bathroom for hours on end. There was England's finest actor, lord of the estate, wandering around its edges, talking to and stroking his trees rather than facing the stream of guests and a wife who would never leave him in peace.[440] There were a lot of answers that Frank and Joan might have given to the question, 'Why don't you two get married?', but obviously nothing very persuasive occurred to either of them.

439 Joan Thring, interview with the author, London, 15 December 2004.
440 Joan Thring, interview with the author, London, 10 January 2005.

Joan and Frank declared their intention to marry in the *Times* on October 15, 1955. Among all the honourables and the daughters of brigadiers and the stately homes, theirs was a starkly prosaic announcement. It had nothing explicitly to do with any parents, and there was no attempt to disguise the fact that they already shared an address. There was to be no long engagement, no round of gifts and parties, no elaborate protocols. It read as a thoroughly modern and mature agreement between the two of them.

> The marriage arranged between Frank Thring and Joan Cunliffe, of 67, Albert Bridge Road, S.W.11, will take place at Stratford-on-Avon on November 21.[441]

Joan, knowing how much his mother had wanted this to happen, said wistfully to Frank when they decided they might as well do it, 'I wish Olive could be here'; Frank, predictably, snapped back, 'I don't'.[442]

Frank wrote to 'the Boys', Ray Mander and Joe Mitchenson, advertising the big event that seemed to everyone else such a surprise:

> Another page of theatrical history will be turned on Monday November 21st when I am married to Joan at Stratford. The cast includes: Larry as deputy-father to the bride and Vivien as Matron of Honour. The list of guests is assuming the proportions of the Royal Command Performance and somewhere down at the bottom are your names. Do keep the day free and we will look forward to seeing you down there.[443]

There was, of course, a strong emphasis on the wedding as a performance, and the casual name-dropping of the two stars appearing in support roles offers confirmation of the importance of their blessing on the occasion. But while his manner was tongue-in-cheek, there was no suggestion that the groom was anything other than proud of his bride and eager for the day.

So Frank married Joan, in the Holy Trinity church at Stratford, where Shakespeare was buried. Larry Olivier gave the bride away, Vivienne Leigh was Matron of Honour. Trader Faulkner had been cast by Olivier to play the best man. The church was filled with people from the *Titus* company

---

441 *Times*, 15 October 1955.

442 Joan Thring interview 15 December 2004.

443 Letter from Frank Thring, 2 October 1955. Mander and Mitchenson Collection, Jerwood Library of the Performing Arts, Trinity College of Music, Old Royal Naval College, Greenwich.

and the wider Shakespeare Memorial Theatre, and there was a big reception at the Welcombe Hotel, with magical lights and music. The path that led to the church before the ceremony was lined with hundreds of residents of Stratford and beyond, who came to stare at the rich and famous. The path that led to the front door of the Welcombe for the reception was lined with large green crystalline rocks, and fifty years later, Joan still had one of them in her Kensington flat that she souvenired that day.

It was quite an occasion. The *Daily Mail*, in the days leading up to the wedding, followed avidly the progress of Joan's dress, a striking coffee-coloured creation in ruched silk designed by the Melbourne coutourier Hall Ludlow. When the paper's social columnist called on Joan with just four days to go, she was hanging about hopefully at the airport, and Frank gave the interview in her place:

> It was midday and he was eating a hearty breakfast in bed, but put a black velvet dressing-gown over his daffodil-coloured pyjamas to come down and see me.
>
> 'We were supposed to collect the dress last night', he told me, 'But the authorities said that livestock has priority over clothes, so I suppose Joan is still waiting for a procession of dogs, snakes and monkeys to come through first'.[444]

The dress arrived, and the day went off in style. Nobody misbehaved too badly, though the presiding Vicar, Canon Prentice, was unable to resist remarking that he hoped that the spirit of Shakespeare wouldn't incline the bridegroom to offer Joan his second-best bed.[445]

It was the supporting cast, naturally, that gave the production most of its lustre: The *Daily Express* covered it with a double-page spread, headed 'Starring Sir Larry in wedding-upon-Avon'. It published four photographs – Sir Larry arriving at the church with the bride on his arm, Sir Larry kissing the bride, Sir Larry scattering the bridal party with confetti, and Sir Larry toasting the bride 'with a well-turned phrase'.[446] It was Olivier's day, and even Vivien found it hard to get into the frame, let alone the happy couple. The honeymoon arrangements, too, bore the mark of their illustrious patrons: the *Birmingham post* reported next day that 'Mr and Mrs Thring spent the

444 'Buttons and Boos', *Daily Mail*, 18 November 1955.
445 Joan Thring, interview with the author, London, January 10, 2005.
446 *Daily Express*, 22 November 1955.

night at Avoncliffe, Stratford, the Georgian mansion which Sir Laurence and Lady Olivier have made their home during the town's Shakespeare season'.[447]

Forty years later, when Joan recalled that occasion in an interview with Clive Stark and Frank Van Straten, she generously saw the blame for the painful times that followed as lying with her alone:

> JT: We got married later in the year.
>
> FVS: This was some wedding, wasn't it?
>
> JT: It was some wedding, yes, even he enjoyed it.
>
> CS: He wasn't bored?
>
> JT: He announced that he didn't like weddings usually, but he liked this one. And it was great fun, more than great fun. Well, for me, it was a proper wedding, and in a way it's a sadness that it changed me, I became a married lady, and Frank wasn't really counting on this.[448]

So many things were working against it, though, that it would be absurd and wrong to see what happened as anyone's fault.

The details of this part of the story are unknowable by anyone other than the two people who lived it. But that didn't stop the almost immediate generation of a number of powerful myths as to what had really happened, and why. How could a man like Frank, whose persona was so outrageously the epitome of camp, even contemplate a heterosexual marriage? How could Joan, who had known him so well for so long, have thought it even remotely a going concern? Could they possibly have been serious?

The marriage was over within a year. It was dissolved on the grounds, as Melbourne's scurrilous weekly the *Truth* gleefully reported in early 1957, of non-consummation:

447 *Birmingham Post*, 22 November 1955.

448 Joan Thring interviewed by Frank Van Straten and Clive Stark, 3LO Nostalgia Show, Melbourne, 5 March 1995.

> The Registrar of Divorce in his judgement said he accepted Mrs Thring's evidence that she and her husband spent their wedding night in a room with two beds – and that Thring insisted on sleeping alone.
>
> He also accepted her statement that her husband had never shown the least intimate interest in her, and that when she asked for children Thring had told her to "go somewhere else and get them."[449]

The sceptics who assumed that it must all have been some kind of macabre joke felt thoroughly vindicated. Rumours about the circumstances of the Thring marriage were there from the beginning, multiplied hugely when it ended, and have kept growing vigorously ever since. Anyone who tries to disentangle fact and fiction, even at a distance of half a century, risks hurting some feelings or spoiling some good stories or both.

The myth takes two forms. The dominant one has Frank's father writing a late codicil to his will, and making Frank's eventual inheritance dependent on his being a married man. It's an unlikely scenario; a man with terminal cancer has more pressing concerns, surely, than the future sexual preferences of his ten-year-old son. The second variant, more plausibly, has the requirement beyond the grave as coming from Olive, who certainly had seen more than enough to doubt that there would ever be another Francis William Thring – or any other Thring at all. It fits the tentative hypothesis that some tensions in this area lay behind those chilling, contemptuous silences at Rylands.

But neither version, as it happens, is true. Neither Frank senior's will in 1936 nor Olive's in 1953 contained any such provision. There was nothing surprising in either document: Frank left everything to Olive, devolving at her death equally to Lola and Frank, but with a thoughtful allowance immediately for his rather marginalised daughter; Olive, after a token acknowledgement of her obligations to Lola and a small remembrance for Ernest the chauffeur and Margaret the housekeeper, left everything, quite unencumbered, to the son she adored.

Frank found the story amusing. He did little to dispel it and, apparently, quite a lot to encourage and embellish it. He may even, in a particularly bleak or impish mood, have invented it, as he did most of the myths that could make a mockery of his life. His clearest statement on the subject came in an interview with Peter Wilmoth in the year of his death:

449 *The Truth*, 2 March 1957.

> When his mother died, she left Thring the Toorak house and contents and a large sum of money. Many years later, there was a rumour that Thring's mother had made his inheritance conditional on his remarrying [sic]. "That was a myth," Thring says now. "Anyway, I was earning more money than she was. She just sat in Toorak and gave bridge parties."[450]

Joan reflected ruefully in 1995 on the inevitable triumph of gossip over truth:

> Well, I always knew it was untrue. Frank and I truly loved each other, and it was just a sadness that I became different, and I couldn't accept what I could accept earlier. So … we'll never know what would have happened had it gone on.[451]

Two years later, though, Mike Walsh, in an interview with Peter Eyres, was one of a number of others keeping the legend alive beyond Frank's death:

> Frank inherited the estate – half when his father died, half on his marriage. So he married the switch-girl from the Princess Theatre in Melbourne, and they went to England, and – Frank was very close to Laurence Olivier in those days, wink wink nudge nudge, and she went over, she knew exactly what the game was about, and she went over there and just had a nice twelve months holiday, which was what he'd said to her, "Let's get married, and we'll have a twelve month holiday in England Pixie." So he got the rest of the money then.[452]

This, with minor variations, remains the received version of the story. As the years passed and the number of people telling the inconceivable story multiplied, its variations and embellishments became more and more comical. There was the persistent whisper that Peter Finch had been summoned to the conjugal bed while the bridegroom, in one version, withdrew to the nether room, in another, had riotous sex with a local lad in the pub. There was the story that Fred Farley possibly passed to Barry Gordon, who probably told it to John Thaw, who certainly gave it to Sheila Hancock:

---

450 Peter Wilmoth, *Sunday Age*, 19 June 1994, p.3.
451 Joan Thring interviewed with Frank Van Straten and Clive Stark, 5 March 1995.
452 Mike Walsh interviewed by Peter Eyres, Sydney, 5 August 1997.

> The rampantly homosexual Thring went through with a grand wedding with all the trimmings, including Vivien Leigh as maid of honour, and as he sashayed down the aisle with his new wife on his arm, he spied a young man in the congregation and squealed, 'You're prettier than the bride, dear!'[453]

The combination of bizarre event with celebrity status at second hand, complicated by the self-parodic impulse of one of the protagonists, refined in the light of a series of excruciating embarrassments, and finally let loose in a game of Chinese Whispers over the next four decades, produced a tale of a wedding unparalleled in its cynicism and grotesquerie. Nobody emerges with much credit from any of the hypotheses. It's a sign, of course, of the improbability of the match that it produced such ingenious explanations. The mythology fits the image of corrosively flippant clown that Frank was increasingly ready to feed.

Joan's explanation fifty years later, as the only other person on the premises at the time, was disarmingly straightforward: 'Frank and I truly loved each other'.[454] Later, almost a decade further on, she suggested an additional motive:

> Frank wanted to be married. He liked the idea of being married. And he wanted children. He would have loved to have a child, though it would probably have had to be a boy. It would have been disastrous, of course, if it had happened. But it couldn't. He found it very difficult. And I harassed him, and made it worse.[455]

Frank's desire to have a child – apart from being a reasonably common human feeling in itself – is consistent with the pleasure he took in his vaguely paternal relationships with a number of young men and women in the second half of his life. With the young men it was often not-very-vaguely sexual in character as well, which complicates retrospective analysis just as it complicated the relationships at the time. But for a man whose experience of his own father was quite limited and skewed, and would inevitably distort his sense of what a father might feel and do, he sometimes showed a surprising predilection, and even talent, for the role.

453 Sheila Hancock, *The Two of Us: My Life with John Thaw*, London, Bloomsbury Publishing, 2004, p.177.

454 Joan Thring interview with Frank Van Straten and Clive Stark, 5 March 1995.

455 Joan Thring, interview 15 December 2004.

In the first months of their marriage, while the fantasy of fatherhood was in the air, Frank was rehearsing and then performing *Peter Pan*. Perhaps Barrie's idealisation of childhood outweighed the taming of all the real children in the stalls; for once in his life, Frank may have felt something in common with Mr Darling, as well as naturally identifying with Hook. By the time he was ranting and roaring his way through Sir Lancelot Spratt, a great deal had changed. Frank was already redefining all that had gone wrong in his marriage in terms similar to Spratt's views on the female sex near the end of *Doctor in the House*:

> SIR LANCELOT: (*To* SIMON) How the devil did you get yourself into this mess, eh?
>
> JOHN: He's not very experienced with women, sir.
>
> SIR LANCELOT: You are, I suppose?
>
> JOHN: Well, I know a little about them, sir.
>
> SIR LANCELOT: And that's all you ever will know. They're a blasted pest, always getting in the way of a man.[456]

He was extricating himself from the mess by regarding the whole thing as an aberration – or at least giving a fair impersonation of a man doing something along those lines.

Joan's account is of a man trying very hard to act something that he couldn't be. Other men of his theatrical acquaintance seemed to manage to have male and female lovers, and wives and children, but Frank could not. It was quite some distance from the testimonies given to the Registrar of Divorce about his callous dismissal of Joan's desire for children, but the seemingly cruel invitation to 'go somewhere else' to find what he could not provide did at least have some place in their dealings with each other:

> It was all very destructive, and I didn't deal with it well. And we talked about it, and we argued about it, and Frank said, why don't you have an affair. And I did, I had this huge affair with Peter Finch, and Frank couldn't bear it. He hated it.[457]

---

456 *Doctor in the House*, Act III, p.105.
457 Joan Thring interview 15 December 2004.

Peter Finch, who had been spotted by Olivier on the Australian tour in 1948 and persuaded to try his luck in Britain, was one actor in Frank's circle who was quite clear and secure as to his sexuality. He had been for several years the lover of Vivien Leigh, and subsequently had highly publicised affairs with Kay Kendall and Mai Zetterling, in addition to the three women he married, and a long list of others. For Australian film audiences, who were inclined to overlook the fact that he was a native Londoner, he epitomised the virile Aussie bloke. He was everything that Frank was not. Frank saw a lot of him in the early part of his stay in London, but then no more; Peter Finch was one theatrical name that Frank, in later years, never dropped.

Joan's relationship with Finch grew rapidly during the eleven weeks that Frank was touring in *Peter Pan*. It was a reasonably public affair, with lots of dinners for two at the fashionable 'White Tower' restaurant. When Joan invited a group of friends, including Peter Finch, to a welcome-home party for Frank on Sunday April 8, only one of those present was not aware of how it had developed: the absent husband. Somehow, during that evening, Frank found out, and there was an angry exchange with Finch, who walked out of the party.

> I didn't know what had happened. I chased after Peter, and asked him what had gone wrong, and he said Frank is going to hit me. And I said of course he wouldn't, but Peter said he was furious and had threatened him, and went home. So I went back in and Frank was so angry. He kept on saying 'Not Peter Finch, of all people, not Peter Finch', and I said to him that he was the one who'd told me I should have an affair and that he had no right to be like that when that's what I'd done. And he said, 'Well, I didn't say Peter Finch', and I said, 'Well, who were you suggesting, the garbage-man?' And he was terribly upset. I think he didn't like the fact that it was someone in the public eye. He hated the fact that everyone would know.[458]

Whatever difficulties were apparent in the nine weeks that Frank and Joan had spent together as man and wife were much exacerbated by the events of the next eleven, and from the night of Frank's return the die was cast. In the ensuing weeks they had a series of terrible rows, always about the same things: sex, and Peter Finch.

458 ibid.

One of those fights blew up at the start of August, while they were visiting Frank's cousin, John Creightmore. Joan pushed Frank, who fell over backwards into a waste-paper basket, and was stuck tight in it. It was a touch of farce that would have delighted the patrons of *Doctor in the House*. Joan, though, didn't find it funny at all at the time:

> I ran out of the house in floods of tears. I went back to the flat. Then John arrived – he was really worried about me. Frank was behind him, and didn't say anything, not a single word. I stopped crying after a bit, and then Frank just looked at me and said 'Ha!' and walked out. I think he couldn't bear seeing that I was all right after all.[459]

That was the night that Joan moved out, for good.

The marriage was effectively over, and less than a year later Frank and Joan gave the *Truth* its delicious expose. Their divorce deposition bent a few of the facts, but was probably quite close to the spirit of the law:

> And so we split up, and then the divorce just happened. It was destructive, and it wasn't going to go anywhere that it hadn't already gone. So we just sort of decided. We made up the grounds.
>
> We said the marriage hadn't been consummated so that we could get it annulled. Which wasn't true, because we had tried. But it just never worked.[460]

The mess and the unhappiness weren't over. Frank planned his return home, and was all set to go when the Shakespeare Memorial Theatre announced its intention to tour a revival of *Titus Andronicus* through half of Europe. Frank took the offer, and left Joan, and the last rites of the divorce proceedings, behind him in London.

Frank was fairly scrupulous about commenting on his ex-wife in the years that followed. They kept in touch, and remained friends; when Joan remarried, Frank liked to refer to her new husband as his 'husband-in-law'. But the likeliest of the hypotheses about the origins of the myth of the will and the sham marriage is still that it came from Frank. It is the kind of

459 Joan Thring interview 10 January 2005.

460 Joan Thring interview 15 December 2004. In an interview with Julia Rose two months after Frank's death, Joan said 'We really meant it to last, and it was, sort of, consummated' ('A Frank Talk with Mrs Thring', *Weekend*, 25 February 1995, p.3).

thing that would have started with a throwaway remark, and was spread and embellished by almost everyone who knew him for decades thereafter. It was an integral part of the incredible tale of the marriage, offering a plausible answer to the obvious question almost before it could be asked.

The joke was not particularly at Frank's expense, or Joan's; it was a joke against the silliness of prejudice and the thought that people might take marriage so seriously when there was money was at stake. Frank in particular, and in some versions of the story Joan too, were presented in the myth as totally in control of what they were doing. It implied that they didn't care at all that it hadn't worked out, that there were no real emotions on the line. How could a man as large and thick-skinned and preposterous as Frank ever be so foolish as to imagine himself able to love a woman, or father a child? It was unthinkable, surely.

So Frank's distress passed into folklore as a comic turn. It was a move completely in keeping with the way Frank the reluctant Grammar boy had dealt with the potential scorn of his classmates; he took each of the elements of his personality that would make him vulnerable, exaggerated them to the point of parody, and made himself look untouchable. Life at school hadn't been so hard, he claimed, 'Not when you're as vicious as I am'. Frank's self-directed humour was part of a strategy of the pre-emptive strike, and while it may not have prevented him from being hurt, it certainly prevented others from seeing it. The failures of the marriage, on Joan's account, had hurt him deeply. He made sure, on returning to Australia, that nobody else would see the whole thing as anything but funny.

The supposition that the myths began with Frank is supported by some of the other tall stories that grew up around the marriage ceremony itself, all of which were verifiably his anecdotes. Larry and Viv were always part of the narrative, as marquee friends, but in some of the tellings all the other guests ceased to be in the picture; it was just the four of them, having a bit of a lark. The announcement in the *Times* five weeks before the ceremony slipped out of some of his versions of the story, too; the wedding was now represented as a sudden whim, a novel way of killing a slow afternoon. The nuptials in the church moved, in most of Frank's remembrances, to the graveyard outside, to Shakespeare's grave, in fact. A marriage in a graveyard was a suitably macabre touch in a tragicomedy. In a final twist, the service moved from just beside the grave to actually astride it, no doubt under the influence of Vladimir's grim reflection on birth, copulation and death in Beckett's *Waiting for Godot*. All these embroiderings of the event are consistent with Frank's refusal to let history get in the way of whimsy, and with the supposition that he needed a good yarn to cover the reasons for the marriage, too.

The final bit of circumstantial evidence that suggests that the myth of the codicil was Frank's own invention is the reminiscence in the story of a key plot element in the comedy that Frank was appearing in during the most painful period of the break-up. Although the medical students in *Doctor in the House* are very susceptible to distraction (beer, rugby, and girls, in roughly that order), all of them except one desperately want to pass the course. Tony Grimsdyke, the perpetual student, has been carefully just-failing for years, because a grandmother with a weakness for doctors left him a legacy for the duration of his course. If going through the motions of something that others might see as a vocation frees him to live the good life, who could blame him? Frank didn't play Grimsdyke in the production, but he showed plenty of aptitude for the role: a man to whom nothing matters but the money is easy to laugh with. A man so clear and unsentimental about what he seeks from life has no soft spots, no fears. The final irony for Grimsdyke was that, under pressure from a girlfriend, he passed his exams, and was condemned to work for a living. The irony for Frank was that the money was his, unentailed, all the time. He was looking for something that it could not buy.

The acrimony in the last months of the marriage gave way to a mutually considerate settlement. The house they had shared was a large one at 19 Westgate Terrace in Earl's Court, at the back of Redcliff Square; Frank and Joan had shared the three bottom floors and leased out the two at the top. After the tragicomic night at John Creightmore's, Joan took a little flat close by, at 5 Trebover Road. It was a reflection of the fact that she felt the need for separation more than he did. After a while Frank suggested they should swap. He gave up the Westgate Terrace apartments, which Joan later turned into multiple flats, ensuring her financial security for her future life in London. Frank took the flat. It might have been a generous gift, an act of penance, a gesture of final closure, a bid for the moral high-ground, or some combination of any or all of these things. Perhaps a practical matter like the division of property was just too boring to bother with. Frank could, occasionally, be very cavalier about money matters; he had been taught very early that it grew inexhaustibly on family trees.

He headed off on the *Titus* tour to Paris, Venice, Vienna, Belgrade, Zagreb and Warsaw. It was a very timely tour, although it ended, inconveniently, in London. Then Frank left again, and this time there was no mystery at all about his leaving.

The *Titus Andronicus* tour in 1957 is not just a tale of six cities, but two very different tales. One is the public story: a whirlwind journey from one triumph to another, where the brilliance of the production and the Bard, combined with the skilful diplomacy of Olivier and the charismatic charm of Vivien Leigh, conquered and united audiences across Europe. The conquests began with the French, traditionally sceptical about all that was not French and especially all that was English, and continued behind the Iron Curtain, where the company was portrayed as turning on the lights at last in cities still oppressed by the physical and psychic legacy of the war. It was a splendid adventure, which added to all the glamour and ceremony of a royal tour the moral and cultural stiffening of missionary zeal.

That story was told through regular breathless bulletins in the press and, most comprehensively, by one member of the company in a long commissioned article for *Plays and Players* – Frank Thring. The other story seeps out in bits and pieces of the diaries, letters and conversations of all the others who were there. That story is about a tired company trying to recapture the energy of its Stratford season two years before, while struggling in unfamiliar languages with tricky protocols and tight political constraints; it is set in often bizarre living arrangements, during a European summer that rarely seemed less than unbearably hot. And it was played out in the shadow of the breakdown of the Olivier marriage, an agony that somehow involved them all.

Frank knew all about the second story, naturally; indeed, his role as an unthreatening confidant to Larry and as a man who could nearly always make Vivien laugh put him quite close to the centre of the drama. But he showed all the tact of a true ambassador in his chronicle for *Plays and Players*, which was certainly no place to start telling the truth. More surprisingly, perhaps, Frank also proved remarkably discreet and trustworthy in the way he talked (or didn't talk) about it in later years. That may have been a token of the quality of his friendship, and his sympathy with each of them in an excruciating situation; it may also have been a consequence of the grisly experience he was still going through in the dismantling of his own marriage.

The article is breezy and enthusiastic, with more than a hint of Frank's fondness for big-noting:

> I flew over with the Oliviers, Tony Quayle gathered up Rosalind Atkinson and drove across in his new-minted Aston Martin, purchased the day before …
>
> The company went on to Venice by train, but Vivien, who can never let a day pass without living it fully, suggested that she, Larry and I break the journey at Florence to lunch with Bernard Berenson, and do a quick tour of the town …
>
> Anthony Quayle and I had good reason to remember our visit [to Yugslavia], for while travelling by road between Belgrade and Zagreb his gleaming new Aston Martin was smashed almost to a pulp. He and I miraculously escaped injury in the front of the car …[461]

The sense in Frank's reminiscences is that he was always right beside the great and the beautiful, and had a front-row seat wherever the action happened to be. There was some truth in this, since the Oliviers enjoyed and perhaps even needed his presence, and he rarely did much socialising with the spear-carriers of the company; moreover, he was, of course, a man who attracted and sometimes created high drama.

Sometimes the manner shifts from that of a man who lives easily with fame to that of a stage-struck fan. Vivien is the star of Frank's tour, constantly opening the doors to a magical kingdom in which the readers of *Plays and Players* can never hope to dwell:

> Larry and Vivien immediately set up house in Bernhardt's charming suite of dressing-rooms, and one by one we went to it as to a museum – the lovely silken wallpaper, the Heath Robinson telephone through which 'le voix d'or' had spoken, the gilded fittings inscribed 'S.B'. …
>
> As she came forward to make her speech [on receiving the Legion d'Honneur] her hair was falling to her shoulders, her white chiffon costume translucent in the spotlights. She looked like a lovely girl

461 Frank Thring, 'Titus Tour was like a Royal Progress', *Plays and Players*, August 1955, p.9.

> receiving her prize. The tears were streaming down her cheeks, and ours too ...
>
> We passed under several bridges [on the Seine]rather precariously only be told as we docked that our helmsman for the last ten minutes had been Vivien herself – steering our course then as indeed she did for the whole tour ...
>
> One night in Zagreb, Larry and Vivien went with some of their Yugoslavian friends to a little village where Vivien wanted to see a local artist's paintings ... two of [the villagers] came up and presented her with one of the artist's paintings which they had taken down from the wall of their own home.
>
> It was obviously one of their most prized possessions, but they begged her to accept it from them with the best wishes of the Yugoslavian people ...
>
> Vivien, on top of her form as always, refused to be fobbed off with Warsaw alone, and decided to pay a visit to Cracow, one of the oldest cities in Poland ...[462]

The glamour and the energy are almost overwhelming. It was part of the truth, too. But Vivien was often not 'on top of her form', and the further the tour went, the more absurdly inappropriate Frank's starry-eyed exuberance became.

Frank paid much more attention to the extra-curricular joys of the tour than he did to the performances themselves, although he noted that in Paris 'the reception at the final curtain, on this [the opening night] and the succeeding nights, surpassed our greatest hopes of success', and relished 'the delightful French custom of turning house-lights on at about fifth or sixth curtain so that we ... could see the people who were so generous in their applause'. Surprisingly, he didn't mention how many more curtain-calls followed that moment; the newspapers in England, though were full of it. 'Seventeen curtain-calls' was the phrase that recurred in every paper, and in the headlines of the tabloids.

It was a tough schedule. Olivier's diary cryptically records the itinerary, every day of it involving receptions and awards and interviews.[463] The

462 ibid.

463 Laurence Olivier, personal diary for 1957, Olivier Collection, The British Library, MS 97976.

movements between capitals are rapid and impressive enough, given the need to transport not only a company of over forty but all the materials of a spectacular and technically demanding production; and given, too, the decision to move the company through Europe always by train or bus, which was prompted by Vivien Leigh's pathological dislike of flying and Olivier's concern to minimise all risks to her fragile state of mind. Frank shared her aversion to aeroplanes, of course, and the fact that he flew to Paris with them for the first leg is a tangible sign of his eagerness to be, in every sense, in their company.

They arrived in Paris at 3.15 on May 13, and the play opened on May 15, playing eight performances concluding on May 25. On May 26 they arrived in Florence by train, en route to Venice which they reached on May 27 and where they opened on May 28, for a season of four performances. They arrived in Belgrade on June 1, opened there on June 2, and played four performances till June 5, taking the bus to Zagreb on June 6, the day of Frank's accident in Quayle's car. Following a rehearsal and party at the embassy on June 7, they opened in Zagreb on June 8 for four more performances. On June 11 they took the train to Vienna, opening on June 12. The rail journey to Warsaw took place on June 16, and following an embassy luncheon on June 19 the production opened that night. The last tour performance on June 21 was followed by a reception at the Ministry of Culture, and the next morning they left for home.

Even Darlington, the critic who had been among the small group of dissenters about the original Stratford season of *Titus*, hailed the whole thing as an unqualified success. He described the tour as 'a triumphal progress around Europe', and viewed the production now as 'a tour-de-force of direction and acting', though he still disliked the play:

> The unaccountable French have preferred it to John Gielgud and Peggy Ashcroft's 'Much Ado About Nothing', thus putting the final seal on their congenial [sic] inability to understand Shakespeare.[464]

The French response, for once, had actually been congenial, but it's likely that Darlington saw their many problems as congenital ones.

There were a few small public hitches. One occurred in Belgrade, when Olivier, who bravely had addressed each opening night audience in their own language made the error that everyone dreads, and that most of us

464 W.A. Darlington, 'The Miracle of Titus', *Daily Telegraph*, 2 July 1957.

probably commit, when trying to communicate in an unfamiliar tongue. In trying to say warmly, 'Ladies and gentlemen, I want to thank you all', he brought the house down by saying 'Ladies and gentlemen, I wish to fuck you all'. Fortunately, the visit had created more than enough goodwill to avoid the potential for an international incident.[465]

Venturing behind the Iron Curtain created some predictable problems of logistics, too. In Warsaw the theatre was too small ('accommodating only six thousand') to meet the demands of an eager public, after half the seats were allocated to party officials,[466] while on the way back to London for the farewell five-week season at the Stoll Theatre, the trucks containing all the set, props and costumes were detached from the train and confiscated at the Czech border; two members of the production team jumped off to try to reclaim them, but were forced back on board by armed guards.[467] But these were relatively minor matters, the natural hazards of campaigns in foreign lands. The production materials arrived just in time for the opening at the Stoll, which was to be the last production at the theatre before it was replaced by a shopping mall. The London season of *Titus Andronicus* sent both the production and the theatre out in style.

So much for the public story, none of it anything but true, but reflecting only part of what took place. The disintegration of the Olivier marriage, and Vivien's own breakdown, were nothing new. The tension and acrimony between them, and her manic depression, had been a part of those elegant weekends at the Abbey that Frank and Joan had savoured two years before. Noel Coward, a friend to both of them, described them in his diary for 1955 as 'eminent, successful, envied and adored, and most wretchedly unhappy', and their life together as 'really hideous'.[468] His sympathies had their limits, too:

> Personally I think that if Larry had turned sharply on Vivien years ago and given her a clip in the chops, he would have been spared a mint of trouble. The seat of all this misery is our old friend, feminine ego. She is, and has been, thoroughly spoiled … Fond as I am of her and sorry as I feel for her, I would like to give her a good belting …[469]

465 Jesse L.Lasky and Pat Silver, *Love Scene: The Story of Laurence Olivier and Vivien Leigh*, London, Sphere Books, 1980, p.249.

466 *Times*, 13 May 1957.

467 *Times*, 25 June 1957.

468 Entry for 7 August 1955. *The Noel Coward Diaries*, edited by Graham Payn and Sheridan Morley, London, Weidenfeld and Nicolson, 1982, p.260.

469 Entry for 19 August 1955, *The Noel Coward Diaries*, p.280.

Kenneth Tynan, his sympathies perhaps similarly complicated by his feelings for the husband in the case, recalled another 'saddening and sur-real' evening at Notley in 1955, when Vivien had behaved outrageously and Olivier had sat morosely in a corner, silent and downing one brandy after another: 'V's manner with L is haughty and derisive. How can he bear it?'[470]

The brilliance of the Olivier court concealed a sickness at its heart. For Trader Faulkner there was always something 'decadent and corrosive' in the air at the charming picnics by the river and the sumptuous parties in the baronial hall,[471] while Anthony Quayle could never enjoy them:

> I could feel the awful tensions beneath the gaiety, like being in a play with undertones running completely counter to the dialogue ... we were all on edge at what our host and hostess might get up to next.[472]

Frank and Joan, in the early stages of their relationship with the Oliviers, may have been so delighted at finding themselves in Camelot that they were less troubled by the subtext. But Frank, particularly, soon had plenty of opportunity to read it all.

Frank not only admired Olivier greatly, but at some level identified with him; in the tales he told in later years about funny things happening on stage there was often slippage between things that had happened to his dear friend Larry and things that had happened to him. Moreover, as a man who similarly liked his relationships to run according to his own rules, he would have felt some identification with Olivier as their marriages disintegrated. He and Larry were both men with elaborately crafted defences that their demanding wives were understood to be continually trying to crack.

The company that reassembled for the tour of *Titus Andronicus* in 1957, most of whom were quite familiar with the tensions and undertones that Quayle remembered from those weekends at Notley, would have been resigned to feeling and hearing more of the same as they journeyed through Europe. This time though, the situation between Olivier and Leigh was unrelievedly bad. Vivien's mind was seriously disturbed, her conflict with her husband was horribly naked, and nobody could pretend not to notice. The tour effectively marked the end of their marriage.

---

470 Entry for 10 April 1973, *The Diaries of Kenneth Tynan*, edited by John Lahr, London, Bloomsbury, 2002, p.133.

471 Trader Faulkner, interview with the author, London, 26 January 2005.

472 Anthony Quayle, interview with Alexander Walker, in Walker, p.303.

Quayle found Olivier extraordinary in his capacity to deal with his private hell throughout that tour and still deliver 'a very great performance':

> Poor Vivien, she was suffering badly from manic depression and had turned against the very man she loved most in the world – against Larry … Standing there beside him while Titus was speaking words of love to poor mutilated Lavinia, she would be cursing him with the most extreme obscenities imaginable, with a piece of bloody gauze tied across her mouth.[473]

The whispered expressions of hate by the woman who was mute began in the Paris season, but became louder and more frequent as the tour wore on:

> During a matinee in Belgrade, Vivien eyed Titus's wailing misery. Quite audibly she pronounced, "You cunt!" The Belgrade audience no doubt took it as a line from Shakespeare.[474]

Several thousand Yugoslavs must have puzzled over the symbolic meaning of Shakespeare's brief, miraculous restoration of Lavinia's voice.

Vivien's behaviour became more and more erratic with each new city. In Zagreb, she managed to evade the guards who seemed to be everywhere, and slipped out of the company's hotel through the kitchen, wearing a green silk evening gown and matching emeralds. No one knew where she was for a day and a night. She was missing for almost thirty hours. An unknown man delivered her back to the hotel on the morning of the play's opening. She walked into the hotel foyer as the company sat down for breakfast, her dress covered in mud. Olivier said nothing about her absence, and gently put down in front of her a tray with breakfast things on it. Vivien threw it against the wall.[475]

When the rest of the company got on the train in Zagreb for the next leg, the journey to Vienna, Vivien flatly refused to board, despite the best efforts of her husband and Otto, the massive local police chief who had been placed in charge of her:

> Finally Larry said, 'I can't stand it'. Then the train began to move and Vivien stood her ground on the platform. And the police chief …

---

473 Anthony Quayle, *A Time to Speak*, London, Barrie and Jenkins, 1990, p.335.
474 Lasky and Silver, *Love Scene*, p.247.
475 ibid, p.248.

> simply picked her up and put her on the train. And she gave him such a shiner, such a smack in the eye.[476]

The next stage of the company's 'triumphal progress' was worse still:

> On the twenty-two hour train journey from Vienna to Warsaw, in ninety-degree heat, she paced the train's corridor restlessly, then began to run up and down it, shouting inanities. When Olivier tried to restrain her, she threw a make-up case at him and smashed the window. He retired, defeated, to the next carriage, leaving protective members of the company to calm her.[477]

Maxine Audley was the first to try, but was driven to lock herself in a lavatory when the fury was turned all on her.[478] Frank was one of those who held Vivien until she was quiet, and suddenly fell asleep on their laps.

They got through the five-week run at the Stoll. Vivien was a little better, and her days became consumed by a passionate crusade to save the St James Theatre, which like the Stoll was scheduled for demolition; she led marches on the House of Commons to disrupt Question Time from the gallery, and the papers all ran photographs of her, once more looking every inch a star, as she advanced down Whitehall. Olivier was there too, though unusually strained and serious-looking, a couple of paces behind her in the background. By that point there can have been no-one in the company who was not longing for it all to end. Frank, with no reason to stay in London and several good reasons to leave, decided to do what he had done in 1947 and in 1954 when the gloss had worn off and he found himself once again alone. He booked his passage back to Melbourne.

There was a little unfinished business to attend to in London, however, which forced him to postpone his voyage home. It grew over the next two years into a career that delayed the return of the prodigal to Rylands until

476 Hon. Colin Clark in an interview with Hugo Vickers. Hugo Vickers, *Vivien Leigh*, London, Hamish Hamilton, 1988, p.246.

477 Anthony Holden, *Olivier*, London, Weidenfeld and Nicolson, 1988, p.321.

478 Alexander Walker, *Vivien: The Life of Vivien Leigh*, London, Orion, 2001, p.317.

the middle of 1959. Frank Thring was about to become a second-level film star on the international screen. It happened almost accidentally, and its first signs were about as unpropititious as one could imagine.

Frank's film career began in the melancholy autumn of 1957 with a minor role in episode twenty-four of a CBS/BBC co-production for television, *Dick and the Duchess*.[479] In the dismal winter that followed he played a couple of other quirkily unpleasant cameos for the cinema in *The Flaming Sword*, directed by Dave Lee, and *A Question of Adultery*, directed by Don Chaffey. These commitments kept him busy and largely out of mischief, which was a good thing at an unhappy time when he was in need of distraction. But they also kept him away from home and, most of the time, in London, which was perhaps the last place in the world where he wanted to be.

The role of Gar, a more than usually malicious warlord in *The Flaming Sword*, came through the *Titus* connection. Maxine Audley recommended Frank when its producers were looking for an actor who could make a memorably sinister impression in a couple of scenes, and who could suggest that cruelty was not just a routine among the Ancient Britons but might be a form of erotic pleasure. It was Saturninus all over again, with just a dash of Herod for old time's sake, and it anticipated the niche market that Frank met in the much more prominent movies that he made for American studios over the following three years. For someone as resistant to almost all forms of physical activity as Frank, the action epic was not the most obvious genre in which to pursue a career. Gar, however, displayed his capacity to play viciousness with the minimum of exertion.

The Flaming Sword starred another Australian, Chips Rafferty, in its leading role as the fighting hero Long Tom. Perhaps that was one of the reasons for the film's almost complete failure to register at the box office. Rafferty was making his bid for international stardom, having established himself as the archetypal lanky, laconic bushman in Australian films such as *Smiley* (1956), and, most iconically, *Bush Christmas* (1946), in which he had

479 *Dick and the Duchess* was a moderately popular comedy-drama which played for twenty-seven half-hour episodes on British and American television in 1957–8. It featured Patrick O'Neal as Dick Starrett, an American Insurance Investigator, and Hazel Court as Jane, the daughter of an English peer whom he marries and who somehow manages to complicate every case. Frank appeared as Wembler in 'The Courtroom', an episode in which Jane gets her driving licence and, after purchasing a car from her Uncle George (Lionel Jeffries) without Dick's knowledge, proceeds to run up a record number of parking fines. The episode went to air on CBS on 8 March 1958, but its UK screening did not occur till 6 September 1959.

played the similarly extended role of Long Sam. The move to seek a wider market in *The Flaming Sword* was disastrous.

A Question of Adultery shaped more promisingly. Its cast was better-known, and its plot relied primarily on drab interiors that suited a shooting-schedule in the English winter much better than a film about battles in fancy-dress.[480] But a number of things made it problematic for Frank, apart from the fact that all his scenes took place in a city he longed to escape. There was the film's title, for a start, which came unnervingly close to circumstances that he knew not wisely, but too well. The question of adultery, as it related to Frank's marriage to Joan, was open. He had countenanced, even recommended, her infidelity, but not precisely with the man she chose. Did that count as an extra-marital affair, or a conditional licence?

The plot was close to the bone, too. Dan Sutherland's stage play, *Breach of Marriage*, on which Anne Edwards' screenplay for the film was based, concerned a couple unable to conceive a child. Mary Loring wanted to try artificial insemination; her pathologically jealous husband Mark disliked the idea, then reluctantly agreed, and finally – after his wife had begun the process – decided to view it as a form of infidelity, and to seek a divorce from his wife. Frank must have reviewed his suggestion that, if Joan wished to conceive a child, she should explore other options than her husband. A discreet medical procedure would have been a lot easier to handle, from his point of view, than a passionate affair with Peter Finch.

The subject was controversial, sufficiently daring to ensure a restricted adult rating in England and to be certified 'Condemned' by the National League of Decency in the United States, which delayed its American release for three years. But the treatment was cautious, even coy. The 'question of adultery' was not only perversely legalistic in the form in which the aggrieved husband chose to raise it, but remained unresolved in the film; the jury was unable to reach unanimity, and the matter was only concluded when Mark, deciding that he loved Mary after all, asked to withdraw the charge and left the court hand-in-hand with his wife. Having marginalised itself as a film about confronting issues, *A Question of Adultery* then alienated its remaining 'serious' audience by ducking or sentimentalising all of its questions.

It failed, although not as comprehensively as *The Flaming Sword*. It was not one of the sixteen thousand films reviewed for posterity in Penguin's *Time*

480 Several scenes involving Flamenco dancers and skiing (ostensibly) in the Swiss Alps in *A Question of Adultery* were a rather unconvincing and clichéd exception to that rule.

Out Film Guide, and, though it is one of the twenty-four thousand movies recorded in *Halliwell's*, is dismissed cursorily as 'Opportunist melodrama ... Not even interesting then'.[481] The critic for the *New York Times* greeted its long-delayed American release without enthusiasm:

> In its present artless, low-budget form, the subject-matter seems designed to invite censorial wrath ... When the husband drops the case and returns to his wife, both seem sorry they brought the matter up in the first place. So was the audience.[482]

More interesting than the film itself was its odd collocation of cast. They were a very eclectic company: Julie London, the husky-voiced American singer imported to play the female lead; the Englishman Anthony Steel as her husband; the Welshman Donald Houston as her attorney; the Scot Andrew Cruickshank as her doctor; the German Anton Diffring as a wrongly suspected co-respondent; and, in the cameo role of the obstreporous juror Mr Stanley, the Australian Frank Thring.

A Question of Adultery was to prove a turning-point in the professional lives of most of the participants. It marked Julie London's most determined assertion of her claims as an actress. It confirmed the complete unravelling of Steel's film career in the wake of his stormy divorce from Anita Ekberg; critics described him as moving 'glumly'[483] through the role of Mark, as though ready to 'chew the scenery'.[484] It cast Cruickshank as the crusty Dr Cameron, by coincidence a character whose name and temperament matched the role he would go on to play in the BBC television series *Doctor Finlay's Casebook* between 1962 and 1971.[485] It was a watershed, too, for its director, Don Chaffey, who afterwards abandoned relationship-dramas for good and moved successfully into making films for children about cute and cuddly animals.

For Frank Thring it was the prelude to a run of four Hollywood epic blockbusters in the next four years. As King Aella in *The Vikings* (1958), Pontius Pilate in *Ben Hur* (1959), Herod Antipas in *King of Kings* (1961), and

---

481 *Halliwell's Film Guide 2008*, ed. David Gitten, London, Harper Collins, 2007, p.937.

482 Eugene Archer, *New York Times*, 6 July 1961.

483 ibid.

484 'Harrison's Reports', 21 February 1959, in *Harrison's Reports and Film Reviews 1959–1962*, volume 14, Hollywood Film Archive 1992, p.30.

485 *Dr Finlay's Casebook* was based on a series of novels by A.J.Cronin, whose Dr Cameron was quite unrelated to the doctor in Anne Edwards' screenplay, or in *Breach of Marriage*, the play by Dan Sutherland on which it was it based.

Al Kadir in *El Cid* (1961), Frank plumbed the depths of sybaritic villainy, won some fame and considerable notoriety, and accumulated anecdotes to last a lifetime. Frank liked to claim, with a rare approximation to the truth, that through this period he was rarely out of a toga, and never appeared in a movie with a budget of less than ten million dollars.[486]

It was a nice irony. The son who had shown virtually no interest in film, who saw himself so completely as a man of the theatre, now found himself borne, so easily that it seemed almost involuntarily, to success in his father's medium.

486 Dunstan, *Ratbags*, p.133.

TRAVELLING FROM LONDON TO STOCKHOLM

British Airways flight, 17 February 1958

Hardangerfjorden. Now there was a name to conjure with. You knew you'd really made it when you shot a film in Hardangerfjorden.

He'd compromised on the flying issue. The Boeing to Stockholm, then the train via Oslo to Bergen. Much less horrifying than the direct flight to Oslo on some flimsy twin-engine contraption, though horrifying enough. It was a paradox, the thing with planes. The bigger they were, the less often they fell. All the same, he hated it, every moment, especially the desperate straining to get off the ground and the perilous wild bounding back onto it. It called for prayer and medication. If God had meant man to fly, he would've replaced his blood with brandy. Salut.

In first class there was plenty of it, as much as one could drink, an irresistible challenge. It was good to have made it. The seats were generous to the larger figure, and a sweet little queen in a tight satin vest ensured that one was never short of a rollmop. Impossible to resist a uniform, even one surmounted by a smile crammed with National Health Service teeth. Adrian, it said on his badge. Naturally.

But he was free of London. Flying away from it at last. There was comfort in that, even if the fucking thing fell out of the sky after all. And he was never going back if he could help it.

It was a nightmare, the whole thing, the whole year really. He'd told her he loved her. It was excruciating to remember. What a fuckwit he'd been. Women couldn't love men like him, not really. Oh, sure, they liked them, of course. Men like him, they were just like their female friends, only bigger, much bigger, and not so smart. They constituted no threat, made no demands.

Men like Finchie, they were a different kettle of fish. They made demands all right, you bet they did. They swam around in their fucking testosterone sea, doing what they wanted, having what they wanted, who they wanted, not much care, no responsibility. While people like Frank, they loved the women the other men used. Always true to you, darling, in my fashion. And they sold out their hopes and screwed up their lives for them and their stupid bloody fantasies, and then they called for another complimentary brandy. Cheap at half the price.

She'd said it was best for both of them. How civil she could be when it suited her. She used every cliché in the book. When he said at first that he was going to go home, she'd told him he was running away. And what if he was. She'd told him he liked being a big fish in a small pool. More clichés. More fucking fish. One more fish metaphor, he'd be obliged to strangle her.

She was wrong. He wasn't going because he liked being anything, least of all because he liked being anything in Melbourne. He was going because he hated being in London. And what a piddling little pool it could be. The man who is tired of London is tired of life, that's what Johnson said. The Good Doctor was, pardon the Francais, a dumb cunt. Un cunt imbecile.

Anyway, now there was this film. He had to go. When a man's got to go, etcetera. So maybe when he came back to Melbourne, whenever that was, they wouldn't all be whispering about how he'd been fucked over by London, and Finch, and Flowergirl. Maybe.

Maybe the laugh would be on them after all, all of them. Presenting The Vikings, starring Tony fucking Curtis and Janet fucking Leigh, for Christ sake. And Frank Thring and Kirk Douglas, of course.

It was all behind him, now. And twenty thousand terrifying feet below. Nothing could reach him, now. The awful thing had been the caring. Once you stopped doing that, it was easy to move on.

He'd played the wrong cards in London. Well, it was a new game, after all; one wasn't thrown over by one's wife every day. But he'd been pathetic. Too many humiliating moments, one too many waste-paper baskets. Too many tears, and admissions he wished he could retract. And after the tumult and the flouncing died, he'd lost her, and his dignity, and any chance of controlling their story.

Hardanger, not a bad name for a fjord. Not impotent rage. Hard, like Finchie. A hard man is good to find, thank you Sophie. Here's to you, and to you, my Flowergirl, with love and kisses from Pansy Boy. May you be happy after all, and all your troubles be little ones. And may your precious Peter and his prime performing prick putrefy in hell.

But he didn't care, not now. Couldn't give a fuck. No, not even to you, Adrian, at least not today. Aeronautical Adrian, a dab hand at getting it up, and an absolute demon at going down. Ah, well. Another day, perhaps, if there was to be another day.

So let's have another drop, AA, with reciprocal compliments to your brandy. A man needs warmth in his heart and his soul if he's to face the Arctic wastes. Sometimes he just needs a bit of fucking help to find it.

Chapter Eleven

RETURN OF THE PRODIGAL

As Frank told the story, his call from Kirk bore a remarkable resemblance to his telegram from Tony:

> Kirk Douglas saw me in some performance in Belgrade or Zagreb or Krakow or … and said, you know, you chop off Larry's hand so beautifully, will you come and chop off Tony Curtis's hand in *The Vikings*? So I said 'Spot on, daddy'. And that was it.[487]

Like Quayle's cheery summons to play Saturninus, Douglas' invitation was perfectly timed. It was, again, an excellent career move; one thing led quite spectacularly to a series of others. Just as *Titus* had given him the chance to work alongside the royal couple of British theatre, in *The Vikings* he was to perform not only with Kirk Douglas (whose own company, Bryna Productions, was making the film), but one of Hollywood's marquee marriages, Tony Curtis and Janet Leigh. In 1955, there had been the added incentive that Melbourne had become less than comfortable; in 1958, escape from London, and from the pain and humiliation that he had felt there, was probably the best of all the reasons to say 'Spot on, daddy', and go.

Frank never came back to London, except very briefly in transit. One of the great attractions of the four epic blockbusters that he made between 1958 and 1961 was that all of them were in suitably exotic locations, a long way from Westgate Terrace. *The Vikings* took him to Norway, to a tiny village on the Hardangerfjorden outside Bergen, and briefly to a mediaeval castle near Munich; *Ben-Hur* was shot primarily in Rome, and *King of Kings* and *El Cid* at more than a dozen sites in Spain. Between *The Vikings* and *Ben-Hur*, and immediately after filming concluded on *El Cid*, he was back in

487 Bill Howie interview, 12 November 1989.

Melbourne. It was a period of fairly constant commuting, which for someone with Frank's pathological aversion to flying was a considerable cost; internal travel in Europe could be managed mostly by train, but the schedule wasn't conducive to leisurely sea voyages like those he had taken on the *Mariposa*, or the *Stratheden*, or the *Arcadia*, in the past.

But it was worth it, for a while. He was living in places that he had never been to, among people whom he had never known before. It was, from every point of view, the beginning of a fresh chapter, on a beautifully blank page. He gained new friends, new names to drop, new anecdotes to tell, and what sometimes seemed a new international notoriety. Making an indelible first impression had never been much of a problem for Frank. How much he thought about the complications he had left behind him in London and Melbourne is anyone's guess; certainly he neither talked nor wrote about any of that messy history to anyone, and gave every indication of being a man completely disconnected from his past and having a wonderful, wonderful time.

In *The Vikings* he played Aella, King of Northumbria, a man keen on a smorgasbord of sadistic delights, with no redeeming humanity whatsoever. The film's plot turns on the conflict between the two sons of Aella's particular enemy, Ragnar (Ernest Borgnine), King of the Vikings: Einar (Kirk Douglas) is Ragnar's legitimate son and heir, and Erik (Tony Curtis) the product of his dalliance with Northumbria's former queen, who has concealed his existence from the murderous Aella. A series of grisly misadventures, and the fact that each falls in love with the beauteous Northumbrian Princess Morgana (Janet Leigh), who is reluctantly betrothed to the vile Aella, cements their deep hostility. Einar captures Morgana, declaring that 'I want her to fight me the first time I take her – and the last'. The princess not surprisingly prefers the gentler wooing of Erik, with whom she flees to England, pursued by Douglas, Borgnine, and most of the rest of the cast.

The film then becomes a parade of deaths and dismemberments. In an early scene, Einar's eye is ripped out by Erik's pet hawk; Douglas was forced to wear an extremely painful plastic shield over the surface of the entire eye in every subsequent scene. And Viking extras are disembowelled or crushed by battering-rams at regular intervals. One of the more shocking visual moments preceded Aella's come-uppance, when Frank was required to tumble into a pit of wolves:

> A very thin piece of glass, 8 feet by 8 feet, was held between Tony and I [sic]. Curtis took a lighted torch and thrust it into my face, causing me

> to fall backward into the pit, when off screen mattresses broke my fall. The glass kept the torch from actually burning my face, but the effect on film was quite realistic![488]

The scene was too graphic for the American censors, however, and was cut from the film. Frank fell less controversially after a simple shove.

Shooting *The Vikings* was for most of its participants a grim business. The weather was a continual problem, with almost daily rain and constant interruptions because of changes in the quality of light; for Douglas, this meant extracting and re-inserting the ghastly eyeball several times each day. Tony Curtis, remembering conditions as 'horrible' from day one, recalled the routine with feeling:

> They put up a kind of tent for us to take refuge under when it rained. We would sit under this lean-to and then run out and do a scene and then run back undercover. In the middle of production, Kirk and I were huddled under that canopy in the miserable weather, waiting for the sun to come out. Finally, just when we thought we were ready to do the shot, it started to pour again. We're sitting there, and he has this awful thing in his eye, and when they came over to take it out, Kirk said, 'Just leave me alone'. The makeup guy went away. Kirk and I kept on sitting under that little lean-to, shivering and feeling miserable, thirty-five days behind schedule, hundreds of people standing around, money going down the drain. Big silence. Then Kirk Douglas looks at me with that bad eye and says, 'Tony, you want to buy a company cheap?'[489]

Douglas and his director, Richard Fleischer, never quite saw eye to eye, good or bad, and retrospectively each blamed the other for the film's shortcomings. Moreover, there were frequent logistical problems, including Viking oarsmen striking for more pay, historically accurate Viking ships that proved too small for twentieth-century bodies and film equipment, and unco-operative wolves.

Douglas, Curtis observed, 'went to tremendous lengths for authenticity'.[490] There were some conscious anachronisms: the ninth century sword-fights

---

488 Frank Thring, quoted in Richard Thompson.

489 Tony Curtis and Barry Paris, *Tony Curtis. The Autobiography*, London, Heinemann, 1993, p.138.

490 ibid, p.136.

were fought on the battlements of decidedly thirteenth-century castles. But he was determined to have real wolves. Unfortunately the wolves he cast initially proved even more ferocious than the script required, so Douglas hired a number of Alsatian dogs instead, and had them painted black. This solved the problem of risk to life and limb, but, as Frank recalled in his interview with Richard Thompson, it did so rather too well.

> The problem was that the 'wolves' ... weren't fierce at all. They were a bunch of perfect sweeties. No matter what we did, we couldn't get an aggressive response out of them. Late that afternoon, one of the experienced cameramen suggested soaking wool rags with methylated spirits and, immediately prior to filming, stick the rags up the dogs' asses. This worked like a charm. The dogs became angry wolves. They snarled, snapped, growled and chased their tails. The scene was shot without incident and seemed very realistic.[491]

It was another triumph for Douglas in his quest for absolute authenticity.

For most of those involved in the making of *The Vikings*, it was a relief when it was over. The film didn't do as well at the box office as Kirk Douglas had hoped, but in the end better than he had feared; it cost 3.5 million dollars and returned precisely twice that sum, and was the fifth highest grossing movie of 1958. Critically, the response was mixed at best, with Bosley Crowther in the *New York Times* dismissing it as a 'Norse Opera', and the Medved Brothers proclaiming it 'a film that did more damage to the Scandinavian public image than any Hollywood development since Muki the Wonder Hound'.[492]

Frank seems to have enjoyed it hugely – the wolves, the eye-gouging, the hand-chopping, the fraternising with the stars, even the ludicrously misnamed Norwegian summer. It fed his strongly developed sense of absurdity. More significantly, it led directly to his casting in *Ben-Hur* and it had nothing to do with London.

---

491 Richard Thompson, 'Frank Thring', *Films in Review*, 1992, p26.

492 Harry and Michael Medved, *The Golden Turkey Awards: the Worst Achievements in Hollywood History*, London, Angus and Robertson, 1980, p.194. Muki was the canine star of the aptly named box-office disaster *Dog of Norway* (1948). The Medveds' list *The Vikings* among a series of 'dull and dismal films' made by Tony Curtis that justify their nomination of Curtis among the contenders for 'Worst Actor of All Time'.

By late June, when *The Vikings* opened in New York, Frank was already engaged in pre-production for *Ben-Hur* in Rome. His original commission in the role of Pontius Pilate required him to be there for five weeks of shooting, but this turned into five months. The spectacular chariot-race in the Circus Maximus between Ben-Hur (Charlton Heston) and Messala (Stephen Boyd), which in the final cut ran for nine minutes, took three months to rehearse and to film; Pontius, whose task was to start the race, was called for the entire process. For Frank, at a loose end through that period with just a few lines to remember, it was a fabulous Roman holiday.

Pilate presented an interesting challenge. His place in the plot of *Ben-Hur* didn't allow a central focus on the agonising and culturally determinative choice that Pilate faced in the story that everyone knew; but it was a less one-dimensional, and certainly less vicious, role than Frank was accustomed to playing. Inevitably, the Thring Pilate was a voluptuary and a glutton, his decadence more the product of a camp aesthetic and moral laziness than a delight in evildoing. William Wyler, the director, was more concerned with the spectacle than with the complexities of a secondary character, and that evidently encouraged Frank to another conflation of his on-stage and off-stage personas.

The Vikings had been big. *Ben-Hur* was colossal, and the phrase 'bigger than *Ben-Hur*' has entered the lexicon as an index of scale impossibly large, in anything from a hit to a reputation, from a shindig to a nose. Roland Rocchecciolі, writing a fond obituary for Frank, even used it as the measure of a life.[493] The statistics for *Ben-Hur* were suitably spectacular:

> 100,000 costumes, 8,000 extras, 300 sets and a staggering budget that in its day was the largest in movie history.[494]

Set construction alone went through forty thousand cubic feet of timber, more than a million pounds of plaster, two hundred and fifty miles of metal tubing, and forty thousand tonnes of white sand from Mediterranean

493 Roland Rocchecciolі, *Australian*, 2 January 1995, p.12.
494 The opening sentence of the blurb for the DVD re-issue of *Ben-Hur*, Warner Brothers, 2001.

beaches.[495] The filming of *Ben-Hur* was the biggest thing in Rome in the summer of 1959. Charlton Heston observed that 'Getting a studio pass was almost on a par with a papal audience'.[496]

Ben-Hur cost a record fifty million dollars, and returned a very healthy eighty million. Just as the 1907 silent version of the story had established Metro Goldwyn Mayer as a major studio, the remake of 1959 rescued it from impending disaster, in an era in which movies were seen as living on borrowed time through the inexorable march of television. The quality of its achievement was acknowledged when the film carried off an unprecedented eleven Academy Awards, including Best Picture, Wyler as Best Director, Charlton Heston as Best Actor in a Leading Role, and Hugh Griffith as Best Supporting Actor.[497] And the critics liked *Ben-Hur* almost as much as its audiences, although unfortunately the most memorable of the film's reviews – one that Cruel Mister Thring, in his days of gay abandon at the *Argus*, would have been proud to claim as his own – was the comedian Mort Sahl's four word dismissal, 'Loved him. Hated Hur'.

Ben-Hur cemented Frank's reputation as a screen villain, and established an unlikely friendship with its star. Heston, whose distaste for homosexuality was as legendary as his passion for guns, became installed as 'dear Chuck' in Frank's pantheon of famous friends, alongside darling Larry and gorgeous Viv. Frank's habit of exaggeration was often as evident in describing his relationships with people as it was in his stories; he is mentioned only once in Heston's autobiography, and then only in passing among a number of 'good Brit actors' cast by Wyler as Romans opposite the American actors who played the Jewish roles.[498] With Larry and Viv, too, there had always been a marked lop-sidedness in the friendship. Frank regularly caught the Christmas mails to send his greetings to the Oliviers, but the reciprocations came late when they came at all. In 1981, for example, Frank shot off a telegram on December 23:[499]

> MY LOVE TO YOU AND YOURS AS ALWAYS
> FRANK THRING MELBOURNE THEATRE COMPANY

---

495 'Ben-Hur' website, www.michaeldvd.com.au/reviews.

496 Charlton Heston, *In the Arena. The Autobiography*, London, Harper Collins, 1995, p.197.

497 That achievement was eventually matched by *Titanic* in 1997 and *The Lord of the Rings: The Return of the King* in 2003.

498 Charlton Heston, p.196.

499 Olivier Collection, The British Library, correspondence folder 79779.

Olivier's cable in reply was sent on January 7:

> DEAREST FRANK SO SWEET TO HEAR FROM YOU SO MUCH LOVE TO YOU FROM ME AND FROM MINE
>
> LARRY OLIVIER

It was a warm response, even if it took a fortnight to send. But the affection had a touch of the foyer embrace about it – Olivier characteristically used 'Dearest' in his correspondence where others would use 'Dear', and the use of 'sweet' and the multiplication of love was also a trademark. There's an inference that the greeting from Frank came as a quite pleasant surprise, a voice from a past that for Frank was still current. Frank's celebrity friends meant much more to him than he did to them.

The friendship with Charlton Heston was similarly a reflection of the way in which Frank tended to luxuriate in glamorous contacts from a golden past while others moved on in their lives. But there was a genuine and improbable connection there as well, which surprised Mike Walsh when he presented Frank to Heston as a 'surprise' reunion on his television show:

> Normally these things were set-ups, of course, with lots of fake sentimentality. But when Frank came on, there was this incredible affection between them. Which was remarkable because, you know, Heston was a bit homophobic, and Frank was about as flabby as you can get.[500]

Frank described Heston with uncharacteristic restraint as 'perfectly nice'.[501] For once, it seems, he didn't need to use the art of delicious malice to keep a new acquaintance at arm's length, or to pre-empt an attack on him. It made the experience of *Ben-Hur* not only the most prestigious but the most pleasant of Frank's toga spectaculars for Hollywood.

The chariot-race was Frank's big scene in *Ben-Hur* and it provided the elaborate stage for his most vivid recollections of the film, in particular the deployment of the extras in the scene. Frank claimed there were ten thousand of them, though the actual number was eight thousand. This was, as Frank's exaggerations went, a relatively modest degree of inflation.

---

500 Mike Walsh interview with Peter Eyres, 5 August 1997.
501 Peter Wilmoth, *Sunday Age*, 19 June 1994, p.3.

> They were lined up 50 deep outside the gates by 5 a.m. As each one came in, someone stuck a beard on him. As he went on, someone else dropped a Roman costume over his shoulders.
>
> They were split into ten groups of a thousand and each group had a deputy director who was bi-lingual, Italian and English … Then anybody who looked faintly intelligent was made a sub group leader, so there was a chain of command right through.
>
> All the sub directors had walkie talkies, so the precision was marvellous. William Wyler would give his radio directions, 'I want section 310 to stand up and cheer. I want seventy-five to jump up and down – forty-two, now leap in front of the chariots', and they would leap.
>
> I can't tell you how slow and tedious it all was. There I was in the Roman heat trying to look lovely in my purple toga. There was a bit of relief. I was in the royal box and under a silk canopy. But you see there were twenty-seven chariots and every time they had a re-take they had to re-lay two hundred tons of sand. Bull dozers had to come in and scrape the whole arena, then they had to call in the Fire Brigade to hose it down. Each time this took about four hours. Every time they raced the track had to be pristine perfect.[502]

Day after day the same set-up, the same routines and frustrations. It was the nearest Frank would come to performing Beckett.

Not all the waiting was in a toga, or even on set, and some of it even Frank could find bearable:

> He has fond memories of cruising around Italy in the late Jack Hawkins' Silver Wraith Rolls-Royce, wining and dining on full pay, phoning in every day or two to see if *Ben Hur* [sic] was still being held up by the rain, a petulant minor star, or a problem with 'the bloody chariot'.
>
> 'It appalled me – mind you, I'm easily appalled – that the money that was wasted could have kept the entire Australian film industry going for 15 years'.[503]

---

502 Dunstan, *Ratbags*, p.133.

503 Graeme Johnstone, 'The Voice holds court with an actor's polish', *Sun Leisure Supplement*, 8 August 1985, p.3.

Arithmetic had never been one of Frank's strengths; no doubt here, as usual, he was using numbers simply as figures of speech. 'The entire Australian film industry' in 1959 was so moribund that it must have seemed beyond resuscitation by any means. The implicit point of comparison was, of course, the Efftee operation, and the mixed feelings he professes here were the ones Frank always thought it appropriate to have when he compared his career with his father's. He loved all the swanning around, but his mocking stories provided a way of expiating, at least retrospectively, a twinge of guilt.

He defined his role in *Ben-Hur* (and indeed in most of his other films) as follows: 'one stands there looking magnificent and does three lines every three hours'.[504] Certainly Wyler's instructions for the chariot race were hardly challenging:

> Director William Wylder [*sic*] had a final chat with Frank, whose turn it was to drop the silk handkerchief which would set Charlton Heston and Stephen Boyd in mortal combat – the one against the other. 'Are you sure you don't want me to do anything?' Frank asked. 'No. Just sit there and give one of your looks', said Wylder.[505]

The preparation for the moment seemed to take forever, but Frank, tucked away cosily under his canopy while the cast of thousands sweltered in the full glare of the Roman summer, found some agreeable ways to kill time. His advice to any fledgling actor setting out on a career of 'looking magnificent' was quite simple: 'Take out your brandy and the ice cubes, and keep it up your toga'.[506] Mostly, this was a strategy that served him well. But in *Ben-Hur* there was a hitch:

> With a 20 camera set-up, the race began. Frank, seated on a throne and wearing a full toga, watched as the race was building to its final dramatic moment. From behind the throne and hidden, Wylder whispered: 'Frank, stand up'. Never one to disobey his director, he leapt to his feet. From the folds of his toga tumbled sunglasses, pieces of chicken, a bottle of brandy, eye-drops, and the other necessities required to help you through a day of filming a Roman chariot race.

504 Peter Wilmoth, *Sunday Age*, 19 June 1994, p.3.
505 Roland Rocchecciol i, *Australian*, 2 January 1995, p.12.
506 Peter Wilmoth, p.3.

> 'Cut', shouted Wylder. The cameras stopped, the chariots ground to a halt, and 10,000 extras stopped cheering and screaming. 'I'm so sorry' said Frank, realising he had ruined hours of preparation and cost the film thousands of dollars. 'Don't worry', said Wylder as he went to salvage the situation. 'It's only money'.[507]

William Wyler, famed for his determination to work within budget and on schedule, must surely have spoken those words through tightly clenched teeth.

Frank was generally dismissive of his work for film. He was of most things, of course, but there was a marked contrast in the ways he spoke of the screen roles that had made him moderately famous and the stage roles that made him genuinely proud. The film roles were about little more than fancy-dress:

> 'All the roles are the same. They wanted me to make a film in Madrid very quickly. I flew over but I learnt the wrong script'. What happened then? 'Well, it didn't matter. Just changed the toga and put on another feather emerald'.[508]

Film, for Frank, was always a little absurd. He was continually dazzled by its technological wizardry and presumption, and continually delighted by the tendency for things to go spectacularly wrong:

> Of course, films, particularly the films with which I have been associated, are veritable hatcheries of disaster.[509]

There were moments, like the one in *Ben-Hur*, when Frank's tendency to play the bull in the china shop contributed quite directly to the hatching of another disaster. Mostly, though, it was a matter of perspective, in which the normal complications of making a movie were refracted through an acute sense of human foolishness:

> You can't be filming in a pit full of wolves in Munich at five o'clock in the morning with Ernest Borgnine, Tony Curtis, Janet Leigh and Kirk Douglas, without getting a giggle somewhere during the day.[510]

---

507 Roland Rocchecciol, *Australian*, 2 January 1995, p.12.
508 Peter Wilmoth, *Sunday Age*, 19 June 1994, p.3.
509 Thring and Rocchecciolli, *The Actor Who Laughed*, Melbourne, Hutchinson, 1985.
510 John Larkin, 'Frank fades into black', *Sunday Press*, 3 July 1988, p.9.

Frank's world view, shockingly cynical in public, profoundly ironic in private, ensured that any film that he was part of would be framed as comic-grotesque. He shared with one of his cultural heroes, Oscar Wilde, the conviction that life was far too important to be taken seriously.

The Vikings and *Ben Hur* made Frank something of a celebrity; not quite as much, perhaps, as he liked to think, but his return to Melbourne in 1959 certainly made more of a splash than his previous homecomings:

> I mean, nobody ever took me … everybody said, yes, he's a marvellous actor, but nobody ever took me seriously until they saw me in *The Vikings* and *Ben Hur* and they said My God he's with Tony Curtis. And Janet Leigh. And Kirk Douglas. And Charlton Heston. There's a star line up for you. And they couldn't give a stuff about me appearing at Stratford on Avon with the Royal Shakespearean [sic] Company with Larry Olivier and Vivien and Quayle and the greatest actors in the theatre. They didn't know about any of that. But the minute they saw me in their Hoyts suburban theatre throwing Tony Curtis into a wolf-pit, they thought My God he must be good. Working with those sparkling people.[511]

This time Frank's return was, literally, a flying visit. He had two commitments to meet with the Union Theatre Repertory Company before heading back to Spain to wear a new toga in *King of Kings*.

His motives for coming back weren't clear at the time. Retrospectively, he would put it down to his hatred of globe-trotting, and his weariness of living in a succession of hotels even when they were luxurious ones. Joan put it down to the fact that he was at heart a 'homebody', and the desire to be a big fish that kept him from swimming in the international pools in which he might look quite small. This time, though, he was contracted to go back to a very large pond in Spain. The trip was rushed enough to compel him to book one of the Qantas flights from Europe that were terrifying enough to think about, let alone to take. And there were no

511 Bill Howie interview, 12 November 1989.

obvious claims of a personal nature to bring him back. Since he set off with *Salome* in early 1954, Frank had spent four years and nine months abroad, and only seven months at home. Many of the important friends and contacts from his youth had, in one way or another, moved on; quite a few were in the hemisphere from which he was flying away. The problem with being 'between engagements' was that it was such a stark reminder of his solitariness. The return to Rylands was in part an escape from that awareness. Frank had seven months to kill, and he had nowhere else to kill them.

Of course, there were the projects with John Sumner and the Union Theatre, though they seemed more a consequence of the decision to come home than a cause. The coolness with John Sumner had eased in April 1957, when they caught up in London. Frank, in the aftermath of the debacle of his divorce, expressed an interest in being part of Sumner's company, which despite its unpromising beginning had proved surprisingly vigorous and durable; it was a handy straw to clutch at. The company's success was confirmed by the project that brought Sumner to London, the tour of Ray Lawler's *Summer of the Seventeenth Doll* under the auspices of Olivier's National Theatre. The play had already been through its English provincial running-in, opening in Nottingham at the end of March. Olivier, who was prevented from attending the British premiere by gout and the need to cram for his role as Archie Rice in *The Entertainer*, was represented by Vivien Leigh; she was accompanied by Joan Thring. Frank, who had nothing particularly to occupy him at the time, might in other circumstances have been there himself, but elected prudently not to attend. Soon after, Frank had found himself caught up in the *Titus* tour, and then four films in rapid succession. But when the gap in his calendar as a tyrant extraordinaire became apparent, he wrote to Sumner offering his services if something suitable was going, and something was.

One was the role of Sergius, the dashing cavalry officer in Shaw's *Arms and the Man*. Playing a procession of vicious sensualists was hardly the perfect preparation, but at least Sergius offered Frank the stimulus of something completely different. The production also gave him the chance to work again with actors like Dorothy Bradley, Moira Carleton and Frank Gatliff, who had been among the pillars of the Arrow. However, while Frank's recent adventures in film did indeed incline some reviewers to think 'My God, he must be good', there was a sceptical counter-tendency to find his performance mannered and overblown. The Shaw season was not the triumphant homecoming for Frank that he and Sumner had in mind.

But the next production, *Moby Dick – Rehearsed*, was everything they could have hoped for, and perhaps a little more. Frank was, for once, the instigator, having seen Orson Welles' play (featuring its author, of course) at the Duke of York in London, and having then left the script that he had procured from Welles with Sumner at that critical London meeting in 1957.

> When I read it I thought it was highly experimental and needed a larger cast than we could afford, but since the whole season was looking hopeful and we needed variety and a good part for Frank, I put it into the repertoire for a risky three weeks.[512]

It was a brave venture by Sumner, who had cut his theatrical teeth in the box-set interiors of English repertory theatre, and who was all too aware that his company was just one conspicuous failure away from oblivion. But the determinedly anti-naturalistic aesthetic of Welles' play proved to be just what the company needed to defy its image as a cautiously provincial theatre, not strikingly dissimilar in its repertoire from the amateur fare at the Little Theatre or the Arrow. The sense of risk was part of the play's dramatic appeal, and it was evident everywhere – in the sophisticated way the script played with the notions of rehearsal, performance and actuality, in the meta-theatricality of design and playing style, and in the emblematic use of elements of the *Pequod* to build a range of distinctive spaces. The self-conscious performativity of the production allowed a performer like Frank (as it had a performer like Welles) to play a little with his stage persona, and to elide Ahab's own egocentricity with the egotism of the actor. Frank's apparent inability to act normality became a significant asset when it came to playing the pathology of obsession.

It helped that the cast was terrific. In addition to Lewis Fiander and the Arrow alumni Dorothy Bradley and Frank Gatliff, who had appeared with Frank in *Arms and the Man*, there were actors of the calibre of Fred Parslow, George Ogilvie and Robin Ramsay, all of whom would share a dressing-room with him frequently over the next twenty-five years. And there was Mary Hardy as Pip, the mad boy, who became one of Frank's more indefatigable drinking-mates as well as a brilliant and dangerous comic presence on Melbourne television.

---

512 John Sumner, *Recollections at Play. A Life in the Australian Theatre*, Melbourne University Press, 1993, p.100.

Moby Dick – Rehearsed was a triumph for the UTRC. It featured among its 'top five' productions in a celebratory retrospective eight years later, and was always in contention when Frank was asked to name the play that had given him the most satisfaction. Ahab was the role he nominated in that tired-and-emotional radio conversation with Philip Brady and Bruce Mansfield when asked to name his favourite role:

> On film, nothing really … They were all so peculiar. But on stage I would say … Captain Ahab in Orson Welles's stage play based on *Moby Dick*.[513]

His answer to that question wasn't always the same. In a taped interview with Barbara Moore three years earlier, he selected the part of the father in Pinter's *The Homecoming*, which he found 'highly satisfactory, because I was on stage for about three minutes before the audience knew who I was'; that was a role in which 'One had to divest oneself of every mannerism'.[514]

Playing Ahab and the Cockney father had two things in common. One was that they compelled him actually to act. His best roles, he said, were

> … the ones that are furthest away from what the popular image of Frank Thring is. I mean we can all come down a forty foot staircase covered in gold togas and do all that, you know, it's neither here nor there … [515]

The other was that they were with the major company in the city that was home to him, and that they were directed by John Sumner. Sumner's relationship with Frank had started on the wrong foot, and over the next twenty-five years developed many of the qualities of a long-running soap opera. There was a good deal of mutual affection and respect, but there was also a generous dash of shared irritation, incomprehension and ironic resignation. The two men could hardly have been more different: Frank huge, histrionic and gay, Sumner none of those things, with an approach to the business of making theatre that was almost ascetic.

> I like a strong and very hard director. That's why Sumner and I got on so well together, because he's a ruthless son of a bitch and so am I. We

513 Brady and Mansfield interview, 1992.
514 Audiotape interview with Barbara Moore, no date recorded, 1989.
515 ibid.

> also happen to be the best of friends. I'd be in the middle of 'Galileo' or Ahab in 'Moby Dick' or whatever it might be, and Sumner would just say: 'Frank, we've seen that, think of something different'.
>
> I'd say, 'you bastard', and go away and think of something different and do it. Then we'd look at each other across the room, and nod. If you don't have a very firm director you simply rely on the old tricks that made you a success in the first place.[516]

Fred Parslow recalled an instance of the process of discovering 'something different' from the early rehearsals for *Moby Dick*:

> Frank was up on the bridge monumental with his cane, glowering out to sea. Sumner mused, 'So what are we going to do with you, Frank?'
>
> Frank looked pensive for a moment, then flung his arms out in a pose that might have been exultation or crucifixion, and offered, 'Well, I suppose I could do this'. Sumner looked at him and said quietly, 'I don't think so, Frank'.[517]

It all sounds like a remarkably gentle instance of 'hardness' in a director, and not a particularly rigorous approach to the reconstruction of a role. But what Frank seemed to relish were the adversarial rites of his relationship with Sumner, partly because, as he readily acknowledged, 'he [Sumner] has drawn from me, as with forceps, the best performances I have ever given',[518] partly because the style ensured that rehearsals were never too boring. Their interaction enlivened the process for the other actors in the room, too:

> During *Cherry Orchard*, Sumner called a break while he went to get his characteristic water and digestive biscuit; Frank wandered into the coffee room, holding a fresh goblet of Ben Ean, and intoned 'Where's the sadistic shit gone to now?' Sumner, immediately behind him, said 'Looking for me, Frank?' 'Ah, there you are, darling', replied Frank.[519]

---

516 Mike Daly, *Age*, 13 December 1988, p.13.
517 Fred Parslow interview, 16 November 2004.
518 Frank Thring, 'Preface' to Geoffrey Hutton, *It Won't Last a Week*, p.ix.
519 Fred Parslow interview, 16 November 2004.

A remark that might have spelt the end of another kind of working relationship became just another whimsical reaffirmation of this one.

Frank's fullest statement of his feelings about Sumner came in the 'Preface' that he wrote to the history of the company's first twenty-five years:

> It hasn't all been sweetness and light. The physical circumstances, plus Sumner's refusal to acknowledge them, have often reduced me to fainting, crying, and on spectacular occasions, haemorrhaging. The dreadful thing is that no matter what you do, Sumner always manages to look worse.
>
> The parchment skin stretches across the cheekbones in a whiter shade of pale, the skeletal hand covered with virile hairs that Alan Hopgood once compared with a lavatory brush either slaps the forehead or caresses the ulcer. Occasionally there are sharp intakes of breath that suggest that oxygen may be needed to sustain him through the torture of your performance. Sandwiches, biscuits and chocolates have to be fed to him regularly to keep death at bay ... it is always a wise ploy to appear more ill than your actors ... I would willingly give him caviare at hourly intervals so long as he keeps producing results ... and, as you may have gathered ... I don't even like the man.[520]

Sumner, who had found Frank 'preposterous' at their first meeting at the Arrow, never really changed that opinion; but, as they somehow bluffed and badgered their way through more than twenty productions together, it was a word that he used with increasing indulgence and warmth.

Moby Dick – Rehearsed received excellent notices in Melbourne,[521] and, on the strength of those reviews and the presence in its cast of a self-styled Hollywood star, was toured to Sydney's Independent Theatre for a three-week season in March of the following year. The critics liked it there, too, though Elizabeth Riddell (under the predictable headline 'MOBY DICK'S A WHALE OF PLAY') wished that the rest of the cast could match Frank Thring's capacity to 'make himself understood when he is bawling to make the eardrums throb, or whispering like a summer breeze',[522] and

---

520 Thring, 'Preface'.

521 Hutton, in *It Won't Last a Week*, recalled the accuracy of his prophecy in the *Age* that it would prove 'one of the most exciting evenings in the theatre that we shall see for a long time', p.45.

522 Elizabeth Riddell, 'Moby Dick a Whale of Play', *Daily Telegraph*, 10 March 1960, p.7.

L.B. in the *Sydney Morning Herald* discerned a straining for effect in all the performances, and especially the lead:

> If he seemed rather more of a conventional tyrant than of a stranger dreadfully tyrannised by impulses within himself, it was nevertheless a portrait for a very large frame. He boomed monumentally; the moments of quiet tenderness, as when the cabin boy goes mad, found him curiously unable to excite much sympathy.[523]

Aella and Pilate, and the role of Herod which Frank was contracted soon to play in Nicholas Ray's film *King of Kings*, may have infiltrated his Captain Ahab; or perhaps it was another instance of the triumph of surface over substance, and the difficulty of suppressing the idiosyncrasies of a massive presence. Given Frank's tendency to grow weary of even the finest roles, it was predictable that the sense of discovery in Melbourne would give way to the habits of recapitulation in Sydney.

It was a gamble to take the play interstate, especially to Sydney where there was traditionally coolness about incursions from Melbourne, if not reflex prejudice. Sumner's cautious scepticism extended to the potential reaction to his flamboyant leading actor:

> I note your remark about the whale for advertising in the absence of company members. I am in your hands about this but do you think Frank Thring would be any drawing power in Sydney. If you feel he will bring anything into the box office, do bill him by all means, but we have not been billing anyone down here as a matter of policy within the Company.
>
> In Sydney it couldn't matter less, but I suggest we only bill people on what could be their merits as box office draws as the other way it gives them swollen heads![524]

Sumner's remarks reflect not just company policy but a sense that his Ahab might be a bit too prone to believe his own publicity. Frank certainly had a well-developed sense of his own importance. He was, as he expected to be,

523 L.B., 'Moby Dick Opens At Elizabethan', *Sydney Morning Herald*, 10 March 1960, p.8.
524 Letter from John Sumner to Robin Lovejoy at the Australian Elizabethan Theatre Trust, 19 February 1960, held in the UTRC Papers, University of Melbourne Archives.

the most highly paid actor in the company: he was on fifty pounds a week for the Sydney tour; Fiander and Gatliff received forty, while Marion Edward and Lyndell Rowe, who doubled as bit-players and assistant stage-managers, were paid sixteen pounds and fifteen shillings.[525] He could have asked for more. Sumner acknowledged with appreciation that Frank had never driven a hard bargain when salaries were discussed. But while he was generously disposed to the Union Rep, Frank's position was probably just as much the product of an upbringing that had taught him to be indifferent to tedious things like a weekly wage, and of a touch of *noblesse oblige*: as the company's biggest name, it behoved him to be kind.

The Hollywood films had transformed Frank from a larger-than-life character into a celebrity. It was a role that seemed to fit him superbly, and not only in his own country, where the badge of success overseas was so irrationally prized. Making expensive movies in glamorous places gave Frank plenty of chances to play the life of the star away from home; and, since behaving like a celebrity is half-way to becoming one, he performed it with some distinction in the capitals of Europe as well.

Diane Cilento, the Australian actress, experienced the full glare of Frank's celebrity presence when she was recuperating from tuberculosis in a hospital in the Vatican, watched over by a vigilant band of nuns. Frank lifted her spirits enormously, and permanently destroyed her reputation in Rome, when he swept in to visit, 'clad in a floor-length cape of purple velvet edged in ermine', and bearing several bottles of Louis Roederer champagne:

> When asked his name, he replied in Italian, hampered by an undershot jaw and a blatant Australian accent.
>
> "Io sono Ponzio Pilato," he rasped darkly … "I've come to see la Principessa Cilento!"[526]

525 Company Salaries Schedule, UTRC Papers.
526 Diane Cilento, *My Nine Lives*, Viking, Camberwell, 2006, p.149.

He had recently finished playing Pilate, of course, so it wasn't exactly a lie. What the nuns made of the invader is impossible to imagine. Even in the Vatican, it is unlikely that they'd been exposed to so much purple and presumption.

Eventually, audacity triumphed; Frank gained entry to the patient, and managed to slam the door on her guards:

> We could still hear the nuns whispering outside. After embracing me for real, Frank continued to make lewd kissing noises into the air, giving me a huge wink.
>
> "Mmmmmmmm ... Yes, darling, yes, I love it! Do it again. Ooooh ... lovely, sweetheart. Oh, oooooooh, yes, that's sooooo good," he began to pant. "Oh, please keep doing it, darling. Ugh! Ugh! Ugh! I think I'm coming! I am! YES! Agh ... agh ... *Ahhhhhh*! *Mmmmmmmmm*. That was so good."
>
> It did not help matters that I could not stop laughing helplessly at his wicked performance. I knew all the nuns standing on the other side of the door were beyond outrage at the imagined scenes of debauchery taking place within. Frank couldn't resist jerking the door open. He offered champagne to the flustered nuns, who fell into the room, but neither of us was surprised when they scuttled out, shaking their heads and muttering invocations. One or two even crossed themselves.[527]

It was quintessential Frank: a virtuoso combination of style and cheek, laced with sexual suggestion, and prompted by a generously comic impulse. It was one way to pass the time when one was at a loose end in Europe.

What that life was like, or seemed like, and what it might have cost in personal terms, is indicated more fully in a reminiscence of a few days with Frank that Robin Hardiman, who had worked briefly behind the scenes at the Union Theatre, sent to John Sumner.[528] To what extent it is a faithful record, to what extent an exaggeration, to what extent a fantasy, is not clear. Not all the terrible tales of Frank were told by the man himself, and people with large personas tend to inspire tall stories in others.

527 ibid.

528 Robin Hardiman, 'The Filmstar's Farewell', unpublished MS loaned to the author by John Sumner. Sumner notes in pencil that 'Hardiman is either writing his memoirs or a boom or a dream'.

Frank left Australia for the filming of *King of Kings* immediately after the end of the Sydney season of *Moby Dick – Rehearsed*, and this time he was able to travel to Europe by sea. He sailed for Rome on the maiden voyage of the Triestino liner *Guglielmo Marconi*, and ran into Hardiman (who had travelled, as befitted an assistant stage manager, second-class) in the Customs Hall at Naples. He took Hardiman literally under one arm and swept him past the tiresome officials; queuing was, for Frank, as much of a thing of the past as embarrassments over Eidy.

The first thing that struck Hardiman was Frank's confidence with the Italian language, which seemed quite unencumbered by any knowledge of it at all:

> Frank claimed to speak Italian but even with the little I knew I was aware of infinite invention. To my astonishment Italians seemed to love this massacre of their tongue. Frank's extravagance of gesture, dress and speech exerted a magnetic power. Being in his company was to have a front row seat in the commedia dell'arte of the streets.

Frank would no doubt have been keen to claim that, in one way or in another, he had never had much trouble picking up a little Italian.

The second of the discoveries was Frank's prodigious capacity for alcohol. They ordered cognacs while waiting for the arrival of the morning train to Rome, and few of the twenty-four hours that they shared when they got there passed without some very conspicuous consumption.

And the third of Hardiman's realisations about his new film-star friend concerned Frank's talent for behaving badly with style. It began on the train, when Frank made the first of many pre-emptive strikes for all the available psychological space:

> We occupied window seats in a small compartment shared with two nuns and two Bersaglieri soldiers. The nuns sat next to the actor, the soldiers next to me. As the jolting journey began, Frank glared balefully and complained that he couldn't sit with his back to the direction in which he was travelling. We immediately exchanged seats. He settled himself comfortably and it seemed to me with a glint of exultation against a handsome soldier's thigh.

What followed was an extraordinary picnic shared by this ill-assorted party of six, in which the nuns supplied sardines, the soldiers knives on which to impale them, and the drinks were on Frank:

> He dabbed at his mouth with a snowy handkerchief and produced a Jensen silver hipflask, releasing heady fumes of cognac. His puckered ruby lips lingered over the tiny spout, his dancing eyes invited the handsomer of the soldiers and that blushing object of his desire moistened his lips and leaned in toward him levelly and close. Eroticism was like a weight and I took refuge from my embarrassment in the pretence of sleep.

It's some performance, even allowing for the fact that the sole testimony is that of a witness who was drunk as well as starstruck. That remains the tone of Hardiman's essay; his magnificent mentor opens a world of unimagined glamour and style to the lad on his first time out of Australia, a world in which every binge is a bacchanale and everything is understood to be exactly what it seems.

The star's story invites a different perspective, though, in which the charades and the hangovers reflect a hollow, and paradoxically quite anonymous, world of desperate diversion. Frank is predictably late for their appointment on the morning-after, but still every symptom remains a performance:

> Then Frank swept in swathed in black cashmere, huge wrap-arounds hiding his tell-tale eyes. He sank onto a seat and complained he was unwell. The hand raised to summon service wavered under its weight of silver – or alcohol induced infirmity – and he seemed to sigh with effort. He groaned and called for Fernet Branca for both of us. I had never heard this brand-name before but I could smell the terrible concoction as it was decanted into glasses. He advised me to hold my breath and throw it down. The effect was immediate and qualified as magical. Hey presto! Headache gone. Next, two enormous Bloody Marys were set before us, breakfast, and Frank invited me to come to lunch.

Frank's spirits revive even more dramatically with a dose of that other staple diet of the celebrity, recognition.

> A contralto chime from the fashion plate seated at the bar attracted Frank's attention and he stared disdainfully. He seemed to forget what he was saying, he massaged his temples and said his headache was back again. Suddenly the woman in black shrieked FRANK! and he raised

> his imperious head, all signs of lassitude gone. To say that he stood scarcely conveys the majesty of his levitation. Arms extended in a kingly gesture, he took her hands and kissed her palms, murmuring to himself in disbelief. He breathed her name in one of those stage whispers heard by the proverbial deaf man in the back row of the gods.

The name Frank breathed was Marie Collier, the renowned Australian opera singer. To the committed celebrity, all recognition is sweet; but celebrity-recognition must be the sweetest of all.

After goblets of Krug champagne and more restorative draughts of the lethal forty-five per cent proof Fernet Branca they set out for a villa once owned by the Emperor Hadrian, at which Frank had arranged lunch. The villa took hours to find, but then turned out to be deserted, and comprehensively locked and barred. They returned to Rome unfed, drank some more, and Frank announced that he was leaving next morning for Spain. Hardiman was shocked:

> I was beginning to like his stars and bars and limousines. With this departure it would be goodbye to highlife and I wanted to protest.

But there was one more night of 'highlife' to be had, and it seems to have been lavishly had, even if the details were a little hazy in the morning:

> I tried to recall the names of the bars we had visited the previous night. Harry's and The Pipistrello, Doney's and the Café de Paris, and not a celebrity (save Frank) in any of them. One celebrity does not a summer make. Nor does it make a party. We had gone in search of the legendary Bricktop's but she was no longer in business or she was no longer in Rome or she was dead or she had gone to Paris – Frank said he could not distinguish between them. People knew Frank wherever we went, at least, they treated him as if they did.

To Hardiman, even the fact that the stars weren't out couldn't dim the brilliance of the filmstar's farewell. To a different observer, that evening, and the days before it, might sound like a nightmare. Take away the persona, and Rome with Frank had all the charm of a pub-crawl, with over-priced drinks and without any friends. Which of those perspectives was closest to Frank's own? There were times, it seems, when he lapped it all up; at other times, he ran away from it, back inside the black walls of Rylands. Frank took life as a sideshow. If it moved between the Giggle Palace and the Chamber of Horrors, that probably represented for him all the fun of the fair.

What is striking about Hardiman's version of this Rake's Progress, apart from the endless drinking and play-acting that struck him, is the loneliness. Frank seems to know everyone, and to be known everywhere; at least, in that world, that's what they all pretend. But the points of contact are all random and external. Friendship in the celebrity scene looks like a set of gestures, about as solid and dependable as a vague invitation to lunch at the Emperor's villa. Love, though it is protested far too much, seems very hard to feel and to find.

It suited Frank's personality, in some ways, to live like this. A childhood in which he was required to become a pint-sized replacement for his father, an adolescence in which he was forbidden to acknowledge the nature of his interests in sex, a young adulthood in which he tried humiliatingly to imitate a husband – all the ways in which Frank played at manhood prepared him well for a life in which he was so recognisable that he didn't need to be known.

Presumably it simplified some things about his relationships with other men, as well. The no-questions-asked, no-undertakings-given kind of affair had always had certain advantages, back in Melbourne under Olive's eagle eye, and even in London, where Joan had to be taken into account. Fleeting relationships could even feel like romances when they had the frisson of a secret society; institutions like theatre foyers, or the bar at the Hotel Australia, or the meetings of the Bread and Cheese Club, provided both opportunities and a kind of security. But Frank as a free agent, travelling alone with fame, wealth, charisma and a completely careless attitude to life, was much more able to pursue sex wherever he could find it.

How much he played his distinctive version of the stereotypical Gay Divorcee is anyone's guess. Frank's own testimony is worthless. He either refused to talk about such matters at all, or talked about them in such lurid and anatomically inconceivable terms that no-one could believe a word. Peter Cooke, who knew Frank well in the late 1960s, could only hazard a guess as to how active he was in this respect:

> He had protégés – not all of them were sexual relationships (even to the degree that Bill Clinton might recognise one), and actually not all his protégés were male, though the ones he liked to take home always

> were. But they were seductive and romantic forms of patronage ... He was probably – for a lot of those years – celibate.[529]

Cooke, who was one of those proteges, thought the stories were 'all rubbish'. John McCallum was inclined to agree; though Frank 'played it [his homosexuality] to the hilt ... I suspect very little went on – it was more talk and fun'. Googie Withers, similarly without first-hand knowledge to draw on, assumed that 'It must have been sailors and people like that'.[530]

In the period of the Hollywood epics, before Frank grew into the role of Grand Old Man of the theatre and began accumulating his proteges, things may have been different. Certainly Frank claimed a number of fleeting conquests, including the star of *King of Kings*, Jeffrey Hunter. But since the latter revelation was made in the context of one of Frank's more scintillating moments of outrageousness, there is a strong argument for suspending belief:

> Fuck, he was a terrible Christ. But Christ, he was a wonderful fuck![531]

Frank's pleasure in playing with words and in scandalising people was such that, had the event in question not occurred, he would certainly have had to invent it.

Speculations of the did-he-or-didn't-he variety have their modest if spurious value of feeding gossip; but their real significance here is in the way all answers corroborate Frank's solitariness, at the height of his fame as at all other times. A life in which all relationships are transitory and the self is continually with-held suited Frank's psychological predisposition, but it left him with little room to grow or to find the love that, though he would never admit to anything so unfashionably sentimental, he clearly wanted very much.

King of Kings put Frank back in Herod's robes, with another seductress trying to engage him with her dance as June Brunel had done six years before. This

529 Peter Cooke, interview with the author, 24 August 2004.
530 Googie Withers and John McCallum interview, 25 August 2004.
531 This has been relayed with relish by a number of people, but Michael Carman is the most reliable source.

time his Salome failed spectacularly to impress her Herod; when Frank talked about the film, the 'frightening 15-year-old from Chicago, who fortunately has faded from public view', was his major preoccupation, alongside of course the pleasures of bedding the actor playing Jesus. Characteristically, the absurdities of *King of Kings* and the disasters encountered in making it seemed much more interesting to Frank than the critical virtues, and this time he got the balance about right.

The 'frightening 15-year-old from Chicago' was Brigid Bazlen, making her first feature film after achieving great success as the star of the children's television hit, *The Blue Fairy*, and the aptly named teenage soap-opera *Too Young to Go Steady*. Suddenly, she found herself in *King of Kings*, trying to attract the sexual attentions of Frank Thring. No wonder she 'faded from public view'. Bazlen's dance was generally panned by the film's earliest critics. Some disliked it because she did not use the traditional Seven Veils at all, others because they found it too sexually explicit; Salome's dance was cut from the first television showings of the film, and MGM decided not to renew her contract because of it.[532]

Brigid Bazlen was at the centre of Frank's favourite disaster-story from *King of Kings*:

> In the course of this marathon, it was decided that she would pull a golden chain that released 500 budgerigars (yes, budgerigars). These tortured creatures were then to flutter about, filling the throne-room and perching on the scantily clad Salome.
>
> Like all Hollywood fantasies, the sequences took days to rehearse. The flaming torches smoked too much, actors fainted with the heat (a thousand extras on a closed set in Madrid in mid-summer), the orchestra couldn't play the barbaric instruments, slaves refused to have their heads shaved and dropped goblets of red wine over $10,000 costumes – in a word, or four, the same old thing.
>
> Eventually we got to the magic moment when Miss Chicago released the budgerigars. As she pulled the chain, a great golden globe was supposed to split apart. It did. And not one budgerigar out of 500 moved a feather.

532 These days, Bazlen (who died young, just two years after Frank's comment about her fading from view) is something of a critical *cause celebre*; her choice about the veils is mostly seen as brave and intelligent, and the sexiness of the dance is regarded as a virtue, not a vice.

> Some days and many conferences later, it was decided to put a hose into their ridiculous globe-shaped container, and, at the moment that Salome pulled the chain, a rocket-like blast of compressed air was to be let loose, literally flushing the poor things out.
>
> It worked like a dream. This incredible blast of cold, compressed air blowing up their little budgerigar bums shot them straight up to the ceiling where, for all we know, they may still be. Certainly they were never seen again. And neither, I am delighted to say, was the Chicago Salome.[533]

There were smaller disasters that survived the final cut; people who love watching movies just to catch the bloopers were thrilled to spot the flapping of the rubber tips of the Romans' spears, and the string attached to the lance thrown at the Jews in the battle sequence.

The initial response from reviewers was less than kind. *Time* magazine proclaimed *King of Kings*

> … incontestably the corniest, phoniest, ickiest and most monstrously vulgar of all the big Bible stories Hollywood has told in the last decade … Christianity, which has survived the Turkish onslaught and the Communist conspiracy, may even survive this picture; but individual Christians who try to sit through it may find themselves longing for extreme unction.[534]

While more recent critics have found some reasons to rehabilitate the reputation of the film – notably, and with exquisite irony, in the sexual edginess of the relationship between Herod and Salome – quite a lot of it seems beyond redemption. Some of this is a product of conflicting agendas: its director Nicholas Ray wanted to make a film about the psychological aspects of the Christ-story, its writer Philip Yordan was fascinated by the complexity of its political context, and its producer Samuel Bronston would have been delighted to have released an epic blockbuster. To the extent that Ray and Yordan were able to shoot the film that they were after, its dismissal is a little unfair.

533 Thring and Rocchecciolli, *The Actor Who Laughed*, Melbourne, Hutchinson, 1985, pp.39–40.

534 Quoted in Harry and Michael Medved, *The Golden Turkey Awards*, p.97.

Partly the problem lies with the Christ-story itself, a plot that is too well known and touches too many points of cultural sensitivity to offer new revelations; partly it's the tendency of that story to encourage treatments that are dutiful rather than dramatic, and to present its central character as a goody-two-shoes whose motives and choices are all pre-ordained. In *King of Kings*, the problems implicit in playing Jesus Christ are exacerbated by the way Jeffrey Hunter approaches the role.

Hunter brought to it good looks and a substantial slice of the teenybopper market. But the good looks were a touch sophomoric, as well as a bit too blond and blue-eyed for traditional tastes, and in combination with Hunter's following encouraged some mischief-makers in the industry to give *King of Kings* an alternative title, 'I Was a Teenage Jesus', from which it could never fully recover. Then either Hunter or Ray or both decided that, to make gentle Jesus suitably meek and mild, he should speak always in a very little voice. To convey the intensity in his soul, all that was needed was a stare from those pretty, vacant eyes; the deeper the passion, the longer the stare. These were not happy choices.

The cheerfully malicious Medved Brothers had enormous fun at Hunter's expense in nominating him for their Golden Turkey for Worst Performance as Jesus Christ:

> When asked by interviewers how he got the part, Hunter fumbled pathetically for convincing answers. He told Louella Parsons: 'Christ was a carpenter and thirty-three years old and I am thirty-three, and I suppose my physical measurements fitted the description in the New Testament'. Had Hunter discovered a little-known passage in the Gospels lost to the rest of the world all these years?[535]

The fact that Hunter renewed his blond rinse for the film, and shaved his armpits to ensure a smooth Crucifixion, made that hypothesis even less likely. Moreover, Hunter had actually turned thirty-five by the time the shooting started. The one actor in the company who was aged thirty-three was Frank Thring, but nobody seemed in a hurry to cast him as the Messiah.

---

535 Harry and Michael Medved, p.96.

Frank's preference, as soon as the last rites of filming *King of Kings* were decently done, would have been to sedate himself on another plane back to Melbourne. This, after all, was the rhythm of life he had already announced as his own, on the basis of a single year in which it had almost happened – a film in the northern summer, followed by a couple of plays at home. It was the life of the busy expatriate, rich and important enough to never have to live through a winter. But his schedule didn't allow it in 1960, as the 'hatcheries of disasters' on *King of Kings* delayed its completion, and the contractual demands of *El Cid* ruled out a return home – as it did, fortuitously, any notion of hanging around with old chums in London. His schedule, or his temperament, never allowed room for that conveniently structured commuting again.

So Frank did his loitering in Spain in 1960, living the life of the celebrity nomad in one luxurious hotel after another. If one had to loiter somewhere, there were certainly worse places to do it in. But as the Spanish summer of *Kings of Kings* gave way to the Spanish autumn and winter of *El Cid*, Frank gave every sign of someone who had already had too much of a good thing.

As Frank would always have enthusiastically agreed, the problem with the life he was leading was its lack of roots – although the film set provided an instant community for the itinerant actor that, if one didn't look too closely, could feel like a kind of home. The company for *El Cid* included a number of people with whom Frank had spent several months on location, and in the world in which he now found himself that almost qualified as a family reunion. Most conspicuously, of course, there was Charlton Heston from the cast of *Ben-Hur*, as another strong, decent and eponymous hero. Miklos Rozsa, who had composed the soundtrack for *Ben-Hur*, was also responsible for the music of *El Cid*. The fact that several of the locations in Spain, and even some of the horses and props had been used in both *Ben-Hur* and *King of Kings* must have made Frank feel, as he slipped into another fetching set of robes, that he had never really been away. There were faces familiar from *King of Kings*, too; Hurd Hatfield, who had played Pilate just a couple of weeks before, was now Arias, while Sam Bronston and Philip Yordan as producer and writer merely transferred their tussle for power to another stage. The most improbable of all Frank's reunions was that with Andrew Cruickshank from the ill-fated *A Question of Adultery*, who was to lend his broad Scots brogue to the Spanish nobleman Count Gormaz.

Sophia Loren's contract for *El Cid* placed on it two significant constraints: the first was that her scenes should be shot in a block at the beginning of the process, the second that her character Jimena, though aging more than twenty years in the plot, should have neither a single line on her face nor a single grey hair on her head to show it. The consequence of the latter was, of course, a mighty blow to the film's credibility; the former meant for the rest of the cast a protracted phase of pre-production, which in Frank's lexicon was just another word for loitering.

The hanging-about was interrupted by a disconcerting incident in which Frank seems to have stabbed somebody with the dagger that he always carried in his not-so-little black bag. The victim was a thief who attacked him in a back street, and Roland Rocchecciolі, to whom Frank told the story, was convinced that that much of it was true. Whether Frank's development of it had any basis in fact is rather less certain; when asked what happened to the man, Frank replied:

> "He died, of course. They had to smuggle me out of Spain – disguised as Sophia Loren!"[536]

The details of this great escape, as in most of Frank's taller tales, are suspiciously vague.

Heston's character, the Castilian knight Roderigo Diaz – the Cid himself – was in his scrupulousness a suitably unbelievable mate for his eternally youthful wife. Diaz single-handedly brings his divided country back from the brink of civil war to repel its Moorish invaders, without ever striking an unfair blow. This feat is often a challenge to his cleverness, but his virtue is never threatened; there is no place for the kind of psychological or moral tension that might make for dramatic interest:

> Heston and Loren make a handsome couple, but their performances are wooden. The plot is high melodrama with few surprises. Diaz is the hero, and he does all the things expected from a knight 'with God on [his] side'. *El Cid* turns more often to the ridiculous than the sublime. Perhaps if the movie didn't take itself so seriously, there wouldn't be opportunities for unintentional laughter, but, from the bombastic dialogue to the stentorian score, *El Cid* is about as self-important as a motion picture can be.[537]

---

536 Roland Rocchecciolі, interview with the author, 21 March 2010.

537 James Berardinelli, on-line review of *El Cid,* 1993, at www.reelviews.net/movies/e/el_cid.html.

Frank's role in *El Cid* was Al Kadir, King of Valencia, a tyrant who added a dash of Pilate's shrewdness and a touch of Aella's barbarity to Herod's lascivious cruelty. Nothing could have come to him more easily. Al Kadir's scenes were few but effective; Frank, who was being in every sense frank when he told an interviewer 'I don't play cameos. I only play big parts',[538] had no fears of being lost in a smaller role. The shooting for once ran smoothly and on time – there were no disasters to blow out the budget or to add to Frank's stock of horror stories.[539] The locations were marvellous, including eleventh century castles in Burgos, Valladolid and Valem. The product, though less successful at the box office and with the critics than his other adventures in a toga, was a thoroughly respectable Hollywood epic. In every way that could be quantified, other perhaps than the odd inconvenient stabbing, Frank's fourth blockbuster in three years was the nearest that film could come to pleasant walk in the park.

Yet he not only came home, but this time came home to stay. He never made another film for Hollywood, and spent only a few weeks of his remaining thirty or so years outside Australia. All the explanations canvassed for his previous homecomings – the sentiments that might bind him to one place, the fears and memories that might drive him from another, and those continually recycled analogies based on fish large and small – no doubt applied in this situation, as strongly as ever. But the experience of living out of suitcases in a foreign country for more than a year, playing roles that he had played before among a throng of best friends he hardly knew, must have concentrated his mind and feelings wonderfully.

When Hardiman trailed him around Rome in the spring, Frank's life looked like a cabaret, providing you didn't look too closely. But even then, it was both literally and metaphorically one long hangover.

In the winter of 1961, Frank Thring came back to Melbourne, and hardly ever went away again. He was still inclined to see the move as part of a neat ritual, in which he would spend half the year overseas adding to his

538 Brady and Mansfield interview.

539 Even the trivia-spotters, ever alert for anomalies, could only come up with the tyre-marks left by the tracking camera in front of the advancing army, and the legendary little red car in the distant background following Heston's farewell to Sophia Loren.

fame, and the other half at home, altruistically enlivening the theatre of Melbourne by his presence. But a number of other choices suggested that, for once, he wasn't just responding to circumstance, but had decided, at last or at least for the moment, the course of the rest of his life.

First, there was his re-establishment at Rylands. Since Olive's death, more than eight years before, the Thring mansion had been empty, except for a couple of occasions when the son of the house was briefly back from a foray overseas or preparing to embark on another one. Joan's mother Edith had kept an eye on the place, and Margaret the cook and Ernest the chauffeur, now apparently married, were ready and willing to swing into action whenever Frank gave them their cue, and as able as the years allowed. Rylands was frozen in time, a mausoleum like Xanadu in *Citizen Kane*. The first conspicuous sign that Frank was back to stay was his radical redecoration of the only real home he had ever known.

He had it painted black. There could hardly have been a more striking and comprehensive way of obliterating his mother's posthumous presence:

> The first thing was to get rid of all that dreadful 1920s clutter – patterned wallpapers, patterned curtains, even patterned carpets – all in autumn tonings.
>
> You can't imagine what it was like. It was one of those homes which didn't quite go as far as plaster ducks on the walls, but it did have those dreadful ebony elephants.[540]

What was 'dreadful' was not simply the taste of the previous generation, but a particular style of expensive vulgarity that for Frank was quintessential Olive. Her carpets were dyed black, her wallpapers stripped away and the walls painted black, her curtains sent off to the Salvation Army and replaced by black ones. The elephants, though they matched the new décor, were banished to a garden shed.

All that Edwardian stuffiness that had proclaimed his parents rich and respectable gave way to a calculated display of difference. Rylands was suddenly a daring piece of set design: Anthony Clarke, in an article entitled 'For Mr Thring, home is part of his stage', declared the house 'as theatrical as the man himself',[541] while a feature in *Woman's Day* noted the way the owner's 'theatrical touch' neatly integrated costume with *mise en scène*:

540 Jo Wiles, 'Black's the Thring', *Woman's Day/Woman's World*, 15 October 1980, p.124.
541 Anthony Clarke, in 'My Home and I', *Age*, 28 October 1980, p.19.

> Not surprisingly, the dominant theme is black. Thring is well-known for dressing only in the shade of mourning.[542]

Clarke noted the same complementarity in Frank's use of dramatic contrast:

> But in most cases it is not an unrelieved or overpowering black. He uses it as a backdrop for vivid splashes of colour and decoration. In the same way as he sets off his monotone clothes with chunky golden rings and pendants, he sets off his walls with richly coloured feature wallpapers, prints and paintings.[543]

The eye for striking detail was evident in the two large zebra rugs, 'complete with tails and tufted manes', that adorned the living room.[544] The flair for brilliant juxtaposition was evident in the way Frank placed his spectacular works of art, each one a cue for a quip or a story:

> Donald Friend's painting, 'Balinese Boy', has pride of place over the fireplace. Friend dedicated his latest book to Frank. Why? 'Because it's pornographic', the actor says.[545]

The delight in a startling splash of colour was on display in the dining-room, which reflected Frank's view that 'Dining rooms should be like theatres – all red plush and gilt'.[546]

It was a spectacular show. But while all its flamboyance seemed to promise an insight into the man himself, perhaps the most revealing aspect of the whole exhibition was the fact that it was so little seen. The oval table in the red and gold room was always set for six, but it was hardly ever used:

> Of course, one likes to have one's friends to come for champagne and nibbles before a show, but not for dinner. We don't have to put on the rubber gloves and get out the Palmolive then.[547]

---

542 Jo Wiles, 'Black's the Thring', *Woman's Day/Woman's World*, 15 October 1980, p.104.

543 Anthony Clarke, in 'My Home and I', *Age*, 28 October 1980, p.19.

544 ibid. Frank, to whom most things were a cue for sexual suggestiveness, couldn't resist noting that 'Those zebra rugs have come in for some hard wear in their time'. He might have been talking about walking, of course.

545 Jo Wiles, p.103.

546 ibid.

547 ibid.

In fact, the gatherings for 'nibbles' were a rarity, and increasingly so. The handsome dinner-setting was a symbol, a gesture for the sake of appearance to a world that Frank had lost and professed to despise: the world of Olive, and her phlock-papered parlour, or of Miss Cavendish in the terrace-house in Hampstead, and the 'best room' that waited for a special occasion that would never happen.

Even when Frank left the black walls of his mansion in Toorak for the white ones of his tiny cottage in Fitzroy, the dining-room remained a place that was important for reasons that had nothing to do with utility:

> But he does eventually invite me into his house, a little workingman's cottage in a narrow Fitzroy street … I follow him into his house as he moves precariously down the corridor, past the dining-room with its table set formally for six, past the many statues and ornaments and artifacts … [548]

The paradox, in both the houses that Frank designed for himself to live in, was that places so performative were at the same time so dedicated to resisting invaders. By the time he reached Fitzroy, the reclusiveness was clearly pathological; there were high wire fences, chains with padlocks, and strands of clumsily wound barbed wire. But at Rylands, too, the defences, architectural and personal, were already thoroughly in place. The lions that bared their plaster fangs at its entrance were a warning and a symptom; the things that really represented Frank's horror of violation were the multiple wrought-iron gates and the elaborate, if invisible, security system. The reporter from *Woman's Day* seemed content to see this preoccupation as understandable enough in a man whose fame and possessions might attract unwelcome visitors, but their only meeting was the one that must have been one of the most disconcerting interviews of her career. To the few people who thought they knew Frank well, the obsessive privacy of this flamboyantly public man was always something approaching psychosis, even in those years back in Melbourne in the 1960s when he was finally, it seemed, thoroughly at home.

Sometimes the sur-real decor and Frank's daemonic persona could run away with the imagination of the visitor. Helmut Bakaitis recalls a young male student who was deputed to drive Frank home coming back with a tale of Gothic nightmare: the place was dark and dank, he said, with holes

548 Peter Wilmoth, *Sunday Age*, 19 June 1994, p.3.

in the roof, perhaps literally bats in the belfry, and dead animals floating in the black pool that were redolent of *Sunset Boulevard*.[549] Nothing could be further removed from Peter Cooke's recollections of Rylands in the same period, where something was always being cleaned and there was always a heavy scent of furniture polish in the air. Everything in the house was immaculate: Frank and his 'wonderful Edith' shared a revulsion at mess of any kind.[550]

When Frank was approached by the Melbourne *Herald* for yet another promotional feature on the family mansion, in the newspaper's 'My Favourite Room' series, he nominated his kitchen. For a man whose culinary specialty, if not his only dish, was scrambled eggs, and for whom dinner mostly defaulted to Chinese take-away, it looked an unlikely and probably mischievous choice. But the bemused interviewer went away wondering whether he might, for once, have been genuine:

> The blackness of the kitchen beyond (even the fridge is black) was uninviting. But framed on a pantry were three marvellous caricatures by newspaper artists ... 'Oh, they're always doing me', he laughed.
>
> Maybe he wasn't playing games. Maybe this really was his favourite room.[551]

Where did Frank feel most 'at home'? Was it in the living-room, where he often reclined on a chaise-longue to welcome unsuspecting visitors? John Preston, a recent and good-looking NIDA graduate, made an appointment to drop off some furniture that Frank had offered to store for him at Rylands, and arrived right on time with his father, who had come to lend a hand:

> Frank was stretched out on a couch, with a fat black cat sitting on his stomach. He smiled and waved at us. 'Forgive me, darling, just take the stuff upstairs, I can't get up while I'm stroking my pussy'. My dad didn't know where to look.[552]

549 Helmut Bakaitis, conversation with the author at NIDA, 24 August 2004.

550 Peter Cooke interview, 24 August 2004.

551 Dorothy Goodwin, 'Thring's decadent décor, DAAAR-ling!', *Herald*, 28 March 1984, p.23.

552 John Preston, conversation with the author, 18 August 2005.

But this wasn't Thring surprised, of course, however much it must have seemed like it to Mr Preston senior; this was Thring prepared. So was the casually surly Thring who indulged the reporters who came to admire his house. So, of course, was the outrageously acerbic Thring who was so easily overheard in foyers and so readily remembered in anecdotes. So was the Thring who gave radio interviews, even when he had drunk enough to put most people under the table. So was the Thring who delighted and scandalised Joan Cunliffe, and the Thring who shepherded Robin Hardiman along the primrose path of celebrity excess, and the Thring who poignantly if seductively introduced a succession of attractive young men to the world of high culture. There are hardly any stories about Frank off-guard.

So, if he wasn't most at home in his lounge stroking his pussy, or in the dining-room where nobody ate, or out in the foyers where there was always an audience, where was Frank Thring most himself? Was it in the bathroom, with its cavernous black bath and its mirrors and exotic pots, which seemed designed to be, as it often was, a photo opportunity? Was it in the room where he stored his private videos, and found inspiration for the shocking tales of sexual ingenuities that he loved to tell? Was it in the bedroom, shared even less often than those other rooms, where after the Nembutal took effect he would finally get some sleep, and where he must have thought longingly of Eidy? Perhaps Dorothy from the *Herald* was right after all. Inside that pantry, behind the caricatures, were the staple supplies of Frank's daily life:

> Frank's pantry was like a supermarket, filled with great piles of all his essentials. A hundred cans of pressed chicken, fifty cans of smoked oysters, dozens of packs of Marlboro cigarettes, cartons of Ben Ean and his favourite brandy, the cheaper, non-VSOP Hennessy's. All of it neatly laid out by Edith.[553]

No doubt a decent reheated honey chicken with special fried rice could make a perfectly satisfying meal, when there was plenty of sweet white wine to wash it down, and three caricatures of Oneself glared down at one to reaffirm one's fame.

553 Peter Cooke interview.

Having remade Rylands in his own image, Frank set about establishing the social patterns and professional routines that would define his life for the next dozen years or so. There would be hardly any dinner parties at the grand table, and not too many invitations to 'champagne and nibbles' before a show, either. But there would be endless importunings to pop in for a few drinks after the show, sometimes with an eye to seduction, always in the hope of deferring the nightly horror of insomnia. And always, in this period, there would be Frank's special guests: the beautiful boys in whom he had a romantic interest that was sometimes probably requited, sometimes certainly not, but always deeply sentimental.

An invitation to go back to Frank's place was always understood to be bristling with possibilities, even when his intentions were relatively innocent. Mike McColl-Jones, a comic writer for Channel Nine during Frank's involvement with the *Noel Ferrier Show*, recalled one such evening:

> Quite often after Frank had been a guest on a show we were doing, he would invite a few of us home for a drink and his specialty at that time of the early morning … an omelette, or scrambled eggs.
>
> I vividly remember one night I was there with Colin Stevenson, Bob Phillips and Peter Smith. On the way in, Pete called me aside and said 'We're all here together … if anyone leaves, we all leave, understand? I don't want to be left alone with him'.
>
> About an hour later, Colin, Bob and I stood up and pretended to leave … Pete nearly went into cardiac arrest.[554]

But Frank was perhaps less predatory than he liked to pretend; he became accustomed, perhaps resigned, to his little overtures being mostly in vain. He was, most of the time, much more pressing about people staying to keep him company than about their joining him in his bed.

That applied to Frank's boys, as well, if that was really the way they wanted it. Paul Karo was the first of them, a young actor who appeared as John in the Melbourne Theatre Company's production of *The Man Who Came to Dinner* in March 1963. Frank was, inevitably, Sheridan Whiteside. Paul Karo remained Frank's regular companion about town until the appearance of Peter Cooke, who lived over the back fence from Rylands, and who from sometime around his eighteenth birthday saw Frank every evening, dined

554 Mike McColl-Jones, *'And Now Here's …'*, Fyshwick, Aerospace Publications, 1999, p.160

with him on most of them, and went out with him to restaurants, functions, films, plays, and the ballet.

> Frank was extraordinarily generous – though in a way very demanding, too; he'd want me to stay with him to talk when we got home, often till four in the morning. Frank was obviously an insomniac – he'd take two Nembutal every night, talk till the tablets kicked in, then sleep till eleven or twelve.
>
> It was all about sexual obsession, of course – I sort of knew that, why Frank was so interested in me, but I was also quite innocent about what that might involve. Frank made no directly sexual advances, or at least none that led anywhere – he'd often touch my arm, or my leg, but that was it.[555]

That relationship lasted for a couple of years, until Peter was sacked by the Melbourne Theatre Company from his casual production job because of 'concerns' that he was too close to Frank; he was never quite sure whose concerns they were, or who they might have been for or about. Peter Cooke went to Sydney to work at NIDA, and was replaced by Hugh Rule, another eighteen-year-old schoolboy who went on the next year to train as a stage manager with the MTC. Hugh was behind the scenes for Frank's roles as Danforth in *The Crucible* and Andrew Undershaft in *Major Barbara* in 1968, and as General Irrigua in Feydeau's *Cat Among the Pigeons*, Azdak in *The Caucasian Chalk Circle*, Robert MacDonald in Phillip Grenville Mann's *Day of Glory*, and Lafew in *All's Well That Ends Well* in 1970; he also shared the stage fleetingly with Frank in a minor role in *Major Barbara* and again in *Henry IV, Part One*, in early 1969, in which Frank played Falstaff.

Hugh Rule's introduction came, quite improbably, at a farm in Lilydale after a game at the local Polo Club. The Jaegers, who hosted the event, had invited their actor-friend Paul Karo to bring along some of his fellow theatricals:

> That first image I had of Frank still lingers: his massive frame bejewelled and dressed in black from head to toe, his voice modulated at a level easily heard 2 acres away, his entire being commanding 'look at me' as he held forth in a room full of polo-playing farmers and their families. …

555 Peter Cooke interview.

> Frank turned his attention to me, drew himself up to his full height, raised his eyebrows and boomed in front of everyone 'Mmmm.... Let's hope you're more than just a pretty face'. Teenage me blushed purple and had not the faintest idea what to say.[556]

In the following year Hugh became installed as Frank's new protégé, or latest flame:

> What proved to be disconcerting is when he invited me to go out with him somewhere .... Frank would make a display of his friendship to me and I'd get quite a few 'looks' from people. I soon realised I was looked upon as the new boy friend. Frank enjoyed this and even used it to tease me. He also took me to the theatre where I experienced the same thing, only more so. Here many people knew him; it was his world. He projected himself as a cross between Orson Welles and Lord Byron and enjoyed vocally displaying his homosexuality, I was viewed by all and sundry as the new boyfriend – why else would I be with him?[557]

For Hugh the evenings at Frank's 'ancestral throne' were like a journey through an all-black *Alice in Wonderland*:

> The meetings at his place always went in a similar fashion. I'd generally go there in the late afternoon after school. He'd serve great quantities of wine or anything else I cared to drink. He'd talk about acting, about life in the theatre, in films. He'd eventually bring the subject of sex into the conversation somehow, then he'd sit on the floor at my feet and either make a physical pass at me (putting his hand on my leg) or ask me if I'd like to go to bed with him.
>
> I always said no. I was scared and the idea of going to bed with a man didn't appeal much – I was desperate to go to bed with girls. But that wasn't proving easy ... [558]

556 Notes emailed to the author, 20 January 2006. All subsequent quotations attributed to Hugh Rule are from this source.

557 ibid.

558 ibid.

They were curious relationships, these romantic liaisons with sometimes unco-operative young men. Frank was persistent, but relatively easily rebuffed, in these situations. The fact that he pursued the connection no doubt had a lot to do with the thrill of the unfulfilled chase, but there was a great deal of affection and generosity in the mix as well. If the violation of innocence was high on the agenda, the adoration and even the nurturing of it were prominently there as well.

In 1970 Frank's favourite ingénue was in fact female: Joanna McCallum, the daughter of Googie and John, had joined the company for the Ben Travers farce *Rookery Nook*, as a very nervous newcomer:

> He took me, like many other young men and women, under his wing; he never said anything nasty to me, though that wasn't true of course for everybody. I think he just liked being around young people …[559]

It wasn't always cosy under that wing: when she asked anxiously what Frank thought of her first performance, he told her 'You were dreadful'. He thought she was 'much better' in her second season, in *Cat Among the Pigeons*, and by the time Joanna played Grusha opposite his Azdak in April 1970 they were firm friends and mischievous playmates:

> Neither of us for some reason thought much of the Storyteller, and during one of his songs John Sumner asked us both to freeze, looking at each other across the stage. In rehearsals Frank made me dissolve into giggles every time; somehow his eyes were able to say just what he was thinking. I was terribly worried that I'd break down at that moment in performances, too – but thankfully I never did, and Frank was always professional whenever there was an audience.[560]

Peter Cooke found 'a kind of sadness' in Frank's 'adoration of youth':

> It must have come from his own awful, deformed childhood. He'd been endlessly indulged, but there wasn't much sign of genuine feeling for his parents – he never spoke about Olive to me. He loved to exercise a kind of parental guidance and power. And he'd be overwhelmed –

559 Joanna McCallum, interview with the author, Chiswick, 13 December 2004.
560 ibid.

> literally moved to tears – by the success of young people, in the theatre or the Olympics, or anything; and by their tragedies ... [561]

To Hugh Rule, those feelings suggested a disjunction between the romanticised sexuality that found expression in his relationships with beautiful youths and the much less sentimental attachments that increasingly came to mark Frank's sexual behaviour:

> I think Frank was more passive sexually than his image suggests. He loved to be overt both vocally and in how he dressed. He loved to make verbal passes at young men, from pretty ones to pretty rough ones.
>
> He used to buy sex when he felt the need. Some of these adventures were definitely quite seedy and a little dangerous. He had three or four unpleasant encounters that I know of – that ended with violence and/or robbery. In general he seemed to latch onto one young man for a while then that would pass and he'd rent another...
>
> As Frank became older, it became harder to get the boyfriends this way and hence the increase in rent-boy use.[562]

The last of Frank's attractive young consorts was Stephen Oldfield, a young actor who as Sister Ines played opposite Frank's outrageous Mother Superior in Eduardo Manet's *The Nuns* (1976). It was a brief revival of the sentimental patronage that had been his primary emotional focus since coming back to Melbourne. When Oldfield went overseas at the end of that year, Frank at fifty gave up on something for good. His relationships with men – some young, some not, some fleeting, some not – were from that point periodical and commercial.

By the mid-1970s, those long nights filled with wine and flirtation had become a rarity. It was from this point especially that Peter Cooke was inclined to see Frank as 'probably – for a lot of those years – celibate', though his stories of sexual conquests became, characteristically, more and more gargantuan. Frank's fantasy world was gigantic. Just as everything in the house was big – massive portraits on the wall, huge bathroom with almost literal throne, giant goblets of creams and perfumes – so his every experience was either 'fabulously brilliant' or 'fucking appalling'. People who were fairly

561 Peter Cooke interview.
562 Hugh Rule notes.

well-off had 'Millions and Millions of Dollars', while Peter Cooke's father who held a minor clerical position with the United Nations was 'A Diplomat'. As Frank's dreams of love dried up, the myths of spectacular sex went forth and multiplied:

> The fantasies that he wove around beautiful young people were in the same territory as the fictions he told about his amazing conquests, and the piles of porn that he had stacked high up in a room at Rylands. He made do with sentimental patronage and porn, and a whole stream of tall stories about suckings and fuckings and massive cocks.[563]

Sometimes, you could get what you wanted by paying for it. But not often. Frank was now, most of the time, alone.

563 Peter Cooke interview.

TRAVELLING FROM ST KILDA TO TOORAK

Embassy taxi-cab, 22 June 1966

Nice to know the night was still young for somebody. It wasn't, sadly, for him. With Mary and her Argentinian deposited safely, more or less, at her hotel, the cab was suddenly much quieter. Just the Showgrounds trots on the radio to break the silence. The driver, a lugubrious person who'd made all too clear his disapproval of all the hilarity in the back seat, was hunched over the wheel, intent on the race – and on pretending his two remaining passengers weren't really there.

He'd been like that since he'd picked them up at Bim's. Something about the group, possibly with the initials F.T., so affronted him he didn't even ask if they followed the footy. One'd have to have a word with Embassy. Not that one gave a fuck what he thought, but a little civility wasn't too much to ask for.

Actually, Peter wasn't absolutely there, either. He'd barely stirred when Mary fell out of the car. The Child was sleeping. Amazing the effect that iced Advocaat could have on a lad, especially when he skolled it as though it was Kool-Spa. Another of life's little lessons. Peter's head lolled against the window, a lock of blond hair tumbled across that unbelievably smooth brow. It was a very beautiful child, even or especially when drunk.

It would be lovely to be young and able to write yourself off like that. To drink, perchance to sleep.

Some girl, that Mary Hardy. She could never get quite drunk enough either, but by crikey, as the lady herself might say, she gave it a fair old nudge. Drunk enough to stumble, that was no problem. Drunk enough to find it hard to stay vertical, though that was unlikely to be a priority when she got inside with her Argentinian. Drunk enough to laugh, laugh like a fucking drain. But never drunk enough to be happy. Never enough to drive the black dog away.

Had he been of another persuasion, she might've been a possibility, Mary. A possibility, as well a pal. She'd looked decidedly fetching as a cabin boy on the good ship Pequod. The bitch would've disapproved, and a spot of rolling in that capacious grave would've been an added enticement. Mary laughed and drank and presumably fucked as though there were no tomorrow. There was a lot to be said for that. But he'd tried all that ten years ago with Flowergirl, though it seemed incredible now, and never again. That was in another country, and besides the wench was in someone else's bed. As he'd been, once in a while.

Mary's Argentinian was fetching, too. Must have been especially so on court, with his pert little South American arse wrapped up in those tight little white shorts. Not much to say for himself of course, nothing one could understand at least, but that could be a tremendous advantage, as Mary no doubt found it. Nothing quite like a pretty boy with a powerful first serve – and an artful second one, apparently. A consummation devoutly etcetera. And the eyes were dark and deep and tempestuous. Or perhaps that was just a cultural difference thing. They've all got eyes that are dark and deep and tempestuous, Argentinians, and some of them surely had to be boring.

Peter's were blue, a vivid blue. Like a bright clear sky. No pain there, not much fear, none of the things he could see in his own. Forty years of shit, still waiting for something to begin.

He'd keep his word tonight, and deliver The Child safely to the bosom of his family. The paternal Cooke had briefly turned his attention from world peace to the nocturnal habits of his boy, and one didn't want to cause trouble in the kitchen. Trusting people, those Cookes.

He hadn't had to reassure them that his intentions were honourable, which was from all points of view a mightily good thing, but he had undertaken to return Peter by twelve, before he turned into a pumpkin, and he would. He hadn't promised their son would be sober, either, which was as well. Perhaps he shouldn't have let The Child become quite so prodigiously pissed, but when one was having a pleasant evening with disreputable friends it was easy to be distracted, and this in loco parentis stuff was still new.

They'd understand, surely. Better send flowers to the mother in the morning, though, just to be sure.

There'd been the yobbos, too, the ones hanging around outside Bim's. He'd heard them saying his name, and was all set to pretend to ignore them. Or perhaps an autograph, since Peter was there. Then he'd made out some of the other words, words like 'poofter' and 'pillow biter', and though he was used to this, and it no longer scared him at all, he'd been thrown. Embarrassed, actually, the thing he tried never to be. Mary heard it, and couldn't care less. Her Argentinian heard it, but in that flat ugly violent Aussie accent the words were probably so strange to his ear that they might just as well have been talking about Melbourne's weather. But Peter heard it all right, and he quickly looked at Frank and then more quickly away, his cheeks suddenly scarlet. It fucked up the evening, for a while, though no-one referred to it. That was what had distracted him, really, not the salted fish and the fun. It'd hurt him, hurt him for Peter. He'd probably downed too many glasses too quickly in consequence.

It was the one thing about coming home that he hated. Strangers didn't do that to him in London, or in Madrid or Valladolid, or in Hardonfjorden or whatever you called it. But people in Melbourne felt they had the right – they knew who he was, he was one of theirs, but he was also One of Them, and they had to let him know that he'd betrayed them, that he was Unaustralian, that he had to be punished for failing to be a true blue bloke, and that they, these pimply stupid vicious boys, were better than him. And he'd been on the telly in their pissy little Housing Commission slum, hadn't he, and that meant they could say what they liked about him. They thought they owned him, these neanderthals, because he was that poof on the seventeen-inch screen who couldn't talk back.

Thing they didn't know was, however much they despised him, he despised them more. And much more intelligently. Just like jolly old Grammar, really, only a different class of scum.

If they'd been worth bothering about, he might've asked them if they knew who he was. He couldn't, of course, because that'd be just another cue for their scintillating wit, and anyway they knew him from the ads. But what he wanted to say was, listen, I'm Frank Thring, you cretins. Frank Thring, the actor. But they didn't see his Ahab, did they, or the Pinter, and Shakespeare was a foreign language you when had a vocabulary of about ten fucking words. So they couldn't know. How could they ever know.

He wanted to say, I'm Frank Thring. The actor. Who I am, what I do. Couldn't really be or do anything else, really.

It was a lesson, though. Salutary. Sobering, one might say, though inaccurately. If he was going to stay in this town, his town, the place he'd grown up in and possibly loved, he was going to need a tougher skin. He was tough, but not yet tough enough. He hadn't reckoned on what it would mean to be known quite so well, though he'd expected to be and felt born to the role. The price of fucking fame.

Frank Thring, the actor. Some might say Australia's finest. Well, there weren't too many other contenders were there. Finch? No. Who else, then, poor old Chips? Frank Thring, the famous actor, the famous son of a famous father. And they thought they could laugh at him, and make him feel afraid. Fuck 'em. Sometimes it almost made you wonder why you dared.

Mr Lugubrious made a sound that was indecipherable. His horse had lost. Maybe there was a God after all. Well, lovey, we've got something in common after all. Welcome to Losers Anonymous. Later tonight, while Peter's sleeping the sleep of the innocent, and Mary and her new doubles partner are shouting Ole, one of us'll be out on the road trying to recoup his losses while the other has a long nightcap and spills his noble seed on a photo in 'Joyboys'. Life, as they say in the serials, Can Be Beautiful.

Clendon Road. Time to wake up, sleepyhead. Yes, you, you silly min. And for fuck's sake try to walk a straight line, and don't mention the advocaat. Or we'll both be up the proverbial gum tree, without the proverbial paddle.

Chapter Twelve

FRANKLY THRING

That was the private story, as far as it is open to inference. What the public saw on Frank's return to Melbourne was similarly definitive in the pattern it established for the next ten years or so, when he would frolic splendidly in the small pool to which he had returned.

His spectacular redecoration of the house in which he lived was accompanied by a comprehensive 'makeover' of the character he was to play. Most of the choices he made about his appearance were a bit too bizarre for the early 1960s, though rather modish a generation later. A man whose hair is thinning as rapidly as Frank's has three options: the unapologetic acceptance of the tonsure, the defensive denial of the comb-over, or the pre-emptive assertion of the shaven skull. Frank chose the third, despite or because of the vaguely sinister associations that it had in the conservative Melbourne to which he had come home. A bit of facial hair, by way of balance or compensation, has often attracted the bald; Frank went for the sculpted whiskers that he had worn as Herod and Saturninus, rather than the fuller beards favoured by others in the 1960s who decided that, when all else failed, one might as well look like an intellectual. In a society easily intimidated by departures from the norm, Frank drew attention to himself in ways that were sure to repel all invaders from taking a prurient or otherwise unwelcome interest in who he really was.

In costume, too, he took some bold initiatives. The new, internationally famous Frank would henceforth appear only in black, the colour of his home and, by provocative inference, his soul. There was no sign of the tweed jackets of his vaguely bohemian Arrow years, some of them, unthinkably now, with leather patches at the elbows; no sign, either, of the ties that – occasionally and reluctantly – he had worn when he had been posturing and poncing around the foyers of the town a decade before.

The restyled Thring was to be not just distinctive, but unique. The starkness of his basic black would always be offset by rings and a bauble of some kind, preferably large and startlingly brilliant, and by the Italian bag in which Frank would carry the bottle (Ben Ean moselle or brandy, depending on mood), the banknotes and the bromide that were indispensable to his days. Frank Thring, Frank Thring's father, was generally credited in the movie industry with the invention of the clapper-board; Frank Thring, Frank Thring's son, may well have invented 'bling' and the 'man-bag', thirty years before either had a name.

Frank the father had spent his money in ways that were designed both to show his affluence and to advance his claims to respectability, but Frank the son seemed to splash it around without a care. He was probably never as rich as he thought he was, but the state of his bank account was something he had no interest in knowing. Peter Cooke found in him 'a strange infantilism', and his attitude to money was one of the areas in which it showed; the pose of the big spender and the careless self-indulgence had their roots in the way Olive had met (or anticipated or created) his various needs and exempted him from all responsibility in meeting them. The stores that he frequented all had running accounts; Frank would choose copious supplies of whatever he felt like, put the bills in an envelope addressed to his accountant, and send it away in an Embassy cab. The mysteries of how they were paid for were for boring people to understand.

That spendthrift persona was only part of the story, though. In some ways, Frank was oddly frugal. He liked drinking Ben Ean because it was sweet, readily available – and cheap. When he went out for dinner, he would characteristically drink Mateus rose, which catered to a similar palate and price-range, while Hennessy's in bulk was his preference among brandies. He also took delight in petty shoplifting, which sprang partly from the thrill of the sport and partly from the sense of the money he was saving. Fred Parslow claimed that Frank, a voracious reader, had hardly ever bought a book: 'He compulsively stole them, on the basis that they were far too expensive'.[564] Peter Cooke recalled the embarrassment of shopping with Frank, given his predilection for slipping something into the little black bag when no-one was looking:

> He'd be at Ford's the Chemist in Toorak, running up his account by selecting a vast array of unguents and medications ('I'll have that, and that, and some of those, and that, and all of those'), and while the pharmacist wasn't looking, he'd sneak a cake of soap or whatever was at hand. Then, in the Embassy cab on the way home, he'd pull out his prize and say 'And look what I got!'. A dollar cake of soap, and that was

564 Frederick Parslow interview.

> the highlight of a massive shopping spree in which he'd spent hundreds. Ford's knew him pretty well, anyway. The extra item would always turn up on the statement at the end of the month.[565]

Frank, who had spent much of his childhood playing a grotesque parody of an adult, spent quite a lot of his adulthood acting like a naughty child.

Perfecting the role he was to play was one priority; there was also the little matter of a career to be attended to. The son and heir of the House of Thring could perhaps afford to be indifferent to the business of earning an income, but Frank's only apparent talent could supply several things that were almost as essential to him as a bag filled with bank-notes: an admiring audience, a community ready to embrace him whenever he felt like being embraced, and a regular diversion from the boredom and melancholy that seemed to be his default condition.

So, within a few days of coming home to stay, Frank set in place the two pillars of his subsequent performance career. One was his stage work, most of it for the UTRC, later the Melbourne Theatre Company. The other was in the medium that had transformed entertainment in Melbourne while he had been away from the place – television.

Frank's work for television had less to do with his skills as an actor than with the force and outrageousness of his presence. He was a 'personality', appearing regularly on variety shows like *The Noel Ferrier Show* in 1964 and *The Ray Taylor Show* in the following year, where his role was always to insult the guests and shock the audience in forgivably delightful ways. On Channel Seven's *Daly at Night*, featuring the American comedian Jonathan Daly, Frank showed his capacity to make the host uneasy too:

> I remember one compere asking Frank "What is the worst TV show you've ever appeared on?" Frank arched his eyebrows and turned to the host contemptuously and said "How about this one, Pixie?"[566]

A decade later, he was interviewed by Channel Nine's principal front-man:

> To a Ray Martin question "What would you like to do now?" Thring replied "Go home."[567]

---

565 Peter Cooke interview.
566 Mike McColl-Jones, *And Now Here's …* , p.159.
567 Peter Wilmoth, *Sunday Age*, 19 June 1994, p.3.

No one, and no subject, was safe when Frank was on camera, and he seemed disconcertingly indifferent to what people might think of him. But he had always had the knack of knowing how outrageous he could afford to be – either stopping tantalisingly just short of 'the line', or crossing it so ambiguously that his double entendres might be given the benefit of the doubt. From his early incarnation as 3XY's kindly Uncle Frankie, inviting those of his young listeners who had a little pussy to look carefully underneath it, Frank had become expert in the art of sexual innuendo.

Television was hardly his medium of choice. He talked about it with the kind of amused contempt that he mostly professed for the cinema – as a form that was all about glib acting and technical whizbangery, and mostly incompatible with art. It had the terrible vice of being popular, too, though even more crassly and availably so than film, and the rhythms of its stories were controlled by ad-breaks rather than narrative logic. There was a lot about it for a man of Frank's style and temperament to dislike. Disdain came easily to the Thring persona, of course, and had never had much trouble co-existing with fascination, and even active involvement, with its object. So despite, or because of, his scorn for Melbourne television, Frank accepted the offer of a periodic column with the magazine *TV Week*, where he resumed the cutting and thrusting that had built his reputation and destroyed others in his reviews for the *Argus* a decade before.

Something about this essay into criticism made its impact less dramatic than the theatre reviewing that had once driven him into the shrubbery in the Fitzroy Gardens. Perhaps it was the availability of the medium, and the fact that while a bad review could keep people away from the theatre it hardly prevented them from casually switching a dial in their own lounge-room. Perhaps it was the fact that, from the beginning, television in Australia was supplied by national networks, and Frank's influence diminished the further one travelled from Melbourne. Perhaps it was the new familiarity that the medium had given to the Thring persona; the fact that Frank was known to be deliberately outrageous, and that his presence was expected to be comic and performative, made his critical bark now much worse than his bite.

Frank reserved his most lip-curling contempt for soap operas, which was probably predictable enough to his readership given the consistent vein of intellectual disdain in his public appearances. He liked to say of *The Sullivans*, the war-time family saga, that it merely showed what a dreary place Melbourne was in the 1940s. When Channel Nine launched the series *Starting Out* with the usual razzamatazz in 1982, Frank responded with total bemusement as to what was going on:

> The Dean's daughter or niece (one loses track) in the flick of an eyelash electrocuted someone trying to work a spin-dryer without paying while standing (where else?) in a pool of water.[568]

The laundromat may have been the natural location for a soapie, but in this case the network pre-empted the reviewers and aborted the show. Frank's next column reflected on its demise in the light of his critique:

> Despite the cancellation of Grundy's latest assault on our senses, I see no reason to alter (apart from tenses) a word of it other than to commiserate with the cast who, in a fit of exuberance, became involved with such drivel. It had to go, and it did.[569]

Frank's reviews often gave the impression that he preferred his television to be awful. Watching 'the box' was a form of cultural slumming, in which all one's low expectations were happily met before one turned the thing off.

For some years in the 1980s he kept a diary of his responses to the shows he watched. It was a big diary, a child's A3 scrap book, in which he scrawled his cryptic splutterings in characteristic thick black capital letters. Perhaps it was to serve as raw material for reviews to come, but little of it saw the light of day, and probably just as well.[570] Frank seems to have found the quiz show *Sale of the Century* (every week night at seven on Nine) compulsive viewing, mostly because of his irritation with its host, Tony Barber. He also watched religiously the same channel's current affairs program *Sixty Minutes*, which Frank renamed (perhaps generously) '49 Minutes' to take account of its ad-breaks. There too his focus was less on the items than on comperes he loved to hate; George Negus appears variously in Frank's notes as 'George Bogus' and 'George Fungus', and the one reference to him under his own name is even less respectful: 'Negus on champagne – like sending Tony Barber to cover the Sistine Chapel'. What emerges from these little glimpses into Frank's dallyings with prime-time trivia is how much time he spent alone in front of his television set, and the fine line between pleasure and pain in his attitude to what he saw.[571]

568 Andrew Mercado, *Super Aussie Soaps: behind the Scenes of Australia's Best Loved TV Shows*, Sydney, Pluto Press, 2004, p.200.

569 ibid.

570 The Scrapbook is kept among unsorted Thring memorabilia in the Performing Arts Museum, Melbourne.

571 Frank not only watched a good deal of television, but, though he rarely admitted the fact, enjoyed a lot of it: the movies, some sport, and the magnificently tawdry series

He even dabbled in a little prime-time triviality himself, deigning to appear in a series of the family show *Skippy* in 1968. The invitation to join the cast came from John McCallum, who had chosen the show about a remarkably clever kangaroo with a penchant for saving lost people and catching crooks to launch his new production company, Fauna Productions. Frank was to be Dr Alexander Stark, a wealthy villain keen to steal Skippy away from the National Park that was her sanctuary, and imprison her in his private zoo. Stark was the enemy of all that was good and straightforward, and therefore the natural antagonist for Sonny, the nine-year-old ranger's son (Garry Pankhurst), Matt his dad (Ed Deveraux), Jerry his avuncular pilot mate (Tony Bonner) and Skippy, his constant companion and closest confidante. In fact, Frank only appeared in three of the ninety-one episodes, which probably reflects the limited permutations of kangaroo-snatching.

Having appeared as supporting villain with Olivier, Heston, Douglas, Curtis and the unrelated Leighs (Vivien and Janet), Frank now found himself consistently upstaged by a kangaroo; more accurately, by a herd of them, since the title role was played at various points by thirty-five kangaroos. Skippy rarely featured among the famous names that he liked to drop.

On his first day on the set, Frank found himself in a scene reminiscent of dismal days in Hardangerfjorden:

> It was very wet and rainy, and we had tents only, no buildings. And we had the kangaroo – the trained one, that we trained for six months, the principal one – in a sack with its head out, you see, as we always carried it like that.
>
> And Frank said, "I don't like the amenities here, John. I'm very worried about my dressing-room, for instance. Especially when I see the star's!" [572]

The weather was so appalling that the owners of Dr Stark's beloved 1930 Rolls Royce Phantom withdrew it from the scene; Frank, who was more familiar with a Rolls than with any other kind of car, was given something more modest to drive. Had the owners known that he had not been behind the wheel since his argument with a brick wall in Banbury in 1955, they might have made the move a little earlier.

---

about sexual relationships in a television studio, *The Box*. Frank rarely missed an episode. Perhaps what particularly attracted him was the ground-breaking depiction of serious and sympathetic gay characters (one played by his friend Paul Karo).

572 John McCallum, 'Googie and John' interview with Peter Thompson, *Talking Heads*, ABC television, screened 8 October 2007.

Stark's efforts to bundle Skippy into his car in episode two provoked a lot of complaints and a formal investigation by the RSPCA, but were, not surprisingly, unsuccessful. He resumed the attempt in episode eighteen, this time getting a couple of henchmen to do his dirty work by paying them to pretend to be animal welfare officers; this neatly recalled the controversy without reviving it, with the bonus of a new plot-line. When that scheme failed, Stark in episode twenty-two developed the idea of impersonation still further with an even bolder plan; by having an actor pass himself off as the noble Matt, he hoped to destroy Matt's reputation, have him and his pesky son driven out of the National Park, and thus leave unprotected Skippy and any other animal he fancied as a candidate for his zoo. Then inspiration clearly ran out for the evil doctor, and he retired from the series.

Skippy consolidated Frank's fame; the variety and talk shows had made him familiar to the late-night adult audience, and now his face and voice could become the stuff of their children's nightmares as well. He made advertisements, too, a string of them. Frank's commercials were designed to keep the viewer watching in the ad-breaks, rather than slipping out to pop on the kettle, and they are well-enough remembered forty years on to suggest that they met the challenge triumphantly. All of them traded on the fact that the Thring persona was not just big and bizarre, but absolutely identifiable. The sinister-looking man who glared at the viewer, threatening all kinds of unspeakable penalties if the television licence was not paid, was that Frank Thring who played cruel tyrants in the movies. The decadently sybaritic chap in gold smoking-jacket who recommended the delights of Martins cigarettes was that Mr Thring who lived like a king in Toorak, and cut people down to size on the telly. The fat bald epicurean who salivated over Huttons hams was that Thring fellow, not just a huge eater but a Genuine Ham. The Devil whose special knowledge of matters combustible made him a natural advocate for Little Lucifers Fire-Starters, was the notorious Thring who no doubt got up to all kinds of mischief that decent people wouldn't even have a name for. The superhero called The Man from Anticol, who hunted down cold and 'flu germs in improbably lumpy latex, was Frank Thring, film-star and self-parodist extraordinaire.

Frank's style in all these commercials had a great deal in common with that of the 'King' of late night television in Melbourne in the 1960s, Graham Kennedy. When Frank described the Kennedy approach to advertising in a *TV Week* review, his comment had the incisiveness of a man who knows the trick inside-out:

> We have had the hard sell and the soft sell: Mr Kennedy has now developed 'the send-up sell', and the ultimate refinement is that he not only sends up the wares he is peddling, but also the public to whom he is trying to peddle them.[573]

The audiences loved it when Graham made fools of his sponsors, even if the joke was partly on them; they loved it again when Frank did it to them, in his own preposterous way.

The unforgettable face and voice became suddenly familiar in the loungerooms of families who had never heard of the Union Repertory, and for whom the theatre was an unknown country that they had no desire to visit. Frank's involvement in television, intermittent though it was, made him recognisable in a way that 'normal' actors, even ones with marquee names, could never be. Now, it seemed, everybody knew his penchant for sneering with style. If Joan Thring was right in her diagnosis of his reasons for coming back to Melbourne, then surely Frank had exactly what he wanted. He told an interviewer for *Listener-In TV* in 1977 about the enduring power of his first venture into television advertising:

> 'Not only did I do it ten years ago but we haven't had licences for six years or whatever. But the minute I set foot outside the front gate a car screeches to a halt and somebody puts their head out of the window ... "Ullo friend, got yah TV licence?' ' And the squirming Thring says 'It's indescribably *very* embarrassing when *one* has to live with *one's* sins'.[574]

For Frank the temperamental recluse, though, the situation was much more complex. Often he would have much preferred to hide, if only there hadn't been so much of him to disguise.

> I'm a very private person ... But you see, when you're surrounded with millions of people, what are they, they look vile ... all day and all night, ... one is dealing with anything up to a hundred or two hundred people a day [in a company] ... one's idea of a holiday is to shut oneself in here. I've got a swimming-pool and a Siamese cat, I've got lots of books to read as you can see, lots of new scripts to read ... And of course the

573 *TV Week*, 14–20 May 1959, p.11.
574 *Listener-In TV*, 1 January 1977, p.5.

> other thing is never to get dressed, wander round in a dressing-gown all day, it's absolute heaven ... I just sit here in absolute silence for six weeks, it's absolute heaven ... I just switch the phone off, I've got a switch on the phone. And I lock the front gate, it's all covered with spikes and barbed wire.
>
> In the city, of course, it is impossible. I can't go into the city. This is where I have to have somebody like Peter [Cooke] to look after me, I mean I can't go shopping in Myer's for six pairs of Jockettes because the entire store comes to a halt. At the cinema, if I'm stuck there at interval we have this, Oh There's the man from Anticol or there's Martin's cigarettes or have you got your television licence Frank, all this thing going on, so the simplest excursion turns into a nightmare.[575]

Being recognisable to a million strangers is a tough fate for anyone, but especially so for an almost pathologically private man. Frank often complained about being a celebrity, even as he continued to play the role to the hilt. It was his favourite resentment, the thing that he dreaded and yet seemed unable to live for long without.

By the mid-1960s, Frank was thoroughly established as a public figure in his home town, indisputably the star of its resident theatre company, and loved or loathed by most of its population. He was doing plays that he wanted, he was thoroughly settled in a house designed to reinforce the myth of his personality, he was unencumbered by family but occasionally able to attract the admiration of beautiful young men. It was a completely familiar world, the world of his childhood where underpants always came from Myers and medicines from Ford's, and Embassy cabs were always on hand to take him to another place he knew. If to people like Joan it seemed regressive, Frank gave a good impression of being past caring what they thought; after all, one had been there and done that, and international fame could be so very tedious. There was little love in this much smaller world, but there was some fondness and plenty of adulation, and Frank was probably, for this time, about as happy as his troublesome mind would allow him to be.

575 Barbara Moore interview.

Then there was the Union Theatre Repertory Company – or, as it became in 1968 when it abandoned the academic and provincial associations of its original name and boldly claimed its position as the major professional company in its city, the Melbourne Theatre Company.

Frank came back in late 1961 and went almost immediately into rehearsals for his role as the bloodsucking Count in *Dracula*. Four weeks after it opened, he was doing *Macbeth*, sporting, as he liked to say, 'Macbeth's ravishing strides' (though John Sumner felt that the Thring legs and knees 'looked pretty horrible' in the outfit that Anne Fraser had designed for him).[576] This was Frank's welcome to the delights and hazards of repertory theatre, and it suited him down to the ground. Headline roles in mostly interesting plays, none running long enough to become tedious. Everyone in *Dracula* popped up again in *Macbeth*, with old pals like Sheila Florance and Leon Lissek and new chums like Reg Livermore and Neil Fitzpatrick to share the general understanding that this was an ongoing ensemble in which Frank Thring was always the star.

He was involved in thirty-five productions with the company after he came back to stay. Twenty-three of those were in the first ten years of his involvement with the Company, fitted around bits and pieces of film, television and commercial theatre; eleven came in the next sixteen years, when he had very little else to do. There is a story in that, of course. But the most immediately noteworthy fact is that, after his first appearance with the UTRC in 1959, Frank worked with the same company for thirty years. There have been very few lives, surely, in which a theatre has provided such a point of stability.

Of those thirty-five productions, twenty were directed by John Sumner. Moira Carleton, one of the stalwarts of the Arrow stage, directed two of the plays in which Frank appeared, *Dracula* and Noel Coward's *Present Laughter* in 1965. So did George Ogilvie (General Irrigua in Feydeau's *Cat Among the Pigeons*, 1970, and the Earl of Caversham in Wilde's *An Ideal Husband*, 1972). Ten others directed Frank once: Wal Cherry (Argan in Moliere's *The Happy Invalid*, 1963), George Whaley (John in Ionesco's *Rhinoceros*, 1967), Tyrone Guthrie (Lafew in *All's Well That Ends Well*, 1970), Rick Billinghurst (Simon in Buchner's *Danton's Death*, 1972), Joachim Tenschert (The Chaplain in Brecht's *Mother Courage and Her Children*, 1973), Mick Rodger (Lord Touchwood in Congreve's *The Double Dealer*, 1975), Ray Lawler (Sir Oliver Surface in Sheridan's *The School for Scandal*, 1977), Simon Chilvers

576 John Sumner, interview with the author.

(Sheridan Whiteside in the remounted production of *The Man Who Came to Dinner*, 1980), and Simon Phillips (the butlers Lane and Merriman in Wilde's *The Importance of Being Earnest*, 1988).

It's an impressive list of roles. But it's also notable that so many of those directorial experiences were 'one-off'. Perhaps the directors were not keen to revisit the pleasure, or perhaps Frank found it even harder to work with them than it was with Sumner. Perhaps it was purely a product of circumstance. But it certainly throws into relief John Sumner's significance in Frank's career. The founding father of the UTRC and the MTC was just two years Frank's senior, but his role was to play the patriarch to his idiosyncratic leading man. Sumner was both model and adversary, the source of all discipline whose approval or disapproval was critical to Frank's self-confidence.

The catalogue of roles on which Frank worked with Sumner is, if anything, even more imposing than the ones above. After Ahab in *Moby Dick – Rehearsed* came Macbeth, the inevitable Sheridan Whiteside (1963), General Burgoyne in Shaw's *The Devil's Disciple* (1963), Old Sam in Peter Ustinov's *Photo Finish* (1964), the Cardinal in Albee's *Tiny Alice* (1965), Max in Pinter's *The Homecoming* (1965), another Cardinal in Hochhuth's *The Representative* (1966), the Right Honourable Joseph Chamberlain in M. Bradley Dyne's *The Right Honourable Gentleman* (1967), Ahab (again) in *Moby Dick – Rehearsed* (1967), Danforth in Miller's *The Crucible* (1968), Andrew Undershaft in Shaw's *Major Barbara* (1968), Falstaff in *Henry IV Part One* (1969), Azdak in Brecht's *Caucasian Chalk Circle* (1970), Galileo in Brecht's *Galileo* (1971), Gaev in Chekhov's *The Cherry Orchard* (1972), Morton Kyle in Buzo's *Batman's Beach-Head* (1973), Sandor Turai in Molnar's *The Play's the Thing* (1973), various roles including a Bunyip in Keith Michell's adaptation of *Peer Gynt*, *Pete McGinty and the Dreamtime* (1981), and, finally and appropriately, the especially tricky role of Frank Thring in Frank's one-man show, *Frankly Thring* (1981).

Again, the imbalance (sixteen plays with Sumner in the first twelve years after Frank's return, just two in the fifteen years that followed) is striking. But Frank could hardly have devised a better repertoire had he owned the theatre; Sumner's company offered most of the charms of the Arrow without any requirement to pay the bills or sew on the sequins. There was no doubt who was this company's biggest presence, either.

One of those thirty-five productions was directed by the man himself. It was the first and last time that Frank tried his hand at directing, which suggests that it proved to be not one of his major talents. The play was

Entertaining Mr Sloane, Joe Orton's bizarre comedy of bad manners, which opened at Russell Street in April 1965, less than a year after its London premiere. The cast (Bunney Brooke, Michael Duffield, Alan Hopgood, and Dennis Miller as the enigmatic Sloane) was strong, and had the extra attraction that all had acted with Frank before, and knew what they were in for. The play fared poorly at the box office, but that probably had less to do with the quality of the production than with its disconcerting sexual ambiguity; Sloane not only has an affair with Kate his landlady which leaves her pregnant, but has a sexual relationship of some kind with her overbearing brother Ed. The possibility that Sloane may be Kate's son produces another little complication. Frank would have liked the tricky subject, and the fact that producing a play by Orton, a writer who presented himself as gay and dangerous, was a daring act of solidarity. But he worked with the company for another twenty-three years, and nobody ever invited him to repeat the experiment. The fact that Sumner doesn't mention it in his memoir, *Recollections at Play*, gives a sense of what he thought of it.

The Company, whatever its name at the time, became the central organising principle in Frank's life. It could be designated his home away from home, except that for so much of his career its habit was, reluctantly, nomadic. Once Sumner's company cut the umbilical with the University, it spent a long time waiting for the lavish facilities that had been promised by the state government at the new Arts Centre in St Kilda Road. Frank's curriculum vitae maps its precariously itinerant operation: ten of his thirty-five productions were staged at the Company's ancestral home, the Union Theatre on the University's Carlton campus; twelve at the Russell Street Theatre, a creaky four-hundred seater with shallow wings and a pronounced proscenium arch; three at the Athenaeum in Collins Street, even creakier, but twice that size; three at the Comedy in Exhibition Street, which had a thousand seats, but a commercial ambience and rental; two at the Princess, the Grand Dame of Melbourne theatres, and a place with which Frank already had many associations; one at St Martins Theatre in South Yarra, where the feel and facilities were much more 'alternative'; one in the courtyard of the Arts Centre on St Kilda Road, which reflected John Sumner's readiness, when politicians were slow and contractors slower, to take refuge in any court in a storm; and one, appropriately Frank's last for the company, at the Playhouse, the state-of-the-art eight hundred seater at the Arts Centre that finally flaunted the company's status as Melbourne's premier maker of professional theatre. He was, by a number of measures, the barometer of its success.

They were all great roles, but which were the great performances? It was relatively easy for Frank to strut his usual stuff, and the MTC subscribers dutifully lapped it up when he did. Probably most of those productions showed a lot more Thring than the character. Sometimes, as in *Macbeth*, the mannerisms were overcome by a virtuosity so passionate that it was almost believable. Sometimes, as in his farewell MTC performance as the two butlers at the Playhouse, there were only the mannerisms. But several of them moved far enough beyond cliché to became the most significant performances of his life.

The three Brechtian plays harnessed Frank's unmistakable presence in the service of a theatrical ideology that made presentational acting not just an engaging vice, but an artistic virtue. Azdak in *The Caucasian Chalk Circle* is written as a performer – his songs with his sidekick Shauwa are a form of manic vaudeville, while his idiosyncratic approach to conflict resolution when it comes to deciding between the competing 'mothers' has as much to do with a fondness for centre-stage and a delight in teasing an audience as it does with gentle worldly wisdom. It wasn't difficult for Frank to find his inner Ham, just as the other Brechtian role he played for Sumner, in *Galileo*, invoked elements of the Thring persona in demonstrating the egoism as well as the courage of non-conformity. Sumner noted, a little ambiguously, that 'Frank bulldozed his way though Azdak, and from the minute he came on in the second half, things were never the same';[577] but there was no hint of equivocation in his comments on the playing of Galileo:

> Frank Thring was dominant as Galileo. From an initial childish delight in the scientist's discoveries, his performance moved through disbelief to pragmatism, then to near-resignation, as he saw the powers gathering against him. The final scenes with Rona McLeod as his daughter were very moving.[578]

Actors often feel insecure about allowing their own experience to inform the way that they play characters in Brecht's theatre; any hint of emotional self-reference can look like the first step on a slippery slope that takes them headlong away from a suitably pious embracing of the *verfremdungeffekt*. For

577 John Sumner, *Recollections at Play. A Life in Australian Theatre*, Melbourne University Press, 1993, p.212.

578 ibid, p.223.

Frank, though, Galileo was a heretically personal performance. It sprang partly from his own oddly clandestine pursuit of the life of the mind:

> Frank read voraciously. Magazines and periodicals especially. He kept up with everything, in the theatre, in books, in world politics. Anything you wanted to know, Frank could tell you.[579]

That wasn't the Frank Thring that the public knew from television chat shows, or *Skippy*, or boozy opening nights. The idea that he might be some kind of closet intellectual was perhaps as discomforting, in its way, as his quite out-of-the-closet sexuality. Frank was attracted to the idea of playing a man whose intelligence was too readily dismissed, as he was to the poignancy of an apparently unfulfilled life:

> Galileo, sitting naked in the wooden bath, centre stage at the old Russell Street Theatre, said: 'I'm 45-years old, and I've done nothing which satisfies me'.
>
> 'I could be talking about my own life', said Frank.[580]

Frank was forty-five, too. He knew what that kind of stock-taking was like.

The Melbourne Theatre Company was on a roll with its succession of 'big shows' between 1969 and 1973, and Frank was very much at its forefront. The company was still itinerant, though, and rehearsals for *Galileo* through the autumn of 1971 – in an abandoned warehouse in South Melbourne that subsequently became its organisational home – were filled with drama:

> For rehearsals we erected some of the set in the new workshop area because we needed space, but I put it in the wrong place and we were frozen among the puddles and bird-droppings. Perhaps to compensate for the cold, one of the actresses managed to set herself on fire when waving sparklers during the carnival scene.
>
> Frank rightly was not too pleased sitting in a bathtub with all the draught; and to top everything, once the klaxon of rush-hour traffic started up, no-one could hear a word.[581]

579 Roland Rocchecciolі, email to the author, 23 March 2010.
580 Sumner, *Recollections at Play*, p.233.
581 ibid, p.223–4.

Still, the MTC was thriving financially with its new subscription model, and the politicians were smiling. Distinguished visiting directors from overseas, like Tyrone Guthrie, who directed *All's Well That Ends Well* in 1970, and Joachim Tenschert, who directed *Mother Courage and Her Children* in 1973, confirmed that the company was significantly raising its stakes.

Playing the Chaplain in *Mother Courage* represented a different challenge from those Frank had faced as Azdak and Galileo, where the stage was indisputably his. The character certainly has a weightily epicurean presence and a keen instinct for survival that might have seemed perfectly Frank, but it was critical that those characteristics didn't distract from the much more developed rat cunning and self-seeking of Mother Courage herself. This was especially so in the context of the Tenschert production, which reflected not only the director's absorption in the discipline of the Berliner Ensemble, but his scrupulous fidelity to Brecht's *Modellbuch* for the play:

> The production was based on that presented in 1949 … Joachim made our cast copy the moves, gestures and inflections from the original, a method of work alien to most of them, but knowing of his reputation they co-operated.[582]

It might just have been Frank's finest theatrical moment. He was used to most things being about him. John Sumner was struck by the fact that he hardly ever complained about the fact that the rehearsal process was less than creative. He hardly ever complained about the fact that the production, night after night after night, was always the same. Frank became, for once in his life, a member of an ensemble.

His performance as the Chaplain was, by Frank's standards, a subdued one. That voice and that massive frame could never disappear into the woodwork, but the familiar strategies for dominating the stage – the milking of pauses, the rolling of eyes, the ad-libbed asides to the stalls – were hardly evident at all. In their place was a stillness that conceded the focus to Gloria Dawn, the Sydney cabaret star who proved a brilliant Mother Courage; the fact that it was widely known that Dawn had been diagnosed with probably terminal cancer gave an added resonance to the play's final scene, in which the tough little woman doggedly dragged her tattered cart into a future that held nothing for her.

582 ibid, p.250.

The role of Falstaff, the buffoon in Shakespeare's *Henry IV* whose mockery of his own absurdities paradoxically confers a power over everyone he deals with, was tailor-made for Frank, and he was predictably outrageous in playing it. He had a lot in common with 'Plump Jack', after all. They shared a massive appetite for most things in life, as well as the habit of self-caricature. Furthermore, as a fond but distinctly self-interested Bad Example to the ingénue Prince Hal, Falstaff mimicked Frank's relationships with Peter Cooke, Hugh Rule and Stephen Oldfield, and a stream of other pretty boys who attracted his attention but didn't hold it long enough or sufficiently reciprocate it. When Prince Hal mocks Falstaff in what purports to be knockabout fun, he uses terms that Frank might see, on a bad day, as not inapplicable to himself:

> ... that huge bombard of sack, that stuffed cloak-bag of guts, that roasted Manningtree ox with the pudding in his belly, that reverend Vice, that grey Iniquity, that Father Ruffian, that Vanity in years? Wherein is he good, but to taste sack and drink it? Wherein neat and cleanly, but to carve a capon and eat it? Wherein cunning, but in craft? Wherein villainous, but in all things? Wherein worthy, but in nothing? (*Henry IV, Part One*, II:4, 439–46)

Frank liked to play the reprobate, in life and on stage. But he was introspective and melancholic enough to ask some of those questions. He must surely have glimpsed in Hal's last cold dismissal of his old playmate the solitude that was becoming a habit, and the lonely years that stretched ahead.

Though it might not have ranked among Frank's best moments on stage – the line between acting and showing-off was often tricky for him to hold – his appearance as Falstaff was certainly among his most memorable. The outdoor locations (initially at the new Octagon Theatre at the University of Western Australia, and then in the Murdoch Courtyard at Melbourne's National Gallery) presented a number of problems. Most of them in Melbourne were caused by competition from the Moomba fireworks, but in Perth, when Falstaff played dead at the Battle of Shrewsbury, he was still lying motionless at the end of the scene. It looked like a heart attack, but soon it was clear that Frank had fainted from dehydration.

> With all the rushing up and down stage and auditorium stairs, and the lack of air-conditioning, the mass of his clothing had been too much. Thank goodness Betty Druitt, the head of wardrobe, was with us. Not

> only a brilliant costume-maker but also a mistress of improvisation, she went to work: armour was modified, balaclava and mittens disappeared, lighter boots were produced, padding was reduced and half the contents of the haversack went … Finally, Margaret [Sumner's wife] suggested that Betty follow Frank with a large jug of water, so he was forced to drink seven pints a day, replacing his sweat. 'But I have been drinking', Frank protested. 'Yes', said Margaret. 'But alcohol doesn't count'.[583]

Some of the people who shared a stage with Frank over the years saw his predilection for passing out on stage as a tactic to cover a loss of lines. Forgetfulness would soon become a recurrent issue for Frank, and falling over an occasional one. But on this occasion it seems, for once, that he wasn't acting at all.

His performance as Gaev in *The Cherry Orchard* was significant, too, and again less because of the quality of the acting than for its revelation of the actor. Sumner encouraged Googie Withers as Ranevsky and Frank as her brother Gaev to play the roles as 'irresponsible, rather stupid, self-centred lovable children'.[584] Stupid Frank was not, but each of the other terms could be applied to the spoilt son of Rylands. The character's eccentricity freed him, dangerously perhaps, to be as whimsical as he wished; Gaev, continually potting imaginary billiard balls whenever he is at a loss, is a guaranteed scene-stealer. But the real revelation of *The Cherry Orchard* in the summer of 1972–3 was not about Frank's character, but his decline as an actor. It had been coming for a while. Lines had never been easy for him, but they were much harder to remember at this point in his career. He had always drunk heavily, but he was drinking more now; Googie Withers estimated that during *The Cherry Orchard* he was knocking back six bottles of Ben Ean a day, yet although he was obviously never sober he was never obviously drunk.[585] The insomnia and the bouts of depression were more frequent, and the only way to find an attractive boy these days was to rent one. The haplessness of Gaev appropriately marked the end of Frank's glory days with the MTC; there would be the uncharacteristically modest performance in *Mother Courage* later that year, and another fifteen years with the company, but just nine plays, and the big roles were behind him.

---

583 Sumner, *Recollections at Play*, p.200.

584 ibid, p.234.

585 Googie Withers, interview with the author, 23 August 2004.

The roles he thought were his best were early ones – his *tour de force* as Ahab in *Moby Dick – Rehearsed* that he gave between movies in 1959, and the vile Max in Pinter's *The Homecoming* in 1965. The latter seemed an improbable piece of casting, especially to Frank:

> When I asked Frank Thring to play the old butcher, he replied: 'You must be mad. That is the most monumental piece of miscasting even you have done'. He was shrewd enough to do it, though, and brilliantly; in fact, on his first entrance it took some people time to realise who he was! For Frank, such a well-known, sophisticated Melbourne personality, that was something.[586]

Frank saw it as his most completely acted role, the one with the smallest amount of Thring. Most people who saw it probably agreed with that estimate, though some were presumably disappointed.

The Homecoming was a risky choice for the company. Pinter's theme seems initially the destruction of innocence, which provides all the frisson as the young and attractive Ruth finds herself in a house filled with predatory men. But the play turns into a walk on the dark side of sexual pathology. Ruth's willingness to become the object of desire – and touch – for any or all of them reflects a perverse longing to become their victim and slave; however, the possibility that she might withdraw her complicity and go gives her a kind of power that is reinforced with every degradation she deigns to allow. All four men are appalling, but Max the butcher is the most appalling of all. He is entirely without charm, humour or affection. For him a woman is just another slab of meat, little more than a vagina with decorative trappings. As patriarch of the family, he sets the tone in this house of horrors.

Frank, who could be charming when he felt like it, was almost compulsively humorous, and was sometimes generous with his affections, was a very different kind of man. He presumably never lusted after the female of the species in his life; old Max thinks of little else. But the actor and the character perhaps had some points of connection, after all. Their tastes in sexual matters were antithetical, but they shared an interest in predatoriness and pornography, and in the outer reaches of sado-masochism. And while Frank could rightly say that some of his best friends were women, there was a streak of misogyny in him, too. While he was proud of his performance as

586 Sumner, *Recollections at Play*, p.173.

Max because it was all acting, he would have recognised the truth that the best acting always draws on something of the self.

Frank seems to have placed the women in his life in three categories. There were, first and foremost, the ones he adored as goddesses of the stage – women of beauty and passionate caprice like Vivien Leigh and Googie Withers whom he knew, or others like Bette Davis or Judy Garland whom he imagined and admired from afar. These were the women he talked most about.

Then there were those he knew as friends, old pals like Joan Harris or younger ones like Joanna McCallum who were kind to him, and mostly forgave him his trespasses, or partial soul-mates like Mary Hardy who could stay with him joke for joke, drink for drink. He was comfortable with them. This group included a number of completely unthreatening older women, too – women like his beloved Nanny, and Edith Cunliff, or Joan Harris' mother who looked forward to seeing him at the Parslow house every Christmas:

> The first time he came round, I was worried what he might say. He could be so cruel to people when he wanted to be. But it was fine. It was always fine. He'd squat on the floor for hours, talking – and even listening – to my very non-theatrical mother. He even seemed to enjoy it. Mum thought he was 'a lovely man'.[587]

The women who forgave him could sometimes be taken too much for granted. Once Joan Harris went backstage to see him during the run of *The Homecoming* at Russell Street:

> He was wedged in the corner at the far end of the dressing-room, taking off his make-up. We'd hardly had time to say hello before a bunch of presumably important people showed up, and Frank instantly rose to welcome them. He did not introduce me, or acknowledge that I was standing there behind him. After a few minutes, I decided to leave. I gave him a very emphatic "Good night Frank", he made no response. Next day a large bunch of flowers was delivered to our house with a card: "Sometimes Frank forgets who his real friends are. With love, FT".[588]

587 Joan Harris, interview with the author, 16 September 2004.
588 ibid.

Sometimes he could be so negligent of those who had cared about him that there would never be a bunch of flowers. Lola, the half-sister who had cuddled and adored him as a child, was now effectively out of his life. It may have suited her as well as it did Frank, of course; the circles she moved in really had no place for a sibling who liked to present himself as the Queen of Melbourne Theatre. It was one of those stereotypical little sadnesses of family life that it was so, though. There had been great fondness there once.

Then there was the third category, the ones who threatened him in ways he resented, and who brought out the least attractive of his attitudes to the Monstrous Regiment of women. If there was fear or a sense of inadequacy in Frank's relationships with them, it was almost entirely masked by a kind of nonchalant aversion. Some women he just grew tired of: Sheila Florance, for example, who had worked with Frank at the Arrow and whose Sunday night soirees he had regularly frequented in the 1950s. Peter Oyston, Sheila's son, who dreaded those evenings and whose sense of theatre people was for a time seriously soured by his disapproval of all that drinking and talking about sex, and the braying laughter into the night, retained a very strong memory of Frank at that time.

> He used to call me Blossom. I'd go and hide in my room. But I could hear them. Frank sang this appalling song, about killing his mother. And once a bottle of champagne erupted, and Frank exclaimed, 'Oh my God, it's just like my first husband!' My mother used to think he was wonderful. But there were always people storming out. I couldn't bear those nights.[589]

Sheila Florance and Frank went back a long way. She had played Jocasta in *Oedipus Rex* at the Arrow in 1953, and even then the tensions were evident:

> They were an extraordinary team. In the miniature theatre there was barely room for the two of them on stage – physically and metaphorically. Sheila had a strong presence but she met her match in Frank, and although they worked more than once together without too many difficulties she couldn't stop herself.[590]

589 Peter Oyston, interview with the author, 29 April 2007.

590 Helen Martineau, *On the Inside. An Intimate Portrait of Sheila Florance*, Melbourne, Australian Scholarly Publishing, 2005, p.109.

Frank probably disagreed with that judgement. But he and Sheila were together again in *The Guardsman* when he was briefly back in Melbourne in 1961. After she shared the stage with him as Lady Macbeth, however, Frank made it clear to John Sumner that he would prefer that she never did so again; he wasn't quite able to forgive her comment about his approach to Macbeth, 'I think he's forgotten he isn't hamming it up in Hollywood now'.[591] Sumner would occasionally tease him with the possibility that he would be working with her, in order to provoke a horrified 'God, you're not going to do another *Guardsman* on me, are you?' from Frank.[592]

Some were natural adversaries from the beginning. Jennifer Claire, who played Ruth in *The Homecoming*, was prepared to call Frank's bluff, and not to find him amusing. Sumner noted her immediate impact on the cast:

> The one woman was Jennifer Claire, who came into rehearsal five days before we opened after another actress dropped out ... She was still and sexy, and unsettled all us men.[593]

She certainly unsettled Frank. The tension in their relationship deepened through a series of productions in which Jennifer Claire played the dark and dangerous female counterpoint to his comic extravagance: *The Right Honourable Gentleman* and *Rhinoceros* in 1967, *The Crucible* and *Major Barbara* in 1968, *Cat Among the Pigeons*, *The Caucasian Chalk Circle* and *All's Well* in 1970, *Danton's Death*, *The Cherry Orchard* and *An Ideal Husband* in 1972, and *Mother Courage* in 1973. It made for a fascinating drama within the drama, and she added a piquant relish to Frank's well-cured ham. But it couldn't last, and their mutual disdain reached its culmination in, of all places, the company cafeteria. Jennifer, in the queue for morning tea, was appalled at the absence of fresh milk; Frank's response was 'You've got a pair of tits. Why don't you use one?'[594]

Frank could sometimes be cruel without any class at all; it was the kind of remark that would have occurred to Max the butcher. Some things can't be fixed by an apologetic bouquet, even if Frank had been inclined to try.

---

591 Helen Martineau, p.161.

592 John Sumner, interview with the author. Frank's veto was successful, though, except for the 'all-hands-on-deck' production of *All's Well That Ends Well* with Tyrone Guthrie in 1970.

593 John Sumner, *Recollections at Play*, p.173.

594 Hugh Rule, interview with the author.

One woman, of course, was all these appalling things: loudly competitive like Sheila Florance, inscrutably so like Jennifer Claire, the representation of all that was mysteriously and hysterically female, and the person for whom Frank reserved his most sustained hatred and contempt. When Frank referred to his mother Olive as 'the cunt' he wasn't simply using an obscenity. He was expressing disgust for her sex.

The woman who, for some time at least, challenged his categories by moving between all of them was Joan Thring. She began as his best pal, the girl figuratively from next door who forgave him more than most; she bloomed, in London, into what John Sumner described as 'an exotic bird, that flew in and flew out',[595] and even stepped briefly into the glorious company of the creatures he adored; then, for a time, in the debacle of their marriage and divorce, Joan was reassigned, to a place near his mother among the enemy that could be so much deadlier than the male. Mostly though, Joan stayed his friend, which said something for Frank's capacity not to be vindictive for long, and a great deal for her genuine loyalty and affection for him.

It might not have been his greatest performance in terms of its acting demands. But of all his roles, the one with which Frank became most closely identified, and the one that had the most interesting connection with the part he chose to play off-stage, was that of Sheridan Whiteside in *The Man Who Came to Dinner.* Frank played Whiteside five times: at the Little Theatre at the age of twenty-four; at the Arrow at the age of twenty-six; at the Russell Street, directed by Sumner for the UTRC, at the age of thirty-six; at the SGIO Theatre for the Queensland Theatre Company at the age of fifty-three; and at the Athenaeum, directed by Simon Chilvers for the MTC, at the age of fifty-four. Eventually, he came close to the age of the character.

From quite early, though, he shared many of the qualities of 'The Man'. Kaufman and Hart created a witty, outrageous egoist, who takes up all the psychological space in any room; others become pallid and timid before the force of his personality and the monstrous scale of his expectations. Frank had just that effect on a lot of people, in a lot of rooms. The Stanleys, who own the large home in the mid-west in which the man who came to dinner

595 John Sumner, interview with the author.

recuperates after falling over outside their front door, are driven to take their meals, and all the business of their daily lives, to their bedroom, leaving the rest of the house to him. Whiteside is a critic, and so accustomed, as Frank professed to be, to being feared and hated. He is '*portly and Falstaffian*' in appearance as Frank had come increasingly to be, but his manner proclaims, as Frank's did, his weariness of the world and his aversion to his kind.

Whiteside's humour is an expression of a jadedness that is profound, almost metaphysical. In his first moments of the stage, he says nothing for some time as he '*looks slowly around, into each and every beaming face*', and then at last pronounces, 'I may vomit'.[596] His eyes are frequently closed, 'as though the pain were too much to bear'; he laments, to no-one in particular, 'Is there a man in the world who suffers as I do from the gross inadequacies of the human race?' [597] But he makes his tragedy a comic turn. He speaks mostly in insults, some of which (like his references to his indispensable assistant Maggie as 'Repulsive', 'you sex-ridden hag', 'you flea-bitten Cleopatra', and 'this aging debutante, ... [whom] I retain in my employ only because she is the sole support of her two-headed brother') are to be understood as terms of grudging endearment, while others (like his remarks about almost everyone else) are every bit as contemptuous as they seem. It was very much the Thring style. Just as Frank could be surprisingly generous, especially to the young, Whiteside is finally a benevolent despot, too: he gives Maggie his blessing in her marriage to Jefferson, and fosters the romantic and career aspirations of the oppressed Stanley offspring, though he makes it clear that disinterested kindness goes against the grain.

So similar was the Whiteside persona to Frank's that it is tempting to see it as a case of life imitating art. The Thring style didn't originate with the role, of course. That set of extraordinary social mannerisms was incubated at Melbourne Grammar, and the distinctive disdainful drawl was heard through the 1940s in places as diverse as the back bar of the Australia, the barracks at Puckapunyal, the foyer on any first night in Melbourne, and the children's program on 3XY; it slowed and deepened with the years, but its essential features remained unchanged. However, finding Sheridan Whiteside confirmed and in a sense legitimised Frank's style. It had always had the character of a pre-emptive defensive strike; after Frank made himself synonymous with Whiteside at the beginning of a new decade, it became

596 Moss Hart and George S. Kaufman, *The Man Who Came to Dinner*, in *Three Plays by Kaufman & Hart*, New York, Grove Press, 1994, p.218.

597 ibid, p.221.

bolder still, a way of meeting the world that seemed to take celebrity for granted. The 'preposterous' figure that John Sumner met in 1953, and the 'extraordinary, flamboyant creature ... like a giant sunflower' who burst into Trader Faulkner's life two years later, were high-camp variations on the man who came to dinner, and acted as if he owned the place.

For a time, the assertion of power had real substance. Through the 1960s and into the next decade Frank drank too much, offended quite a few people, and behaved scandalously from time to time, but mostly got away with it all magnificently; he was the biggest name in Melbourne theatre, he was a man of apparently infinite means, he was known to everybody who owned a television set, and evidently afraid of nobody. He had some claim to fame in Hollywood. He was a success. Not everything in his life was as he would have desired it, but in most respects he seemed to be living it idiosyncratically on his own terms.

Though he was much in demand at the Melbourne Theatre Company, Frank found time for the occasional commercial production. In 1966 he even appeared in a musical, *Robert and Elizabeth*, in which he played the heavy Victorian father to June Bronhill's Elizabeth Browning, in the tale of her legendary love for Robert Browning (Dennis Quilley). Mercifully, the patriarch of Wimpole Street was a largely non-singing role. The piece played successfully at an old Thring stamping-ground, Melbourne's Princess Theatre, and then much less so at Sydney's Tivoli. But it was, for Frank, enormous fun. Mr Barrett was splendidly melodramatic, and Frank had learned domestic tyranny literally at his mother's knee. June Bronhill, who enjoyed a convivial off-stage glass and a dash of on-stage mischief, was a wonderfully compatible leading lady. She remembered the show and 'lovely Thring' with great affection, and recounted gleefully in her memoirs the private joke that began when she distracted him with an unusual ring, and resolved to 'do something silly with the ring situation' thereafter:

> The first thing I did was get some of those awful big pearls you buy at Woolies with great big holes that you thread through. I threaded it on string and tied it underneath my finger. When he looked down, he couldn't believe what he saw. After that, at each performance he'd look down to see what I had on my finger. I'd lull him into a false sense of security and then do another. Next I put a Bandaid around my finger and on the top of it, I put a bit of glue and stuck red glitter all over it. Once again he went completely sky-high. I did all sorts of evil things

> and he got to the stage where, even if I didn't do anything silly, he still had the giggles![598]

It would have taken Frank back to the glory days of glued-down props and whoopee-cushions at the Little Theatre. Life on the commercial stage could be so much more relaxed than it was under Sumner's beady eye.

There were other shows scheduled for the Tivoli circuit, none of them a success: *Waltzes of Vienna* didn't make it to Sydney at all after a brief and disastrous season at the Palais in St Kilda; *Hadrian VII* did make the journey, following its solid Melbourne premiere at Her Majesty's, but just in time to close the Sydney Tivoli forever. Frank's ventures into the commercial theatre did no damage to his reputation, however, and it suited him that they didn't last too long. Big shows, short runs, hardly ever out of rehearsal, and always another commitment to go to. It was just the way Frank had always wanted his career to be.

There were films, too – smaller ones than Frank was accustomed to, but each of them prestigious in its way. He played Godfrey, the madly gay art dealer, in *Age of Consent* (1969), an adaptation of Norman Lindsay's self-referential novel about an ageing artist whose inspiration is rekindled when he meets a nubile muse on a beautiful Queensland beach.

Frank was in distinguished company: James Mason had been imported to play the lead, and the Englishman Michael Powell to direct, while Helen Mirren, the great discovery of the previous season at the Royal Shakespeare Company, played the fetching Cora. There were high hopes for the film, in which Mason had invested a good deal of his own money, but the script was hampered by the limitations of Lindsay's story. Its modest claims to fame rested on its visual attractions – the startling beauty of its locations on the Great Barrier Reef, and Mirren's notorious nude scene; Mason's retrospective advice to potential viewers was, 'Don't bother looking at me on screen. Just look at Helen Mirren's bottom'.[599] Even an accomplished scene-stealer like Frank could not stand up to that kind of competition.

He appeared in another British venture down under, *Ned Kelly*, directed by Tony Richardson with the large-lipped Rolling Stone Mick Jagger debuting in the title-role, later that year. Frank was Redmond Barry, the judge who sent Ned the bushranger to the gallows; the film, with its romantic if rather glum acceptance of Ned's status as outsider-hero, allowed no room for

598 June Bronhill, *The Merry Bronhill*, North Ryde, Methuen Haynes, 1987, p.115.
599 Ivan Waterman, *Helen Mirren. The Biography*, London, Metro Publishing, 2003, p.33.

Barry's character to develop any of the complexity of the historical man. This suited Frank well enough. Barry was written as just another variation on despotism, which he could do with panache even without a toga, and he had always preferred a light preparation.

Ned Kelly, too, had a disappointing reception. Frank probably spared a thought, as it sank with *Age of Consent* slowly below the critical horizon, for the time and effort that his father had put into building reciprocal relationships with overseas studios. At least on these occasions all the money floating down the drain was English.

Frank's third film in Australia enjoyed a better fate, though it relied on the late-night drive-in audience to do so. *Alvin Purple Rides Again* (1974) was the sequel to *Alvin Purple* (1973), the first Australian film to take advantage of new censorship laws that had introduced an R (restricted to audiences of eighteen years and over) classification and, not at all coincidentally, a film that set new records at the box-office. The original was a cheerful sex romp, starring Graeme Blundell as a hapless and improbable sex object no female can resist; it was a clever reversal of sexual stereotypes, but as Alvin desperately tried to escape from hordes of smitten schoolgirls, randy wives and outraged husbands, Tim Burstall's film also found plenty of opportunities to play with soft-porn fantasy.

The sequel had less going for it. Alvin spent much less time in bed, for a start, despite the promise of its subtitle, *Foreplay: The Prequel*, and its American title, *Alvin Rideas Again, and Again! And Again! And Again!* But there was also a risible cops-and-robbers plot, in which Alvin finds he has a double, the crime boss Balls McGee, whose identity Alvin takes over for reasons that are unbelievably complicated. It was in Balls' seedy world, rather than in some titillating corner of Alvin's sexual progress, that Frank's character Fingers did his manipulating. The part was small, but suitably depraved; its effectiveness turned, like Frank's television advertisements, on the fact that the actor was so recognisable that he brought with him all the baggage of roles and notorieties that had nothing to do with the colourful tale of Alvin.

Then, quite suddenly, things started to change. It was in *The Cherry Orchard* that it first became clear that the bigger roles were becoming too much for his memory. He had bluffed his way through Azdak and Galileo well enough, despite the proliferation of funny stories about his habit of falling over whenever the mind went blank. Those stories were indulgent, because they assumed a stage personality big enough to survive the occasional hitch. The Stage Manager's report for an early performance of *The Cherry Orchard* still presented Frank's little lapses with lines as a charming eccentricity:

> Gaev to Liubov: I used to sleep in this room when I was a child, and now I'm 21!!! How strange it seems!
>
> – otherwise a super show … [600]

What the audience made of that very 'strange' remark from the middle-aged Gaev is not recorded; presumably they saw it as a symptom of mental debility in the character, not the actor. But Sumner was reading the signs. Frank remained a part of the company, but the offers of roles became fewer and further apart. In *The Double Dealer* in 1975, Frank confirmed that the strategy of the timely collapse was well and truly established:

> Frank covered the loss of his lines by passing out onstage at the Athenaeum Theatre … He lay there like a beached whale until the revolve took him out of sight to a round of applause from the audience.[601]

Sumner cast Frank as Shylock in *The Merchant of Venice* in the following year, but it was a great mutual relief when Frank withdrew from the role: 'he just knew he couldn't do it any more'.[602] In future he would be confined to quirky cameos like the butlers in *The Importance of Being Earnest* or the Leading Bunyip in *Pete McGinty and the Dreamtime*, or to material that he could be presumed to know already, like the return of Sheridan Whiteside in 1980, or Frank's appearance as absolutely himself in *Frankly Thring*.

What went wrong had a lot to do with the drinking, no doubt. The six bottles a day that Googie Withers claimed got him through *The Cherry Orchard* were no longer enough. Sumner decreed that Frank should be rehearsed only in the mornings, because there was no point in working with him after lunch. Since Frank was still sedating himself on Nembutal in the small hours of the morning, an early call was the last thing he needed. So the problem with lines may have been in part a product of increased intake, in part a consequence of the years he had devoted to wiping out brain cells.

Then there was the labyrinthitis. When and how this began, how precisely it was related to the failure of his memory, how much it was a cause or a symptom of his profound loss of self-confidence in these years, where it stood in the spiral of drinking and depression that seemed his only resource,

600 Stage Manager's Report, *The Cherry Orchard*, 2 February 1973, Melbourne Theatre Company Papers, University of Melbourne Archive.

601 Roland Rocchecciolli, email to the author.

602 John Sumner, interview with the author.

whether it was ever 'real' – these questions lead only to other questions. Frank thought it was real, though. He needed some explanation for what he could feel happening to him.

> This is a recognised clinical condition. The actor who suffers from it cannot get on stage. Thring … found himself trying to get ready for his cue, but instead bumping into walls in the backstage corridors. It was, in his words, agony.
>
> Labyrinthitis means that actors deep down do not want to do a play any more, or even worse, that they have lost their nerve.[603]

Frank dated the condition from *Pete McGynty*, but there were warning signs well before he began bunyipping. Most people diagnosed it as a case of Ben Ean, or at least the best part of one. Perhaps Frank saw the uncertainty about cues and his route to the stage that way too, for a while. But, whatever this condition was, it was no temporary thing, and nor was the crisis of confidence that might have been its cause or its symptom.

Through the late 1970s, Frank found a number of projects to fill in the time, and to compensate in some measure for the fact that he had largely destroyed his credit with his beloved MTC. There was a memorably excessive *Othello* for the South Australian Theatre Company in 1975, in which someone unfortunately decided that Frank's Moor should be caramel for the occasion; Frank's performance was accordingly dubbed 'the cappuccino Othello'. He remembered enough from Shakespeare's script and his own grandstanding at the Arrow to bluff his way through the season, but it was touch and go. Then in 1978 he played a manservant in the Googie Withers/John McCallum commercial vehicle, *The Kingfisher*. For Googie Frank's performance only confirmed how far he had slipped; for her husband, it was a graphic demonstration of how essentially limited his acting had always been:

> As an actor he always played front. It was very irritating to work with on stage though I don't think it was deliberately competitive. All he knew was to play to the audience, right to the edge of the stage, sometimes leaving you stranded up the back. When my agent Ronnie Waters saw *The Kingfisher*, he said "What an extraordinary performance by that

603 John Larkin, 'Thring Fades to Black', *Sunday Press*, 3 July 1988, p.59.

> Thring fellow. Supposed to be your manservant and he never even looks at you. So much for deference!"[604]

It wasn't all grand sham. In rehearsal at the Comedy Theatre in Melbourne, John heard that Frank was in a terrible rage with the wardrobe department. Assuming that Frank found his butler's uniform too unbecoming for his outlandish tastes, John went to his dressing-room to find out what was the matter. At first it seemed that he was right. Frank was jumping up and down on the new grey jacket he had been given to wear. But the problem wasn't its drabness; Frank's tantrum was all about authenticity:

> "This thing has come straight from the tailor's, John! I've been your manservant for years – I can't wear a brand-new jacket!" All for the cause of reality! Bit strange coming from Frank … [605]

It might have been a rare and belated moment of homage to Stanislavski. More probably, it was another symptom of an actor who had lost his self-belief, and was trying, in roughly equal measure, to assert some residual personal control and to blame somebody else for the problem he was unable to face. The jacket was not, in the end, the issue. When Frank was, for undisclosed reasons, unavailable for the revival tour of *The Kingfisher*, Ron Frazer replaced him, much to the relief of the producer and star. 'And he was much better, of course. Frank was a turn. Ronnie was an actor'.[606]

In 1979, largely through the persuasive powers of Peter Cooke, the Queensland Theatre Company agreed to mount a revival of *The Man Who Came to Dinner* with Frank again as Whiteside, and Frank after a lot of coaxing and a lot more grumbling agreed to do it. Finally, the company and Frank were brought together for the first reading. It was a disaster:

> There was a reference in the script to Sheridan Whiteside being partial to the Sherry Netherlands. Poor John Krummel, the director, interrupted to ask Frank whether he drank sherry. Frank was appalled. "It's a fucking hotel, you stupid fucking min. It's one of the finest fucking hotels in fucking New York." He turned to me and shouted,

---

604 John McCallum, interview with the author.
605 ibid.
606 ibid.

> "This is simply fucking absurd. What am I doing in this fucking room? Get me out of here."[607]

Peter didn't, and he stayed, and the season ran. But Frank's inability to remember the lines that he had played so often before made each performance a tense affair; fortunately, the fact that Whiteside was in a wheelchair throughout the show made it mostly manageable. Frank had no need to worry about cues for moves since others made them for him, and the chair was fitted with a special tray for his script, so that he could read the lines whenever he had to. The same strategies got him through his fifth and last incarnation as Whiteside when the Melbourne Theatre Company revived it in the following year. Frank was fifty-three, but he was being treated – by the theatre companies, by his anxiously protective friends, by the beautiful young men who caught his perpetually roving eye – as an old man. A Grand Old Man, certainly, a man who had once been and done something. But a man who was past it, whatever 'it' was.

Frank's powers as an actor had begun to decline in his early forties, and by the time he was fifty, they had largely gone. It was a terribly cruel irony, however self-inflicted the wound. Frank had reached the kind of age that he had been playing for years. For another actor of his type – a Monty Woolley, a Robert Morley, a Peter Ustinov – it would have been the beginning of his finest decade. But not for Frank. It was cruel, too, given the way in which his social and emotional life had shrunk. The theatre was where he lived. The theatre was where he found his friends, his purpose, his sense of his role and himself. The theatre was, really, all he had.

A number of people noticed when Frank gave his finest performances, as Ahab or Max or Galileo or even Sheridan Whiteside, and almost everybody seemed to know when he was past his best. The question that remains, though, is just how good he was at his peak.

To the generation that grew up on episodes of *Skippy* and Frank's outrageous ads, it would have been inconceivable that he was ever a serious actor; the Thring they saw could only do self-caricature, and the notion of

607 Peter Cooke, interview with the author.

that amalgam of affectation playing Macbeth or Othello or Oedipus was absurd. Frank's sometime friend, employer and role model Laurence Olivier once asked 'What is acting but lying, and what is good lying but convincing lying?'; Frank was a serial liar, and probably a good one, but was he ever 'convincing'?

The best answer to the question about whether he was ever a genuinely good actor is probably the one that Frank was inclined to give when filling in forms that enquired as to 'Sex': 'occasionally'. On the available evidence, occasionally, as in *Galileo* or *Moby Dick – Rehearsed*, there was an intensity that suggested not only that he had inhabited the role, but that he had grasped its intellectual context. Occasionally, as in *The School for Scandal* or *Salome*, and perhaps even *The Man Who Came to Dinner*, the size of his presence found a suitable match in the style of the play. Occasionally, as in *The Ideal Husband* or *The Play's the Thing*, he could be brilliantly funny:

> Frank excelled at farce. He had impeccable timing. Frank really understood the difference between comedy and farce.[608]

Occasionally, as in *The Homecoming*, he lied so convincingly that he seemed for a while to disappear into the role. As he said to Roland Rocchecciolі, not only did the audience not recognise him as Max the butcher, but, extraordinarily in more ways than one, 'they actually believed that I wanted to fuck Jennifer Claire!'[609] It helped, of course, that in the Pinter play Frank's idiosyncratic line in menace was camouflaged by a cloth cap and a Cockney accent. He was usually a lot harder to hide.

The question is complicated by the profound shifts in attitude during Frank's career as to what acting, and especially very good acting, was understood to be. A resonant voice and an imperious command of the stage were still eminently desirable when Frank began his career at the Little Theatre in 1946; all the reviewers noted with approval the power of The Voice and the size of The Presence in those precocious early appearances, as though that was what the game was all about. But within a decade the game was becoming quite a different one. While Frank was successfully strutting his stuff on a grand scale in *Titus Andronicus*, the new wave of actors were playing in quite another key. Osborne, Pinter and the other bold new voices in British theatre set their plays in seedy

608 Roland Rocchecciolі, interview with the author.
609 Roland Rocchecciolі, email to the author.

interiors, where taut conversations took place in relentless close-up and usually in provincial accents. The plays of Williams and Miller were taking the American theatre into the territory of suburban neurosis, where the structures of bourgeois domesticity cracked and disintegrated under the weight of the lies that had created them. Actors in these plays needed to seem like real, even ordinary, people; The Voice and The Presence were antithetical to that purpose.

Frank was a theatrical throwback to the age of the Grand Thespian. Olivier was born in 1907; Richardson and Wolfit in 1902, Gielgud in 1904, Quayle in 1913, Guinness in 1914, Welles in 1915. All of them were a decade or two older than Frank. The actor to whom, from the age of nineteen, he was most often compared, Monte Woolley (born 1888) was nearly as old as Frank's father. Some of them were capable of the self-effacement that the new age seemed to demand of them: Olivier managed the transition to a period in which unpolished accents and the art of the television close-up suddenly ruled his profession with an apparent ease that absolutely confirmed his greatness. Frank, though, was never going be unobtrusive, or even (noticeably, at least) subtle. Even on the Australian stage to which he came back in the 1960s, Frank was starting to look like a man born out of his time.

Moreover, that Australian theatre was undergoing its own highly political version of the painful transitions bequeathed to it by what was happening in London and New York, and in defiantly anti-establishment little theatres on their fringes and elsewhere. Suddenly, at the end of the 1960s, a bold, rambunctious New Wave represented by local playwrights like David Williamson transformed the repertoire of even mainstream companies like the MTC forever. It was a kind of theatre driven by the energy of the local vernacular. Australian culture was its focus, warts and all, and there was no role for manicured upper-class English vowels except as the occasional butt of an easy joke. A number of Australian actors were unable to rediscover, or even to affect, the accent that they had so determinedly tried to lose. Frank, whose accent had never been other than uniquely his own, was never going to be part of that revolution.

But while the recognition that his theatrical style was out of alignment with the time and place in which he found himself explains a lot, it also concedes too much. It denies him his claims to occasional greatness by seeing him simply as the self-caricature he increasingly became, which was precisely that of the Grand Anachronism. The critics who saw Frank recognised those moments, just as they noticed when he was coasting, when

The Voice and The Presence were all that seemed to be asked of him, and all that he was inclined to offer his audience.

Thus Phillip Adams, who farewelled Frank with an obituary more disparaging than an actor's worst nightmare:

> Frankly, Frank couldn't act his way out of a wet paper bag. Oh, he'd rave and rant and posture, spraying the front stalls with his serpentine sibilance ... But the performances were essentially hollow. There was only one role in which he was at all convincing. That of himself. And even then, he over-acted.[610]

The same Phillip Adams, however, had twenty-five years earlier, when Frank was in what most critics agreed was his prime, greeted his performance as Falstaff in *Henry IV, Part One* as a revelation:

> I never expect to see ... a finer Falstaff than Frank Thring. He seemed the perfect embodiment of 'that trunk of humours, that bolting hutch of beastliness, that swoln parcels [*sic*] of dropsies'. Rolling obscenely around the stage or dimpling like an innocent cherub, he was a delight to watch and hear.

It didn't seem necessary, apparently, with the old role-player safely dead, to explore the disparity between those perceptions, or to ask what might in a quarter of a century have led a critic so completely to change his mind – or perhaps, simply, to forget.

Thus, too, Leonard Glickfeld, who a year before had dismissed his performance as Azdak in *The Caucasian Chalk Circle*, and indeed Sumner's whole production, as 'a Christmas panto', but who felt that he was seeing something much finer in *Galileo*:

> The proof of Frank Thring's performance as Galileo is that it shows that it is not the scientific genius who is important, but his effect on other people: the true "star" performance highlights the ensemble.
>
> Thring delivers the monologues with an enchantment that is like music, and his final scene is among the best of his career. Subdued, hoary, large gestures now curtailed to minuteness, he scrutinises his submission to

610 'Frankly sssspeaking', *Australian Weekend Review*, 21/22 January 1995, p.2.

> the old order with a grim, ennobling honesty. The fingers of the failed, broken hero continue to grasp with unconscious furtiveness betraying the incorrigible animal in his nature.[611]

There's not much trace in this description of the preposterous old fraud, dispensing his lavish and distinctive servings of ham, which is all that some of his audience can now remember of him. This sounds for all the world like a highly intelligent and committed actor, bringing all his gifts to bear on a challenging role, giving generously to the actors that surround him, and delivering a powerful and moving performance. None of those qualities was part of the Thring persona. But, as we have seen, Frank characteristically mocked or denied the things that meant most to him. Acting truthfully, sometimes, might well have been one of them.

The first of the handful of performances that he really prized, that as Ahab in the UTRC's first production of *Moby Dick – Rehearsed*, evoked a similar response. None of the reviewers failed to notice the scale of the performance; it was hard to miss. But A.S.J., in the *Bulletin*, moved past the inevitable Voice and Presence to register how sensitively both were being harnessed in the interests of the character and the play:

> Whatever its roots, Ahab's obsession certainly invested him with a terrifying intensity ... Nonetheless, as superbly played by a scowling, limping Frank Thring, the captain's dominance of the play was rarely more than it should have been – which is not always the case with a Thring characterisation.[612]

The critic noted the way the central performance enabled the subsidiary ones, who were 'surprisingly' able to avoid 'becoming entirely lost under the shadow of Thring's magnificent Ahab'. Geoffrey Hutton was similarly struck by the disciplined power of the playing:

> Frank Thring is a gift for the role. There is no question of overplaying in this flamboyant portrait of obsession: the roaring voice, the intent scowl, the stumping wooden leg all belong to Melville's authentic figure.[613]

---

611 Leonard Glickfeld, *National Times*, 17–22 May 1971, p.20.

612 *Bulletin*, 25 November 1959, p.23.

613 *Age*, 17 November 1959, p.3

In reviewing the reviewers of Frank's work with the MTC, it's striking how often words like 'disciplined' and 'authentic' recur; they're not the kind of adjectives that came to be associated with his image and reputation in the last two decades of his life. To the critics of Melbourne, from the days of the Arrow to his astonishing Galileo in 1971, there was no doubt that Thring was a fine actor, one of the few in the country who could take on the biggest of roles, a man 'whose personal wealth alone seems to prevent him from seeking "a major international career"'.[614] From that point, the affection in which Frank was held as a celebrity oddity grew in inverse proportion to the decline in respect for the way he pursued his vocation.

This may have been partly a consequence of the repertory model of the Melbourne Theatre Company. The pattern of performance that saved Frank from the nightmare of the long commercial run, that stopped him becoming too bored and possibly kept him mostly sane, was also one that encouraged bad acting habits. A lot of the shows, after all, were of the kind in which style and charisma were not only essential, but might almost be enough; on a tight schedule, it must have been tempting, perhaps even necessary, to play the old familiar tricks, the old familiar public self. Frank closed in *Dracula* on a Saturday night in March 1962, and opened in *Macbeth* on the following Tuesday. For the three preceding weeks, he had rehearsed the Scottish play by day, and played the blood-sucking Count five nights a week; there was no space for thinking his way into the character of Macbeth, and a terrible risk not only that Macbeth would be left to Voice and Presence, but that he might contain a fair bit of the psychopath that Frank embodied by night.

Partly, of course, the decline in status as in career was attributable to bad luck. The forgetfulness, the labyrinthitis, the succession of ailments – all conspired to end his growth as an actor, and to incline him to fall back on his stock-in-trade, performing Frank Thring. But in all these things, he was in some degree complicit; Frank had done the damage to his mind and his body that had left him where suddenly he found himself.

Frank was complicit, too, in the triumph of his persona over his art. He was a victim, at the same time; the public liked the preposterous role he played for them, all of its dangerous subversiveness turned harmlessly into comedy, and increasingly he gave them just what they wanted. In life, it seemed that it was impossible that one could be loved without uncovering the self; on the stage and the celebrity circuit, Frank found repeatedly that the more self-protectively he played the more they loved him. It was

614 John Cargher, review of *The Caucasian Chalk Circle*, *Bulletin*, 16 May 1970, p.47.

very easy, very seductive, this adulation. Who could blame him, then, for performing the role that not only made so many people happy, but kept him safe?

It was Frank's choice, though, to be the prisoner of his concocted self. And the more he played it, irrespective of the character or the show, the further he moved from the intelligent self-forgetfulness that had sometimes let him know what it was to truly act, the more impossible he made it that he would ever feel that again.

Frank liked to make a distinction between two kinds of actor. He used it in an interview with John Larkin to mark the Melbourne Theatre Company's five hundredth production in 1982:

> "There are tigers, and there are pussycats. Sybil, of course, was a pussycat. Googie's a bit of a pussycat, but she can be a tiger. Larry, or Bette Davis, automatically came on thinking: 'You don't think I can do this play, do you? I'll show you!' and the audience has got a tiger loose."
>
> And which is Thring? He answered without even thinking: "Tiger", he growled, and sat back and smiled like a pussycat.[615]

He liked it so much that he repeated it quite regularly over the years. The distinction had less to do with a particular style of acting than a particular attitude to the audience. The tiger-actor's relationship with his public is adversarial, even malicious, and that is the source of its intensity:

> FT: If you say here are fifteen hundred people who have paid a lot of money to see me play Othello at 8.15 tonight, you'd better be on the ball.
>
> BH: Do you think people come to see Othello, or do they come to see Frank Thring?

615 John Larkin, 'Melbourne Theatre Company. Then … and Now', *Sunday Age*, 16 October 1988, p.58.

> FT: Both. They come to see Frank Thring fail as Othello.[616]

Fighting them, beating them, is the actor's triumph. But it's a battle for personal survival that is repeated with every performance of every play, and it begins, and recurs, in terror.

Long before Frank had ever heard of 'labyrinthitis' as a condition, he was all too familiar with stage-fright as a set of physical symptoms. Bill Howie recalled Bunney Brooke's story from the early days at Melbourne Repertory, about how she and Frank held hands in the wings to comfort each other, both shaking with fear:

> BH: I was surprised, because you seem so confident.
>
> FT: Well, that's acting, baby.
>
> BH: And you still get nervous?
>
> FT: Petrified. And it becomes worse and worse and worse.[617]

Frank's fear of performance lay behind his sense of its fundamental absurdity, and his horror of the extended run. Both, like the nervousness, became worse and worse and worse.

> Then if you are in a successful show you have to work eight times a week for months and months and months. And always you've got this thing hanging over you. That's what makes actors eccentric. You have to be mad. So one wakes up on a perfectly nice day in Melbourne and at 8 p.m. one murders his father, fucks his mother and gouges out his eyes with a hat pin.
>
> That's *Oedipus Rex*. All that happens just at a time when one should be finishing one's dinner, sipping a good port and taking in a nineteen forties Bette Davis movie.[618]

And the fear spread out to encompass all forms of travel that ended in another opening of another show. Steve Cossar interviewed Frank just after his forays to Adelaide for *Othello*, to Brisbane for *The Man Who Came to*

616 Bill Howie interview.
617 ibid.
618 Keith Dunstan, *Ratbags*, p.136.

Dinner, and to most capitals for *The Kingfisher*; it was a tour that, for a variety of reasons, was agony for him from the start :

> SC: Do you like having to move around like that all the time?
>
> FT: I hate every moment of it.
>
> SC: Why do it?
>
> FT: Well, that's what one's paid for. I mean, do you like sitting here at this ungodly hour of the morning? And having to cope with me?[619]

It seemed to be almost an allergy. But though he presented it as a form of existential weariness, an aversion to recycling acting choices that had once been fresh and inspired, Frank's hatred of recapitulation must always have involved some element of cost analysis; the pain of overcoming the terror could be justified when the creative gain was new, but when the passion and the novelty had passed and the pain was still as keen, the game was no longer worth the candle. It was probably a bit like sado-masochistic sex. Frank would have understood that analogy.

The tiger was created in the theatre out of his conquest of terror. But when his fear could no longer be conquered, and the audience's malevolence turned to sympathetic indulgence, the tiger could hardly be expected to burn brightly anymore. He could do nothing but roll over, and hope for their affection. And having his tummy tickled had never been the kind of acceptance Frank had been after.

In the summer of 1981–2 there were two striking symbols of the taming of Frank Thring. One was Sumner's initiative to make the MTC's Christmas show for that year a one-man show, *Frankly Thring*, in which Frank chatted to the audience about his career, his family, and pretty much anything he cared to talk about. The other was his appointment as King of Moomba, the festival that invites the citizens of Melbourne each March to 'get together and have fun'. The crowds that lined Swanston Street to cheer their King on his motorised float, surrounded by glamorous girls in minimal clothes, had no desire to watch Frank Thring fail; nor did the people who filled Russell Street Theatre to listen to Frank's stories about his life. They came to declare a strange but quite powerful affection.

619 Steve Cossar interview.

There were jokes, of course, about kings and queens, but there was little malice in them. Frank probably made most of them himself. Somehow, without wanting it, let alone seeking it, the unpredictable predator had been transformed into domestic pet. The tiger had become a pussycat.

Frankly Thring was to be the celebration of a theatrical life. The minutes of a planning meeting in July strike the festive note very clearly:

> Moves are being made to gain permission, then promotion for wine to be served in the interval. We were looking for a way to make this sensible, bearing in mind the small size of the Russell Street Theatre foyer. I suggested that the under-ceiling of the theatre could be hung with balloons (the whole night will be a party anyway) and at the appropriate time a number of the balloons – say 50 – could be released and those people who obtained one could be entitled to a drink.[620]

The structure of the show was to be organised as a loose autobiography, but it allowed plenty of scope for him to read poems and to play music that he liked, or to tell some of his favourite tales.

It was to be not just a tour of the 'real' world according to Thring, but a journey into his imagination, even – alarmingly – into his dreams.

> Frank frequently used the word Cubist … One of the items he was thinking of doing was taking place in an opium brothel. He wondered if something could be done with gauze walls.[621]

Still more dangerously, Frank conceived the evening as largely unscripted. In an interview just before rehearsals began, he was comfortably, if alarmingly, vague about the shape it might take:

> "Each night will be different. It's not going to be glamorous like *Betty Blockbuster*, or Barry Humphries. I'm not spending the whole evening in suspender belts. More of a quiet little family affair."
>
> Although nothing has been written yet, he intends to perform a selection of pieces that will stay the same from night to night. "They won't be from plays, because most of the plays I've wanted to do I've

620 'Frankly Thring. Notes from a Discussion with Frank Thring, 9.7.81', Melbourne Theatre Company files, University of Melbourne Archive.
621 ibid.

> done. They will be things that don't fit into plays. Things that I would like to share with the audience."[622]

In the end the readings were a very mixed lot: recitations of 'Flannan Isle' and 'The Pigtail of Li Fang Yu' that he had been forced to learn at Melbourne Grammar, a reading of a much-abridged version of 'The Infanta' that reflected his immersion in Wilde during interminable delays in the shooting of *King of Kings*, and a little poem by Dorothy Parker that he claimed had been a great resource when he had been plunged deep into gloom on finding that nothing could be done about his speech impediment:

> SUICIDE
>
> Razors pain you
> Rivers are damp
> Acids stain you
> And drugs cause cramp
> Guns aren't lawful
> Nooses dive
> Gas smells awful
> You might as well live

There were bits of film footage – Frank's fleeting film debut in *The Sentimental Bloke*, half a minute of *Diggers*, the pit of enraged wolves in *The Vikings*, and some smart toga action from *Ben Hur* – and two of his commercials, for Hutton's hams and Anticol. But mostly, in the end, it was Frank chatting about his life.

The life that he told began with his father, whose deeds filled perhaps the first fifteen minutes of the performance. It did not include his mother. Frank told the stories about how his father had exploited him as he did everyone else – the publicity stunt with the snake in the Regent foyer, the appearances as an unpaid extra in *Diggers* and *The Sentimental Bloke* – and he indulged his favourite comparison with Simon Legree. But these memories were recalled, this time, with unmistakable admiration and affection.

In the early performances, until the show's length became so embarrassing as to require radical surgery, Frank included a poem about Frank Thring Senior, which he said had been sent to him anonymously after his father's

622 Kate Legge, 'A life in the day of Frank Thring', *Theatre Australia*, volume 6, number 3, November 1981, p.10.

death. The poem, 'To F.T.', was actually the work of C.J. Dennis (with a significant debt to Rudyard Kipling), and had been presented to its subject at a dinner on the eve of his strangely solitary departure for England in 1932:

> If you can steel your heart against the wailing
> Of these your fiends who sit about this board,
> When from the quay tomorrow you go sailing
> To carry culture to old England's horde -
> If you can dry your tears, yet still remember
> Our thoughts are with you through all stress and storm,
> And, reaching London in the chill November,
> Still let enthusiasm keep you warm -
>
> If you can banish yearnings sentimental
> At leaving us, and battle on alone,
> Forgetting pleasures of the occidental
> And woes of cutting room and microphone -
> If you can, like a hero and a free man,
> Meet troubles in the first and second reel
> And still face English coldness like a he-man,
> With bland diplomacy – <u>and</u> sex appeal -
>
> If you find action slowed down to a crawl, but,
> Keeping impatience sternly on the leash,
> Break barriers with the polish of a Talbot
> Combined with the aplomb of a McLeish -
> If you can show them that you're no alien,
> Coming to force his product on their screens,
> But ever of the Empire, and Australian
> Setting its ideals in Australian scenes -
>
> If you can wade through seven reels of trouble
> And see no prospect of the happy end,
> While worries wax and difficulties double
> And none about you seems to stand your friend -
> If, in that hour when you feel most forsaken,
> You can still battle and 'put in the boot',
> Then, Big Boy, you'll be bringing home the bacon;
> Go after it! ... Lights! Camera! Action! Shoot![623]

623 Thring Papers, Performing Arts Museum, Melbourne.

The poem is not of interest for any insight in particular that it gives into F.T., although it is tempting to see the rather odd sideways glance at his improbable 'sex appeal' as a reference, for those in the know, to the importance in his travel plans of Donalda Warne. Nor does it have much distinction as occasional verse; in fact, it's precisely the mediocrity of the piece that makes Frank's insistence on reading it in full so significant. He chose it not because it was funny, but because it was a tribute to his father, and the act of including it in *Frankly Thring* made the tribute his own.

The familiar tall tales about his own career were in the show, too, of course – Frank paying the papers to run the headline 'Oliviers send for Thring', Frank marrying Joan astride Shakespeare's grave, Frank charming the chaps with poems at Puckapunyal. So were the familiar inflations – of numbers, of successes, of absurdities, of horrors; Whiteside's line 'Is there a man in the world who suffers as I do from the gross inadequacies of the human race?' was never quoted, but the thought was the premise for the humour of the show. Most of it had a grain of truth, but it was a very selective telling of the tale, and the characteristic layers of self-parody made it a typically self-protective one, too. Frank wisely had no intention of appearing in a suspender-belt. In fact he had no intention of baring anything at all.

The response to the show each night confirmed how completely Frank had parodied himself into acceptability. The MTC subscribers loved it, and – obviously – him. To restore some of the air of informality that Frank's original improvisatory model had envisaged, there were questions from the stalls each night. Most of these were 'plants', of course, but now and then a genuine one sneaked through.

The bank of set-up queries included a number that were innocently banal ('What do you have for breakfast?', 'Mr Thring, what kind of tea do you get and where do you get it?', 'What does the gold medallion around your neck mean?'), but could still produce some racy answers. Others were more explicitly framed to lower the tone hilariously:

> Is this show the biggest ego trip imaginable or do you propose a sequel?
>
> Like Gordon Chater, have you ever been co-ersed [sic] into playing a nude scene?
>
> I come from Shepparton and I don't know your hangouts – please give directions.
>
> When you buy this theatre if you don't already own it will you please replace the seats?

> Dear Frankly, Who irons your shirts? Are you concealing a love-bite?
>
> Were the school dances at Melbourne Grammar as bad as they are today?[624]

If it was the basis for a 'quiet little family affair', it was a funny old family. But it was a happy family, and it wasn't little at all. Frank could forget things in such company, and would always be forgiven.

Not everyone was caught up in the mood of celebratory compassion. Bob Crimeen, the theatre critic for the Melbourne *Sun*, described *Frankly Thring* as 'the most self-indulgent happening in Melbourne theatre in living memory', but this wasn't the prelude to one last gesture of magnanimity:

> It climaxes with a series of written questions, allegedly submitted by audience members, which set new standards of banality …
>
> If only Frank Thring, and not Ernest Borgnine, had been thrown into The Vikings wolf pit.[625]

There were probably others in the audience who found the self-indulgence unforgivable. Most did not.

The argument about who first fed whom to the wolves in that pit in Hardangerfjorden became oddly important in the critical cut and thrust about its subject's actual status that surrounded *Frankly Thring*. No doubt Frank had Bob Crimeen and others in mind, and not just his addressee, Peter Coster of the *Herald*, when he made his final bid for the veracity of the record:

> I am shocked and hurt that such a fan of mine could confuse my cinematographic triumphs.
>
> It is true that in THE VIKINGS I ended up in a pit full of wolves, but not before I had already consigned the chunky Ernest Borgnine to a similar fate, and in passing, chopped off Tony Curtis' hand.
>
> In EL CID, I was not only thrown from a 300 foot wall, but on hitting bottom, was cannibalised by an eager multitude of starving Spanish peasants.

---

624 Handwritten questions for designated members of the audience at *Frankly Thring*, Thring papers, Performing Arts Museum, Melbourne.

625 Bob Crimeen, *Sun*, 3 December 1981, p.24.

> In KING OF KINGS and BEN HUR, I simply decapitated John the Baptist and crucified Christ.
>
> In such troublous times I think that matters of such importance as these should be recorded with absolute accuracy, don't you?
>
> FRANKLY THRING.[626]

The tone made it clear that these 'matters of such importance' really didn't matter at all. The films, the stars, the whole career, were to be treated with all the reverence they deserved, and, accordingly, to be treated as a joke.

At one level, Frank in his one-man show was simply lodging an ambit claim to his right to his own tall story, in an attempt to discourage liars with less entitlement than his own. At the same time, of course, he was registering that the story that almost everybody knew, the story that involved winning an international reputation and then trading on it for as long as one could at 'the arse-end of the world'[627], was essentially not only comically unheroic, but ironic.

Frankly Thring was all about Frank, but it was also about a very unusual man's relationship with the place he came from, and the people who lived there. It was the perfect prelude to the announcement in the following month that he had been chosen to be King of Moomba.

It said something for Melbourne's growing sophistication as a city that Frank was enthroned. Nobody acknowledged it explicitly at the time, but everyone knew, of course. Frank Thring in 1982 was still in most respects the antithesis of Melbourne's public values: he was gay, he was rude, he had nothing to do with home or family or sport. But somehow he was no longer threatening, and somehow he had become appropriated as the face of a modern Melbourne that could comfortably absorb all the kinds of difference on which Frank had constructed his career and his sense of self. He had ceased to be unpredictable, and could now be installed as a kind of kept iconoclast, a sign of how wonderfully adaptable the niceness of 'the world's most liveable city' could be. Frank probably despised that accommodating complacency as much as he did the provincialism that he had found so suffocating, and had intermittently escaped, two decades before.

But he had come home, and home had adjusted to embrace him, and there was almost nothing he could do any more to become disreputable. It

---

626 Letter from Frank Thring to Peter Coster, Melbourne Theatre Company archives, B53/1/7.

627 This phrase was used, probably not originally but certainly (for the first time) iconically by Australia's Prime Minister, Paul Keating.

was galling for him, surely, and the kind of irony that only the gods could find amusing.

It was also, of course, exactly the kind of recognition that another kind of actor, another kind of public personality, would have celebrated as the pinnacle of his career. How many actors have been invited to perform a one-man show about their careers? Come to that, how many lives of actors alive or dead have become subjects for theatre? How many cities, moreover, would honour a stage actor, even one much more conformist than Frank Thring, as King of their annual festival of frivolity? His reign was sandwiched between those of the soapie star Paul Cronin from *The Sullivans*, and the ex-Collingwood footballer and sports media personality Lou Richards, in 1980 and 1981, and the variety compere Daryl Somers and recently retired Richmond goalsneak Kevin Bartlett in 1983 and 1984. They were, as he possibly noted, odd bedfellows for Frank.

In the event, it rained on his parade. Moomba in Melbourne on the Labour Day weekend of 1982 was one of the wettest in memory. Frank performed the regal wave with determined good cheer, smiling benignly at the sodden throng though he could barely see it through his rain-spattered spectacles. Naturally he recalled it with Bruce Mansfield as yet another of the grotesqueries that, excruciatingly, made up the story of Frank Thring's life.

> BM: Was that a happy occasion for you?
>
> FT: Absolute agony. Poured with rain, the whole thing was a nightmare … Absolutely absurd.
>
> BM: But it was good coverage and publicity.
>
> FT: I don't need that.[628]

The *Herald*, Melbourne's then evening newspaper, ran the news of the day with a banner headline – 'Pour old Moomba'. Dominating the front page was a photograph of King Thring grinning almost convincingly; nearly enough, perhaps, to support the Pollyanna perspective in the report:

> By the end of it all, skimpy costumes clung to wet bodies, carefully constructed hair styles had collapsed and paint ran from some of the floats.

---

628 Interview with Philip Brady and Bruce Mansfield.

> But nothing could wash the smiles from those who took part – and those who watched.[629]

He said it was 'agony'. Was that what he really felt, or what the sardonic persona required him to say? When the people who listened to 3AW at night heard him say that, did they believe him? Or did they smile sentimentally (as befitted a program called 'Remember When') and think that dear old Frank was being naughty again, and of course he didn't really mean it? And as he looked at all those wet, smiling faces, gazing up at him in his regalia and cheering him along the way, did he feel the appreciation – or, more challengingly still, the love – that they seemed to have for him? If he did recognise it, what did it make Frank feel – for them, for the town he had come home to, for the dying career that he had played out before them? Probably he felt both the absurdity and the poignancy of the situation, and in roughly equal measure. He was keenly attuned and attracted to both, after all. The role of Moomba King required just the kind of high-camp posturing that he loved, and represented exactly the kind of bourgeois vulgarity that he deplored. The weather added another twist to the plot. It showed that the gods were smirking, too.

Frank's reign on the Moomba throne became the stuff of legend. An interview in the *Sun*, the morning stablemate of the *Herald*, three years later noted that 'He added a whole new dimension to the job of King of Moomba'. It went on to confirm how much a part of the furniture the old scapegrace had become. The mellowness that now seemed to enfold his public reputation extended to Frank's own musings about his long career:

> "Maybe it could've been more successful. I don't know.
>
> "But I've been everywhere. I've been with the best, met everybody, been in the most glamorous productions, been in lots of plays.
>
> "That's not bad for a little boy from Melbourne Grammar."
>
> Indeed not.
>
> Melbourne without The Voice would not be Melbourne.[630]

The disconcertingly valedictory tone of the piece would have seemed a little odd to someone who had not been observing Frank's decline over the

629 *Herald*, March 1982, p.1.
630 Graeme Johnstone, *Sun Leisure Supplement*, 8 August 1985, p.3.

preceding decade. He was not yet sixty, after all. There should have been plenty more opportunities for the little boy from Melbourne Grammar to demonstrate how far and how stylishly he had travelled.

But Frank was in the process of giving up – on his career, on his provocative public roles, on any hope that sex and affection might ever come into alignment. Those things had been unravelling slowly enough to allow some acceptance of their loss, however tentative, bitter and inadequate it was. He was also about to give up on Rylands, though, the only home he had known, and the powerful symbol of the bizarre heritage that had always defined who he was and who he could not be. That break was sudden, and partly for that reason harder to deal with than those other evidently more important things. Frank consigned his family mansion to the developers, and moved to a little workman's cottage in Fitzroy, a working-class suburb undergoing a process of 'trendification'. In that single choice, Frank determined how much smaller everything would be from now on, and closed much more than a chapter in his life.

TRAVELLING FROM TOORAK TO NORTH FITZROY

Embassy taxi-cab, 17 October 1987

Peak-hour traffic on a Friday afternoon. Getting from Toorak to Fitzroy was harder than it looked in a Melways. Not that one had ever actually looked in a Melways.

So, Fitzroy. What else could you do, what was left to say, when your bank account was as sick as his, and your body even sicker? The Thring family fortune, one had to say, was permanently stuffed. He'd lost Rylands. Going, going, gone.

Still, no-one to leave it to, was there? No more little Thrings. The end of the tree, the end of the line. The end of the House of Thring. The agent talked about the place being renovated, but everyone knew they'd pull it down. Nice metaphor, really; Mr Whelan crashing one of his dirty great balls into the House of Thring, and nothing left but rubble.

Crossing the Yarra, and not even a visa. They said people really did live on the other side. Hard to imagine. One was moving to meet the working-class, whoever they were, and that was enticing. Or perhaps not, though one'd had some competent tradesmen in one's time.

He'd kept some things. No idea how they'd fit into the cottage, but the truck was on the road somewhere with them. So was the unsinkable Wilma Bird, and she'd find a way to organise things. There was a lot to be said for practical people, sometimes.

Just as well, probably, that poor little Wuddles had gone to the great cattery in the sky. There was no room to swing her in Fitzroy.

He'd paint it white. White in every nook, white in every cranny. Suitably angelic, and besides it'd make the place feel bigger. And a touch of hospital sterility was just the job for a man who was coming apart. Fucking feet, fucking leg, fucking throat, fucking bladder, fucking rectum. Just as well nobody wanted to see him these days, because he looked as though he'd been done by Picasso. Most of the mirrors, fortunately, had been too big to take. Safely sold by Wilma and the House of Joel. For this relief, much thanks.

How long? That was the question. Now, of course, it meant something different. And not even how long till Mahoney Street. Now it was the biggest of questions. Sixty years old, and the body was dying. How long, O Lord. Fucked. Stuffed. Rooted. All those verbs, what different meanings they could have. They call it irony, you stupid min.

An inside run, and they were in Fitzroy. A large green sign proclaimed 'Queens Parade'. As they did. And what a wonderfully appropriate boulevard to bear him to his less than ancestral home. He fumbled with the roll of banknotes in his bag, and had to pull out the Ben Ean to get at them. Still half full, which was a nice surprise, but not for long.

He peeled off two tens, and, since it was a special occasion, let the driver keep the twenty cents change. Might encourage him to take some English lessons, possibly even shave. And so to the next challenge, getting out of the car. Predictably not much help forthcoming from the Turkish quarter. Should've kept that two bob after all.

There was too much of him for the back seat of a Commodore, and the stick, and the fact that most of his bits and pieces weren't functioning, compounded the problem.

A walking argument for euthanasia. Mind you, he'd always been in favour of that. Youth in Asia, youth in Europe, and in Australia, if it came to that. One had never been inclined to the cultural cringe. All those beautiful, beautiful boys.

Well, an almost walking argument. One foot after the other, a hand on the roof, and up we go, like a crippled gazelle.

Emoh Ruo. It was, one would have to say, small, distinctly small, though the agent preferred to call it compact. He called it charming, too, and that wasn't true either. A charming period home, needing just a little love, for which read a shitload of money and some rational plumbing.

But it was good enough to live in, and presumably any place'd do to die in. You'll learn to love it in the end, as the actor might have said to the bishop. Or vice-versa, probably.

It needed a bigger gate, and a decent lock. And a steel security door, and some wire, barbed wire. This charming, compact cottage lacked a lot, but most of all it lacked defences.

Chapter Thirteen

A THRING OF SHREDS AND PATCHES

In 1988, Frank Thring gave to the *Sunday Press* one of his increasingly rare interviews. The occasion was the morning after the first episode of *The Gerry Connolly Show* on ABC television, in which Frank had appeared in a cameo. Frank was doing what was expected of an actor who had been well-paid for a few minutes work and the loan of his name, though these obligations, which had rarely been less than excruciating, were these days almost unbearable.

> When asked, he admitted: "I am not having a particularly good time at the moment."
>
> In the theatre, or in his life?
>
> "Both. The theatre is my life."[631]

The interviewer chose to follow up his question, oddly but perhaps considerately, in terms of the relativities of government subsidy for the arts. But that wasn't what Frank was talking about, at all.

Later in that bicentennial year, on returning to the Melbourne Theatre Company after a seven-year absence, he went through the motions again:

> Frank Thring as a *butler*? Two butlers, actually. What are the Melbourne Theatre Company and director Simon Phillips up to in their forthcoming revival of Oscar Wilde's classic comedy, 'The Importance of Being Earnest'?

631 John Larkin, 'Thring Fades to Black', *Sunday Press*, 3 July 1988, p.59.

> Picture the scene, in the house of Lady Bracknell (Ruth Cracknell). Enter the menacing figure of Thring, eyes glistening beneath that broad, domed forehead. Through clenched teeth he hisses: 'Dinner is served'. One almost expects him to bring in the head of John the Baptist on a silver salver.[632]

It is very doubtful that any production of *Earnest*, before or since, has been promoted primarily on the roles of Merriman and Lane.

Frank gave little away about what precisely he would bring to the roles:

> Mr Thring merely smiled enigmatically and said, 'That's for you to make up your mind. I'm only playing a butler – I don't think I've got eight lines. But wait till you see how I play them'.[633]

It wasn't so very unpredictable, really. Frank did with his nearly eight lines just what he was employed to do, and what the loyal patrons of the MTC had come to see. He delayed. He glared. He arched his eyebrows, and curled his lip. He elongated every vowel, and snapped off the consonants like a steel trap. He made it clear – as Merriman, as Lane, as Frank Thring – that the last place in the world he wanted to be was here, in this room, with these people. He made the action of the play turn on the demeanour of its two least significant characters, and they loved it.

The old dog was still playing the old tricks; he could play them in his sleep, and possibly did. But where Thring the tiger had played contempt as a perverse offering of love, Thring the pussycat was hardly pretending at all.

> ... he played the two men-servants, and stole the show, much to his delight. But it was an unhappy time for him – there were tensions backstage and he found the grind of touring and eight performances a week too much. His stamina had gone. When the show closed in Albury, Frank had a taxi waiting at the stage-door to drive him the 350km back to Melbourne. It was a sad finale to a remarkable on-stage career.[634]

It wasn't promoted as Frank's farewell performance, but there was a tacit understanding that in giving him these grossly inflated moments the MTC

632 Mike Daly, *Age*, 13 December 1988, p.17.
633 ibid.
634 Roland Rocchecciolli, 'Wicked ways of Thring ...', *Weekend Australian*, 31 August-1 September 1991, p.7.

was saying goodbye to its biggest, most durable, most outrageous presence. The way the audience cheered his bad habits suggested that they knew it, too. Frank possibly didn't, although the fact that he found playing sixty-four lines a week 'too much' must have alerted him to that possibility.

Although he was doing it tough, and the *Earnest* company in general was not a particularly happy one, Frank could still be an idiosyncratically engaging travelling companion. Cracknell as Bracknell enjoyed the novelty of his acquaintance, and relished the story of Frank's progress through the dusty back-blocks of the Wimmera:

> Touring was not a special joy for Frank, and the Thring groan was much in evidence. One town on our schedule was Nhill – a bit to the west in Victoria. Way out in Frank's view.
>
> He threatened to sell one of his pictures so he could buy the house and bypass Nhill – an offer not taken up by management.
>
> When he knew we would be staying at the Zero Inn his misery was total. 'Zero Inn in Nhill', he groaned. 'And I suppose that's located in Fuck All Street'.[635]

If there was one thing about Frank that could still be relied on, it was his quotability. Ruth Cracknell sensed an unhappiness behind all that world-weary wisecracking that was more than just a reflection of a tiring tour and his failing powers as an actor.

> Frank always looming over one, with his strange, sonorous, sibilant voice. Black eminence. Did Frank garb himself in black to match that core of tragedy within? I often thought so.[636]

She was not alone in that thought. Of course, the tragic clown was always a tempting stereotype, and people had been speculating about it even when he his style and success had made him seem impervious to the usual kinds of human sadness. Now that things weren't going so well, the observation was a common one, and Frank had to work hard to be funny and arch enough to refute it.

---

635 Ruth Cracknell, *Ruth Cracknell: A Biased Memoir*, Viking, Ringwood, 1997, p.208.
636 ibid.

His career on the stage was dead, but film was still a possibility. Instead of fronting up, night after night, to an unknown audience rustling and murmuring in the dark as they waited eagerly for one to fail, instead of cues and lines from an entire script that had to be dredged somehow from one's treacherous memory, film made things easy. The roles were small, the calls were short, one hardly ever had to hold more than a dozen lines in one's head at a time. And once the thing was done, once the scene was shot, it was all over. Definitive, for better for worse, to be shown to audiences one would never have to see or hear. Film, which had once seemed to Frank a diversion from the main game, was suddenly the one kind of acting he could do.

After he made a decadently decent fist of Fingers in *Alvin Purple Rides Again*, Frank had prominent minor roles in four films (*The Man from Hong Kong* in 1975, *Mad Dog Morgan* (1976), *Mad Max: Beyond Thunderdome* (1985) and *The Marsupials: The Howling III* in 1987), and the most fleeting of appearances in two others (as an unnamed television producer in *At Last … Bullamakanka The Motion Picture* in 1984, and as an unnamed religious preacher in *Death of a Soldier* in 1986). It was, in some ways, a far cry from his work in the Hollywood blockbusters in the early 1960s. They had been big studio films, in which he played kings and emperors, powerful men who deserved to be acted with theatrical extravagance and flair; if the performance was a little larger than life, so much the better – the character was, too. The bit-parts that he played in the action adventures and horror-films were characters conspicuously too small for his style, and that seemed to be the point.

These films all contained in some measure a fair serve of self-mockery, whereas the great toga-dramas had never taken themselves less than very seriously. Frank was now trading on a presence that was not just excessive but anachronistic; in plots where everyone was camping it up, Frank offered camp on a scale grand enough to make others seem almost believable.

They were, most of them, once, twice or three times removed from the original. *Alvin Purple Rides Again* was (roughly speaking) a prequel, *Mad Max: Beyond Thunderdome* was the third part of a trilogy that was stretched into a tetralogy, while *The Marsupials* succeeded *The Howling II: Werewolf Bitch*. Some acts are hard to follow because they are so good they can't be emulated, some, like *Werewolf Bitch*, because it's hard to go much lower. The knowledge that each of them was a spin-off aspiring to be a rip-off must for the actors have informed the general sense of pastiche and parody that was already there in the screenplay. It was freeing in a way, that there was no need to be make a performance that was authentic, or intelligent, or prepared; freeing, too, that there was no need to worry, or even, really, to care. But it was a long way from what Frank had done, let alone what he had hoped. It was a long way, too, from his father's attempts to make films that said something about Australia, or Australians, or humanity.

In *The Man from Hong Kong* Frank played the straightest of the roles that made up the ten-year post-script to his acting career in films. He was Willard, a crook in a suit and tie, smooth but surprisingly subdued. The film around him was bizarre, a martial arts extravaganza in which most people ended up dead, usually as a result of a fiendishly brilliant kung fu manoeuvre. It was a Hong Kong/Australian co-production, set in Sydney (where the Harbour was rarely out of view), with Jimmy Wang Yu as the hang-gliding, high kicking Inspector Fang, and George Lazenby, the sometime James Bond, as the drug baron he has come down under to find.[637] Though Inspector Fang is regularly delayed in his quest by the need to have sex with attractive Sydney girls, he gets his man in a brutal chop-down-drag-out finale, prompted by his enemy's taunt, 'I never met a Chinese yet that didn't have a yellow streak'.

Mad Dog Morgan, like *Ned Kelly*, celebrated – and, of course, condoned – one of Australia's most notorious bushrangers. Like *Ned Kelly*, it imported an unconventionally attractive and notoriously badly behaved star to confirm its hero's status as counter-cultural rebel against an oppressively authoritarian society. Morgan was played by Dennis Hopper, whose career had hit a bumpy patch since he shared an open road with Peter Fonda in *Easy Rider* (1969). Frank's role was to represent, as unsubtly as possible, the evils of the ruling class. As Superintendent Cobham, he scowled and tyrranised on cue, and had the advantage of the best line in the script: 'I want his spleen on my desk by sundown'. It was Frank's kind of sentiment.

In his last film, *The Marsupials: The Howling III*, Frank played a film director, Jack Citron, who was distinguished primarily by the affectation of his manner and the proliferation of chains around his neck. It was, even by Frank's standards, a remarkably broad and florid exercise; but to play anyone who was certifiably human in this film was to be consigned to a kind of comfortable ordinariness. The plot began with a scientist's quest for the Australian werewolf, and his hypothesis that it might be descended from the extinct Tasmanian tiger. It became a little more complicated when he fell in

637 George Lazenby, an Australian actor, had been plucked from relative obscurity to play Bond in *On Her Majesty's Secret Service* (1969). He was not quite what the producers were looking for.

love with the female marsupial who became the focus of his research. Jerboa, the object of his affections, is a marsupial with one or two problems, as she discloses in the confessional:

> Priest: You should not run away from home.
>
> Jerboa: I don't like home.
>
> Priest: Why, child?
>
> Jerboa: Because my stepfather tried to rape me and he's a werewolf.

When the lovely Jerboa is shown giving birth, and the little one crawls up over her furry belly to slip into her pouch, the film is close to disintegration. For Philippe Mora, a talented film-maker who had directed Frank in *Mad Dog Morgan*, this episode of *The Howling* represented an improbable step down from his work on *Werewolf Bitch*.

Beyond Thunderdome, the third of George Miller's apocalyptic action films, had the highest profile among Frank's last films. Initially this had more to do with the success of *Mad Max* and *Mad Max II: The Road Warrior*, and its marquee names, than with the script; but the elaborately mythic plot has gained it not only a cult following but perhaps more enduring interest than either of its predecessors. The first *Mad Max* had set the Australian actor Mel Gibson on his way to becoming an international super-star, and *Road Warrior* had confirmed his arrival; playing opposite him in death-defying epic number three was Tina Turner, first famous in the pop music world as the other half of Ike and now a mature screen siren and soul diva in her own right. Frank was in celebrity company again, though that was the only respect in which making movies in the 1980s was just like the good old days.

Max in *Beyond Thunderdome* finds himself in a harsh, bleak part of Australia that has survived a nuclear apocalypse. His journey takes him through a number of archetypal locations: Bartertown, a society governed on crudely capitalist lines by Auntie Entity (Turner), who rules the place from a rickety tower; Thunderdome, a vast dust-bowl arena in which Max must confront the massive Blaster, and his own moral values; and Crack in the Earth, a secluded oasis where a tribe of feral children await the messianic Captain Walker, who they believe will lead them to Tomorrow-morrow Land. Where the popularity of *Mad Max II* was founded on relentless brutality, the third film in the series found its form of excess in allegory.

Frank played Entity's aide-de-camp, The Collector, the gatekeeper of her town's economy. The character didn't offer Frank the regalia or the chances for gratuitous cruelty that his Hollywood roles had provided, but he did have a compatible sense of ill-humour:

> THE COLLECTOR: If you have nothing to trade, you got no business in Bartertown.
>
> MAX: An hour on the inside, that's all.
>
> THE COLLECTOR: Next!
>
> MAX: I got skills, I could trade them.
>
> THE COLLECTOR: Sorry. The brothel's full.

Of all the films that Frank made in the 1980s, *Beyond Thunderdome* gave him the nearest approximation to an opportunity to act. He was hairless and oiled, and splendidly sinister, but rather than try to trump all the over-actors around him, Frank chose to hold back; The Collector's chilled, incisive speech patterns stood out in a film where others snarled or mumbled. He even had a rare piece of physical business to challenge him, when his character was foolish enough to attempt to split Max with an axe.

The conditions, as they so often seemed to be when Frank was involved in a film, were terrible. George Ogilvie, who had directed Frank in two plays at the Melbourne Theatre Company, had acted with him in half-a-dozen more, and in the previous year had directed the mini-series *Bodyline* with Frank in a featured role, was co-director with Miller on *Beyond Thunderdome*. He noted that Frank's capacity for comically making the worst of tough conditions was stretched by the searingly hot days and bone-chilling nights on location at Coober Pedy:

> His caustic wit kept things lively on the set but even he was subdued by the night shoots when, by three o'clock, the weather closed in. We all froze. The romance of making a movie very quickly vanished as we stamped around in our overcoats creating scene after scene of torrid desert weather.[638]

638 George Ogilvie, *Simple Gifts: A life in the theatre*, Currency House, Strawberry Hills, 2006, p.286.

Frank made the most of his discomfort, though, finding not only a rich vein of anecdote but some agreeable coping strategies:

> Tina, Mel and I got up on a 40-foot scaffolding and got pissed ... That was the simplest way out of that. Nobody could get at us. We were up there and we couldn't get down.[639]

It sounded like a cosy little arrangement, but it had its disadvantages, especially after one had been drinking on Auntie Entity's tower for a while:

> Nobody could have a piss. We were all in chain mail and any time you needed to go to the loo it involved a sort of journey to Shangri-La and half an hour with a pair of pliers.[640]

Taking the piss was Frank's stock-in-trade, of course, and there may have been a smidgin of exaggeration in the story. As there was in his account of the weather:

> 'Oh, it was a nightmare', says Thring. 'Being stuck in a caravan at Coober Pedy in 45 degree heat. It was so hot even the film melted in the camera and all the hundreds of extras were wilting'.[641]

Well, at least it was in the vicinity of the truth. Being accurate with facts and figures was for Frank the stuff of commerce, not conversation.

Frank's other notable screen performance in the 1980s was in *Bodyline*, the seven-part mini-series made by the ABC about the legendary 1932–3 Test Series, in which the visiting Englishmen implemented their notorious plan to dim the brilliance of Bradman. Frank played Lord Harris, chairman of the Marylebone Cricket Club, and the man who encouraged the architect of the scheme, the English captain Douglas Jardine (Hugo Weaving), and betrayed its principal agent, the Northants miner Harold Larwood. The series, produced by Kennedy-Miller, the makers of *Beyond Thunderdome*, worked on a classic mythic opposition of Old World duplicity and the New World innocence that shone in the clear blue eyes of Don Bradman (Gary Sweet). Frank's patrician style

---

639 Peter Wilmoth, *Sunday Age*, 19 June 1994, p.3.
640 ibid.
641 Corrie Perkin, *Age Good Weekend*.

and accent made him very persuasive as a predatory Pom, and exuded a certainty that he had been born to rule, and to win.

Frank found an unusual degree of pleasure in the role. He was hairier than he had been for some considerable time: as Harris, he sported not only an expansive handlebar moustache, but a fetchingly curled toupee. But he thought Harris 'wasn't a bad egg',[642] and almost enjoyed watching himself in action:

> I'm the one who said: 'If you have trouble, don't bowl at the wicket, bowl at his head' ... I thought I was very good in that. I usually hate myself.[643]

He was still as inclined as ever to disparage the acting demands of the part, and to express his sense of the absurdity it required him to do:

> 'I clap, politically', he said.
>
> Did he ever play cricket?
>
> 'No. I hate it', he said. 'It bores me to tears'.[644]

He found the process of making the film physically unbearable as he always had, even though, for once, the locations seemed quite civilised:

> 'Sydney was vile', he said. 'Rushing about perspiring and panting from functions to parties and being holed up in a Kings Cross studio in that humidity'.[645]

It may have occurred to Frank that there were doubtless some people in the world who had endured worse kinds of hell. But of course for him hell would always be a more colourful option than the other place.

There were other bits and pieces in this coda to a career. There was the guest appearance on ABC television's *The Gerry Connolly Show* in 1988, in which Frank played in three segments a character remarkably like himself. There was a cameo in 'Bayou', an episode of the prime-time American action series *Mission Impossible* in 1989, in which Frank appeared improbably as a white slaver, trafficking in young girls in New Orleans. Finally, he was heard briefly in 1993 as a voice-over in the spoof *Hercules Returns*, among

642 Dorothy Goodwin, *Herald*, 8 March 1984, p.22.
643 Mike Daly, *Age*, 13 December 1988, p.17.
644 David Dark, 'Odd – Frank seems to be a no body', *Sun*, 5 June 1984, p.13.
645 Dorothy Goodwin, *Herald*, 8 March 1984, p.22.

characters with names like Testicula and Labia; Michael Carman, an actor who does a very fair facsimile of Frank Thring, played the role of the stylishly unpleasant Englishman that Frank might have played in the days when his health and his memory were up to it.

The two butlers in *The Importance of Being Earnest* were Frank's last roles as an actor. There was some appropriateness in that, given the place that Wilde had had in developing Frank's capacity to out-Herod Herod. But finishing up by playing a couple of servants was also an irony that might have given some perverse pleasure to a man whose patrimony had helped him to so many of the plum roles.

The patrimony, of course, was gone, at least in terms of the things that made it tangible. Rylands was sold in 1985. Frank put the best possible 'spin' on the decision to sell the family estate; it was too much of a 'bloody nuisance' to maintain, he told a journalist from the *Sun*, especially for a man as busy as he was:

> I love it as a home, and have a sentimental attachment. But if it has to go, it has to go.
>
> It really is like an ageing parent – you just have to put it down.[646]

He was serenely pragmatic in conversation with the *Age* two months later, when the auction was imminent:

> I can't think of anything else until I get rid of it. But I have to sell. It's too big for one to look after, especially as one is seldom here.[647]

Rylands was no bigger to look after than it had always been, of course. Actually, the trouble was that 'one' had never been more frequently there than one was in this period of Frank's life. There had been the little excursion

646 Graeme Johnstone, *Sun*, 8 August 1985.

647 Corrie Perkin, 'Frank Thring "won't retire until he is a spastic wreck"', *Age Good Weekend*, 2 October 1985.

to Coober Pedy for the filming of *Mad Max III: Beyond Thunderdome*, which had by astonishing coincidence opened in Melbourne on the day of Frank's interview in the *Sun*; and there had been the 'nightmare' of several weeks in Sydney the year before that. But the truth was that there was all too little to take him away from home.

It 'had to go' not because it had become an irritating encumbrance to Frank, what he would have called a black elephant, but because he couldn't afford to live there anymore. What had happened to the Thring fortune was a mystery. Finances had always been a mystery to Frank, but this one perplexed members of Lola's branch of the family, too. Properties seemed to have been sold off at the bottom of the market, but they still brought in a lot of money; and while Frank's taste for expensive artifacts and his spectacular consumption of cheap wine were a continual drain on family funds, even his huge appetites could not account for the shortfall. And Frank, of course, was no longer earning very much. Really, he never had. In his sixtieth year, for the first time in his life, it occurred to him that he should probably consider what he could afford when he thought about what he might like to do.

In mid-1985, Frank rang Joan Harris with a melodramatic announcement to make: 'I'm going to live in Ballarat. It's all I can afford. You've got Lake Wendouree and the Begonia Festival. What more could I want?'[648] He was struck with a similar whim in his interview in the *Sun* ('Ballarat would be nice'[649]); where it had come from is anyone's guess. It was a passing fancy, and for Frank, a quintessentially urban man, that was probably just as well. The move to a little cottage in Mahoney Street, Fitzroy, represented a significant shrinkage in the parameters of his life. But it was ten minutes from the Melbourne GPO It kept him in touch, if he wanted still to be in touch, with his city.

He painted the cottage white. He brought in white carpets and white curtains. That decision might have been an aesthetic choice, an attempt to make the new place feel as spacious as possible. It might have stemmed from the desire for a complete change from the house that had been his home since he was born. But he brought with him what he could of the Rylands décor:

> 'I took everything I wanted with me', he said. 'Nothing escaped that I couldn't live without'.[650]

---

648 Joan Harris, interview with the author.
649 Graeme Johnstone, *Sun*, 8 August 1985.
650 Mike Daly, *Age*, 13 December 1988, p.17.

He brought to the two-bedroom cottage the habits of a lifetime, pared down to a suitably smaller scale. Joan Thring was shocked to find the old rituals, grotesquely, survived:

> The first time I came back to Melbourne, he gave me a key to that awful little place that he'd moved to, and I let myself in. The first thing I saw in the ghastly front room on the left of the hallway was the table, all immaculately set, just like the much grander one at Rylands. Waiting for guests that never came.[651]

The white dining-room at Mahoney Street was as superfluous as the red and gold one at Rylands. And in Fitzroy there were hardly any visitors to admire even it from the doorway.

It suited him to be reclusive. It had for a very long time. When *Woman's Day* had been treated in 1965 to one of those periodical tours of the weird and wonderful that made Frank's family home such a paradoxically safe subject, his version of the Greta Garbo syndrome had looked like a quirk, a decidedly romantic kind of solitariness:

> At sundown he sends Margaret off home, padlocks the great wrought-iron gate, bolts the door, prepares his own dinner, with only elegant cats, snow-white Puffkins and oyster-grey Squeeky [*sic*] for company.[652]

But Frank's obsession with security had grown. Even at Rylands he had begun in the 70s to lock the door of his bedroom at night, and to keep knives by his bed in case an intruder attacked him. Two decades and several cat-generations later, at North Fitzroy, it was far worse. He barricaded himself in, against not only those who might do him harm, but people like Joanna McCallum who meant nothing but good:

> I found out where he was living, and caught a cab there. There were chains across the gate and front door, and the opening of the letter box was sealed with tape. You wouldn't know if there was anyone living there or not. And I shouted outside the gate to try to get his attention, but he never came to the door. In the end I wrote a card giving him my love, and the nice Greek taxi-driver clambered over the high fence and

651 Joan Thring, interview with the author, 14 December 2004.
652 Interview with Joanna Parsons, *Woman's Day*, 6 September 1965, p.102.

> slid it under the front door. I never heard if he received it, and I never heard from him again.[653]

The condition was never less than pathological, but on some days it was more severe than others. Sometimes it looked like paranoid delusion. On the day of Joan Thring's return to Melbourne, she at first found Frank in better health and spirits than she had expected; his new house might be 'an awful little place', but its owner seemed in better shape. They went out to a show together, just as they'd done so often before, in Melbourne and in London. When they went back to Fitzroy, for the inevitable eggs and a glass or four, it felt like a fitting end to a pleasant evening:

> When he got back from the theatre, we chatted away for a couple of hours about all sorts of things – until something terrible happened.
>
> Frank got up suddenly, looming over me, and said, 'I don't know you. Who are you? You're not my Joan. You're an imposter'. He started shoving me, pushing me out of the house. I'd taken off my shoes, and I didn't even have time to grab them before he slammed the door on me. The concrete was freezing under my feet. I'd left my suitcase in the room, too. But I knew I couldn't argue. Frank just stood in the doorway, watching me go.
>
> I found a cab, and didn't know where to ask him to drive; I got the driver to just drive me around for ten minutes, and then I – very apprehensively – asked him to stop outside Frank's house. He was there again, at the top of the steps, and as I walked up the path toward him he spread his arms to embrace me. He knew now who I was, and was very contrite. I wondered what medication he was taking. I actually wondered whether he was going a little bit mad. The whole thing was terrifying.[654]

Joan saw him again before she left Melbourne, but the abiding image that she took home with her to London was of that giant, grotesque figure standing over her, consumed with fury and hatred. Frank had sublimated a lot of the pain and anger of that last year or two in London; when he referred to it at all it was in a crudely comic way. But what came bubbling up in that moment was clearly not the bitter resentment of what had been done to him by the person who had known him longer and perhaps more intimately than

---

653 Joanna McCallum, interview with the author, 13 December 2004.
654 Joan Thring, interview with the author, 14 December 2004.

anyone else in his world. It was a primal panic, and it came when he found himself in the midst of nightmare without any awareness at all that he had left waking reality behind. It must have been 'terrifying' for him, too.

Frank had lived on his own for a long time – since the days at Westgarth Terrace, really, more than thirty years before. Even when there had been someone to share his bed and his fantasies, there had hardly ever been anyone waking up beside him in the morning. It was hard to be clear about the line between dreaming and remembering, especially when one was never quite sober, and especially now, when the cocktail of medicines mixed with the moselle, and the brandy, and the pain, and the possible dementia, and the bitterness of years blurred things and distorted them as they did.

The pain and the prescriptions had a number of sources. Frank had avoided the medical profession reasonably successfully until the mid-1980s. There had been a need to see a doctor periodically for repeats on his nightly Nembutal, but that was standard. No doubt he was warned that he was drinking far too much, but Frank was perfectly aware of that.

He had sought help for the memory lapses and the labyrinthitis in the early 1970s, but all they could do for him was tell him again what he already knew. He did visit a surgeon to see whether something could be done about his sagging jowls, but that did nothing to encourage his faith in modern medicine either:

> He had a face-lift in the early eighties. They neatly filleted his throat, but the job only lasted three weeks. Frank was aghast. 'Look at this! The fucking thing's back!'[655]

But there was a lot more wrong with Frank than a bit of facial droop. The first problem to be diagnosed was with his liver, which had taken a fearful pounding for nearly five decades. To deal with the problem Frank was required to take a number of pills, which he did fairly religiously, and to give up drinking, which he had no intention of doing; the pills affected his balance and slowed his speech, and both effects were exacerbated by the continual bibbing of Ben-Ean. There was the circulation problem, too, which made Frank fear for a time that he might lose a leg, and eventually led to the amputation of several toes; that was another product of his drinking, and the side-effects of those tablets too were worse for him because of the way

655 Fred Parslow, interview with the author.

he chose to wash them down. Finally, in every sense, there was the cancer of the oesophagus. It was the thing that had killed his father, and it had its source in one of Frank's relatively minor vices, Marlboro cigarettes. Little secondary spots appeared, quite quickly; almost everywhere, it seemed.

In his last five years, nothing much in Frank's body was doing what it was supposed to do any longer. He was quite ready to see his smorgasbord of symptoms as the wages of sin, but there was never a suggestion that he wished he had done things differently. As a walking, or nearly walking, advertisement for the wisdom of wowserism, Frank was defiant to the end.

He had several strategies for dealing with the disintegration of his body. One, the most consistent, was a profound embarrassment, which confirmed his habit of reclusiveness. He disliked people seeing him as he now was most of the time; at his worst, when he was incontinent and immobile, he wanted nobody near him. Joan Thring, hearing a few weeks before his death that he was about to go into hospital, wrote to Frank that she was getting on a plane and coming to Melbourne; she left five telephone messages, too, none of which ever received a response. Joan came anyway, and found him, in a ridiculously skimpy hospital gown and minus several toes, 'intensely ashamed of what had happened to him'.[656] That desire to become invisible was related to a second set of reactions, in which he embraced his depression, or fumed ineffectually at the way his body had betrayed him, the doctors and nurses pestered him, and life had let him down.

The best way of coping with unhappiness, as it had always been with Frank, was with corrosive humour. Somehow, almost all of the interviews he gave in his sixties came down to death in the end:

> Is he frightened of death? 'It's pointless, isn't it?'
>
> What does death mean to him? Is it the beginning of another life? 'I don't think so. I think you die. One only hopes that one doesn't die in excruciating agony, that's what one dreads. Months in a hospital bed, dragged up and down, blood pumped into you, blood pumped out. One can live without that'.
>
> How would he like to go? 'Champagne and caviar and a handful of Nembutal, waft away into the middle distance with Dr Death'.[657]

656 Joan Thring, interview with the author 14 December 2004.
657 Peter Wilmoth, *Sunday Age*, 19 June 1994, p.3.

When Frank died, less than six months later, it wasn't as smooth a transition as he had hoped for. It was weeks, rather than months, in hospital. But there was agony, and there were blood transfusions, and champagne and caviar were never on the menu at the Epworth Hospital.

Among Frank's papers was a handwritten poem, originally by W.H. Auden, significantly tweaked by J.B.S. Haldane, and carefully adjusted by Frank to suit his own straitened circumstances. It was a nice reflection of the way that irony could almost make the unbearable bearable:

I wish I had the voice of Homer
To sing of rectal carcinoma
Which kills a lot more chaps, in fact,
Than were bumped off when Troy was sacked.
I noticed I was passing blood
(Only a few drops, not a flood).
Not feeling faint, nor too coy,
I stopped off en route to Fitzroy;
I asked a doctor, now my friend,
To peer into my hinder end,
To prove or to disprove the rumour
That I had a malignant tumour.
They pumped in Ba S O
Till I could really stand no more,
And, when sufficient had been pressed in,
They photographed my large intestine.
In order to decide the issue
They next scraped out some bits of tissue
(Before they did, some good pal
Had knocked me out with Pentothal,
Whose action is extremely quick,
And does not leave me feeling sick).
The microscope returned the answer
That I certainly had got cancer.
So I was wheeled into the theatre
Where holes were made to make me better.
One set is in my perineum
Where I can feel, but can't yet see 'm.
Another made me like a kipper,

Or female prey of Jack the Ripper.
Through this incision, I don't doubt,
The neoplasm was taken out,
Along with colon, and lymph nodes
Where cancer cells might find abodes.
I'll swear, without the risk of perjury,
It was a snappy piece of surgery.
My rectum is a serious loss to me,
But I've got a very neat colostomy,
And I hope, as soon as I am able,
To make it keep a fixed timetable.
I know that cancer often kills,
But so do cars and sleeping pills;
And it can hurt one till one sweats,
So can bad teeth and unpaid debts.
A spot of laughter, I am sure,
Often accelerates one's cure;
So let us patients do our bit
To help the surgeons make us fit.
My final word before I'm done,
Is 'Cancer can be rather fun'.

'Fun' it never could be. But the poem shows the importance to Frank of 'a spot of laughter', and, while to say that it 'often accelerates one's cure' was wishful thinking, it helped sometimes to distract one from, or dull, the pain.

Apart from the jokiness, two things threw some shafts of light on the otherwise grim last act of Frank's tragicomedy. One was his surprising readiness to become involved in the Fitzroy counter-culture, especially with the community radio station 3RRR, and through the connections he gained there, with Melbourne's fringe film culture. He found some new friends, which was handy when so few of the old ones seemed able to do him much good. Barbara Moore asked Frank a very astute question in her interview in 1989:

> BM: Because of your fame, have you found it difficult to form any deep and lasting relationships ... real, lasting ones ...?
>
> FT: Lots of them, I'm delighted to say, because it doesn't take you long to sort out the hangers-on ... No, I've got, there's some very good, long-lasting relationships ... For example, in the last five years, I've met some young film-makers ...[658]

It was a very revealing slide – almost an explicit concession. Frank's decision to cite his most recent relationships as examples of having formed 'real, lasting' ones was strong testimony to the importance of those new friendships, but it said little for the current relevance and resilience of the enduring relationships that had always defined the parameters of his world.

Fitzroy gave him a community that was in some sense his own, where Toorak had always been defined by the tastes and habits of his parents. There was nothing of Olive in Fitzroy. Where Toorak was a seemingly changeless world of gracious affluence and smart shops, Fitzroy was a world in transition; not just a place where people went home to sleep, but one in which activists were forging a new, collaborative cultural identity. It was exciting to be around; 'they', the 'young film-makers', were exciting to be around. They liked Frank, too, it seemed; they respected what he had done and who and what he was, including the iconoclastic humour and unconventional sexual behaviour that had never quite fitted the conservative assumptions of S.E.2.

The interview with Peter Wilmoth in which Frank talked of his feelings about death and dying ended on a quietly positive note that came from the sense that Frank, having left 'Rylands' after a lifetime, finally felt at home:

> Only once in our time together does Thring dispense with the realm of darkness, irony or extreme weariness, and that is when we are outside talking about the houses in his street. He has shuffled out here in his socks. He thoroughly enjoys living in Fitzroy with its cafes and energy and history ... He looks over at the street sign and wonders aloud which local dignitary it was named after. This is the warm Frank Thring that the people who know him talk about. The wheezy misanthrope is suddenly gone.[659]

---

658 Barbara Moore interview.
659 Peter Wilmoth, *Sunday Age*, 19 June 1994, p.3.

The image of the old man shuffling in his socks is not one that Frank would ever have been keen to cultivate; nor does it suggest a man inclined to stray far from his front door. But Frank did take the walk down to the 3RRR studio on the corner of Brunswick Street, where he recorded free of charge promotional sound-bites for the station ('Subscribe – or die!'), and pursued those 'very good, long-lasting' connections with 'young film-makers', though they were actually quite new, and destined to be brief.

That they were young was important to Frank. It probably wasn't important in quite the same way as it had been at other times in his life; now it was as unconceivable that Frank would reveal his worn and dysfunctional body to an attractive youth as it had always been unlikely that a youth would do the same for him, at least without a serious inducement. The fantasy was probably there still, somewhere in the background; Frank's body might have almost given up on him, but his pornographic imagination was apparently as vivid as ever.

Now, the rumour went, rent-boys were his most regular, and almost his only, guests. There were all sorts of shocked whispers about the bizarre masochistic manoeuvres that they were required to perform. And Frank was, as ever, their most enthusiastic source:

> One weekend, according to the Thring website, he went missing.
>
> His friends phoned and knocked on his door, but received no answer. By Sunday, a group of them came together and went to the back of Thring's house to investigate.
>
> Through a window, they saw him sitting naked, bound, gagged, and tied to a chair.
>
> They broke in and hurriedly loosened his bonds, afraid he had been robbed.
>
> When they removed the gag, all he could say was: 'What a fantastic weekend'.[660]

Frank, who died too soon to discover the joys of the internet though he might have used it enthusiastically and disgracefully had he had the chance, would have been gratified (or, in his own parlance of innuendo, 'tickled pink') to have seen the results of googling the name 'Frank Thring' in the new millennium. In a gesture of *homage* that was ironic on more levels than a single sentence

660 Adam Zwar, 'The Thrings people say', *Sunday Herald Sun*, 25 March 2001, p.87.

could suggest, one of the world's most prolific pornographers had taken Frank's name and had put together a list of credits that made Frank's career, in all its arenas, look not only modest but unadventurous in scope.

This Frank Thring of the twenty-first century, who sometimes used the less flamboyant alias of Arthur Potts, had on last count produced more than a hundred skinflicks between 1998 and 2009, ranging from the relatively direct (*Legs Wide Open,* 2009) to the intriguingly exotic (*Secret Delights of Baroness Kinky,* 2003). This Frank Thring confined himself to sexual interactions between men and women, though that was a field that turned out to be much wider than most people imagine. Although the interests of the Australian actor from whom he stole the name Frank Thring took a different path, that Frank would have thought it, with his insatiable delight in the parodic, an entirely appropriate legacy.

But the Australian Frank Thring, dying a little more every day in Fitzroy and excruciatingly aware of it, would also have felt the unfairness of it all. What he would have recognised as truly ludicrous was the fact that, beyond all the violations real and imagined, all the wilful degradation, the romance of youth itself, youth with its smooth complexion and its enthusiasm and its lack of fear, was enormously attractive to him still. It was now about as disconnected from sexual desire as it could ever be.

The beauty of youth was the second thing that cut through the gloom which generally characterised so much of Frank's time at Mahoney Street. One incident, Frank's visit to NIDA in Sydney to address the graduating class of 1988, is particularly revealing about his susceptibility to its poignancy, as well as its more evident charms. Frank waxed eloquent about it in an interview with Mike Daly in the *Age*:

> 'So I was social and charming and witty and brilliant, and then, having got through all that, the kids put on a show.
>
> I thought I was in for a night of horror. You know, 25 appalling dramatic students and I have to be polite and nod at the right times.
>
> 'But I was stunned by it. They were breathtaking … the timing, the lighting, the dancing were just sensational. That's how they are training them: every young actor nowadays has to be able to do everything. I just sat back and thought, 'My God. They're a bloody sight better performers than I've seen in London or New York".[661]

661 Mike Daly, 'The Importance of Being Frank and Earnest', *Age*, 13 December 1988, p.11.

It was a generous story, both in its appreciation of the talents of 'the kids' and in its acknowledgement of the prejudices that had led him to see the whole occasion as a chore rather than the privilege it turned out to be. But it was a good deal less than half of the truth, which is more revealing still.

Peter Cooke had set up Frank's visit with a fair bit of trepidation, and from the beginning all his misgivings seemed to be confirmed. Frank had hated the flight up from Melbourne. He was fairly drunk on arrival at the airport at around eleven, and complained of not feeling well. He was irritable all the way into town, and loathed the whole idea of the official lunch with various senior people and distinguished guests that he was required to attend. Once there, he was about as far from being 'social and charming and witty and brilliant' as it was possible to be. Through the meal he was truculent and morose, and drank even more than Peter, who knew Frank's ways all too well, had allowed for.

Frank was particularly obstreperous about the performance he now found he was supposed to attend after the ceremony. He was insistent that he wouldn't go. That was awkward enough; but Peter hadn't told him about all that he was in for at the degree ceremony:

> I couldn't face telling him about the other major tension that day, which was that one of the students was receiving his diploma posthumously. He'd died suddenly from a brain haemorrhage on a performance tour in Singapore, and his parents were coming to collect it for him.
>
> Frank behaved well enough during the early part of the ceremony, doing the right things, congratulating them all appropriately – he wouldn't do anything to offend all those beautiful boys and girls.
>
> But when the name of the dead boy was announced, and the circumstances surrounding the whole situation, Frank was overwhelmed. He turned to watch the special video of the dead boy's work at NIDA that was on the big screen behind him, and he began to weep. His shoulders were heaving, he couldn't control the tears. Then, when the boy's parents came up to the stage together, Frank turned around, spread his arms wide open, and engulfed them in an embrace. The three of them just stood there for several minutes, holding each other, and crying.[662]

---

662 Peter Cooke, interview with the author.

This was the emotional frame for the 'breathtaking' performance that followed. Frank could be cruel and cutting about the things that other adults found tragic about their lives, but he was the softest of touches when it came to the tragedies of youth.

Peter Cooke's tale of excruciating dangers negotiated is much closer to the truth than Frank's of a perfect day as an account of NIDA's graduation ceremony in 1988. But there is another dimension of the story that Peter Cooke could hardly have imagined. The great fear was that Frank would forget, would dwell on the tedious formalities rather than the bright faces of the graduates, would refuse to take it seriously, would embarrass himself and Peter and turn the whole affair into a debacle. These were entirely appropriate anxieties; Frank had 'form', poor form, on every front. But he remembered, and prepared, and faced up to all his responsibilities, as much as anyone could have hoped; more, perhaps, given the way his own insecurities had grown, than was in NIDA's interests, or Peter's, or his own.

Frank spent a lot of hours thinking about the speech he might give to the students, and the importance of its occasion. The notes he kept are a record of elaborate preparation: preparation that was fairly drunk and disorderly, certainly, but perhaps even more passionate for that. Frank's jottings are typically in bold capitals, but thicker and messier than the comments he wrote in the child's scrapbook about Melbourne television just a few years earlier. These look like the work of a thumbnail dipped in tar. There are multiple crossings-out, there are blots and bloopers everywhere, but not one of them comes from carelessness; they come from a wrestling with a task for which he feared he was inadequate, and a desire to give something worthwhile to his young audience, something they might remember, and something worthy of their trust. It probably wasn't a particularly good speech, in the end. But it came, painfully, from the heart.

In his notes, Frank began, as he often did when he was trying to be funny, with word-play. The notion of GRADUANDS quickly gave way to GRADU/ANTS, and then to NIDANTS; the qualities of those, if not all, ANTS ('work hard – swarm – sugar') developed into an association that seemed relevant to actors ('white ants … can bring down the house') and to designers (who were categorised – unfairly – as 'bull ants').

But then things started to fall apart, as the pen became thicker, the lines became erratic, and even the spelling (one of Frank's consistent strengths) became unpredictable. At some point, late in the night or early in the morning, he tried to say what mattered to him about his art:

> A KID IN THE AUDIENCE WILL [illegible] BE WRAPT IN YOUR PERFORMANCE AND HE WILL DECIDE HE WANTS TO BE [illegible] LIKE YOU – HE WILL KILL TO BE IN NIDA. AND THAT IS THE INFLUENCE YOU HAVE – USE [illegible] IT WISELY – MAY I WELCOME YOU TO RESPECT THE PROFFESSION [sic] WITH ADMIRATION AND LOVE …[663]

But now the lines were running into each other. It finished up a proverbial dog's breakfast, and who knows how much of it, if any, was actually said at the lectern that day at NIDA. What the students would remember most clearly, anyway, were the tears and the hug.

What the notes tell us is that this was a guest speaker who was emotionally very committed to his commission. Frank arrived in Sydney drunk, defensive and disagreeable not because he didn't want to be part of the occasion, or didn't take it seriously, but because he still believed intensely in what he was doing, and was afraid that he had lost the words and the confidence to communicate it.

Of course, being drunk, defensive and disagreeable was by 1988 Frank's default condition, so it would be foolish to sentimentalise his behaviour simply as that of a man who cared too much. But then, he was a very sentimental man; as Joan Thring observed, 'Frank would cry at anything sad. He was a great big softie'.[664] He devoted a good deal of his public persona to denying that, by saying the terrible tasteless things that other people merely thought, or by professing to be a man without a heart. As he got older though there seemed no convincing argument for disguising it:

> I'm hopeless. I'll just cry. And this is why I won't go to a public screening of *Gallipoli* because I will be a wreck, they'll have to drag me out of the theatre … I don't necessarily cry at sad things. I cry at magic moments … I cry at comedy. I must say I think I'm a bit strange at times.[665]

As he was, of course.

---

663 Frank Thring, miscellaneous notes, Performing Arts Museum, Melbourne.
664 Joan Thring, interview with the author, 2004.
665 Barbara Moore interview, 1981.

TRAVELLING FROM FITZROY TO THE EPWORTH HOSPITAL, RICHMOND

Ambulance, 26 December 1994

There had to be a better end for it all than this. This was demeaning, and not just because of the slapstick routine that was getting one up off the floor, or even the shit one'd been lying in.

The perfect anti-climax, banal and complete. No supernatural white light, no choirs and trumpets. No tragic tumble into the pit or the stalls. Just the lousy fucking pettiness of death.

They'd cleaned him up in the end, literally enough. And they'd done a Baby Cheeses on him, rather appropriate, wrapping him in swaddling-bands and laying him on a stretcher. None of it Thring-size, but dignity had long ceased to be an issue in this matter. They'd left behind his fucking bag. He told them he never went anywhere without his fucking bag. Bring me my bucking fag, as the good doctor Spooner would say. Now that'd be a hospital worth visiting. Thing of the past now, anyway, like most things. Past even a Thring joke, actually.

They didn't know yet, they said, what had made him black out. So much wrong with him it could be anything. The rot went all the way through. What an irony if it was that sneaky little thing in the throat that got him after all. It got your dear old Dad, Frankie, got him in four weeks. His'd popped up, what, five or six weeks ago; not a bad run, then, one might say, given the family history. There you go. Like father, like son.

Sixty-eight. Not such a bad innings, really, when the old man was gone at fifty-three. Fuck. Only someone fool enough to use cricket-metaphors could think that was fair enough, for either of them. It wasn't.

Fuck, fuck, fuck.

The ambulance person had asked him, once he was safely tucked into the manger, whether he was 'the' Frank Thring. How many do you think there are, you stupid min? That's what he'd wanted to say.

But he was too sick to make all those sounds, so he just made the obvious reply, in what was barely a stage whisper. 'Possibly'. Yes, no, occasionally – please tick appropriate box. One might've said all that, and Happy Boxing Day. But no time. Not enough.

Come on, sweetie, you know me, you know that you know. Look at the face, listen to the voice, what's left of them.

Well, fuck me dead.

There's only one Frank Thring, baby.

I'm him. Frank Thring. Can't you tell?

Epilogue

MY FATHER'S SON

Joan Thring knew something had happened to Frank when the phone didn't ring in her Knightsbridge flat:

> He rang every Christmas morning – I knew there was something wrong … So I rang Joan and Fred and found that he hadn't turned up as expected for Christmas dinner. Then I rang the young man who lived next door, and somehow he climbed in and found Frank lying on the floor …[666]

After a decade of defying his doctors and teasing the grim reaper, the decline was swift at the end. Frank had come round for a meal with the Parslows a couple of weeks before his death. Joan thought he 'looked terrible', but he managed to turn a short lunch into seven hours laughing about the times that they had seen; the aesophagal cancer that was Frank's latest curse prevented him from laughing with the old abandon, though, and all he could manage to eat was a little soft pudding with ice-cream.[667]

There's not much to tell about Frank's last few days. Two of them he spent, unconscious, on the floor of the cottage in Fitzroy. The last three, until his death on December 29, were spent in a bed in Epworth Hospital. Like his father's, those final days passed in a haze of morphine, interrupted occasionally by painful consciousness. It was, like the immediate cause of the deaths for the two Frank Thrings, one of the rare points at which the details of their lives coincided. Like father, like son.

Biographies tend to end, naturally enough, with deaths. It's not simply the end of the subject that drives the closure; there's a morbid curiosity,

666 Joan Thring, interview with the author, 2004.
667 Joan Parslow, interview with the author, 2004.

even a kind of prurience, about those final moments, which is probably an aspect of our anticipating our own mortality. There's a desire, as well, to find in the nature of that conclusion an element of resolution, or a trace of pattern, that might give the whole thing at least symbolic meaning. When the end comes with cancer, and is shrouded by morphine, making sense of it is almost as difficult for the observer as it must have been for the person who has shrunk to a patient. When there are two deaths at issue, though, the contrast allows room to manufacture a structure in which to accommodate them both.

Frank the son, dead at sixty-eight, had been aware for at least a decade that he was living his final chapter. There was too much wrong with him to ignore, and too little expectation left for him to feel particularly cheated at the prospect of dying. What he dreaded and resented was the agony and the gross indignity. He didn't quite manage the swift and smooth release he had declared as his preference: instead of 'champagne and caviar' there was hospital pap that didn't require chewing, and instead of 'a handful of Nembutal' to let him 'waft away into the middle distance with Dr Death' there were massive doses of morphine to counter the recurrent pain as he stumbled his way over the line. But in a number of ways Frank had conceded that his time had passed. The man who boasted that he had set himself to take the London stage by storm before he was thirty and to become a Hollywood star by thirty-five (and who could claim, with just a little characteristic exaggeration of the truth, that he had done so) had no aspirations in particular beyond that. In his forties, he established just the kind of stage career in Melbourne that suited him: good roles for short runs to susceptible audiences. By the time he was fifty, though, his career was beginning to stall; at fifty-three, the age at which his father had died, Frank was, by general agreement including his own, washed up.

As Frank the father had imagined his life's narrative, his sixth decade was to be his finest. This would be the time when he would rewrite the history of Australian film, and transform it from a short story about struggle into a grand and glorious epic about individual daring and the cultural maturity of a nation. He died with his head filled with dreams and deals, triumph so close that he believed he could almost touch it. The reality, of course, was more complex than he could ever publicly acknowledge. Frank's last three years were marked by impulsive changes of plan and direction, by projects vigorously begun and lightly cast aside, and by an air of continual frustration. The evidence suggests a man whose energy is undiminished, but who has lost all certainty as to how to direct it. The image he cultivated, however, and in which he always professed to believe, had the simplicity of all heroic myth. He had spent his twenties and thirties positioning himself to become a man of substance. In his forties, having established the substance, he worked out what it was that he wanted to do with it. The showman stepped out from behind the numbers man he had been impersonating, and set out to impose his vision on the world of cinema. Three years into his great decade he was dead. Fifty-three is too young for anyone to die, but for Frank Thring the father, when the climax of his career seemed to lie before him, it was the most vicious of ironies. He would certainly have felt cheated, and with good reason. The thought that at fifty-three he too might have been washed up would never have occurred to him, even in his darkest hours.

There are suggestive contrasts, too, in the ways in which their deaths were publicly handled. Both events were accorded their generous share of newsprint, but their memorials could hardly have been more different.

For Frank senior, there was a big funeral; Olive ensured that he was sent off in a style befitting a famous man, a man whose initials made a film studio, who owned Rylands and Arden and who played golf badly with the rich and powerful. The Tallises and the Taits were there, and most of the members of the Athenaeum Club. Gladys Moncrieff and George Wallace were there, as was Tom Holt, the colleague and friend whom he could surely never have imagined as the man soon to become his son-in-law; so was Stuart Doyle, who flew down from Sydney to farewell his old adversary, bearing a large bouquet. At the back of the crowded chapel stood men like Arthur Higgins, Alan Mill and Bert Nicholas, who had made Efftee's machinery work. The funeral of Frank Thring the father was a significant public event.

He had left clear instructions for his earthly remains, too, which, though they must have seemed to her rather perverse, Olive faithfully enacted. So Frank Thring the father was buried beside his own father, whose narrow and humble world he had left so far behind; and buried at Burwood not among the dead of the Catholic faith into which he had been born or those who observed the Anglican rites in which he had married Olive, but as a Presbyterian, the religion he had briefly adopted for the purposes of marrying Grace. The headstone is still there, expanded to include Olive seventeen years later, though it is not clear that that was part of Frank's plan in securing a double plot at all. For Frank senior, monuments were important. So were connections; hence his desire to be buried beside the father to whom he had never been close in life.

Frank Thring the son wanted no funeral, and no memorial. He rang Joan Parslow a little while before his death with his last instructions: 'When I go, I want Freddie to hire a Tiger Moth and scatter my ashes over the bay'.[668] When it came to the point, that seemed a little too dangerous; quite apart from the perils of low flying in a small plane, Joan and Fred had visions of little bits of Frank falling on unsuspecting fishermen below. So instead they took the urn to Queenscliff:

> Hugh Rule hired a four-wheel drive vehicle, and he and Joan [Thring] and I headed down with it. We took some champagne (no one could contemplate Ben Ean) and a sheaf of tuberoses. We were joined, much to our surprise, by that woman from Ernst and Young – she had driven down for the occasion with her daughter, who didn't even know Frank. Joan and I were furious.[669]

'That woman' was Wilma Bird, the accountant who had managed Frank's messy finances over the preceding decade, and who had come to exert – sometimes proprietorially, but mostly helpfully – a good deal of influence over all his arrangements. She was genuinely fond of Frank, and keen to protect him from the world and himself. For the two Joans, it seemed an insensitive intrusion on their very private farewell to a very private man. But they went ahead with the ceremony, nonetheless:

> We walked out to the end of the very long pier, trying to calculate the direction of the wind. It was very blustery, and the waves were choppy. Each of us took a turn to cast Frank on the waters, trying not to get him all over us. Then we realised that the tide was surging in, and watched as the ashes and the roses rode the waves in till they all washed up on the shore.[670]

Frank would have found it a fitting finale. There was the little band of friends, to represent the only slightly larger circle of people who had managed to stay close to him: Joan Thring, his sometime soulmate and wife, Joan Parslow, who had been his friend for almost as long, and Hugh Rule, one of the beautiful young men with whom he had been obsessed. With bizarre appropriateness,

668 Joan Parslow, interview with the author, 2004.
669 ibid.
670 ibid.

there were two uninvited guests at this intimate occasion – his accountant and a young girl he had never met; Frank liked disruptive presences, and he had always depended on the kindness of accountants and strangers. He would have been amused by the potential for black comedy in the affair, too, as all five of them did all they could to avoid his ashes in a scene that he would have found reminiscent of the farcical funeral in Edward Bond's *The Sea*. Most of all, he would have found in that last dispersal to the winds and waves a perfect culmination of his disconnection from family, friendships, audiences and all. It was the final anonymity. 'Wafting away into the middle distance with Dr Death' was a playful fancy; at the end, Frank knew that one wafted away alone.

He had been insistent that there should be no memorials, no eulogies, no monuments. But people never take notice of these things completely. NIDA, to whom he had bequeathed his papers and the scraps that remained of the Thring fortune, named a scholarship after him, and placed a bust of Frank in the foyer of its home on Anzac Parade. And a large number of old theatre acquaintances met at the Playhouse on the first Sunday afternoon in March 1995, some ten weeks after his death, for 'A Tribute to Frank'. There were tributes from Alan Burke, George Fairfax, Alan Hopgood, Paul Karo, Leo McKern, Keith Michell, Irene Mitchell, Joan and Fred Parslow. John Sumner sent an affectionate message on video from Oxford. Hugh Rule wrote a poem, entitled 'Frank Thring, tribute in 400 words', which not only covered a long career with impressive succinctness but offered some personal observations as well:

> And that barbed wit was legendary
> the stare withering – especially when
> leveraged by about 7 feet and 18 stone.
> Oh so very adept at driving away
> friends and colleagues and strangers alike.
> Yet carefully concealed under that imperious bearing
> a soft-hearted man, kind and generous to boot.[671]

A lot of the stories were funny, and most were very tall. Frank would have liked it that way. A lot of the gossip in the foyer, however, focused on whether Frank would have liked the event to happen at all:

671 The order of proceedings for the memorial event is preserved in the unclassified Frank Thring papers, Performing Arts Museum, Melbourne.

> 'Frank would have hated us being here, he loathed sentimentality', more than one speaker told the 800 people who attended yesterday's two-hour tribute to the actor at the Playhouse Theatre.[672]

Those who knew him best would have recognised this as a simplistic answer to a complex question. Frank loathed sentimentality all right, but he could also be very sentimental – about old friends (sometimes), even those whose names were not worth dropping; about the triumphs and tragedies of young people (almost always), whether he knew them or not; about himself (increasingly), as his own life came more and more to lack an audience. In the same way that he both courted celebrity and longed to be left alone, the question of how and how much Frank wanted to be remembered points to self-contradictions in him that were never resolved. There were always two Frank Thrings, as several commentators observed, even when his father wasn't one of them:

> We never got close to Thring, we never learnt much about him – despite his misleadingly titled one-man show *Frankly Thring* – yet he remains a figure of fascination and a magnet for genuine affection.
>
> I suggest this has little to do with any specific roles he played – how many theatergoers remember his superb Galileo, or the butcher in *The Homecoming*? – and everything to do with the general role he cultivated offstage: the imperious raconteur who was perpetually tired of life – and always larger than it.[673]

Phillip Adams, in his defiantly irreverent obituary for the *Australian*, softened his general dismissal of Frank's style and career as a grand anachronism to admit a similar distinction between the performed self and the 'real' one:

> Frank liked to flash his teeth, and to close them slowly as he gave one of his reptilian hisses. He liked capes, togas, he liked to preen and parade. He liked to bully and bellow. But just as the Wizard of Oz turned out to be a little bloke pulling a few levers, the bloke beneath the Thring persona (if you could ever be bothered shining a torch into a crevice in his carapace) was a likeable human being.[674]

672 Greg Burchall, 'Farewell to Thring – a memorable scene-stealer', *Age*, 6 March 1995, p.7.
673 Simon Plant, 'Frankly, the legend lives', *Herald Sun*, 4 March 1995, p.29.
674 Phillip Adams, 'Frankly sssspeaking', *Australian Weekend Review*, 21/22 January 1995, p.2.

That suggestion was another over-simplification, of course. The roles that we play are rarely so neatly separable from the selves that we are, and those selves are ambiguous and shifting, too; 'inner selves' can be as hard for us to know or acknowledge as they are for others to read in us, even if we can be certain they are there. The 'little bloke' glimpsed inside Frank Thring might be more likeable and seem more vulnerable than the big bloke wearing the persona, but his fears and insecurities could make him every bit as mean and vicious, surely, as the public performer; and when the big bloke on the outside cried tears of compassion, or made little gifts of kindness, as he did surprisingly often, he could look awfully like a likeable human being, too. The Thring performance was always imperfect, always a complex set of transactions between different kinds and degrees of self-exposure. That was what made it an exciting show to watch.

Frank the son was certainly never inclined to be sentimental about his mother. But his feelings about his father were more explicitly complex. Some time in the late 1980s, the film-maker John Lamond took him and Fred Parslow to the house of a cinema buff in Carlton, who had some rare newsreel footage that featured Frank Thring senior, including images of Frank as a child returning from an overseas jaunt with his parents. The images on the screen were awkward, even a little comical, but Frank made no comment, and no-one was inclined to laugh; his uncharacteristic silence imposed itself on the others in the room, too:

> When the lights were turned on, Frank was in tears. He took a while before he could speak. Then he turned to me and said, 'I don't know. I just – I think the old man was pretty jazzy'.[675]

It wasn't a word that Frank the father would have selected for himself, but from his son it was quite a compliment. It was about as close to an unambiguous declaration of love as Frank the son could ever allow himself.

And what would 'the old man' have made of him? The image that Frank found so 'jazzy' was that of a wealthy conservative man, trussed up tight

675 Fred Parslow, interview with the author.

in a credibility suit. It was that of a man with the air of the patriarch, accompanied by his wife and the son who bore his name. He was a man who spoke with a strong Australian accent, though some of its rough edges had been smoothed in the interests of social advancement; his manner when speaking in public reflected his confidence that he was important enough to demand attention, but also the diffidence of the serious man of action about performing in public. His son, in shaved head and black skivvy, festooned with chains and sporting a handbag, looked like the apotheosis of camp; when he opened his mouth, the ludicrous affectation of the voice proclaimed his sexuality, as well as how much he savoured, and insisted on, holding the floor. Surely no generation gap has ever been wider.

It was a question that must have often occurred to the younger Frank. Would his father have accepted his son as he was, had he lived long enough to find out? How far was paternal love unconditional, and how much did disapproval and disappointment come with the territory? Not only had Frank had no child of his own to experiment on; he hadn't known his own father long enough to have an informed opinion.

'The old man' was ahead of his time in entrepreneurial matters, but his social and moral assumptions were a fair reflection of the spirit of the age he lived in. Moreover, he had the particular concern for respectability in behaviour and appearance of the man who has a past he wants to live down. Acceptance might have been just too hard for him. That Frank was homosexual would have been bad enough; the fact that he flaunted it would surely have been too much. His father would have blamed Olive, of course. The boy had had no male role model to guide him at the critical time, and a mother who spoiled and smothered him. Too many women in a house was a sure recipe for disaster. For a man of Frank senior's generation, Rylands after his own death provided a classic scenario in which a young fellow might lose his way.

For his son, of course, there were no such 'extenuating circumstances', because there was no need for them. It was the one thing for which he never thought to blame his mother, since blame was as irrelevant to the case as choice. Frank Thring the son never gave the slightest sign that he was unhappy to be gay.

Frank the son liked to portray his father as 'evil', a Simon Legree who would stop at nothing to get what he wanted. But he didn't talk about him in those terms to express disapproval, or even distance; there was always humour, mostly admiration, and often affection in those remarks. That running joke was very different in tone from his references to the Volumnia of Toorak and Lucretia Borgia, the terms he applied to the mother he 'finally got rid of'. Whatever Olive had done to him, it could never be forgiven, and he hated her. His father had done nothing worse to him than die. That was a considerable grievance. But it did remove any possibility of all the resentments that would otherwise, surely, have come.

In fact, the last of the Frank Thrings did choose to tread in some of those large paternal footprints, despite deviations along the way that would have appalled his father. A career that began in the studios of 3XY and ended with appearances in optimistic Australian film projects that came to a disappointing end, and featured in the middle a series of variations on Simon Legree for Hollywood and a sustained involvement in the theatre of his own town, was hardly a story of complete filial rebellion. It could even look disconcertingly like a bid for approval.

Perhaps there were some things about his son, in the end, about which Frank Thring the father might have been well pleased.

Appendix

EFFTEE FILMOGRAPHY

Compiled by Chris Long

This list of the productions by Efftee Films is an expanded revision of its author's article in *Cinema Papers*, December 1982. It confirms the Efftee studio's amazingly prolific output over barely three years of production, from March 1931 to May 1934.

The running times listed here are those of the original Australian prints as recorded in contemporary censorship records, not from the cut-down British release prints frequently circulated by Australia's National Film and Sound Archive.

The technical crew on all films listed here is as follows, unless otherwise stated:

Direction: Mostly F.W. Thring, but a couple of the earliest featurettes were directed by E. A. Dietrich-Derrick. Assistant director on some early features was Raymond Longford, notably on Efftee's talkie version of *The Sentimental Bloke*. The dialogue director on many of the pre-1933 films was Gregan McMahon, the founder of the semi-professional Gregan McMahon Players in 1929. In spite of screen credits to the contrary, some Efftee shorts were directed by the people featured in them, notably George Wallace on *Oh! What a Night*, Ada Reeve on *In the Future*, and the Bert Nicholas/David Fleahy combination on the *Efftee Film Magazines*.

Casting: Raymond Longford or Roy Steyne shot extensive screen tests of hopefuls.

Camera: Arthur Higgins, previously involved with Austin Fay in the production of Australia's first part-talkie feature *Fellers* (1930); Bert Nicholas, formerly a newsreel cameraman with Australasian Films' Melbourne branch; occasionally Roy Driver from Herschells Films was brought in to cover larger crowd scenes. Damien Parer, who can be seen holding the clapper board on several outtakes from Charles Chauvel's *Heritage*, was a camera assistant on a few scenes of Efftee's later films. Tasman Higgins assisted briefly with commissioned camerawork on Efftee's Sydney travelogue, then came to Melbourne to supervise camerawork on *Heritage* at Wattle Path late in 1934. Efftee's electrical and lighting expert was Don Harris, who published an article on the subject in *The Electrical Engineer and Merchandiser* (Melbourne) on 16 November 1931, pp.299–301.

Sound: RCA Photophone monolateral variable-area optical recording system, with no noise reduction, which was installed in the majority of British studios at that time. Initially Dan J Bloomberg, the RCA engineer sent out from America with the'J2' film recorder was in charge. He previously worked on sound for the pioneer British talkie based on the SS.'Titanic' disaster, *Atlantic* (E A Dupont for B.I.P., 1929). By the end of 1931, the locals, previously assisting and taking instruction, took over: Alan Mill (formerly of DeForest Phonofilms in Sydney), Jack Murray, R. Alan Stuart and occasionally John Heyer on later films.

Musical direction: Usually Harry Jacobs, then leader of the Palais Pictures Orchestra in St Kilda; occasionally Art Chapman with his band from the Rex Cabaret for some popular music and jazz interludes. The latter band appears with George Wallace in the cabaret sequences of *A Ticket in Tatts.*

Sets: W.R. Coleman (chief), Harry Whiting, George Kenyon, Franklin Hughes (Hughes on *Clara Gibbings* only).

A. Feature Films *(listed chronologically)*

Note on script copyrights: At Australian Archives' Mitchell repository, ACT, the bound indexes from which scenario registration numbers are obtained is in series A1961/1. All citations below refer to this Index.

Films Made at His Majesty's Theatre Studio, Exhibition Street:

(1) A Co-Respondent's Course – 44 minutes, released 6 November 1931. P.C.: Efftee. Dir. E. A. Dietrich-Derrick. Marital farce starring John D'Arcy (Snr.), Patricia Minchin, Donalda Warne. Produced from a script by Montague Grover. Shooting locales: His Majesty's Theatre studio; a home in Orrong Road, Toorak; Nepean Highway, Mordialloc; Flinders Street Station; Frankston Hotel; Portsea beach/hotel; and 'London Bridge' at Portsea Back Beach. The first Australian film with optical sound to be completed. Copies of the script are at NFSA; its literary copyright material is at registration number 21467.

(2) Diggers – 69 minutes, released 6 November 1931. P.C.: Efftee. Dir. F. W. Thring. Wartime comedy-drama starring Pat Hanna and his 'Diggers' dramatic company. Shot entirely at His Majesty's Theatre studio, Exhibition Street. Copyright material held at registration number 21189 under the title of 'Old Soldiers Never Die.'

(3) **The Haunted Barn** – 43 minutes, released 29 November 1931. P.C.: Efftee. Dir.: E. A. Diettrich-Derrick and Gregan McMahon. Mystery-drama with comic elements. Stars Keith Desmond, Donalda Warne, Phil Smith, John Cameron, Thelma Scott (in her first film). Shot entirely at His Majesty's Theatre Studio, Exhibition Street. Copyright material held at registration number 21466.

(4) **The Sentimental Bloke** – 92 minutes, released 26 March 1932. P.C.: Efftee. Dir.: F. W. Thring. Elaborate talkie adaptation of C J Dennis poem, starring Cecil Scott, Ray Fisher and Tal Ordell. Location shooting at: St Kilda beach, Collins Street, Victoria Market, Fitzroy, farm scenes shot at Eltham. Studio scenes all shot at His Majesty's Theatre studio, Exhibition Street. *Note: the NFSA has the British release print, cut to 72 mins.*

(5) **His Royal Highness** – 90 minutes, premiered Regent, Brisbane, 1 October 1932. P.C.: Efftee. Dir.: F. W. Thring. Lavish musical comedy of an Australian down-and-out who dreams that he is the king of a small Ruritanian country. Stars George Wallace, John Dobbie, Marshall Crosby. Nearly all of the film was shot inside the His Majesty's Theatre studio, with the exception of a brief shot of the distant 'palace' (a glass matte shot) taken in The Botanic Gardens, Melbourne. The script's copyright material – possibly the script for this film's stage prototype – is held at registration number 20048 'REVUE – His Royal Highness.' *Note: the NFSA has the British print, renamed* 'His Loyal Highness' *and cut to 85 minutes. The local 16mm print circulated by the NFSA around 1980 has at least one extra song, a romantic duet performed by Donalda Warne and Frank Tarrant.*

(6) **'Harmony Row'** – 82 minutes, released 11 February 1933. P.C.: Efftee. Dir.: F. W. Thring. George Wallace as an incompetent but lovable policeman. The least successful of the Wallace films, adapted from several of his stage sketches placed back-to-back. The script's copyright material – possibly the script for this film's stage prototype – is held at registration number 20045 'REVUE – Harmony Row'. *Note.: the NFA print is cut to 67 minutes.*

(7) **'Diggers In Blighty'** – 78 minutes, released 11 February 1933. P.C.: Pat Hanna Productions. Dir.: Pat Hanna and Raymond Longford. Wartime comedy starring Pat Hanna. A sequel to *Diggers*. Produced at the His Majesty's Theatre studio. The script's copyright material is held at registration number 23381.

(8) **'Waltzing Matilda'** – 87 minutes, released 2 December 1933. P.C.: Pat Hanna Productions. Dir.: Pat Hanna and Raymond Longford. Comedy of returned

servicemen in Melbourne. The stars were mostly members of Pat Hanna's 'Diggers' company, including a notable 'walk-on' part by Coral Brown. The script's copyright material is held under registration number 23858.

(9) **'Sheepmates'** – unfinished feature, in production late 1933. P.C.: Efftee. Dir.: F.W. Thring. About 9,000 feet of silent negative and 1000 feet of sound was exposed before Thring suspended production after viewing the rushes. *Sheepmates* was an adaptation of William Hatfield's bestselling novel of the same name (Angus and Robertson, 1931), dealing with an Englishman's arrival in outback Australia. *Everyones* 4 October 1933 announced the cast of the film: Campbell Copelin as Atherton (based on Hatfield's own life), George Wallace, Frank Harvey, Henry Wenman, and Harold B Meade, Guy Hastings, Marshall Crosby and Darcy Kelway. Over 8000 feet of unedited outback footage was shot on a major expedition to cattle stations in North-Western New South Wales for subsequent usage via back-projection in the studio (the first Australian usage of this optical technique).

(10) **A Ticket In Tatts** – 91 minutes, produced late 1933, released 6 January 1934. P.C.: Efftee. Dir.: F. W. Thring. George Wallace horse-racing comedy. According to copyright registers in the Mitchell Archives, Canberra, the film was based on a combination of Jock McLeod's scenario 'High Stakes' and George Wallace's script 'High Heels', scenario copyright number 21969. This was the last film produced entirely at the Her Majesty's Theatre Studio.

(11) **Collits' Inn** – unfinished feature. P.C.: Efftee. Producer: F.W. Thring. Director: Claude Flemming. An Australian operetta set in the Blue Mountains in 1828, the book by T. Stuart Gurr and the music by Mrs Varney Monk. Only film sound recordings of musical numbers survive. About 35 minutes of the soundtrack survives, probably dating from the Australian summer of 1933–34, now held by NFA. These songs had been recorded optically on reels of 35 mm film, about four songs to each reel. They probably were recorded either at Her Majesty's Theatre during rehearsals late in 1933, or (rather less likely) at the Wattle Path studio, St Kilda Upper Esplanade during the show's run, early in 1934.

Films Made at the 'Wattle Path' Studios, Upper Esplanade, St Kilda

(1) **'Streets Of London'** – 71 minutes, in production January–February 1934 but never publicly released in Australia as it did not satisfy the quota act's 'quality' clause; apparently released in England as a 'supporting feature' under the Empire Quota c1935. P.C.: Efftee, Dir.: F. W. Thring. Filmed 19th century stage melodrama, played chiefly as farce, complete with scenes of the audience entering the theatre. Stars Frank Harvey, Phyllis Baker, Campbell Copelin.

Partly shot at Gregan McMahon's Garrick Theatre, South Melbourne, where the 'live' theatre production opened on 11 November 1933 – but mostly filmed at Efftee's newly opened Wattle Path studio.

(2) **'Clara Gibbings'** – 88 minutes, released 13 October 1934. P.C.: Efftee. Dir.: F.W. Thring and F. Harvey. Society melodrama starring Dorothy Brunton and Campbell Copelin. Shot entirely at Wattle Path studio. Dorothy Brunton had been a musical comedy star and a pin-up of the Australian troops at the First World War. By the 1930s she was getting a little old for romantic parts, so that considerable effort was made by Arthur Higgins to shoot her close-ups through gauze screens.

(3) **'Heritage'** – 98 minutes, released 13 April 1935. P.C.: Expeditionary Films. Dir.: Charles Chauvel. Stars Peggy Maguire and Franklyn Bennett. Chauvel's epic attempt at an Australian equivalent of *The Birth of a Nation*. Only indoor scenes and the sound track were done at the Efftee studio. Some outdoor scenes were shot in New South Wales, Mrs Elsa Chauvel briefly seen in the role of Mrs Governor Macquarie.

B. The 'Efftee Entertainers' Variety Shorts

This series is unique in the annals of Australian film, though it had strong parallels in America and Britain. The 'Efftee Entertainers' series of vaudeville 'shorts' was modeled on similar series produced abroad, notably by British Pathé, but also by several of the major American film producers. Collectively, these 'shorts' provide a fascinating record of a theatrical era whose passing was principally caused by the talking picture medium used to record it.

Warner Brothers' pioneering *Vitaphone Varieties* sound shorts were the prototype for this type of film, produced in the earliest days of the 'talkie' with synchronised sound recorded on big gramophone discs (1926 – 1930). The later RKO Headliners, and the many vaudeville shorts made by Paramount followed in the peak production years of Paramount's east coast 'Astoria' studios on Long Island (1928 – 1932). The major attractions of the earliest talkie shows often was their 'Vitaphone Prologue' [the 'sound shorts'], rather than in the feature that they nominally supported. Initially, there was more recorded dialogue in these 'shorts' than in the features.

In England, the filming of vaudeville 'shorts' with sound began when DeForest Phonofilms (circa 1925–28) opened a tiny studio for making demonstration talkies at Clapham Junction in the mid-1920s, but British Pathé was the principal producer of vaudeville shorts at the dawn of the 'talkie', with the *Pathé Pictorial* and *Pathétone* series (1929–40). Gainsborough also produced a *Gainsborough*

Gems and *Sugar and Spice* series (both 1930) and in the same year B.I.P. produced the feature-length revue picture *Elstree Calling* starring the Sydney-born Cicely Courtneidge. Most of the copious surviving British Pathé material is available for preview, sale and download from their excellent website, www.britishpathe.com.

In Australia, a production scale commensurate with our smaller population resulted only in the production of Efftee's series of vaudeville shorts. Cinesound in Sydney produced no similar series. However, they did make one similar featurette early in 1934, *Cinesound Varieties*, a 50-minute film made at the Dog Pavilion in the Sydney Showground, starring Sydney vaudevillians in offbeat routines. Its director, Ken Hall, often recalled this as the worst production effort of his career, and is rumoured to have destroyed much of the footage. However, the surviving parts of *Cinesound Varieties* reflect Hall's appreciation of the unique potentialities of adapting stage routines to the cinema, in stark contrast with Thring's stolid technique, where the camera is mostly used as a recording instrument for a theatrically conceived scene. A video selection of these 'Efftee Entertainers' shorts compiled by Chris Long was released by the NFSA in 1989.

The Efftee Shorts *(in approximate chronological order)*

(1) **Will Cade and his Regent Theatre Orchestra in Selections from 'The Desert Song'** – 5 minutes, filmed prior to July 1931, shown as a support to *Diggers*. Melbourne's Regent Theatre Orchestra plays 'One Alone' and 'Ho' (The Riffs' Song) from Romberg's hit musical comedy *The Desert Song*, which was one of the first talkies.

(2) **Jack O'Hagan – Vocalist Composer** – 7 minutes, filmed prior to 4 November 1931, shown as a support to *Diggers*. Pioneer broadcaster and local song composer O'Hagan sings a selection of his own compositions, including 'Carry On', 'By the Big Blue Billabong', 'In Dreamy Araby', 'After the Dawn' and 'The Road to Gundagai'. This was the first (and possibly the only) occasion on which O'Hagan recorded 'Gundagai', his most famous composition.

(3) **Cecil Parkes' Strad Trio in Selections from their Repertoire** – 8 minutes, 1931, shown as a support to *Diggers*. Trio of violin, cello and piano playing a selection of ballads and light classical items. These include 'Toselli's Serenade', 'La Ronde Des Lutins' and numbers from the Evelyn Laye/John Boles filmed operetta *One Heavenly Night* (early 1931).

(4) **Athol Tier as Napoleon** – 7 minutes, filmed prior to 4 November 1931, shown as a support to *Diggers*. The only short solo film by the radio comedian Athol Tier, later famous as half of the radio comedy team of Mrs 'Arris and Mrs 'Iggs, with Dan Agar. This film was of a rather bizarre vaudeville turn, apparently well known at the time. The routine was contemporaneously recorded by Tier

at 'Vocalion' Records under the title of 'Napoleon, The Only'un'. Tier later was featured in the Efftee film 'The Sentimental Bloke' (1932) as 'Artie'.

(5) Keith Desmond in Recitations [No.1] – 3 minutes, filmed in 1931. A short film released in March 1932 to support *The Sentimental Bloke.* Desmond recites the poem 'On The Stairs' in typical turn-of-the-century declamatory style, impeccably dressed in a stiff collar and tails – apparently before growing the beard he used as the Bush Uncle in *The Sentimental Bloke.*

(6) Keith Desmond in Recitations [No.2] – 6 minutes, filmed in 1931. A short film intended for release in March 1932 to support *The Sentimental Bloke.* This short exists at the NFA only as a picture negative, and may not have been released. Desmond appears in Cockney costume, with a cloth cap – probably reciting his well-known item *'A Cockney version of 'The Death Of Nelson'* which he recorded locally for the 'Broadcast' gramophone record label.

(7) The Sundowners – Harmony Quartette [No.1] – 5 minutes, filmed late in 1931. A short film released in March 1932 to support *The Sentimental Bloke.* Pioneer broadcasters and popular vocal quartette from radio 3LO consisting of: Tom Semple, tenor; Bert Gillard, bass; Herbert Sanderson, baritone and Bob Allen, counter-tenor (or alto) with piano accompanist Cecil Fraser. All are dressed in white tennis outfits, carrying racquets for good measure! Songs include 'In Apple Blossom Time' and 'I Haven't Told Her, She Hasn't Told Me'. Fraser was then the conductor of the ABC Radio Dance Orchestra on 3LO.

(8) The Sundowners – Harmony Quartette [No.2] – 5 minutes, filmed late in 1931. A short film released in March 1932 to support *The Sentimental Bloke.* Vocal quartet from radio station 3LO with Cecil Fraser on piano. All are dressed in dinner suits, singing a selection of children's songs, including 'The Wedding of the Three Blind Mice' and 'Sleepy Town Express'.

(9) Lou Vernon – Character Songs [No.1] – 4 minutes, filmed late in 1931. A short film released in March 1932 to support *The Sentimental Bloke.* Lou Vernon (1888–1971), veteran character actor and creator of the radio character 'Dr. Mac', sings and delivers the monologue 'That's My Idea of a Lady'. Vernon was well-known as a performer in JCW musicals during the 1920s. and appeared prominently in George Wallace's *His Royal Highness.*

(10) Kathleen Goodall – Songs at the Piano [No.1] – 4 minutes, filmed late 1931. A short film released in March 1932 to support *The Sentimental Bloke.* A character actress and singer, then appearing in 'Songs at the Piano' at King's Theatre in Russell Street. Kathleen Goodall was an adaptable singer and actress, equally comfortable in panto, Gilbert & Sullivan and even Ernest C. Rolls' racy musical variety shows. Here she sings the First World War hit, 'Widows are Wonderful'.

(11) Kathleen Goodall – Songs at the Piano [No.2] – 4 minutes, filmed late 1931. A short film released in March 1932 to support *The Sentimental Bloke*. Kathleen sings the cloying children's song 'Little Mr. Baggy Breeches'.

(12) Kathleen Goodall – Songs at the Piano [No.3] – 4 minutes, filmed late 1931. A short film released in March 1932 to support *The Sentimental Bloke*. Kathleen sings 'Little Mary Fawcett', an insinuating lyric with elements of double entendre.

(13) George Wallace, Australia's Premier Comedian – 7 minutes, filmed late 1931, shown as a support for *The Sentimental Bloke* on 26 March 1932. George Wallace's first motion picture appearance, filmed after his touring company reached Melbourne in late October 1931. Patter, dance and song, featuring 'Down at Donovan's Store' and 'The Dance of the Wounded Wombat'.

(14) Melody and Terpsichore – 7 minutes, filmed early 1932, shown as a support for *The Sentimental Bloke* on 26 March 1932. Violinist Hermia Barton leads a corps de ballet of dancing lady violinists and solo dancer Dorothy Hutchison. A spectacular but naïve routine in which ten coiffured violinists and dancers in 18th century costume emerge in Freudian profusion from beneath the voluminous hoop skirt of the solo violinist.

15) Stan Ray and George Moon Jnr., Speciality Dancers [No.1] – 3 minutes, 1931–32, shown as a support for *The Sentimental Bloke* on 26 March 1932. Tap dancers with Art Chapman's Dance Orchestra playing the popular tune 'There ought to be a Moonlight Saving Time'.

(16) Stan Ray and George Moon Jnr., Speciality Dancers [No.2] – 4 minutes, 1931–32, shown as a support for *The Sentimental Bloke* on 26 March 1932. Eccentric dance in blackface to the musical number 'I Want to be Bad' (DeSylva, Brown & Henderson) from the 1930 Paramount film *Follow Thru*. Accompaniment probably by Art Chapman's Rex Cabaret Dance Orchestra.

(17) Melbourne's Chinese Orchestra in Selections – 3 minutes, 1932. Chinese orchestra with ethnic instruments, from the Little Lonsdale Street ('Chinatown') precinct behind His Majesty's Theatre. The film was cut to half its original length by Jack Murray just before its initial screening, in a last-minute decision by Thring, and would sound very disjointed to a Chinese audience.

(18) Minnie Love, Impressions of Famous Artists [No.1] – 3 minutes, 1932. This veteran stage performer (1890–1967) was brought to Australia by JCW 1914–1920, and returned in the early 1930s when these films were made. She was very popular at the time of the First World War. In this 'short' she does an impression of the British music hall star Lily Morris singing 'The Old Apple Tree'. Piano accompaniment is by Stan Rafael.

(19) Minnie Love, Impressions of Famous Artists [No.2] – 5 minutes, 1932. Impressions of Gracie Fields singing 'A Coople O'Dooks' and of Maurice Chevalier singing 'Valentine' from *Innocents of Paris* (1929).

(20) Minnie Love, Impressions of Famous Artists [No.3] – 4 minutes, 1932. Impression of Randolph Sutton singing 'Over the Garden Wall' and of Maurice Chevalier singing 'You Brought a New Kind of Love to Me' from his recent Paramount film *The Big Pond* (1930).

(21) Peter Bornstein, Celebrated Violinist – 5 minutes, 1932. Bornstein, formerly leader of Pavlova's theatre orchestra, plays a selection of classical items, with the locally famous composer Henri Penn providing piano accompaniment. All filmed in one long tracking shot, without cut-aways. Filmed prior to March 1932.

(22) George White (cellist) – film of unknown length, 1932. Short of unknown content, now apparently lost. Listed in an issue of *Everyone's*, March 1932.

(23) Miss Ada Reeve – Comedienne [No.1] – 4 minutes, 1932. Filmed to support *His Royal Highness*. Famous British musical comedy and revue star Ada Reeve (1874–1964) in her first talkie 'shorts'. Here she delivers the sentimental monologue 'Ain't yer Jim' with accompaniment from Harry Jacobs' Palais Theatre Orchestra. Ada sings to her baby about its future life – though, at the age of 58, her credibility in this role had worn a little thin.

(24) Miss Ada Reeve – Comedienne [No.2] – 5 minutes, 1932. Filmed to support *His Royal Highness*. Sings 'I Never Forget I'm A Lady' carrying a large feather fan, in the manner of her music hall appearances forty years earlier – with accompaniment by Harry Jacobs' orchestra. She also recorded this song for Columbia Records in Sydney in 1930.

(25) Miss Byrl Walkley, Soprano – 5 minutes, 1932. Newcastle-born star of *His Royal Highness*, *Collit's Inn* and other JCW and Efftee productions sings 'Love is Best of All' and 'Trees'. Accompanied by Alaric Howitt, co-composer of music for *His Royal Highness*.

(26) 'Somewhere South of Shanghai' Rendered by Marshall Crosby – 4 mins, 1932. Filmed to support *His Royal Highness*. This local Jack Lumsdaine composition is sung by character actor Marshall Crosby (1881–1954), father of the Australian character actor Don Crosby, who appears to be performing on the ship set from *His Royal Highness*.

(27) Neil McKay, Scottish Comedian – 7 minutes, 1932. Filmed to support *His Royal Highness*. Glasgow-born comic filmed on his second visit to Australia, for the Tivoli Circuit. Sings 'The Sea's the Life for Me' in a thick Scottish dialect with some rather clichéd patter, and briefly plays the bagpipes. Again apparently filmed on the ship set from *His Royal Highness*.

(28) Williamson Imperial Grand Opera Co. Orchestra – Overture from 'Carmen', by Bizet – 3 minutes, 1932. Filmed to support *His Royal Highness.* The orchestra from Melbourne's Theatre Royal in Bourke Street, conducted by visiting Italian maestro Wando Aldrovandi during its Melbourne Opera season (2 July – 23 September 1932).

(29) Williamson-Imperial Grand Opera Co. Orchestra – Overture from Gounod's 'Faust' – 4 minutes, 1932. Filmed to support *His Royal Highness,* and again conducted by Aldrovandi.

(30) Williamson-Imperial Grand Opera Co. Orchestra – Selections from 'The Barber of Seville' by Rossini – 7 minutes, 1932. Filmed to support *His Royal Highness.* The J. C. Williamson 1932 Opera Season orchestra conducted – again – by Aldrovandi.

(31) Signor Apollo Granforte and the Williamson-Imperial Grand Opera Company Orchestra – 5 minutes, 1932. First shown at the Capitol Theatre, Melbourne, September 1932. The internationally renowned baritone and HMV red-label recording artist sings 'Largo al Factotum' from Rossini's *The Barber of Seville* by Rossini.

(32) Lou Vernon – Character Songs [No.2] – 5 minutes, 1933. Elaborate short with Vernon as an Italian fruit-stall owner singing 'Italiano'. Brief introductory exterior of the fruit vendor's pushcart in Melbourne's city streets.

The 'Non-Stop Variety' Film Series (Shorts)

These were a rearrangement of the above 'Efftee Entertainers' shorts into groups of two or three, apparently for British release only. The original vaudeville shorts were sometimes clumsily edited in the process of rearrangement:

Non-stop Variety No.1. First half only of 'Melody and Terpsichore' (short 8); first half only of 'Moon & Ray' (short 9); Ada Reeve in 'Aint yer Jim' (short 23, complete); last few feet of 'Melody and Terpsichore' (short 8).

Non-stop Variety No.2. Ada Reeve in 'I Never Forget I'm a Lady' (short 24); small section only of 'Cecil Parkes' Strad Trio' (short 3).

Non-stop Variety No.3. Middle section only of 'Melody and Terpsichore' (short 8); second half only of Byrl Walkley' short (short 25).

Non-stop Variety No.4. Williamson 1932 Grand Opera Orchestra – 'Carmen Overture' (short 28); 'Minnie Love in Impressions' (short 14); 'Sundowners Harmony Quartette' (short 16, complete).

Non-stop Variety No.5. Lou Vernon – 'That's My Idea of a Lady' (short 17); 'Peter Bornstein, Violinist' (short 21, incomplete); Minnie Love – 'The Old Apple Tree' (short 12, complete).

Non-stop Variety No.6. Grand Opera Orchestra – Faust Overture (short 29); Kathleen Goodall 'Mr Baggy Breeches' (short 19); Melbourne's Chinese Orchestra (announced here as 'Ting a Ling and his Rattling Good Din-Copaters') (short 11).

Non-stop Variety No.7. Marshall Crosby – 'Shanghai' (short 26, complete); Minnie Love –'Coople o'Dooks'(first half only, short 13); Moon & Ray – 'Moonlight Saving Time' (short 9, second half only) followed by a brief clip from short 10.

Non-stop Variety No.8. Lou Vernon –'Italiano' (short 32, complete); Sundowners – 'I Haven't Told Her' (last half only, short 15); Byrl Walkley –'Love is Best of All' (first half only, short 25).

Non-stop Variety No.9. Minnie Love – Chevalier Impression (last half only, short 13); Cecil Parkes' Strad Trio (section only of short 3); Kath Goodall – 'Little Mary Fawcett' (short 20, complete).

Non-stop Variety No.10. Sundowners –'Apple Blossom Time' (short 15, first half); Kath Goodall – 'Widows'; (short 18, complete); Parkes' Strad Trio – 'La Ronde des Lutins' (section of short 3).

Two-Reel 'Efftee Shorts' – One Act Plays

On a couple of occasions, Thring made 'shorts' that were longer and slightly more elaborate than the usual 'Efftee Entertainers' series, to preserve complete one-act plays or comedy sketches that had been 'hits' in live performance. Of these, one holds up quite well, the other not so well…

(1) Oh, What a Night! – 14 minutes, filmed prior to its listing in the Melbourne 'Argus' on 11 August 1932 (p.8). P.C. Efftee. Direction: nominally F.W. Thring, but Jack Murray maintained that Thring wasn't anywhere near the set, that the film was actually directed by George Wallace himself and completed in three days at His Majesty's in 1932. An excellent domestic comedy with Wallace as an errant drunk, based on a comedy sketch performed by him on stage since about 1928. Also stars Wallace's blonde live-in lover, the actress Maida Jones, in her only film appearance (uncredited), as Wallace's wife; with Marshall Crosby as the Irish neighbour and John Dobbie as the gay policeman. A British print is held by the National Film Lending collection. Chris Long restored this film to its full original length on video from 35mm nitrate negatives and print materials for the 1989 NFSA video compilation *Efftee Entertainers*.

(2) In the Future – 12 minutes, filmed prior to 18 October 1932, the film's censor screening date in New Zealand. P.C. Efftee. Direction: nominally F.W. Thring, but according to Thelma Scott, the direction was almost totally under Ada Reeve's control. A love triangle farce based on sexual role-play reversal. The women go out to make a living, smoke cigars, and carouse; while the men are left at home to raise the family. According to Thelma Scott, Ada Reeve presented this sketch on stage for many years before Efftee committed it to film. Stars Ada Reeve (the wife), Thelma Scott (the lover), Leonard Stephens (the husband) and John Dobbie (the butler).

The Pat Hanna Variety Shorts

Imitating Thring's success in producing 'unit programs' of a feature and supporting shorts, Pat Hanna made a series of shorts in support of the two early sound films he made after appearing in Diggers, when he 'went independent'. Hanna used Efftee's studio and crew for all of his films, including these 'shorts'.

(1) Joe Valli and Charlie Albert in 'Long Lost Son' – 9 minutes, November 1932. Direction: Pat Hanna. Joe Valli plays a shambling actor who applies for a job to Charlie Albert, a Labor Exchange manager whom he mistakes for a theatrical manager. Valli appeared in many Australian films as a supporting comic, while Charles Albert's career on stage stretched back to 1893.

(2) George Randall and Babe Scott in 'The Imposter' – 10 minutes, November 1932. Direction: Pat Hanna. Babe Scott was George Wallace's half-sister, and a noted vaudevillian in her own right. Apparently filmed on the haunted house set built for *Harmony Row*.

(3) Lavender and Lace – 4 minutes, 1932. Direction: Pat Hanna. Features Ern Kopke (tenor) and Frances Ogilvy (solo dancer) with the Ostend String Trio. Song and dance in 18th Century costume, and charmingly quaint. Kopke had been a long-term member of Hanna's 'Diggers' concert party. He is heard in the last reel of *Diggers*, singing 'Mademoiselle from Armentieres'.

(4) Pat Hanna in 'The Gospel According to Cricket' – length unknown, no print known. Direction: Pat Hanna. Short film now lost, listed in *Everyone's*, 14 December 1932. Pat Hanna as a religious cleric, preaching the fate of 'Australia's Eleven' in ecclesiastical declamatory style from the pulpit. Based on Hanna's famous gramophone record of the monologue of the same name (released by Vocalion in February 1930).

The Efftee Documentaries

The earlier Efftee documentary shorts are now among the slickest and most interesting products of the whole company output, but with the later Tatler Social Newsreel items, where the films were to be shown at only one venue, the accent was on economy. They were released with scant editing from the original negatives, other than the addition of titles and a narration track.

(1) Cities of the Empire Series – Melbourne Today – 10 minutes, filmed prior to November 1931. P.C.: Efftee Films. Direction: F.W. Thring. First and best of the Efftee documentaries. Excellent camerawork by Arthur Higgins, with skilful use of fades, dissolves and transitional devices. The narration was written and spoken by Norman Campbell, editor of Melbourne's *Punch* magazine, and was charmingly evocative of the period. The Fitzroy Gardens, we are told, is a place to which 'busy workers come … for an hour's sylvan treat' while 'students muse over their books and lovers whisper sweet nothings'. Musical backing by Cecil Parkes' Strad Trio.

(2) Cities of the Empire Series – Ballarat – 8 minutes, 1932. P.C. Efftee Films. Direction: F.W. Thring. Standard program travelogue. Narration spoken by F. W. Thring. Fine pictorial shots of the city, the Old Curiosity Shop, Lake Wendouree, the old gold diggings etc. Includes an interesting shot of Depression-pinched miners desperately digging for gold in the gutters of Humffray Street North. Musical backing by Cecil Parkes' Strad Trio.

(3) Cities of the Empire Series – Sydney – film lost, length unknown – 1932. Direction: F.W. Thring. Camerawork by Arthur and Tasman Higgins. According to Jack Murray, Tas Higgins was originally commissioned to shoot this film in Sydney, but his initial results were 'newsreel stuff – nothing pictorially satisfying or attractive'. Arthur Higgins then went to Sydney to reshoot this travelogue almost in its entirety; no print of this film has so far been found.

(4) Dear Old London – 40 minutes, 1933. Initially released in support of the feature *A Ticket in Tatts*. P.C. Efftee Films. Direction: Claude Flemming (Britain) and F.W. Thring (Melbourne). By far the longest of the Efftee travelogues, and made in response to a similar travelogue of London released by Cinesound, this film was a tourist's view of London in four reels, shot by an English crew under Claude Flemming's direction for Efftee.

(5) Efftee Film Magazine Series: 'The Wedge Tailed Eagle' – 3 minutes, 1934. P.C.: Efftee Films. Direction:Frank Harvey. Narration: Frank Harvey. Technical Assistance: David Fleahy. Camera: Bert Nicholas. Part of a 'no-frills' nature series shot by Bert Nicholas late in 1934.

(6) Efftee Film Magazine Series: 'The Echidna' – 3 minutes, 1934. P.C.: Efftee Films. Direction: Frank Harvey. Narration: Frank Harvey. Technical Assistance: David Fleahy. Camera: Bert Nicholas. Other parts of this series, now lost, featured the koala, the emu, the platypus etc.

The Tatler [Theatrette] Social Newsreel Series

P.C.: Efftee Films. Direction: F.W. Thring. Narration: F.W. Thring, Peter Newmarch and/or Frank Harvey (1934). According to Jack Murray and Bert Nicholas, about a dozen 'newsreels', chiefly of upper-crust social gatherings and topical items rather than news events, were made from May to July 1934 specifically for Thring and Matear's new Tatler Newsreel Theatrette. It was one of Australia's earliest newsreel theatres – in the basement of the Australia Hotel, 266 Collins Street, with seating for 300 people. This was a continuous one-hour show, open daily from 25 May 1934, 10:30 am to 11:00 pm. The Tatler Newsreel items were almost all shot by Efftee's assistant cameraman Bert Nicholas, with script and narration by Peter Newmarch of Melbourne's Truth newspaper.

(1) **Tatler Social Newsreel Number 1** (?) released 25 May 1934, the date of the Tatler Newsreel Theatre's opening. Synopsis unknown. No print known.

(2) **Tatler Social Newsreel Number 2** (?) released 1 June 1934. Synopsis unknown. No print known, though a workprint of one item survives (see below)

(3) **Item from 'Tatler News No.2'** [clapper board composite negative and 16mm print held by NFSA, possibly unused and unreleased] – **Dr William Maloney, MLA.** (filmed c. May 1934). Maloney, 'the Little Doctor' (1854–1940), a friend (and frequently a portrait subject) of many of the Heidelberg School impressionists reviews his own political career in a full lip-sync talk to camera around the time of his eightieth birthday.

(4) **Tatler Social Newsreel Number 3** (?) released 7 June 1934: On the Lawn at Moonee Valley; Big Business Ball; Melbourne's Riding Schools. No print known.

(5) **Tatler Social Newsreel Number 4** (?) released 11 June 1934: With the hounds at Ballarat; Flemington Spring Carnival Fashions; Melbourne's Riding Schools. No print known.

(6) **Tatler Social Newsreel Number 5** (?) released 21 June 1934: Joyce Macbeth, World Champion Skater; Don Cameron's Horse-Riding School; Dog Parade at Show Ground; Toorak Party 'etc'. Narration by Peter Newmarch and Frank Harvey.

(7) **Tatler Social Newsreel Number 6** (?) released 28 June 1934: R. G. Menzies (Australian Prime Minister 1949–1965) in a major speech at the Younger Set's Ball at Rumpelmayer's. No print known. The speech probably concerned Menzies' move from State to Federal Politics, and the launching of the new United Australia Party, which were both much in the news at the time.

(8) **Tatler Social Newsreel Number 7** (?) released just before 5 July 1934: Exclusive views of the Grand National Candidates; St Kilda versus Carlton football match; highlights of The Bowery Ball at the Rex Cabaret. No print known.

(9) **Tatler Social Newsreel Number 8** (?) released 7 July 1934: Grand National Steeple favourites; A Dip with Melbourne's Early Morning Swimmers; Latest Lingerie Fashions on Display. No print known.

(10) **According to the Efftee crew, there may have been up to four further Tatler Social Newsreels.** If this were the case, they would have ceased production in August 1934, but no Efftee-Tatler newsreels after number 8 are listed in the Tatler's programs printed in the *Argus* newspaper.

(11) **Eucharistic Congress Procession Special**, filmed specifically for the Tatler Theatrette by Arthur Higgins in December 1934, listed in *Everyones* 12 December 1934 p.80. No print known.

The 'Australian Educational Films' Shorts

The Sydney-based musician and amateur naturalist Noel Monkman produced two micro-cinematography items for the Fox Movietone Newsreel in 1930–31. Always alert to local film production potential, Thring offered to employ Monkman to make similar nature films as supports for his Efftee features. Monkman was a rugged individualist and a bit of a loner, and rejected the offer. Thring then fell back to offering him an equal collaborative role in a new production partnership, so 'Australian Educational Films' was formed as a joint company between Thring and Monkman in 1931.

Monkman used Efftee's technical and post-production facilities to produce eleven nature shorts, chiefly (though not entirely) in Queensland, in two series. The first series of five were shot on the Barrier Reef between June and December 1931, according to a report in the Melbourne *Argus*, 29 January 1932. Monkman's latter nature shorts shot in collaboration with Thring, the 'Monkman Marvelogues' were more varied and occupied a longer period of production, from 1932 to 1934. Their production saga was later recorded by Noel Monkman in two autobiographical books, *Escape to Adventure* (1956) and *Quest of the Curly-Tailed Horses* (1963). After Monkman's death in 1969, his wife Kitty published her own book on their film making experiences, *Over and Under the Great Barrier Reef* (1975).

Series 1 – The Barrier Reef Series

(1) **Ocean Oddities** – 11 minutes, 1931. Life histories of Barrier Reef animals including the green turtle, bêche-de-mer, stonefish and crown of thorns starfish. Script, direction and photography by Monkman. Narration spoken by F.W. Thring. Music by Cecil Parkes' Strad Trio.

(2) **Coral and its Creatures** – 9 minutes, 1931. On coral reefs, and the creatures that inhabit them. Visually rich item, but only picture negative held by

NFSA. Sound could be recovered from a release print in the Davidson collection.

(3) **Secrets of the Sea** – 10 minutes, 1931. Microscopic life of the Barrier Reef. Sound lost on existing library print.

(4) **Strange Sea Shells** – 9 minutes, 1931. Molluscs, microscopic diatoms, and the unusual creatures which inhabit them. Sound lost on existing NFSA print.

(5) **Birds of the Barrier Reef** – 9 minutes, 1931. Rookeries on the Barrier Reef, with life histories of the gannet and mutton-bird. Sound lost on existing NFA print.

Series 2 – The Monkman Marvelogues

(1) **People of the Ponds** – 11 minutes, 1933. Microscopic life from the rock pools of an extinct Queensland volcano. Narration by F.W. Thring.

(2) **Catching Crocodiles** – 9 minutes, 1933. Life with the crocodile hunters on the Gulf of Carpentaria. Narration by F.W. Thring.

(3) **Nature's Little Jokes** – 9 minutes, 1933. Unusual and bizarre plants and animals of Queensland. Narration by F.W. Thring.

(4) **The Cliff Dwellers** – 9 minutes, 1933. Life history of an Australian native bee, found living in burrows at Red Bluff, Victoria. Narration written by Tarlton Rayment, spoken by F.W. Thring.

(5) **The Winged Empress** – 10 minutes, 1934. The science of bee keeping, the social life of bees, and their manufacture of honey. Narration written by Tarlton Rayment, spoken by Frank Harvey. Direction and photography by Noel Monkman.

(6) **You'd Never Guess** – 9 minutes, 1934. Micro-cinematography used to explain some lesser-known natural history phenomena. The beating heart of a fly larva; the ways wasps store fresh food; water beetles which dive with trapped air bubbles to breathe under water; etc. Direction and photography by Noel Monkman. Narration by Frank Harvey.

[7] **[Ants and their Antics]** – film not released, 1933–34. This project was completed by Monkman but the majority of the film negative was destroyed in a processing accident. The script was reworked by Monkman as a chapter of his book *Quest of the Curly-Tailed Horses* (1963).

On 12 February 1936, the magazine *Everyones* stated that Thring and Monkman were linking up in a new company to make an initial feature to be shot partly in the tropics with the title *Typhoon Treasure*. Thring's death soon after delayed the production of this picture, which was completed independently by Monkman.

Miscellaneous Efftee Shorts

(1) Frank M. Forde, Minister for Trade and Customs. Speech opening the Efftee studio at Her Majesty's Theatre, filmed on 2 June 1931. This was privately screened at the 3DB theatrette at the Capitol Theatre building one hour after its production, with other shorts including one of Melbourne's Regent Theatre Orchestra, and 'rush' tests of actors auditioning for Thring's film of *The Sentimental Bloke*. Forde's speech was politically interesting, supporting the infant Australian film industry and Thring in particular, and was subsequently used to introduce the film *Diggers*. On the death of John Curtin in 1945, Forde became, for one week, interim Prime Minister

(2) Lord Somers – Speech (film lost, filmed 3 June 1931). One of the first filmed speeches shot by Efftee, made for British Dominion Film distributors (BDF), on the subject of Empire trade and Empire Preference. Somers was then the Governor of Victoria. The film was shown in a special all-British film program, headed by the British feature *Canaries Sometimes Sing* at the Melbourne Athenaeum on June 5, 1931. The first short film ever released by Efftee and shown publicly.

(3) Arrivals at the Melbourne 'Athenaeum' Theatre prior to showing of an all-British Film Programme (film lost, shot June 5, 1931) The film included speeches by Prime Minister Scullin and Victorian Premier Hogan. It was rush-processed and shown at the Athenaeum at the conclusion of the night's film program.

(4) Miss Dorothy Fricke attains her majority (21st birthday party – 1931). Silent, survives at NFSA. A single long filmed shot of the dancers at the party shot by Arthur Higgins after his crew blocked the driveway entrance to the hall in which the party was held, in Mordialloc, for the filming of the garage scene in *A Co-Respondent's Course*, 1931. Thring sent a 35mm movie print of the birthday party dancers to Fricke's family as a gift afterwards.

(5) Mr F.W. Thring – Speech (3 minutes, 1931). Opening film for the first Efftee unit program in November 1931, introducing Efftee stars Donalda Warne, Pat Hanna, George Moon, Cecil Scott and Rae Fisher. The film was included in the NFSA video release *Efftee's Australia*.

(6) Mr F.W. Thring (film lost, 1932). Filmed speech for the initial screening of *The Sentimental Bloke*, reported by the late Harry Davidson – who may have confused this with *His Royal Highness – Prelude*, which consisted of the opening music for the George Wallace film accompanied by a rolling caption written by Thring, explaining the making of the film.

(7) **Efftee Contract Advertisements.** A large number of these were made under contract to the Robyns theatre advertising company. They included radio personality Norman Banks advertising the Direct Supply Jewellery Company, and several ads for the 'Antigen B' Cough Remedy.

(8) **Test Films.** Many screen tests, outtakes and so forth, were made for Efftee productions. They include the first Australian tests of Howard Hughes' Multicolor bi-pack color system in 1932 and a screen test of a local 'Hollywood beauty contest' winner, Gwen Munro, filmed by Arthur Higgins in 1933.

(9) **A deleted musical item from *His Royal Highness*** (1932) survives as a workprint in the Davidson collection.

(10) **'Advertising 'Trailers'** were made for most of the Efftee and Hanna films, including *His Royal Highness, The Sentimental Bloke, Diggers in Blighty, Waltzing Matilda, A Ticket in Tatts, Clara Gibbings* and *Harmony Row* – the last is included in the video compilation *Efftee's Australia.*

(11) **Promotional film for J.V.M. Wood, political candidate for the Seat of Evelyn, 1934** – 'The Farmers' Representative' (about 7 minutes). A filmed speech by the candidate, and a tour of his farm at Doncaster in outer suburban Melbourne.

(12) **Film Sound Recordings.** Several of these were made on Efftee's RCA film recorder for subsequent replay on radio broadcasts. According to the assistant sound recordist Jack Murray, several complete radio plays were recorded on film and broadcast over 3XY in this way around 1935–36, from the original studios in the upper floors of the Princess Theatre.

(13) **Outtakes from 'Heritage'** (1935) – a reel survives at NFSA, Canberra. Part of this has a declamatory speech by Victor Fitzherbert in the part of William Charles Wentworth: close inspection of the man holding a clapper board in this scene will reveal the face of a young Damien Parer in his first film job.

(14) **Efftee 'blooper' reel.** Sadly. not known to survive. Its existence was confirmed several times by Jack Murray and Bert Nicholas. It included Raymond Longford trying to make a donkey buck for a scene in *Diggers* by shoving a stick up its anus. Also included the many attempts to film the scratching, urinating, grumpy koala for the Efftee trademark.

Newsreel Items Pertaining to Efftee Films

(1) **The Australasian Gazette** (silent, c. 1928) F.W. Thring and W A Gibson, disembarking from an ocean liner at Port Melbourne. Held by NFSA on viewing print NA553; included in the NFSA video 'Efftee's Australia' (1989).

(2) **Movietone News Vol.2, No.20.** Released May 5, 1931. One of the micro-photography items shot by Noel Monkman in 1922, the basis for Thring's

offer of partnership in Australian Educational Films: 'Looking at a Smaller World. Subtitle 1: Magnified one thousand times under the eye of a microscope'. This item has survived.

(3) **Movietone News Vol.2, No.27.** Released July 7, 1931. 'Strange Monsters in a Drop of Water' 'Movietone takes another peep through the fascinating lenses of Noel Monkman, Australian micro-photographer'. This item survives in Movietone Library can A-002, V/A-012. Monkman takes a specimen of water to view back in his lab. Views of a mosquito larva follow, with Monkman's voice-over describing the details.

(4) **Movietone News Vol.2, No.46.** Released November 14, 1931. This contains a brief item titled 'Australian Talkies a Fact At Last!' ...'Gala premiere at Plaza Melbourne draws notable throng to see first all home grown movies.' The item, which survives at the National Film Archive, shows F.W. Thring, Olive Thring, Donalda Warne and others giving speeches at the foyer of the Plaza Theatre, Collins Street on November 6, 1931, at the premiere of *Diggers* and *A Co-Respondent's Course*. Item survives in Movietone can A-006 V/A-034.

(5) **Melbourne Herald Newsreel No.21.** Released March 23, 1932. This included an item titled 'How They're Made – Melbourne: Newsreel camera gives intimate glimpses of F.W. Thring directing big studio scene'. The item was filmed by Roy Driver of Herschell's Films while he was working as third cameraman on the ballroom scenes of 'His Royal Highness'. No copy of this item, which was 3 minutes in duration, is known to survive.

Other Material Relating to Efftee Films

(1) **F.W. Thring – filmed speech made at Fox studios, Hollywood, September 1929.** This short, now probably lost, was made during a tour of Fox studios, while Thring was finalising a big film distribution deal for Hoyts. According to the local film industry magazine 'Film Weekly', it was shown at the Melbourne Regent Theatre in October 1929.

(2) **Alan Mill in Hollywood** (1930–31) – test film on Thring's newly purchased Mitchell gear made by Arthur Higgins in Hollywood and featuring Alan Mill, late 1930. It was held by Mill's son in Sydney in 1979. A brief shot is included in Film Australia's 'Now You're Talking' (1978).

(3) **Now You're Talking** (Film Australia, 1978). Compilation film on Australian Cinema in the 1930s. Many clips from Efftee productions, Thring at his November 1931 premiere, etc.

(4) **Harry Jacobs' Home Movies** – 9.5mm silent films taken by Efftee's musical director in the early 1930s. Includes shots of Melbourne, the Palais Theatre

Orchestra, Ada Reeve etc. Formerly held by Harry's daughter, Wendy Selover, now at NFSA.

(5) **"The Coming of Sound"** – ABC radio series (audio only, 1978) – three documentary radio programs, each 45 minutes in length, made by Chris Long for the fiftieth anniversary of the Australian advent of talking pictures. The third program in the series dealt entirely with Efftee films, interviewees including Jack Murray, Thelma Scott and Patricia Minchin.

(6) **Efftee Entertainers** (1989). Compilation videocassette of complete Efftee vaudeville 'shorts' by Chris Long for National Film and Sound Archive, Canberra. Includes 'Will Cade and his [Melbourne] Regent Theatre Orchestra in Selections from 'The Desert Song'; 'Jack O'Hagan – Vocalist composer'; 'Kathleen Goodall – Songs at the Piano' ('Little Mary Fawcett'); 'The Sundowners Harmony Quartette' (both of their shorts); 'George Wallace, Australia's Premier Comedian'; 'Oh, What a Night!'; 'Ada Reeve – Comedienne' ('I Never Forget I'm a Lady').

(7) **Efftee's Australia** (1989). Compilation videocassette of Efftee-related documentary 'shorts' by Chris Long for National Film and Sound Archive, Canberra. Includes 'Australasian Gazette – F.W. Thring meets W A Gibson'; 'Melbourne Today (1931) – Cities of the Empire Series'; 'Catching Crocodiles' (Monkman/Australian Educational Films); 'Cities of the Empire Series – Ballarat'; 'Signor Apollo Granforte with Williamson-Imperial Grand Opera Orchestra'; 'Trailer for 'Harmony Row'; 'Efftee Film Magazine – Wedge Tailed Eagle'; Dr William Maloney MLA from Tatler News No.2; Mr F.W. Thring – speech.

(8) **Celluloid Heroes (Parts 1 & 2)** (1992). A 'new' history of Australian cinema, directed by Robert Francis for Film Australia, and produced by Anthony Buckley. Made in preparation for the so-called 'Centenary of Cinema' celebrations in 1995–96. The series was originally intended to replace Film Australia's earlier historical compilations on Australian cinema, but the 'new' material included actually supplements and compliments it. *Celluloid Heroes* included some coverage of Efftee, but Thring's contribution is heavily overshadowed by a focus on Cinesound. An interview with sound engineer Jack Murray is included, claiming that the clapper board was invented by Alan Mill and Harry Whiting at Efftee.

(9) **'Funny by George' – The George Wallace Story** (2000). TV documentary written by Jim Murphy, directed by Don Percy for Onkus Productions. Includes many 'Efftee' clips and – for the first time – segments from 'George Wallace Screen Test for Efftee Films' (1931). Also includes interviews with Efftee sound engineer Jack Murray and researcher Chris Long.

INDEX

(Note: Page numbers in bold indicate photographs, and page numbers followed by *n* indicate footnotes.)